D1607127

CROWS OF THE WORLD

CROWS OF THE WORLD

By DEREK GOODWIN
Illustrations by
ROBERT GILLMOR

PUBLISHED IN COOPERATION WITH THE
BRITISH MUSEUM (NATURAL HISTORY) BY
COMSTOCK PUBLISHING ASSOCIATES, *a division of*
CORNELL UNIVERSITY PRESS / *Ithaca, New York*

First published 1976 by Cornell University Press.

International Standard Book Number 0–8014–1057–6
Library of Congress Catalog Card Number 76–20194

PRINTED AND BOUND IN GREAT BRITAIN BY
STAPLES PRINTERS LIMITED AT THE GEORGE PRESS, KETTERING NORTHAMPTONSHIRE

CONTENTS

COLOUR PLATES

INTRODUCTION

The crow family, Corvidae, is a numerous, diverse and successful group of passerine birds. It includes such familiar species as the Rook in England and the Blue Jay in eastern North America and also others, such as the Sooty Jay and the African Bush-crow, about which little is known. Corvids range in size from the little lark-sized Hume's Ground Jay to the Raven, which is the largest of passerine birds. Some are dull or uniform black in hue, others are among the most colourful of the world's birds.

Most members of this family are, as passerine birds go, medium to large in size; have the tarsus large, strong, scutellated in front and booted behind; ten primary wing feathers, the outermost not greatly reduced in size; and the nostrils more or less (usually completely) covered with nasal bristles or nasal plumes. The colour patterns of their plumage are usually rather simple although often highly ornate.

Characteristic corvine behaviour patterns are: feeding of the female of a pair by the male; hiding surplus food and covering it from sight; nest-building by both sexes but incubation and brooding by female only; holding large or awkward food items under one or both feet while breaking or tearing them with the bill; and carrying food for the young in the throat or gular pouch.

None of these traits is uniquely corvine. One of them, incubation by female only, does not hold good for the nutcrackers, in which both sexes incubate. All the same, the general similarity in behaviour is such that anyone familiar with, say, the Rook and the Jay would, I think, when visiting a zoo, never doubt that such exotic species as the Green Magpie or Thick-billed Raven were correctly placed in the same family with them. Conversely any such person would only have to watch an Australian Magpie, *Gymnorhina*, for a short time to be convinced that its resemblances to the Corvidae were superficial.

The members of the crow family include the large black typical crows of the genus *Corvus*, the sandy-hued ground jays with trim black and white markings, the richly ornamented jays and magpies, and the tree pies with their long and sometimes bizarrely-shaped tails. The majority are to some extent arboreal. Many get most or all of their food from the ground and use trees for nesting, roosting and (sometimes) for resting in by day. Others usually obtain their food above ground in trees, shrubs or creepers. Some species, however, live in treeless areas.

Any or all of the crow family are often, quite correctly, referred to as 'crows' by ornithologists. Unfortunately the term 'crow' without qualification is also, equally correctly, used to indicate a member of the genus *Corvus* as distinct from members of other corvine genera. It is in this sense that it is usually understood by the layman. I therefore use the term 'corvid' when the meaning is a bird belonging to any genus of this family. The names 'pie', 'magpie', and 'jay' have been applied to various corvids according to whether their shape approximates most nearly to that of our British Jay or our Magpie and without much regard for real affinities. The Black Jay is, for example, more closely related to the tree pies than it is to the jays of the genus *Garrulus*. The blue and green magpies are, on the other hand, probably closer to the jays than they are to the Magpie, *Pica*.

In this book I have tried to give facts, so far as known, about all living corvids. It does not include any detailed anatomical study, as a work on comparative anatomy of the Corvidae would need to be written by someone with greater knowledge of that subject. The first part of the book discusses such subjects as behaviour, coloration, etc., in reference to birds of the crow family. These are, therefore, dealt with shortly and in descriptive terms under the species headings. In the species section forms believed to be most closely related to each other are placed together in so far as this is possible within the confines of linear arrangement. For each group, such as the American jays or the typical crows, its general characteristics and the relationships of the forms within it are discussed first. Under the species heading is given a description together with a black and white drawing except, sometimes, where the bird closely resembles in shape and markings some other species that is illustrated, or where it is illustrated on a colour plate, and a synopsis of what is known of its behaviour and biology.

The drawings, by Robert Gillmor, are from sketches that he or I have done from living birds or from photographs, where this was possible. For some species, however, such material was not available and

1

Mr Gillmor had to base his drawings on sketches I had done from museum specimens.   Lists of measurements are apt to be misleading to those unused to measuring bird skins.   I have, therefore, described size and shape in reference to seven well-known species; the Raven, Hooded Crow, House Crow, Jackdaw, Magpie, Jay and Blue Jay.   Outline sketches of these and the measurements of the individual specimens from which the sketches were made are given here.

FIG. 1.   Outline sketches, for size comparisons, of (top left to bottom right) Raven (wing from carpal joint 424 mm, tail 246 mm, tarsus 67 mm, bill from forehead 77 mm); Hooded Crow (w. 340 mm, t. 195 mm, tar. 60 mm, b. 62 mm); House Crow (w. 278 mm, t. 186 mm, tar. 54 mm, b. 55 mm); Jackdaw (w. 245 mm, t. 130 mm, tar. 54 mm, b. 37 mm); Magpie (w. 190 mm, t. 260 mm, tar. 49 mm, b. 39 mm); Jay (w. 185 mm, t. 143 mm, tar. 40 mm, b. 30 mm); Blue Jay (w. 134 mm, t. 123 mm, tar. 36 mm, b. 29 mm).

Most of the references fall into two main categories, which are not always mutually exclusive.   There are those where part or all of the information given is derived from one or a few sources only or where some piece of information seems questionable as being possibly based on an isolated or misinterpreted observation.   Secondly, for species or subjects on which a great deal has been written, the references given are to those papers which I have found of most use or that appear to me likely to be particularly worth the reader's while to consult.   The context should make the type of reference clear.   An enormous amount has been written on some species, such as the Rook and the Raven.   It should not, therefore, be concluded that any paper not mentioned among the references has necessarily been judged irrelevant or lacking in interest.

The dendrograms show what I believe to be the most likely phylogenetic relationships of the forms in question.   In these dendrograms the length of a 'stem' indicates degree of divergence; members of the same superspecies are connected by one dotted line; very distinct and geographically separated races of the same species are connected by two dotted lines.   Parallel lines between the 'stem' of a species and its 'branch' indicate that its derivation is uncertain but is thought to be, most probably, this branch.

The distribution maps indicate the approximate geographical areas inhabited by each species.   It is, of course, to be understood that any bird is only likely to be found in suitable habitat within the given range.   At any particular time a species is as likely to be increasing or decreasing in numbers and extending or contracting its geographical range as to be static in these respects.   In Britain the recent decrease of the Chough and increase of the Jackdaw are examples of this.   I have sometimes used the word 'India' in a geographical sense for the Indian subcontinent of (politically) India, Pakistan and Bangladesh.

The American Museum of Natural History authorities have been most helpful in sending specimens to me on loan.

I have little hope that I have not missed some published information that should have been included. Some may disagree with my opinions on relationships or interpretations of behaviour.   I shall be glad to have any omissions pointed out or to receive constructive criticism.   It must be emphasized that one of the book's purposes is to indicate what is *not* known.

I hope it will encourage readers to record their observations on any of the less well-known forms that they may come across; also that the information given here on the better-known species will make them of greater interest and less liable to be dismissed by the birdwatcher with some mental paraphrase of Aesop's 'It's only a crow and that signifies nothing!'

ACKNOWLEDGEMENTS

While preparing this book I have had much help and encouragement from my friends and colleagues in the Sub-department of Ornithology of the British Museum (Natural History) and from many ornithologists and others elsewhere who have contributed valuable information or helpful discussion.

I am particularly indebted to Dr Dean Amadon, Professor Russel P. Balda, Dr Franklin Coombs, Mr and Mrs John Field, Professor J. W. Hardy, Mr David Holyoak, Dr Leon Kelso, The Hon. Miriam Rothschild, Mr Ian Rowley, Dr Kenneth Simmons, Mr Kenneth Spencer, Dr Charles Vaurie and Dr C. E. Woolfenden; also to Mr Peter Olney, Curator of Birds at the London Zoo, for allowing me facilities to study birds in his charge.

CHAPTER 1
NOMENCLATURE: GENERA, SPECIES, SUB-SPECIES
AND VARIETIES

Here I shall try to define such scientific and popular terms as are likely to concern the average person interested in crows or other birds and to define the sense in which certain terms, which might otherwise be ambiguous to some readers, are used in this book. Those wishing to delve at all deeply in avian taxonomy will, however, need to consult one of the many works dealing specifically with the subject.

Birds of the crow family belong to the order Passeriformes: the passerine birds. This order is, in an evolutionary sense, relatively recent and highly successful. The resultant large number of contemporary passerine species has been one factor that has influenced ornithologists to divide up this order into very many different families. The differences between passerine families are usually less marked than those between other bird families. Also, as would be expected, the passerines show a number of species whose familial affinities are in doubt.

The corvids, as here envisaged, are usually (e.g. Blake & Vaurie, 1962) treated as a separate family, Corvidae. It has been suggested (Amadon, 1944) that it might be better to treat the crow family only as a subfamily, Corvinae, and to include in the Corvidae the birds-of-paradise, bell-magpies, orioles, drongos and possibly, helmet-shrikes. In the present state of knowledge I do not think this has much to commend it. Comparative studies of passerine egg white proteins suggest that the Corvidae are probably more closely related to the shrikes, Laniidae, than to any other group (Sibley, 1970). I concur with Amadon and Stonor that the wattled crows, *Callaeas*, of New Zealand and the West African *Picathartes* should not be included with the corvids.

The Corvidae have sometimes been subdivided into two subfamilies, Corvinae and Garrulinae, but such subdivision of them is, in my opinion, unnecessary.

Below the subfamily the term 'tribe' is sometimes used for groups of closely related genera. A term of more concern to the non-taxonomist is the genus (plural genera). A genus is a group of species that are related to each other and all of whose members appear to be more closely akin to other species within the same genus than they are to any species in other genera; for example the choughs, genus *Pyrrhocorax*, or Old World jays, genus *Garrulus*. As would be expected, authorities often disagree as to what constitutes a genus, some (the 'lumpers') preferring to recognize large genera, and others (the 'splitters') to put in the same genus only very close relatives. Unfortunately an almost equally good case can too often be made out for either course, especially within the crow family. It must be recognized that genera are, to some extent, units of convenience and decisions as to whether to recognize a particular genus must often be arguable or arbitrary, or both. Naturally, for Nature has no regard for man's convenience, there are sometimes species that are intermediate between those in one genus and those in another.

The categories of sub-genus, species-group and species sub-group are sometimes used to denote (in that order) degrees of relationship within a genus. They are not, however, formal categories in the scientific nomenclature. Below them comes the superspecies, but this is better discussed after dealing with the species category.

The species is the basic category of classification in the sense that the species concept is more closely related to observable facts than are most other categories. The term 'species' has been variously defined, and most definitions have been objected to by someone on some grounds, good or otherwise. So far as corvids and other birds are concerned, one might, I think, say that a species consists of a number (usually a very large number) of individuals, all of which show more resemblances to each other than to any other species, interbreed freely wherever they come in contact with each other, and do not normally breed with individuals of other species. The Raven, Rook, Jackdaw and Magpie, are for example, obviously 'good' species. In scientific nomenclature a species is designated by a specific name, *not* capitalized, following the generic name. Thus *Corvus corax* (the Raven), *Cissa chinensis* (the Green Magpie) and so on.

In different parts of its range a species of bird may, like man, show geographical variation. For example, the Magpies of Arabia have larger bills and less white on the wings than our English Magpies, those of Kamschatka have smaller bills and more extensive white areas on the wings, those of the Tibetan uplands have proportionately larger wings. Such differing populations are termed races or subspecies. They are given a third scientific name (tri-nomial) which in the case of the first described or nominate form is a repetition of the specific name. Thus the Magpie of southern Scandinavia and much of western Europe is *Pica p. pica*, the Arabian Magpie is *Pica pica asirensis* and so on.

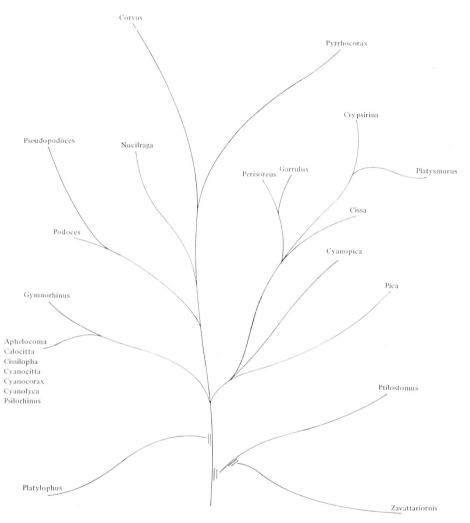

FIG. D.1. Presumed relationships of corvine genera. In this and subsequent dendrograms parallel lines between the 'branch' of a genus, species or group, and its 'stem' indicate that its derivation is highly uncertain but thought to be most probably as shown.

The form of the species that was first described and named in some publication is usually called the nominate form or nominate race. Sometimes it is called the typical form because the first specimen so described is known as the 'type' of the species. Typical form (or race or subspecies) can, however, be misleading as it may wrongly suggest that the form first described is, somehow, more typical (using the word in its everyday sense) of its species than are others that happened to be discovered and described later.

Unless they are separated by natural barriers, such as the sea or areas of country unsuitable for the species to inhabit, subspecies intergrade with each other, and many individuals – indeed all of them in some areas – will be intermediate in character. Also, of course, some subspecies are more distinct than others. Many of them have been named by over-zealous taxonomists because of very small average differences. Under the species headings in this book I have in many cases described and named only the more distinct of such geographical races. By doing this it is possible to give a general idea of what the species looks like and the degree of difference that it shows in different parts of its range. On the other hand, to describe all the many subspecies that have been named on very slight differences of size and colour would confuse rather than clarify the position for the average reader and would take up too much space. Any subspecies that has not been described here is very similar indeed to one or other of those that have been.

Geographic races may in time come to differ so much from their parent stock that they evolve into new species. Usually, perhaps always, such speciation can take place only if they are isolated from other populations. This may come about in many ways. Some members of a species may invade an island whither others of their kind do not follow. A species may disappear from large areas of its range through alteration of the habitat, leaving isolated populations separated by areas of country no longer suitable for it. If, after such a period of isolation, something happens to cause the two populations to come together again they may now have become so different that they will no longer interbreed. Each has, in fact, become a separate species.

They may, however, interbreed when they meet again but if the resultant 'hybrid' offspring are for any reason less viable than the 'pure' members of both populations then selection will favour any characters that tend to prevent mating between the two stocks. Such characters as a tendency to prefer different types of country when breeding (which would tend to re-isolate the two stocks even though they were in the same geographical area), or the development of different colour patterns (which, by imprinting, would discourage pairing between the two) might, for example, be 'seized on' and developed by natural selection in such circumstances. In this way full specific status may be achieved only after a period during which there has been some interbreeding between the two reunited forms.

Where two similar forms, which are clearly derived from a common ancestor, now occupy different geographical areas and appear too distinct to be treated as races of one species, they are commonly given specific rank but within the same superspecies. A superspecies is, as its name suggests, a form whose geographical representatives have evolved to the point where they are best considered as species rather than races. Perhaps it would be more correct to say that they have evolved to a point between the category of race and that of species but, in scientific nomenclature, are considered best treated as species and given specific names. Occasionally the term 'semispecies' is used for such members of a super-species, but there is as yet no particular designation for them in the scientific (Latin) terms. Sometimes the geographical representatives of a form have diverged considerably. In such cases they are not usually classed as members of a superspecies even although this is, or at any rate was, their relationship. I have in this book used the term 'geographical representatives' to indicate the status of all such forms.

Naturally there is sometimes doubt as to whether the geographical representatives of a form should be considered as species within a superspecies or as races of one species. This cannot always be decided solely on the amount of visible difference between its members.

For example, some of the subspecies of Steller's Jay, *Cyanocitta stelleri*, differ more in appearance from one another than do such related species as the Australian Raven and the Little Crow, *Corvus coronoides* and *C. bennetti*. In these cases there can be little doubt as to the correctness of this treatment as the most different forms of Steller's Jay are connected by intermediate ones; the Australian Raven and the Little Crow live in the same areas without interbreeding. Where there is considerable doubt as to whether a form should be given specific or only subspecific rank I think it is preferable, in a book of this type, to take the former course, in order to ensure that any available information can be unambiguously attached to the form concerned.

In the case of the Jay, *Garrulus glandarius*, some very distinct forms occupy different geographical regions. Most of these are, however, connected by forms which show some degree of intermediacy. Such information as is available does not suggest that there are specifically significant differences of behaviour or biology between even the most different-appearing forms. I have, therefore, treated them as conspecific but dealt with each main group of forms separately. The Green Jay, *Cyanocorax yncas*, has been treated in the same way for like reasons. Because of their very distinct appearance and their having different vernacular names in most European languages, like treatment has been used for the conspecific Hooded and Carrion Crows.

The status of the various forms is discussed in the introduction to the group to which they belong, where the taxonomy and relationships within each group are dealt with.

Where two closely-related species whose ranges overlap or adjoin are very similar in appearance they are often termed sibling species. Needless to say there are different opinions as to what degree of resemblance must be shown before this term should be used. The term 'variety' is sometimes incorrectly used when species or race is meant. The word variety should be used only for those aberrant individuals that differ markedly from the norm of their species; such as silver-grey Carrion Crows or white Magpies. In a wild state such varieties are usually less viable than normal individuals and tend soon to die or be killed. Under modern conditions they have even less chance of survival than they otherwise would, as they usually attract the attention of the man with the gun.

The term 'breed' means a well-established domesticated variety that has been 'fixed' by artificial selection so that it 'breeds true', more or less. This term can, therefore, only be used in reference to domesticated creatures and not to wild species such as all the Corvidae still are.

Throughout this book the terms 'group(s)' and 'form(s)' are used in a general sense as convenient. Their meaning in any particular case will be clear from the context. The term 'hybrid' is used, as in other ornithological books, for the offspring resulting from the interbreeding of distinct races of the *same* species, that have secondarily come into contact after presumed geographical separation; as well as in its everyday meaning of the offspring of two *different* species. The context makes clear which is meant.

REFERENCES

AMADON, D. 1944. The genera of Corvidae and their relationships. *Amer. Mus. Novit.* No. 1251.
BLAKE, E. R. & VAURIE, C. 1962. *'Peters' Check-list of birds of the world*, vol. 15. Cam. Mass.
SIBLEY, C. G. 1970. A comparative study of the egg-white proteins of passerine birds. *Peabody Mus. Bull.* **32**.

CHAPTER 2
ADAPTIVE RADIATION AND SOME ADAPTIVE CHARACTERS

The differences found within the crow family as a result of speciation and adaptation have been broadly indicated in the introduction. Here I propose to discuss more fully the adaptive radiation found within the Corvidae, its geographical distribution, and some characters that seem correlated with such adaptations.

The amount of adaptive radiation and consequent differentiation found within the Corvidae surpasses that within many passerine families, and equals that within others such as the babblers (Timaliidae), warblers (Sylviidae) and estrildines (Estrildidae). It falls, indeed, not far short of that found within some of the most numerous and versatile of the presumably older non-passerine groups such as the pigeons and parrots. The majority of corvids are at least partly arboreal but some have emancipated themselves from dependence on trees.

Forms which nest and roost in trees but obtain part of their food from the ground are found in all parts of the world where corvids occur, except for treeless areas and possibly some areas of dense jungle. Some species that are primarily ground feeders but usually nest in trees can adapt themselves to treeless country, nesting on cliffs, bushes or even on the ground, as do the Hooded Crow, North-western Crow, Rook and Magpie in parts of their range. Among the *Corvus* species the ravens of Africa and Eurasia have gone a step further in this direction. Some of them over much or, in some species, all of their ranges are typical cliff nesters and quite independent of trees. The same is largely true of the Jackdaw, *C. monedula*, although perhaps only as a result of man's alteration of habitats.

The choughs, *Pyrrhocorax*, are birds of rocky mountainous or coastal regions. They sometimes perch on trees when these are available within their habitat. Choughs are restricted to the Palaearctic region with a small outpost, or remnant, of one species in Ethiopia.

In the steppe deserts of central Asia and the high uplands of Tibet the Corvidae have evolved terrestrial forms in the ground jays or desert choughs, *Podoces* and *Pseudopodoces*. These bear a convergent resemblance to some of the larger larks and to the Australian quail-thrushes. They often nest in and perch on trees and bushes although otherwise ground dwellers. Hume's Ground Jay has diverged furthest from the more typical arboreal corvids. It is very small, entirely terrestrial and digs out its own nest cavity in earth banks.

Corvids that are highly arboreal and obtain most or all of their food above ground occur in the tropics and sub-tropics of both Asia and America but are, rather surprisingly, entirely absent from Africa. The Ethiopian region is singularly poor in corvids, especially in comparison with its richness of species in many other passerine families. No forest-dwelling corvid occurs in Africa south of the Sahara. Temperate woodlands, whose trees bear no fruit and harbour few insects in winter, generally support only species which are sufficiently versatile to find food, or to hide and later recover it, on or in the ground as well as in the branches. It is, however, likely that the grey jays of the northern forests obtain most or all of their winter food and hide their stored food above ground except when a fortuitous campsite or remains of a carcass killed by wolf or man supply food at ground level.

Relatively long wings with medium or shortish tails are characteristic of forms that often undertake fairly long-continued flight. In forms which spend much time soaring and gliding, relatively long wings may be correlated with a rather long and graduated tail, as in the Raven and the Thick-billed Raven, or with a much shorter tail as in the White-necked Raven. This latter tendency is carried still further in the Fan-tailed Raven with its broad wings and very short tail. Comparative studies on the flight behaviour of these four species in relation to their different tail and wing proportions would be of great interest.

Long tails, in which the central two or four feathers often greatly exceed the others in length, are found especially in forms that tend to keep in or near cover. In some cases, as with the highly developed spatulate tails of some of the tree pies, they are used as balancing organs. It is, however, possible that very long ornate tails are not so much functional adaptations to a highly arboreal way of life as display plumage which can only be 'afforded' if the owner keeps in or near cover or has few avian predators.

KEY TO PLATE 1

Some old world corvids, to show diversity within the family.

(1) Hooded Racquet-tailed Tree Pie, *Crypsirina cucullata*; (2) Green Magpie, *Cissa chinensis*; (3) Formosan Blue Magpie, *Cissa caerulea*; (4) Azure-winged Magpie, *Cyanopica cyana*; (5) Siberian Jay, *Perisoreus infaustus*; (6) Hume's Ground Jay, *Pseudopodoces humilis*; (7) Henderson's Ground Jay, *Podoces hendersoni*; (8) Nutcracker, *Nucifraga caryocatactes*: the very distinct form *multipunctata*; (9) Chough, *Pyrrhocorax pyrrhocorax*.

PLATE 1

Robert Gillmor

Less extremely long tails, such as that of the Magpie, may be largely functional as, judging from this bird's agility and quick reactions when mobbing predators, its long tail and rounded wings enable it to fly up or dodge with great speed. The same may be true of the Piapiac. The Magpie's tail does, however, appear to incommode it when flying a distance in the open, at least by comparison with *Corvus* species or even with the Jay *Garrulus glandarius*. The more *Corvus*-like proportions of the Tibetan race of the Magpie, with its relatively long wings and short tail, seem to be correlated with the appreciable distances which it more often flies over open country.

Differences in size and shape of bill are, without much doubt, usually correlated with differences of food or feeding methods. Where there are minor differences from the 'typical' stout, slightly hook-tipped bill, much further study is needed in most cases before we can be sure how far these are correlated with different feeding habits. For example, the small sharp hook and notch at the tip of the Jay's bill seems adapted to biting open and breaking up acorns, but this hooked tip is less developed in the other *Garrulus* species and almost absent in some New World jays, all of which also feed largely on acorns. This shrike-like bill tip, which is seen more markedly in *Platylophus*, may therefore, as in the shrikes, be a prey-disabling mechanism that has been put to use on acorns, at a later stage in evolution, by the *Garrulus* species.

The strong pointed bills of nutcrackers are used in prising loose the seeds from conifer cones, and the hard ridge inside their lower mandibles in cracking them. Those forms of the Eurasian Nutcracker that habitually feed on hazel nuts tend to have stouter and heavier bills, probably as an adaptation to breaking these very large and hard-shelled seeds. The ground jays and the Chough have long curved bills with which the latter certainly and the former probably dig and probe in a Hoopoe-like manner when seeking food.

In general, Gloger's rule (that in a given species, forms in warm and humid areas tend to be most heavily pigmented) and Allen's rule (that extensions of the body tend to be longer in warmer areas) apply to most corvid species with wide geographical ranges. They are particularly well illustrated in the Magpie if a specimen from, say, Kamschatka, is compared with one from Arabia. As with other birds, forms inhabiting cold climates usually have noticeably thicker, fluffier plumage and proportionately smaller bills and feet than those from warmer regions. Such plumage is very evident in the grey jays and in the northern forms of *Garrulus*. In contrast to these, the nutcrackers, which are also birds of cold boreal and montane woodlands, have rather short close-fitting plumage which must, presumably, be equally effective for insulation.

In America the corvids show a lesser degree of divergence than in the Old World where they almost certainly originated. Only the genera *Corvus*, *Nucifraga*, and *Perisoreus* are common to both Old and New Worlds. No forms comparable with the choughs or the ground jays exist in the Americas.

Otherwise, adaptive radiation of the American jays has to a considerable extent paralleled that of Old World forms. They are, however, more numerous in species, have developed fewer long-tailed forms and show more species obviously intermediate between the most divergent forms. It would seem possible that during the presumed longer time that corvids have been evolving in the Old World many previously-existing species, some of them probably just such 'connecting links', have become extinct.

Crests of various types and erect or fan-forming nasal or frontal plumes have apparently evolved independently in several groups. There may be considerable difference in crest or nasal plume development between forms of a single species, as in the Green Jay. In Steller's Jay length of crest is positively correlated with relatively open habitat. However, no corvid of really open country is crested, although this may merely reflect the general arboreal tendencies of the family.

The South American jays include some large and rather crow-like forms, that show both a relatively simplified colour pattern and in some cases a tendency to fly freely over open country. It is probably at least partly the absence of *Corvus* species that has permitted this development.

KEY TO PLATE 2

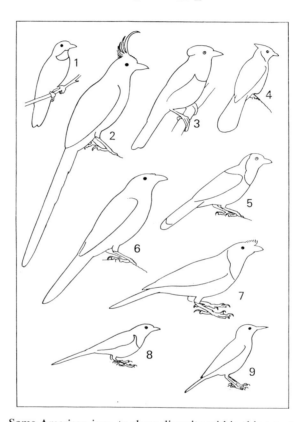

Some American jays, to show diversity within this group.

(1) Silver-throated Jay, *Cyanolyca argentigula*; (2) Magpie-jay, *Calocitta formosa*; (3) Plush-capped Jay, *Cyanocorax chrysops*; (4) Blue Jay, *Cyanocitta cristata*; (5) White-tailed Jay, *Cyanocorax mystacalis*; (6) Brown Jay, *Psilorhinus morio*; (7) Azure Jay, *Cyanocorax caeruleus*; (8) Green Jay, *Cyanocorax yncas* (Yucatan form); (9) Piñon Jay, *Gymnorhinus cyanocephala*.

Plate 2

Robert Gillmor

CHAPTER 3
PLUMAGE AND COLORATION

Coloration of plumage and soft parts

In many different bird families there is a tendency for the smaller species to be most cryptically coloured and the largest species most conspicuous but at the same time most simply patterned. This general tendency is shown within the crow family which, however, appears to have been less influenced by the need for concealing coloration than many other groups of birds. Only in a few species, such as some of the ground jays, does there appear to have been strong selection for cryptic plumage. The plumage of some other species may, however, aid concealment from a bird-of-prey looking down from above. This seems probable for those corvids with relatively dull-coloured upperparts. It may also apply to some relatively bright species, which may be cryptically coloured in their natural environments.

Corvids tend to have relatively simple although often highly ornate plumage patterns. None of them show cryptic streaked plumage patterns of the kinds that are so widespread in passerine (and other) birds. These streaked patterns are particularly evident in and adapted for the concealment of species that live or feed among grass although, in their less extreme forms, they occur also in some partly arboreal species.

Some plumage patterns that are conspicuous at close range or in the open may be disruptive and thus have a concealing function when the bird is in cover. The white wing patch of the European forms of the Jay, for example, is used in display but, at least to human eyes, often appears as a spot of light among the foliage and makes the bird more difficult to pick out.

In every species of bird whose behaviour is known, all bright or very conspicuously contrasting areas of plumage serve a social function. Either they are exhibited by special movements in hostile, sexual or self-assertive displays, as with the black malar stripes of the Jay or the white shoulder patches and shining secondaries of the Magpie, or else they are shown automatically when the bird spreads its wings or tail. These latter types of markings, such as the white tail feather ends of the Lanceolated Jay or the white rump of the Jay, serve to alert conspecifics and, under appropriate circumstances, to stimulate or enable them more easily to follow the bird that has taken wing. The terms 'display plumage' and 'signal markings' are often used for both types of conspicuous markings, but the former is best restricted to such as are 'deliberately' displayed and the latter to markings that are automatically shown by movements used in taking wing, alighting or so on. The same feathers may, however, function both as display plumage and as signal markings.

What has been said above concerning conspicuous plumage areas does not imply that all markings that appear beautiful to us must have a social function. This is not always the case. For example, the very lovely and, at close quarters, quite strikingly patterned inner secondaries of the Lanceolated Jay do not appear to be used in any display, so it seems likely that they may function as a disruptive pattern and aid concealment, especially for an incubating bird, from aerial predators.

In very many birds, forms long isolated on islands or in montane forests often show partial or complete loss of bright markings that their nearest relatives living elsewhere possess. This is presumably because one of the functions of such markings is to ensure species recognition and, once the birds are isolated from close relatives, their advantages may not compensate for their disadvantages in making the bird more conspicuous. The corvids, however, show few examples of this. The coloration of Lidth's Jay is one example, if we assume its ancestral form to have been, like the related Lanceolated Jay, more clearly and brightly patterned. So also may be the very dull and concolorous Sooty Jay of the montane conifer forests of eastern central Asia.

The corvids show particularly well the not uncommon situation in which a species which does *not* co-exist with closely related species nevertheless retains conspicuous markings. The Jay, the Blue Jay and the Magpie, for example, have no sympatric relatives over most of their present ranges. A comparison of related species gives the impression that partial or complete obliteration of ornate markings through the spread of black or dark pigment has occurred among several different groups of corvids, sometimes, as with the American jays, in spite of sympatry with related forms. This has been carried to an extreme in the all-black plumage of typical crows and choughs.

There are perhaps physiological advantages in having entirely black plumage. Those parts of feathers that have heavy deposition of dark melanin pigment are less susceptible to wear and tear than unpigmented or less heavily pigmented parts of the same feathers. It has also been proved (Heppner, 1970) that black plumage is more efficient at absorbing solar energy. It is therefore likely that black-plumaged birds are able to maintain body heat more efficiently at low temperatures, if sunlight is available.

There are also possible social advantages in all-black coloration. It enables the bird to be readily seen against most backgrounds and recognized at a distance by conspecifics. It is no accident that the typical crows and the choughs are mostly birds of open country and/or travel considerable distances on the wing in their everyday life. In this connection, those crows which have grey or white areas on neck or body hardly constitute an exception, as they are, in most situations, as conspicuous as all-black forms.

It has been suggested (Cody) that birds of two different species may evolve closely similar colours and markings because it is advantageous to one or both of them to show some of the normal intra-specific behaviour towards members of the other species, and vice versa. This might enable species with similar feeding or other requirements to maintain separate territories, instead of both species competing with each other in overlapping territories. It might also facilitate sharing of abundant food supplies or harrying of mutually harmful predators.

Interspecific territorial exclusion apparently exists between some similarly-coloured woodpecker species. It does not, however, occur to any extent in those concolorous crow species whose behaviour is known. Many pairs of Rooks or Jackdaws often nest within the breeding territory of a single pair of Carrion Crows; many pairs of Carrion Crows may hold breeding territories within that of a single pair of Ravens. A similar state of affairs appears to exist with *Corvus* species in Australia and elsewhere. Breeding pairs of one species may attack or harass crows of other species within their territories but they seldom show hostility to the same degree as they do towards conspecifics and they do not usually prevent them from breeding there.

That different species of crows may associate on newly sown fields, garbage tips and other feeding grounds, spend the night at a communal roost, or fly together when on migration, is common knowledge. Such behaviour is at least partly brought about because the similar black plumage attracts or elicits a following response in related species as well as in conspecifics. It is, however, much less certain that the presumed advantages of this have been responsible for sympatric *Corvus* species developing or (more probably) retaining similar colouring. Prior to man's pastoral and agricultural activities it is likely that there was less overlap of feeding sites between *Corvus* species than is now the case. All the species concerned appear, as one would expect, to show a preference for following or associating with conspecifics rather than congeners of other species in most situations. The strongest interspecific attraction seems to be between the Rook and the Jackdaw although the advantages to either are far from clear and would repay study. There seems no evidence that either fares less well in the few places where it is found plentifully but the other is rare or absent.

The *Corvus* species show clearly that it is sometimes possible for related species to exist in sympatry even when they are similar or identical in plumage colour, not greatly dissimilar in size, have no conspicuous or distinctive species-specific markings, and have some similar and some identical agonistic and sexual displays. Differences of voice (sometimes not very marked to a human ear), behaviour, and the minor differences of appearance are sufficient to prevent interspecific pair formation in a wild state. In captivity Rooks often readily form mixed pairs with Carrion or Hooded Crows and the same would probably prove true of the many less strongly differentiated sympatric *Corvus* species.

In view of the frequency of black display plumage in many birds, including some corvids, it is probable that the all-black glossy *Corvus* species appear anything but dull to avian eyes. Also, of course, by differentially erecting areas of plumage, by movements of wings and tail and by drawing white nictitating membranes over the eyes, they can greatly alter their appearance when displaying.

Most corvids have black or dark legs and feet. Their bills vary from ivory-white to black but are most often dark or black in colour. Bright yellow or red bills and legs occur in the green and blue magpies and the choughs, having apparently evolved independently in these two groups, as it seems unlikely that they are more closely related to each other than each is to forms with blackish bills and legs. The Yellow-billed Magpie, *Pica nuttalli*, has the bill so coloured. Partially pink or pinkish bills occur in three rather aberrant *Corvus* species and in the immature Piapiac.

Dark brown is the commonest iris colour in the crow family, although some corvids have white, blue, violet, reddish, yellow or golden eyes. Some of the dark-eyed forms have white or pale nictitating membranes which are drawn over the eyes in certain displays.

Sexual differences and the differences of juveniles and immatures are discussed in the section on plumage sequences and age differences. In most species the juveniles do not differ greatly in colour from the adults.

REFERENCES

CODY, M. L. 1969. Convergent characteristics in sympatric species: a possible relation to interspecific competition and aggression. *Condor* **71**: 223–239.
HEPPNER, F. 1970. The metabolic significance of differential absorption of radiant energy by black and white birds. *Condor* **72**: 50–59.

Plumage sequences and age differences

Newly-hatched corvids usually have a very sparse amount of nestling down or are naked. The nutcrackers have the nestling down more profuse, presumably an adaptation to early nesting in cold climates. The nestling down (when present) is replaced by the juvenile plumage, to the tips of which it adheres for some little time, as in other birds.

The cover feathers of the juvenile plumage are usually looser and more 'woolly' in texture than the adult feathers, often to a marked degree. The wing and tail quills are often slightly weaker and shorter than their adult counterparts but not to any appreciable extent. In some long-tailed forms the central (longest) tail feathers may be much shorter in the juvenile plumage.

In most corvids the juvenile plumage is very similar in colour and pattern to the adult's, usually differing only in being slightly duller. Black, grey or vinous brown of adults may be replaced by very dark smoky grey, brownish grey and rufous brown in the juvenile. In a few forms, however, such as the Canada Jay and the Yucatan Jay (see col. pl. 3) there are striking colour differences between adult and juvenile plumages. The remarkably un-corvine juvenile plumage of the Crested Jay, *Platylophus*, is discussed elsewhere.

The moult of the juvenile body plumage usually starts within a month or two of leaving the nest. The juvenile wing and tail quills are, as in many other passerines, usually retained until the second moult when the bird is from 12 to 20 months old. In some forms, however, the tail quills may be regularly or sometimes moulted and in at least one species, the Azure-winged Magpie, the wing quills are sometimes, probably usually, replaced at the first moult.

Although striking differences of colour or pattern between adult and immature plumages are unusual in corvids, appreciable differences in appearance are less uncommon. The juvenile's iris, bill and mouth are usually different in colour from the adult's. In many species the young bird, even after it has become independent and passed its first moult, is distinguishable at a glance from an adult by its differently coloured bill or eye. In such cases the bill is usually rather similar to what it was in the young juvenile but the iris colour often differs from that of both younger and fully adult birds. Such differences of

KEY TO PLATE 3

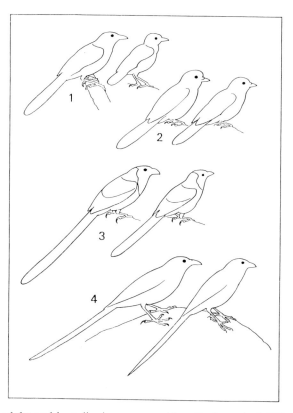

Differences between adults and juveniles in some corvids. Such marked differences in appearance between adult and juvenile as are shown by the Yucatan and Grey Jays are most unusual in the family.

(1) Yucatan Jays, *Cissilopha yucatanica*; (2) Grey Jays, *Perisoreus canadensis*; (3) Southern Tree Pies, *Crypsirina leucogastra*; (4) Piapiacs, *Ptilostomus afer*.

PLATE 3

Robert Gillmor

bill and iris colour may be retained until the bird is about two years old. For example, in Australian crows the irides are at first bluish or grey (as with most or all *Corvus* species), then become brown for a considerable period before changing to the white or white and blue of the adults. In the Piapiac first-year birds have a pink, black-tipped bill, very like that of a fledgling juvenile, which at once sets them apart from the adults whose bills are entirely black.

In the Rook adult and first-year birds show no colour differences but are nevertheless usually different in appearance owing to the bare whitish faces of the former and the feathered or still partly feathered faces of most of the immatures. From a Rook's eye view, facing a potential mate or rival, this difference is probably just as immediately noticeable in the eastern form in which only the forehead of the adult is bare.

Where marked differences in appearance between adult and immature corvids occur they seem correlated with highly social habits or with the likelihood of food supplies being very limited in distribution at certain times. Thus those American jays which show marked age differences in bill colour tend to live in rather closely integrated flocks and, in some species, more than two individuals are involved in feeding each brood of young.

It seems likely that in such cases the immediately visible age differences help to lessen or prevent serious fighting, either through partially inhibiting adult aggressiveness (in conjunction with appeasing displays by the immatures) or through discouraging the younger and usually weaker immatures from challenging an adult, or through both these traits working together. Appeasing displays from young Canada Jays at a food source are usual, and immature Rooks at a breeding rookery often respond to any aggression near them, whether directed at them or not, with the appeasing display.

It is possible that adults of such species may find birds with immature characters less attractive sexually. If so, an adult that was unpaired for any reason would not pair with an immature bird unless no suitable adult were available. This might be an additional function of any striking differences between adults and immatures if the latter are likely, on average, to be less efficient parents. Nor would this necessarily be to the ultimate disadvantage of the immature that had been passed over. Since corvids, as well as some other birds, are often at greater risk when caring for young, a bird that failed to get a mate and had an extra year or two to increase its experience of life and learn details of its habitat might well end by producing more viable young than one that acquired a mate and started breeding at an earlier age.

Except for the length and texture of the juvenile wing and tail quills (if retained), the plumage of the first-year birds does not usually differ from that of adults, although in some American jays there are differences of colour or pattern of the head markings. Once the adult plumage has been acquired it is renewed without any alteration yearly. Unpigmented, abnormally coloured or otherwise defective feathers may, as with other birds, be produced at any moult as a result of sickness, inadequate diet or injury.

Corvids moult completely once a year. The main stages of the moult are always after the nesting season but casting and renewal of the primaries may, especially in the larger species, begin in spring. In species, such as the Raven, which fly considerable distances in their everyday life, moult of the larger primaries proceeds rather slowly so that the flying ability is never impaired. Moulting and the feeding of young may take place concurrently, especially in northern species in which full advantage must be aken of the short summer. There may be differences in the timing and duration of moult between different populations of the same species, especially when it has a wide latitudinal range. No attempt is made in this book to give full details of the moults of individual species but references to some detailed moult studies are given in the species sections.

Although feathers are usually said to fall out during the moult, it may be added that in Jays at least, the large quills of wings and tail usually seem to be pulled out by the bird when preening. As the Jay attempts to draw a wing or tail feather between its mandibles, the loosened feather comes away in its bill. When this happens the bird appears surprised and completely at a loss; it usually holds the feather for some seconds before discarding it.

No corvids show marked sexual differences of size or colour. The females tend to be very slightly duller in colour or smaller in size, this being perhaps most marked in some of the American jays. Such differences are found in the majority of birds in which the sexes are usually described as 'alike'. These slight differences are, on the whole, less in corvids than, for example, in tits or pigeons.

Female corvids also tend to have proportionately smaller bills than males and this may sometimes be correlated with a tendency to take smaller prey, thus possibly decreasing competition between the members of a pair.

Even in species, such as the Jay, in which size differences overlap and big females are larger than small males, there seem to be no recorded instances of *wild* pairs in which the male was smaller than the female. I have seen many pairs of Rooks, Jays and Carrion Crows in which male and female appeared, in the field, to be of equal size and many others in which the male appeared larger but never the converse. It is probable that this is because male dominance, at least initially and in a psychological sense, is a factor in normal pair-formation.

In many species, perhaps all, there are some sexual differences in voice and postures. Certain calls or displays may be used only by one sex. There is also some evidence that in many species most calls may be uttered with differences of pitch by the two sexes.

CHAPTER 4
BEHAVIOUR

Feeding habits

That birds of the crow family tend to be omnivorous, and versatile in their methods of obtaining food, has been emphasized by many writers. Even the most omnivorous are, however, only so within limits. They are no more capable of utilizing large amounts of bulky and un-nutritious vegetable food than are most other birds. The idea that because such species as, for example, the Carrion Crow, eat a great many different things they can therefore 'live on anything' is far from true, as the poor condition of all too many captive crows bears eloquent witness. For versatility and initiative when seeking food it is probable that at least the typical crows of the genus *Corvus* do surpass most birds of other groups, although some non-corvine species, such as the House Sparrow and the Common Grackle, probably equal them.

Particular feeding methods of different groups or species are described under their respective headings, but a general account is attempted here.

Corvids seek their food either on or above ground. They exploit such varied terrains as high alpine slopes and cliff ledges, plains, cultivated fields, the woodland floor, the sea's edge at low tide, the conifers of the northern forest, and the intertangled creepers of tropical jungles. Some species extend their feeding sites even further by catching flying insects on the wing, picking up floating food from the sea or inland waters, or catching fish in the shallows. In general, however, corvine birds feed either on the ground or in trees. No species relies to any great extent on flycatching, flotsam or fishing.

Many corvids seek food both in trees and on the ground. A few, so far as is known, forage only on the ground or only in vegetation above it. Some of the tropical or subtropical tree pies and jays have not been seen taking food from the ground but, bearing in mind the versatility of most corvids, it is rather unlikely that they *never* do so. The converse may apply to the Chough, the ground jays, and some species of typical crows that have been recorded feeding only on the ground. Of species whose feeding habits have been much observed, the Rook and the Alpine Chough are primarily ground feeders that at certain times and places regularly take, respectively, acorns and walnuts from trees, and berries from shrubs or bushes. If, as is the case with many less well-known species, we had only a few intermittent observations on them we might easily and wrongly assume them to be obligatory ground feeders.

Of our British species all the typical crows seek most of their food on the ground although all, with the possible exception of the Raven, take some food from trees. The Magpie is also mainly a ground feeder while the Jay habitually seeks food both on the ground and in trees or shrubs. For obvious reasons no bird that relies on such foods as large insects, seeds or fruits can be a year round arboreal feeder in temperate regions. This is, however, possible in the tropics where some species of tree or other is always bearing fruit, seeds or nectar-holding flowers and where some insects and other small arboreal creatures are always active.

All corvids whose feeding habits are known take both animal and vegetable foods, usually a variety of both kinds. Some, such as the Nutcracker and the Piñon Jay may, however, be very largely dependent on one or two foods and would be unlikely to survive were their principal food plants to be exterminated.

As well as looking keenly about for visible food items most, and probably all, corvids discover concealed foods in various ways. They dig in loose soil with the typical side to side flicking of the bill used by many passerines and some other birds, tear off loose bark or tear open adhering leaves, flip over bits of wood, cow-dung or other objects lying on the ground. They also try to open up any small hole, crevice, or rolled-up leaf by the movement termed 'Zirkeln' in German, which has been translated as 'openbilled probing'. The bird inserts its closed bill into the hole or crevice and then forcibly opens or tries to open it. The tipping over of flattish objects lying on the ground is often achieved by an apparent combination of the 'Zirkeln' and a vigorous upward and forward heave as the bill is opened.

19

Food that requires breaking up, de-husking, or tearing to pieces is held down under one or both feet and torn, bitten or hammered with the bill. Sometimes food items are rubbed about on the ground or perch, or placed in some cleft or depression and there broken up with the bill without use of the feet. Some, perhaps all, species dislike using the feet for any food that is at all sticky or slimy. They prepare such foods for eating with the bill alone if it is possible to do so. Dry foods may, however, also be broken up with the bill alone.

Many species of typical crows have been seen to carry food in their feet although they do not usually do so. Frank Finn, writing on the House Crow in India, says he saw it drop inedible objects from its bill and catch them with its feet, but it did not risk using its feet for anything so valuable as food! This has been my impression with other crows. I have seen Carrion Crows and Rooks use their feet to catch and sometimes to carry twigs or pine cones when playing with them but have not seen them or any other corvid carry food in its feet. The Piñon Jay also sometimes uses its feet to carry food and has been seen to catch small birds by seizing them in its feet.

Crows sometimes place food objects in water before breaking them up and/or eating them. This dunking of food is commonly practised by (all?) individuals of many (but not all) species of *Corvus* in captivity and has been seen done by wild individuals of some species, such as the Carrion Crow. It seems especially prevalent in forms that often seek their food near water. It is generally interpreted as being a means of softening hard food, presumably because the Carrion Crow and House Crow have often been seen dunking hard crusts of bread. I do not believe this is the case as I can think of no hard natural food of any crow that could be quickly softened by dipping or placing it in water. From my experiments feeding various foods to captive corvids and to wild Carrion Crows I believe that any suggestion of stickiness in the food is the most potent stimulus to elicit dunking.

I think one function of food dunking is to prevent soiling of the bill or plumage with such substances as glutinous mud or egg white. It probably also makes the food easier to break up and swallow. It seems analogous to the 'washing' of their prey that is such a common habit of many waders when feeding on muddy ground near to water. Crows that are in the habit of dunking food objects seem to do so whenever these appear to be, for any reason, difficult or unpleasant to deal with. It is very probable that such birds may learn that hard bread is softened by this process. Hard human foods may also be sticky and observers may not always have appreciated this. For example, over-burnt bread crust is often 'tacky' to the touch, hard pastry may be smeared with jam or treacle. I have seen a Carrion Crow carry a large piece of jammy pastry about 450 metres to dunk it. Many species that have not been observed dunking food often drink immediately after eating any slightly sticky food (Holyoak *in litt.*, pers. obs.).

A tame Magpie that I kept for many years dunked only meat and any small birds or mammals she caught. The dunking of a live mouse has been recorded for a wild Yellow-billed Magpie. Here the wetting of the prey certainly made for quicker and more efficient plucking of the fur or feathers. Further observations are needed to show whether dunking is specific or individually learned behaviour. I think the latter is unlikely as captive crows seem uninfluenced in this matter by the example of their fellows. I have never seen a Pied Crow, *Corvus albus*, at the London Zoo, dunk anything, although its cage mate, a Collared Crow, *C. torquatus*, dunks everything that is not suitable for immediate swallowing. The latter bird habitually takes its official ration, a minced-up mixture of meat, biscuit, and possibly other substances, by the billful to the edge of its pool, places it in the water and then carefully dissects it, eating only the more palatable items.

Some *Corvus* species, and possibly also the Magpie, sometimes manage to rob larger predators of food. As this behaviour is usually correlated with predator mobbing it is discussed in the chapter on anti-predator behaviour.

The curiosity with which young corvids investigate any new objects that do not inspire considerable fear functions primarily to enable them to discover food supplies. It is shown, as with other birds, especially at the stage when the young bird can fly well but is still being supported mainly or entirely by its parents. Although at this stage the bird appears prompted by curiosity rather than hunger (very hungry individuals cease such inquisitive behaviour and beg from the parent if it is within sight) the movements used are essentially those employed in finding and dealing with food objects. In adult life such investigations are largely incorporated with or superseded by deliberate food-seeking, except sometimes by tame individuals. These, if adequately fed by their owners, may continue to show strong investigatory behaviour, no doubt because it provides an equivalent for the food-seeking which takes up so much of a wild corvid's time, interest, and energy.

Just as young wild corvids, especially when they begin to follow their parents about, pay particular attention to the feeding behaviour of the adults and thus, apparently, learn the appearance of many foods and where to find them, so hand-reared young assume that anything their owner, in his role of parent, examines or handles with interest must be edible. It is for this reason and not because of any 'love of destructiveness' that they often try to tear to pieces cameras or other possessions prized by their human owner.

The breaking open of food by dropping it on hard surfaces is known, within the Corvidae, only from some species of *Corvus*, which deal with shellfish in this way.

Indigestible food remains are usually disgorged in the form of rather friable pellets which soon disintegrate.

Food storage

The hiding or storing of food is widespread in the crow family; it may well occur in all species. It is sometimes said or implied that it is confined to forms dwelling in cold or temperate regions but this is not the case. Some tropical and subtropical species are known to hide food in captivity and it is most unlikely that they never do so when wild. Although the habit may be more useful in climates with cold winters, the fact that it has been most often observed in Europe and North America may merely reflect the greater number of bird watchers in these regions.

The food-hiding behaviour of each species is noted, where known, in the species section; here I shall discuss some general principles to avoid needless repetition. Although the term 'storing' is used for such behaviour it must be emphasized that, although a great number of food objects may be hidden fairly close together, wild corvids very seldom hide a large number of food objects in exactly the same place. Caged individuals who have only one or two possible hiding places available may do so of necessity.

Food storing is commonly shown when the bird has more food available than it is able or willing to eat at once, especially if the food is of a kind that will keep edible for some time. These two factors operate at both specific and individual levels. Thus the nutcrackers and some jays, which periodically find themselves presented with a temporary superabundance of acorns, nuts or conifer seeds are intensive food storers. At the individual level a Carrion Crow foraging in a field for small invertebrates usually swallows each capture as soon as found but if it suddenly finds some sandwiches left by a picnic party it will usually hide them away.

The movements used when putting food into a hiding place are essentially similar to, or identical with, those used when feeding young. Typically the food is held in the bill or throat, often having first been brought up from deeper in the gullet, throat or sublingual pouch. The bird then pushes its bill into the chosen hiding place. This may be the ground, among matted vegetation, or some crevice, hole or niche. If the food has been held in mouth or throat it is then ejected with the aid of the tongue and the bill is withdrawn. The food is then hidden from sight. This is done by raking or pulling over adjacent soil or vegetation with sideways movements of the bill similar to those used when digging for food, or by placing one or more stones, leaves or other objects on top of it. Where feasible both these methods are usually employed. Often the bird will go several feet from the hiding place to fetch an object to cover it with. The digging of holes in which to bury food by the Rook (Andrew), the use of bill and feet to prepare a hiding place by the Piñon Jay and the use of saliva by the Grey Jay are dealt with under the species headings. Unless otherwise stated in the species sections food-hiding methods are as here described for all corvids in which the behaviour is known.

Lorenz states that if no other material is available the Raven will cover its booty with some totally inadequate object such as a tiny bit of paper that makes it more, not less, conspicuous. I have, however, never seen this or any other corvid fail to cover completely the food it was hiding when it had the opportunity of doing so. Captive corvids in zoos, that are given no facilities for food storing, usually show much apparent mental stress at not being able to conceal from sight the food they try to hide. That hiding food is innate and that species which hide food will, therefore, try to do so even under conditions that make it, from a human viewpoint, pointless is undoubtedly true. On the other hand, many of them show some apparent insight in this connection. Lorenz records that tame Ravens that have been robbed a few times by their owner will learn to hide food out of his reach and will also try to hide it out of sight of other Ravens. He implies that smaller and allegedly less intelligent corvine species do not show such behaviour but this is not always so. Jays try to hide food out of sight of other Jays that are socially dominant to them. If a Jay sees a potential 'thief' near one of its caches it will often remove the hidden food and hide it again in a different place. In this situation it may either first drive away the other bird or, if this is a Jay dominant to itself, may loiter in the vicinity until the opportunity occurs to take out its booty before the other can interfere. I have also seen similar behaviour from the Rook.

Although, in general, food-hiding is correlated with a temporary superabundance of food, corvids do not always or even usually eat to repletion before beginning to hide food away. A Carrion Crow that comes upon several lumps of bread will often at once begin to hide them and only eat some when it has the last load ready for transportation. The voracity with which it then feeds often shows that it must have been extremely hungry (Goodwin, 1955). Gwinner found that Ravens store food more intensely when they are hungry and, in at least one instance which he cites, a Raven began to store before beginning to eat.

That the function of food-hiding is to provide a reserve for the hider which must, therefore, recover at least some of its hidden food, would appear self-evident. It is known that the Nutcracker relies very largely on its stores for food during the winter and spring (Swanberg). The Jay feeds extensively on acorns that it has previously hidden. Where it feeds much on scraps of human food the Carrion Crow habitually recovers and eats food which it has previously hidden, although to what extent it and most other species rely on food stores under natural conditions is not known. It would not, of course, be necessary for a species to feed largely on its hidden stores for the food-hiding habit to be selected for. If a bird only occasionally saved itself or its dependent young in a period of food shortage by this means the habit would be highly advantageous. I think it is likely that in all food-storing species the individual does make use of its stores. It is, however, possible that some species may retain the habit, at least to the extent of showing it under certain conditions, even though at their present stage of evolution they no longer make use of it.

Two other suggestions have been made as to the function of food-storing. One of these suggestions is that it serves to plant food trees and thus to perpetuate a habitat in which the species can thrive. That this effect is produced is unquestionable: the Jay is probably the chief factor in the natural spreading and perpetuation of oaks and the Nutcracker fulfils a similar function for *Pinus cembra* and some other conifers. In view of the time elapsing between the 'planting' of an acorn or conifer seed and the production of seeds by the resultant tree, any selective advantage of the food-hiding habit would presuppose that descendants of the original 'planter' were still inhabiting the area. It seems more likely that recovery of the hidden food by the individual that hides it has been the reason for the development and maintenance of food-storing.

Hardy makes the novel suggestion that the value of food-storing in the Blue Jay may be to remove surplus food from the territory and thus discourage other Blue Jays from trespassing in search of food and, perhaps, later competing with the territory owners when food is in short supply. It is possible that this might be a beneficial side-effect of food-storing in the Blue Jay but I think that, even in this species, it is not likely to be its main function. It cannot apply to such species as the Jay and Nutcracker which habitually carry food from a distance back to their living areas or to the Rook which will carry acorns from the trees (where it does not feed except when collecting them) to the fields where it usually feeds and bury them there (Chettleburgh; Goodwin; Richards; Simmons; Swanberg).

Swanberg (1951) has shown that the Nutcracker is able to return to and dig up a very large percentage of the nuts it has hidden and it can do so even when the ground has been covered by snow. The Jay and Carrion Crow frequently recover hidden food by flying straight to the spot and digging, or probing into a crevice for it, in an assured and confident manner. So does the Magpie (Hayman). The Jay will sometimes fly from a distance to drive off some bird, such as an innocent Blackbird or Wood Pigeon, that by chance is close to one of its caches, then dig up the hidden food and at once take it and hide it again elsewhere. These facts suggest that hidden food is sometimes, if not always, discovered by a remarkable memory or recollection of the exact place where it was hidden. Richards has suggested the possibility that a sense of smell might be used and cites the situation in the Grey Squirrel which appears to remember the approximate areas in which it has hidden food but locates the exact position of the buried food by its sense of smell. I know of no recent works on the sense of smell in corvids but the behaviour of corvids recovering their stores shows nothing comparable to the very obvious 'smelling out' of the Grey Squirrel when thus engaged.

Haftorn's observations on food storage by the Crested Tit suggested that this species finds the seeds it has hidden by trial and error searching but that it remembers the general area in which it has hidden food, or tends to seek food in its favourite hiding area, and so each bird finds a greater percentage of its own stores than other tits do. The Marsh Tit, however, evidently remembers the actual hiding places and goes straight to them (Löhrl). Jays often appear to indulge in trial and error searching, which sometimes results in their finding an acorn. This might be due to the bird remembering the area but not the exact hiding place; to growing vegetation, disturbance of the ground by man or other creatures, or some other cause having altered the immediate appearance of the hiding place; or through the Jay at such times being actually in search of food that its mate, or some other Jay, has hidden. The behaviour shown is certainly identical to that when a Jay *has* seen another hide food and at once tries to find it without, apparently, having been able to mark the exact spot. I have seen such attempts at robbery of food that a conspecific has just hidden by Carrion Crows and Rooks also, and have been impressed at the difficulty the bird has (usually it does not succeed) in finding food hidden by another, even when it has located the place to within a few yards, compared with the immediate success of a Crow or Jay when recovering food it is known to have hidden itself.

Bossema found that, in his study area in Holland, Jays fed on acorns in June and July. At this time acorns 'planted' the previous autumn had developed into baby saplings several inches high, with three or more leaves, but with the cotyledons of the acorns still attached, in excellent condition and hardly diminished. Jays dug up and removed the cotyledons from such saplings and, from the bill-prints on the stalks, appeared to have first grasped and tugged at the saplings. Bossema concludes that Jays re-discover hidden acorns by locating the saplings growing from them and seems to doubt the possibility of Jays recovering acorns without such clues.

Whilst there can be no doubt that Bossema is correct in deducing that Jays find some acorns by seeing the growing sapling and investigating it, it is certainly also true that Jays recover a great many acorns before the young oaks are showing above ground. Swanberg (1969) has seen Jays recover hidden acorns when they had to dig through snow to do so. Also, in such places as the London Parks, where Jays feed partly on human foods, they hide and recover bread, cheese and meat, of which there can be no question of future growth revealing the hiding places. Indeed, it seems to me very likely that Jays may *learn* to associate oak saplings with the presence of the cotyledons of the acorn through discovering them when they return to a cache rather than having a, presumably innate, tendency to selectively investigate oak saplings. Such learning would, of course, enable them to find the stores of others as well as their own.

It may be mentioned that although it is very easy to see food-hiding behaviour in tame captive corvids (one need only distribute peanuts or bits of cheese to those in any zoo where they have any possibility of hiding food in their cages) it is often less easy to see its recovery. This is sometimes partly because the birds are reluctant to retrieve hidden food in the presence of a social superior, in which light they often consider the human, but usually it is because they are conditioned to expect food from people. In the presence of a potential food provider they seek to obtain food from him and in his presence seem 'never to think' of returning to and using their own stores. The situation seems similar to that with many young birds at the stage when they will feed themselves when alone but will only beg for food if their parent, or a human fosterer, is close.

It seems pertinent to discuss here the 'stealing' and hiding of jewels and other bright objects with which birds of the crow family, especially the Jackdaw and Magpie, have long been credited. I know of no proof of wild corvids behaving in this manner. Some of the tales one hears or reads involve valuables being re-discovered in the *nests* of the birds where, of course, they do not normally, if ever, store food.

The hiding of bright objects, when it occurs, is, I think, an extension of or substitution for normal food-hiding behaviour. Young corvids, especially during the period when they are able to fly well but are still being largely or entirely fed by their parents, investigate almost every object they come across and 'test' its possibility as food. Like most other birds they tend to peck particularly at any small objects that contrast with the background. During this period the food-hiding behaviour may be indulged in with inedible objects.

In a wild state corvids learn to restrict their investigations largely to more or less 'serious' food-seeking and do not normally hide inedible objects. Tame or captive individuals, with food supplied but lacking the normal outlets for food-seeking activity, often continue to investigate and 'meddle with everything' even in adult life. Under these conditions they sometimes, Magpies in particular, show great interest in any object, such as an enamel dish, that makes a loud clatter when dragged about, tipped over or hurled off a ledge. I have not seen a such a bird spontaneously hide inedible objects but this may sometimes occur. Birds that are used to being offered tit-bits by hand usually assume that anything so offered 'ought' to be edible. This sometimes causes the bird to treat such an object as if it were of value and be reluctant to relinquish it. This is especially the case if the object has been presented by someone to whom the bird is emotionally attached. In these situations the object may be hidden.

I doubt if shining objects necessarily have the intense attraction for corvids that is often suggested. I have not, for example, seen Carrion Crows, Rooks, or Jackdaws, when foraging on garbage tips or investigating the contents of a litter bin, pay any particular attention to such things as bits of tin foil. Nor did I observe any special interest in such objects from a Jackdaw, several Magpies and many Jays and Lanceolated Jays that I kept at different times. I think it is possible that where jewels, rings and similar trinkets have proved highly coveted by tame corvids this may have been the result of their having been prevented from examining such things in the course of their early investigatory behaviour. The way in which a human may refuse to allow a tame corvid to pick up a valuable trinket must strike the bird as behaviour that could only have reference to food and thus increase its determination to seize it as soon as it has opportunity. It is possible that in some such cases a permanent 'fixation' on glittering objects may result although I have not myself come across an instance of it.

Some corvids have structural adaptations that are of use in transporting food for storage. These are the antelingual enlargement of the lower buccal cavity of the Hooded Crow, Rook, Jackdaw, Magpie and Jay, involving modification of the muscles of the tongue and hyoid structure (Eigelis and Nekrasov, in Turcek and Kelso), the very distensible gullet of the Jay, and the sublingual pouch of the Nutcracker. It is probable that such distensible buccal cavities and/or gullets are possessed by most corvids.

Whether these organs evolved originally in connection with food storage is debatable. All these birds also use them to carry food to their young and, as homologous distensible gullets and sublingual pouches have developed in some species that do not store food, it is possible that they originally developed in connection with parental feeding. There is, however, little doubt that their more extreme development in some corvids has been due to their use in transporting food for storage.

REFERENCES

ANDREW, D. G. 1969. Food-hiding by Rooks. *Brit. Birds* **62**: 334–336.

BOSSEMA, I. 1968. Recovery of acorns in the European Jay (*Garrulus g. glandarius L.*) *Proc. K. Ned. Adad. Wet.* Series C, **71**, No. 1.

CHETTLEBURGH, M. R. 1952. Observations on the collection and burial of acorns by Jays in Hainault Forest. *Brit. Birds* **45**: 359–364.

—— 1955. Further notes on recovery of acorns by Jays. *Brit. Birds* **48**: 183–184.

FINN, F. 1919. *Bird Behaviour*, p. 59, London.

GOODWIN, D. 1951. Some aspects of the behaviour of the Jay *Garrulus glandarius*. *Ibis* **93**: 414–442.

—— 1955. Jays and Carrion Crows recovering hidden food. *Brit. Birds* **48**: 181–182.

—— 1956. Further observations on the behaviour of the Jay. *Ibis* **98**: 186–219.

GWINNER, E. 1965. Über den Einfluss des Hungers und anderer Faktoren auf die Versteck-Aktivität des Kolkraben (*Corvus corax*). *Vogelwarte* **23**: 1–4.

HAFTORN, S. 1954. Contribution to the food biology of tits especially about storing of surplus food. Pt. 1 the Crested Tit (*Parus c. cristatus L.*). *Det. Kgl Norske Videnskabers Selskabs Skrifter* 1953, No. 4.

HARDY, J. W. 1961. Studies in Behaviour and Phylogeny of Certain New World Jays (Garrulinae). *Univ. Kansas Sci. Bull.* **42**, No. 2.

HARRISON, C. J. O. 1954. Jays recovering buried acorns. *Brit. Birds* **47**: 406.

HAYMAN, R. 1958. Magpie burying and recovering food. *Brit. Birds* **51**: 275.

LÖHRL, H. 1950. Beobachtungen zur Soziologie und Verhaltensweise von Sumpfmeisen (*Parus palustris communis*) im Winter. *Z. Tierpsychol.* **7**: 417–424.

LORENZ, K. 1932. Betrachtungen Über das Erkennen der arteigenen Triebhandlung der Vögel. *J. Orn.* **80**: 50–98.

RICHARDS, T. J. 1958. Concealment and recovery of food by birds, with some relevant observations on squirrels. *Brit. Birds* **51**: 497–508.

SIMMONS, K. E. L. 1968. Food-hiding by Rooks and other crows. *Brit. Birds* **61**: 228–229.

—— 1970. Further observations on food-hiding in the Corvidae. *Brit. Birds* **63**: 175–177.

SCHUSTER, L. 1950. Über den Sammeltrieb des Eichelhähers (*Garrulus glandarius*). *Vogelwelt* **71**: 9–17.

SWANBERG, O. 1951. Food storage, territory and song in the thick-billed nutcracker. *Proc. 10th Int. Orn. Congr.*; 445–454.

—— 1969. Jays recovering buried food from under snow. *Brit. Birds* **62**: 238–240.

TURCEK, F. J. & KELSO, L. 1968. Ecological aspects of food transportation and storage in the Corvidae. *Communications in Behavioural Biology*, Part A, **1**: 277–297.

Drinking, bathing, sunning, anting and preening

So far as is known all corvids drink regularly. The better-known species appear to be obligate and fairly frequent drinkers. Many other passerine birds are known to be capable of going without drinking for considerable periods if they can obtain food, such as some fruits and insects, with a high water content. Some corvids of arid regions may also have this faculty, which has been claimed for the Grey Ground Jay.

Like many other birds some corvids will eat snow and probably some may depend largely upon it for their water supply in winter. Alpine Choughs have been seen to come regularly to running water to drink in winter so they, at least, appear to prefer water to snow when given a choice. Corvids drink in the usual passerine manner, by dipping and then lifting the head. Although it is often said that this makes use only of the lower mandible to scoop up water and of gravity to let it run down I think that suction is also involved (Goodwin, 1965).

So far as is known all corvids bathe in water and none take dustbaths. I have, however, not been able to find information on the bathing of the ground jays which seem the only forms that might be likely to have developed dusting instead of or additionally to water bathing.

Bathing takes place while the bird stands in shallow water with its feet on the bottom or gripping a submerged branch or other object. When the bird is bathing in some artificial container it may be reluctant to hop *down* into the water, or the water be too deep, and may bathe as best it can from the edge. The preliminary stages usually involve much hesitation and apparent nervousness before the bird settles down to bathe in a determined manner. This probably serves to lessen the danger of the bird starting to bathe in earnest near a lurking predator.

The bathing movements are the same as those of most other passerines. Ducking of head and breast with a violent side to side shaking of the bill and upward flicking movements of the wings alternates with the head and foreparts being raised, the tail lowered on or into the water, and the wings beaten in and out of the water and flicked transversely over the back so that water is showered up over the body. During this phase the bird often tilts to one side, then to the other. Once determined bathing has begun, but not during the nervous preliminaries, the plumage is erected so that the water can get between the feathers and, presumably, reach the skin also. Simmons (1964) has described bathing and other aspects of feather care in passerine and other birds in detail.

After bathing the bird usually gets quickly on to some relatively safe and elevated perch to dry itself. The drying movements, in crows and other passerines, consist mainly of ruffling and shaking the plumage, vibrating wing and tail tips together, drooping the wings and somewhat spreading the primaries then vibrating them and making a rapid side to side movement of the tail. These drying movements are used when the bird has got wet by accident in rain, mist or wet foliage as well as when it has deliberately bathed.

Preening and oiling are performed in the usual passerine manner (see Simmons, 1964 for full details). Corvids normally scratch the head 'indirectly', the bird lowering one wing and then bringing the leg on that side up over the shoulder to the head. David Holyoak (pers. comm.) has, however, seen direct head scratching by the Raven, White-necked Raven and Carrion Crow although these species also usually scratch the head indirectly. One use made of head scratching is to apply preen oil to the head feathers. The bird obtains oil from the preen gland, transfers some of it, by scratching the oily bill, to the foot and then scratches its head. Allo-preening, as the preening of one individual by another is now usually called, is always concentrated on the head and upper neck which cannot be reached by the bird's own bill. Allo-preening has, however, social as well as practical aspects and is not universal among the Corvidae.

During preening previously applied preen oil, feather exudates and ectoparasites are removed and usually swallowed. It is probably true of corvids, as it is known to be for some other birds, that although healthy individuals usually have some ectoparasites sick individuals have more, and that birds with deformed or injured bills nearly always harbour great numbers of ectoparasites. This clearly shows that one function of the frequent preening is to control ectoparasites. During the moult, wing and tail quills are often removed by the bird when preening. At such times the loosened feather comes away as the bird tries to preen it.

Corvids, like other passerines, clean their bills by stropping them vigorously against their perch. They also sometimes rub their faces against the perch, apparently to remove contaminating substances or to allay irritation.

Sunbathing or sunning is practised by corvids as by many other birds. When sunning at fairly high intensity the bird usually positions itself sideways on to the sun and erects its feathers, especially those on head, belly, flanks and rump. The oil gland is exposed by this feather erection. The bird leans a little to the far side, slightly droops the near wing and somewhat spreads its primaries. A rather similar posture with back to the sun, both wings often partly spread and tail somewhat spread is also used, but I think less often by corvids than by some other passerines. Sunbathing seems most often and regularly indulged in by moulting birds.

It is also commonly seen during a sunny spell after or during a period of cold or inclement weather. Jays often come out on to the edge of a wood to sun themselves in a wind-sheltered 'sun trap'. The functions of sunning seem to be as yet uncertain; some of the evidence as to how far birds can compensate for dietary deficiencies by, apparently, ingesting irradiated preen oil from the feathers is conflicting (Kennedy).

It has, however, been claimed that the action of sunlight (irradiation) on preen oil causes it to become a source of Vitamin D (Simmons, 1964) and it is highly likely that some such deficiencies, especially or perhaps only of vitamin D, can thus be made good. Sunning may also function to disturb ectoparasites and make them easier for the bird to capture; preening usually follows or intersperses sunbathing. Some sunbathing, especially when the bird adopts no special posture but merely sits quietly with somewhat fluffed out feathers, may serve simply to warm the bird. This in itself may, of course, be 'useful' in a physiological sense quite apart from being, presumably, pleasant for the bird.

Intense sunbathing postures are sometimes shown by birds forced to endure heat in experiments, or by brooding or incubating birds exposed to the sun. This does not, I think, indicate that all sunbathing is just a reflex and involuntary reaction to heat. The fact that birds deliberately seek a suitable place, or revisit one that they have previously found, shows that sunning can be at least as purposive as eating or drinking.

The now well-known habit of anting is widespread, but not universal, among passerine birds. It does not appear to occur in birds of other families (see Simmons, 1957) but is shown by many corvids; possibly all of them will be found to practise it. When anting the bird applies ants to the plumage in such a way that the defensive or other body fluids of the ants are applied to the feathers. The ants used are usually workers of those species which eject acid (Formicinae) or pungent anal fluids (Dolichorderinae), when molested. Stinging ants are not normally, if ever, used for this purpose. Corvids have been recorded 'anting' with fire, hot ashes and burning cigarette ends. Various other pungent or burning substances or insects that produce fluids of such nature are also known to have been used by some other passerines (Simmons, 1957).

In typical or active anting the bird picks up and bites one or more ants, holds them in the bill tip and almost at the same moment contorts into the characteristic anting posture. One wing is brought forward, the primaries usually somewhat spread. The angle of the primaries may be changed from normal so as to present them edgeways for treatment. At the same moment the tail is jerked forward, on the same side, and the bird, with a quick quivering movement, runs the bill down the underside of its primaries, or of one primary. Often the eyes are partly closed and the nictitating membranes drawn across them. Some corvids (see species section) apply ants to other parts of the plumage, but in general it is to the ventral ends of the primaries that the ant secretions are applied; possibly also to the head as it brushes against already treated feathers during the performance. The apparent function of the forward position of the tail is to steady the primaries while ants are applied to them although, especially if anting on the ground, the bird may tread on its tail and overbalance. Ants may be used one at a time or the bird may pick up one after another and ant with a ball of crushed ants in the bill. After use the ants are usually discarded but may be eaten. It should be mentioned that even species like the Jay, which do not usually if ever eat worker ants, will eat the winged males and females and especially ant pupae. These latter are, however, seldom available to a bird anting in the wild.

Passive anting is shown by many corvids; it may alternate with periods of active anting. When anting passively the bird may wallow among the ants, flopping, grovelling or lying among them with wings spread and tail either raised or pressed against the ground. This gives the ants opportunity to crawl over and among the plumage.

The Jay, the Green Magpie and the Red-billed Blue Magpie use a form of passive anting in which both wings are thrust forward at once, and the primaries brush the ground and, at high intensity, are almost fully spread in front of the bird. This bringing forward of the wings is accompanied by a convulsive shuddering movement. The tail movement is the same as in typical anting. These three species do not (or, at least, never have when I watched them) take up ants in the bill although they may appear to the casual observer to be doing so. They use similar head movements to those used in active anting but do not actually pick up ants. The Azure-winged Magpie uses the same wing movements as the Jay and the *Cissa* species, but it picks up ants in its bill and applies them to its primaries in the usual manner.

Supposed differences between the anting movements of individuals of the same species are usually, and perhaps always, due to different intensities at which the birds have anted. There are, however, apparent individual differences in the amount of anting that different individuals of the same species will indulge in. These differences are, at any rate, more influenced by factors not discernible to the observer than are, for example, preening or bathing. One Magpie, which I kept for three years, never anted although it had many opportunities to do so and often saw Jays anting. As a species, however, the Magpie certainly ants. I have often seen anting by other tame Magpies. Some wild-caught captive Lanceolated Jays anted eagerly the first time I offered them ants but never did so again during the many years that I kept them, only making a few very low-intensity anting movements on rare occasions. On the other hand, I saw high-intensity anting several times from three Lanceolated Jays in a zoo.

The anting movements are innate. Those of active anting are similar to and probably derived from the movements used for high-intensity preening and oiling of the primaries (Simmons, 1964). Some or all of the movements of passive anting may be derived from sunning or bathing postures. Birds appear to have to learn to use ants or rather to recognize that they are the 'right' objects to use for anting. In-experienced birds show no signs of anting at the sight of ants and do not do so until they have, in the case of active-anting species, picked up one or more ants experimentally or, in the case of passive-anting species, until the ants have begun to climb up their legs or into their plumage. It seems probable that, as Simmons (1964) suggests, active-anting species react initially to the acid, pungent or burning taste of the ant's fluids and/or to their chemical effect on the nasal organs. Experienced birds, on the other hand, react to the sight of ants. Tame Jays that have anted before will often start the typical anting movements when they see their keeper approaching with the container he carries ants in.

It is probably this learning element that is responsible for birds anting with objects other than ants. Possibly some of these may supply a supra-normal stimulus. This may be the reason that individual corvids that have first become accustomed to anting with fire or cigarette ends may thereafter remain indifferent to ants.

There has been much dispute over the possible functions of anting. It has sometimes been suggested that it is merely a means of getting rid of formic acid or other unpleasant fluids before eating the ant. This is certainly not the case. The movements used are quite different from those used by feeding birds to incapacitate dangerous insects or to remove slime from molluscs. In many cases the ants are dis-carded and not eaten after use. Captive birds may be short of insect food and so more ready to eat worker ants than wild birds might be, and ants are often presented to them in a mass of nest debris which contains also the highly edible pupae. These facts have caused some people to assume too close a correla-tion between anting and feeding.

It seems likely that anting helps to maintain the feathers in good condition and to discourage ecto-parasites. The ventral ends of the primaries are the parts especially anointed with ant fluids by most birds when anting; these are just the parts of the plumage least accessible to passerines when preening. Formic acid (Simmons, 1966) is known to kill or harm ectoparasites. Bathing, preening and oiling the plumage commonly follow anting. In Jays they always do so if the bird has opportunity; a captive Jay that has anted shows apparent distress and discomfort if water for bathing is not immediately available.

Birds anting at high intensity do so with great apparent concentration and, like sunning birds, give an impression of being less alert than usual to other stimuli. If this is truly so it might account for the rela-tive infrequency of anting, as compared with other feather-care activities, by some of the species that practise it. It also suggests the possibility that anting may once have been universal among passerines but in some has already been and in others is now being eliminated by natural selection where its dangers outweigh its advantages. Simmons (1957) makes the pertinent suggestion that the active anting move-ments of most passerines may be 'mere relics of a once more widespread anointing which proved harmful in some way'. So far as is known no non-passerine birds ant although some of them, such as the Green Woodpecker and the Wryneck, specialize in feeding on ants and their pupae.

During anting a bird may perform movements which are not specifically connected with anting. A common one is to rub the side of the head and eye on the carpal joint of the wing. This appears to be done when the bird has accidentally got formic acid or some other ant fluid in or near its eye. Precisely the same movement is used to try to remove irritation from the eye under other circumstances and by some species which do not ant.

Stretching and similar movements are often termed 'comfort movements' but they may well have important physiological functions also. Those of corvids resemble those of other passerines (Simmons, 1964). To sleep, corvids, like other passerines, 'tuck their heads under their wings'; that is, they turn the head round so that it rests on the back with the bill tucked into the scapulars or between folded wing and body. The fluffed out feathers then largely obscure the head, giving a rounded outline. Fluffing out the plumage and then shaking is used not only when drying or when the plumage has been dis-arranged but also in many situations where the stimulus seems to be mainly or entirely psychological. It appears to be done at moments of relief or relative relief from fear or nervous tension.

REFERENCES

ELDER, W. H. 1954. The oil gland of birds. *Wilson Bull.* **66**: 16–31.
GIBB, J. 1947. Sunbathing by birds. *Brit. Birds* **40**: 172–174.
GOODWIN, D. 1953. Interspecific differences in the anting movements of some corvine birds. *Ibis* **95**: 147–149.
—— 1965. Remarks on drinking methods of some birds. *Avicult. Mag.* **71**: 76–80.
HEINROTH, O. 1938. Das Baden der Vögel. *Orn. Monatsb.* **46**: 97–100.
IVOR, H. R. 1941. Observations on anting in birds. *Auk* **58**: 415–416.
—— 1943. Further studies of anting by birds. *Auk* **60**: 51–55.
—— 1956. The enigma of bird anting. *Nat. Geog. Mag.* **110**: 105–118.
KELSO, L. 1946. Irradiation, Vitamin D, preening and anting. *Biol Leaflet* **35**: 1–2
KENNEDY, R. J. 1969. Sunbathing behaviour in birds. *Brit. Birds* **62**: 249–258
NICE, M. M. 1955. Blue Jay anting with hot chocolate and soapsuds. *Wilson Bull.* **67**: 64.
SIMMONS, K. E. L. 1957. A review of the anting-behaviour of passerine birds. *Brit. Birds* **50**: 401–424.
—— 1964. Feather Maintenance. *A New Dictionary of Birds* (edited by A. Landsborough Thomson): 284–286.
—— 1966. Anting and the problem of self stimulation. *J. Zool. (London)* **149**: 145–162.
WYNNE-EDWARDS, V. C. 1947. Sun-bathing by birds. *Brit. Birds* **40**: 256.

Having dealt with certain aspects of behaviour which are observed in corvids as individuals, I propose in the following sections to discuss in general terms some of the behaviour that corvids show in various encounters with others of their species and some displays that are common to many species. The three last sections of this chapter are concerned with reproduction and with some particular behaviour patterns characteristic of corvids. Even widely distributed behaviour patterns and displays may be, and usually are, shown in slightly different form by different species and these differences, where known, will be described for each species under its own heading.

Sociability and flocking

Most, possibly all, corvids are gregarious to some extent. The degree of sociability may vary from that of species like the Rook in which even the breeding adults are highly social, usually nesting in colonies with many nests only a few feet apart in the same tree and only a tiny territory defended against neigh-bours, or some of the New World jays in which a group of birds share a territory and cooperate in rear-ing young, to others, like the Raven, in which breeding adults usually maintain an extensive territory (in which non-breeding Ravens may be tolerated) but landless younger birds are more sociable.

If the term 'flock' is taken to imply some degree of cohesion or unison of action among its members then it is rather difficult at times to say whether a number of corvids together constitute a flock or simply an aggregation of pairs and individuals. Migrating or pre-roosting flocks of Rooks or Jackdaws may, for example, show considerable cohesion. On the other hand flocks of either of these species on their home ground may be found, on watching, to be composed of birds which, unless frightened, often pay very little heed to individuals other than their own mates. One may see a Rook fly up from such a 'flock', to be at once followed by its mate but ignored by other individuals. The pair may then fly a little distance, join another 'flock' of food-seeking birds, or by alighting in a Rook-less field, form the nucleus of a 'new' flock when others join them. If the acorn crop is poor or localized, Jays may gather in large numbers at such trees as are bearing fruit to collect and carry off acorns, but the only social cohesion shown is between paired birds, who tend to arrive and depart together, or rather one straggling some way behind the other in the usual Jay manner. With species that commonly live in pairs, cohesion between male and female is often, probably usually, relatively weak when the birds are sexually inactive.

Sociability tends to be strongest when roosting, when flying for some distance (especially when on migration over unfamiliar territory), in times of acute food shortage and, to a lesser extent, when idly preening, sunning or bathing. Immature birds and those without territory tend to be more highly social than territory-holding adults of the same species, although the latter do, of course, normally have their own mates as more or less constant companions.

The above facts suggest that corvids, like men and pigeons, feel most in need of company when they are bewildered, ill at ease, lacking in self-confidence or slightly afraid. Their behaviour under such circumstances is suggestive of that of the fledged young of some species which, after they become strong on the wing, closely follow a parent on its flights until they are independent or at least more familiar with the district. Lorenz (1931) has remarked on the similarity between the behaviour of migrant Jackdaws in apparently unfamiliar surroundings and that of young Jackdaws without an adult to guide them.

Flocking, using the term in its widest sense to include all gatherings of birds of the same species, may have many functions. It probably facilitates the discovery and maximum use of food supplies that are plentiful in quantity but uneven in distribution, especially perhaps in species like the Chough and Rook, in which flocks tend to split up into small groups or pairs which later come together again and gather or circle together before again seeking food. Probably at such times birds which have been unsuccessful follow others that, as a result of previous success, fly in a decisive manner back to their feeding places. It enables young or inexperienced birds to benefit from the initiative or knowledge of local dangers, food or water supplies possessed by older or more experienced birds. This of course will apply less to species in which the adults maintain large territories. Flocking also probably facilitates the meeting and subsequent pairing of unrelated individuals, although in some species special gatherings for this purpose seem to have evolved. Flocking may act as a significant check on predation, especially in the case of inexperienced or underfed birds that would be otherwise most vulnerable to it. Two dozen eyes are more likely than two to spot the approach of a predator and a large number, by mobbing and confusing it, are more likely to be able to frustrate its purpose than is a single individual. Although some of the larger corvids have relatively few predators, other than man, this is in some cases due to man's having destroyed or reduced the numbers of the larger birds of prey and predatory mammals.

The extent to which individuals of some social species tend to follow, alight near or feel secure in the presence of another of their species that acts in a determined or self confident manner is often very clearly revealed if one has a tame corvid that follows one about. When I had a tame Jackdaw I was repeatedly astonished at the way in which, if it was walking about on the ground near me, wild Jackdaws would often swoop down to join it. Sometimes they did not notice my presence until after they had alighted and very often not until they were within a few yards of me. Lorenz (1931) gives some striking examples of this, involving Hooded Crows as well as Jackdaws. Jays, although less highly social and, when adult, never following other individuals closely or blindly (except in moments of intense aggressive or sexual excitement), evidently at times watch and follow the movements of other individuals as seems proved by the speed with which, in a bad acorn year, any oaks that have a good crop are discovered by large numbers of Jays.

It seems hardly necessary to state that the terms 'social', 'sociable' etc., as used here, do not necessarily imply that the more highly social species or individuals are more peaceable or friendly towards conspecifics than are less social forms. Indeed the reverse is often true; the individual pairs of a dense rookery or the competing individuals of a hungry feeding flock are likely to be involved in more aggressive encounters than are individuals of species that rest and feed less close to one another.

Territory

'Territory' is usually defined as an area which an individual, pair or group of birds defend against others of their species. In some corvids, such as the Nutcracker (Swanberg), actual defence by overt aggression appears not to have been observed but, nevertheless, pairs are able to maintain their living area free from intrusion. With these possible part-exceptions all corvids whose behaviour is known are territorial when breeding although in colonially-nesting species, such as the Rook, only the nest site and a tiny area around it may be defended. In other species breeding adults may hold very extensive territories in which the pair spend most of their time and find most or all of their food throughout the year. The boundaries of such territories may be poorly defined and the influence of its owners diminish outwards from the central area or from the nest site. In some American species group territories are held and other individuals of the group assist the breeding pair(s) to rear their young. In species which hold large territories some other individuals of the same species may be, and often are, permitted to enter and even forage in the territory. The tolerance of the owners tends to lessen or vanish as they come into breeding condition, however, and is probably at all times contingent on submissive behaviour being shown by the trespassers in any encounter. Any individuals known to be or suspected of being sexual or territorial rivals are usually fiercely excluded. Deliberate meeting of neighbours on the borders for mutual self-assertive display, and possibly in some cases for non-hostile social contact, may occur regularly.

It is not known whether migratory individuals of territorial species hold territory in their winter quarters (as many other migratory passerines do). There is circumstantial evidence to suggest that in some cases individuals return to the same area where they have wintered before. It has sometimes been claimed that Rooks and Jackdaws hold feeding territories and that only members of a particular colony or clan are permitted to use its feeding grounds. I know of no evidence for such behaviour and all that I have seen makes me think that it does not occur. Evidence from ringed birds suggests that some Polish-breeding Rooks may wander over a considerable area and move in flocks from one country to another during the winter (Busse). Wintering Rooks do not appear to be excluded from the feeding grounds of resident birds and such fighting as does take place is either individual quarrelling over food items or sexually motivated, as when a third bird interferes or tries to interfere with a courting or copulating pair. Indeed, it is very noticeable that even in the less sociable species really superlative feeding sites appear to be either impossible to incorporate with an individual pair's territory or impossible to defend if they are. Any productive garbage tip is likely to be regularly visited and fed on by scores or even hundreds of Carrion Crows, Ravens or whatever other 'territorial' species of *Corvus* is found in the area. In Carrion Crows trespassing by neighbours can often be induced by supplying conspicuous food, such as chunks of white bread, inside a pair's territory.

Some corvids maintain large territories whose main function seems to be to provide or safeguard a food supply. The territory may supply much or all of the pair's food throughout the year; it almost certainly supplies readily available food for the young in the first week or so of their lives when they probably need frequent feeding as well as almost constant brooding. Additionally or alternatively the territory may serve as an area where food obtained elsewhere can be hidden with a relatively greater expectation that the pair will be able to retrieve what they have gathered than if they hid it elsewhere. In some species territory size is known to be correlated with availability of food: in districts where food is abundant territories are smaller than in those where food appears to be relatively scarce. There is some evidence to suggest that this reduction of territory size may be related to the number of birds that the general area supports rather than to the food supplies available in *each* individual territory.

In territorial species the young may be tolerated in the territory for a long time, sometimes until the parents breed again. It is probably extension of such tolerance that has brought about the system, practised by some American jays, where one pair of adults nests more or less in company with several, usually younger, individuals who help the pair rear its young. Since it has evolved or, if it was the primitive corvine behaviour, has been perpetuated, this system presumably has advantages for the species that practise it. It might, for example, enable young to be reared in an environment poor in food supplies or in a period of food shortage, as several adults would be able to find more food, and in the aggregate spare more from their own needs, than two. This situation obtains in some arid parts of Australia where in many (non-corvine) passerines several individuals help the breeding pair to rear their young (Harrison, 1969). Several adults may also be better able to repel nest predators than are a single pair. However, it looks as if, in the Corvidae, this system is on the whole not advantageous. As Crossin (1967) suggested, it may keep too many potential breeding birds involved with a single nesting attempt. So far as is known, in the most abundant, successful and widely ranging species, including the colonial nesters, each brood is normally cared for only by its own parents.

Colonial nesting, as in the Rook, seems primarily an adaptation to allow maximum use of available nesting sites. Before the advent of agricultural man it is likely that the Rook was a bird of open steppe. It would therefore have been advantageous for it to develop the ability to cram its nests close together in such relatively few clumps of trees as were available. The birds could then, not holding feeding territories, exploit wide areas of the surrounding grassland. A second possible function of colonial nesting, that of defence against predators, is perhaps more valid for the Rook and other corvids than for many smaller and weaker colonial nesters. Kites, *Milvus milvus*, and, it is said, Grey Squirrels take young Rooks and eggs respectively but their methods of doing so appear not to have been observed. I think, however, that with colonial corvids as well as with smaller colonial species, the need to exploit suitable nest sites fully has been most important in originating and maintaining colonial nesting.

It is interesting in this connection that the only behavioural or psychological adjustments that the Rook appears to have evolved in adaptation to colonial nesting are to be ready to make do with a very tiny territory around the nest, whilst at the same time retaining or even increasing its readiness to defend such territory as it does hold; and to continue to fear other Rooks on their own little territories. These are obviously the minimal requirements, without which colonial nesting would be impossible. Jackdaws are said to have a pattern of communal defence to prevent one of their number from interfering with the nest of a weaker individual (Lorenz, 1931), although this does not seem to have been observed in the wild. Rooks show no such behaviour. They habitually trespass and rob any temporarily unguarded nest of its constituent materials, sometimes destroying it in the process. When doing so they fight other trespassers readily yet all flee before the owners as soon as they reappear (Goodwin, 1955).

Colonial nesting is usually highly disadvantageous if man becomes a predator on the species practising it. This has been true of the Rook in some parts of Europe, where rookeries have been exterminated as they very easily can be if consistent and ruthless attacks are made on them. In Britain, and possibly elsewhere, young Rooks have been killed off at some rookeries while other rookeries have been protected or partially protected for sentimental or humanitarian reasons. Many rookeries in Britain have long persisted in spite of regular or intermittent shooting of the fledglings. This does not, as is often claimed, prove that shooting can have no effect on ultimate numbers but only shows that, in those particular cases, the number of young Rooks killed has been insufficient for it to do so.

It is thus possible that, in the Rook, colonial nesting may still be advantageous and still be selected for. It enables a maximum number of Rooks to breed in places where they may receive at least some protection. The more or less communal feeding habits enable the birds quickly to find and to exploit food sources. It is very noticeable that, where conditions are suitable, the colonially nesting Rook and Jackdaw are able to exist in much greater density than are the non-colonial species.

Communal roosting

Communal roosting is frequent or usual in many species of corvids, as in many other birds. Individuals that are dispersed in pairs or small parties during the day may gather in larger numbers to pass the night together. Roosts of one species may be shared by or immediately adjacent to a roost of another species, sometimes even to one of quite unrelated birds, such as parrots. Generally speaking, the tendency to roost in company is strongest in birds that are sexually immature, not holding territory, wintering in an area at a distance from their breeding grounds, or unpaired; and weakest in paired adult birds in breeding condition that are holding territory.

The psychological implications of this have already been suggested when discussing sociability and flocking behaviour in general. Their behaviour suggests that many diurnal birds find the approaching darkness slightly frightening, especially when the environment is hostile or unfamiliar. Everyone who has kept birds will know how a bird, placed in an aviary or cage new to it early in the day, may seem to settle down and be at ease only to show renewed signs of uneasiness and attempts to escape in the evening.

Communal roosting may be advantageous in several different ways, which are not mutually exclusive. It may enable relatively safe roosting places to be used by the greatest possible number of individuals. The number of birds present may decrease the chances of predators approaching unobserved. Modern man with his explosives, contact poisons and shotguns can, and sometimes does, wreak havoc on communally roosting corvids and other birds, but their behaviour evolved long before such hazards came about. Communal roosts may, however, even give protection from human predation, if they are in places that cannot be reached without difficulty or are on the property of some person who does not allow other humans on his land.

Communal roosting permits many individuals to share a site that gives some protection from the elements. This is perhaps less important for corvids than it may be for smaller species. Some shelter from the wind does, however, often seem to provided by the communal roosting sites of, for example, the Magpie, and this may sometimes be a factor influencing the choice of a communal roosting place.

Communal roosting may facilitate the meeting and subsequent pairing of unrelated individuals. It may also enable the greatest possible use to be made of scattered or localized food supplies during periods of food shortage. At such times it is probable that birds which have found adequate food the previous day will return to the same feeding ground and that their decisive manner when so doing will stimulate others, which have been less successful, to follow them.

Little appears to be known about how and why a particular site is first 'chosen' as a communal roost. Once such a roost is established it is easy to see how new members may be recruited, through the tendency of young or insecure individuals to follow those older or more decisive in manner. New communal roosts are, however, quite often formed. Anyone able to study the formation of such a roost from its earliest stages would almost certainly be able to make new and interesting observations.

Individual distance

This is the term used for the behaviour shown by many otherwise social species in which each individual normally maintains a certain distance between itself and other conspecifics. This may be achieved by attacking, threatening or moving away from any individual that comes too near. Individual distance can be particularly well seen in resting flocks of Black-headed Gulls or roosting Starlings. Within a species, individual distance may or may not be shown, according to circumstances. The individuals of some species that otherwise maintain it do not do so in reference to their mates or dependent young; when suffering from fatigue, hunger, or cold some species which normally maintain individual distance, such as the Swallow, *Hirundo rustica*, and Starling, *Sturnus vulgaris*, huddle together, and so on.

Some corvids, like the Jay, maintain individual distance to a fairly high degree. Even the members of a pair only have physical contact when one is feeding the other or during copulation. They seldom or never approach very closely to one another without one or both showing some appeasing or threatening behaviour. In the Jackdaw, on the other hand, the pair habitually perch side by side in contact with each other and also indulge in allo-preening. A somewhat intermediate situation is found in many *Corvus* species, in which members of a pair do not usually show signs of fear or aggression when near each other but which, nevertheless, do not normally perch closely enough to be in contact with each other. Such species, such as the Carrion Crow and Raven, may indulge in allo-preening, but when they do so the active partner stands a little away from the other and reaches forward or to one side to preen it, instead of perching in bodily contact with it as an allo-preening pigeon or estrildine would usually do.

Even in species which maintain individual distance the recently-fledged young seldom do so and, especially after they can fly, may often rest side by side with one or more of their siblings. There appears to be some correlation between the degree to which individual distance is usually maintained between members of a pair and the distance apart which they habitually fly when going anywhere together. Colonial nesting, which usually means that the individual pairs have a very restricted nesting territory, and hole-nesting with its even stronger tendency to make physical contact difficult to avoid, might seem likely to facilitate or encourage tolerance of mutual contact between at least the members of a pair. There are, however, too many exceptions to generalize. To give but one contrary example, few birds maintain individual distance more compulsively than many woodpeckers, all of which are hole-nesters.

A possible function of individual distance is that it would enable the bird to take wing without being knocked or hindered by another close alongside it in an emergency. This certainly applies in the case of roosting or resting flocks, but for species that do not associate in numbers in the open it is difficult to think that this is very important in view of the fact that, at least in some species, the recently fledged young, which are likely to be most vulnerable to predation, do not maintain individual distance.

As the maintenance of individual distance is correlated with a tendency to keep apart when seeking food as well as, and usually to a rather greater distance than, when perched or resting, it seems possible that it could be advantageous in feeding situations. By keeping habitually a little apart from other individuals when seeking food the weaker or more submissive member(s) of flock or pair might have a much better chance to swallow or carry off any food morsel before it could be robbed by another individual. Both in corvids and other birds that sometimes feed socially I have the impression that, on the whole, species that feed mainly on small items that are easy to swallow before thay can be snatched away, tend to forage nearer to each other than do species that feed much on large food objects. This possible function would correlate well with the lack of individual distance in dependent juveniles, which, in the course of learning to fend for themselves, closely approach parents and siblings to investigate when the latter have found or are seeking food, and thereby learn or reinforce their innate recognition of foods and feeding sites.

Dominance and social rank

It is well known in the Domestic Fowl, and some other species of birds, that if a number are confined together in an enclosure a 'peck-order' soon develops. As a result of the outcome of their first hostile encounter(s), one of every two birds afterwards habitually gives way to the other, does not 'hit back' if pecked or threatened but often 'passes the punishment on' to another that is below it in the hierarchy. This hierarchy may not be a straight linear arrangement: bird A may, for example, be dominant over B, who is dominant over C, who is nevertheless dominant over A. At the bottom is usually some wretched specimen that is subordinate to all. This type of peck order does not necessarily develop if a number of birds are confined; much depends on their species and condition. In some species a single pair will become completely dominant and dominate or harry to death all the rest; in others several pairs or individuals may each become dominant in its own mini-territory as happens, for example, with Domestic Pigeons in a crowded loft. Because the 'classical' peck order situation so closely resembles that often prevailing in human groups there is, perhaps, a tendency to interpret bird behaviour in such terms even when the evidence does not justify it.

Corvids in captivity usually form a social hierarchy, at least if none of them are in breeding condition. In Jays and Lanceolated Jays the dominance of the superior(s) is then very mild. Subordinates have to wait their turn at the food dish and submit to having food they have hidden stolen by the dominant bird (if it has seen them hide it), but they are very seldom attacked and usually only mildly threatened. When, however, one pair of Jays in such a forced association comes fully into breeding condition they usually show greater intolerance and begin to harry the others. As I have always removed the latter at this point I cannot say whether they would be finally attacked and killed, or tolerated after vain attempts to drive them away.

Lorenz found that his hand-reared Jackdaws formed a hierarchy in which the top birds were jealous of and quarrelsome towards those just below them but tolerant and peaceable towards those much lower down in social rank.   His Jackdaws, although allowed to fly freely at times, were apparently shut up at night and by day also for part of the year.

It seems doubtful whether such firm hierarchies form among wild corvids.   At their nesting colonies wild Rooks and Jackdaws usually give the impression that each nesting pair is dominant within its own tiny territory and that all the breeding adults are dominant over any non-breeding yearlings that visit the colony.   With corvids which hold a larger territory, the owners are normally dominant over other individuals within their territory, even when they tolerate their presence there.

In species which, like the Rook, feed much in company in the open, attempts to drive other individuals from sources of food or to rob them of food they have found are frequent, especially in times of food shortage.   Similar behaviour may be seen in less social species if, for example, a number of individuals are visiting a bird table.   Under such circumstances it is common for individuals to give way when threatened by others at a food source; occasionally they drop food they have already seized, without resistance.   As would be expected, in times of food shortage there tends to be a rather greater readiness to defend food but even then some individuals will give way without resistance.

It has been suggested (Lockie, 1956) that such competition over food may function in conjunction with the presumed social hierarchy to ensure that in times of food shortage the lowest-ranking individuals starve while the higher-ranking remain well nourished.   Thus, at any one time, only a few individuals (those lowest in social rank) are seriously short of food.   These soon die, to be replaced, if the food shortage continues, by those next above them in rank, but unless the situation becomes lastingly acute many well nourished individuals will survive.   There does not, however, appear to be concrete proof for this theory.   In many parts of Britain there is little evidence that winter, when such competition for food is most observed, is in fact a time of relatively high mortality for corvids.

Competition for food and the robbing or exclusion of weak individuals need not imply the existence of a hierarchy.   Probably, in many instances, especially when large flocks or gatherings are concerned, the situation is not that there is a permanent or semi-permanent hierarchy in which each bird knows every other as well as 'knowing its place', but that in any encounter an individual bird is able to estimate the condition and determination of its opponent, and usually gives way if it judges the other to be its superior.   The speed with which social rank may change in captive corvids, without any physical fighting, suggests that these birds are very competent at judging the physical and psychological condition of others. If, for example, the dominant of two or three captive Jays becomes very slightly ill or sustains a small injury it is usually at once relegated to subordinate rank.

David Holyoak informs me (*pers. comm.*) that he found, during his long-term field studies of corvids, that the individual encounters over food, involving displacement of one individual by another, that took place within a large flock of Rooks known to be composed of several smaller flocks each of which was known to represent a different breeding rookery, were apparently identical with those occurring earlier in the day when these small flocks were feeding alone.   This agrees with my own impressions that behaviour in these circumstances is not necessarily, and probably not usually, based on a rigid social hierarchy and that it need not involve individual recognition.

To what extent intraspecific competition of this kind actually results in the death of the weaker or lower-ranking individuals does not appear to be known.   Holyoak (pers. comm.) found no evidence of it when studying Rooks, Carrion Crows and Jackdaws near Tring.   Dominant individuals may succeed better in preventing subordinates from feeding under unnatural conditions, as for example when Rooks or Jackdaws are feeding from a garbage bin, bird table or pig trough, than they would as members of a party seeking insects or seeds in open country or woodland.   Even under entirely natural conditions dominant individuals of carrion-eating species would presumably be able to make subordinates keep away from or await their turn at a carcass.   Here, however, a point to bear in mind is that, except where man has killed them off, other carrion feeders such as vultures, eagles, wolves, jackals or foxes might play a more important part than conspecifics in preventing corvids feeding from a carcass. Some fighting over food and food-robbing does of course occur even in species which, under natural conditions, feed on seeds or small invertebrates.

In captivity females of many corvid species are lower in the hierarchy than males, except sometimes during a limited part of the breeding cycle, or at the nest, or if a male becomes ill or injured. If, as is certainly sometimes the case, wild females are also subordinate to males, then, if competition between individuals of feeding flocks resulted in numbers of birds dying of starvation, one might expect an excess of males among the survivors. This phenomenon has been observed among introduced Pheasants, *Phasianus colchicus*, in North America (Nelson and Janson), but I know of no evidence for such differential survival for any corvid.

When feeding pairs of wild Jackdaws, Carrion Crows and Jays, I have repeatedly observed that the female does not try to take food from the male or to share his food with him. She will approach and stand very near, ready to pick up any morsel she can if he is, for example, pecking bits off a large piece of bread held with his feet. In the case of the Jay the female may be driven, albeit usually only with mild threat, even from somewhat scattered food. In the Jay at least, the male may sometimes rob his mate of food which she has hidden and he very often attempts to do so if he suspects where she has hidden food.

For much of the breeding cycle and especially when she is laying or incubating this dominance and 'selfishness' of the male is clearly counterbalanced by his regular feeding of the female. Even although the pair usually stay together, however, feeding of the female is, generally speaking, absent or much less frequent during the summer, autumn and winter. Theoretically one might suppose the female of a corvid pair to be in some jeopardy from her mate, as a potential competitor, during periods of food shortage. There seems no evidence to suggest that she does in fact ever suffer starvation from this cause. Presumably her being able to seek and store food in the territory which is mainly defended and held by her mate, or her being allowed to feed more closely to him without interference than are other conspecifics, provides an adequate margin of safety for her. In some species competition between members of a pair may be lessened by the smaller-billed female tending to take more small food items.

Species recognition and imprinting

Some (possibly all) corvids either do not recognize others of their own species instinctively or else, as is known to be the case with many species of ducks (Schutz, 1965), innate species recognition can be obliterated or suppressed by conditioning in early life. They appear to learn the characteristics of their species from their parents, and sometimes also from their siblings or other members of their species with whom they associate in early life. This learning of the creature's own species, when restricted to a definite early period, is called 'imprinting'. Siblings may only have this effect with human-reared birds. Some waxbills and grassfinches, if reared with conspecifics but by an allied species, become imprinted solely on the foster-parents' species (Immelmann; Goodwin, 1971).

Under natural conditions imprinting ensures that the young bird will recognize and respond to its own kind. Schutz's work on ducks has shown that in some (probably all) species in which only the male is brightly and distinctively coloured, such as the Mallard, females recognize males instinctively and usually show sexual preference for males of their own kind no matter what species they have been reared by or with. Males, on the other hand, if reared by other species of waterfowl (or reared with them, being cared for by humans) usually become imprinted on this other and 'wrong' species and when adult show sexual preference for them. In many cases they show sexual behaviour only towards them. On the other hand in ducks, such as the Chilean Teal, in which both sexes are nearly alike and are cryptic and inconspicuous in colour, *both* sexes become sexually imprinted on other species if they are reared alone with or by them.

It thus seems that under natural conditions the function of imprinting is to supplement or reinforce innate species-recognition. It is probably especially important when the birds in question are very similar in general appearance to allied sympatric species, as is the case with females (but not males) of such sexually dimorphic ducks as the Mallard, both sexes of many tropical or southern hemisphere ducks such as the Chilean Teal, and many of the black or predominantly black crows of the genus *Corvus*. It is understandably easier to evolve a 'built-in' innate recognition of and sexual response to, say, a male Mallard rather than to the very differently-coloured and equally unmistakeable males of Pintail, Shoveller or Gadwall than it is to evolve an innate response to the relatively slight differences in appearance between the females of these species.

Most of the information on imprinting in corvids is based on European species and on the American Crow. In the following remarks, therefore, references to *Corvus* are based on information on the Raven, Carrion (and Hooded) Crow, American Crow, Rook and Jackdaw. It is, however, highly likely that they will prove broadly true for other *Corvus* species. Similarly, the information on imprinting in the Jay and Magpie may apply also to such genera as *Perisoreus*, *Cissa*, and *Cyanopica*.

Corvus species that have been taken at an early age, that is before they are about half-feathered, and reared by hand, usually become completely imprinted on man and show no recognition of their own kind in later life. This may occur even if they have been reared and subsequently kept in company with others of their own species or where the bird has been taken at a later age from the nest but then for a period had only human company. Where the bird is hand-reared but kept with others of its kind, or where it is taken at a fairly late stage but allowed to contact others of its kind shortly after fledging, it may later react socially to both humans and its own species. I know, however, of no instance where a young *Corvus* has been taken at an *early* age, hand-reared *alone*, and later responded normally to its own kind.

Lorenz (1931) had a Jackdaw which, through imprinting, became sexually and socially fixated on humans but which responded to Hooded Crows (which it had met shortly after it was able to fly) as flying companions and habitually flew with them when they were on the wing in its vicinity. He suggested that this might indicate an innate recognition of black corvine wings in flight. I once, however, had a human-fixated Jackdaw which never showed the slightest interest in its own or other *Corvus* species, whether in flight or not. Possibly the age at which the bird first comes into contact with flying crows may be critical here.

Jays that are hand-reared singly may become imprinted on man and show no recognition of their own species. Whether this is always the case is uncertain as I know for sure of only four birds which were thus treated, a very small sample. Jays that are hand-reared and kept together with other young of their own species usually react socially and sexually both to Jays and to humans. This they may do even if they have been taken from the nest quite late; a young Jay that flew from the nest when I was taking her and had to be chased and caught later responded to humans as well as to Jays and paired (in different years) both to Jays and to me (Goodwin, 1956). Sometimes, however, Jays that are hand-reared in company with other Jays later show social and sexual reactions only to Jays. There would appear to be individual differences in the effects of imprinting even under apparently identical conditions, as Schutz's detailed and comprehensive studies proved to be the case in the Mallard.

Of several Magpies that, at different times, were hand-reared (some by me and some by others) together with siblings of their own species, none reacted socially or sexually to humans in later life and all appeared to be reacting normally to their own species. One female that I hand-reared alone became fixated on Domestic Pigeons which she had constantly seen and with which she consorted as soon as she was able to feed herself (Goodwin, 1951). Another female Magpie was taken as a fledgling and hand-reared. She was taken daily to a crowded office where she was fed and talked to by many other people beside her owner. This bird was given to me when about three months old. She was, and remained to the end of her life, completely fixated on humans. She never showed any social or sexual reactions to the wild Magpies that visited the garden daily or to a second tame one that was kept with her once for a period of several months. Lorenz (1931) on the other hand had a hand-reared Magpie which, although it never saw others of its kind until fully adult, then showed completely normal recognition of its own species ('völlig ungestörtes Artbewusstsein'). However, Lorenz's description of the behaviour of this bird suggests that it was also reacting socially to the Jackdaws with which it had been kept as a young bird.

From the above it will be seen that imprinting seems rather more important and more far-reaching in its effects in the *Corvus* species than it usually is in the Jay or Magpie. This is readily explicable, as the former coexist with allied species, which are similar in colour, whereas the latter do not. Indeed, the extent to which imprinting is still potent in Jays and Magpies suggests that they may, in fact, formerly have coexisted with more closely allied and similar species which are now extinct.

When comparing imprinting in corvids with that in other birds one point needs bearing in mind. No corvid has been domesticated and care and some trouble are needed to breed them in captivity. Hence imprinting experiments (whether deliberate or accidental) with them have all involved either human foster parents, or other species which they have associated with but which have *not* stood in a parental relationship to them. It is known that ducks imprint most easily on species fairly similar to them in general appearance, less readily on those that are greatly dissimilar. In view of the relative ease with which all the corvids mentioned above may be imprinted on human beings it is likely that if they were (through human intervention) fostered under other species of corvids they would become even more readily and firmly fixated on their foster parents' species. In view, however, of the almost inevitable frustrations to which such birds would be doomed (unless the experimenter cross-imprinted an equal number of two species) such an experiment would have much to be said against it.

Some aspects of the pair-bond

In all corvids whose behaviour is reasonably well-known the breeding adults live in pairs, although such pairs may, in some species, be members of an integrated group. Often there are indications that some landless immature birds are also paired. It is likely that pairs once formed usually endure until one partner dies or is killed but the evidence for this, taking the corvids as a whole, is mainly circumstantial or based on captive or tame individuals. The members of a pair sometimes tend, as would be expected, to associate more loosely at times of year when their gonads are regressing or inactive.

Captive corvids of some species (and this will probably prove true for others) appear to pair more readily with strangers introduced to them at an appropriate time than they do with conspecifics which they have been reared and constantly kept with. The same is true also of some other birds. This may be relevant to the fact that in some species, such as the Jay, Blue Jay and Magpie, noisy gatherings of several or many individuals occur just before and in the early part of the breeding season. At these gatherings much sexual and self-assertive display takes place and, at least in some cases, pair-formation results. In the Jay and Magpie it is known (Raspail) that killing one member of an established pair may result in one of these gatherings shortly taking place, after which the survivor has a new mate.

Sometimes Magpies whose mates have been shot obtain new ones without a gathering taking place. This does not, I think, disprove the presumed function of such gatherings. Presumably much depends on local population and individual circumstances. It is possible that, where corvids suffer much persecution from man, some of their more conspicuous social behaviour may become reduced, inhibited or distorted.

In some species pair formation sometimes appears to come about rather gradually within the loose flocks of immature or landless birds. This is sometimes the case in the Carrion Crow (Holyoak, in prep.). As, however, in some of such species, gatherings that appear very like those of Jays and Magpies also occur, further information is needed. In some other birds, for example, the Marsh Tit, Blackbird, Stonechat, and Bullfinch, it is known that two individuals which associate during the autumn or winter do not necessarily stay with each other for the breeding season. In the conspicuously sexually dimorphic Bullfinch it is very readily apparent that a minority of the autumn and winter 'pairs' consist of two males or two females whereas in spring only heterosexual pairs are to be seen. The possibility that corvids, especially young birds in flocks, that are apparently paired in autumn or winter, may not always remain permanently with the same partner, must be considered if the birds are not individually recognizable by the observer. The speed with which established adults apparently obtain a new mate when bereaved suggests that among the landless individuals there must be many that are either unpaired or are willing to desert a mate that has no established territory for one that has. As, however, such observations have mostly been made on unmarked individuals, it is possible that in some cases a new *pair* may have driven the widow or widower from its former territory.

Feeding of the female by the male appears to be almost (but not quite) universal among corvids. It takes place most frequently and regularly at periods during which the female is laying, incubating, or brooding young nestlings. In many species, however, it may be indulged much earlier in the breeding cycle, even, sometimes, in autumn and winter. The giving of food may be accompanied or prefaced by juvenile-type begging by the female but this is not always the case. In the Jay, for example, such feeding may involve food-begging, the quivering display, the male's sexual (pre-copulatory) display, or simply the passing of food and the utterance of a particular version of the appeal call, different to that uttered in juvenile-type food begging.

In the Rook and the Jay (perhaps in other species) the female may feed the male, or food may be passed from one to the other several times, usually to be finally eaten by the female. In captive birds a complete reversal of the feeding rôles may occur if the male is less fully in breeding condition than his mate. For example, in late winter I put an adult (three-year-old) male Jay together with a widowed female. That spring he persistently begged from and was fed by her. In spite of this reversal of rôles and the male's lack of cooperation in building, the female nested and laid eggs, which were infertile. The following year the male came into full breeding condition, behaved normally and reared a brood with this female. A female Rook belonging to a friend of mine would, in the breeding season, always feed her owner if she begged from her with open mouth, imitating the Rook's begging call.

It is highly unlikely that such complete reversals of the normal rôles in connubial feeding would take place in the wild. The captive females had an unlimited supply of food which did not have to be searched for. Under natural conditions a main function of connubial feeding is to supply the female with food, or at least to augment her food supply when she has relatively little time for seeking food or is needing extra food for the eggs she is producing. It is, I think, significant that when I have seen wild female Jays or Rooks give food to their mates or pass back food given to them, this has nearly always been in the early part of the breeding cycle and not when the female was incubating, laying or (to judge from the progress made with nesting) likely to lay within a week or so. Once, however, a wild male Jay begged to his mate who flew to him, fed him and solicited, whereupon the male mounted her and copulated.

Feeding of one bird by another usually seems to imply some degree of dominance by the feeder. This may be of a very transient nature but nevertheless be indicated. For example, when a pair of Rooks or Jays are passing a food morsel back and forth to each other, each bird as it receives it usually goes into the submissive quivering display, although usually only a low-intensity version of it. However, in such circumstances the bird that first offers the food may also go into this display. Also feeding of the female may, at least in captive corvids, take place at periods when she is dominant over the male.

Observations of wild corvids suggest that, except sometimes at or near the nest, the male of a pair is usually dominant. In the Jay this dominance may be expressed by such overt acts as robbing the female's stores in spite of her obvious but powerless displeasure. Even in species like the Jackdaw, in which the pair appear much more loving and inseparable to the human observer (and may well truly be so), the male usually seems to take the initiative in deciding when and whither to take flight. Apart from his feeding of the female, which is part of his innate pattern of behaviour, the male corvid does not usually seem willing to share food with his mate. In my experience, not even the male Jackdaw will do so.

Threat and fighting

Threat in corvids and other birds, as in man, may be used either when the threatening individual is somewhat afraid or for some other reason inhibited from attack or else, towards known inferiors and usually only in mild form, when the dominant individual realizes that it does not need to attack to make the other withdraw.

Threat may consist of approach with head held up, often with the bill pointing upwards and the plumage sleeked. This seems to be derived from the intention-movement of flying up to attack. Postures in which the bill is raised and the throat presented to another bird may, however, have an appeasing function. Snapping of the mandibles may be used as a threat. Horizontal postures or postures with bill pointing down and some erection of the plumage usually indicate elements of defensive-threat or self-assertive display, which are discussed further on.

Actual physical combat may occur either in sexual or territorial contexts or over food. Typically the latter tend to be shorter-lived and less serious. Fighting corvids grapple with their feet and peck with their bills. They often bite hard, twisting and wrenching, appearing to use the same movements as those used in feeding but with much more vigour and violence. It is of interest that corvids that are very hungry, but not to the extent of having been weakened by hunger, may feed with the same violent vigour in their movements as is usually shown only when fighting. Sometimes during a fight two temporarily exhausted birds may lie on the ground grasped breast-to-breast. This has evidently been the origin of the mistaken but widespread notion that corvids copulate in this manner and not (as they do) ventro-dorsally like other birds.

The old saying 'One crow does not peck out another crow's eyes' has more foundation. Although corvids sometimes (though relatively rarely) injure one another in fights, they appear not to attack their opponent's eyes. In some species it is certain that there is a definite inhibition against pecking the eyes of conspecifics (including humans to whom the birds are reacting socially) and it is likely that this will prove to be the case with all species.

Defensive threat display

In situations where a corvid is threatening defensively and is at least momentarily inhibited from attacking or from moving from its position, all the plumage tends to be erected. This is often especially evident in the feathers of head and back. The bill is usually partly open and the bird faces its enemy. Sometimes its wings may be spread. It may move with great speed if it attacks but even then, perhaps because of the absence of tail or wing flicking on alighting, gives an impression of inhibited movement. This form of threat is shown in its most typical form in nest defence, where it may be combined with inhibition from actually fighting (see section on nesting and parental care). It may, however, be seen, usually in less intense forms, in other hostile contexts.

Self-assertive display

The above seems the best term for the display that is shown in certain contexts either to the mate or to a sexual or territorial rival. Often there are significant differences in the details of this display according to its precise context. Because of specific differences apparently homologous displays of this nature have, in different corvine species, been given such names as 'bowing display', 'lateral display', etc. When given to the mate, or when the pair display together, the self-assertive display seems to function as a greeting, to augment the bond with the mate, or to stimulate or 'back up' the mate in reference to mutual enemies. It is, however, essentially defiant or hostile when given to rivals. As I wrote when discussing the Jay (Goodwin, 1956) the psychological factors involved seem rather similar to those associated with laughter in man. Laughter seems basically aggressive, as it is so often shown in response to stimuli which would otherwise arouse anger or be expected to. It is often used in a hostile sense accompanied by feelings of anger or dislike. When we laugh *at* another person or they laugh *at* us this arouses strong feelings of anger or resentment, unless the people involved love and completely trust each other. When, however, another person, even a stranger, laughs *with* us, it arouses feelings that deepen or even initiate a bond between us.

In self-assertive display different areas of plumage are erected to a different extent. The displaying bird may, according to species, present itself either frontally or laterally. Especially in sexual situations it may move round the bird displayed to. In long-tailed species the tail may be twisted (out of the median line of the body) towards the bird displayed at. Tail or wings (or both) may be tilted and/or partly spread to display their colours or markings. Whereas in those Old World genera whose displays are well known there are clear differences between their self-assertive displays in spite of many obvious similarities, those of some of the American jays appear from descriptions to be to some extent intermediate between those of such Old World genera as *Garrulus* and *Pica*. It is possible that this may indicate that such species are phylogenetically closer to the (presumed) common ancestor of such Old World genera than they are to any contemporary Old World genus.

Quivering or submissive display

Rook in quivering display

Some (probably all) species of *Corvus* and *Garrulus* and at least some other corvids have a display in which the tail or wings, or both, are quivered. Usually the bird adopts a horizontal posture with tail and rump slightly raised. The wings are held slightly or partly open and often drooped. In *Garrulus* the wings are widely spread and presented frontally when the display is given at high intensity. The tail, with the upper tail coverts where they rest upon its base, is quivered; often it also makes lateral or oscillating jerking movements. In *Garrulus* the wings are also quivered. In *Corvus* the wings are usually drooped and only slightly opened and there is commonly no noticeable wing quivering. Apart from variations caused by intensity, there may be individual differences, at least when low-intensity display is given. At such times Jays may quiver the wings and not the tail, or vice versa, tail quivering may occur without the usual crouching posture being adopted, and so on. Very similar and probably homologous tail-quivering displays are shown by the waxbills and grassfinches.

This display is the female's invitation to coition. In the Jay and Rook (and probably in other species) it is sometimes used by paired birds when exchanging food or inedible objects. I have seen it used by a yearling Rook, at a breeding rookery, whenever a fight broke out in its vicinity. It is frequently given by the male Rook if the female refuses to allow copulation, but only if the male is courting his own mate, not when he is attempting to rape a female to whom he is otherwise indifferent. In captive Jays, Lanceolated Jays, some *Corvus* species, and the Red-billed Blue Magpie it is also used towards social superiors and by tame birds towards human beings in what appears to be an appeasing or imploring sense. In these situations it is not correlated with the reproductive condition of the bird showing it. A tame Jay may give this display to a human who is doing something that frightens it a little or to a dominant Jay when the latter is stealing food the displaying bird has hidden.

A common factor in all the situations in which the quivering display may be given in apparently non-sexual situations, is that it appears always to be shown as an alternative to either attacking or fleeing. I do not infer by this that these alternatives are then possible for the bird: quite the contrary. This display appears to be given when impulses to attack and to escape seem likely to be in conflict, but only if the creature responsible is a feared or 'respected' fellow-member of the species, or a human that is regarded by the displaying bird as a conspecific.

It seems likely that this display first evolved as the receptive female's signal of her desire for copulation, and later came to be used, by some species, as an appeasing display in other situations. Presumably it must have some inhibiting effect on any aggressive tendencies of the dominant bird involved. It does not, however, make the latter desist from robbing the subordinate of its just-hidden food. I have never seen a dominant individual show any signs of a sexual response, whether overt or symbolic, in response to the quivering display, except when this was given by its mate in an obviously sexual context. In view of the persistence with which male Rooks, at a rookery where I was watching, attempted (as they habitually do) to rape incubating females, I was surprised that when a yearling gave the tail-quivering display, no attempt was made by others to copulate with it.

Pigeons, humans, and many other creatures tremble in many situations in which they are afraid but are, for various reasons, inhibited or prevented from fleeing. Jays may also tremble under such circumstances but their trembling may not be visible. I was once feeding a tame Jay on her nest (she was at that time 'paired' to me) when a stranger (to her) entered the aviary. She at once cowered in the nest as a wild Jay does if a man approaches, facing him with partly-opened bill. I put my finger to the tip of her bill and found that she was trembling, although I could not see this. I think the tail-trembling or wing-trembling of corvids may have originated from relatively simple trembling due to fear which later became exaggerated and ritualized to serve as a sexual and, secondarily, as a social signal. Even in the corvids the quivering display may still, however, be given in situations that have certain aspects in common with those that evoke non-ritualized trembling in pigeons and man.

It may be significant that in some of the *Corvus* species, in which one has the impression of there being more mutual confidence between the members of the pair than in, for example, the Jay, copulation may take place in response to only a very slight degree of display by the female. In some non-corvine birds, such as the waxbills, the tail-quivering display is used in solicitation even although the members of the pair show little or no signs of uneasiness in each other's presence. It is possible, however, that in these species the mutual confidence of paired birds is a later acquisition in the evolutionary history of the species than is this display. It is also possible that in certain specific states of sexual excitement these birds do in fact feel a 'primitive fear' at the close approach of the mate.

Juvenile-type begging

In this the bird begs with flapping or fluttering wings and utters calls identical with or very similar to those of a begging fledgling. At low intensities, or as an individual variation, the begging call may be uttered without wing movement but this is not usual. At least in *Garrulus* and *Corvus* the wing movements are very different from those used in the quivering display. In some and perhaps all corvids this behaviour is characteristic of females during the period when they are laying or incubating. It may, however, be shown in other circumstances and by both sexes. I have seen wild male Rooks beg to their mates, but rarely, except in the case of a yearling male that had paired to an adult female. This bird frequently begged to his mate when she begged to him. On the rather infrequent occasions when he did feed her he often begged immediately after (Goodwin, 1955). I have never seen a wild female Rook feed her mate in response to this type of begging although I saw one respond by symbolic feeding. Mutual bill fondling followed. I once, as has been described, saw a male Jay fed by his mate when he had begged to her and I have seen other wild male Jays beg in this manner when apparently trying to entice the female to a selected nest site.

In captivity tame female Jays, when laying or incubating, will beg from their owner in this manner if they regard him as their mate. Both sexes will often beg to a human if they are very hungry, particularly eager for some favourite tit-bit, if they are in full moult, or if they are ill. It thus seems that this display is linked with feelings of dependence or infantile reliance on the creature begged from. It may be shown by either sex at any time, if for any reason the bird is in this dependent mood. With captive Jays at least, and the same is no doubt true for other species, there is much individual variation in the amount of stimulus necessary before they beg in this manner to their owner. Tame Rooks and Hooded Crows, probably also other *Corvus* species, will also beg to trusted humans in this manner if very hungry.

The flapping or fluttering wing movements are usually considered to be the now ritualized intention movements of flying toward the parent although, as Lorenz (1935) long ago pointed out, a young bird, when actually begging, is inhibited from flying towards the parent, a fact of which anyone who has ever tried to recover a tame young corvid that has perched out of reach will be vividly aware. It has been suggested (P. Marler, *pers. comm.*) that the wing flapping when begging might represent intention movements of fleeing from rather than approaching the parent or mate. In any case these wing movements have now become completely emancipated from their original motivation, if this was one of escape or approach. They are, as is well known, shown by nestlings still incapable of flight.

Displacement movements and redirected aggression

'Unnecessary' bill-wiping and pecking at or fiddling with various inanimate objects are commonly shown by corvids in moments of excitement or apparently mild tension. In situations where there appears to be a strong conflict between anger and fear, as with birds threatening each other at a territorial boundary, more vigorous movements are used. These usually seem to be derived primarily from movements used by the particular species when feeding: hammering with closed bill, pecking and tearing to pieces of leaves or other objects, digging in the ground and so on. They are usually performed with much greater violence than in normal food-seeking and clearly indicate redirected aggression. Should food then be very near the bird may eat it but in such cases it seizes and swallows the food with the same angry, violent movements.

I once had a Lanceolated Jay that, if uneasy at my close presence, used to pull at the ring on his leg. I was reminded vividly of a man fiddling with his tie under comparable circumstances.

Reactions to the sick or injured

It is well known that many vertebrates, including some birds, have a tendency to attack conspecifics that are sick, injured or behaving in an aberrant manner. Goethe (1940) gives many examples for different species. In birds aberrant behaviour must suggest incapacity or injury to elicit attack. In man, of course, aberrancy of behaviour that does *not* suggest incapacity tends also to elicit attack from his fellows but this is probably a relatively recent 'refinement' of the same basic behaviour.

In considering this behaviour we must distinguish between attacks that appear to result solely because of the sickness or injury of the victim and others. Observations on captive birds can be very misleading if this is not kept in mind. For example, if a sick or injured bird is put in a cage, together with another that regards the whole cage as its territory, it will be attacked because it represents a potential rival. The attack may ,of course, be pressed home more fiercely as a result of the lack of adequate defence and consequent encouragement of the attacker. Also, a captive bird may find release for anger or frustration, aroused by some other cause, by attacking any available unresisting conspecific. There are many observations of such behaviour by birds in a wild state, though rather few on corvids.

Jays and Lanceolated Jays show not the slightest tendency to attack ill or injured conspecifics, even in captivity. They exploit their weaknesses to the extent of becoming dominant over them but I do not think this can be considered in any sense as an attack. With Rooks, however, there are strong tendencies to attack the incapacitated. When I was watching at a rookery (Goodwin, 1955) I found that a one-legged female (who had a nest and eggs) was constantly being attacked by different individuals. Unlike all the other Rooks in the colony she was not safe from attack even when standing on the edge of her own nest. These attacks were definitely aggressive, not the attempted sexual assaults to which all incubating female Rooks are liable. Kramer (1941) observed that Rooks that had been caught on migration, very roughly handled, and then ringed and released were attacked by other migrant Rooks as they sat miserably or flew weakly about. There are some observations which suggest that Choughs, Alpine Choughs and Carrion Crows may sometimes show similar behaviour, but the accounts that I have read or heard have been ambiguous and other interpretations were possible.

The contrasting behaviour of Rook and Jay tempt one to speculate that attacking the sick or crippled may be correlated with a high degree of sociability and its lack with less strongly gregarious habits. However, Jackdaws seem not to persecute sick or crippled individuals (Goethe, 1940, pers. obs.). This behaviour may possibly lessen the danger of disease by driving off infective individuals. It does not, however, always obtain this end. In the case of the crippled Rook mentioned above no such result was achieved. It has been suggested that crippled birds might endanger others by attracting predators. Predators certainly selectively attack the weak and injured but they must be around anyway, to spot them, and the injured individuals, by falling victims themselves, safeguard rather than endanger their fellows.

This behaviour often seems to be provoked by the sight of an incapacitated conspecific and to stimulate attack from an individual that appeared previously in a 'neutral' state. Possibly, especially in some social species, the very frequent hostile intraspecific encounters and the ability, whether learned or innate, to 'size up' an opponent, may make an individual unable to resist attacking another whose degree of incapacity is such that it realizes that it can safely do so. I do not, of course, suggest that the realization of the opponent's helplessness is at all conscious. In man, however, where this behaviour *is* subject to conscious realization, it is widespread.

Individual differences

Observers with limited experience of a species sometimes attribute to innate individuality differences of behaviour which are, in fact, caused by the different degrees of health, sexual activity, or conditioning due to past experience, of the birds concerned. Because of such frequent misinterpretations of observed behaviour, it has sometimes been thought that no individual differences can exist between wild birds of the same sex and species if their health, condition and past experiences are similar.

Some individual differences of behaviour of genetic origin may, however, occur. Although observed differences of the 'same' behaviour patterns are most often due to nongenetic factors, the possibility that some may represent innate individual differentiation within the species cannot be excluded.

REFERENCES

BUSSE, P. 1963. Bird-ringing results in Poland. Family Corvidae. *Acta orn., Warz.* **7** (7): 189–220.
CROSSIN, R. S. 1967. The breeding biology of the Tufted Jay. *Proc. West. Fdn. vert. Zool.* **1**, No. 5.
GOETHE, F. 1940. 'Über das "Anstoss-Nehmen" bei Vögeln'. *Z. Tierpsychol.* **3**: 371–374.
GOODWIN, D. 1951. My Magpies, past and present. *Avicult. Mag.* **57**: 10–15.
——— 1955. Some observations on the reproductive behaviour of Rooks. *Brit. Birds* **68**: 97–105.
——— 1956. Further observation on the behaviour of the Jay, *Garrulus glandarius*. *Ibis* **98**: 186–219.
——— 1971. Imprinting in cross-fostered cordon-bleus. *Avicult. Mag.* **77**: 26–31.
HARRISON, C. J. O. 1969. Helpers at the nest in Australian passerine birds. *Emu* **69**: 30–40.
HOLYOAK, D. Ecology, behaviour and territory of Carrion Crows. *Bird Study* (in press).
IMMELMANN, K. 1970. The influence of early experience upon the development of social behaviour in estrildine finches. *15th Cong. Int. Orn. Abs.*: 21–23.
KRAMER, G. 1941. Beobachtungen über das Verhalten der Aaskrähe (*Corvus corone*) zu Freund und Feind. *J. Orn. Festschr. Oskar Heinroth*: 105–131.
LOCKIE, J. D. 1956. Winter fighting in feeding flocks of Rooks, Jackdaws and Carrion Crows. *Bird Study* **3**: 180–189.
LOHRL, H. 1950. Beobachtungen zur Soziologie und Verhaltensweise von Sumpfmeisen (*Parus palustris communis*) im Winter. *Z. Tierpsychol.* **7**: 417–424.
LORENZ, K. 1931. Beiträge zur Ethologie sozialer Corviden. *J. Orn.* **79**: 67–127.
——— 1935. Der Kumpan in der Umwelt des Vogels. *J. Orn.* **83**: 138–213 and 289–413.
NELSON, B. A. & JANSON, R. G. 1949. Starvation of Pheasants in South Dakota. *J. Wildlife Management* **13**: 308–309.
NICOLAI, J. 1956. Zur Biologie und Ethologie des Gimpels. *Z. Tierpsychol.* **13**: 93–132.
RASPAIL, X. 1901. Cérémonie de secondes noces chez les Garruliens. *Bull. Soc. Zool. France* **26**: 104–109.
SCHUTZ, F. 1965. Sexuelle Prägung bei Anatiden. *Z. Tierpsychol.* **22**: 50–103.
SWANBERG, P. O. 1956. Territory in the Thick-billed Nutcracker, *Nucifraga caryocatactes*. *Ibis* **98**: 412–419.

Nesting and parental care

The nesting places chosen by corvids vary not only between species but also according to the particular environment, opportunities, and experience of individual pairs. Most nest on or among branches of trees or shrubs. Some, however, nest in holes, on rock ledges or even on the ground.

Branch-nesting species tend to choose a site where there is a fork, preferably multiple in character, that they can crouch in; a firm support beneath; or twigs that offer some screening and support all round. They will push sticks down into a vertical fork until (if they are lucky) some hold firm and form the basis for the nest, and so they do not have to rely entirely, as do pigeons for example, on being able to build around themselves while squatting in the selected site. Species such as the Rook, that have in the course of evolution often had to make the best of a paucity of sites, seem more able, or more willing, to build in a site that appears to present some difficulties and which often involves considerable delay and much wasted effort before the first foundations stay in place. There may be minor differences in the site usually chosen between species that otherwise nest in similar places. For example, Rooks and Carrion Crows both often nest in the peripheral branches of trees but Rooks far less often nest on a stout branch below the canopy or against the main trunk than Carrion Crows do. This is possibly because a lower situation than most of the other nests might have some disadvantage for the colonially-nesting Rook whereas, so long as the site is sufficiently open to permit the parents to come and go readily, this would be no drawback for the Crow.

One requisite for a nest site seems to be that the birds should feel relatively secure and at ease there. The type of site that fits this requirement for any particular species is, of course, predetermined by heredity to a greater or lesser extent. The need to feel secure is, however, probably responsible for some of the local or individual differences in the type of nest site chosen that are sometimes found within a species. I have described elsewhere (Goodwin, 1956) how a pair of Jays in an aviary would not begin nesting until the site was screened around by conifer branches, although wild Jays often build where there is no side screening of the site. Similarly, in aviaries where birds on the floor are subject to constant disturbance, some species of waxbills, *Estrilda* spp., that in a wild state nest on the ground, choose nest baskets high up on the wall in preference to similar baskets on or near the ground.

From nesting in sites that are screened and which give a firm support for the squatting bird, it is but a short step to nesting in niches and hollows of trunks or large branches. The three species of typical jays of the genus *Garrulus* show apparently different stages in this shift to hole-nesting. The Lanceolated Jay nests, so far as is known, only in the branches of trees or shrubs. The Jay usually does so and often sites its nest against the trunk or within a tangle of honeysuckle. Sometimes, however, especially when it is living in relatively open parkland or orchards, the Jay nests in hollows in trees. Lidth's Jay habitually nests in tree hollows.

The Hooded Crow and the Raven nest either on cliffs or in trees according to the habitat and, probably, sometimes according to individual choice due to conditioning of the birds concerned. When on cliffs their nests, especially those of the Raven, are usually in recesses or on well-sheltered ledges. This is probably because protection from the worst of wind is both more needed and more readily obtainable on a cliff than in a tree in wooded country. A recess is also perhaps less liable to predation or more easily defended from predators than an open ledge.

As thoroughgoing cliff and mountain birds not of a size able to repel most possible bird predators, the choughs have evolved the habit of nesting in deep crannies, on ledges in caves and similar sites. Jackdaws nest, as is well known, in holes in all sorts of places. It seems most likely that they evolved as tree hole nesters and later took to nesting also in cliffs and buildings.

The extreme development of hole-nesting in the Corvidae is found in Hume's Ground Chough which digs its own holes. This condition is foreshadowed in the Jackdaw which, when nesting in chalk cliffs, often enlarges holes and crevices by removing debris.

Typically nests of corvids consist of a base or platform and outer shell of sticks or large stems and an inner lining of softer substances. Usually an intermediate binding layer, very often largely or entirely of fibrous bark, is more or less interposed between the outer shell of sticks and the inner lining. Some species use earth or mud as well as the more usual materials. The inner part of the nest is usually more or less cup-shaped and open at the top. Only a few species build a canopy over the nest.

Different types of nest are clearly adapted to their situation and habitat. Forms that nest in fairly dense cover in temperate or tropical woodland, such as the Jay and the blue magpies, build relatively small and slight nests. The nutcrackers and the grey jays, that nest early in the year in cold northern or montane forests, build thick-walled, softly-lined nests. The Jackdaw will carry enormous quantities of sticks to fill up a large hollow but contents itself with a scant lining when nesting in a very small hole. The thick-walled nest of the magpies of the genus *Pica*, with its canopy of sticks, seems to be a special adaptation for defence against nest-predators such as crows, *Corvus* spp,. and some birds-of-prey. It is probably one factor that has enabled *Pica* to spread so successfully over wide areas and to inhabit relatively open areas where, although some scrub or trees provide refuge for the adult magpies when attacked by birds-of-prey, their nests may often be hard to conceal from view.

In all species which have been observed in detail both sexes build. In some the females have been recorded as doing more building than the male or as doing most of the work on the interior of the nest. It is, however, possible that some observers may have inferred that the bird doing most building, or most concerned with the interior of the nest, must have been the female, without any proof. Both of these statements have, for example, been made about the Rook, for which they are certainly not true. Although in some individual pairs of Rooks the female may do more work than the male, the reverse seems more often the case. In the Rook, Magpie, and Jay it is, however, true that there are authentic records of females building complete nests without any help from their mates. The birds concerned were widowed wild Rooks, a captive Jay whose mate was not in full breeding condition, another Jay and two tame Magpies 'paired' to humans or domestic pigeons, and a tame Rook 'paired' to its human owner. There seems to be no record of a male corvid building a complete nest without any help from his mate. This difference seems due not, as has sometimes been claimed, to the male being unable to build at all stages (for he habitually does so when normally paired) but to his lacking the impulse to do so unless he has an adequate partner.

The building movements used are those common to most (perhaps all) passerines, and to many non-passerines also. Sticks are usually held by the point of balance, after some juggling to ascertain this. Loose bark, and sometimes also side twigs, are often removed from sticks before carrying them to the nest site. When fixing a stick the bird thrusts it into position and then makes a shuddering side to side movement. If this results in the stick becoming anchored in the site or in the other material already there, the bird leaves it; if not it usually takes it out and tries again, often in another place. This shuddering movement has special names – *Einnesteln* and *Einzittern* – in German.

At first the framework is often concentrated at one point, if the sticks happen to fasten more easily there. This is rectified by the bird turning as it builds around itself and tending to pay most attention to the gaps. Rooks, and presumably also other species nesting in fairly open forks of trees, often have to work for many days before they manage to get the first sticks to stay in place, but once a foundation has been secured, however small, progress is much quicker.

The cup of the nest is shaped by the bird crouching in it, pressing against it with breast and carpal joints of the wings, and crouching and kicking backwards with the feet while pressing the tail down on the nest rim. So far as is known, corvids lack the weaving movements used in building by some passerines. Soft materials are carried 'bundled' in the bill, those for the inner lining of the nest being first carefully prepared. A Raven will, for example, painstakingly pull a lump of wool into fine pieces and then 'bundle' them for carrying; a Jay given a tangled mass of fibres will carefully hold them underfoot and pull out single strand after single strand until it has as many as it can carry.

Clutch size varies but is seldom less than 2 or more than 7. Eggs are usually laid at daily intervals or at intervals of a little over 24 hours. In many (probably most) species they are laid early in the morning and the female roosts on the nest the night before laying. She may do so for two or three nights before the day on which the first egg is laid. The time at which true incubation begins varies between species and possibly sometimes between individuals. As a rule, however, a parent sits on the nest for much of the time, even if it does not actually incubate, as soon as the first egg has been laid.

In most species whose behaviour is known the female alone incubates and is fed on or near the nest by the male. In some of these the male may stand or crouch over the nest or sit in it for short periods. Records of males of such species incubating are few and probably mostly erroneous but some may refer to aberrant behaviour by individual males. Such individually variant behaviour could, presumably, be selected for and lead to regular male incubation, if environmental conditions made it more efficient for the sexes to share incubation than for the female to incubate alone and the male to provide her food as well as his own.

The only corvids in which this has apparently occurred are the nutcrackers, *Nucifraga* spp., in which both sexes incubate in turn and have well-developed brood patches, and probably the Hawaiian Crow. In the case of the nutcrackers it is generally thought, most probably correctly, that this is correlated with the importance of food stores during their breeding seasons, which makes it more efficient for each sex to feed itself from its own stores. It remains to be discovered whether their food stores may not prove equally important to some other forms, such as the grey jays, *Perisoreus*. If so, incubation and self-feeding by both sexes would prove not to be an essential correlate of reliance on stored food when breeding.

The eggs of corvids are usually some shade of blue or green with darker markings, and usually with pale grey or lilac underlying markings. Erythristic eggs, in which the ground colour is buff or yellowish and the markings reddish, occur as occasional variants in many species but are normal in the African Black Crow, *Corvus capensis*. It is possible that the colours and markings of corvid eggs, which in most cases make them inconspicuous at a little distance, may have some protective function, even though they are seldom left unguarded and most egg-eating birds thoroughly investigate any nest they find whether the contents are conspicuous or not. There can, however, be little doubt that the conspicuously pale eggs of the hole-nesting forms have survival value by rendering them more visible to the parents. The eggs of the Jackdaw are noticeably paler than those of most other species of *Corvus*. Holyoak showed that when the eggs of Jackdaws nesting in dark holes were artificially darkened many of them were broken accidentally by the parents. The correlation of pale eggs with hole-nesting has reached its extreme development in the pure white eggs of Hume's Ground Jay.

Rook carrying food for young

At hatching time the eggshells are removed, and usually eaten, by the incubating parent. In the Raven, and possibly other species, the female may help to free the young from the shell and membranes. The newly-hatched nestlings are usually naked or clad only with a little sparse down. The parents induce them to gape for food by uttering a soft call and, sometimes, by lightly touching or prodding them at the gape edges. Food is carried to the young in the gullet or the sub-lingual pouch and regurgitated into the throats of the young. The parent often thrusts its bill so deeply into the nestling's throat that the observer almost winces in fear lest it go too far and cause injury, which of course it never does. The food given is prepared ready for swallowing, great care being taken with preparation of food for very young nestlings, much less with that for older young.

The faeces of the young are either removed or swallowed by the parents. The adult usually takes the faecal sac direct from the nestling's cloaca. The female, perhaps sometimes also the male, removes any drop of excreta, rain water or any other foreign matter from the plumage of the young and then carefully preens the feathers that have been soiled. Probing in the nest and shaking and tugging at the nest lining may serve to aerate the nest or to allow scurf or other debris to fall free of the young. Often, however, these activities seem to be performed when the female is catching or attempting to catch ecto-parasites. The young are fed by their parents for some time after leaving the nest. The female may cease to feed them before the male does but there is no division of the brood as with some other birds in which male and female feed different individual young after fledging.

The above observations are based on what is known of the behaviour of a few species: especially the Raven, Rook, Carrion Crow, Jackdaw, Magpie, Jay, Lanceolated Jay and Blue Jay. There is, however, reason to think that they will hold good, generally, for most of the Corvidae. Precise differences between species are described, where known, under the species headings.

Magpie carrying food for young

Some New World jays differ from the general pattern outlined above in that other individuals besides the breeding pair may assist in nest-building, in feeding the incubating female and, especially, in caring for the young. In some species this cooperation of several individuals in rearing a single brood is the usual pattern. No Old World forms are known to behave in this manner but as some of the tropical and subtropical species have been very little studied it is possible that they may.

Commonly but by no means invariably the number of young corvids fledged from an otherwise success-ful nest is fewer than the number of eggs laid. Sometimes this is due to young dying during the nestling period as a result of food shortage. The asynchronous or partly asynchronous hatching ensures that in times of dearth the older, and therefore larger and stronger young get most of what food is brought to the nest. At this stage the young appear not to be recognized as individuals and the parent feeds first whichever begs most vigorously and stretches up highest when begging. As a result the oldest young may suffer little or not at all while the youngest weaken and then die. When some eggs fail to hatch they are not usually removed for at least a week after hatching, probably not unless they are accidently broken by the growing young. Conspicuously damaged eggs are, as with many non-corvine species, usually eaten by the incubating parent.

At times young disappear without trace within a day or two of hatching, or one finds a nest containing fewer small young than it did eggs a few days previously. A possible explanation, and the one usually accepted, is that owing to lack of sufficient food some nestlings have died and then been eaten or removed by the parents. It is, however, difficult to believe that in all such cases the parents have been unable to secure sufficient food for, say, four newly-hatched young, when this is certainly less than will be required even a few days later for, say, the two which are successfully reared. I think it is possible that under some circumstances, perhaps when it is weakly or for some other reason does not present quite the 'right' stimuli, a newly-hatched or hatching nestling may be swallowed or removed by the brooding parent in the same manner as the eggshells, remains of the allantois and other débris of the hatching process.

When complete clutches of eggs disappear from nests predation is sometimes, and perhaps usually, the cause. However, with some corvids in captivity the parents are sometimes responsible for such disappearances. The eggs of wild corvids, and of Reed Warblers (Brown and Davies, 1949), also sometimes vanish under circumstances that suggest that the parents are responsible. Corvids, like other birds, normally have an inhibition against injuring intact eggs or young in their own nests. In at least some cases this holds good even for eggs very different from their own if these are experimentally placed in their nests. On the other hand, if their own eggs are presented to them outside the nest they will break and eat them readily. It seems at least possible that some psychic upset, perhaps caused through disturbance by a frightening predator, may sometimes cause a temporary failure of this inhibition and result in a bird destroying its own eggs. I have discussed this more fully elsewhere in reference to the Jay (Goodwin).

Perhaps connected with the inhibition against eating eggs in its own nest or even using hurried movements that might injure its eggs or nestlings, is a tendency for the incubating or brooding bird to be inhibited from attacking when at the nest, although not when a little way from it. I found that my tame female Jays would attack me fiercely until I reached their nests but when I was right at the nest the Jay, in defensive display, only made slight intention movements of pecking and would not even bite hard if a finger was pushed into its open bill. Similar behaviour at the nest has been recorded for wild individuals of the Florida Scrub Jay (Amadon, 1944) and Clark's Nutcracker (Dixon). These forms have relatively little fear of man but, although they often fight fiercely when handled elsewhere, the incubating or brooding bird is 'gentle' when handled at the nest.

To what extent such behaviour is shown towards natural predators by corvids appears to be unknown. I have seen a pair of Song Thrushes, *Turdus philomelos*, furiously mobbing and attacking a Jay that was approaching their nest, suddenly cease their outcry and perch quietly watching it as soon as it had reached the nest, renewing their attacks when, egg in bill, it flew away. Comparable behaviour has been seen from a Great Grey Shrike when its nest was robbed by a Magpie.

The function of such behaviour is a little puzzling and may well differ between species. In such cases as that of the Song Thrushes and the Jay it could be beneficial, as, once the predator has reached the nest, the chances of permanently deflecting it are almost nil, certainly not worth the risk of getting injured by continuing the attack. With corvids it is possible that this behaviour may have reference to conspecifics or to predators not dangerous to the adult. If so there may have been selection for a very strong inhibition against actual fighting at the nest because of the risk of injury to its contents or of their being taken should the adult move from its guarding position above them. It is, however, very likely that this inhibition against attacking at the nest site has facilitated the parasitism of some corvids (and other birds) by cuckoos; but there seem to be no first-hand observations on precisely how the cuckoos which parasitize corvids manage to get into their nests to lay.

Further information on this inhibition is badly needed and it is hoped that any readers who make observations on it will publish their notes. It must be emphasized that this lack of active defence against an enemy that is right at the nest, although perhaps more widespread than at present realized, is not universal. Some species of birds will attack predators and humans who are right at their nests or will trample heedlessly over their eggs and young when fighting or expelling trespassing birds of their own species.

REFERENCES

AMADON, D. 1944. A preliminary life history study of the Florida Jay. *Amer. Mus. Novit.*, No. 1252: 1–22.
BROWN, P. E. & DAVIES, M. G. 1949. *Reed Warblers*. London.
DIXON, J. B. 1934. Nesting of the Clark Nutcracker in California. *Condor* **36**: 229–234.
GOODWIN, D. 1956. Further observations on the behaviour of the Jay. *Ibis* **98**: 186–219.
HOLYOAK, D. 1969. The function of pale egg colour in the Jackdaw. *Bull. B.O.C.* **89**: 159.

Voice and vocal mimicry

The corvids, like most passerine birds, have an extensive vocabulary. Typically, however, many or most of their innate calls tend to be specifically distinct, at least from those of other sympatric species. Most species have a number of fairly distinct calls which tend to be linked by intermediate utterances. Basically similar calls can, as with many utterances of the Carrion Crow, be greatly modified according to the stress or intensity with which they are given and express different moods of the caller. It is often very much easier for a person familiar with a particular species to understand differences in the nuances of its calls than it is for him to describe or explain them!

That the hearer's subjective impression of stress, fear, anger, perplexity or tenderness in a corvid call is not always (if ever) sheer anthropomorphism is often clearly shown when the accompanying or subsequent actions of the calling bird are observed.

I have attempted, in the species sections, to give some idea of known calls by means of letter combinations. The limitations of this method are, of course, considerable but sound spectrographs would be equally so for many readers. Where possible reference is given to sound spectrographs where these are known to exist. It must, however, be borne in mind that comparisons between species, or even between races, sexes or individuals of a single species, can be misleading unless it is certain that homologous calls given at a similar intensity are being compared.

For the most part corvine calls that appear to express rage, terror or frustration (and some that do not) are harsh and loud, hence the proverbial reputation for unpleasant voices which these birds have with mankind. Often the alarm call which is given when mobbing a predator, and also in many other situations where there appears to be intense arousal but also conflict between opposing impulses (most often between fear and aggression), is stated in books to be the 'usual' call of the corvid in question.

Calls that apparently express self-assertive well-being and may function as territorial advertisement, the advertising calls of unpaired or widowed individuals, high intensity food-begging calls, and social contact calls are also often very loud and sometimes, to human ears, discordant.

Hawk-alarm calls, given in response to a *flying* and potentially dangerous bird-of-prey are often difficult to 'pin-point', as are the hawk-alarm notes of other birds.

Many species of *Corvus* and the Jay (probably some other corvids also) utter harsh guttural grating sounds at the moment of attacking or countering the attack of a bird-of-prey or some other formidable bird.

In many species, of different genera, the females utter guttural mechanical-sounding clicking or rattling calls in sexual or self-assertive situations. Although these calls differ between species and genera, as do the postures in which they are uttered, it is highly probable that they are homologous.

In some cases similarity of calls is almost certainly correlated with close phylogenetic relationship, as with the Raven and the White-necked Raven, *Corvus corax* and *C. albicollis*, for example. This is not always true, however, where a general similarity between only one or a few calls of two species is concerned. Nor does dissimilarity in one or two calls necessarily indicate that the two birds in question are not, phylogenetically, closely related.

Song or its equivalent in corvids usually approximates rather to the subsong or whisper song of other passerines. It is typically given by a bird perched alone, or flying alone, and seems to have no territorial function. Such song often consists of a medley of the various calls in the species' repertoire, sometimes with the addition of vocal mimicry (q.v.). Frequently corvid song is rather quiet, uttered *sotto voce*, but it may sometimes be quite loud. A Rook or Jackdaw flying alone often utters an astonishing babble of sounds.

Calls used in appeasing contexts between two individuals, when offering food to mate or young, or when begging food at low intensity, tend to be soft and tender in tone. In some species, and possibly all, calls uttered by both sexes may be given at a slightly different pitch or in a slightly different form by male and female even when uttered at an apparently comparable intensity. Such sexual differences are sometimes difficult to distinguish from individual differences which may also be present.

Boswall gives references to many papers by himself and others which list available gramophone records and tape recordings of bird sounds. These include many featuring calls of European and some non-European corvids.

Vocal mimicry is widespread in the Corvidae. On present knowledge one can roughly divide corvine (and other) vocal mimics into two main classes. Firstly there are species, like the Raven and Magpie, in which tame hand-reared birds usually or habitually practise vocal mimicry but which in a wild state do not commonly, if at all, utter recognizable imitations of other species or of non-animate sounds. Secondly there are species, like the Jay and Lanceolated Jay, which habitually practise vocal mimicry in a wild state and in which adult birds will, at least in some instances, continue to add new copied sounds to their repertoires. It may be added that, whereas among other passerines that are vocal mimics, we find both these categories represented, so far as is known all parrots come into the first category and do not practise extra-specific vocal mimicry when wild.

With the species that do not usually practise vocal mimicry of other species in a wild state or which never do so, their learning of human words or whistling seems to depend on an emotional attachment to human beings. Such birds have, as a rule, initially accepted a human as a parent substitute and later show social behaviour towards humans. These hand-reared individuals usually mimic the human voice, to an individually varying extent. Some of the species in question are known to imitate the individual nuances and variations of some or all of the calls uttered by their parent(s) or mates in a natural state.

In some cases (see esp. Gwinner & Kneutgen) when the members of a pair of birds of such species are separated, whichever of the two is left in its home area will soon begin to utter calls or song phrases that are normally used only or mostly by its mate. This has the effect of 'calling the mate home' if it is in a position to return. Thus in such species the ability to mimic is not, as was once thought, merely latent under natural conditions. It is, in fact, practised and used by wild individuals, but as it then only involves minor differences in individual species-specific calls it is difficult for the human hearer to recognize it as mimicry.

Although this interpretation fits well with the vocal mimicry of a species like the Bullfinch (Nicolai), many and possibly all corvids that appear otherwise to come into this first category do not entirely restrict their vocal mimicry to human sounds when tame and reacting socially to humans. They also usually copy other sounds, some of them of non-living origin. The same is true of parrots. It is possible that in some instances such noises may be associated with humans or human actions by the mimicking bird and that one could, so to speak, say that it 'thinks' they are human calls. This is, however, very unlikely to hold good in all cases. It seems more likely that such extensions of vocal mimicry to sounds made by creatures or objects that the bird is *not* reacting to socially is because the tame bird, especially if it is a captive, has more 'spare' time than a wild individual and makes use of its mimicking ability to relieve the tedium. It is also possible that once the bird has begun to imitate sounds not normally in the species' repertoire, because of its social reactions to humans, this utterance of and interest in sounds unlike the specific calls inevitably leads to the bird being more receptive to other alien sounds. It should perhaps be mentioned, in connection with the suggestion that the captive bird has more 'spare' time, that wild corvids may at times be able to spend much time in apparently idle resting. It is however probable, as a result of their exertions when food seeking, escaping danger so on, that, like humans in comparable conditions, they are more ready to be inactive than is the safe well-fed but possibly bored captive.

Of corvids that are habitual vocal mimics in a wild state the Jay is the best known. It seems pertinent to discuss its mimicry further as, in all probability, other habitual corvine mimics will be found to behave very similarly.

Both sexes mimic but males usually indulge in more persistent and extensive mimicry than do females. A great many different sounds may be copied, ranging from the creaking of gates, the cawing of the Carrion Crow, and the 'Frank' call of the Grey Heron, to the trillings and warblings of small passerines. Tame Jays are particularly apt to imitate (usually to perfection) human whistling, although this bears little resemblance to any of their innate calls. I have never heard Jays attempt to mimic any calls of pigeons or doves even when they have been kept with them from an early age. It is, therefore, evident that it is not the frequency with which a sound is heard that determines whether or not the Jay will try to copy it.

Copied sounds may be rendered with considerable accuracy, sometimes, at least to my ears, with absolute fidelity. At other times the Jay may, however, render its mimicries in a quieter tone than the originals or it may 'refine and polish' a copied sound but finally render it more loudly than the original. I have known Jays do this with imitations of small passerine song phrases and of distant dripping water. At times Jays will produce what might be called 'a symbolic interpretation' of a sound or sounds.

Persistent mimicry, the use of mimicry when the bird is quietly resting or foraging, and the continual adding of new items to the repertoire and discarding of others are particularly characteristic of young, unpaired individuals. At least this is so with captive birds and circumstantial evidence suggests the same is true in the wild. Second-year (or older) individuals, that have paired, largely restrict their vocal imitations to what they have already learned, or part of it. They may, however, add a few new items to their repertoire from time to time. David Holyoak informs me (pers. comm.) that he has heard 'song' from known first- and second-year Carrion Crows but not from individuals known to be older.

Vocal mimicry may occur in self-assertive contexts and be incorporated in one or more of the individual's display phrases. Although the Jay will at times copy mechanical sounds of whose origin it must be in ignorance there can be no doubt that it often makes some mental association between a sound and the creature that produces it. Tame male Jays, when reacting aggressively to their keeper, invariably defy him with display phrases consisting partly or wholly of words or whistles that he has often used in their hearing, usually those with which he customarily greets them.

I have on several occasions seen a (different) wild Jay utter an imitation of the call of the Grey Heron on catching sight of one of these birds in flight. My tame jays, both this species and *G. lanceolatus*, often used to bark if a dog came into the garden and 'miaow' if a cat appeared. At such times I was reminded of a small child greeting an animal with an imitation of its cry. Imitations of the Tawny Owl are often given when mobbing owls, usually, however, not by the most active mobbers but by individuals more or less in the background. Löhrl observed how a party of Jays came to a Tawny Owl's habitual roosting place and, not finding it, some of them uttered imitations of its hootings before they flew off to another owl roost to mob the bird there!

The utterance of a particular sound seems often to be correlated with a particular emotional state, presumably similar to that under which the Jay first heard it. Thus on very many occasions when I have been examining Jays' nests containing young the parents have uttered vocal mimicry, either interspersed with their own screeches as they mobbed me or else more quietly as they waited in cover at a little distance. In these circumstances the copied sounds uttered have been the calls of the Tawny Owl and Carrion Crow (and rarely of domestic cat also) and the *alarm* calls of smaller species. Thus in a situation when the young are (in the Jay's estimation) in danger the mimicries uttered by the parent are all sounds that, if heard 'naturally' near the nest, would indicate actual or potential danger for the young.

Such other corvids as are known to mimic habitually in a wild state probably do so in similar circumstances to the Jay. Further information about their mimicry will be needed before definite statements can be made. In some non-corvine passerines that are frequent or habitual mimics, vocal mimicry may be incorporated in the territorial song. This is done, for example, by the Crested Lark, *Galerida cristata*, and the Skylark, *Alauda arvensis*.

The function of habitual vocal mimicry is perplexing and, in my opinion, none of the attempted explanations appears adequate. It is possible that, as with such birds as Ravens and parrots, previously discussed, individuals may be recognized by particular 'signature tunes' and perhaps recalled by the mate using them when they are absent. This does not, however, explain why most individuals of such species should practise extensive vocal mimicry of other species when wild for, as we have seen, Ravens and parrots do not do this. I might mention, incidentally, that on the two or three occasions when I have experimentally separated paired Jays, the temporarily bereaved individuals did not imitate their mate's personal display phrases but uttered innate calls.

Marshall, discussing vocal mimicry mainly in relation to Australian passerines, notes that there the most accomplished and persistent mimics tend to be territorial species that keep much to cover. He suggests that 'lack of visibility places a premium on sound . . . it is biologically advantageous for individuals to make more and more sound' and that some species achieve this by 'supplementing their natural notes with a "borrowed" repertoire'. That uttering frequent loud sounds may be of use to cover-haunting species I do not doubt but, like Thorpe (1964), I cannot see how this end is better achieved by vocal mimicry. There are very many noisy, cover-haunting species that do not practise it. Its use may aid recognition of individuals but individually recognizable nuances and variations of specific calls or songs are achieved by most species without its aid. It is difficult to see what biological function could be achieved by habitual vocal mimicry of other species that could not be equally well, and perhaps less ambiguously, achieved by the bird concentrating on its own specific sounds.

It may be significant that some species such as the Blackcap, *Sylvia atricapilla*, with fine specific songs into which they do not usually interject vocal mimicries, indulge in vocal mimicry at moments of intense sexual excitement and also when the young appear to be in danger from man (Howard, pers. obs.). The Jay's mimicry of owls and other predators suggests that under some circumstances vocal mimicry may possibly function to convey a more precise indication of the nature of the danger to other individuals than would be possible by the use of innate calls, but we have as yet no evidence that it does so function.

REFERENCES

BOSWALL, J. 1969. A bibliography of wild life sound recording. *Recorded Sound* **34**: 466–470.
GOODWIN, D. 1951. Some aspects of the behaviour of the Jay *Garrulus glandarius*. *Ibis* **93**: 421–425.
—— 1952. A comparative study of the voice and some aspects of behaviour in two Old World jays. *Behaviour* **4**: 301–302.
—— 1956. Further observations on the behaviour of the Jay. *Ibis* **98**: 213–214.
GWINNER, E. & KNEUTGEN, J. 1962. Über die biologische Bedeutung der 'zweckdienlichen' Anwendung erlernter Laute bei Vögeln. *Z. Tierpsychol.* **19**: 692–696.
HOWARD, E. 1909. *British Warblers* **1** (3): 63.
LÖHRL, H. 1968. *Tiere und Wir*. Berlin.
MARSHALL, J. 1950. The function of vocal mimicry in birds. *Emu* **50**: 5–16.
NICOLAI, J. 1959. Familientradition in der Gesangsentwicklung des Gimpels (*Pyrrhula pyrrhula* L.). *J. Orn.* **100**: 39–46.
THORPE, W. H. 1964. Mimicry: in *A New Dictionary of Birds*, London, pp. 473–476.

Escape, mobbing, and some other anti-predator behaviour

Birds of the crow family usually appear to have relatively few non-human predators, by comparison with smaller passerines, pigeons or game-birds. This impression is almost certainly correct where the larger species are concerned but may not be for many of the smaller ones. Conditions in Britain and some other countries, where the larger predatory birds and mammals have long been either exterminated or reduced to very small numbers, may however be very different from what they once were or from the situation in countries where predators have been less persecuted. Even the typical crows are liable to be killed by such birds as the Goshawk and Eagle Owl. A tame Tawny Owl has been known to kill a healthy adult Hooded Crow and it is possible that wild Tawny Owls may take other *Corvus* species, besides Jackdaws which they have been known to kill. Crows may possibly be killed, and are certainly sometimes kept away from food, by predatory mammals; and their eggs or young are vulnerable to a greater range of predators than are the adults.

With one or two possible exceptions the larger corvids are not concealingly coloured. The black or piebald crows of the genus *Corvus* and the Magpie, *Pica*, are conspicuous in most surroundings. The colour patterns of some forms, such as that of the Jay, *Garrulus glandarius*, are to some extent disruptive when the bird is in dappled light and shade among trees or shrubs. The largely grey, brown or green upperparts of some species may also have protective value, by making them less conspicuous to a bird-of-prey looking down from above. The coloration of such species as the Siberian Jay and Hume's

Ground Jay may be primarily cryptic. Many quite small species, such as the Blue Jay, are however highly conspicuous, allowing for the fact that in fairly dense cover almost any bird is difficult to pick out.

Jays and Lanceolated Jays may react to the sudden or close appearance of a flying Sparrow Hawk, *Accipiter nisus*, by darting into cover or by 'freezing' in a crouching posture. While its head and body remain absolutely still the jay's eyes move to a surprising degree within their sockets as it tries to keep the hawk in view or, if it has gone out of sight, to discover its whereabouts. If closely pursued by a hawk, a Jay will sharply change direction and dodge round, under or over boughs, usually staying within a small area and among the branches. I have seen this behaviour on a few occasions when a Sparrow Hawk has tried to catch one of a number of Jays that were mobbing it. That they are normal escaping tactics can be inferred from their being used in apparent play by immature Jays. Such play in birds usually involves movements which, when used in earnest, are used in attempts to escape from or when attacking predators.

It is probable that other woodland corvids behave similarly but little seems to have been recorded of their purely evasive behaviour towards predators. The Magpie, when in danger from birds of prey, tries to get into cover and stay there. Falconers indulging in the sport of Magpie-hawking apparently have great difficulty, even with the aid of whips and sticks, in driving the quarry from a bush or hedge in which it has taken cover.

Crows of the genus *Corvus* seem seldom to be observed taking cover although they will do when hard pressed, and sometimes keep in or under cover when a dangerous bird-of-prey is near. A frequent reaction even to those birds-of-prey which they greatly fear is to gain height in the open and try to get above and behind the hawk. This behaviour is shown by the Carrion Crow towards the Goshawk, and has been studied in detail by Löhrl (1950).

Crows of the genus *Corvus* frequently attack flying birds-of-prey by swooping down at them, usually at a steep angle. Sometimes the crow appears to try to peck its adversary or strikes and bounces off it with outstretched feet but more often the hawk turns over and presents its talons or dodges to one side at the crucial moment. As it attacks, and also when it parries an attack, a crow usually utters a short hard grating call (*Stossquarren* in German). With the Carrion Crow and with the Jay (which has an equivalent call) I have the impression that the variations of tone and emphasis of this grating call are correlated with the degree of fear or anger felt. Löhrl (1950) states that this grating call is never given by a Carrion Crow when it swoops at the greatly feared Goshawk, as it is when the crow attacks a Buzzard, Kestrel or some other less dangerous enemy. He concludes from this that the grating call indicates that the crow is not very frightened. I think another possibility is that the grating call depends on an emotional state that is only felt (and which seems often to involve fear) when the crow is almost or quite in contact with its foe. Possibly it does not, in its attacks on the Goshawk, dare to come close enough to its enemy to feel impelled to utter this call.

I have twice seen a Jay (a different one each time) very closely pursuing a Sparrow Hawk high in the air. In each case the birds were flying almost 'bill to tail', I saw no actual attacks by the Jay, and it soon dived down at great speed into a tree. In neither instance did I see the start of the pursuit. It seems very likely that the Jay was crossing an open space when it first saw the hawk and then got behind it for safety, only to dive to cover at first opportunity, rather than that it had deliberately followed the hawk into the open.

The function of the above-described behaviour of a corvid towards a flying bird-of-prey is clearly that the former tries to keep in positions where it cannot be successfully attacked. Its own attacks may possibly discourage the predator from hunting in the vicinity or from trying to catch corvids. Corvine attacks are not restricted to those species of hawks which are serious predators, some which represent little or no danger, such as the Kestrel, may be harried in this manner. Grey Herons are often treated in the same manner by Carrion and Hooded Crows, probably because their appearance and movements in flight suggest those of large birds-of-prey.

Some crows of the genus *Corvus* will very fiercely chase and harry such birds-of-prey as Kestrels and

Kites when these are carrying food.   Here robbery appears to be the chief motive but it is probable that the normal tendency to mob birds-of-prey is also involved.   It seems possible that such behaviour may develop, in the individual crow, from incidents of ordinary mobbing of a bird-of-prey in flight in which the crow is emboldened by the bird-of-prey being hampered by the food it carries, through the crow's having in such a situation been able to snatch up food which the hawk had dropped to defend itself. Similarly, the tendency to attack Herons may be reinforced by the fact that these birds sometimes disgorge food when harried by crows.

Like many other passerine and some non-passerine birds, corvids habitually mob predatory mammals, perched birds-of-prey and owls discovered by day.   Such predators usually present no danger to a bird capable of flight, so long as it has them in sight.   The details of mobbing may vary according to differences in species, of both mobber and mobbed, and many other factors.   It always, however, involves approaching the predator and uttering loud calls that usually attract the attention of other corvids of the same species, and often of many other birds.   Very often attacks are made on the predator.   The mobbing birds or some of them, usually one at a time, dive at it from behind and either peck at it, hit it with their feet as they 'bounce off' to safety, or swerve upwards or sideways through fear getting the better of anger before making actual contact.   When magpies or typical crows are mobbing a predator on the ground one often walks or hops up quietly behind it and pecks or pulls at its tail when its attention is fixed on a bird in front of it.   Corvids that are breeding, and especially such as have dependent young either in or out of the nest, usually mob predators much more fiercely and persistently than do non-breeding individuals.   They also continue mobbing longer; non-breeding birds usually lose interest after a few minutes mobbing, especially if the predator remains still.

Although unfamiliar creatures that are harmless, and apparently harmless birds-of-prey, are sometimes mobbed, as a general rule only species which sometimes prey on a corvid or bear considerable resemblance to species that do are regularly mobbed by it.   For example, I have on several occasions seen Jays taking no notice of a Little Owl perched near them and have never seen this species mobbed by Jays.   Even a Jay initially attracted by smaller birds mobbing a Little Owl merely hopped up close, looked at it from a few inches away without any signs of alarm or anger and then flew off.   Nor, so far as I am aware, does the Little Owl prey on Jays.   On the other hand, the Tawny Owl is habitually mobbed by Jays and some Tawny Owls take roosting or brooding Jays when they get an opportunity.

It is said (see Seitz) that some individuals of both Red and Silver Foxes catch Carrion or Hooded Crows by feigning death and then suddenly springing at the nearest of the approaching birds.   It is not certain from the descriptions whether in these cases the Crows were mobbing the fox or approaching it to feed on a supposed corpse.   Further observations are needed.   It is possible that wrong interpretations of the behaviour involved might have arisen if, for example, a person had at one time seen Crows approaching or mobbing a dead or quiescent fox and, at another, a fox which had caught a crow in some other manner (such as by finding it sick, injured, in a gin trap, or tethered as a decoy) being mobbed by other Crows as it carried its prey.

I think the primary functions of mobbing are to alert conspecifics to the presence and whereabouts of the predator and to impress its appearance on inexperienced young individuals.   In some species there may be little or no innate recognition of some or even of any predators.   Even when there is some innate recognition, it is likely that finer specific and behavioural details have to be learned.   Other possible functions of mobbing are to discourage the predator from staying or hunting in the vicinity, or to discourage it from attacking the species mobbing it.   It is probably only under certain circumstances, such as with wandering or migrating predators, that such effects may be achieved.   It is, for example, rather unlikely that a Tawny Owl, mobbed at its roosting site by Jays during the day, is thereby discouraged from hunting in the neighbourhood at night or from taking a roosting or incubating Jay should it find one.

The motivation prompting mobbing seems to be conflicting feelings of anger and fear.   Curiosity may also be involved, especially with inexperienced individuals.   Mobbing birds seem often under some kind of compulsive attraction, perhaps comparable with that which prompts many humans to gather and stare at accident victims or to look at, and very often also to tease or torment, any captive or helpless animal of a species they fear. Jays have been seen (Löhrl, 1968) to come to a Tawny Owl's roosting place, apparently with the deliberate intention of mobbing it and, not finding it at home (it had been caught and removed), to fly straight to the next nearest Tawny Owl's roosting site and mob the owl there!

Some species of *Corvus* often rob predatory mammals and birds of food they are eating or about to eat. One bird approaches from behind and pecks or pulls the predator's tail. If it turns round, and especially if it runs or flies after its tormentor, the crow or crows in front try to snatch up the food and often succeed in doing so. As with the attacks on birds-of-prey carrying food on the wing, it is probable that this behaviour often or usually originates in and evolves from simple predator-mobbing. These tactics may be accompanied by actual mobbing behaviour and where they are not it is probably because the crows have learned not to fear the species in question. Such food robbery has been most often observed with domestic dogs or Black Kites, *Milvus migrans*, as the victims, probably because these two scavenging predators are so abundant in many inhabited areas.

It has often been implied or claimed (e.g. Finn, 1919; Seitz, 1950) that two or more crows will deliberately cooperate, the one that attacks from behind doing so 'in order' that its mate or companions shall have an opportunity to snatch the food. This may sometimes happen and is difficult to disprove, but there is no need to assume this explanation. The behaviour is essentially similar to that shown at times by crows that are harrassing a foodless predator, or by a single crow. The fact that one or more of the birds in front seize their opportunity when another crow attacks from behind is no proof that the latter is acting on their behalf.

I once had a good demonstration that the tail-pulling tactics can be effective even when only one crow is involved. A Whistling Kite, *Haliastur sphenurus*, carried a rabbit's leg into a gum tree and began to feed from it. Suddenly, to my astonishment, the shining black head and white eyes of an Australian Raven appeared from among the foliage behind the Kite. The Raven circled, hopping and walking along the main branch and on subsidiary ones. The Kite endeavoured to face it but twice the Raven managed to get behind it and tweak its tail. The second time this happened the Kite itself knocked the rabbit's leg off the branch as it moved round to face its foe. It did not seem conscious of what it had done as, for several minutes after the Australian Raven had gone down, picked up the food and flown away with it, the Kite continued to peer about on the branch in a puzzled manner.

Many, possibly all, corvids react with mobbing behaviour, or some elements of it, to situations in which a conspecific or closely related species appears to be in acute danger from a predator. With some (perhaps all) *Corvus* species, this mobbing response is usually elicited when anything crow-like is carried by another creature. Lorenz, in detailed experiments with Jackdaws, concluded that the stimulus releasing this response was anything black and more or less shiny in appearance being carried by any creature. Later experiments with Carrion Crows and Lorenz's own later observations (Kramer), however, suggested that the basic stimulus needed to elicit the response was any situation in which a conspecific appeared to be in danger. Thus wild Carrion Crows mobbed Kramer when he carried a tame young Crow perched on his head or shoulder. Wild Jackdaws often give their mobbing call if a human closely approaches their young (Lorenz, in Kramer 1941, pers. obs.) although Lorenz's tame Jackdaws only did so when their young were handled.

Captive Jays that were reacting socially to humans did not give a mobbing response when I held a struggling and screaming Jay in my hands in full sight of them. Jays bred in captivity but reared by their own parents and which were, therefore, not reacting socially to man (as were their hand-reared parents) at once mobbed me when they saw a struggling Jay in my hand (Goodwin, 1952, 1956). It appeared that to the Jays which were reacting socially to me, the situation when I held a Jay in my hand was in the nature of 'Jay being ill-treated by another Jay' whereas to Jays that did not regard me as a conspecific it was 'Jay being held by a predator'. Some of Lorenz's observations on his Ravens make it seem likely that the same applies to this species. It seems evident that in many birds there are, as in man, differences between the feelings aroused by and the consequent responses to situations in which another of the same species has been seized by a predator and one in which it is being illtreated or killed by a higher ranking conspecific.

It must be added that corvids (including Jays) that are reacting socially to a human may mob or attack him if he holds their mate or young or arouses parental, sexual, or territorial aggression in some other way. Some corvids, such as the Raven and the Magpie, will, if a human they are friendly with tries to catch or seizes another creature, even if it is a conspecific, often 'join the hunt' and attack or attempt to attack the 'victim'. This reaction is not, however, connected with predator mobbing. It is not shown unless they regard the human concerned as 'one of themselves'. It is not, incidentally, shown by the Jay.

Where man is seldom seen corvids may mob him at close quarters as they do other predatory mammals. Where he is omnipresent but does them no harm they usually show little fear of him. Where they are persecuted by man they usually show considerable fear. Naturally, any sort of intermediate response may be shown in less clearly defined circumstances than those described above.

In areas where they have been frequently shot at, corvids (and many other birds) appear to recognize that man (unlike any other mammalian predator) can strike at a distance and they usually try to keep well out of shot-gun range. Even when they mob him, they usually do so from a safe distance. Jays, for example, often mob a human with what are basically the same calls as they use when mobbing other predators but, instead of approaching closely as they would to an owl or fox, they *first* flee to cover and stay there while calling. This behaviour shows remarkable adaptation to a totally 'unnatural' type of danger. It appears to involve the combining of aspects of both normal reactions to dangerous flying birds-of-prey and those to mammal predators, together with an increase of the 'flight distance'. Comparable behaviour towards man is shown not only by other relatively intelligent corvids but also by, for example, pigeons and thrushes. It is of great interest and, obviously, of great importance for the survival of certain species.

Corvids that are reacting socially to humans can recognize individual men and women, apparently chiefly by their faces and voices. This is not surprising as they can also recognize individual conspecifics, who show much less marked differences from each other than do humans of western European stock. Wild crows, at any rate some species of the genus *Corvus* (Goodwin, 1946; Kramer, 1941; Ryves, 1948) can, however, also quickly learn to distinguish individual humans. This is, of course, of great benefit to them in areas where humans are abundant but only certain individual humans are dangerous to them or provide food for them.

It is frequently claimed that crows can learn to recognize a gun and fear a man with a gun more than one without. There seems to be some circumstantial evidence for this, at least with the Rook, American Crow and Carrion Crow, but it is difficult to evaluate as other factors may be involved. The man with the gun may, for example, be recognized individually with or without his weapon although *he* may only notice that the birds are particularly shy of him on occasions when he is trying to shoot them. The movements of a man hunting or stalking some creature, particularly his tenseness and his tendency to fix his eyes on his prospective victim, are characteristic of many predators and tend to arouse alarm and suspicion, gun or no gun. Any unusual extension from the human body is frightening to birds familiar with the latter, especially if it extends upwards. Otherwise completely tame corvids can be (to varying degrees dependent on varying factors) frightened or intimidated if one lifts up a stick or any other elongate object so that it projects above one's head.

Corvids, like other birds, usually become alarmed if, when they are close to a human, he fixes his eyes on them, even at a distance at which they would not otherwise fear him. The lifting up and focusing of binoculars on them will (at least in Britain) usually alarm Carrion Crows, sometimes also Rooks, Jackdaws and Magpies, at a considerable distance. It would be of interest to know whether this response is because the action appears to the bird similar to that of raising and aiming a gun, and is a learned response caused by shooting. When I was in the grounds of the Colombo Zoo, in Ceylon, I found that the House Crows and Jungle Crows there paid no attention when I looked at them through binoculars, presumably because they had never been persecuted. Both these species are known to learn fear of humans, or of particular humans, very quickly where they are shot at.

Ravens and some other corvids are often very frightened at any alteration in their accustomed surroundings, or of any new object that has been introduced to it. It is not easy to see what non-human dangers such behaviour would help to circumvent but it has probably 'pre-adapted' the birds to avoiding traps. Indeed it may well be that this tendency has only developed in those species which have for very long been associated with man. In this connection it must be remembered that man has been trapping and snaring birds much longer than he has been shooting them with guns. However, they sooner or later become accustomed to most new things, if these have not meanwhile proved harmful. There seems no evidence that wild birds often, if ever, have this fear of something unusual aroused to the same extent as captive birds that have been long kept in an impoverished and unaltering environment. These latter sometimes show prolonged and intense fear responses to even quite small changes of their surroundings.

It is sometimes said that corvids that feed in company deliberately post sentinels to warn the feeding individuals of approaching danger. Similar claims have been made for cockatoos, geese and other birds. I think that such claims are based on wrong interpretation of the behaviour involved. At least as regards the Rook, of which such stories are often told, I am convinced that this is so.

When a number of Rooks (or any other species) are seeking food, some individuals may at any particular moment be less hungry or more suspicious than the rest, or temporarily sated. Such birds often perch on some tree or fence where they can get a good view around. These often see approaching danger before their comrades on the ground do, and their flying off in fear or their cries of alarm may cause the feeding birds to follow or alert them to the danger. The temporarily perched individuals may thus function as sentinels but they are not appointed nor do they appoint themselves as such.

Selous gives several instances where an apparent 'sentinel' Rook, having seen his approach from a distance, flew off 'in good time' without any signs of alarm and, as a result, did *not* alert other Rooks feeding nearby out of sight of him. I have had similar experiences with both Rooks and Carrion Crows. On several occasions, when I have been watching unconcealed at a rookery, a male Rook coming to feed his sitting mate, suddenly noticing me, and apparently taking fright, has turned in flight and either circled round or settled in a tree further from me than that in which his mate was on her nest. One might expect that then, if ever, one Rook might deliberately try to warn another but it does not. Either the apparently puzzled female's repeated begging towards her mate finally induces him to come to the nest and feed her or, more often, when he does not do so she flies to him. He then feeds her and makes no attempt to stop her returning to the nest as, of course, she does immediately afterwards.

Similar behaviour can be seen in other species. In those which do not nest colonially the male is usually even more reluctant to come to the nest if he is at all frightened or suspicious. In some (probably most) species that live in more or less territorial pairs when breeding, the male often spends much time on some look-out perch while the female is incubating or seeking food. Should he see danger approaching his calls and movements usually alert her to it or induce her to follow him and thus avoid it. In at least one species, the Piñon Jay, sentinel-like behaviour seems to be at a higher level. Feeding flocks commonly have several 'look-outs' who always give loud warning of danger (Balda & Bateman).

In these cases also there seems to be no evidence that there is any deliberate giving of information or attempt to do so. The male simply expresses his own feelings of alarm, anxiety, or hostility at the sight of danger approaching himself or his mate. She may, and usually does, become alarmed or anxious through seeing or hearing him and, as a result, discovers the danger for herself or flees in good time. The processes involved, as with those in many other social situations, have much in common with the way in which humans often unintentionally infect other men or women with their own feelings of joy, fear, suspicion and so on, but little or nothing in common with the deliberate giving of verbal information by one human to another.

REFERENCES

BALDA, R. P. & BATEMAN, G. C.   1971.   Flocking and annual cycle of the Piñon Jay, *Gymnorhinus cyanocephalus*. *Condor* **73**: 287–302.

FINN, F.   1919.   *Bird Behaviour*, p. 260.   London.

GOODWIN, D.   1946.   Odd hours with Brown-necked Ravens.   *Avicult. Mag.* **52**: 90–97.

——1952.   A comparative study of the voice and some aspects of behaviour in two Old World Jays.   *Behaviour* **4**: 293–316.

——1956.   Further observations on the behaviour of the Jay *Garrulus glandarius*.   *Ibis* **98**: 186–219.

KRAMER, G.   1941.   Beobachtungen über das Verhalten der Aaskrähe (*Corvus corone*) zu Freund und Feind.   *J. Orn.* **89**: Sonderheft: 105–131.

LÖHRL, H.   1950.   Verhalten der Rabenkrähe (*Corvus c. corone*) gegenuber dem Habicht.   *Z. Tierpsychol.* **7**: 130–133.

——1968.   *Tiere und Wir*, p. 41.   Berlin.

LORENZ, K.   1931.   Beiträge zur Ethologie sozialer Corviden.   *J. Orn.* **79**: 67–127.

RYVES, B. H.   1948.   *Bird Life in Cornwall*.   London.

SEITZ, A.   1950.   Verhaltensstudien an Caniden.   *Z. Tierpsychol.* **7**: 33–46.

SELOUS, E.   1901.   *Bird Watching*.   London.

CHAPTER 5
THE CROW FAMILY

Man and crows

Corvids, of one species or another, are characteristic and common birds of many parts of the world where man has long been established. They are usually conspicuous and their quick-wittedness often enables them to profit from opportunities created by man's activities and largely to frustrate any attempts he may make to get rid of them.

It is, therefore, understandable that they often play a part in folklore, legend and literature. Nor, in view of man's intolerance of food-competitors, or creatures that he regards as such, is it surprising that many of the references to them are uncomplimentary: 'Crows are never whiter for washing themselves', 'Khrishna's name in a crow's mouth' and so on. It is, however, at least partly factors other than the actual damage that they do or are thought to do to man's interests, that are responsible for much of the hostile attitude that man often shows towards them.

Darkness is connected in the human mind with ideas of death or other disaster. There are good reasons for this. Man's inability to see effectively in the dark meant that through long ages he necessarily associated darkness with danger from beasts of prey. When, in the course of his increasing technical ability, this danger became, over much of the world, non-existent or relatively small, his own species, with some group or individual of which he was all too likely to be at enmity, represented an equal danger, as indeed it still does today, even in some of the most supposedly civilized cities of the world. It is, therefore, not surprising that even the modern child still instinctively fears the dark. A second, possibly less potent, reason for the feeling of apprehension at darkness is that there is a very basic association of darkness with dominance in vertebrates. In many species of mammals and birds the adult males, and in some instances breeding adults of both sexes, are darker than those phases or age-classes of their species that are usually subordinate to them, or have black areas of pelage or plumage which they display in threat or self assertion. Human clothing often makes this principle abundantly clear. Examples are the black (or near-black) uniform and helmet of the policeman and the black gown of the old-time schoolmaster. It is significant that the latter is usually discarded now that schoolmasters no longer have so dominant a status in relation to their scholars.

The typical crows of the genus *Corvus* with their entirely or predominantly black plumage and harsh voices, epitomized by the Raven with its deep gruff calls and carrion-eating habits, must surely have made a deep impression. In Norse mythology the Raven was sacred to the god Odin, whose two Ravens, Thought and Memory, flew about the world all day and at evening returned to their master's shoulders to tell him all that was going on. The Raven's small degree of sanctity was not, however, sufficient to prevent it being sometimes made use of as a land-finding bird, carried at sea to be released and followed in the hope that it would find land when the crew had lost their bearings. According to tradition Iceland was first discovered in this manner.

The Raven's reputation as a bird of evil omen may have been heightened by its association in much of western Europe, including the British Isles, with the Viking raiders and invaders who are said to have used as their emblem representations of this species. Some of the reproductions of such emblems that I have seen struck me, however, as at least as suggestive of Great Skuas, *Catharacta skua*, as of Ravens. The Raven played a similarly ungrateful part in the floods of both Noah and his earlier prototype Gilgamesh. English literature is full of baleful references to it and other crows. By some of the Alaskan tribes the Raven is, or at least was, more happily credited with bringing light to the world, although the combination of magic and trickery by which it achieved this laudable end might not commend itself to the moral purist. I have been unable to trace the recorder of this last legend, which I read in 1941, when at sea. Armstrong (1958), however, in his comprehensive book on bird folklore, quotes a rather similar legend, besides much else of interest on the mythology of the Raven.

The tendency for corvids, like many other birds, to persist from generation to generation in suitable territories has, presumably, been responsible for the many legends about their supposed longevity. The

60

House Crow of India has been popularly credited with immortality; the old folk saying holds that 'a Crow lives three times as long as a man, a Raven lives three times as long as a Crow'; Medea used 'the head and beak of a Crow more than nine generations old' in rejuvenating broth (Ovid). I believe the greatest age recorded for a captive Raven was twenty-nine years, for the late Miss Frances Pitt's famous 'Joe', (Pitt, 1946). As this bird apparently died of senile decay, it is doubtful if wild ones often live longer.

In Europe the harsh notes of the Jay and Magpie (their softer ones have not been much noticed by writers or poets) have often been picked on to illustrate the doubtful hypothesis that good looks indicate a lack of deeper or more endearing qualities. Goldsmith, for example, after acknowledging the beauty of the Magpie, adds that it 'has too many of the qualities of a beau to offset these natural perfections'. In La Fontaine's fable of the Nightingale and the Blackcap the latter's claims for singing ability were scornfully dismissed because the Jay upheld them.

In technically 'advanced' countries man has now got the upper hand over birds-of-prey and such large mammals as once plagued him, but not, or not to such a great extent, over the corvids. The rise of intensive game-bird and wildfowl 'preservation', which got under way by about the middle of the last century, coincided with a growing appreciation of and sentimental affection for *small* passerine birds. The popularity of killing game-birds and feeding small birds has since continued, having been rather enhanced than diminished by the partial replacement of the Lord of the Manor and his guests by syndicates and societies of shooters and by the ever-growing web of officialdom, technology and machinery encompassing the average man or woman in town or suburb.

As a result the corvids, as predators on the eggs and young of both game-birds and song-birds, have been and still are under fire, both literally and metaphorically, from bird-shooters and bird-lovers. Our more robust and forthright ancestors expressed their dislike with pungency and wit: 'The crow is a fungus of city life, a corollary of man and sin' (Eha); their modern counterparts are apt to talk about 'the need to control corvine birds', but so far as the crows, jays and magpies are concerned the effects are the same. It is, however, a measure of corvine achievement that this hostility persists. Once man's efforts against a bird species have been crowned with success, as with the Red Kite in Britain for example, his attitude, at least publicly, usually changes to one of vain regret and an assiduous cossetting of any last pitiful survivors.

The northern or grey jays of the genus *Perisoreus* seem to have sometimes aroused affection and interest, sometimes hatred and persecution by their lack of fear when visiting camps and their tendency to fly off with any portable food and to tear to bits any that they cannot carry. It is interesting that both the Lapps of Europe (Carpelan) and some of the American Indians (Turner, in Bendire) believed that serious bad luck would follow if anyone saw the nest of a northern jay, let alone interfered with it. At least with the Amerindians this belief was not correlated with any inhibitions against killing the adult jays when they showed themselves in camp.

Corvids, like many other birds, may cause damage to crops. It was claimed that in the early 1940s Rooks in Britain were taking about £3 million worth of grain a year. Many other corvids take grain, although probably few to the same extent as the Rook. Carrion Crows, Ravens and Australian Ravens sometimes kill weakly lambs and are often found feeding on the carcasses of lambs that have died or been killed by other predators and so get blamed for their deaths. The Brown-necked Raven may do much damage to date crops at the edge of desert oases. In parts of eastern Europe the Jay takes ripening maize, and so on. It is quite possible that, at least in some cases, the number of insects and small mammals taken by corvids compensates or outweighs the damage to human foodstuffs. Such possible benefits are, however, difficult to evaluate and seldom so obvious as the damage done.

Perhaps partly because man is a hunter by instinct but only a grower of food by virtue of reason and necessity, the damage done or thought to be done to sporting interests earns the corvids much more dislike than does the damage they do to agriculture. This at least is the case in Britain and, apparently, throughout much of Europe and North America. It is likely that, in terms of human food, the Rook is the most harmful, or least useful, of British corvids. As, however, it is believed to be much less harmful to game and wildfowl-shooting interests than the Crow, Magpie or Jay it is seldom so consistently persecuted and, unlike its relatives, has a very large body of people in favour of it.

Birds of the crow kind have often been locally used for food, young Rooks in England, Choughs in parts of the western Himalayas, *Corvus* species in the West Indies and so on. They have, however, seldom been so widely popular as human food as have game-birds, waterfowl, doves or thrushes. Peoples' tastes in foods vary culturally, racially and individually and birds of the same species can (to the same person) taste good or bad according to the food they have themselves lately fed upon. It is, therefore, not easy to say whether or to what extent corvids are inferior as human food to some other forms. What is certain is that the scavenging and carrion-eating habits of some of the typical crows have caused *Corvus* species to be regarded as unclean and unfit for food in many different parts of the world. This, although it may have done them some harm in alienating human sympathy, has probably been largely advantageous to the crows. Only peoples who are relatively rich and well-fed, or very greatly incommoded by them, are usually willing to spend money or time killing or catching crows that can be neither sold nor eaten.

Prophecies are notoriously liable to error. It is, however, of interest to speculate as to the possible joint future of man and crows. It seems rather unlikely that, as a family, the corvids will be extirpated by man or his activities. Some forms may become extinct through destruction of suitable habitat. This fate may already threaten the Florida race of the Scrub Jay. Others may be locally wiped out or much reduced in numbers by direct persecution, especially if modern poisoning techniques are used on a large scale. Should man suffer reverses which drastically decrease his numbers, it is likely that a corresponding drop in the numbers of some presently very successful corvids would take place. If man's numbers continue to increase until all those parts of the earth productive of food for corvids are either built over or rendered barren by contamination, the crow family will, of course, become extinct. It is, however, questionable whether man will be able to increase to and survive at such densities. If he does not the corvids would seem likely to have as hopeful a chance for future survival as most other birds and a much better chance than some of them.

REFERENCES

ARMSTRONG, E. A. 1958. *The Folklore of Birds*. London.
BENDIRE, C. 1895. Life Histories of North American Birds. *U.S. Nat. Mus. Spec. Bull.*
CARPELAN, J. 1929. Einige Beobachtungen über Lebensweise und Fortpflanzung des Unglückshähers im nördlichen Finnland. *Beitr. Fortpfl. biol. Vög.* **5**: 60–63.
'EHA', E. H. AITKIN. 1881. *The Tribes on my Frontier*. Bombay.
GOLDSMITH, O. 1728–1774. *A History of the Earth and Animated Nature* vol. 2. London.
OVID,. *The Metamorphoses*.
PITT, F. 1946. *Birds in Britain*. London.

The typical crows

The typical crows of the genus *Corvus* are, with two or three possible exceptions, all birds that anyone would at once recognize as 'some sort of crow'. Ravens, Rook and Jackdaw are, of course, crows in all but name. Some workers have divided these species into several genera but, as the late Col. Meinertzhagen (1926) wrote, 'Students of any area may stand aghast [at including the Thick-billed Raven and the Jackdaw in the same genus] but if they examine all the intermediate forms they will find it difficult to disagree'.

The typical crows are all, as compared with other corvids or, for that matter with other passerines in general, fairly large to very large in size. They have strong legs and feet, strong and usually rather large bills, large wings, tails usually of moderate length, sometimes short, sometimes rather long and somewhat graduated but never to an extreme degree. They are all black, black and grey, black and white, or some shade of grey in colour. Some (perhaps all) of them have white or pale blue nictitating membranes which are drawn over the eyes in some displays. Often they have beautiful purple, blue, green or silvery sheen on the plumage but otherwise, except for the red or pink mouths of young birds, they are completely without bright colours.

A very basic pattern in the genus seems to be that in which the face, forehead, crown, throat, wings and tail are a very intense or glossy black and the rest of the plumage, especially on the neck and sides of the head, much less so. This pattern is seen well developed in the House Crow and the Jackdaw but is visible on close inspection in many forms that appear more or less uniform black at a little distance. Often the feather bases, especially on the neck and mantle, are extensively white.

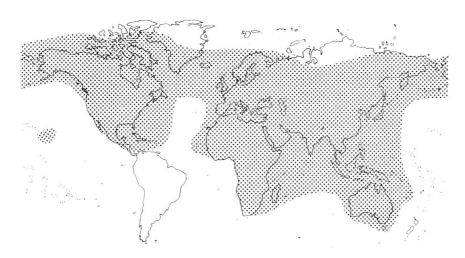

Many species of *Corvus* have the feathers of the throat elongated or bifurcated at the tips. Every intergradation occurs between species whose throat feathers show one or both of these characters to a marked degree and the opposite extreme in which the throat feathers are short and silky, hairy, or bristly.

The typical crows are lively, intelligent and often adaptable and highly successful species. They are almost cosmopolitan in distribution but are not found in South America, New Zealand, or the Antarctic. An extinct crow, *Palaeocorax*, is thought to have once been common in New Zealand but it seems possible, as Amadon (1944) suggests, that the subfossil remains involved may be those of a crow-like cracticid rather than of a corvid.

Members of the genus *Corvus* inhabit all types of country from forest to tree-less tundras and deserts but they are typically birds of more or less open but tree-grown areas: savanna woodland, natural or artificial parkland, wood edges, steppeland with forest islands or at least occasional trees, and cultivated areas. It seems likely that 'Proto-Corvus' evolved from some more jay-like form in the course of adaptation to life in more open country, these adaptations then enabling it to spread more widely over the world than any of its relatives. Dorst has suggested that its wide distribution indicates that *Corvus* is an old genus. If this is the case, the relative homogeneity of the species within it could indicate either the success of the basic 'crow' type or a relative lack of further genetic mutability once this type had evolved. I think, however, that it is rather more likely that *Corvus* is a relatively young and very successful genus whose members have been and perhaps still are successfully adapting and speciating to fill various mostly rather broad niches, mainly but not entirely in the sort of habitats to which the prototype became adapted. It is, however, very likely that having lost the ability to produce carotenoid pigments or structural blue (one or both of which are possessed by so many other corvids) they are now willy-nilly circumscribed to a narrow range of plumage hues.

Within the Corvidae, *Corvus* is usually considered as being closest to the choughs, *Pyrrhocorax* (see esp. Amadon). It is certainly likely that the choughs represent an offshoot of *Corvus* or rather proto-*Corvus* stock that became adapted to rocky, mountainous regions, and are thus the closest relatives of the typical crows. It is, however, also possible that the choughs and crows may represent relatively unrelated stocks, within the same family, that show some convergent similarities – large wings, black plumage, gregariousness – through both becoming adapted to largely open habitats. The similarity

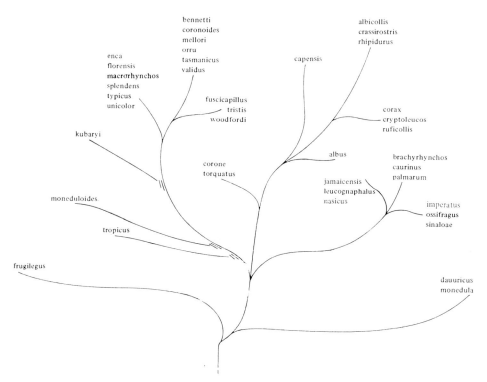

FIG. D.2.   Presumed relationships of the typical crows of the genus *Corvus*.   Owing to the number of species, groups are arranged in alphabetical order and members of superspecies are not indicated as such.

of some calls of the Chough to some calls of the Jackdaw is striking but might possibly be due to convergence.

Most, probably all, of the typical crows are omnivorous, with insects and other invertebrate animals usually comprising an important part of their diet. A few tropical forms are frugivorous so far as is known but it is extremely unlikely that they confine themselves entirely to fruit, especially when rearing their young.   The Raven is largely a predator of birds and small mammals and a carrion feeder in parts of its range and a few other species hardly less so.   Most species have the nostrils covered with a stiff mat of nasal bristles.   Those that do not are species known to be largely arboreal and frugivorous in feeding habits and it is possible that these might, therefore, be in less need of having their nostrils protected against dust or sharp stems of grass and the like or, alternatively, that they might be more incommoded by the bristles becoming gummed up with viscous juices.   The Rook, with its completely bare nostrils, is in a different category and it is possible that in its case there has been selective value in loss of nasal bristles (and some of the facial feathers) in the adult, to enable the age groups to be immediately identifiable.

Many, perhaps all, *Corvus* species store food but, so far as is known, none of them relies on its stores to the same extent as some jays and the nutcrackers do.   Food is held underfoot to be torn or hammered with the bill.   One or, less often in most species, both feet may be used to hold down food.   When one only is used it is more often than not the right foot.   Dunking of food (see p.20) occurs commonly in this genus.   Some species sometimes carry objects in their feet.

All species whose habits are known are more or less social.   Typically breeding pairs hold territory from which they may or may not exclude immature and non-breeding individuals. These latter often go about in loose flocks although they sometimes hold territory.   Even territory owners often join neighbouring pairs at the boundaries and may go to a communal roost at night.   Some species nest colonially or semi-colonially.   This habit has apparently evolved in response to living in open country with ample feeding space but with only sparsely-scattered clumps of trees suitable for nesting, or to using holes or caves as nest sites.

In all species whose breeding habits are known both sexes build; the male feeds the incubating female; both sexes feed the young; only the female regularly incubates but the male may stand in or over the nest to guard eggs or young while the female takes a brief flight. Incubation by the male has been recorded in a few species but further evidence is needed before it can be accepted that these records do not refer to aberrant behaviour or errors in sex identification. Tail quivering in both sexual and appeasing contexts occurs in many, probably all, species. Juvenile-type begging is shown by adults in some situations. Allo-preening between members of a pair, sometimes between siblings also, occurs in many species, possibly in all.

Crows of the genus *Corvus* are characteristic and common birds of inhabited regions over most of their range. Their being naturally (for the most part) birds of more or less open country and largely omnivorous has pre-adapted them to many of the types of habitat created by man. Furthermore their intelligence, suspicion and learning ability have enabled them to thrive in spite of persecution by man except when this has been very intensive and persistent. Indeed, until man had modern firearms and modern poisons, he was not usually able to make any serious reduction in the numbers of his corvine neighbours even when he wished to do so. This is vividly indicated in the illustration of sowing in the Luttrell Psalter (*c.* 1340) where the sower's dog is shown chasing off one crow from the new-sown field while another helps itself from the grain bag.

Crows, *Corvus orru* and *C. coronoides*, scavenge around the camps of some of the present-day Australian Aborigines and it is extremely likely that many species of *Corvus*, in different parts of the world, became camp-followers of man when he was at the hunting and food-gathering stage. Possibly his dogs were the original attraction. Where these animals live largely as scavengers they still attract the attention of crows as potential food competitors and predators to be mobbed but also as indicators of the probable presence of food. In parts of Britain today the fox, *Vulpes vulpes*, plays this dual role in the life of the Carrion Crow.

Any crows that had started to hang around man in his hunting stage would have had little difficulty in continuing to do so when he turned to herding or farming. Scraps from killed wild animals would be replaced by wastage from the slaughter of domestic ones or their death through neglect and ill-treatment. There would also be insects, such as various coprophagous beetles and their larvae, to be found in or under the droppings of his cattle. When and where man took to agriculture instead of or in addition to stock-keeping or herding, this resulted in two other sources of food: grain, when it was sown and when it was ready for or spilled after harvesting, and the insects and other small creatures exposed by cultivation. It was probably not until man had reached this stage that the less carnivorous species, such as the Rook and the Jackdaw, began to associate with him.

At all cultural levels, at least until very recent times, battles provided carrion in the form of both human and animal bodies for the Raven and, probably, some other species as well. The Raven's leading place in Norse mythology appears to be due as much to its former almost invariable presence on battlefields as to its ominous black plumage and sepulchral voice.

Crows have successfully populated towns, but appear only able to do so in numbers where the town is either small enough for them to forage freely outside it also or is so situated that the breeding crows can find enough natural food to rear their young, and where the human population is not seriously hostile. This last may be a more important factor than is commonly supposed. For example, the Carrion Crow is a moderately common although hardly numerous species in London and some other towns but because of its fear of man (due to past or present persecution by him) it cannot exploit all food sources that would otherwise be available to it. One has only to compare the way in which the Carrion Crow in London restricts its scavenging to roof tops, large open spaces and the river's edge, only sometimes coming down into small gardens, streets and so on when they are temporarily deserted of people, with the behaviour of the conspecific Hooded Crow in Egypt, to say nothing of that of the House Crow in India, to realize how much man's feelings towards it can affect a bird's behaviour and consequent opportunities.

Owing to the general similarity of most *Corvus* species, the little that is known of the calls and behaviour of many of them, and the high probability that some resemblances are due to convergence within the genus, speculations as to relationships must be tentative in many cases. For similar reasons it is often difficult to decide whether to treat certain forms as 'good' species or not and, on present knowledge, many such decisions must be arbitrary and may later be proved wrong.

The Carrion Crow, *Corvus corone*, and the Hooded Crow, *C. cornix*, of Europe and Asia are now usually treated as conspecific and this seems correct. In spite of their considerable differences of coloration, presumably evolved during the last ice age when their respective ancestors must have been separated (see Meise 1928), they show no significant differences of voice or behaviour and interbreed or hybridize freely where their ranges overlap, as in northern Scotland. It has been suggested that the relative narrowness of the hybrid zones indicate that on either side of them selection is working respectively against black or hooded individuals or hybrids carrying their respective genes. It is, however, worth emphasizing that at present most of the more divergent types of habitat and climate within their joint ranges are occupied by black crows in one area and grey in another. Those who talk of the Hooded Crow being better adapted to hills and the Carrion Crow to lowlands have only to go as far as central Europe where they will find Carrion Crows in the alps and Hoodies on the Danube plain.

Differences in voice, or at any rate accent, certainly exist between some populations of Hooded Crows and some of Carrion Crows, but these appear to be no greater than those existing between some Carrion Crow populations. I have the impression that most of the calls I have heard from Hooded Crows in Scotland have been rather less clear and vibrant in character than comparable calls from Carrion Crows around London, but Dr C. J. F. Coombs, who has kept and studied both forms, informs me that he noticed far greater vocal differences between Spanish and Cornish Carrion Crows than between the latter and Scottish Hoodies.

The very distinct pale Iraqi form, *C. corone capellanus*, is sometimes considered a full species. Apart from the extreme pallor of the 'grey' parts of its plumage, it also differs from other forms of the Hooded Crow in having, on average, longer throat hackles, a larger bill and slightly more graduated tail. It has, however, precisely the same plumage pattern as *cornix*, one which differs markedly from the more usual colour pattern of most black and grey or black and white *Corvus* species in that the same shade of grey extends down the back and underparts to the upper and under tail coverts, instead of being more or less restricted to the mantle and lower breast as in other particoloured species. *C. corone sharpii* is, moreover, intermediate in appearance between *C. c. cornix* and *C. c. capellanus* although nearer to the former. Vaurie (1959) states that Hooded Crows from the southern slopes of the Zagros to Luristan show signs of intergradation between *sharpii* and *capellanus*. On present evidence it seems, therefore, best to consider *capellanus* conspecific with other forms of *corone* (*cornix*).

The Collared Crow, *C. torquatus*, of the low-lying regions of China, seems most likely to be a geographical representative of the *corone* group. Although the pattern of its plumage differs from that of the Hooded Crow, and is more close to the 'typical' *Corvus* pattern, it agrees with *cornix* in having a similar demarcation of light and dark plumage on the neck and upper breast, in details of feather shape and texture and in body proportions. Its ecology is also similar; it is, admittedly, particularly prone to forage on wet ground and at the edge of shallow water but such situations are characteristic feeding places for *corone* where they exist within its range, even although it is not dependent upon them.

The Collared Crow overlaps geographically with the eastern race, *orientalis*, of *corone* and although their breeding areas do not, apparently, overlap, there would seem fair presumptive evidence that *torquatus* has reached specific level. It is possible, though I think unlikely, that its resemblances to *corone* are due to convergence. It is worth noting that both *torquatus* and *corone orientalis* have a wide geographical overlap with (different races of) the Jungle Crow, *Corvus macrorhynchos*. In both cases there is ecological separation, *corone* and *torquatus* inhabiting chiefly open cultivated country and *macrorhynchos* chiefly more hilly and wooded country.

The American Crow, *Corvus brachyrhynchos*, bears a considerable overall resemblance to the Carrion Crow, and some ornithologists (e.g. Dorst 1947, Dementiev & Gladkov 1954) treat them as conspecific. The American Crow differs in the laxer texture of its relatively glossless head and throat feathers (and to a less extent the rest of its plumage) and in its smaller size. Its calls, or at least those of them that I heard during a few weeks' stay in New York State, differ appreciably from those of *corone*. I concur with Blake in thinking that the American Crow should be treated as a separate species. I am, indeed, doubtful whether it is as closely related to *corone* as its appearance and ecology might suggest.

The Northwestern Crow, *Corvus caurinus*, is almost certainly a very close relative of *brachyrhynchos* but has reached specific level. Its calls and behaviour differ from the American Crow's more than does its appearance which is largely intermediate between the American Crow and the Fish Crow, *Corvus ossifragus*. The latter's shape and coloration closely approach the Mexican Crow, *Corvus imperatus*. This last species with its relatively small bill, small size, slender appearance and the rich gloss on its silky plumage, shows remarkable convergence towards some of the American blackbirds in the family Icteridae.

The Sinaloan Crow, *Corvus sinaloae*, is not separated from *C. imperatus* in current checklists because there is no clear-cut taxonomic difference between them. Davis (1958) has, however, shown that they differ in voice and ecology and also in wing–tail ratio. The latter does not always seem to provide a clear distinction but I treat them separately here for the following reasons. Firstly, by doing so the information available on each can be unambiguously assigned to its possessor. Secondly, the example of the American, Northwestern and Fish Crows strongly suggests that, in North American crows at least, differences of voice and behaviour have been of more importance in speciation than differences of appearance which are still very slight to human, and probably also to avian eyes. The Mexican and Sinaloan Crows appear to show an early, but probably most important, stage of divergence. They are at present allopatric but, should their ranges ever meet, it seems quite likely that they would behave as good species.

The White-necked Crow, *Corvus leucognaphalus*, of Hispaniola and Puerto Rico, and the Cuban Crow, *C. nasicus*, agree in having a bare rictal region and sub-orbital patch and the nasal bristles directed so that the nostril is more or less exposed. Although it is probably best to give them specific rank they can certainly be considered as members of a superspecies. That the feather-bases of *leucognaphalus* are white and those of *nasicus* grey indicates how unimportant a character this may sometimes be rather than any great gulf between them. I do not think that the white neck-feather bases of *leucognaphalus* indicate relationship to the American White-necked Raven, *C. cryptoleucos*, the only other American *Corvus* species possessing this character. It is possible that both *leucognaphalus* and *nasicus* were derived from a 'raven' rather than a 'crow' ancestor, but I think more likely that they represent a rather early offshoot from the same stock as produced the American crows, *C. brachyrhynchos* and its allies. In spite of its smaller size and duller coloration I think the Jamaican Crow, *C. jamaicensis*, is closely related to and should be included in the same superspecies as *leucognaphalus* and *nasicus*. It has similar bare areas on its face and, so far as one can ascertain from descriptions, similar calls.

The Palm Crow, *Corvus palmarum*, overlaps both the White-necked and Cuban Crows. It is, I think, more closely related to *brachyrhynchos* and its allies and represents a more recent invasion of the West Indies whereas *leucognaphalus* and *nasicus* probably represent an earlier invasion.

Although the House Crow, *Corvus splendens*, of the Indian region, has a very Jackdaw-like colour pattern it is no close relative of the Jackdaw, but probably most closely allied to the Jungle Crow, *Corvus macrorhynchos*. It is everywhere a close associate of man and relies in part on food thrown away by or 'stolen' from him. Other crows have become scavengers and hangers-on of man where allowed to do so but none to the same extent as this species. It appears often able to supplant other species in the town scavenging niche when it reaches or is introduced to new areas. I have not been able to find any record of it occurring away from mankind. Presumably the House Crow's original habitat was early overrun by man and it became completely adapted to living with him. Although it takes natural foods such as insects and fruits when available, it seems to be able to succeed in competition with any other crows in town or village environments, as it manages to achieve a greater density of numbers in such environments than any competing *Corvus* species. It would be interesting to know whether, as I suspect may be the case, it is able to thrive on a diet less rich in vitamins and animal proteins than other crows can.

The range of the Jungle Crow, *Corvus macrorhynchos*, now almost completely overlaps that of the House Crow although extending much further to the north-east and south-east. I think, however, that the two are rather closely related and derived from a common ancestor two stocks of which became isolated, the ancestors of the House Crow developing commensalism with man to a much greater extent than those of the Jungle Crow. The latter is, nevertheless, an habitual scavenger, particularly but by no means exclusively in those parts of its range where it does not have to compete with the House Crow in this rôle. The paler races of the Jungle Crow show precisely the same pattern of plumage as the House Crow although, being darker, much less conspicuously. The two species show, on the whole, comparable geographic variation in size and depth of pigmentation, although *macrorhynchos* is everywhere larger and darker than *splendens*.

I concur with Vaurie (in 'Peters', 1962) in thinking *Corvus philippinus* is best considered a race of *macrorhynchos*. Stresemann (1943) gives it specific rank and remarks on its more slender bill and relatively long tail. These differences are, however, rather slight. In all races of the Jungle Crow, as with other *Corvus* species, there is in any case a fair amount of individual variation in bill size, and bills of males average larger than those of females. I can find nothing recorded on the voice or behaviour of *philippinus* to suggest that it is specifically distinct. Indeed there seems more difference between the eastern races of the Jungle Crow, *japonensis*, *colonorum* and *mandschuricus*, and the form from peninsular India, than between the Philippine and the nominate forms. The Jungle Crow of peninsular India and Ceylon, *C. m. culminatus*, is said to have different-sounding calls from the Himalayan form *C. m. intermedius* and it is possible that it is now specifically distinct.

It is of interest that in those parts of its range where it overlaps with either the Carrion Crow or the Raven, the Jungle Crow is typically a bird of wooded rather than open country whereas the reverse seems to be the case where it overlaps with the Slender-billed Crow of the Malayan and Philippine regions. This latter species, *Corvus enca*, is almost certainly a close relative of the Jungle Crow, which it much resembles, but is now sympatric with it through most of its (*enca's*) range. Suprisingly, they nevertheless show similar geographic variation in size, gloss and texture of plumage and bill size. As its name implies, *C. enca's* bill is proportionately rather more slender and has a less arched culmen than that of *macrorhynchos*, when specimens of both from the same geographical area are compared. The little recorded of their habits suggest that the Slender-billed Crow may feed more on fruits and insects taken from the branches than does the Jungle Crow.

Throughout its range in the Indonesian and Philippine islands the Slender-billed Crow shows much geographical variation in bill length. The forms from Ceram and the Philippines have been considered a separate species, *Corvus violaceus*, by Stresemann and Dorst. They have shorter bills and a more pronounced matt-looking violaceous sheen on the plumage. If compared with the form of *enca* found in Malaya and Sumatra, *C. e. compilator*, the difference in length of bill is striking. However, the nominate form, *C. e. enca*, from Java and Bali, is intermediate in this respect. The little available information does not suggest any significant differences of voice and behaviour between any of these forms. McGregor stated that the voice of *samarensis*, from Samar and Mindanao, was 'entirely different' from that of *pusillus* from Balabac, Palawan and Mindoro, but he did not give any description and may perhaps have been comparing different calls. On present evidence it seems best to treat all the above forms as races of *enca*.

The Celebes Pied Crow, *Corvus typicus*, closely resembles the shorter-billed forms of *Corvus enca*, from which it differs chiefly in its pied plumage. It almost certainly originated from the first (or first successful) invasion of the Celebes by *enca* or proto-*enca* stock, which diverged sufficiently not to interbreed with the second *enca* invasion which produced the present day *C. e. celebensis* with which *typicus* is now sympatric.

The Banggai Crow, *Corvus unicolor*, has been sometimes considered, as by Vaurie (1958), a race of *enca*. It is not sympatric with any other *Corvus* species but the races of *enca* that come nearest to it geographically, *C. e. celebensis* from the Celebes and *C. e. mangoli* from the Sula Archipelago, are much larger and longer-billed. On the other hand *unicolor* agrees with its other neighbour, *C. typicus*, in everything but colour and in this respect it differs in its grey feather bases from both *enca* and *typicus* as well as more obviously from the latter in its lack of visible white areas of plumage. I think *C. unicolor* is closer to *typicus* than to *enca* and best considered as forming a superspecies with it.

The Flores Crow, *Corvus florensis*, has sometimes been considered a race of *C. enca*. Rensch argues against this decision because of its larger nostrils and grey feather bases. I have not seen examples of this rarely-collected form, which, at least till more is known about it, seems best given specific rank.

The Long-billed Crow of the Moluccas, *Corvus validus*, is very similar to the larger-billed forms of the Slender-billed Crow and still more to some forms of the Jungle Crow. It differs, apart from its rather longer bill, from these and all other south-east Asian and Indonesian crows and agrees with the Australian crows, *orru*, *bennetti*, *coronoides* and *mellori*, in having whitish eyes. This suggests that it may be most closely related to the New Guinea form of *Corvus orru* and represent a first invasion of this stock into the Moluccas. It is now sympatric with *orru*. Its much greater bill length presumably indicates that the two have different feeding habits but these have not been recorded.

Four Australian crows, the Little Crow, *Corvus bennetti*, the Australian Crow, *C. orru*, the Australian Raven, *C. coronoides* and the recently discovered Little Raven, *C. mellori*, are probably all more closely related to each other than they are to any other species with the possible exception of *C. validus*. They show conclusively how in this genus specific level may be reached by forms that show only very slight morphological differences.

The Forest Raven, *Corvus tasmanicus*, is sometimes treated as conspecific with *C. mellori*. On the evidence given by Rowley (1970), however, it would seem to differ at least as much from *mellori* in voice and behaviour as the latter does from *coronoides*. S. Parker, who has seen and heard both forms in the field, tells me (*in litt.*) that he is convinced they are specifically distinct. For these reasons I have, provisionally, given *tasmanicus* specific rank.

The Solomon Islands Crow, *Corvus woodfordi*, and the Brown-headed Crow, *C. fuscicapillus*, of the West Papuan and Aru Islands, seem closely related and, in spite of differences in size and plumage colour, can be considered as members of a superspecies. They have in common large bills with deeply curved culmen and pale eyes. *C. woodfordi* with its silken, dense, glossy plumage shows a certain resemblance to some of the birds-of-paradise. The Bare-faced Crow, *Corvus tristis*, of New Guinea differs strikingly from them in its largely naked face but otherwise much resembles *fuscicapillus*. In colour, size and shape of tail *fuscicapillus* is largely intermediate between *woodfordi* and *tristis*, which latter is, I think, very closely related to *fuscicapillus* and *woodfordi* and can be considered a geographical representative of the same stock, if one disregards the possible overlap in the one area of the north-western New Guinea mainland where the Brown-headed Crow is known to occur.

All these have pale eyes and probably represent an early offshoot from the same stock as produced the other pale-eyed forms. They have become largely adapted to fruit-eating and would appear to be more highly arboreal than most other *Corvus* species.

The Micronesian Crow, *Corvus kubaryi*, is probably nearest to *enca* and its relatives but this is speculation based on distribution as *kubaryi* could, on appearance, be derived from any *Corvus*. It shows the somewhat lax and hairy plumage that is so often characteristic of island forms. The rather long and slender bill contrasts with those of the New Caledonian and Hawaiian Crows.

The New Caledonian Crow, *Corvus moneduloides*, has an unusually-shaped bill with nearly straight culmen ridge and sharply angled gonys. On geographical grounds it might be linked with the Australian species but in appearance it is very distinct from them. The much larger Hawaiian Crow, *Corvus tropicus*, is often considered a close relative because its bill is shaped like that of *moneduloides* although to a much lesser degree. The Hawaiian Crow is larger and has dull lustreless lax plumage very unlike that of *moneduloides*. Although they may be derivatives from the same stock this seems by no means certain. The rather similar bill shape could well be adaptive. Detailed information on behaviour, voice and feeding habits of these and other crows will be needed before one can do more than guess their affinities.

The Raven, *Corvus corax*, has the widest distribution of any corvine species, being found widely throughout the cold, temperate and subtropical regions of both old and new worlds. The fact that throughout this vast area it shows only relatively slight racial differences suggests that it may have spread only comparatively recently into much of its range. It is pre-eminently a crow of open or montane country, but occurs locally in wooded areas. It is much more a carrion feeder and predator on birds and mammals than are most *Corvus* species, with the possible exception of its closest relatives.

The Brown-necked or Desert Raven, *Corvus ruficollis*, was for long considered a race of *corax* but is now usually given specific rank. Vaurie (1954) states that the 'morphological differences are sharp' and that in specimens of *corax* (race *subcorax*, syn. *laurencei*) and *ruficollis* from Palestine which he examined the former differed in wing formula, having the third and fifth primaries more or less equal instead of the third distinctly longer than the fifth, much larger bill and, when birds in similar plumage state were compared, much less coppery brown tinge on head and neck. Dr H. Mendelssohn (in Vaurie, 1954) states that in Palestine the ranges of *ruficollis* and *corax* meet but do not overlap, the former being a bird of the desert and the latter of the more humid coastal region. I have not been able to observe *ruficollis* in areas where its range met that of *corax*, but in Egypt I repeatedly noticed how rigidly the Brown-necked Raven kept to the desert and the desert edge, never, so far as I saw, entering the cultivated areas although sometimes flying over them.

Although the wing formula holds good for the Middle East specimens of *corax* and *ruficollis* that I have been able to examine, it does not hold good for the Indian region where out of a large series of *C. corax subcorax* many have a wing formula similar to that of *ruficollis*. There is, however, no correlation between this and other characters; specimens of *corax* with a longer third primary are not otherwise closer to *ruficollis*. On the other hand, Indian specimens of *subcorax* are, in appearance, certainly intermediate between the larger, blacker races of *corax* and *ruficollis*. The only places in the Indian region from which the British Museum has specimens of both *subcorax* and *ruficollis* are Quetta, in Baluchistan, and Kandahar, in Afghanistan, from each of which we have one specimen only of *ruficollis* and several undoubted *subcorax*. The two *ruficollis* are an alleged male from Kandahar (British Museum no. 1886.3.1.103) collected on 12 Sept. 1879 and an unsexed bird Quetta (B.M. no 1860.4.16.523). Both these, although agreeing best with *ruficollis* on their taxonomic characters, have bills rather larger than the average for that form and the possibility that they might represent (especially should the Kandahar bird be wrongly sexed) unusually small and brownish individuals of *subcorax* stock, or genuine intergrades or hybrids, cannot be excluded.

There is, however, no positive evidence of interbreeding between *corax* and *ruficollis;* they normally frequent different habitats (although the statement sometimes made that *corax* nests only on cliffs and *ruficollis* only in trees is incorrect), and at least some of their commoner calls appear to differ. It thus seems likely that *ruficollis* is now specifically distinct and it is certainly more convenient to treat it so. The possibility that some specimens currently referred to races of *corax* in collections might represent *corax*-like individuals or populations of *ruficollis* cannot be excluded. Further studies on living birds are needed.

The Brown-necked Raven shows much individual and local variation in size and still more in length, curvature and depth of bill. Of the many specimens that I have examined, those from western Arabia and Khartoum, Sudan, were largest. The two from Khartoum, both males, have rather long and very slender bills so that although their bills (culmen lengths 65 and 73 mm) are, in one case only, slightly longer than those of birds from elsewhere they appear much longer than they are because of their slenderness.

Specimens from Sokotra island are on average large, they have the largest average length of bill (68.5 mm), and their bills are rather thick. It is just possible that the Sokotran form might be racially separable but it seems better not to split up into unnecessary races a species in which so much individual variation exists. The only readily separable race is *C. ruficollis edithae* from Somaliland, Eritrea and adjacent parts of Ethiopia, which averages smaller in size and has a shorter bill, its culmen length (from skull) ranging, in those I have measured, from 50 to 57 mm as against 60 to 73 mm in *ruficollis*. It is often stated that *edithae* also differs from *ruficollis* in having the feather bases white instead of dusky but this is not always so. Both show a fair amount of variation, due, I think, largely to age of feather not age of birds. In *ruficollis* the feather bases vary from dusky light grey to greyish white and, in a few specimens, nearly pure white; in *edithae* the feather bases are usually white but sometimes greyish white. A bird from Lodwa, Turkana, Kenya, where the population is probably intermediate, agrees with *edithae* in bill size (56 mm) but is rather large and has light grey feather bases. Beals (1966) saw two larger-billed, brown-headed *Corvus*, together with four blacker, smaller-billed individuals, at Assab, Ethiopia. He believed them to be, respectively *ruficollis* and *edithae*, which he therefore considered specifically distinct. The possibilty that they were adults and immatures of the *same* form cannot, I think, be excluded.

The Pied Crow, *Corvus albus*, is found throughout most of Africa south of the Sahara and in Madagascar. In these areas it appears to fill a similar ecological niche to the Carrion and Hooded Crows in Europe. Because of this and the general resemblance of its colour pattern to that of the Hooded Crow it is often thought of as the geographical representative of *corone*. This may be the case, as in spite of its being rather Raven-like in some calls and displays in others it approaches the *corone-torquatus* group; like them too, and unlike *corax*, it has the habit of flirting up its folded wings when uneasy or after alighting. In some ways it suggests a link between the 'crows' and 'ravens', and it may possibly prove to be conspecific with *ruficollis* (*edithae*).

There is firm evidence (Kleinschmidt, Smith, Blair) that Pied Crows interbreed with 'black crows' that are presumably, but not on present evidence provedly, *C. ruficollis edithae*. All the records for this come from the Arussi region of Ethiopia and the Eritrean coast. Kleinschmidt examined and figured specimens showing various intermediate types of plumage between that of typical *albus* and typical *edithae*. He considered that these were more probably dark phases of *albus* than hybrids but was, perhaps, influenced by his conviction that *albus* belonged to the same polytypic species (Formenkreise) as *corone* and was no close relation of the 'noble Raven'.

Blair collected in 1958 an adult female that is streaked (broad brownish black central streaks) on the white parts of the breast and mantle. On its mantle many of the feathers in this area are largely black so that the streaked area is less extensive than the white in normal *albus*. This bird had been paired for three years with a black male (Blair). On the same day and locality, 21 January 1958, at Robi, Arussi, Blair collected a male nearly identical in coloration to the female described above but, rather surprisingly, makes no mention of this individual in his paper. In 1955 he collected two young from the streaked female and the black male (which was not collected). These two juveniles are much darker than their mother, having the feathers of the 'white' parts of the breast largely suffused with brownish black and those of the mantle brownish black (with white bases) with russet or creamy tips. He noted that birds similar to those he collected were frequently seen although usually in much smaller numbers than black individuals. Popov (in Smith) collected a black male that was paired with a pied (*albus*-type) female but did not keep the specimens after he had identified them to his own satisfaction as, respectively, *C. edithae* and *C. albus*.

North (1962) stated that most of the calls of *albus* and *edithae* are extremely alike and the 'typical call' of each is a caw like that of the Rook. He thought this indicated that *edithae* and *ruficollis* were specifically distinct and that the former was a crow, not a raven. However, Meinertzhagen (1940) describes a call of *ruficollis* as like the caw of a Rook and I remember that its mobbing call struck me as Rook-like in Egypt. The two intermediate adult specimens in the British Museum collection, mentioned above, certainly look more like aberrantly coloured specimens of *albus* than *albus-edithae* hybrids as they have little or no trace of brown (certainly no more than on pure *albus*) on head and neck.   On the other hand intermediates pictured by Kleinschmidt are as brown as typical *edithae*.

It is unfortunate that none of the black individuals actually paired to pied or intermediate birds appear to have been collected *and* preserved.   Thus the question must remain open as to whether these birds are *C. ruficollis edithae* and therefore this form interbreeds with *albus* where their range meets in north-eastern Africa, or whether *albus* has all-black and intermediate forms, which are specifically distinct from *edithae*, in the north-east of its range.

It is probable that *albus* and *ruficollis* are fairly close relatives although until the above question is resolved, and more known about the behaviour of both, their degree of relationship must be questionable.

The American White-necked Raven, *Corvus cryptoleucos*, is almost certainly close to *corax* and probably derived from an invasion of the new world by *corax*, or '*proto-corax*', stock prior to the arrival of present-day *corax*.   It now overlaps geographically with *corax* to some extent but is ecologically separated.   In ecology it seems to fill much the same niche in the New World, and to present similar contrasts to *corax*, as *ruficollis* does in the Old World.   It has, however, diverged further from *corax* in behaviour than has *ruficollis*, as is shown especially by its more sociable habits.

The Fan-tailed Raven, *Corvus rhipidurus*, the White-necked Raven, *Corvus albicollis*, and the Thick-billed Raven, *Corvus crassirostris*, form a species group and were probably geographical representatives in the relatively recent past.   The Fan-tailed and Thick-billed Ravens now overlap in range in Ethiopia although typically they occur in rather different habitats and at different altitudes.   There is some apparent geographical overlap between Fan-tailed and White-necked Ravens but I can find no evidence of their occurring in precisely the same locality, although both have been recorded on Mount Elgon, in East Africa.

Owing to their very deep bills with strongly curved culmens *albicollis* and *crassirostris* have sometimes been put in a separate genus *Corvultur*.   However, as has been pointed out by Meinertzhagen and others, *rhipidurus* is to some extent intermediate in bill shape between these two species and *corax* and, although all black on the visible parts of its plumage, has white feather bases on nape and hind neck.   The White-necked Raven has a much shorter tail and smaller bill than the Thick-billed Raven and thus comes nearer in proportions to the smaller-billed and very short-tailed *rhipidurus* than does *crassirostris*.   It is possible that the greater differences between the partly sympatric *crassirostris* and *rhipidurus* are due to adaptations to different ecological niches.   It has been suggested that the large deep bills of '*Corvultur*' are adapted for scattering the dung of large mammals in search for grubs.   I think this rather unlikely as other species of *Corvus*, e.g. *corone*, *frugilegus*, *monedula*, habitually use their 'normal' bills for this purpose.   It is more probable that the '*Corvultur*' bill has evolved either for predation, perhaps on tortoises, or primarily as a display organ.

The Fan-tailed Raven overlaps widely with the Brown-necked Raven.   Their ecologies differ in that cliffs and crags seem essential to *rhipidurus* for nesting purposes whereas *ruficollis* nests freely, and in the areas of overlap usually, in trees.   Both scavenge at camp sites and garbage tips but although little is recorded in any detail of their feeding habits it is likely that they do not normally compete when taking natural foods.

The White-necked and Thick-billed Ravens seem to fill a similar role in the Ethiopian region to that of *corax* in the holarctic regions.   They, and *rhipidurus*, are probably much closer to *corax* phylogenetically than their appearance would at first suggest.   In *albicollis*, calls and many aspects of behaviour are remarkably similar to those of *corax*. The same may be true for *crassirostris* and *rhipidurus* of which I have not, however, been able to observe live individuals.

The Black Crow, *Corvus capensis*, shows considerable superficial resemblance to the Rook, *Corvus frugilegus*, having a similar but more extremely developed long, rather straight and slender bill.   It differs from *frugilegus* in being larger, in the different texture of its feathers, especially on the throat, which more resemble those of other African *Corvus* species, and in the nesting pairs holding extensive territory.

I think its resemblance to the Rook is due to convergent adaptations for feeding in a similar manner by probing and digging for invertebrates.   In the coloration of the visible parts of its plumage it is very similar to *ruficollis*. I think it is more nearly related to *ruficollis* and *albus* than to any Eurasian species.

The Rook, *Corvus frugilegus*, is so distinct that its relationships within the genus cannot be deduced on present evidence. It presumably evolved as a bird of open country, probably somewhere in the grass steppes of Eurasia, developing the long, probing bill and colonial nesting, the latter as an adaptation to shortage of nesting sites. Later it spread west and east following agricultural man as he destroyed the forests and made fields in which it could obtain food.

The bare face of the Rook is often instanced as an adaptation for probing or digging. That this is its primary function seems doubtful as, if this were the case, it would be difficult to understand why it develops only when the bird is from ten to fifteen months old and why the bare area is much more extensive in the western form, *frugilegus*, than in the eastern form, *pastinator*. It is possible that its late development is correlated with the *adult* bird's need to obtain large quantities of animal food for its young. I think, however, that it may function socially, to indicate at once the age and potential status of the individual. Young Rooks, still with feathered faces, that pair and try to breed sometimes seem relatively inept and inefficient. It is possible that their feathered faces, by making them at once distinguishable, may prevent them getting mates except when no others are available. This might be of advantage to the individual young bird by preventing it (as a rule) from shouldering the extra risks and stresses attendant on trying to raise a brood in its first year, and to the species by preventing experienced adult birds from accepting a biologically inferior partner when choice was available.

The jackdaws have sometimes been placed in a separate genus *Coloeus* which Hartert differentiated as having a sharp indentation on the inner web of the first primary, loose-textured neck feathers, less rounded ends to the tail feathers, eggs paler in colour with fewer and larger spots, and a musky scent differing from that of other *Corvus* species. With the exception of the last these differences are of degree rather than of kind. To them might be added the habit of nesting in holes. In spite of these differences the jackdaws are obviously related to the other *Corvus* species, their colour patterns are quite typical of the genus. I think it preferable to regard *Coloeus* only as a subgenus, within *Corvus*.

The Daurian Jackdaw, *Corvus dauuricus*, replaces the Jackdaw, *C. monedula*, in much of eastern Asia. It is sometimes treated as a race of *C. monedula*, as by Meise (1934) who quotes Stegmann as saying that a hybrid zone exists in eastern Siberia. On the other hand Vaurie (1954) gives evidence indicating that both forms are sympatric in the region east of the Yenisei and quotes Johansen, who found only one specimen that appeared to be a hybrid in the extensive collections in the Academy of Sciences in Leningrad. Vaurie also claims that there is a clear-cut difference in wing formula, *dauuricus* having the outer primary shorter than have Asian specimens at *monedula* and the second primary shorter than the fifth instead of being equal to it.

The specimens in the British Museum (Natural History) do not differ so sharply in wing formula as those Vaurie examined; on the contrary some specimens of *dauuricus* agree quite well with *monedula* in this respect. I agree with Vaurie, however, in thinking that present evidence suggests that the two jackdaws have probably reached specific level. A further character, one that might well inhibit pair formation between them, is their difference in eye colour. The Daurian Jackdaw has a dark brown iris like most other crows, the Jackdaw a silver-grey or whitish iris.

REFERENCES

AMADON, D. 1944. The genera of Corvidae and their relationships. *Amer. Mus. Novit.*, No. 1251.
BEALS, E. W. 1966. Sight additions to the Avifaunal list of Ethiopia. *J. E. Afr. Nat. Hist. Soc.* **25**: 3 (112): 227–229.
BLAIR, C. M. G. 1961. Hybridisation of *Corvus albus* and *Corvus edithae* in Ethiopia. *Ibis* **103a**: 499–502.
BLAKE, E. R. 1962. *'Peters' Check-list of Birds of the World*, vol. 15. Camb., Mass.
DAVIS, L. I. 1958. Acoustic evidence of relationship in North American crows. *Wilson Bull.* **70**: 151–167.
DEMENTIEV, G. P. & GLADKOV, N. A. 1954. *The birds of the Soviet Union* 5.
DORST, J. 1947. Révision systematique du genre *Corvus*. *L'Oiseau* **17**: 44–87.

HARTERT, E. 1910. *Die Vögel der Paläarkitschen Fauna*, vol. 1. Berlin.
KLEINSCHMIDT, O. 1906. Beiträge zur Vogelfauna Nordostafrikas: Gattung *Corvus*. *J. Orn.* **54**: 78–99.
McGREGOR, R. C. 1909. *A Manual of Philippine Birds*. Manila.
MEINERTZHAGEN, R. M. 1926. Introduction to a review of the genus *Corvus*. *Novit. Zool.* **33**: 57–121.
—— 1940. Autumn in Central Morocco. *Ibis* **4**, 14th Series: 124–125.
MEISE, W. 1928. Die Verbreitung der Aaskrähe (Formenkreis *Corvus corone* L.). *J. Orn.* **76**: 1–203.
—— 1934. Die vogelwelt der Mandschurei. *adh. Mus. Dresden.* **18**, 2, 12–13.
NORTH, M. E. W. 1962. Vocal affinities of *Corvus corax edithae*. *Ibis* **104**: 431.
RENSCH, B. 1931. Die Vogelwelt von Lombok, Sumbawa und Flores. *Mitt. Zoolog. Mus. Berlin* **17**: 588.
ROWLEY, I. 1967. A fourth species of Australian Corvid. *Emu* **66**: 190–210.
—— 1970. The genus *Corvus* in Australia. C.S.I.R.O. *Wildl. Res.* **15**: 27–71.
SMITH, K. D. 1957. Birds of Eritrea. *Ibis* **99**: 326.
STRESEMANN, E. 1943. Die Gattung *Corvus* in Australien und Neuguinea. *J. Orn.* **91**: 121–135.
VAURIE, C. 1954. Systematic notes on Palearctic birds. No. 5 Corvidae. *Amer. Mus. Novit.* 1668.
—— 1958. Remarks on some Corvidae of Indo-Malaya and the Australian Region. *Amer. Mus. Novit.* 1915.
—— 1959. *The Birds of the Palearctic Fauna* vol. 1. London.
—— 1962. '*Peters*' *Check-list of Birds of the World* vol. 15. Camb., Mass.

JACKDAW   *Corvus monedula*

Corvus monedula Linnaeus, *Syst. Nat.*, ed. 10, 1, p. 106, 1758.

Description Forehead, crown, front of face, throat, wings and tail black, richly glossed with bluish and purplish on the forehead, crown, secondaries and secondary coverts, and with mainly greenish or greenish blue on the throat, primaries and tail. Feathers of the cheeks, nape and neck light grey to greyish silver in colour and lax and silky in texture. The feather tips at the sides of the lower periphery of this silver-grey area usually silvery white, forming a fairly conspicuous whitish bar or partial collar. The rest of the plumage is greyish blue-black above (greyish fringes to bluish black feathers) and dark slate-grey below. Irides greyish white or silvery white. Bill, legs and feet black. Females average less silvery on the neck than males. Juvenile duller with much less contrast between black and grey areas. Irides of juveniles are at first bluish, then change to dull brown and slowly to dull white before, at about a year old, becoming silvery white or pearl grey. Nestling has conspicuous pale yellow gape flanges. Newly-hatched young naked except for a little greyish down.

The above description is of the nominate form *C. m. monedula*, from Norway, Sweden and northern Denmark. The Jackdaws breeding in eastern Europe and Asia, *C. m. soemmerringii*, usually have the whitish bar or patch below the grey of the neck more emphasized; those from most of western Europe and the British Isles, *C. monedula spermologus*, are darker, especially on the underparts, and usually lack the whitish mark at the border of the grey 'collar'. Those from Algeria, *C.m. cirtensis*, are paler and duller with less contrast between black and grey areas. Except in the case of the Algerian birds all populations intergrade, however, and there is much individual variation, as well as differences due to wear of plumage.

Field identification Commonest calls diagnostic. When in company with other *Corvus* species smaller size, quicker wing-beat (both flight and silhouette more pigeon-like) and shorter bill identify it. Whitish iris of adult also diagnostic.

Distribution and habitat Europe and Asia eastward to Ussuriland. In the north to about 66° latitude in the west and about 60° in Siberia and to the middle Amur in the east. Southward it occurs to the Mediterranean region, Near East, Iran and north-western Himalayas and in the east of its range to the Sayans, north-western Mongolia and western and central Altai. Also locally in Morocco and Algeria. The northern populations are migratory and the species occurs in winter south of its breeding range, in Sinkiang, north-western India, southern Iran, Iraq and the near East. Said to have occurred in Egypt.

Inhabits wooded steppes, river valleys with open or intermittent woodland, cultivated country, parkland both natural and artificial, villages and towns (especially small towns surrounded by agricultural or pastoral areas), and coastal or inland cliffs in vicinity of pasture land or cultivation. Although thriving in agricultural regions and tending to spread into new areas when forests are destroyed and turned into farmland, it is, at least in Britain, much less dependent on grain than the Rook appears to be and occurs plentifully in some areas where no grain is grown.

Feeding and general habits Seeks food mostly on the ground but also in trees. Typically feeds in fairly open areas where the ground is covered only with short or scattered vegetation or is more or less bare, such as pasture land, ploughed or harvested fields, areas of short grass about cliffs, parks and similar places. Coastal populations often forage on the shore at low tide. Regularly scavenges on garbage tips. Where not persecuted will readily take food from gardens or bird tables. In some towns takes food from the streets, litter baskets and even quite small yards and enclosed spaces; tends to do so most frequently in the early morning or at other times when people are fewer and traffic less dense. Its greater agility and less extreme caution often enable it to compete successfully with the stronger Rook and Carrion Crow when scavenging in towns or gardens. The Jackdaw will dash down, seize the food and bounce up and away with it while a Rook or Crow is still hesitating to fly down.

Takes insects and other invertebrates, grain, and weed seeds; also, but usually to a lesser extent, acorns, fruit, berries, eggs, young birds, walnuts and chestnuts. Readily eats bread, cheese and many other human foods when available. Sometimes scavenges or steals fish at seabird colonies.

When seeking food turns over small objects and scatters animal dung. Also digs and probes crevices and interstices in the grass-sward but appears to obtain more by picking from the surface than does the Rook (Lockie, 1955: pers. obs.). It takes far fewer earthworms than the Rook. At nests in Switzerland the young were, however, fed to a large extent on cockchafer grubs (Zimmerman, 1951), which are normally deep among the grass roots. Food that requires breaking up is held under one or both feet. Carrying of food in feet has been recorded but is rare. Eggs are carried by inserting the under mandible into the uppermost part of the shell and then closing the bill (Lorenz, 1931; Zimmerman).

Food hiding recorded (Lorenz, 1932; Simmons) for both semi-captive and wild birds. Both these observers imply that food is hidden in the typical manner, but Strauss (1938) found that his Jackdaws never covered the food they hid. I have not seen food storing in wild Jackdaws, in spite of trying to elicit it by methods which invariably succeed with wild Carrion Crows.

Usual gait a brisk walk but sometimes runs or hops. Flies with quicker wing beats and hence its flight appears more pigeon-like than that of other *Corvus* species. Indulges in spectacular gliding, twisting, swooping and diving aerobatics, especially in the vicinity of its breeding places.

Gregarious at all seasons but pairs or single birds (the latter mostly in spring when the mate is sitting) often forage by themselves and at all times the pair appears to be the basic social unit. When a flock of Jackdaws is flying or resting paired birds usually keep noticeably closer to one another than they do to other individuals.   Often associates with Rooks, especially when on migration or flying to or from feeding or roosting places.

Perches freely in or on trees, cliffs and buildings.   Roosts communally, usually in trees but sometimes in reed beds or on cliffs.   Communal roosts may be used throughout the year.   Some breeding birds, however, are known to roost near their nests (Rittenbach, 1951).   Where both species occur, roosts are usually shared with Rooks.

An impressive example of individual adaptability in a Jackdaw which, with human help, adapted to blindness is given in the most interesting book *Blind Jack* (Ryder, 1960).

Nesting   Usually nests colonially but the spacing out of nesting pairs depends largely on the sites available, and some pairs may nest a considerable distance from their nearest neighbours.   The nest is placed in a hole, crevice or other cavity in a tree, cliff or building; less often in a hole in the ground or at ground level, in or on the old nest of some other species, in a mass of twigs and other debris lodged in a tree, or among the branches of thickly-foliaged conifers or other evergreens.   Cliffs, quarries, groves of old trees, and ruined buildings are typical sites for nesting colonies.   In many places Jackdaws habitually attempt to nest inside the chimneys of inhabited houses.

Nest built of sticks, woody stems and similar materials, lined with fibrous bark, fur, hair, wool, rags or other soft substances, with dry mud or earth incorporated.   Soft materials and earth are added to the nest throughout the incubation and brooding periods.   Both sexes build and sometimes (Zimmerman), probably usually, each takes an equal part in all stages, although in a tame pair (Lorenz, 1931) the female alone lined the nest.   Nests built in a small cavity may, of necessity, consist only of lining material and sometimes very little of that.   Where the material permits cavities may be enlarged by the birds themselves. Unwanted material, such as the old nests or droppings of pigeons, are removed before building begins. Twigs for the nest are usually broken off the trees.   Loose hair is plucked from living deer or cattle, several pairs often perching in a row along the back of an apparently quite unperturbed deer or cow to do so.

Eggs 3 to 7, usually 4 or 5, pale greenish blue to bluish white, sparsely spotted and flecked with blackish and light grey.   Incubation period 17 to 18 days, exceptionally 16 or 19 days.   Young fledge at 30–35 days. Incubation and brooding by the female only, fed on or at nest by male.   In one pair the male frequently entered the nest when the female had come out on his arrival and flown off, but uncertain if he incubated while there (Lorenz, 1931).   Both sexes feed and care for young.   At nests observed by Zimmerman in Switzerland the female alone fed the young for the first few days, with food brought by the male.   After about ten days only the male brought food and fed the young.   Elsewhere both sexes have been observed collecting and bringing food (Lockie; Lorenz); probably much depends on the local food situation.   The faeces of the young are not always enclosed in a gelatinous sac and when not are removed by the parents together with the adjacent nest-lining material.   As soon as they are strong on the wing the young follow their parents closely.   At this stage the vicinity of the breeding colony is often deserted until autumn. Some Jackdaws, possibly most, do not breed until 2 years old but some have been proved to breed in their first year (Zimmerman).

Insects are carefully pulled to pieces and the bill meticulously cleaned before feeding small young. This behaviour ceased in one pair when their oldest young were 6 and the youngest 3 days old (Lorenz, 1931).

In Britain, most of Europe, and Kashmir, eggs are laid from mid-April to late May, most in late April and early May.

Voice   Most calls are short and rather high-pitched, but less explosive than those of the Chough (q.v.). The well-known 'tchak', from which the bird takes the first part of its name, seems equivalent to the appeal call of *Garrulus* species.   It appears to be used as a contact call and in many other situations, and is subject to much variation: 't'yak', 'k'yow', 'tchak-ak' etc.   Lorenz (1952) distinguishes between the call given when a bird is in a mood to fly away from home or when flying on migration, 'kia', and a deeper-toned 'kiaw' which indicates a homeward-flying mood.

Flying Jackdaws often utter a long-drawn 'kraare' or 'chaairr!' which is usually prefaced and/or followed by a burst of variously modulated 'tchak-ak' notes. Whilst uttering the long-drawn call the bird glides or swoops on downward-held wings. In flight the wings appear not to move but when this call is given by a perched bird it bows forward, half opens and droops its wings and vibrates them as it calls.

The predator-mobbing call is a long-drawn, harsh, somewhat grating 'kaaarr', very similar to the homologous calls of Rook and Carrion Crow but perhaps rather more nasal in tone. It sounds to my ears different in tone from the 'chaair' but the latter may, perhaps, be a 'playful' variant of it. Lorenz describes birds giving it while leaning forward and beating their wings. I have not noticed this wing movement in birds mobbing me when I was at their nests or handling fledged young, possibly because the wild birds were more afraid of me than Lorenz's tame ones were of him.

The food-offering call is a short somewhat muffled-sounding version of the usual 'tchak' and appears to be produced by the bird uttering the 'tchak' call with bill closed and throat pouch full. However, the bird sometimes utters it when the throat pouch is empty but still with bill closed.

Lorenz distinguishes a sharp, repeated 'zik', which is uttered as a nest call and serves to repel other males and attract females, and a rather similar 'yip' or 'yep' (Jüp) which is used in defensive contexts by paired birds. I have not been able to distinguish properly the calls in this series which always sound to me to have no 'ts' or 'z' sound in them, but I have only heard them from wild Jackdaws and not at very close quarters from individually-known birds.

The begging call of adults and well-grown young has about it something of the usual nagging, imploring tone of most other corvids' begging calls, but also much of the common 'tchak' note. It could perhaps be written 'kyaay' or 'tchaaayk'.

Strauss describes a complaining, high-pitched squeaking, given by paired birds feeding one another, growling notes that may also be used in the same context, and a hissing puff ('Fauchen'), given sometimes when warding off another Jackdaw or the too-importunate mate. This latter sound was always made by a tame Jackdaw I once kept if I handled it in darkness. Strauss also describes a few other calls most of which seem to be variants of those described above.

The song consists of a medley of any or all of the calls, with a great variation of loudness and inflection. Lorenz says that copied sounds are also included, but in spite of trying I have never been able to recognize the call of any other bird in the songs of the very many wild Jackdaws I have listened to. The Jackdaw sings when alone, whether perched or flying, and the volume of noise that is produced and its variability are surprising. One often has the impression that a flock of Jackdaws are calling and answering one another and, looking up, is astonished to see a lone individual in flight. The gestures that normally accompany certain calls are also used when they are uttered in song.

Display and social behaviour In self-assertive display the head feathers, especially those on the nape and hind neck, are erected and the bird, usually with head held up but bill horizontal or rather downward, and body more or less horizontal, stands or walks well up on its legs. This display is shown, as usual, in sexual as well as hostile contexts.

In defensive threat, used when a Jackdaw is determined to hold its place, usually at its nest site, it erects its feathers, particularly those on head and back, somewhat spreads and lowers its tail, lowers its head and presents itself laterally to its rival.

When soliciting allo-preening the head feathers are raised and the bird usually presents its nape to the partner. Lorenz describes a similar posture, with strongly bent legs and upright body, used in purely submissive contexts between unpaired individuals.

In the quivering display the bird usually crouches and slightly lowers the wings but only the tail is noticeably quivered. At presumed lower intensities the tail may be, and very often is, violently quivered without any crouching or wing drooping. This display is used by the female when soliciting coition but also very frequently in other contexts and by both sexes, especially at or near the nest site.

The lateral jerking and quivering of the tail may be performed in flight. It is then used (*fide* Lorenz) by a bird that wishes another to fly with it, the displaying bird flying low over its companion (whether Jackdaw or human) and making this tail movement as it passes.

In quarrels not involving nest sites or perching places the usual threatening posture is with sleeked plumage and uplifted head, the preparatory movements of flying or leaping to attack. The various displays have been well illustrated by Lorenz (1952) and some also in photographs by Strauss.

Lorenz (1931, 1952) found a remarkable communal defence of any colony member attacked at its nest site. When the weaker bird gave its 'yep' call all the others would gather and, if the aggressor persisted, attack and drive it off. Usually, however, the latter joined in with the 'defenders', giving the bowing and tail-fanning movements characteristic of this response. It is not known to what extent such defence of weaker individuals obtains in wild colonies.

At small colonies, both wild and tame, strange Jackdaws are attacked and driven off during the breeding season (Lorenz; Zimmerman). The situation at large colonies, which may number many hundreds of pairs, is apparently unknown.

Other names Chough (formerly used for this species, as by Chaucer and sometimes by Shakespeare), Daw.

Note Around the turn of the century pure white Jackdaws were on sale yearly in London. They were imported from Europe, presumably from some (now unknown?) district that produced unusual numbers of these beautiful freaks.

REFERENCES

CROSS, A. E. 1948. Open-beaked probing of Rook, Carrion Crow and Jackdaw. *Brit. Birds* **41**: 342.
GRIFFITHS, J. 1955. Jackdaw roost continuing throughout the breeding season. *Brit. Birds* **48**: 139.
LOCKIE, J. D. 1955. The feeding and breeding of Jackdaws and Rooks with notes on Carrion Crows and other Corvidae. *Ibis* **97**: 341–369.
—— 1956. Winter fighting in feeding flocks of Rooks, Jackdaws and Carrion Crows. *Bird Study* **3**: 180–190.
LORENZ, K. 1927. Beobachtungen an Dohlen. *J. Orn.* **75**: 511–519.
—— 1931. Beiträge zur Ethologie sozialer Corviden. *J. Orn.* **79**: 67–127.
—— 1932. Betrachtungen über das Erkennen der arteigenen Triebhandlungen der Vögel. *J. Orn.* **80**: 51–98.
—— 1952. *King Solomon's Ring.* London.
RITTENBACH, H. E. 1951. Notizen über eine Dohlenkolonie. *Orn. Beob.* **48**: 47–51.
RYDER, S. R. 1960. *Blind Jack.* London.
SCHIEMANN, K. 1940. Vom Erlernen unbenannter Anzahlen bei Dohlen. *Z. Tierpsychol.* **3**: 292–347.
SIMMONS, K. E. L. 1968. Food-hiding by Rooks and other crows. *Brit. Birds* **61**: 228–229.
STRAUSS, E. 1938. Vergleichende Beobachtungen über Verhaltensweisen von Rabenvögeln. *Z. Tierpsychol.* **2**: 145–172.
VOOUS, K. H. 1950. The post-glacial distribution of *Corvus monedula* in Europe. *Limosa* **23**: 281–292.
WITHERBY H. F. *et al.* 1938. *The Handbook of British Birds* vol. 1. *London.*
ZIMMERMANN, D. 1951. Zur Brutbiologie der Dohle, *Coloeus monedula* (L.). *Orn. Beobachter* **48**: 73–111.

DAURIAN JACKDAW   *Corvus dauuricus*

Corvus dauuricus Pallas, 1776, *Reise d. versch. Prov. Russ. Reichs*, 3, p. 694.

Description Size and proportions as Jackdaw, but with the first and second primaries averaging a little shorter. Nasal bristles blackish but with pale grey or white shafts giving a streaked or grizzled effect. Ear coverts, feathers behind and above the back of the eye, and sometimes also those of the nape, tipped or intermixed with white giving a silvery effect. Most of the underparts (see sketch) and a broad band around the hind neck creamy-white, more or less tinged with pinkish grey in new plumage and with the feather bases grey. Rest of plumage bluish black, glossed intensely with bluish and purplish on the forehead, crown, secondaries and secondary coverts and rather less intensely with bluish-green and greenish on the throat, centre of breast and (visible parts of) primaries, primary coverts and tail. Greyish fringes to feathers of tibia and under tail coverts and, less prominently, to those of back and rump. Irides dark brown. Bill, feet and legs black.

Females average a little less glossy than males and some have the white parts considerably suffused with grey. Juveniles like adults, but except on wings, tail and top of head, which are like adult's but less strongly glossed, the black parts are a dull blackish grey and where the adult is creamy white they are light fawnish grey.

A dark colour phase occurs, in a majority in some areas, which was formerly given specific rank as *C. neglectus*, in which the areas that are white in the pied phase are greyish black or, especially on the underparts, more or less mottled dull creamy grey and sooty dark grey. I think the black phase is the first year plumage as all the many specimens in the British Museum (Natural History) that I have examined appear to be yearlings and Kleinschmidt & Weigold state that they collected specimens moulting from juvenile plumage into the black first year plumage and from the latter into the pied adult dress. On the other hand Koslova recorded seeing pied adults feeding both dark and light young. Dementiev and Gladkov also treat the black form as a colour morph.

Distribution and habitat Siberia from about Kansk district eastward to Amurland and Ussuriland, north to about Olekminsk but only to the middle of the Zeya River Valley in Amurland, south to Mongolia, and China south to northern Szechwan, Kansu, Eastern Tibet (now eastern Tsinghai and Sikang) and eastern Yunnan. In winter in China south to Fukien, Russian Turkestan, Korea, Formosa and, irregularly, Japan. Summer resident in the more northern parts of its range and at high altitudes but sometimes winters as far north at least as Harbin (Piechocki).

Inhabits open woodland, wooded river valleys in open or hilly country, cultivated areas and pasture land with some trees, old buildings or cliffs. Not normally in dense woodland, but sometimes in clearings in such forest. Presumed non-breeding flocks may occur in open country far from any possible nest sites (Schäfer).

Field characters Smaller size and proportionately shorter bill distinguish the pied phase from Collared Crow; pied coloration from all other sympatric *Corvus* species.

Black phase probably not distinguishable from Jackdaw in the field unless iris colour visible, from other crows distinguished by shorter bill and small size.

Feeding and general habits Probably similar if not identical to those of Jackdaw (q.v.). Known to take cultivated grain, weed seeds, insects and berries. In parts of China and eastern Tibet feeds chiefly on stubble fields in winter, largely on grain and seeds. Has been observed turning over the droppings of Yaks and other domestic animals in search of insects. At one colony in Manchuria recently fledged young were being fed largely on the caterpillars of *Cirphis unipuncta* (Piechocki).

Out of the breeding season (and perhaps during it to some extent) roosts communally. In China roosts are commonly in town trees, in company with Rooks. In eastern Tibet Schäfer found it roosting, but never nesting, in old ruined walls and buildings, together with Choughs and Eastern Rock Pigeons.

Nesting Nesting habits appear to be similar to those of *C. monedula*. In eastern Tibet, however, Schäfer found that it nested only in holes in trees, never in holes in cliffs or buildings as it often does elsewhere (La Touche; Koslova; Zieger), although non-breeding birds roosted in such places. Koslova found many nests built in the branches of trees; she implies these were built entirely by the Daurian Jackdaws, not on the foundations of old nests of other species. Piechocki also found it nesting freely in colonies on branches of trees where holes were not available.

Eggs like those of the Jackdaw. Eggs have been taken as early as February 18th in China. Near Yekundo in eastern Tibet (now Sikang) Schäfer found it incubating in late May. Recently fledged young in numbers in Manchuria (Kungchuling) in early July.

Unafraid of man where not persecuted, breeding freely near or even in houses and following the plough in search of food.

Voice I can find no detailed description of its calls. Such few general descriptions as I have seen suggest that its voice is similar to that of *C. monedula*.

Display and social behaviour No information. Probably as Jackdaw.

Other names Pied Jackdaw, Black Jackdaw (the dark phase), Chinese Jackdaw.

REFERENCES

DEMENTIEV, G. P. & GLADKOV, N. A. 1954. *The birds of the Soviet Union*, 5.
KLEINSCHMIDT, H. & WEIGOLD, O. 1922. Zoologische Ergebnisse der Walter Stötznerschen Expedition nach Szetschwan, Osttibet und Tschili. *Abh. u. Ber. Mus. Dresden* **15**: 3: 2–3.
KOSLOVA, E. V. 1933. The birds of south-west Transbaikalia, northern Mongolia and central Gobi. *Ibis* (13) **3**: 60–61.
LA TOUCHE, J. D. D. 1925–30. *A Handbook of the Birds of Eastern China*, 1: 11–13.
MEISE, W. 1934. Die Vogelwelt der Mandschurei. *Abh. Mus. Dresden* **18**, 2: 12–13.
PIECHOCKI, R. 1956. *Beiträge zur Avifauna Nord und Nordost-Chinas* (*Mandschurei*): 123–124. Dresden.
SCHÄFER, E. 1938. Ornithologische Ergebnisse zweier Forschungsreisen nach Tibet. *J. Orn.*, **86**: Sonderheft May 1938. 261–262.
ZIEGER, R. 1967. Kleine Beobachtungen aus der Mongolei. *Beiträge zur Vogelkunde* **13**: 116–124.

ROOK   *Corvus frugilegus*

Corvus frugilegus Linnaeus, 1758, Syst. Nat., ed. 10, 1, p. 105.

Description A little smaller than Hooded Crow. Tail somewhat graduated but less so than Raven's. Feathers on the head, neck, upper breast and upper mantle (and to some extent elsewhere) with a very soft, dense, lax, silky texture. Whole of face in front of the eyes bare of feathers (except for aborted feather sheaths, which form a pimply surface, and degenerate bristles and filoplumes) and greyish white in colour. Throat covered with short, woolly, degenerate downy feathers which wear off, or are shed, six months or so after the moult, leaving the throat like rest of face. Rest of plumage black with a very intense gloss which is, in most lights, predominantly greenish blue, purplish blue and purple on head and wings, and purplish blue and purple elsewhere. When the bird is facing observer its head and foreparts may look dark blue-purple and the wings silvery green. In bright light the whole bird may look silvery. On old museum skins the gloss is often mainly purplish red but I have never seen a live Rook appear this colour. Bases of hind neck feathers grey. Irides dark brown. Bill, the skin-covered nasal area excepted, black. Legs and feet black.

The juvenile is duller, and often has a patch of white feathers at the base of the lower mandible. It has a fully feathered face and nasal bristles covering the nostrils in a dense mat as in most *Corvus* species. The bare face is acquired between about 10 and 15 months of age. Irides of fledgling juvenile a smoky bluish grey, inside of mouth pink or pinkish red.

The above description is of the nominate form *C. f. frugilegus*. The form from eastern Asia, *C. f. dastinator*, is a little smaller, has much less bare skin on the face and fully feathered throat (see sketches).

Field identification Bare face of adult diagnostic and gives characteristic apparently high foreheaded profile in flight. Loose feathers around thighs give a shaggier outline than Crow's. Young Rooks walking about feeding are usually distinguishable from Carrion Crows by this feature but it is not always obvious in perched or resting individuals. Wing beat is usually quicker than Carrion Crow's. Calls also differ but this feature is of use only to one familiar with the many utterances of both species. Identifications based on supposed solitary habits of Carrion Crow and gregariousness of Rook are useless and misleading.

Distribution and habitat Europe and Asia. South of about 60° to 63°N. latitude in Scandinavia and Russia to about 56° in Siberia, eastward to the lower Amur but north along the Lena to Yakutsk, south to central France and the foot of the Alps in Italy, Balkans, Caucasas, northern and western Iran, Russian and Chinese Turkestan to the Tian Shan, Mongolia, Manchuria and China south to the Yangtze. Some populations are migratory. A summer resident in the more northerly parts of its breeding range. Less marked or less regular movements may occur also in other parts of its range.

Inhabits open country: agricultural and pastoral regions with clumps of trees or small woods, wooded steppe or open steppe with clumps of trees or bushes, and wide river valleys with open grassy areas. Usually most abundant in low-lying areas. In Britain, and probably elsewhere in western Europe, appears only to thrive well where there is both arable and pasture land. Where little or no grain is grown it is seldom abundant, unlike the Jackdaw. Often in villages and towns but only where these are adjacent to suitable countryside. Does not normally occur as a breeding or resident species in extensive built-up areas.

Feeding and general habits In Britain, and probably in many other parts of its range, earthworms and cultivated grains are the most important foods, in terms of amounts taken and the number of Rooks taking them. Also eats insects and their larvae, including beetles, moths, caterpillars, grasshoppers, crane flies, and especially their larvae (leatherjackets); also other invertebrates, including both land and shore molluscs and crustaceans. Vegetable foods, other than grain, include acorns, walnuts, potatoes, cultivated roots, cherries and other fruits (but not usually in any quantity). Small mammals such as Field Voles, eggs and young birds (mostly of field-nesting species), are taken. Very readily learns to eat bread, meat, cooked potatoes and other human foods, also many foods fed to farm stock.

Feeds largely in pasture and arable fields and other open areas with short or sparse vegetation. On many shores and estuaries regularly feeds along the tide line and on exposed rocks, mud or sand at low tide. When seeking food digs and probes in the ground to a greater extent than most other crows but also picks food from surface, turns over objects, scatters animal dung, and makes quick jumps to capture moving insects. When probing uses the usual method of inserting the closed bill and opening it (*Zirkeln*).

Seeks food also in trees but usually only when taking acorns, walnuts, swarming caterpillars, or cock-chafers.   Regularly scavenges on garbage dumps; locally also around railway stations, on picnic grounds and in town streets.   Scavenging in towns takes place mostly in early morning, before many people are about, and before the previous night's litter of discarded food remnants is removed.   Some regularly visit gardens and bird tables for food; in Britain this habit seems usually confined to relatively few indivi-dual Rooks but around Vienna it is widespread in winter (Steiner).

Stores acorns and such artificial foods (when available) as bread and peanuts; possibly other foods as well.   Food is hidden in or on the ground, usually (perhaps always) in some area which the individual hiding it regularly visits.   Acorns may be carried up to two miles to such a place (Richards).   In some areas the cones of conifers are regularly carried off and hidden (Andrews).   It is likely, but apparently not proven, that the seeds of such conifers are used as food.   Food is often hidden in the typical manner but sometimes the Rook, unlike most other corvids, first digs a hole in which to hide it (Richards; Sim-mons; Andrews).   I have seen a Rook that had just hidden a piece of bread wait its opportunity to remove it and carry it off when a superior searched for it, and Simmons noted that one, to which he fed peanuts, would bury them in the immediate vicinity if it was alone but carry them off to hide elsewhere if other Rooks were present.   It is not known to what extent Rooks depend on previously hidden food.

Large food objects are held under one or (less often) both feet while being broken or dissected with the bill.   Food for the young is carried in the buccal pouch; food for storing either in the buccal pouch or bill.   Has been recorded dropping mussels to break them but this does not seem common (Priestley, 1947).   Dunking of food has been recorded (Strauss, 1938) in captivity but not all captive Rooks do it often (pers. obs.).

Gregarious but, except possibly with immatures or with birds migrating or wintering away from the breeding areas, the pair is the basic unit.   When Rooks are foraging an individual that leaves one field to fly to another is usually followed by its mate (probably always if it has one) but often by no other individuals.   At least near the breeding rookeries, and not only in the breeding season, individuals and pairs may forage by themselves.   Members of a pair roost close together even when using large communal roosts (Coombs, 1960).   In late spring and summer family parties may forage by themselves (this is, of course, merely an extension of the pair unit) although more often than not in the proximity of other Rooks.   In autumn and winter young Rooks may form flocks of their own and such flocks sometimes roost separately.   Other immatures accompany adults.

Roosts communally, in autumn and winter at large roosts which are usually based upon a rookery but to which birds from other breeding rookeries also come.   In spring adults roost at their breeding rookeries although they may not start to do so until after the eggs are laid.   Winter roosts are usually used also by Jackdaws (at least in Britain) and often by Carrion Crows, and where they occur, Ravens. Repeated apparent panics in which some or all birds leave their perches and fly around before re-settling are a characteristic behaviour pattern at large roosts and may take place when it is nearly or quite dark as well as earlier.

Migrating Rooks fly by day, interrupting such flights to descend and feed.   Night flying has been suspected (Waterston) but, as Schuster points out, perhaps incorrectly.   On migration often accompanied by Jackdaws.   Migrating flocks may split up, some individuals descending to feed and later joining other flocks, some flying on, indicating that such flocks are not always, and probably never, cohesive social units.

Both passive and active anting is shown by captive individuals and anting by wild Rooks has been recorded.   Anting with fire was practised regularly by a tame individual (Burton).   The 'smoke-bathing' of wild Rooks on chimney pots, which is common in some places, seems usually only an attempt to get warm.

Nesting   Nests colonially; usually in or near the tops of tall trees, less often in smaller trees, shrubs or bushes; exceptionally on buildings and a solitary nest on the ground once recorded (Scott).   Rookeries are usually situated in clumps or avenues of trees, or small woods in otherwise fairly open country.   In Britain tall trees in villages, around farmhouses or manors and in small towns in agricultural districts are typical sites of rookeries. Will use either broad-leaved or coniferous trees. There are commonly several or many nests in each tree but some pairs may nest at a little distance from the main body. Where the Rook is very numerous individual rookeries may be connected by scattered nests to such an extent that most of the tall trees of the district seem to comprise part of an enormous far-flung Rookery.

Nest site selected by either or both sexes; in one instance in which cock and hen chose different sites the nest was finally built at the male's (Coombs). In Britain (and probably elsewhere where the species is resident) the breeding rookery is visited daily by the adults except for a brief period in summer (Marshall and Coombs) when the gonads are in a refractory state and sometimes during periods of food shortage in winter. Nest site selection may take place in autumn or spring (or late winter). Some carrying of nest material usually occurs from autumn onwards but serious building seldom starts, in Britain, before March.

As with other colonial birds sudden mass flights of most or all individuals in apparent alarm occur frequently during the early stages of the breeding cycle. Sometimes, and perhaps always, these 'dreads' or 'out flights' are sparked off by alarming sights or sounds (Coombs).

Both sexes gather material and build with what they bring, much less often one may present the other with material. Female Rooks are capable of making a complete nest (Goodwin; Coombs) by themselves but normally the male does as much as or more work on the nest than the female. The female is usually more reluctant to leave the nest site and does not go so far afield for nest material as her mate does (Coombs). Sticks and twigs are broken from the trees, material for lining the nest mostly taken from the ground, but both are stolen from other Rooks' nests whenever opportunity occurs.

Nest built of sticks and twigs, solidified with grass tufts, earth, leaves, fibrous bark etc. and lined with grasses, moss, fibrous roots, leaves, straw or similar materials, rarely with some wool or hair. The typical passerine nest-building movements are used by both sexes (see p.46, and Coombs for detailed description of nest construction). The building Rook appears to make few or no intelligent adaptations in reference to the type of stick or site when trying to get the foundations of a nest built but it does seem to be aware of the danger of material falling. If it notices a stick begin to fall or slip it will at once try to seize it in time. Sticks that fall are not retrieved from the ground. The female (and possibly also the male) of a pair whose nest broke apart, resulting in the loss of two of their three young, repaired the nest, using twigs only and no lining material. She (or they) did this in late April and early May at a time when gonad regression was well advanced (Coombs). It is difficult to interpret this behaviour as lacking in insight and purposiveness.

Once building begins in earnest the female is reluctant to leave the vicinity of the nest, and any prolonged absence by both sexes normally leads to its being partly or entirely dismantled by other Rooks seeking nest material. When incubation begins the female does not normally go more than a few yards from the nest; if she does, the male remains to guard it.

Eggs usually 3 to 5, sometimes 2, up to 9 recorded. Light green, greyish green or light bluish green; speckled and/or spotted or blotched with greyish brown, olive brown or dark brown and with underlying greyish markings. Eggs are usually profusely but sometimes quite sparsely marked. Exceptional erythristic eggs are pinkish buff with reddish brown and pinkish lilac markings. In Britain eggs are laid from late February to late April but mainly in March. Young are usually in the nest in very late March and April when the main rearing foods, earthworms and moth larvae, are abundant. Annual variations in laying dates are correlated with changes of temperature in the pre-laying period, mild weather encouraging early laying (Owen). In northern and north-eastern China eggs are usually laid in April (La Touche). Exceptionally, in Britain, Rooks lay in autumn, but I have seen no record of autumn-hatched young being successfully reared.

Female alone incubates and broods, fed at nest by the male. Incubation period 16 to 18 days (Witherby et al.). Incubation begins before the clutch is complete, in large broods (4 to 6) one or more of the later-hatched nestlings commonly die, presumably of under-nourishment. Both sexes feed and tend the young. The male brings food in his sublingual pouch and usually gives some to one or more of the young and some to the female. Sometimes he may give all to the female but sometimes, especially after the first week or so, he may neglect the female in favour of the young. At least during the first week the female usually gives to the young part of the food the male brings her. She remains at the nest, guarding or brooding the young, until apparently forced by hunger to seek food for herself. Thus the time at which she does this varies according to the success of the male in obtaining food and his willingness or otherwise to give her some of it. When there are only one or two young in the brood and food is plentiful the female may remain at the nest until they fledge at about 32 to 33 days. Where Rooks are fed by man near their nests females will leave the nest for a few moments to collect food and (sometimes) feed their young with it. Faeces are taken either from the nest or directly from the young, carried in the throat pouch, or less often in the bill tip, and dropped away from nest. The young are fed for some time after leaving the nest and may still be dependent on parental feeding in August.

Voice The most commonly heard call is the familiar 'caw', which could better be written 'kaah!' It is usually said to be less raucous than the cawing of Carrion Crow but to my ear tends to sound harsher and flatter than the usual calls of *C. corone*. With minor variations it is given in many situations which involve some social or sexual excitement. It accompanies the bowing and tail-fanning and is used as a greeting between mates when one returns after a short absence.

The alarm call, used when mobbing a predator, differs only in being louder, more vehement and perhaps a little harsher.

A very high-pitched call, 'kraa-a' or 'koo-a' may also be given with bowing and tail-fanning. It seems largely aggressive but Dr Coombs (1960 and *in litt.*) believes it usually also indicates some degree of alarm. He has often heard it as a prelude to flight out from the rookery when there has been some disturbance. Probably human presence at a rookery is often the factor eliciting it.

A similar high-pitched 'kroo' or 'kew-u' is given by the female in defensive threat when she is molested by other Rooks while incubating or brooding.

The begging call is rather similar to the usual 'kaah' call but has the unmistakeable nagging, pleading tone that characterises it in some other species of *Corvus* and in *Garrulus*. It is given by the female and fledged young when begging for food and by both sexes when begging in other contexts. At a rookery at Windsor one female habitually begged with a much higher pitched call than the usual rather hoarse flat tone.

When building, particularly and perhaps only if the stick or other material gets temporarily jammed in an unsuitable position, the Rook often utters a long drawn-out, hoarse call with an almost human tone of exasperation and complaint. The same call is often heard (Coombs *in litt.*, pers. obs.) from one or more of a number of birds involved in attempted rape or interference therewith. When a zoo keeper took one of a pair of tame Rooks in his hand the other (which was an albino) at once flew onto the bird in his hand, pecking it and attempting to copulate with it. One of them (but I could not be sure which) uttered the long complaining sounding call as this was going on.

Mechanical sounding deep clicking sounds with some (individual?) variation are probably homologous with the clicking notes of the Jay and many other corvids. The version given by a ten years old tame female was a singly-uttered, deep but rather liquid-sounding glottal click. From wild Rooks (sex unknown) perched alone I have heard series of run-together glottal clicks, very like the clicking of female Jays but deeper in tone. These clicking calls are given with the forward movement of the bowing and tail-fanning display, but the degree of tail-spreading is slight and the head plumage is arranged so that erected feathers form two 'ears' at either side of the head as in some displays of *C. corax* and *C. coronoides*.

The song consists of a medley of much or all of the Rook's repertoire, usually given rather more softly than in other contexts. Various soft cawing, gurgling, rattling and crackling calls are uttered and the general effect is very much like that of a singing Starling, only louder. Song is usually given by a Rook at a little distance from others, often when perched alone on a telegraph pole, fence post, television aerial or similar place. While singing the bird's head moves forward and back and it may pivot one way or another (Coombs). Singing seems correlated with a rather low state of sexual arousal. It is most often heard in early spring, late winter or autumn. In late winter, in 1946 in northern Yorkshire, a sudden thaw after about a week of frost and heavy snow cover set a great many Rooks singing. I saw and heard many individual Rooks singing in the sun, although the snow had not at the moment melted sufficiently to bare the soil and so it was unlikely that they had fed better than during the previous days.

Strauss distinguished ten different calls from a captive Rook, most of which seem referable to or variations of those described above, but additional to which were a growling call of contentment when feeding or preening and a higher pitched and more 'crackling' sounding version of the begging call.

Display and social behaviour   The display postures (and some others) have been beautifully and accurately illustrated by Coombs.

The bowing and tail-fanning display accompanies many situations which appear to involve social or sexual excitement.   Coombs found that it was seldom or never shown (in his study area in Cornwall) in May, June and July, when the gonads are in a refractory condition.   In this display the bird slightly or partly droops and/or opens its wings, raises and spreads its tail, bows forward and calls.   The head and open bill are not usually much, if any, below the horizontal at the lowest point of the bow.   Often the head movement appears to me more forward than downward and to be oriented towards another individual.   This display seems to be largely self-assertive in character; it is given as an apparent greeting to the mate as well as in hostile situations.   Usually the head and flank feathers are somewhat erected. It may be given when the Rook is somewhat alarmed and then the accompanying call is higher-pitched and the plumage, except for the crown feathers, tends to be sleeked down (Coombs).

A movement in which the wing tips are quickly lifted from the back and the tail slightly spread, without head movements or calling, is possibly a low intensity version of this display.   Both forms appear as if they might have been derived from flight-intention movements, although they do not usually occur immediately before taking flight.

The pre-copulatory display of the male is similar to but more exaggerated than the bowing and tail-fanning.   The wings are lifted more slowly and are partly spread, the head is raised with the bill pointing downwards, the feathers on crown, nape and flanks are fully erected.   If the female is sideways-on to the displaying male, his tail and body are tilted so that the upper surfaces of the wings and tail are towards her.

This display is (in my experience) directed by the male only at his own mate; it does not precede sexual attacks on other females.   Coombs found this display was given 'only occasionally' on the ground or away from the rookery.   I have seen it quite often in such situations so that it is possible there may be regional or individual differences, perhaps linked with the amount of interference at the nest site experienced by the pairs concerned.

In the quivering or submissive display the bird crouches with its wings partly opened and (usually) drooped, its head more or less on a level with the back, but sometimes looking up, and its tail slightly or (more rarely) appreciably raised above the horizontal.   The tail is rapidly vibrated, there may be slight quivering of the wings also (more often not), and the nictitating membrane may be repeatedly drawn across the eye.   At low intensities the bird will merely crouch still with little or no tail movement.

This is the female's invitation to coition.   It is, however, used by both sexes in what appear to be appeasing contexts.   It may be given, often alternately, by members of a pair passing food back and forth, by the male when his mate has refused to allow copulation, by a yearling in the presence of aggressive or fighting adults, and so on.   Coombs states that on every occasion that he has seen it given the other individual, whether male or female, has attempted to mount the displaying bird.   I have, however, on several occasions seen it given, by individuals away from a rookery passing food to each other, by yearlings at a rookery, by a male to his own mate at the nest site and (once) by an adult that had just been trespassing towards the nest owner that had driven it away, without eliciting any mounting attempts.

Copulation between the members of a pair may take place either at the nest or on the ground, sometimes at a little distance from the rookery.   I have the impression that some pairs deliberately go onto the ground at some distance from other Rooks in order to try to avoid being disturbed, in which they are not, however, always successful.   Coombs says that at most rookeries copulation nearly always takes place on the nest but that there is local variation, Gilbert White recorded it as commonly occurring on the ground.   I have seen Rooks copulating on the ground many times in Surrey (Virginia Water, Windsor, Guildford) and a few times in Yorkshire.

Male Rooks, including many or all of those with sitting mates of their own, habitually attempt to copulate forcibly with incubating females. Commonly but by no means always the male flies or drops onto an incubating female from above and Coombs suggests that seen from above such a female appears very similar to one in the precoitional display. Males do not, so far as I have seen, ever attempt to rape their own mates in this way, although I once saw a male attempt copulation with his own mate as an apparently automatic response to finding himself on top of her after he had driven off her attackers.

The female defends herself with fluffed out plumage and wings held loosely, moving with curiously 'floppy' jumps if, as often happens, she leaves the nest to attack an approaching male. She does not show these postures, so far as I have seen, when her own mate attempts unwelcome copulation, then merely stepping aside to prevent him.

Other Rooks, usually and perhaps always males, habitually interfere with copulation attempts. They fly at the mating pair and often peck fiercely at the female as well as trying to dislodge the mounted male When this occurs at the rookery many birds may be quickly involved and any male that finds himself on top of the female attempts copulation with her. The belief that only 'illicit' matings are interfered with in this way is incorrect. It seems unlikely that raping attempts ever result in actual insemination of the obviously unwilling and uncooperative female, who has, in any case, already laid her eggs.

Coombs has observed attacks on males performing the precopulatory display and once on an anting Rook. He suggests that any action suggestive of mounting may elicit attack. In apparently non-sexual situations it may be difficult to say whether a suggestion of copulatory behaviour or of injury is what sparks off aggression in the observers. The Rook has a tendency to attack individuals who, through injury or weakness, are apparently recognized as being unable to retaliate (Goodwin; Kramer).

Begging with fluttering or flapping wings, juvenile-type begging calls and, usually, a somewhat hunched and crouching posture, is characteristic of the female shortly before and during incubation. Such begging is an appeal for food but it seems also to express a degree of dependence. It may be shown by the male towards the female, sometimes immediately after he has given her food. I have seen wild female Rooks respond to male begging by a brief insertion of the bill but have not seen them feed the male in this context. The begging of an injured captive male seemed an important factor in stimulating its mate to take a partly male role in nesting (Coombs) and a tame female Rook I know will feed her owner if the latter presents her open mouth and imitates the begging call. Tame captive Rooks of either sex will beg to humans when hungry.

In display flight the wing beats are slower and more emphasized than in normal flight. The wings are raised to a greater angle above the horizontal and the flapping may be interspersed with short glides with the wings at a fairly steep angle above the horizontal. Display flight is most frequent at and near the Rookery, especially during pursuit flights. It seems to have both sexual and self-assertive significance.

Pursuit flights are common in autumn, late winter and early spring. Two or (usually) more Rooks fly around the nest trees, using the display flight much or all of the time. They often appear to be chasing and dodging but the order may change when a pursuing bird overshoots the leader. Either sex may be the 'pursued' but most often a female (Coombs). These flights often take place after quarrelling and may be, at least in some cases, connected with pair formation.

It is probable that pair-formation, at least in Britain, takes place in autumn during the morning visits to the nesting rookery. Adults whose mates are shot may acquire new ones in the breeding season but some females at least sometimes fail to do so. Possibly, owing to their relative boldness when they have to find food for the female and young, more male Rooks than females are shot, trapped and poisoned. The relatively rare cases of male Rooks with two mates also probably arise from this cause.

Allo-preening, in which most attention is paid to the partner's head and neck, whose feathers are parted by the typical food-seeking movement of inserting and then opening the bill, occurs between members of a pair, especially in late summer, early autumn and early spring.

The territory consists only of a small area around the nest. Immediate neighbours are recognized and other individuals are not usually allowed to approach so closely. Thus a pair of Rooks may sometimes appear to be deliberately defending a neighbour's nest. It is probable (see esp. Coombs) that most pairs of Rooks have a territory that has been invaded or compressed by the establishment of other pairs nearby. Their potential territory is larger than that which they defend from known neighbours and 'strangers' may be excluded also from the potential territory.

Each pair of Rooks is usually feared and respected by all others at its own nest. This alone stops the pilfering of nest material from getting completely out of hand and preventing colonial nesting. Rooks robbing a nest may fight each other for position on it but give way at once to the owners and flee from them when they return. Crippled birds may, however, be attacked even in their own territories (Goodwin).

Other names Crow (not uncommonly in non-ornithological literature and by the many people who do not distinguish between this species and the Carrion Crow).

REFERENCES

ANDREWS, D. G. 1969. Food-hiding by Rooks. *Brit. Birds* **62**: 334–336.
BURTON, M. 1957. Phoenix reborn. *Illus. London News* 231, nos. 6161 and 6167.
COOMBS, C. J. F. 1960. Observations on the Rook *Corvus frugilegus* in southwest Cornwall. *Ibis* **102**: 394–419.
DUNLOP, E. B. 1917. Polygamy among Rooks. *Brit. Birds* **10**: 278–279.
GOODWIN, D. 1955. Some observations on the reproductive behaviour of Rooks. *Brit. Birds* **48**: 97–105.
KRAMER, G. 1941. Beobachtungen über das Verhalten der Aaskrähe (*Corvus corone*) zu Freund und Feind. *J. Orn. Festschr. Oskar Heinroth*: 105–131.
LA TOUCHE, J. D. D. 1925-1930. *A Handbook of the Birds of Eastern China*: 9–11. London.
LOCKIE, J. D. 1955. The breeding and feeding of Jackdaws and Rooks, with notes on Carrion Crows and other Corvidae.
—— 1956. Winter fighting in feeding flocks of Rooks, Jackdaws and Carrion Crows. *Bird Study* **3**: 180–190.
—— 1959. The food of nestling Rooks near Oxford. *Brit. Birds* **52**: 309–311.
MARSHALL, A. J. & COOMBS, C. J. E. 1957. The interaction of environmental and behavioural factors in the Rook *Corvus frugilegus* Linnaeus. *Proc. Zool. Soc. London* **128**: 545–589.
OGILVIE, C. M. 1947. Observations in a rookery during the incubation period. *Brit. Birds* **40**: 135–139.
—— 1949. Observations in a rookery in winter. *Brit. Birds* **42**: 64–68.
—— 1951. The building of a rookery. *Brit. Birds* **44**: 278–279.
OWEN, D. F. 1959. The breeding season and clutch-size of the Rook *Corvus frugilegus*. *Ibis* **101**: 235–239.
PRIESTLEY, C. F. 1947. Rook feeding on mussels. *Brit. Birds* **40**: 176.
RICHARDS, T. J. 1958. Concealment and recovery of food by birds, with some relevant observations on squirrels. *Brit. Birds* **51**: 497–508.
SCOTT, R. E. 1959. Rook nesting on ground. *Brit. Birds* **52**: 388.
SIMMONS, K. E. L. 1968. Food-hiding by Rooks and other crows. *Brit. Birds* **61**: 228–229.
SCHUSTER, L. 1949. Review of and comments on a paper by Waterhouse, (see below) in *Vogelwelt* **70**: 125–126.
STEINER, H. M. 1967. Zunehmende Verstädterung der Saatkrähe in Wien. *Egretta* **10**: 34–35.
STRAUSS, E. 1938. Vergleichende Beobachtungen über Verhaltensweisen von Rabenvögeln. *Z. Tierpsychol Berlin* **2**: 145–172.
VAURIE, C. 1959. *The Birds of the Palearctic Fauna: Passeriformes*: 166–167. London.
WATERSTON, M. J. 1949. Rook and Jackdaw migrations observed in Germany. *Ibis* **91**: 1–16.
WITHERBY, H. F., JOURDAIN, F. C. R., TICEHURST, N. F., & TUCKER, B. W. 1913. The sequence of plumages of the Rook. *Brit. Birds* **7**: 126–139.

AMERICAN CROW   *Corvus brachyrhynchos*

Corvus brachyrhynchos Brehm, 1882, Beitr. Vögelkunde, 2, p. 56.

Description Between Hooded Crow and House Crow in size, similar to former in shape but with proportionately slightly smaller bill. Black with slight dark purple and blue iridescence. The feathers of the mantle, back, rump and inner wing coverts have their tips glossless and thus appear blacker at close quarters when, in some lights, as with the Carrion Crow but to a less extent, they appear shiny purplish or bluish laced with black. Bases of neck feathers grey. Irides dark brown. Legs, feet and bill black.

Juvenile duller, at first with greyish eye and inside of mouth red.

The form from western North America, *C. b. hesperis* is smaller, with a proportionately smaller and more slender bill; that from Florida, *C. b. pascuus*, is also smaller than the nominate form but with a proportionately larger bill; *C. b. paulus*, from elsewhere in the southern U.S.A., is similar to *pascuus* but has a smaller bill.   Newly-hatched young are fleshy or pinkish with sparse tufts of dark greyish-brown down on head and upperparts.

Field characters   Easily distinguished from Raven by the only very slightly rounded instead of wedge-shaped tail, different calls and much less frequent gliding or soaring when in flight.   Also much smaller but this is only useful if another bird of known size is also present.   From Fish Crow and North-western Crow (q.v.) by differently-sounding voice.   From all the American blackbirds (*Icteridae*) by larger size and different proportions.

Distribution and habitat   North America: from inland British Columbia, south-western Mackenzie, northern Saskatchewan, northern Manitoba, northern Ontario, central Quebec, and southern Newfoundland south to Baja California, central Arizona, north-central New Mexico, Colorado, central Texas, the Gulf of Mexico, and southern Florida.   Uncommon in the Great Basin area.   The northerly breeding populations are partly migratory, wintering further south.
   Inhabits many types of open country, farmland, wood edges, open woodland and parks.

Feeding and general habits   Feeds largely on the ground but also in trees.   An extensive investigation (Kalmbach) showed about 28% of the food of the adult crows to be of animal origin.   Animal food consists largely of insects, especially beetles and their larvae, grasshoppers, locusts and crickets; and other invertebrates such as spiders, millipedes and small crustaceans; also small reptiles, frogs, small mammals, eggs, young birds and carrion.   Vegetable food includes much cultivated grain, especially maize, but also wheat and sorghum where available, some wild seeds, especially of the Arrow Alum, *Peltandra virginica*, and wild and cultivated fruits and nuts, especially pecan nuts.   Scraps of human food readily taken when available.   Habitually scavenges on garbage tips and around slaughterhouses.
   Locally it may forage on the shore, drops shellfish to break them but, on the whole, much less a shore feeder than the Fish Crow or North-western Crow.   Hiding of food and other objects has been observed regularly in tame birds (Criddle, in Bent) but it is uncertain to what extent food is hidden in the wild.
   Adults usually in pairs, or male foraging alone when his mate is sitting, during breeding season, but in autumn and winter usually in small or large parties.   Considerable numbers may gather at good feeding grounds and en route for the very large communal roosts that form in winter in areas where the species is abundant (see esp. Haase and Bent).   The flight to the roost begins well before sunset.   As with some other birds, the habit of communal roosting results in heavy predation by modern man, many thousands being killed by officially organized bombing of the roosts.   In very cold weather the American Crow has been recorded leaving its previous roosting perches and roosting on the ground nearby, presumably to conserve body heat more readily (Widmann, in Bent), but such behaviour appears not to be usual.
   Very wary, nervous, and suspicious of new objects, especially where persecuted by man.   Will desert a major source of food when only a very small number of crows have been killed with poisoned samples of the food in question (Bent).   Mobs birds-of-prey and other predators in typical manner.

Nesting   Nests in trees, shrubs or bushes, sometimes on the cross-arms of telephone poles and, exceptionally, on the ground.   Usually nests singly but sometimes, at least in the western parts of its range, in small colonies. Bendire found three occupied nests in one small tree although there were other suitable trees nearby.

Usual crow nest of sticks or tough stems with an inner binding layer of fibrous bark and similar materials, sometimes (or usually?) with some mud or earth, and lined with fibrous bark, fine roots, hair, fur, moss, fine grasses, etc.

The 3 to 6 eggs, usually 4 or 5 are very variable, bluish green, pale olive, pale green, or greenish white, mottled, blotched, speckled and/or streaked with drab and olive brown, and with grey or lilac underlying markings. Erythristic eggs with a pinkish buff ground and reddish markings exceptionally occur. Incubation period 18 days (Bent), the young fledge at about 35 days. Both sexes are said to incubate (Bent; Bendire) but it seems at least doubtful whether they normally do so. Further observation is desirable.

Voice Davis describes the 'usual call' as 'a short "caah" with a quick rise in inflection at the beginning and almost as quick a fall at the end'. The descriptions of may other observers agree with this, as did calls that I heard from a few individual American Crows in New York state. They sounded shorter than and not much like any of the usual calls of the Carrion Crow known to me; as was the case with various recorded calls (Kellogg & Allen) of this species that I have heard. The begging call that I heard from recently-fledged juveniles was, however, a nagging 'caa a' or 'caa, caa', very like that of young Carrion Crows.

Chamberlain & Cornwell discuss the functions and give descriptions and sound spectrograms of many (but, they state, not all) of the species' calls. The following is condensed from their information, using their terminology for the different calls, with my comments or presumptions in brackets.

The *assembly call* is an intense and raucous call containing long notes. It is given when a predator is seen or heard nearby. It apparently functions to call together a group of crows to mob a predator. It is given at night, by crows at communal roosts, as well as by day. It may be given while diving at a flying bird-of-prey. When giving this call from a perch the crow holds its tail slightly spread, flicks it up and down below the body plane, and moves its wings rapidly up and over and back down to a closed position. On hearing this call other crows usually fly to its source with a rapid wing beat. (This call appears homologous in all respects with high intensity alarm or mobbing calls of many other corvids.)

The *simple scolding call* is more sharply staccato and continuous, and not as raucous as the *assembly call*. It is subject to a good deal of variation, (apparently according to the crow's estimation of the degree of danger). It is uttered at all times of the year and both by day and night. It is given when the crow hears an unseen predator or when it is approaching a distant predator that it can see. Its primary function is to announce the presence and location of a predator. It attracts other crows to the source of the call but they sometimes come using leisurely flapping and gliding instead of the rapid flapping flight. (This would seem to indicate similar but less intense motivation to that eliciting the *assembly call*.)

The *modified scolding call* closely resembles the *simple scolding call* but all its notes are inflected. It is elicited by the sound or distant sight of a predator. (Apparently this call does not differ in function from the *simple scolding call* but perhaps indicates a lesser degree of arousal.)

The *alert call* is variable; its distinctive feature is the number of notes per call, which rarely exceed 7 and are usually fewer than 6. Its function is also to warn other crows of danger. It may, in differing forms, be uttered either in immediate danger, as when a crow on the ground is suddenly surprised by a predator, or in situations of only slight risk, as when the crow sees a distant predator. Crows hearing the *alert call* commonly respond by giving *scolding* or *assembly calls*, and searching for the predator.

The *dispersal call* is the extreme degree of the *alert call*. Its notes are generally sharper and delivered closer together, the first note in the series is often inflected. This call is given by a crow in immediate danger, as at the sudden appearance of a Great Horned Owl or a crow-hunting human. Other crows usually respond by flying directly away from the sound, often then to ascend and gather in a circling flock high in the air. (This call appears very largely equivalent to the hawk alarm call of the Carrion Crow.)

The *squalling call* is given by a crow struggling to escape from a predator. This call functions to warn others of the predator.   Other crows usually fly to the sound's source, uttering the *assembly call* or *scolding calls*.   They will do this even at night.   (This type of call, and the reactions to it, other than the flying towards it at night, are widespread in corvids and other passerines.)

The *moribund call* consists of a more raucous and gurgling version of the squalling call.   Other crows responded in individually differing ways to a broadcast of this call.   The *moribund call* is said to be 'a definite communication' and 'not a sound produced mechanically or incidentally in the process of dying'. (It might, however, be produced whenever dying is accompanied by pain or terror.)

The *threat call* is the most variable of the American Crow's calls.   *Threat calls* may be screams, cackles, growls, staccato, or rattling notes, coos and a variety of other sounds.   They are uttered in threat, both aggressive and defensive, and in both interspecific and intraspecific contexts.   They are often given with head and body plumage erected.   (It seems likely that at least some of the above are equivalent to the grating rattle of the Carrion Crow and Jay; possibly others may be vocal mimicry given in moments of stress.)

Immature hunger and feeding calls resemble the *squalling call* but are not so protracted or wailing.   They are uttered by young birds when begging for food.

The *contact call* may consist of 3, 4 or more notes, but is usually a 4-noted sequence uttered by one crow in note-pairs.   It functions to maintain contact between the members of a pair or group, both when in flight and when they have become separated at a roost.

The *announcement call* is used by individuals flying to join a number of others at a roost, feeding ground etc.   *Announcement calls* are variable and resemble *simple scolding* and *assembly calls* but are usually much shorter.   They function 'as a form of recognition and contact'.

Rattling notes generally consist of 5 to 20 sharply delivered, staccato notes in a single utterance, suggestive of a woodpecker tapping.   They may be given perched or when a bird in flight dives downward either near its mate or to enter a roost or a feeding group.   (It seems possible that calls homologous to the clicking or rattling calls used in self-assertive display by some other corvids and others corresponding to the grating rattle given in intraspecific situations by the Jay and Carrion Crow may here have been included under one heading).

Chamberlain & Cornwell also describe many other calls heard from smaller numbers of crows, some of which may represent vocal mimicry, which they state is commonly practised.

Display and social behaviour   A tame bird displayed to humans by spreading its wings, bowing and mimicking the human voice (Warne).   Young taken early from the nest imprint readily on human beings and may completely ignore their own species in later life as a result (Cruickshank).

Other names   Crow, Common Crow (the usual names in America), Western Crow (the western race), Florida Crow (the Florida race).

REFERENCES

BENDIRE, C. E. 1895. Life histories of North American birds. *U.S. Nat. Mus. Spec. Bull.*
BENT, A. C. 1946. Life histories of North American jays, crows, and titmice. *U.S. Nat. Mus. Bull.* No. 191.
CHAMBERLAIN, D. R. & CORNWELL, G. W. 1971. Selected vocalisations of the Common Crow. *Auk* **88**: 613–634.
CRUICKSHANK, A. D. 1939. The behaviour of some Corvidae. *Bird Lore* **41**: 78–81.
DAVIS, L. I. 1958. Acoustic evidence of relationship in North American crows. *Wilson Bull.* **70**: 151–167.
HAASE, B. L. 1963. The winter flocking behaviour of the common crow. *Ohio J. Sci.* **63**: 145–151.
KALMBCH, E. R. 1939. The Crow in its relation to agriculture. Revised ed. *Farmer's Bull. U.S. Dep. Agriculture* No. 1102: 1–26.
KELLOGG, P. P. & ALLEN, A. A. 1959. *A Field Guide to Bird Songs of Eastern and Central North America.* Boston.
WARNE, F. L. 1926. Crows is crows. *Bird Lore* **28**: 110–116.

NORTHWESTERN CROW   *Corvus caurinus*

Corvus caurinus Baird, 1858, in Baird, Cassin, and Lawrence, Rep. Expl. and Surv. R. R. Pac., 9, p. 559; 569.

Description   Very similar to the small western race of the American Crow but rather smaller, a little smaller than a House Crow, and with proportionately smaller feet and more slender bill. Calls and behaviour (q.v.) more distinctive than appearance.

Distribution and habitat North-western North America: Coastal areas and off-shore islands from southern Alaska south to Puget Sound and Long Beach, Washington.

Inhabits shores and beaches and their immediate vicinity. Abundant in and about villages.

Field characters Differently-sounding calls, quicker wing-beats in flight and greater sociability distinguish it from western race of *C. brachyrhynchos.*

Feeding and general habits Very similar to the Fish Crow (q.v.). Takes stranded fish, shellfish, crabs, mussels, edible refuse around villages, grasshoppers and other insects, berries and fruits. Habitually carries mussels into air and drops them on hard surfaces to break.

Sociable; commonly in parties or flocks which resemble Jackdaws in their general liveliness and quick social responses.

Nesting Sometimes nests in small, loose-knit colonies of about half a dozen pairs, sometimes in single, scattered pairs. Two occupied nests have been found in one tree (Bowles, in Bent) but this is unusual. Nests in trees, shrubs or bushes; sometimes in recesses of rocks or banks, or on the ground under overhanging boulders.

Nest of usual crow type with an outer part of sticks or sticks and mud, the inside bound and consolidated with fibrous bark, pine needles, dead grass and similar materials and the inner cup lined with hair, fibres, fine grass and the like.

The eggs do not differ in colour from those of the Fish Crow (q.v.); 4 or 5 are usually laid in May or June.

Voice Observers agree that the calls of this bird differ markedly from those of the American Crow but disagree as to *how* they differ, some describing them as lower-pitched and others as higher-pitched than the usual calls of *C. brachyrhynchos.* Brooks describes a 'caw' higher in pitch than that of the American Crow and a musical cackling 'wok-wok-wok' given by members of straggling flocks when in flight. Bailey says that the most characteristic note is a sound like a cork coming out of a bottle which is given with a sharp upward movement of the previously lowered head. Lawrence (in Bendire) recorded a guttural rattling, obviously homologous with the similarly mechanical-sounding rattling calls of other corvids, a 'koo-wow, koo-wow' with the last drawled and emphasized, and a noisy 'caw, caw'. Bailey's statement that they are 'the best imitators of their family in Alaska' implies vocal mimicry but he does not give specific instances of it. Davis gives sound spectrograms of some calls of this and other American crows. Recorded calls that I have heard (Kellogg & Allen, 1962) included an 'ark ark ark', deeper and hoarser than Fish Crow's, and a longer 'caaar' very like the begging call of a Carrion Crow.

Display and social behaviour Little information. The rattling call is evidently made with similar posturing to that of some other corvids as Lawrence describes how the bird utters it 'with a slight spreading of the shoulders and the tail, the head being down and the tail drooped'.

REFERENCES

BAILEY, F. M. 1927. Notes on the birds of southeastern Alaska. *Auk* **44**: 351–367.
BENDIRE, C. E. 1895. Life histories of North American birds. *U.S. Nat. Mus. Spec. Bull.* No. 3.

BENT, A. C. 1946. Life histories of North American jays, crows, and titmice. *U.S. Nat. Mus. Bull.* No. 191: 269–275.
BROOKS, A. 1942. The status of the Northwestern Crow. *Condor* **44**: 166–167.
DAVIS, L. I. 1958. Acoustic evidence of relationship in North American crows. *Wilson Bull.* **70**: 151–167.
KELLOGG, P. P. & ALLEN, A. A. 1962. *Field Guide to Bird Songs of Western North America.* Boston.

FISH CROW   *Corvus ossifragus*

Corvus ossifragus Wilson, 1812, Amer. Orn., 5, p. 27, pl. 37, fig. 2.

Description   Very similar to the North-western Crow but slightly smaller.   Bill smaller and slimmer, but with some overlap of measurements.   Plumage denser and more silky in texture and more glossy, with a strong bluish or greenish-blue sheen on the upperparts and greenish or bluish-green sheen on the under parts.   Bases of neck feathers light grey.   Tail a little more rounded on average.   Irides brown.   Legs, feet and bill black.

Field characters   Voice difference distinguishes it from the American Crow.   Only if both species are present together are the Fish Crow's smaller size and thinner bill diagnostic.

Distribution and habitat   Eastern North America: The Atlantic and Gulf plains of the eastern United States from Rhode Island, Connecticut and New York south to Key West, and from south-eastern Texas and Louisiana eastward.   Also along the major river systems to north-western Louisiana, east-central Oklahoma, north-western North Carolina, south-western South Carolina, central Virginia, District of Columbia, central Maryland, central Pennsylvania and central-eastern New York.

Inhabits coastal marshes and beaches, shores of inland lakes and marshes, river banks and adjacent areas.

Feeding and general habits   Feeds largely on the ground but also in trees, most commonly along the shores of the sea or inland waters.   Readily and frequently picks food out of the water and has been recorded doing so with its feet (Wilson, in Bent).

Takes small crabs, shrimps and other crustaceans, stranded or dead fish, also small live fish if circumstances enable it to capture them, insects and probably other small invertebrates, eggs and young birds, small reptiles, berries and fruits of both native and introduced trees, some seeds, especially of wild rice, cultivated grains and peanuts.   Does not appear to have been recorded taking scraps of human food but probably does when they are available.

Sociable and gregarious, but the pair would appear to be the basic unit as in other *Corvus* species.   Forms large communal roosts in winter.   Flight quicker (or with quicker wing-beats?) than that of American Crow and it glides more often during flight.   Often hovers above the water's surface when seeking food.

Nesting   Nests in trees, often high up but sometimes as low as 2 metres or less from ground.   Often nests in small colonies but with the nests well spaced out, not several in one tree.   Nest of usual crow type; of sticks and twigs with much fibrous bark or similar material binding the outside of the central cup which is lined with pine needles, fibrous bark, hair, grass, and similar materials.   Many nests are described as being lined partly with animal dung but possibly this is sometimes used to bind the middle part of the structure rather than as a lining.

Usually 4 or 5 eggs are laid. They are bluish green, pale green, greenish white or greenish buff, variously mottled, speckled, or blotched with drab and olive brown. They have underlying greyish markings but, in the specimens I have seen, these are less prominent than is usual in crows' eggs and may be nearly absent. The eggs appear usually to be laid in May.

It has been said (Bendire) that both sexes 'assist in incubation' but further information is needed. It seems unlikely that both sexes normally incubate.

Voice Usual calls are described as shorter, hoarser and more nasal than usual calls of *C. brachyrhynchos*. I transcribed calls I heard as a short deep nasal 'ark ark ark'. They are variously transcribed as 'car', caa-ah', 'ah-uk' etc. Distinct, apparently, from the above is a querelous 'maah, maah' or 'whaw, whaw', possibly a begging call. Davis gives sound spectrograms of the usual call of this and other American Crows. Calls of this species are available on a record by Kellogg & Allen.

Display and social behaviour No detailed description. Said to indulge in sexual fighting, gliding flights and to 'have a playful, captivating manner in mid air' during the early spring (Dickey, in Bent).

REFERENCES

BENDIRE, C. E. 1895. Life histories of North American Birds: 415–418. *U.S. Nat. Mus. Spec. Bull.* No. 3.
BENT, A. C. 1946. Life histories of North American jays crows, and titmice: 275–283. *U.S. Nat. Mus. Bull.* No. 191.
DAVIS, L. I. 1958. Acoustic evidence of relationship in North American crows. *Wilson Bull.* **70**: 151–167.
KELLOGG, P. P. & ALLEN, A. A. 1959. *A Field Guide to Bird Songs of Eastern and Central North America.* Boston.

SINALOAN CROW   *Corvus sinaloae*

Corvus sinaloae Davis, 1958, *Wilson Bull.*, 70, p. 163.

Description Does not differ in appearance from the Mexican Crow, *C. imparatus*, with which it may be conspecific, but its tail is said to average slightly longer so that the wing-tail length ratio is always under 1.63 (Davis).

Field characters As Mexican Crow (q.v.) from which it can only be identified by its voice and locality as they do not occur together.

Distribution and habitat The Pacific coastal slope of Mexico, from Sonora to Colima. Inhabits coastal regions, riversides and semi-desert woodland, ranging inland in the hills to elevations of 300 metres or more. Common in coastal towns and villages.

Feeding and general habits Feeds both in trees and on the ground; where living on the coast habitually forages on the shore at low tide. Known to take fruits, insects, small crabs and shellfish. Turns over bits of wood and other objects in search of food.

Nesting Nests in trees, including thorny *Mimosa* trees and tall coconut palms. Nest and eggs said to be similar to those of American Crow but smaller.

Voice   Said (Davis) to be strikingly different from that of *C. imparatus*.   The 'usual call' is 'a clear "ceow" ' (Davis).   Davis gives sound spectrograms of this and comparable calls of other American crows.

Display and social behaviour   No information.

Other name   Mexican Crow (by many authors who, possibly rightly, consider this bird and *C. imparatus* conspecific).

REFERENCES

DAVIS, L. I.   1958.   Acoustic evidence of relationship in North American Crows.   *Wilson Bull.* **70**: 151–167.
SALVIN, O. & GODMAN, F. D.   1879–1904.   *Biologia Centrali-Americana* **1**: 488–489.

MEXICAN CROW   *Corvus imparatus*

Corvus imparatus Peters 1929, Proc. Biol. Soc. Washington, 42, p. 123.

Description   A little larger than a Jackdaw; very similar to Fish Crow in appearance but usually slightly smaller and more slender, with appreciably more slender bill and a much richer gloss on its very soft and silken plumage.   Black, richly glossed with purple, blue and greenish blue above and with green and bluish green below.   Both its size, proportions and rich iridescence show a strong convergent resemblance to many of the American blackbirds (Icteridae).   Irides brown.   Legs, feet and bill black.   Juvenile duller and less lustrous but with more iridescence than is usual in juvenile crows.

Field characters   Glossier plumage and different voice may serve to distinguish it from American Crow with which it is not usually sympatric.   Voice alone differentiates it from the possibly conspecific Sinaloan Crow.   Less slender than the male Boat-tailed Grackle, *Cassidix mexicanus*, and has an only slightly rounded tail, the grackle's being strongly graduated.   Has longer bill, wings and tail than the Giant Cowbird, *Psomocolax oryzivorus*.

Distribution and habitat   Mexico: from China, Nuevo Leon, eastward to the lower tip of the Rio Grande Delta and southward to about 24 km south of Valles, San Luis Potosi, and to the northern borders of Veracruz, near Tampico, Tamaulipas.

   Inhabits semi-desert scrub and brushland, including towns, villages, farms and ranches in such country. Also in open areas in more humid woodland, but not normally in forests, true deserts, mountains or on the seashore.

Feeding and general habits   In late winter Sutton found Mexican Crows associating in 'close-knit' flocks, perching and flying up together.

Nesting   No information.

Voice   Its typical calls are very different from most other crows.   Davis, who gives sound spectrograms for this and other American *Corvus* species, describes its voice as 'burry, low-pitched, relatively low in volume . . . something like a frog croaking softly . . .'   Sutton heard from flocking birds a 'surprisingly feeble cry which resembled the syllables 'gar-lic'."

Display and social behaviour   No information.

Other names   Tamaulipas Crow.

REFERENCES

DAVIS, L. I.   1958.   Acoustic evidence of relationship in North American crows.   *Wilson Bull.* **70**: 151–167.
SUTTON, J. M.   1951.   *Mexican Birds.   First Impressions* 102–103.   Oklahoma.

WHITE-NECKED CROW   *Corvus leucognaphalus*

Corvus leucognaphalus Daudin, 1800, Traité Orn., 2, p. 231.

Description   Between Hooded Crow and House Crow in size.   Rather long bill with a smoothly curving culmen.   Bare rictal area and sub-orbital patch.   Lower rictal bristles directed somewhat upwards so that nostrils are partly or quite exposed.   It is possible, however, that in life these bristles are partly mobile.   Feathers at base of culmen and between the eye and bill short and rather stiff, appearing some-what plush-like and of a more intense (lustre-less) black than elsewhere.   This condition is common to most *Corvus* species but more fully developed in *leucognaphalus*.   Plumage black with some bluish and purplish gloss, chiefly on upper parts.   Bases of neck and other contour feathers snow-white.   The bare facial skin looks, on museum specimens, as though it was dark or blackish in life and as observers do not describe it this seems likely.   Irides orange-brown to orange-red.   Bill, legs and feet black.

Field characters   Bond says it can be distinguished from the Palm Crow by its more graceful, leisurely flight and very different voice.

Distribution and habitat   The West Indian islands of Hispaniola (Haiti and Dominica), and Puerto Rico, Inhabits forest and woodland, including pine forest.

Feeding and general habits   Little information available.   Feeds largely on fruits and berries, including the drupes of *Dacryodes excelsa*.   Remains of a tree toad and a passerine nestling were found (once each out of twenty specimens) in the stomachs of shot birds.   It probably takes insects and other small creatures when available.

Often gregarious, in small or sometimes large parties, that sometimes fly high with much gliding and soaring.

Nesting   Wetmore found nests with both eggs and well-grown young in March in Puerto Rico but they were all in high trees and inaccessible.

Voice   Evidently loud and loquacious but I can find no detailed information.   Its calls are variously described as 'Raven-like', loud, high-pitched, and gabbling.   Bond transcribes a common call as 'culik-calow-calow'.   Probably has many calls, like most corvids.   May be a vocal mimic also.

Display and social behaviour   No information.

REFERENCES

BOND, J.   1960.   *Birds of the West Indies:* 164.   London.
CORY, C. B.   1885.   *The Birds of Haiti and San Domingo.*   Boston.
WETMORE, A.   1927.   *The Birds of Porto Rico and the Virgin Islands* 479–482.   New York.
WETMORE, A. & SWALES, B. H.   1931.   The birds of Haiti and the Dominican Republic.   *U.S. Nat. Mus. Bull.*
No. 155: 325–328.

CUBAN CROW   *Corvus nasicus*

Corvus nasicus Temminck, 1826, Nouv. Rec. Pl. col., 2, livr. 70, p. 143.

Description   Very similar to the previous species, *C. leucognaphalus*, with which it may be conspecific and from which it differs in being smaller, about the size of a House Crow or rather less, and with grey instead of white bases to the contour feathers.

Field characters   Said not to be certainly distinguishable in field from Palm Crow except by voice (Bond), but the latter species is rarer in Cuba.

Distribution and habitat   Cuba, the Isle of Pines, and Grand Caicos Island in the Bahamas.   Inhabits forests and wooded areas but comes into settlements and villages where trees are plentiful.   Said to be dependent on heavy forest and unable to maintain itself where this has been destroyed (Barbour).

Feeding and general habits   Apparently little known, comes into plantations to take fruit and grain (Barbour).

Nesting   No information.

Voice   Apparently very similar to those of the Palm and White-necked Crows.   Bond describes it as 'parrot-like squawks and guttural jabbering'; Barbour says 'this crow babbles and chatters in infinite variety like the Jamaican Crow'.

Display and social behaviour   No information.

REFERENCES

BARBOUR, T.   1943.   Cuban Ornithology.   *Mem. Nuttall Orn. Club. No.* **9**: 102.
BOND, J.   1960.   *Birds of the West Indies.*   London.

JAMAICAN CROW   *Corvus jamaicensis*

Corvus jamaicensis Gmelin, 1788, Syst. Nat., 1 (1), p. 367.

Description Between House Crow and Jackdaw in size. Proportions and bare rictal and post-orbital areas as in the White-necked and Cuban Crows to which it is closely allied. Plumage rather loose and soft in texture. General colour dark, dull slate grey deepening to greyish-black with a slight gloss on the wings and tail and to black on the forehead, face and throat. Irides greyish-brown. Bill, legs and feet black.

Field characters The only crow on Jamaica. Voice distinctive.

Distribution and habitat Jamaica. Inhabits woodland and park-like country.

Feeding and general habits Both Gosse and Cruz record that it feeds largely on fruit and berries taken from the trees and also takes insects. Fruits include those of *Picrasma excels*, *Ficus trigonata*, *Laetia thamnia*, *Daphnosis tinfolia*, bananas, plantains and pimentos. Probes in bromeliads, under bark and in rotting wood in search of invertebrates (Cruz). Said to take eggs and young of wild pigeons, and small birds caught in snares. Hiding of inedible objects has been observed in captive individuals (Gosse).

Commonly in pairs, sometimes in small parties. Much given to perching on high, bare boughs of tall trees. Flight rather slow and heavy in appearance; the members of a pair flying one a little way behind the other as with most crows. Mobs flying hawks of the genus *Buteo* in typical manner.

Gosse is the only person, who seems to have studied this crow at all and the above notes, and those on voice, are mainly compiled from his observations.

Nesting Little available information. Robinson (in Gosse) says they nest on tall trees and elsewhere that 'they are said to build in hollow trees'. Four eggs, probably laid by different individuals, in the British Museum (Natural History), are pale greenish-blue, greenish-white or yellowish-green spotted, blotched and flecked with dark drab and olive brown and with underlying greyish markings.

Voice Frequently utters series of loud jabbering sounds that are suggestive of the human voice. To quote Gosse: 'So uncouth and yet so articulate, so varied in the inflexions of their tones, are these sounds, that the wondering stranger can with difficulty believe he is listening to the voice of a bird, but rather supposes he hears the harsh consonants, and deep guttural intonations of some savage language '... These strange sounds are generally poured forth *in sentences*, of varying length, from the summit of some lofty tree'.

Gosse also describes a monotonous cawing heard in late May and early June, 'somewhat like the note of the Rook, but uttered more pertinaciously, and more *impatiently*'. It seems possible that this is the begging call of the female or juvenile. Bond records a 'harsh "craa-craa" ' as well as the jabbering sounds.

Display One was seen feeding another, which begged with shivering wings, by one of Gosse's servants.

Other names Jabbering Crow.

REFERENCES

BOND, J. 1960. *Birds of the West Indies.* London.
CRUZ, A. 1972. Food and Feeding behaviour of the Jamaican Crow, *Corvus jamaicensis.* *Auk* **89**: 445–446.
GOSSE, P. H. 1847. *The Birds of Jamaica.* London.

PALM CROW   *Corvus palmarum*

Corvus palmarum Wurttemberg, 1835, Erste Reise N. Amer., p. 68.

Description   About size of Fish Crow (rather smaller than House Crow) but not so slender and with more rounded wing and proportionately larger bill, with longer nasal bristles. Plumage relatively coarse and harsh in texture. Black, more or less glossed with purplish and bluish and tending to fade to a brownish lustre-less black in worn plumage. Bases of neck feathers grey. Irides brown. Bill, legs and feet black.

The above description is of the nominate form. The Cuban form, *C. palmarum minutus*, is appreciably smaller and has a proportionately shorter and stouter bill.

Field characters   In flight its wings appear shorter than those of the White-necked Crow and it flies with a steadier flapping. Calls different.

Distribution and habitat   Cuba and Hispaniola. Now scarce and local in Cuba. Mainly inhabits wooded areas, often in villages or cultivated places where trees are numerous.

Feeding and general habits   Feeds both on the ground and in trees. Known to take beetles, including the genera *Prepodes* and *Calosoma*, caterpillars, cicadas and other bugs, lizards, snails, and fruit.

Nesting   Nests in trees. Eggs have been collected in late April; they are very pale greenish or yellowish-green, speckled, stippled and blotched with olive brown and dark drab and with underlying greyish mauve markings.

Voice   Bond describes its usual call as a harsh 'craa-craa' reminding him of the Fish Crow and Carrion Crow. All observers emphasize the difference between the voice of this species on one hand and *leucognaphalus* and *nasicus* on the other.

Display and social behaviour   No information.

REFERENCES

BARBOUR, T. 1943. Cuban ornithology. *Mem. Nuttall Orn. Club* No. 9.
BOND, J. 1960. *Birds of the West Indies.* London.
WETMORE, A. & SWALES, B. H. 1931. The birds of Haiti and the Dominican Republic. *U.S. Nat. Mus. Bull.* No. 155.

HOUSE CROW   *Corvus splendens*

Corvus splendens Vieillot, 1817, Nnouv. Dict. Hist. Nat.; nouv. éd., 8, p. 44.

Description Between Hooded Crow and Jackdaw in size but slimmer than either. Feathers of the throat and central part of upper breast long, glossy and bifurcated. Forehead, crown, front of face, throat and central part of upper breast black and richly glossed; this iridescence is mainly greenish on the throat and upper breast, bluish-green, bluish or purplish on the top of the head. Neck and lower breast fawnish-grey with a slight pinkish tinge, shading into greenish-black on the back and blackish-grey on the belly. Wings black, richly glossed with green, bluish-green, purple and blue; the blue and purple gloss being mostly on the coverts and secondaries. Tail rounded or very slightly graduated, black glossed with green or greenish-blue.

Irides dark brown or blackish-brown. Bill and legs black. Juvenile duller and with the inside of the mouth fleshy red, not black and grey as adult's.

The above description is of the nominate form, *Corvus s. splendens*, which is found throughout India except in the north-west. *C. splendens zugmayeri*, from Kashmir and north-western India, is even more beautiful as it has the grey parts of a very pale milky grey that contrasts strongly with the iridescent black of the head and wings. *C. splendens protegatus*, from Ceylon, and *C. s. maledivicus*, from the Maldive and Laccadive Islands, are very similar to nominate *splendens* but a little darker. *C. s. insolens*, from Burma, south-western Thailand and western Yunnan is darker still, having the grey parts a very dark grey; it also tends to have a more strongly arched culmen.

Field characters A slender, shining crow, frequently seen with puffed-out throat. Smaller size and greyer neck distinguish from Jungle Crow; longer bill, dark eyes, very different voice and slimmer less compact shape from Jackdaw.

Distribution and habitat India and Pakistan, Ceylon, Maldive and Laccadive Islands, Burma south to Tenasserim, south-western Thailand, coastal southern Iran and on Kharg Island off Bushire, Iran. Introduced, or possibly in some cases self-introduced to Malaya, in Klang district or Selangor; East Africa, in Zanzibar and Port Sudan; Arabia, in Oman, and the northern United Arab Emirates on the north-eastern coastal strip, Aden and Egypt, at Port Tewfik. Has occurred several times in Australia through self-introduction via ships (e.g. Hylton, 1927) but has not, so far, succeeded in establishing itself there, probably because of human persecution.

Always found near human habitations. In all types of inhabited country, but the presence of some trees probably essential for its permanent establishment in any area. In the Indian regions found up to 1500 metres, 2100 metres at Darjeeling, but typically a bird of lower elevations. In eastern Arabia only (so far) where there is a fairly narrow coastal belt 'backed' by mountains.

Feeding and general habits Feeds largely on scraps of human food discarded by or taken from man; also takes insects, and other small animals including lizards and young birds, eggs, grain, nectar and fruits. Seeks food largely on the ground but also in trees and in or on buildings, as chance offers.

Tame and bold where not persecuted but wary and quick to take alarm.   It is said soon to learn to recognize a gun as dangerous although perhaps it is a combination of the hunting behaviour of the shooter and the gun's presence which are noted by the bird.   Jerdon recorded that it not only attended any people eating out of doors but that 'a fire, or rather its smoke, even in some place far from normal crow haunts' would at once attract House Crows which would then, if they found cooking in progress, wait for the leavings.   Has been seen catching water insects by hovering and plunging in a kingfisher-like manner, seizing the insects with its bill and sometimes plunging its head and half its body under water in doing so (Dodsworth).   Has been observed dunking hard pieces of bread and toast but it appears not to be known what natural foods are so treated.

Storing of food, in usual manner, has been observed in captive individuals and presumably is practised in the wild also.   Young House Sparrows that have left the nest but are not yet strong on the wing are often preyed on intensively by individual crows, particularly when these have young of their own to feed.

Usually in pairs or family parties by day but large numbers gather at sources of food.   Roosts communally; perches freely on buildings by day but roosts in trees.   Mobs predators in similar manner to that recorded for Raven and Magpie, attacking from behind at moments when the predator is distracted by another crow in front of it.   Can sometimes in this way more or less immobilize such creatures as cats and snakes for a considerable time (Eates, MSS).   Creatures which are, or may be later, used as food are also sometimes attacked cautiously from behind, the attacking bird approaching, pecking hard and retreating at once, to repeat the process with greater boldness and persistency if no effective counter-measures have been taken by the victim.

Nesting   Pairs usually nest singly but Lamba found up to 9 occupied nests in one large tree and saw no territorial behaviour.   Nest of sticks and twigs, sometimes bits of wire; inner cup of very fine twigs, roots, fibres and sometimes other soft materials.   Eggs 3 to 6, usually 4 or 5, bluish-green to greenish-blue, less often whitish; speckled, flecked and blotched with brown, dull reddish, greyish and/or blackish.   The markings are usually profuse but may be sparse, especially on eggs with pale or whitish ground colour.   The nest is usually in a tree, less often in a bush or shrub and relatively rarely on a building.   Husain observed a nest inside the verandah of a house.   The female would not come to the nest while people were near although once on it she sat tight until someone looked directly at her, when she fled at once.   The young died and it is suggested that the House Crows' sensitivity to humans near the nest is a reason they normally only nest on trees.   It is, however, possible that a nest in a verandah where the human occupants were totally *un*interested in the crows might have fared better.

The House Crow is parasitized by the Koel, *Eudynamis scolopaceus*.   The latter is attacked when near the crow's nest but possibly as a potential egg eater (which it is) rather than or as well as for its parasitic habits.   Dewar provides evidence that the male Koel lures the parent crows away and, while they are chasing him, his mate lays in their nest.   Eates, on the other hand claimed, on three occasions to have seen a female Koel and a Crow on a nest in the late evening.   Each time there was some flapping and apparent jockeying for position, and calls rather like a young House Crow being fed were uttered.   The Koel was not attacked but suddenly dived out and flew off.   In each case Eates then found one or two Koel's eggs in the nest but was unable to say whether one had been laid at that visit or not although it seems extremely likely.   Once the male Crow appeared after the Koel left and seemed at first alarmed, but in no case was the male, or any other House Crow, attracted by the calls and movements at the nest.

Breeds in western India from April to June, in Bengal earlier; in the heavy rainfall areas of south-western India breeding is usually over before the onset of the south-west monsoon in May (Ali).   In Kashmir begins to breed in May (Bates & Lowther); in Africa recorded breeding in February in Sudan and from October to January in Zanzibar (Mackworth-Praed & Grant); in Burma nesting may begin as early as January but the eggs are probably not usually laid until March and late nests, perhaps second attempts after failures, can be found as late as June and July (Smythies).

Incubation by the female only, fed at nest by the male.   Some writers have implied that both sexes incubate but I have seen no first-hand evidence for this and it seems unlikely.

Voice   One of the commonest calls is a flat, rather harsh 'caaa, caaa . . .' variously modulated.   Like the

Raven, and to a lesser extent the Rook, and unlike the Carrion and Hooded Crows, this species often calls very frequently as it flies about. I have, however, only been able to observe it for a few hours on a few occasions.

Display and social behaviour Allo-preening between members of pair recorded.

Other names Splendid Crow, Town Crow, Indian Crow, Ceylon Crow, Grey-necked Crow.

REFERENCES

ALI, S. 1941. *The Book of Indian Birds*, p. 2. Bombay.
BATES, R. S. P. & LOWTHER, E. H. N. 1952. *Breeding birds of Kashmir:* 6–8. Oxford.
DEWAR, D. 1907. An enquiry into the parasitic habits at the Koel. *Journal Bombay Nat. Hist. Soc.* **17**: 765.
DODSWORTH, P. L. T. 1911. Crow and its food. *Journal Bombay Nat. Hist. Soc.,* **21**: 248–249.
EATES, K. R. (unpublished). *Memories grave and gay of a field naturalist.* Section 4, Crows (*In British Museum (Nat. Hist.) files*).
HYLTON, C. G. 1927. Colombo Crows reach Australia. *Emu* **2**: 44.
HUSAIN, K. Z. 1964. House Crow's nest in a house. *Bull. B.O.C.* **84**: 9–11.
JERDON, T. C. 1863. *The Birds of India* 298–300. Calcutta.
LAMBA, B. S. 1963. The nidification of some common Indian birds. *Journal Bombay Nat. Hist. Soc.* **60**: 121–133
MACKWORTH-PRAED, C. W. & GRANT, C. H. B. 1955. *The African Handbook of Birds*, ser. 1, Vol. 1.
SMYTHIES, B. E. 1953. *The Birds of Burma*. London.

JUNGLE CROW   *Corvus macrorhynchos*

Corvus Macrorhynchos Wagler, 1827, Syst. Av., Corvus, sp. 3, ex Temminck MS.

Description In size from somewhat larger than Hooded Crow to only a little larger than House Crow. As compared with a Hooded Crow's its bill is proportionately longer and deeper with more strongly arched culmen, and longer, slightly graduated tail. Throat hackles well developed and usually with many or most of them bifurcated. Irides dark brown or blackish-brown. Legs, bill and mouth black. Fledglings have crimson red mouths and bluish eyes (Wilder & Hubbard). Usually with base of culmen ridge more or less covered by rictal bristles. Feather bases on hind neck dark grey to greyish-white.

The form from the Kuriles, Sakhalin and Japan, *C. m. japonensis*, is the largest and has a very large bill with deeply arched culmen. The general coloration is black, richly glossed with dark purple and dark purplish-blue on back, wings and tail, and with greenish or greenish-blue on throat, forecrown and forehead and outer webs of primaries. Hind crown, hind neck, lower parts of sides of neck and, to a lesser extent, breast and underparts with feathers of a denser and softer texture, greyish-black to very dark grey in colour with little or no iridescence. The pattern of the glossy black and the less glossy, not quite black, areas is identical to that shown by the House Crow although the contrast is not so great in the present species. Bases of hind neck feathers dark grey.

The form from Amurland, Manchuria and Korea, *C. macrorhynchos mandshuricus*, is slightly smaller with a slightly shorter bill. The form from much of China and Indo-China, *C. m. colonorum*, is smaller and less intensely iridescent, with the dark grey on neck and underparts more pronounced. The form from the western Himalayas, *C. m. intermedius*, is large with relatively dull, grey-tinged body plumage. That from the eastern Himalayas east to the mountains of western China, *C. m. tibetosinensis*, has darker and glossier plumage and a proportionately larger bill. The nominate form, from the Malayan regions, *C. m. macrorhynchos*, is all black with the hind neck, nape etc. only a less intense and shining black than the forehead, throat and wings, and the bases of the neck feathers whitish-grey. The form from the Indian Peninsula, *C. m. culminatus*, is smaller, being appreciably smaller than a Hooded Crow, and is a deep, shining black all over but still with the iridescence less intense on those areas that are dark grey in the more northerly forms. Its bill is proprtionately shorter. Its neck feather bases are dark grey.

The form from the Philippine Islands, *C. m. philippinus*, is similar to nominate *macrorhynchos* but has a proportionately rather longer and more graduated tail, whiter bases to the neck feathers and usually a smaller and less strongly arched bill.

In all forms the juveniles differ in having a less lustrous body plumage of a woollier texture. Newly-hatched young (of the S. Indian form) are naked and light flesh-coloured. Neossoptiles (*prepennae*) appear at 2–3 days old (Lamba).

Other races have been recognized that are similar to or intermediate between those described here.

Field characters Larger size and more uniformly black plumage distinguish it from House Crow in areas where both occur. From Carrion Crow by larger bill with more arched culmen and more graduated tail; from Raven by slightly smaller size and less graduated tail; from Slender-billed Crow by larger and thicker bill. Typically in rather different habitats (q.v.) from the last three species but there is some overlap and when only one species is seen identification may not be easy.

Distribution and habitat Asia from Afghanistan (Safed Koh and Kafiristan), southern Tadzhikistan, southern Transcaspia and eastern Iran, east and south-east through the Himalayas and India to Amurland (middle Amur north to the Zeya River and lower Amur to the gulf of Uda), Ussuriland, Manchuria, Korea, China, Japan, Riu Kiu Islands, Ceylon, the Andaman Islands, Burma, Thailand, Indo-China, the Malay Peninsula, Greater and Lesser Sunda Islands to Timor and Wetar, the Philippine Islands (not Palawan). Recorded a few times from Borneo.

Inhabits woodland of many different types, parkland, semi-cultivated country, open country with some trees and, in many places, villages and towns. In cultivated regions of Tibet and Western China may be found above the tree-line up to 5000 metres (Schäfer). Individuals may also forage above the tree-line away from cultivation. Its northernmost limits in the Tibetan region are, however, the northernmost limits of the trees.

In those parts of its range where it overlaps with the Carrion Crow or Raven, it is mainly a bird of wooded and they of more open regions (but with some overlap) whereas in the south-east of its range, where it overlaps with the Slender-billed Crow, the latter is the forest crow and the Jungle Crow largely replaces it in more open areas.

Feeding and general habits Feeds both on the ground and in trees. Known to take insects, lizards, frogs, land crabs, eggs, small mammals, young birds, centipedes, grain, carrion and fruits. Also readily takes scraps of bread, meat and other human foods. Appears to be a rather more frequent killer of young Domestic Fowls than is the Carrion Crow, at least in regions where both species occur. Habitually follows caravans (although it is unlikely that individual birds often follow further than their normal foraging ranges) and investigates camp sites for scraps.

Wary, and quick to take alarm when persecuted, but otherwise bold and persistent when seeking food in camps, towns or villages. Adults usually in pairs and sedentary. Numbers may congregate at good feeding places and there is some evidence suggesting that immature, unpaired or 'landless' birds may form loose flocks and wander about. Sometimes roosts communally.

Normal flight direct with slow and regular wing beats, often glides. Yamashina states that the Japanese form seldom soars but Ali (1961) notes the Himalayan form as fond of soaring in thermals.

Nesting Nests in trees, usually high up, with an apparent preference for pine or fir trees when available. Both sexes collect material and build. Usual crow nest, chiefly of sticks and twigs, the cup lined with hair, wool, fibres, thin wiry roots and similar materials. Has been seen collecting wool and hair from living cattle and sheep. Eggs, 3 to 5, of usual *Corvus* type, light bluish-green to light blue, blotched and speckled with blackish-brown, olive brown and greyish and showing considerable variation. Rarely with few or no markings, and exceptionally buffish-white with reddish-brown markings. Incubation period 17–19 days, usually 18.

Breeding usually begins early in spring. In peninsular India normal breeding season is between December and April, north of the Ganges and in Assam and Burma later (Ali, 1941). Also nests early in the year in Malaya (Robinson); in Kashmir fresh eggs have been found from late April till early June but most are laid in the end of April and May. Building and more particularly the carrying of material to the nest site may, however, take place two months or more before laying begins. Often parasitized by the Koel, *Eudynamis scolopaceus*. In Japan breeding starts in March in Honshu and April in Hokkaido, continuing into July (Austin & Kuroda). It has been claimed that both sexes incubate but further evidence for incubation by the male is needed.

Voice I can find no detailed account of this bird's calls. It evidently has various cawing calls, some or most of which are deep and resonant; several observers describe its voice as being deeper than the Carrion Crow's and House Crow's. Has a song or subsong of gurgling and chuckling sounds. A repeated 'kro-kro-kro-kro' is uttered during the display flight (Jahn).

Ali (1961) notes that the voice of the Himalayan form *intermedius* differs from that of the low level (Indian) form *culminatus* in being more like that of the Raven and including many bell-like notes.

Display and social behaviour Jahn records a display flight in which the bird circles with strange short wing beats. This sounds very similar to a display flight of the Australian Raven, *C. coronoides*, which I have seen.

Kuroda saw much apparently insightful behaviour from a pair with fledged young. In the first few weeks after the young fledged the parents would not leave for the communal roost unless the young were settled quietly to roost. If, on looking back, they saw them still active and noisy, they would fly back to them, feed them again and sometimes roost with them. Two young went to the communal roost with the parents 19 days after leaving the nest and never returned to the nest area with them. The third remained with its parents until 94 days after leaving the nest and 75 days after it first went to the communal roost with them.

Other names Thick-billed Crow, Indian Corby, Black Crow.

REFERENCES

ALI, S. 1941. *The Book of Indian Birds*. Bombay.
—— 1961. *The Birds of Sikkim*. Oxford.
AUSTIN, O. L. & KURODA, N. 1953. The birds of Japan, their status and distribution. *Bull. Mus. Comp. Zool.*, **109**, 4: 503–505.
BATES, R. S. P. & LOWTHER, E. H. N. 1952. *Breeding Birds of Kashmir*.
JAHN, H. 1942. Zur Oekologie und Biologie der Vögel Japans. *J. Orn.*, **90**: 73–75.
KURODA, N. H. 1969. Post-fledging family behaviour in Jungle Crow. *Misc. Rep. Yamashina Inst. Orn.* **5**: 640–658.
—— 1974. Some behaviour and vocalization of Jungle Crow. *Misc. Rep. Yamashina Inst. Orn.* **7**: 427–438.
LAMBA, B. S. 1965. The nidification of some common Indian birds – Part 2. *Journ. Bombay Nat. Hist. Soc.* **62**: 425–433.
ROBINSON, H. C. 1927. *The Birds of the Malay Peninsula*, **1**: 264–265.
SCHÄFER, E. 1938. Ornithologische Ergebnisse zweier Forschungsreisen nach Tibet. *J. Orn.* **86**: Sonderheft May 1938; 258–259.
WILDER, E. D. & HUBBARD, H. W. 1938. Peking Nat. Hist. Bull. April 1938: Handbook No. 6. *Birds of Northeastern China*: 126.
YAMASHINA, Y. 1961. *Birds in Japan*. Tokyo, Japan.

SLENDER-BILLED CROW   *Corvus enca*

Fregilus Enca Horsfield, 1882, Trans. Linn. Soc., London, 13, p. 164.

Description   A little smaller than a Hooded Crow.   Very similar to the nominate form of the Jungle Crow (q.v.) but with proportionately more slender bill with less strongly arched culmen, shorter and only slightly rounded tail, glossy throat feathers much less developed and all plumage softer in texture and with less intense iridescence which is predominantly of a greyish-violet sheen.   Bare post-ocular patch more developed than is usual in *macrorhynchos*.   Base of ridge of culmen not covered by rictal bristles. Bases of hind-neck feathers white.   Irides dark brown.   Bill and feet black.

The above description and the sketch are of the form *Corvus enca compilator* which has the widest distribution, being found throughout the greater part of the species' range.   The nominate form, from Java, Bali and the Mentawi Islands, is smaller, between Hooded Crow and Jackdaw size, with a proportionately shorter bill and rather blacker and more iridescent plumage.   *C. e. mangoli*, from the Sula Islands, is like nominate *enca* but has, on average, a longer bill.   *C. e. celebensis*, from the Celebes, is similar but with a shorter and thicker bill.   *C. enca violaceus*, from Ceram, has a still shorter bill and a more pronounced and curiously matt-looking mauvish sheen, and its irides vary from dark greyish-brown to dark reddish-brown.   It may have reached specific level.   *C. e. pusillus* from the Philippine islands of Balabac, Palawan and Mindoro is very similar to *violaceus* but a little larger and a shade darker and more glossy.   *C. e. samarensis*, from Samar and Mindanao, is like *pusillus* but smaller.

Juvenile duller and greyer on body.   In juveniles of *compilator* and *enca* the body feathers are dark grey with, on the upper parts chiefly, blackish tips.

Distribution and habitat   Malaya, Rhio Archipelago, Sumatra, Simalur, Nias, Borneo, Mentawei Islands, Java, Bali, Celebes, Butung, Tukang Islands, Banggai Islands, Mangoli Island, Sula Islands, Ceram (Seram) and probably Buru and the Philippine Islands of Balabac, Palawan, Mindoro, Samar and Mindanao.

Inhabits both primary and secondary forest, perhaps more common at forest edge along rivers and in other semi-open areas than in denser forest.   Sometimes in mangroves.   Not usually near human habitations or in open areas where it is replaced, in the regions where they are sympatric, by the Jungle Crow. In Borneo however, where the Jungle Crow is very rare, it is found in semi-open areas (Nisbet).

Field characters   Usual calls are higher in pitch, and tail is proportionately shorter than Jungle Crow's but more information is needed on valid field characters of both where they are sympatric.

Feeding and general habits   Lizards, large beetles and fruit recorded.   Probably largely omnivorous and may feed more in trees than most *Corvus* species.   Said usually to be shy of man but this may merely mean that it cannot compete successfully with the Jungle Crow in inhabited areas.

The Ceram form, *C. e. violaceus*, has been recorded gathering in flocks to feed on ripening maize.   It (this probably applies equally to other forms) has a heavy and noisy flight (Stresemann).

Nesting   Two nests, each with 4 eggs, found by Bernstein in Java, were built of dry twigs, roots and large stems with an inner cup of stems, fine roots and fibres. The substructure of coarser materials was much smaller than in nests of *macrorhynchos*. Eggs pale bluish-green to off-white with olive brown and greyish, or greyish and blackish spots and speckles. The only clutch of eggs of the form *violaceus* that I have seen were white, sparsely speckled with pale brown. Stresemann describes eggs believed to be of this form as white, finely spotted with yellowish-brown.

Voice Smythies records a rather high-pitched caw and, accompanying the display (?) flight, a harsh 'kark-kark' which shortens and rises in pitch to a series of chuckling sounds. Stresemann describes the voice of *violaceus* as high-pitched and Jackdaw-like. Van Bemmell describes a 'ka-ka-ka', much higher pitched than call (? all calls) of Jungle Crow, and Whitehead, for the form *pusillus* a 'ka-ka-gug-gug-'.

Display and social behaviour No information.

Other names Violaceous Crow (the Ceram form).

REFERENCES

BERNSTEIN, H. A. 1859. Über Nester und Eier einiger javascher Vögel. *J. Orn.* **7**: 261–281.
GORE, M. E. J. 1968. A check-list of the birds of Sabah, Borneo. *Ibis* **110**: 165–196.
NISBET, I. C. T. 1968. The utilisation of mangroves by Malayan birds. *Ibis* **110**: 348–352.
ROBINSON, H. C. & CHASEN, F. N. 1939. *The Birds of the Malay Peninsula* **1**: 346. London.
SMYTHIES, B. E. 1960. *The Birds of Borneo*: 511–512. London.
STRESEMANN, E. 1914. Die Vögel von Seran (Ceram). *Nov. Zool.* **21**: 153.
VAN BEMMELL, A. C. V. (19?) *De Plagen van de Culturgewassen in Indonesië, Aves.* Bandoeng.
WHITEHEAD, J. 1893. *Exploration of Mount Kina Balu, North Borneo*: appendix: 256. London.

CELEBES PIED CROW   *Corvus typicus*

Gazzola typica Bonaparte 1853, Compt. Rend. Acad. Sci. Paris 37: 828.

Description Slightly smaller than a House Crow but in shape and structure similar to the smaller and shorter-billed forms of the Slender-billed Crow, *Corvus enca*, to which it is closely allied. Neck, upper mantle, lower breast and belly white, tinged and intermixed with greyish-brown on the flanks. Rest of plumage black, glossed with purple and blue but inclining to a glossless brownish-black on upper mantle, throat and under tail coverts. Bases of neck feathers dark grey. Throat feathers rather hairy in texture and with no suggestion of hackling. Irides dark brown. Legs, feet and bill black. Juvenile duller, with white parts suffused with greyish-brown.

Distribution and habitat Central and southern Celebes and Butung Island. Inhabits forest edge and woodlands broken by clearings or other open spaces. Found at heights up to 1200 metres.

Feeding and general habits Probably omnivorous but food apparently unrecorded. Described as restless, shy and lively.   Has a swift, whistling, pigeon-like flight, reminiscent of that of birds-of-paradise of the genus *Lycocorax*.   Has been observed in families or small parties.

Nesting   No information.

Voice   Said to be cheerful and Starling-like.   Has a whistling strophe, often uttered from the top of a tree, which consists of three tones and which rises in pitch and ends in a crowing sound.   Also has many creaking and trilling notes and a 'Jay-like' call.

Display and social behaviour   No information.

REFERENCE

STRESEMANN, E. & HEINRICH, G.   1940.   Die Vögel von Celebes.   *J. Orn.* **88**: 16–18.

BANGGAI CROW   *Corvus unicolor*

Gazzola unicolor Rothschild and Hartert, 1900, Bull. Brit. Orn. Cl., 11: 29.

Description   Like the Celebes Crow, with which it may be conspecific, but entirely black, glossed with bluish or greenish, and with grey bases to feathers of hind neck.

Distribution and habitat   Banggai Islands, in the Sula Islands off Celebes.

Feeding and general habits   No information.

Nesting   No information.

Voice   No information.

Display and social behaviour   No information.

FLORES CROW   *Corvus florensis*

Corvus florensis Büttikofer, 1894, in Weber's Reise Nederl. Ost.-Ind., 3: 304.

Description   A small, Jackdaw-sized crow, all black in colour with an even, dull violet sheen and smoke-grey bases to the cover feathers.   Nostrils nearly twice as long as those of *C. enca*.

   I have not seen a specimen of this apparently rare little crow.   The above description is taken from Rensch.

Distribution and habitat   Flores, in the Lesser Sunda Islands.

Feeding and general habits   No information.

Nesting   No information.

Voice   No information.

Display and social behaviour   No information.

REFERENCE

RENSCH, B. 1931. Die Vogelwelt von Lombok, Sumbawa und Flores. *Mitt. Zool. Mus. Berlin* **17**.

LONG-BILLED CROW   *Corvus validus*

Corvus validus Bonaparte, 1851, Consp. Av., 1 (1850), p. 385.

Description   Very similar to the large form of the Slender-billed Crow, *Corvus enca compilator*, but with a longer and deeper bill with the nasal bristles almost or quite covering the base of the culmen ridge. Upper parts and wings usually more richly glossed and looking darker; texture of plumage more like that of Jungle Crow, *C. macrorhynchos*, but in some lights feathers appear to have greyish fringes, giving a scaled effect.   Throat and cheeks usually with a more greenish gloss than either Jungle Crow's or Slender-billed Crow's.   Bases of neck feathers snow white.

Irides whitish-blue; even juveniles are said to have irides of this colour (Stresemann), but the possibility that this may refer to the bluish colour (or a paler version of it) common in the irides of nestling crows and that in this as other species it may turn dark shortly after fledging cannot, perhaps, be discounted. Bill and feet black.

Field characters   Much longer bill would distinguish from *Corvus orru*, the only sympatric species. Probably there are vocal and behavioural differences also that would serve as field characters.

Distribution and habitat   Moluccan islands of Morotai, Halmahera, Kajoa, Batjan (Batchian) and Obi.

Feeding and general habits   No information.

Nesting   No information.

Voice   No information.

Display and social behaviour   No information.

REFERENCE

STRESEMANN, E. 1943. Die Gattung *Corvus* in Australien und Neuguinea. *J. Orn* **91**: 121–135.

AUSTRALIAN CROW   *Corvus orru*

Corvus orru Bonaparte, 1851, Consp. Av., 1, (1850), p. 385.

Description   About size of Hooded Crow but rather more massively built with proportionately stouter bill and longer legs.   Tail very slightly graduated.   Plumage deep black glossed with dark purplish and purplish-blue. Throat feathers glossy and bifurcated, with a greenish or greenish-blue sheen. Bases of neck feathers snow white. Irides pale blue, white, or bluish-white, normally with a bluish inner ring. Juvenile duller with brownish eyes (blue in nestling). The iris becomes white at a little under a year old (Rowley).

The above description is of the best known form, *C. orru ceciliae* of Australia. Nominate *C. o. orru*, from New Guinea and the Moluccas, has a relatively shorter tail and more violet sheen on the plumage; *C. orru insularis*, from New Britain, New Hanover, New Ireland, Rooke and Vidua Islands, is slightly smaller and has light blue eyes as a nestling and in its first year as well as when adult (*fide* Heinroth); *C. orru latirostris*, of Tenimber and Barbar Islands, is similar to the New Guinea form but has a slightly stouter bill.

Field characters Rowley states that a rapid nervous 'shuffling of the wings above the back before they are settled to the side' is particularly characteristic of this species and will often serve to identify it.

Distribution and habitat The Moluccan islands of Morotai, Halmahera, Ternate, Tidore, Mare, Moti, Makian, Bisa and Obi Major; western Papuan Islands and islands of Geelvink Bay, New Guinea, D'Entrecasteaux islands, Trobriand Islands, Woodlark Island and the Louisiades; New Britain, New Ireland, New Hanover, Rooke, and Vitu Islands; Tenimber and Barbar Islands; Australia except South Australia, New South Wales, and Victoria.

Inhabits savannah woodlands, open country with some trees, cultivated regions and seashore, locally in tropical rain forest (Deignan). In Australia it frequents two very different main regions, the summer rainfall tropics and the dry interior.

Feeding and general habits Known to take cultivated grains, fruits and berries, beetles, caterpillars, grasshoppers and other insects, and scraps of meat and other human food where available. Presumably also takes stranded fish, crustaceans and other marine life as in places it habitually seeks food along the shore.

Commonly in pairs or small parties, large numbers may aggregate at garbage dumps or other food sources, but it seems doubtful if these are usually cohesive flocks. In Arnhem Land, Deignan found it numerous about Aboriginal encampments and 'quite fearless *until* someone approached with a gun, the significance of which it seemed thoroughly to comprehend'.

A free-living tame individual hid surplus food in the usual manner (Heinroth).

Nesting Usual crow nest of sticks lined with finer materials. In Australia Rowley notes that nests of this species are much frailer than those of *C. coronoides*. Possibly there may be differences dependent on site chosen and materials available; nests of *C. orru* in New Guinea are described as 'bulky' by Rand & Gilliard. The two to four eggs are similar to but tend to be paler than most eggs of other *Corvus* species, being light greenish-blue or off-white with rather scanty darker markings, often almost unmarked or with longitudinal olive-brown streaks. It is, however, possible that especially in Australia where most eggs seem to have been taken, darker clutches may not have been recognized as those of *C. orru* (Rowley).

In north-western Australia breeds from June to September (Serventy & Whittell); in Queensland eggs have been taken in October, in New Guinea in late January, and in the Bismarck Archipelago (Heinroth) in February and March.

Voice   Rowley describes the most usual call as a nasal high-pitched clipped 'uk-uk-uk-uk-uk' or 'ok-ok-ok-ok'.   Serventy and Whittell similarly say that it is short, higher-pitched than calls of *C. coronoides* and with an 'o' not an 'a' sound in it.

Heinroth, who observed *C. orru insularis* and kept a tame, hand-reared individual of this form, noted that the usual call resembled the native name for the species, 'kottkott', but it also uttered a kind of song, 'krah, krah, kroaaaa' with a comical emphasis on the drawn-out final syllable.   His tame bird would 'taik' to him for a quarter of an hour at a time, uttering a variety of 'deep and high-pitched, soft and loud' notes.

Display and social behaviour   Heinroth's hand-reared bird was evidently completely imprinted on humans. It recognized the human mouth as the equivalent of a bird's beak and showed the usual inhibition against injuring eyes.   It was also very gentle when investigating its owner's mouth.

Other names   Papuan Crow, Crow.

REFERENCES

DEIGNAN, H. G.   1964.   Birds of the Arnhem Land Expedition.   *Rec. Amer.-Aust. Sci. Exped. Arnhem Land*, 4·
HEINROTH, O.   1903.   Ornithologische Ergebnisse der '1. Deutschen Südsee-Expedition von Br. Mencke'. *J. Orn.* **51**: 69–71.
RAND, A. L. & GILLIARD, E. T.   1967.   *Birds of New Guinea.*   London.
ROWLEY, I.   1970.   The genus *Corvus* in Australia.   *C.S.I.R.O. Wildlife Research* **15**: 27–71.
SERVENTY, D. L. & WHITTELL, H. M.   1948.   *Birds of Western Australia.*   Perth.

LITTLE CROW   *Corvus bennetti*

Corvus bennetti Noath 1901, Victorian Nat. 17: 170.

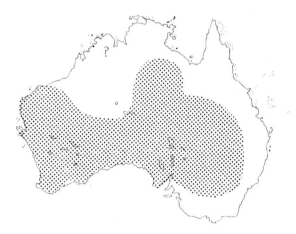

Description   Very similar to the Australian form of the previous species, *C. orru*, but slightly smaller in size and tending to have a proportionately smaller bill.   Small individuals of *orru* may, however, be no larger than some individuals of the present species.

Irides white with a blue inner ring or with a bluish tinge on inner and outer zones.   Nestlings have bluish-grey irides which turn brown, then brown and white, and become the adult colour at about two years old.

Field characters   Common calls, and, if the wind blows the neck feathers awry, their white bases distinguish it from *C. coronoides* and *C. mellori*.   Probably not distinguishable from *C. orru* except by observers very familiar with both species.   Smaller size only useful for identification when another species is near for comparison.

Distribution and habitat   Western and South Australia to western New South Wales, central Australia to western Queensland.   Possibly also the Gulf of Carpentaria to Cape York.   In 1964 Shane Parker (*in litt.*) found a small breeding colony at Burketown, north-western Queensland, where the species does not appear to breed regularly.   The nomadic habits of the species and possible confusion with *C. orru.* may have led to some errors of distribution records (Rowley).

Inhabits mulga scrub and open country.   Common about some towns and other inhabited areas and in cultivated regions.

Feeding and general habits   Commonly in loose flocks.   Feeds mainly on the ground.   The Rook-like flocks of these birds in some agricultural parts of Western Australia contribute much to the very 'English' appearance of the landscape.   Nomadic.   Flocks often perform spectacular aerobatics.   This habit (*fide* Rowley) is confined to *bennetti* among Australian crows.

Takes insects and other invertebrates, cultivated grain, and some other seeds.   Habitually scavenges for scraps on garbage heaps and similar places.   Less of a carrion eater than *C. coronoides*, and possibly when foraging around dead or dying cattle it may be principally interested in obtaining insects.

Nesting   Usually nests in small, loose colonies but with nests 45 metres or more from each other (Serventy); but not colonial in the same sense as, for example, the Rook.

The nest differs from that of other Australian crows in having mud or clay placed between the stick base and the lining of fibrous bark, hair, wool or other soft materials.   It is placed in a tree or shrub, sometimes, and commonly in treeless areas, on a windmill platform or the cross-bars of a telephone pole.

The 3 to 6 eggs are similar to those of *C. coronoides* but smaller.   According to the rains the birds may breed in spring or autumn, whenever conditions are suitable.

When disturbed from the nest by man habitually flies around calling loudly and often attacks if the young are handled (Hobbs).

Voice   Rowley says that the 'characteristic call' is a very nasal 'nark-nark-nark-nark'.   During brief observations of this species in South Australia I noted: 'usual call "kah! kah!" flatter and higher-pitched than calls of *coronoides*.   Also has a long drawn-out and muttering call very like that of *coronoides* but less miserable and human-sounding, a creaking call and a tremulous repeated call given with a display flight like that of *coronoides*.'   Hobbs also notes that 'the usually short note of the Little Crow may become a little protracted'.

Display and social behaviour   I have seen an apparent display flight with the wings held below the horizontal and beaten through a small amplitude, similar to that described for *C. coronoides* (q.v.).

Other names   Bennett's Crow, Crow.

REFERENCES

HOBBS, J. N. 1962. Defence of the Nest by the Little Crow. *Emu* **62**: 172–173.
ROWLEY, I. 1970. The genus *Corvus* in Australia. *C.S.I.R.O. Wildlife Research* **15**: 27–71.
SERVENTY, D. L. & WHITTELL, H. M. 1948. *Birds of Western Australia*: 339–340. Perth.

AUSTRALIAN RAVEN   *Corvus coronoides*

Corvus Coronoides Vigors and Horsfield, 1827, Trans. Linn. Soc. London, 15, p. 261.

Description   Between Raven and Hooded Crow in size.   Shows much convergent resemblance to the Raven (*C. corax*) in appearance but is a more slender bird with less strongly graduated tail, proportionately less massive bill with much less strongly curved culmen and the inter-ramal area is largely bare so that the baggy gular pouch with its long, lanceolate throat feathers is even more prominent.   Glossy black, the gloss mainly purplish and bluish-purple on the mantle and back and greenish-blue or purplish-blue elsewhere.   Irides white, with a narrow blue inner ring, and strikingly conspicuous in life.   Bill, legs and feet black.   Base of neck feathers dark brownish-grey to pale grey.

Western Australian specimens tend to have shorter throat hackles and S. Parker (*in litt.*) is in favour of separating them subspecifically as *C. coronoides perplexus*.   The irides of nestlings are bluish-grey; they turn brown in the juvenile, then mottled brown and white and finally white when the bird is nearly three years old (Rowley).   Juvenile duller in plumage than adult.

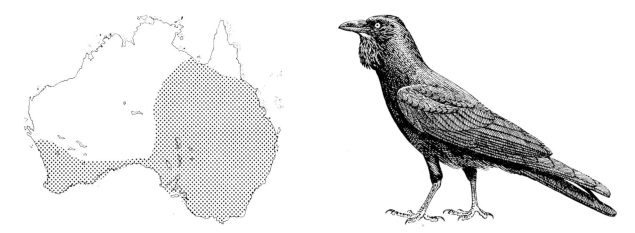

Field characters   Very conspicuous gular pouch, and the characteristic call with long 'dying away' gargling finish (see voice) are characteristic and said by Rowley (1967a) to be diagnostic for this species.
Distribution and habitat   Eastern and south-western Australia.   Inhabits savannah woodland, gum creeks and various types of fairly open country.   The presence of some tall trees seems essential for nesting.
Feeding and general habits   Feeds mainly on the ground but also in trees.   Eats insects and other invertebrates, lizards, carrion, grain, seeds, fruit, nestlings and eggs.   Sometimes attacks newborn (and usually sickly) lambs but even in areas where it habitually feeds on dead lambs it is responsible for less than 5% of lamb casualties.   Very readily takes human foods and in some places regularly investigates camp sites and roadside cooking fires as soon as the people leave.   Food storing by both captive and wild birds has been observed (Boehm; Rowley, 1970).

Usually in pairs or small parties but large numbers may congregate at a good feeding place.   Adult breeding pairs are highly territorial, maintaining territories of about 120 hectares in which they obtain their food (Rowley).   Immature birds, and possibly also unpaired or unsuccessful adults, form nomadic or semi-nomadic flocks which are, however, seldom so big or so integrated as flocks of *C. mellori* and *C. bennetti* commonly are.

Nesting   Nests in trees, nearly always about 12 m or more above ground.   Nest of sticks lined with fibrous bark, grass, wool, hair or similar materials.   Does not place mud in its nest as does *C. bennetti* (Rowley, 1970).   Eggs 3 to 5, average clutch 4; green, greenish-white or greenish-blue, speckled, blotched or clouded with drab, olive brown, or blackish and with underlying markings of grey, violet-grey or light olive drab.   They are typical *Corvus* eggs and show the usual amount of variation.

Incubation by the female only, presumably fed by the male.   Incubation period 20 days on average. The young fledge at about 45 days.   They are fed by the parents for long after leaving the nest and remain in their parents' territory for about four months.   In southern New South Wales breeding begins in mid-July (Rowley, 1967b).   Eggs believed to be of this species have been taken in New South Wales and Queensland in September and October but in view of the recent discovery of *Corvus mellori* (Rowley, 1967a) identities of clutches in museums are suspect in some cases.
Voice   The most striking call is used (*fide* Rowley) in aggressive and territorial situations.   I transcribed

it, from birds heard in South Australia, as 'gwaaar, gwaa-aar, aaar, aaaaaaaaar', long drawn out and loud, but getting lower in pitch as it lengthens, and dying away in a long gargling or muttering. It has a terribly human-sounding tone of despair and protest, quite unlike the calls of any European crow. Rowley transcribes it as 'aah-aah-aah-aaaaaaaaahh' the last note drawn out and dropping in pitch.

Individuals that I heard, in South Australia, often uttered a series of stuttering sounds very like the bleating of a sheep or goat but deeper in tone. I had the impression that these were homologous with the clicking sounds made by many other corvids. I frequently heard this species utter a hoarse creaking call, so like the creaking of a branch in the wind that I did not at first realise that a bird had made the sound. I also heard a nagging, querulous 'aa, aa, aa', like the begging of a Carrion Crow, but am not completely sure that this species was involved as *C. mellori* was present in the area (not then recognized) and I did not hear this querulous call from a bird also seen to give the long call.

Vocal mimicry, of Domestic Fowl, has been recorded from a captive (Ramsey, in Chisholm).

Display and social behaviour When giving the long moaning territorial call the bird adopts a horizontal posture with the gular pouch apparently distended and the throat hackles erected to form a shaggy dew-lap like that of the Raven, *C. corax*, only more so. Sometimes the bird giving this call raises the feathers immediately above its eyes to form two little 'ears' precisely as some Eurasian *Corvus* species do in some hostile contexts. I saw this from two calling birds when two pairs had both flown into a tree with a nest in it.

Rowley says that it has an 'aerial chase' that is used in courtship but rather rarely. I have seen a presumed display flight in which the wings are held below the horizontal and beaten through a small arc, giving an odd, fluttering effect suggestive of the flight of the Common Sandpiper, *Tringa hypoleucos*.

Other names This, like other species, is known simply as 'Crow' by many laymen.

REFERENCES

BOEHM, E. F. 1949. The Australian Raven in relation to other species of birds. *South Australian Ornithologist* **19**: 26–27.
—— 1962-3. *C.S.I.R.O. Annual Report: Wildlife Research:* 13–14.
CHISHOLM, A. H. 1965. Further remarks on vocal mimicry. *Emu* **65**: 57–64.
ROWLEY, I. 1967a. A fourth species of Australian corvid. *Emu* **66**: 191–210.
—— 1967b. Sympatry in Australian Ravens. *Proc. ecol. Soc. Aust.* **2**: 107–115.
—— 1970. The genus *Corvus* in Australia. *C.S.I.R.O. Wildlife Research* **15**: 27–71.
—— Unpublished manuscripts and letters.

LITTLE RAVEN   *Corvus mellori*

Corvus marianae mellori Mathews 1912 Nov. Zool. 18: 443.

This species was only recently discovered (Rowley, 1967a), having formerly been thought conspecific with *C. coronoides*.

Description Very like the previous species, *C. coronoides*, from which it differs in appearance only in having the inter-ramal area fully feathered; the glossy throat feathers shorter, and many of them bifurcated at the tip. It is also a little smaller in size as a rule but measurements of the two species overlap. Its behaviour and ecology differ. Its irides become white at 2 years old (Rowley 1970).

Distribution and habitat South-eastern Australia; in southern South Australia, New South Wales and Victoria. Inhabits scrub and woodland, cleared or partly-cleared grazing lands and agricultural regions.

Feeding and general habits Nomadic and rather highly social. Both adults and young leave the nesting territories and migrate or wander after the breeding season. Commonly in parties or flocks. Breeding pairs feed very largely outside their territories on communal feeding grounds. Seeks food largely on the ground, especially on open grassland.

Feeds much on insects, especially lepidopterous larvae, and is thought to take rather more vegetable food than does *C. coronoides* (Rowley, 1967b), but otherwise is probably omnivorous to a similar extent to other large *Corvus* species. As its specific distinctness has only recently been recognized it is uncertain whether much previous information on feeding habits refers to this species or to *coronoides* (Rowley, 1967a).

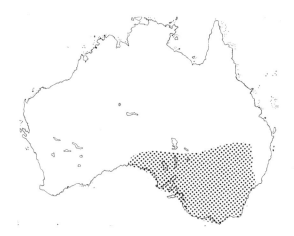

Nesting Often nests semi-colonially. The average territory size is about 4 hectares (Rowley) but pairs may tolerate others breeding very close to them. Rowley found, for example, 15 active nests in a plantation of sugar gums 270 × 45 m. There are often several nests of this species within the breeding territory of a single pair of *C. coronoides*.

Nest in trees or shrubs, usually lower than about 12 m. Where suitable trees are lacking this species will nest on the ground, or very near it on a tangle of wire, the remains of a fence or other building or the skeleton of a large mammal (Hobbs). Nest and eggs similar to those of *C. coronoides* but breeding starts later, in early August where the two are sympatric in the western Riverina of New South Wales (Rowley, 1967b).

Young fledge at 36 days, about 9 days earlier than young *coronoides*. They follow the parents to feed with others on communal grounds within two or three days after fledging. All birds, young and old, associate in nomadic flocks when breeding is finished.

Voice The most usual call is described by Rowley (1967a, 1970) as a very guttural 'kar-kar-kar-kar' or 'ark-ark-ark-ark'. He gives a sonagram of this call together with the comparable call of *C. coronoides* (Rowley, 1967a).

Display When calling this species habitually gives two or three rapid up and down flips of its folded wings, apparently very similar to those given by many other *Corvus* species (sketches in Rowley, 1967a) but not by *C. coronoides*.

It also has a display very similar to the pre-copulatory posturing of the Rook and Carrion Crow in which one bird slowly promenades past another with wings drooped and tail erected at an angle of more than 45°.

REFERENCES

HOBBS, J. N. 1962. Ground-nesting of the Raven. *Aust. Bird Watcher* 1; **7**: 202–203.
ROWLEY, I. 1967a. A fourth species of Australian corvid. *Emu* **66**: 191–210.
—— 1967b. Sympatry in Australian Ravens. *Proc. ecol. Soc. Aust.* **2**: 107–115.
—— 1970. The genus Corvus in Australia. *C.S.I.R.O. Wildlife Research* **15**: 27–71.

FOREST RAVEN   *Corvus tasmanicus*

Corvus marianae tasmanicus Mathews, 1912, Novit. Zool., 18, p. 443.

Description   Like the Little Raven, *Corvus mellori*, but averaging a little larger and with a proportionately more massive bill and slightly shorter tail.

The above description is of nominate *C. t. tasmanicus* from Tasmania, and mainland Australia on Wilson's Promontory and the Otway Ranges in Victoria.   *C. m. novaanglica* Rowley, from eastern New South Wales, has slightly larger wings and tail.

Distribution and habitat   Tasmania; south-eastern Australia on Wilson's Promontory and in the Otway Ranges.   An isolated population in and near the forested areas of the northern tablelands of north-eastern New South Wales.

In Tasmania, where it is the only crow, it inhabits most types of country: forest, open woodland, grazing lands, cultivated and coastal areas and around town edges.   The presumably relict Australian populations appear to be largely confined to wet sclerophyll forest or its near vicinity.

Feeding and general habits   In Tasmania known to take insects and other invertebrates, including worms, carrion and fruit.   So far as is known its habits appear very close to those of *C. coronoides* with which, on the mainland, it appears to have been in unsuccessful competition which has resulted in its present very restricted distribution (Rowley).

Nesting   Nest and eggs similar to those of *coronoides*.   Nest site in a tree.

Voice   The most usual call is distinct from that of *C. mellori*, being given more slowly and much deeper in pitch.   Rowley transcribes it as 'korr-korr-korr-korr', with a tendency to draw out the last note, similar to *C. coronoides*.

Display   No information.

REFERENCES

ROWLEY, I.   1970.   The genus *Corvus* in Australia.   *C.S.I.R.O. Wildlife Research* **15**: 27–71.
SHARLAND, M.   1945.   *Tasmanian Birds*.   Hobart.

SOLOMON ISLANDS CROW   *Corvus woodfordi*

Macrocorax woodfordi Ogilvie-Grant, 1887, Proc. Zool. Soc. London, p. 332, pl. 27.

Description   Between Hooded Crow and House Crow in size, with short square-ended tail, large bill with strongly curved culmen and ridge of culmen bare at the base.   Inter-ramal area partly bare and purplish-red.   Plumage of head and upper part of neck with a very fine, silky texture.   Black in colour, glossed strongly with dark oily green on head, throat and upper breast, and with purple or bluish-purple on upperparts.   Underparts dull black with a slight greenish gloss.   Irides grey or greyish-white.   Bill yellowish-white, more or less tinged with pink and usually shading through pale bluish to purple at base, with black tip. Legs and feet black, soles of feet orange in some (probably all) individuals. Bases of neck feathers greyish-white.

The above description is of the nominate form of the species, which is found in the Central and southern Solomons. The form from Bougainville and Shortland Islands in the northern Solomons, *C. w. meeki*, which may have reached specific level, differs in having a black bill, with the nasal bristles more or less covering the base of the culmen ridge, and dark brown irides.

Field characters A smallish crow with rather rounded wings and proportionately large head and bill, and short tail. The contrasting pale bill of the nominate form is conspicuous.

Distribution and habitat The Solomon Islands of Choiseul, Isabel, Guadalcanal and the northern Solomon Islands of Bougainville and Shortland Island. Inhabits forest, said seldom to come into the open (Mayr). The black-billed form is said (Mayr) to occur only on lowland forest but the white-billed form was found by Cain and Galbraith on Guadalcanal in hill and mist forest, where it spent much time on top of and flying about the canopy.

Feeding and general habits Known to eat beetles and various fruits. Feeds in and on trees; does not appear to have been recorded feeding on the ground but probably does so at times.
Often or usually in small parties.

Nesting No information.

Voice Cain and Galbraith noted a 'very loud, rather high-pitched, AO...AO...AO'. S. Parker (*in litt.*) describes the typical call as like that of *Corvus orru* but higher-pitched and faster.

Display and social behaviour No information.

Other names White-billed Crow (the nominate race), Bougainville Crow (the black-billed race).

REFERENCES

CAIN, A. J. & GALBRAITH, I. C. J. 1956. Field notes on birds of the Eastern Solomon Islands. *Ibis* **98**: 262–295.
MAYR, E. 1945. *Birds of the Southwest Pacific*. New York.

BROWN-HEADED CROW   *Corvus fuscicapillus*

Corvus fuscicapillus Gray, 1859, Proc. Zool. Soc. London, p. 157.

Description About size of Hooded Crow. Rather short, somewhat graduated tail, large bill with strongly arched culmen. Throat feathers bristly, feathers of upper breast and neck lax and somewhat hair-like in texture. Forehead, face and throat brownish-black shading to dark, dull brown on nape, neck and upper breast. Underparts brownish-black with slight gloss. Upperparts black glossed with purple and purplish-blue, especially on wings and tail. Bases of neck feathers white. Irides blue. Bill black in the male and yellow with blackish tip, and sometimes some black at base also, in female.   Legs and feet black.   (Note: further observations on soft part colours are desirable, especially to determine whether the difference in bill colour is always sexual and not connected with age or breeding status.)

Juvenile paler and browner, with white feather bases largely visible, bill yellow.

The above description is of the nominate form; *C. f. megarhynchus*, from the western Papuan islands, has a somewhat smaller bill.

Field characters   Brownish head and neck and very deep bill with very strongly arched culmen distinguish it from the all-black *Corvus orru*.

Distribution and habitat   New Guinea: known only from the Aru Islands and lower Memberano River (Taua), and from the western Papuan islands of Waigeu and Geimen.   Inhabits forest.

Feeding and general habits   Bernstein recorded that the specimens collected by him had been feeding 'almost entirely' on tree fruits.   It seems likely that some insects and other small animals are also taken.

Bernstein found it only in woodland, never foraging on the shore with *C. orru*.

Nesting   No information.

Voice   Bernstein states that its voice is much deeper than that of *C. orru*.

Display and social behaviour   No information.

REFERENCES

BERNSTEIN, H. A.   1864.   Ueber einen neuen Paradiesvogel und einige andere neue Vögel.   *J. Orn.* **11**: 401–410.
RAND, A. & GILLIARD, E. T.   1967.   *Handbook of New Guinea Birds.*   London.
STRESEMANN, E. & PALUDAN, K.   1932.   Die Vögel von Waigeu.   *Novit. Zool.* **38**: 139–140.

BARE-FACED CROW   *Corvus tristis*

Corvus tristis Lesson and Garnot, 1827, Bull. Sci. Nat. (Férussac), 10, p. 291.

Description   About size of Hooded Crow but very different in shape with long, somewhat graduated tail, scanty nasal and rictal bristles and largely bare face.   Coloration varying from brownish-black above and dark dull brown below, glossed with purple on wings and tail, to light drab brown with whitish head and underparts.   Even dark specimens, or perhaps especially such, are liable to have pale feather fringes and grizzled white or off-white areas on the inner webs of wing and tail quills.   Both dark and pale types of plumage are much liable to fading so that moulting birds appear more or less mottled light and dark.   In fact in all its variants this species strongly resembles in colour (and correlated tendency to extreme bleaching) the brown, grey and grizzled individuals that appear as occasional freaks in other crow species.

Irides pale whitish-blue to sky blue.   Bare facial and orbital skin pinkish-white to flesh pink.   Bill variable: pinkish-white; pinkish-white with darker tip; pale bluish on upper mandible, pinkish on lower, with dark tip; or pale bluish with darker tip, or dark bluish-grey.   Legs and feet white, pinkish-white or pale yellowish, often with some dark or black markings. In general the palest-feathered individuals have the palest bills and *vice versa*. Sexes alike but, if the smallish series of sexed specimens in the British Museum is representative, relatively more males than females are dark in colour.

Juveniles (only a few examined) appear on the whole to be paler and browner.

Field characters Longish tail, bare pinkish face and usually 'washed-out' plumage colour distingish it from all other crows. Has a superficial resemblance to the Channel-bill Cuckoo.

Distribution and habitat New Guinea and the nearby islands of Salawati, Batanta, Ron, Japen (Jobi), and the D'Entrecasteaux Archipelago. Inhabits lowland and hill forest, up to 1350 m. Found in both original and secondary forest.

Feeding and general habits Feeds both in trees and on ground. Known to take fruits, particularly that of a climbing arum, but almost certainly takes other foods as well. When seen foraging in sandy and shingly river beds it has been assumed to be taking grit or about to drink but it may well have been searching for some form of live food. Other crow species often take water insects, small frogs etc. from such places. Has also been seen on an air strip, apparently searching for insects (Schodde & Hitchcock).

Usually in small parties of about 4 to 8 individuals that move about through the tree tops and through native gardens keeping rather loose contact with each other. Noisy and excitable.

Nesting I have only seen one clutch, of 2 eggs, that was taken in Mysol in 1862. These are a very pale greenish-cream with dark brown and grey flecks and spots sparsely scattered over most of the shell but coalescing to form a dark cap at the large end.

Voice Gilliard records a hoarse, weak 'ka', a whining caw and excited outcries of hoarse calls.

Display and social behaviour No information.

Other names Grey Crow.

REFERENCES

GILLIARD, E. T. & LECROY, M. 1967. Annotated list of the birds of Adelbert Mountains, New Guinea. *Bull. Amer. Mus. Nat. Hist.*, 138, Art. **2**: 72.
OGILVIE-GRANT, W. R. 1915. *Ibis* Jubilee Suppl., No. 2.
RAND, A. L. & GILLIARD, E. T. 1967. *The Handbook of New Guinea Birds*.
SCHODDE, R. & HITCHCOCK, W. B. 1968. *Contributions to Papuasian Ornithology*. Div. Wildlife Tech. Paper No. 13, C.S.I.R.O., Aust.

GUAM CROW   *Corvus kubaryi*

Corvus kubaryi Reichenow, 1885, J. Orn. 33: 110.

Description About size of House Crow but wings shorter. Bill rather long and becoming slender towards the tip. Plumage rather lax and hairy in texture, coal black with only slight hints of iridescence. Bases of neck feathers dull white.

Field characters   Only crow within its range.

Distribution and habitat   The Micronesian islands of Guam and Rota.   Inhabits forest.

Feeding and general habits   Apparently little known.   Marshall observed it feeding on the ground beneath dense woodland canopy.   The stomachs of five specimens that he collected contained grass-hoppers and other insects, lizards, buds, flowers and other vegetable matter.

Nesting   No information.

Voice   'Their "caw" has conversational variations' (Marshall).

Display and social behaviour   No information.

REFERENCE

MARSHALL, J. T.   1949.   The endemic avifauna of Saipan, Tinian, Guam and Palau.   *Condor* **51**: 216.

NEW CALEDONIAN CROW   *Corvus moneduloides*

Corvus moneduloides Lesson, 1830 or 1831, Traité Orn., p. 329.

Description   About size of House Crow or very slightly larger; tail rather long, rounded or slightly graduated; bill unusually shaped with nearly straight culmen and sharply angled gonys.   Rich black, glossed with purple and dark blue, and sometimes slightly with green on the outer webs of the primaries and primary coverts.   Irides dark brown.   Legs, feet and bill black.   Throat feathers hairy in texture.

Distribution and habitat   New Caledonia and Loyalty Islands.   Inhabits forest.

Feeding and general habits   Recorded (by the Layards) taking locusts and other insects, snails of the genus *Bulimus*, candle-nuts, and seeds and flowers of *Erythrina*.   Often takes night-flying insects at dusk, catching them in the air with great agility; also said to feed from human corpses placed in trees and to take the eggs and chicks of domestic poultry.   Candle-nuts and snails are said to be dropped on stones, hard roots and similar surfaces to break them and, from the accumulations of shells at suitable places, it is certain that the crows either drop them or break them by beating on such anvils.   Orenstein saw one of a pair repeatedly probe under bark and into hollows with a twig, in a manner reminiscent of that of the Woodpecker Finch.

Nesting Nest described as 'a platform of sticks', placed in a fairly high tree. Usually 2 eggs per clutch; pale bluish green to greenish white with profuse olive-brown and grey speckles, spots and small blotches. Eggs laid from September to November.

Voice A 'not unmusical', soft, 'wa-wa' may be a ground-predator alarm or mobbing call, as the Layards say the bird gives it at sight of man, flies towards him, and is thereupon joined by its companions. Orenstein (*in litt.*) heard 'a soft, hoarse waaaw, rather high-pitched . . .' a louder, high-pitched 'wak! wak!' and a similarly high-pitched but more drawn-out 'aaup'.

Display and social behaviour Orenstein (*in litt.*) found it commonly in pairs, sometimes singly but never in large groups.

Other names Wa-wa.

REFERENCES

LAYARD, E. L. & E. L. C. 1882. Notes on the avifauna of New Caledonia. *Ibis* **6**, 4th series, pp. 520–522.
ORENSTEIN, R. 1972. Tool-use by the Caledonian Crow (*Corvus moneduloides*). *Auk* **89**: 674.

HAWAIIAN CROW   *Corvus tropicus*

Corvus tropicus Kerr 1792, Animal Kingdom, 1, pt. 2, p. 640.

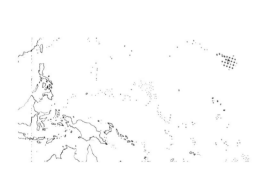

Description About size of Hooded Crow, with rather more rounded wings and much thicker bill. Nasal and rictal bristles well developed. Plumage soft, lax and slightly hairy in texture. Throat feathers long and bristly. Brownish-black, sometimes fading to dark brown on worn feathers. Outer webs of primaries light dull drab. Bases of neck feathers light dull grey. Irides unrecorded. Feet, legs and bill black.

Field characters   The only crow.   Large size and black coloration distinguish it from all other Hawaiian birds except the dark phase of the Hawaiian Hawk, *Buteo solitarius.*

Distribution and habitat   Island of Hawaii; found only in Kona and Kau districts (western slopes). Inhabits edges of montane forest and open park-like country between lava flows.   Found in both the wet belt and the upper dry forest.   It had already decreased from its former abundance when Perkins wrote in 1903.   So far as is known, however, its range was always restricted for no obvious reason, since it appears, from Perkins' observations, to be as potentially adaptable and as strong-flying as most *Corvus* species.

Further decreases have since taken place but it is still fairly common locally at high elevations.   Baldwin gives detailed observations on its past and more recent distribution.

Feeding and general habits   Apparently seeks food both in trees, shrubs and creepers and on the ground. The fruits of *Freycinetia* and the berries of *Physalis* are eaten extensively.   Has been seen feeding on flesh of dead horses and is said, probably correctly, to take the eggs and young of some of the introduced birds.   Perkins, from whose observations the notes on its food and habits have been compiled, implies that it takes other foods when, talking of its feeding on carrion, he says '. . . nor (before the white man's arrival) could it have obtained some other kinds of food to which it is now partial'.

Not wary and relatively little afraid of man (Tomich), formerly perhaps even 'tamer' than now.   In early spring it often soars high on the wing, fighting or playing.   Not aggressive towards smaller species feeding near it on the same fruits.
Presumably takes some invertebrates as it has been seen prising off loose bark as other corvids do in search of insects.

Nesting   Nests in trees, sometimes in relatively exposed sites, at others in dense masses of the creeper *Freycinetia*.   Nest trees described have been either growing scattered in park-like country or in groups of large trees adjacent to open areas.   One nest was found only 3 m up in a dead shrub (Baldwin).

The nest is built by both sexes, of sticks with an inner cup of grass stems and blades, flexible strands of *Cocculus ferrandianus* and sometimes also small pliant twigs.   A nest built only of twigs was found by Baldwin.   At the nest watched by Tomich the five eggs were laid in the first half of April.   Perkins found many nests containing young in the summer months.

Both sexes incubated in the case of the only pair that appear to have been watched at the nest (Tomich). The male and female changed over several times in the course of the day and the bird 'off duty' spent much time perched on the nest rim.

Voice   Baldwin records a 'two-toned caw', a screech and 'strident low-pitched calls suggesting the grossly magnified "meow" of a cat'.   Those recorded calls (Kellogg & Allen) that I have heard struck me as reminiscent of some calls of the Carrion Crow but given in high-pitched, almost shrieking, tones.   Tomich, however, thought its usual calls 'mellow and musical' in contrast with the 'usually coarse and raucous' calls of the American Crow.   He describes a variously inflected 'cawk', a sharp 'ca-wak' given in apparent alarm, a muscial, ringing 'caw-awk' and a low-pitched 'churk'.

Display and social behaviour   Members of a pair watched by Tomich were seen to preen each other.

Other names   Alala (the Hawaiian name).

REFERENCES

BALDWIN, P. H.   1969.   The Alala (*Corvus tropicus*) of Western Hawaii Island.   *Elepaio* **30**: **5**: 41–45.
BRYAN, E. H. & GREENWAY, J. C.   1944.   Contributions to the ornithology of the Hawaiian Islands.   *Bull. Mus. Comp. zool. Harvard* **94**: **2**: 122.
KELLOGG, P. P. & ALLEN, A. A.   1962. Field Guide to Bird Songs of Western North America.   Boston.
PERKINS, R. C. L.   1903.   *Fauna Hawaiiensis or the Zoology of the Sandwich (Hawaiian) Isles:* 1, pt. 4.   Cambridge.
PETERSON, R. T.   1961.   *A Field Guide to the Western Birds.*   Cambridge, Mass., U.S.A.
TOMICH, P. Q.   1971.   Notes on nests and behaviour of the Hawaiian Crow. *Pacific Science.* **25**: 465–474.

CARRION CROW   *Corvus corone* (*corone* group)

Corvus Corone Linnaeus, 1758, Syst. Nat., ed. 10, 1, p. 105.

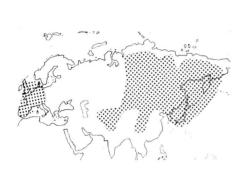

Description Size of Hooded Crow. Black, more or less glossed bluish, bluish-green or purplish but less intensely so than Rook. Little or no gloss on back and sides of neck, cheeks, and underparts below breast. Glossless black fringes to the feathers of mantle, back and inner wing coverts give a laced or scaled effect at close quarters in some lights. Bases of neck feathers grey. Irides dark brown. Bill, legs and feet black. Juvenile duller with at first greyish or bluish eyes and red inside mouth.

The above description is of the nominate form from western Europe. The east Asian form, *C. corone orientalis*, is slightly larger but does not differ in appearance.

Field characters To one not familiar with both can easily be confused with the immature Rook if only one species present. Plumage of Carrion Crow's underparts usually looks sleeker and its bill rather shorter, giving different outline. Flies, typically, with slower wing-beats than Rook's. Calls differ and most are more resonant than Rook's but both have many calls and voice differences are of little use unless all calls of one are known.

Distinguished from Jungle Crow by smaller, shorter and less strongly arched bill; from Raven by shorter wings and ungraduated tail; and from the conspecific Hooded Crow by its all-black plumage.

Distribution and habitat England, southern and central Scotland, western Europe south to the Alps and northern Italy, occurs further south in winter or on passage. In Asia in eastern Iran, south-eastern Transcaspia and oases of Russian Turkestan west to the eastern coast of the Aral Sea; northern Afghanistan west to north-western Himalayas to Kashmir and western Tibet, south to North West Frontier Province and northern Baluchistan, mountains of Russian Turkestan in the Pamirs and Tian Shan to Sinkiang, north to the Altai and Kuznetzk Mountains then northward along western side of Yenisei throughout central and eastern Asia to Anadyrland, Kamchatka and parts of the Gobi, and China south to south-eastern Yunnan and north-western Tonkin. In winter south to Fukien, north-western India and southern Afghanistan.

Replaced in northern and eastern Europe and western Asia by the conspecific Hooded Crow with which it interbreeds.

Inhabits very varied types of country; arable and farmland, moors, parks, sea coasts, river valleys, hills, saltmarsh, villages, suburbs, towns, wood edge, open woodland, and semi-deserts. Its habitats usually have some trees or shrubs. Not found in dense and extensive forests. Where its range overlaps that of the Jungle Crow, as in Tibet and Japan, the latter tends to replace it in heavily wooded and mountainous country and the Carrion Crow is mainly confined to low-lying agricultural regions. In western Europe, and perhaps particularly in Britain, it is characterized by the wide range of different habitats in all of which it is plentiful; it is found in the typical habitats of *all* the other British species of *Corvus*.

Feeding and general habits Feeds mainly on the ground but also in trees. Regularly feeds in taller grass or other vegetation than the Rook or Jackdaw normally do although also, like them, commonly on bare or nearly bare soil and short-grazed pastures. On sea coasts and estuaries seeks food on the shore at low tide. Will pick dead or dying fish and other floating food from the water, scavenges on garbage dumps and similar places, and in towns often takes food from roofs and gutters. Where not persecuted by man will seek food in gardens and around human dwellings but is wary of doing so where much afraid of man.

Takes insects and other invertebrates, small reptiles, frogs, mice and other small mammals, eggs, young and injured birds, stranded or dying fish, rarely healthy fish snatched from shallow water, shellfish, small crustaceans, grain, potatoes, cherries and sometimes other fruit, green walnuts, carrion, and scraps of bread, meat and other human foods when available. Adaptable (within limits) and experimental; the above list of foods is indicative rather than comprehensive. Despite its English name carrion is not usually a significant part of its food, except perhaps in hill sheep country in winter. It occasionally eats acorns, but does not do so, at least in England, to any appreciable extent even when they are super-abundant.

When seeking food picks from surface, probes into grass, earth or small crevices and then opens bill; also uses same movement while bringing bill back towards body at the same time. Thrusts bill into grass, roots etc., and then pushes them to one side. Turns over clods, stones, bits of bark and other objects. Worms are sometimes, and perhaps usually, seized by the head end with a quick forward lunge. A crow that I watched very closely through binoculars from almost directly above, as it fed on the tidal mud of an estuary, would suddenly lunge forward and downward to seize a small worm by the head end. It caught four (and missed one) in about a minute. I was not able to see the worm before the Crow pulled it out on any occasion, but I presume its head or a betraying movement must have been seen by the bird.

Mussels and other shellfish are often dropped and thus broken. Carrion Crows may carry a mussel some distance to drop it on a hard surface. Food that needs breaking or tearing with the bill is held under one or (less often) both feet. Bread and pastry, if hard or sticky, are usually carried to water and dunked before eating. Habitually hides and later retrieves surplus food in typical manner.

Sometimes appears to 'play' with inanimate objects such as twigs and fir cones, dropping and then catching them as they fall. Such things are often, but food rarely, carried in the feet in flight.

I have often put out lumps of bread for wild Carrion Crows and observed that they usually go about hiding them in a systematic manner. The Crow picks up a piece of bread, puts it down again, brings a second piece to the first, continues this till it has as many as it can carry, then flies off with them, hides them and returns for more. It usually estimates correctly the amount of bread it will be able to pick up (often only with difficulty after several attempts) and it usually brings other pieces back to the first it picked up, instead of taking the first to the second and so on. Usually it does not eat until the last load is ready to transport, even though the eagerness with which it then eats shows it must have been hungry before. If two or more Carrion Crows arrive together each bird endeavours to seize, carry off and hide as much as possible as quickly as possible and the behaviour appears much less deliberate and systematic, as it may also if the birds are suspicious and afraid. Croze proved that Carrion Crows quickly learn the appearance of camouflaged prey and that, in any particular area, they search specifically for the kind of food they have learnt to expect to find there.

The more successful adult Crows live in pairs and are territorial, but territory size (which varied from 14 to 49 hectares in one area of Germany (Wittenberg)) and degree to which other crows are excluded varies considerably. Defence of territory is strongest near the nest and declines progressively further from it. Territorial aggressiveness is most intense during the nest building period. Some individual Crows may be tolerated on occasions, quite near the nest while others are driven away from further off. Territories may overlap and 'strangers' may be driven out of neighbours' territories.

The territory probably functions to allow nest building and copulation to take place undisturbed, or relatively so, and to increase the likelihood of the adults having food supplies near the nest when the young are small and need constant brooding and guarding. Yom-Tov proved that ample food supplies *near* the nest increase breeding success.   Adults usually obtain food largely within their territories but may also feed outside, especially when food is scarce.   Non-breeding birds in their first year may also hold territories (Holyoak).

Adults that have failed to obtain territory and non-breeding immature birds roam about in small parties or loose associations.   They sometimes tend to stay in the vicinity of breeding pairs, which show varying degrees of tolerance or intolerance towards them.   They sometimes rob the nests of breeding pairs and may prevent their breeding successfully (Charles, in Yom-Tov).   Such landless birds often form the bulk of the large gatherings at garbage tips, sewage farms, recently drained lakes, and other sources of abundant food.

Established adult pairs usually roost in their territories but may, especially outside the breeding season, leave them to go to a communal roost each evening.   At such roosts they often associate with or are adjacent to roosting Rooks and Jackdaws.   In autumn and winter Carrion Crows may begin to gather on open ground or in trees near the communal roost as early as mid-afternoon but actual settling down at the roost takes place much later, many birds coming in after sunset.   Crows usually leave the roost correspondingly early.   This early rising is equally or even more characteristic of pairs that roost in their own territory.

Mobs predators such as foxes and some birds-of-prey.   Frequently makes swooping attacks or mock-attacks on flying birds-of-prey and, but less often, on harmless species.   May press home attacks on the latter if they show signs of sickness or injury.   Sometimes robs gulls, Rooks, Kestrels or other birds of food; often remarkably successful in finally obtaining a large piece of bread initially carried by a gull in spite of many other gulls also being in pursuit.

When anting 'wallows' on the ants, flopping about, grovelling and lying down with wings outspread, tail raised or pressed down.   Water bathing frequent.   Scratches head directly at times (Holyoak, *pers. comm.*) but usually by the indirect method.   Sometimes rubs side of head on perch and may rub nape on perch between feet.

Nesting   Nests usually in trees, sometimes in shrubs or bushes, on ledges or recesses of cliffs, banks or old buildings; such alternative sites usually only where there are no suitable trees.   In some areas, in Europe, now nests regularly and successfully on electricity pylons, even where trees are at hand.

The nest consists of a foundation and outer wall of sticks or woody stems of heather, seaweed or other tough-stemmed plants.   Inside this, and to some extent mixed with it, is a binding layer of fibrous bark, finer twigs, tough runners of couch grass, etc.   Then moss, grass, grass roots, and lumps of earth; then an inner lining of hair, wool, finer fibrous bark or other soft materials.

Both sexes bring material and build.   In some pairs the male may bring more material and the female do more building, especially in later nest-lining stages (Holyoak), but in other pairs both sexes build at all stages.

Eggs 2 to 7, commonly 4 or 5; greenish-blue, light green, greenish-white or pale olive; speckled, blotched, or clouded with dark and lighter olive-brown and with underlying greyish and (sometimes) pale olive markings.   Very variable; some eggs have only very sparse spots or blotches, others are so thickly marked as to appear olive-brown.

Eggs usually laid early in spring, in England from late March onward but with a majority laid in mid-April (Holyoak, 1967) but many in early or late April.   In northern Germany also the peak laying period is in mid-April (Wittenberg).   Single-brooded, but if eggs or young are lost the pair may make one or even two repeat attempts.   Eggs usually laid daily.   Incubation by female only, fed on and near nest by male.   She also leaves the nest for short periods and may then find food for herself.   The female usually spends much time on the nest from the time of laying of first egg and roosts on the nest two or three nights prior to laying.   Incubation period 17 to 19 days.   True incubation appears to begin at varying stages but perhaps most often with the second egg.

Female broods the young, with decreasing intensity, from 12 to 15 days but may start to collect some food for them as early as the 8th or 9th day.   Young are fed and tended by both parents, the male at first bringing all or almost all the food for both female and young.   Food is brought in the throat pouch;

large items may be carried in the bill to vicinity of nest but are then broken up before feeding to young. The late Miss Frances Pitt saw (and photographed) a Carrion Crow feed a whole frog to one of its nestlings but this would appear to be unusual behaviour.

Young fledge at 32 to 36 days. Regular parental feeding stops about 4 weeks after fledging but occasional feeding of young may occur in 5th week or, less often, later. Young associate with their parents for a considerable time, sometimes to some extent until the following breeding season. While thus associating with them they gain from the parents' knowledge of local food sources and dangers. They sometimes snatch or steal food from them.

Wittenberg saw what seems to be remarkable parental behaviour: when a young Crow fell from its roosting perch on a high tension mast both parents at once flew down to it and spent the night on the ground with it. It is astonishing that the parents' concern should impel them to do this as it is difficult to believe they could have achieved anything except endanger their own lives had a fox or other predator discovered them during the night. It is, however, well known that Carrion Crows will often come close to man and enable themselves to be shot, if their fledged young are roughly handled and cry out in fear.

Many nests lose some or all of their eggs or newly-hatched young. Wittenberg obtained circumstantial evidence, but no proof, that parties of immature non-breeding Crows are implicated. While one was being chased by the breeding female another flew to and looked into the nest. This was, however, only seen after the nest had already been robbed. At other times Wittenberg saw other breeding birds fly quickly to a neighbour's temporarily vacated nest, look into it, then return to their own territories without having harmed the eggs. In Scotland Charles (in Yom-Tov) had evidence of nest robbing by non-breeding individuals.

In each territory there are usually several look-out posts on high trees that the male uses especially while the female is sitting. At any alarm or disturbance in the vicinity the male usually flies at once to one of his look-out posts to watch for and try to discover the possible danger (Löhrl).

In the spring of 1973, in Devon, two pairs nested in the same tree. Both reared young, in nests less than 10 m apart (G. H. Gush, pers. comm.). Such sociability must be extremely rare.

Voice The usual 'caws' are more vibrant and resonant than the most typical calls of the Rook. The descriptions below are compiled from my own observations, those of Mr David Holyoak (in press and pers. comm.) and the published accounts of Wittenberg, Kramer and Löhrl. These latter suggest that the calls of German and English Carrion Crows are essentially the same. There is, however, some geographical variation; Dr Coombs (*in litt.*) tells me that he noticed considerable vocal differences between Carrion Crows in Spain and those in Cornwall. Hand-reared Carrion Crows may indulge in vocal mimicry but this has not been recorded from wild individuals.

The usual caw could be written 'kraa', 'karaa', 'aaarr' etc. It is subject to much variation but typically resonant and with a vibrant quality about it, and is given with somewhat variable head and body movements. A very common variant is a loud harsh 'kraar kraar kraar', repeated two to four times, given with a movement in which head is lowered, then jerked up, the nictitating membrane drawn over the eye, the throat feathers fluffed, the wings opened slightly at the shoulders and tail partly spread as each note is given. This appears to be a self-assertive call, especially of the male. It is commonly given in territorial situations. Softer variants are often given by the female in response to self-assertive calling of her mate but may also be given by both sexes.

Hoarse asthmatic-sounding calls that lack any resonance, and odd calls sounding very like some motor-car horns are commonly uttered. Their significance is uncertain and some of them may well be alternative or individual variants of the self-assertive call.

An emphatic, angry-sounding 'kar, kar' or 'ark, ark', usually given two notes at a time, is uttered in territorial disputes, particularly by a Crow that has just seen an interloper as it flies quickly towards the trespasser to chase it away.

A loud, harsh, repeated 'kaaaar', like the usual caw but harsher, flatter and longer drawn out, is the typical 'alarm' call used when mobbing ground predators or perched birds-of-prey. It seems motivated by conflict between fear and aggression, or fear and curiosity. It is given also when another crow appears to be in danger or at the sight of remains of *Corvus* species or what, apparently, appear to the crow to be such.

A very similar call, not to my ears clearly separable, is given when several Crows are attracted to food put out for them. Possibly in this situation most of the calls are from individuals that are in a conflict state through suspicion or through frustration at the presence of competitors. This call (in both situations) attracts other Crows to the vicinity.

Wittenberg describes a bleating call with an up-and-down cadence. It is uttered when returning to the nest after territorial strife or, later in the breeding season, when the pair return to an empty nest, whether it is empty as a result of predation or because the young have successfully fledged.

The begging call of fledged juveniles and of the incubating female is a loud 'caaa' or 'aaa, aaa', very similar in its eager, pleading tone to the homologous call of the Jay, although deeper in tone. Wittenberg describes as the 'nest call' a short 'rarr', with the 'r' sound not audible at a distance and rather nasal in tone, which may be uttered in apparent pain by the female when laying, or when the male comes with food, in which case it may carry over into the begging call. He also describes a loud 'raerraeraerr' given by one bird, he thinks the female, during copulation.

A mechanical rattling 'klok-klok-klok', suggestive of machine-gun fire or the clicking call of the female Jay, is given by the female (only?) in some territorial situations, at social gatherings, and sometimes in response to display or self-assertive calling of her mate. When I have seen the calling bird it has lowered its head similarly to that of a clicking female Jay but Holyoak (*pers. comm.*) has seen this call uttered with no appreciable head movement or with a movement similar to that when uttering the self-assertive call.

A short, grating rattle (German *stossquarren*) is given when attacking flying birds-of-prey, as the Crow swoops at them, and, usually less intensely, in apparently semi-playful attacks on other Crows. Löhrl observed that in his experience, it was never uttered when such diving attacks were made on the greatly feared Goshawk, but only when less dangerous birds-of-prey were involved.

The hawk alarm call is described by Löhrl as a series of short, high-pitched, breathless-sounding notes that lack any resonance. It is given at the appearance of a *flying* Goshawk, probably also at sight of other flying birds that are dangerous to adult Crows, and appears to express great fear. On hearing it other Crows at once fly up, bunching together, and seek to gain height. They fly *from* the source of the cry unless this is at a considerable distance. If it is they fly to a high perch and keep watch. Kramer heard this call given by one (only) of a pair of Hooded Crows at an Eagle Owl which he had placed near their young.

A soliloquy of very variable calls that seem to represent low-intensity versions of most of the innate calls and, possibly, some vocal mimicry, is given as song or sub-song. I have heard it only from immature birds. It has also occasionally been heard from sitting females.

Display and social behaviour Bowing, each bow followed by and accompanied by an upward head-jerk, drawing over of the nictitating membranes and spreading of the tail, is equivalent to the bowing display of the Rook and the lateral self-assertive display of the Jay (q.v.). While thus displaying the bird may or may not call. Sometimes both members of a pair will display in this manner to each other, sometimes with head feathers fully erected, prior to the female going over into the quivering display or begging to be fed. Often two hostile males will stand close together or walk side by side displaying at each other. Particularly at such times the body and spread tail may be tilted towards the bird at which the display is directed.

In another version of self-assertive display the head plumage is fully ruffled and the bill held pointing downward. This seems to indicate more inhibition against attacking or more definite sexual motivation. The bird may strut about in this posture, or even maintain it for some time while food-seeking, if a sexual or territorial rival is in the vicinity. In pre-copulatory display the body plumage is more fully erected, the wings somewhat lowered, and the tail partly spread.

The feathers above the eyes are sometimes erected to form 'ears' as in some other *Corvus* species. Holyoak (*pers. comm.*) thinks this usually indicates a lesser degree of arousal than the fluffed-headed bill down posture but I think it may merely indicate less conflict and a greater readiness to attack, as with the

Raven (q.v.). Rival males sometimes, however, bow repeatedly side by side with 'ears' erected, without physical attack following.

The female solicits with partly open and lowered wings and quivering tail (probably the wings are more fully opened and also quivered at high-intensity) and this display is, as usual, also used in an appeasing context by both sexes.

Copulation usually occurs on the nest or in its vicinity. It may take place without any conspicuous prior display. Probably with established pairs mutual understanding and communication by glances and slight posturing develops at the 'expense' of the more fully stereotyped and 'impersonal' display patterns. Attempts by males in neighbouring territories to rape sitting females have been observed (Wittenberg).

In display flight the Carrion Crow uses very deliberate wing beats, the wings seeming to pass through a wider arc than in normal flight.

Social gatherings apparently similar to those of *Garrulus* and *Pica* are common in late winter and early spring. Wittenberg could find no obvious function for them other than serving as an outlet for social impulses. Some of such gatherings, that I have seen, involved self-assertive display between neighbouring pairs. Both Wittenberg and Holyoak consider that pair formation takes place among the flocks of immature non-breeders but I think the possibility should be kept in mind that it might, at least sometimes, be established or initiated at spring gatherings.

Neighbouring territory owners frequently keep in contact by calling and answering each other. This may express rivalry as well as sociality.

Feeding of female by male is regular during incubation but less frequent prior to this, or at least much less often observed, than in the Rook or Jay. When hungry, the female begs with flapping wings like a juvenile.

Allo-preening takes place between members of a pair and also between immature siblings.

Perch hammering, pulling and tearing objects and so on are shown, as usual, in redirected aggression or frustrated rage. 'Stare down', in which the Crow suddenly lowers its head and looks at or between its feet, is also shown in conflict situations.

Other names Corby, Black Crow, Crow.

REFERENCES

CROZE, H. 1970. Searching image in Carrion Crows. *Z. Tierpsychol.*, Beiheft 5.
GOODWIN, D. 1955. Jays and Carrion Crows recovering hidden food. *Brit. Birds* **48**: 181–183.
HOLYOAK, D. 1967. Breeding biology of the Corvidae. *Bird Study* **14**: 153–168.
—— 1970. Sex-differences in feeding behaviour and size in the Carrion Crow. *Ibis* **112**: 397–400.
—— in prep. Ecology, behaviour and territory of Carrion Crows.
JAHN, H. 1942. Zur Oekologie und Biologie der Vögel Japans. *J. Orn.* **90**: 73–75.
KRAMER, G. 1930. Stimme von Raben- und Nebelkrähe. *Orn. Monatsb.* **38**: 146–147.
—— 1941. Beobachtungen über das Verhalten der Aaskrähe (*Corvus corone*) zu Freund und Feind. *J. Orn.* **89**: Sonderheft: 105–131.
LÖHRL, H. 1950. Zum Verhalten der Rabenkrähe gegenüber dem Habicht. *Z. Tierpsychol.*, 7: 130–133.
PITT, F. 1946. *Birds in Britain*: 99. London.
SCHÄFER, E. 1938. Ornithologische Ergebnisse zweier Forschungsreisen nach Tibet. *J. Orn.* **86**: Sonderheft, May 1938.
WITTENBERG, J. 1968. Freilanduntersuchungen zu Brutbiologie und Verhalten der Rabenkrähe (*Corvus c. corone*). *Zool. Jb. Syst.* Bd. **95**: 16–146.
YOM-TOV, Y. 1974. The effect of food and predation on breeding density and success, clutch size and laying date of the Crow (*Corvus corone* L.). *J. anim. Ecol.* **43**: 479–498.

HOODED CROW   *Corvus corone* (*cornix* group)

Corvus cornix Linnaeus, 1758, Syst. Nat., ed. 10, 1, p. 105.

Description Head, central part of breast, wings and tail black, glossed slightly on head and breast and strongly on wings and tail with bluish and greenish, the greenish gloss mainly on outer webs of primaries. Upper tail coverts blackish or black and grey, with grey tips. Rest of plumage medium to light grey. The grey feathers have dark or blackish shafts and some of the breast feathers, on periphery of black area, are parti-coloured. Irides dark brown. Bill, legs and feet black. Juvenile duller, with usual 'woolly' texture of contour feathers and with inside of mouth (at first) red, and greyish or bluish eyes.

The above description is of *C. corone cornix*, which is found in the British Isles and throughout most of Europe. The form from the Mediterranean islands, the adjacent areas of southern and south-eastern Europe and the Egyptian delta, *C. corone sardonius*, is slightly smaller, with the grey parts of the plumage slightly paler and the feathers of throat and upper breast tending to be more lanceolate and more richly glossed. Hooded Crows from western Siberia, Caucasas, Iran and (in winter) Turkestan, north-west India and southern Afghanistan, *C. corone sharpii*, are, on average, a still paler grey and more strongly iridescent. These forms all intergrade and there is not only some individual variation but birds in worn and bleached plumage are much paler than fresh-plumaged specimens. The most distinctive form is *C. corone capellanus*, from Iraq to south-western Iran. This is as large as the nominate form with, on average, a slightly larger bill with more curved culmen, longer lanceolate feathers on the throat and a more graduated tail. The grey parts of its plumage are a very pale silvery grey with, in life, a faint vinous-pink tinge when new; they fade to a pale milky-grey or nearly white in worn plumage. In life, at a little distance, it appears black and white.

Field characters The grey or whitish body, contrasting with the black of the head, central upper breast, tail and wings at once distinguish it from the conspecific Carrion Crow and all other species. When colour not visible characters as Carrion Crow (q.v.).

Distribution Ireland, Isle of Man, northern Scotland, Orkneys, Shetland and Hebrides. Europe north and east of, and Asia west of the range of the Carrion Crow, south to Iraq and south-western Iran and the Egyptian delta south down the Nile Valley to about Aswan. Northern populations partly migratory, in winter regular in western Europe, eastern England, Turkestan and north-western India. The accompanying map shows approximate breeding distribution as the winter range overlaps that of the black forms. There is evidence that in the past several decades the winter ranges of the northern populations have largely shifted nearer to the breeding grounds and more northern birds remain all year near or at their breeding areas (Holyoak).

Feeding and general habits As Carrion Crow. Wendland gives detailed notes on reactions of Hooded Crows to various predators. He found they reacted with the same fear and intense mobbing to Goshawks and to martens; most birds-of-prey from the Hobby to the Honey-buzzard were treated alike and mobbed with less apparent fear and concern, but the Sea Eagle was never mobbed and seemed to be regarded as a food provider by the Hoodies which followed it in winter to feed on remains of its kills.

Nesting As Carrion Crow (q.v.) but later or earlier where appreciably further north or south. In Scottish

Hooded Crows incubating females are said to obtain most of their own food, and later most of that needed for their young (Yom-Tov).   In north-western Russia, Estonia, Shetland and Faeroes nests with eggs have been found from mid-May until mid-June, in Estonia sometimes in late April.   In the Persian Gulf the form *capellanus* often has full clutches as early as late February.

Voice   As Carrion Crow (q.v.).   There appear to be geographical variations in voice but there is no evidence that these are correlated with all-black or black-and-grey colour pattern.   The 'most extraordinary rattling call' of *C. c. capellanus* (Moore & Boswell) is probably the same as that of nominate *corone* but more detailed comparative studies of the very distinct *capellanus* are needed.

Display and social behaviour   As Carrion Crow but owing to the colour pattern the erection of the head feathers gives a more striking effect.

Other names   Grey Crow, Hoodie, Scotch Crow, Danish Crow, Irish Crow, Rob Roy Crow, Pied Crow (*C. corone capellanus* only).

REFERENCES

ABSHAGEN, K.   1963.   Über die Nester der Nebelkrähen.   *Beitr. Vogelk.* **8**: 325–338.
HOLYOAK, D.   1971.   Movements and mortality of Corvidae.   *Bird Study* **18**: 97–106.
KUHK, R.   1931.   Brutbiologische Beobachtungen am Nest der Nebelkrähe (*Corvus corone cornix* L.).   *J. Orn.* **79**: 269–278.
MOORE, H. J. & BOSWELL, C.   1956.   Field observations on the birds of Iraq.   *Iraq. Nat. Hist. Mus. Publication* No. 10 (See also references under Carrion Crow).
WENDLAND, V.   1958   Einiges vom Verhalten der Nebelkrähe   *J. Orn.* **99**: 203–208.
YOM-TOV, Y.   1974.   The effect of food and predation on breeding density and success, clutch size and laying date of the Crow (*Corvus corone*). *J. anim. Ecol.* **43**: 479–498.

COLLARED CROW   *Corvus torquatus*

Corvus torquatus Lesson, 1830, or 1831, Traité Orn., p. 328.

Description   About size of Hooded Crow or slightly larger; wings, tail and bill a little longer in proportion.   Culmen usually (but not always) straighter.   Hind neck, upper part of mantle and a broad band extending thence around lower breast white.   These white feathers have grey bases and, especially on the peripheral parts of the white areas, often greyish shafts.   Rest of plumage glossy black, throat feathers lanceolate; gloss in most lights appears mainly purplish and greenish on head and throat, greenish on outer webs of primaries and purplish or bluish elsewhere.   Irides dark brown.   Bill, legs and feet black.

Juvenile duller, with usual woolly texture of body plumage.   Feathers of the white parts tipped or fringed with dark grey and usually more or less suffused with greyish at the peripheral areas.   Irides and inside mouth probably differently coloured from adults', but information lacking.

Distribution and habitat   Eastern and central China from Hopeh south to Tonkin, northern Annam and Hainan, inland to Shensi, southern Kansu, the 'red basin' of Szechwan and eastern Sikang.   Does not normally occur north of Peking but has been observed in south-western Manchuria and has occurred in Formosa.

Inhabits plains and low-lying river valleys, usually below about 60 m.   Typically in fairly open, cultivated areas and a characteristic bird of rice-growing areas.   Relatively rare in temple gardens, wooded hills and built-up areas, where its place is taken by the Jungle Crow.

Field characters   White neck and breast band at once distinguish it from all similarly-sized oriental crows; proportionately longer bill and black belly from Daurian Jackdaw.

Feeding and general habits   Seeks food on the ground, particularly near and in shallow water, along canal banks, the edges of flooded rice fields and so on.   Known to take insects, molluscs, crustaceans, grain (rice) and edible refuse but its food does not appear to have been investigated in detail.   Apparently much less of a carrion feeder and predator on young poultry and other birds than the Jungle Crow. Captive birds habitually dunk food, particularly anything in the slightest degree sticky, in water and then break it up or dissect it; doubtless wild ones do the same.   Food objects may be held under either foot.

Gait and flight apparently much like those of Carrion Crow.   When flying short distances often lets its legs hang down (Rickett).

Nesting   Nest of sticks, plastered with mud (Wilder & Hubbard) and lined with soft materials.   In trees, commonly but not always fairly high up.   2 to 6 (usually 3 or 4) eggs, pale bluish green to blue, speckled and blotched with olive brown.

Voice   The alarm call of a captive bird was a loud 'kaaarr', repeated several times.   Very similar to the homologous call of the Carrion Crow (and most other *Corvus* species) but rather less vibrant and more nagging in tone than is usual with *corone* in southern England.   Lower-pitched and quieter variants were also heard from the same individual.   An apparently self-assertive 'kaar! kaar!' was given with an upward movement of head and bill and tail-spreading, much as in Carrion Crow.

A mechanical-sounding snipping or clicking sound was regularly uttered by a captive bird during its bowing display (q.v.).

Others have described both cawing and creaking calls, less deep and harsh in sound than the calls of the Jungle Crow.

Display and social behaviour   In response to the head raising display and accompanying 'klok, klok' calls of a Pied Crow with which it was then apparently beginning to form a pair, a captive Collared Crow would fly or walk to its side with raised head and, at about the same moment as the Pied Crow next gave its display, would bow forwards, check momentarily and utter a 'snippy click' with its bill about horizontal, then continue the movement till the head was deeply bowed.   At the lowest point, when the bill was at or near vertical, another similar but not identically sounding click was uttered.

In self-assertive display the head feathers were raised, the bill depressed and the bird marched towards the companion it wished to impress or intimidate.   Whereas in the bowing display the white nape is exposed and the black face hidden, in self-assertive display the white parts of the head are concealed from the other bird.   All displays seen appeared similar to and homologous with those of the Carrion Crow.

Other names   Ring-necked Crow, White-necked Crow.

REFERENCES

La Touche, J. D. D.   1952.   *A Handbook of the Birds of Eastern China* 1: 9.   London.
Piechocki, R.   1956.   Beiträge zur Avifauna Nord- und Nordost Chinas (Mandschurei): 123.   Dresden.
Rickett, C. B.   1908.   *Notes on the Birds of Fohkien Province.*   (bound manuscript in British Museum Natural History, Sub-dept. of Ornithology library).
Schäfer, E.   1938.   Ornithologische Ergebnisse zweier Forschungsreisen nach Tibet.   *J. Orn.* **86**: Sonderheft May 1938: 260–261.
Wilder, G. D. & Hubbard, H. W.   1938.   *Peking Nat. Hist. Bull.* Handbook No. 6, Birds of Northeastern China: 127.

BLACK CROW   *Corvus capensis*

Corvus capensis Lichtenstein, 1823, Verz. Doubl., p. 20.

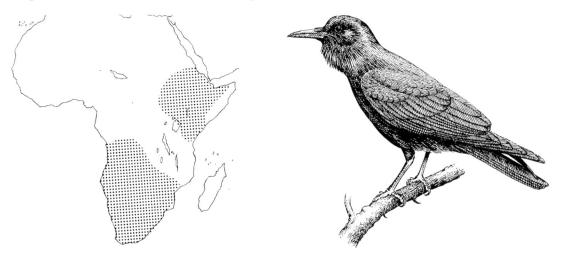

Description   Slightly larger than Hooded Crow, with proportionately rather longer legs and wings and much longer, straighter and more slender bill.   Feathers of throat shining, rather long and many of them bifurcated.   General coloration black, glossed with purplish and bluish, but brownish black with a purplish coppery gloss on crown, nape and sides of neck.   In worn plumage may fade and bleach to dark, oily brown and a lighter, more chocolate tinge on back of head and neck.   Bases of hind neck feathers dark grey.   Irides dark brown, light brown once recorded (? sick bird).   Bill, legs and feet black.   Juvenile duller with the contour feathers perhaps even more lax and woolly in texture than in young of most other *Corvus* species.   Inside mouth of fledgling scarlet.   Day-old nestlings have skin reddish orange (turning red by second day) with mouth and gape edges deep pink.   They have short grey down on crural tracts, flanks and wings, short bristles at end of rump.

   The above description is of the nominate form from southern Africa.   Birds from north-eastern Africa average rather smaller in size, often slightly smaller than Hooded Crow, and are sometimes racially separated as *C. capensis kordofanensis*.   There is, however, much individual variation in size, as in most species of the genus.

Field characters   Entirely black plumage distinguishes it from all other sympatric *Corvus* species except the Brown-necked Raven.   It is not likely to be found in the same localities as the latter but should it be, its straighter and more slender bill would probably serve as a field character.

Distribution and habitat   Africa, from Somaliland and the Sudan south of about 13°N., south to Cape Colony.   In west, north to southern Angola.   Inhabits open grassland, moorland, and agricultural country with some trees or patches of woodland or wooded gullies.   Tends to thrive and increase where arable farming is practised, often in spite of human persecution.

Feeding and general habits   In feeding habits, although not in other aspects of behaviour, very much the African counterpart of the Eurasian Rook.   Takes insects and other invertebrates, grain and seeds, including cultivated maize whose cobs it opens before they are fully ripe, frogs, fruits and berries (esp., in South Africa, *Scutia myrtina*, *Opuntia* sp. and *Royena pubescens*), bulbs of *Cyperus* and probably other bulbs and nutritious roots.   Has been recorded killing young domestic poultry up to a pound in weight (Skead).

   Feeds mostly on the ground.   Digs regularly for food with strong downward stabs of the bill. Probes in and turns over the droppings of cattle and other large mammals in search of insects.   Sometimes takes eggs of domestic poultry and, presumably, ground-nesting wild birds.

In a detailed study on this species in the eastern Cape Province of South Africa Skead found the adult land-owning pairs to be strictly territorial. Each pair's territory was about 60 hectares in extent; the owners did not trespass into adjacent territories even when food was abundant there. They attacked and drove away trespassers or 'escorted' them out of their territory. Flocks of 20 or more trespassers were attacked as boldly as were single individuals. Other Black Crows flying high over their territory might, however, evoke only self-assertive calls from the resident pair.

Birds without territory, probably largely immatures and unpaired individuals, form flocks of up to 50 which roam about in search of food, keeping usually within an area of a few square kilometres, and roost communally. Breeding pairs roost in their territories. The less detailed observations of others do not suggest any significant differences in the behaviour, voice and display of the species elsewhere and the information given here on these subjects is derived from Skead's work except where otherwise indicated.

Nesting Nests in trees, usually near the top, less often in shrubs or large bushes. Skead describes the nest as consisting of a cylindrical basket-work of large dead twigs open top and bottom, an intermediate lining of grass stems, roots etc., and a pad of coarse grass, sedge etc. occupying the central core; about 60 cm deep and in diameter and with the central hollow 23 cm in diameter. Dung of various animals was always incorporated in the nest.

Other observers (Archer & Godman; Hoesch & Niethammer, 1940) record nests lined with hair, old bits of cloth and similar material, and do not suggest that it differs essentially from any other *Corvus* nest in its construction. As Skead refers to the lining as 'resting on the supporting branch' it seems possible that the type of nest he describes, in which the outer framework is bottomless, is built only when there is a firm support beneath.

The eggs are unusual in that they are coloured like the rare erythristic varieties of other crows' eggs. They are buff, buffish white or pale pinkish, speckled, spotted and blotched, usually profusely, with brownish red or brown and with underlying purplish grey markings. Clutch 3 to 4; Skead found 4 the usual clutch in eastern Cape Province but that never more than 3 young were fully reared. The breeding season of this species is more prolonged than that of most Eurasian crows and it will make repeated attempts to breed if eggs or even large young are destroyed. In eastern Cape Province may breed from June to December. In south-west Africa nests with eggs have been found in November and February; in Namaqualand in August; in the north-east of the species' range, in Sudan and Somaliland, in March and April.

Godfrey and Skead (Skead) both observed only one bird of a pair building and carrying material. Both sexes are said to incubate but Skead's description of the changeover does not give positive indication that the bird leaving the nest was not the one that had come to it.

Incubation period 18–19 days. Young fledge at about 38 days. Both sexes feed and tend the young, which may remain with their parents for over five months. A young bird that had fledged on October 20th was seen being fed by both parents on January 18th although it had been finding some food for itself long before this date.

Voice Skead distinguishes the following calls:-

(1) A cawing 'krrah . . . krrah . . . krraah' (Steyn transcribes it 'kah-kah-kah'). Used as an advertisement call or to express apprehension (perhaps with a different intonation not readily distinguishable to human ears?). When danger threatens the 'krraahs' become louder and faster and the calling bird uses the display flight (q.v.).

(2) A soft, liquid, throaty but far-carrying bubbling sound, 'ker-lollop', single or in a series. Sometimes varied to 'kolla-*lol*lop', rather like a large air bubble bursting up through the surface of the water. A challenge call to conspecific intruders. May be given in display flight or from a perch, with the wings partially opened and the throat and head feathers erected. A slower, quieter version, without any apparent aggressive motivation, may be given by the bird when alone or with its mate.

(3) A calm, quiet and slow 'cwrr' used for interrogative apprehension. A 'growl of uncertainty'.

(4) A curious bubbling 'voerrr' followed by an explosive 'click'. When giving this call the bird slowly

bows the body, depressing the bill against its throat. This vocalization is given after excitedly chasing some predator or intruder from the territory.

A call sounding like 'how-aaar-you', a throaty, crackling noise and a throaty chuckle were also heard by Skead. Other observers record croaking, gurgling and cawing calls which may well refer to those described above. Vocal mimicry has been heard from a free-flying tame individual (Hoesch, 1937).

Display and social behaviour   Skead describes a display flight in which the bird glides with wings 'arched in an inverted bow, with the open-fingered primaries quivering rapidly'. This flight is used in various agonistic situations, some or all of which appear to involve actual or frustrated aggression. It is given when chasing an intruder from the territory, sometimes when a predator is in sight and when a man is near the nest or young (Steyn).

It is probable that the bowing that accompanies the 'voerr-click' (see 'Voice') could be considered as a self-assertive display.

Touching of bills has been recorded but not, apparently, feeding of the female by male. Allo-preening occurs, in which, at least at times, the feathers are lifted up by the preening bird in the same manner as by the Raven and White-necked Raven.

Other names   Cape Rook, African Rook.

REFERENCES

ARCHER, G. & GODMAN, E. M. 1961. *The Birds of British Somaliland and the Gulf of Aden.* **4**: 1386–7. London.
CHEESMAN, R. E. 1936. On a collection of birds from North-western Abyssinia. *Ibis* **6**, 13th series, pp. 163–197.
HOESCH, W. 1937. Das Honiganzeigen von *Indicator*. *J. Orn.* **85**: 202.
—— & NIETHAMMER, G. 1940. Die Vogelwelt Deutsch-Südwestafrikas. *J. Orn.* **88**, Sonderheft, pp. 314–315.
SKEAD, C. J. 1952. A study of the Black Crow *Corvus capensis*. *Ibis* **94**: 434–451.
SMITH, K. D. 1957. Birds in Eritrea. *Ibis* **99**: 326.
STEYN, P. 1965. Distraction behaviour in the Black Crow. *Bokmakierie* **17**: 16–17.

PIED CROW   *Corvus albus*

Corvus albus P. L. S. Muller, 1776, *Natursyst.*, Supplement, p. 85.

Description   About size of Hooded Crow or slightly larger with, proportionately, rather longer wings, legs and bill, more strongly curved culmen and more rounded tail. Well-developed broadly lanceolate 'hackled' feathers on throat and front of neck. Hind neck, upper mantle, lower breast and sides of upper breast snow-white. Rest of plumage glossy black, the gloss being, in most lights, purplish or bluish and most conspicuous on throat, wing coverts and secondaries. Irides dark brown. Bill, feet and legs black. Juvenile duller and often with many of the feathers of the white areas having blackish tips or suffusions.

Field characters   Conspicuously black and white. Much smaller bill and white on underparts distinguish it from White-necked and Thick-billed Ravens, piebald plumage from other African crows.

Distribution and habitat   Africa south of the Sahara, from Senegal, Sudan, northern Ethiopia and Somaliland southwards. Also on Madagascar, the Comoro Islands, Assumption, Aldabra, Zanzibar, Pemba, and Fernando Po. Widespread but often surprisingly local, rare or absent in some of the dryer parts of south-west Africa and the Congo Forest. Evidence of migration within Africa, in some areas (Elgood *et al.*).

Inhabits various types of more or less open country with trees, and clearings in forests. Typically in association with man in cultivated or pastoral regions, and in and about villages and towns. In Eritrea also occurs in uninhabited arid regions (Smith, 1955, 1957), and has been recorded interbreeding with *C. ruficollis edithae* (but see p. 71).

Feeding and general habits   Seeks food largely on the ground. Takes insects and other invertebrates, small mammals, small reptiles, eggs, young birds, grain, peanuts, the oily husk of palm nuts, carrion, and scraps of human foods when available.   In a recent study this species was found to take a preponderence of vegetable food (Brooke & Grobler).

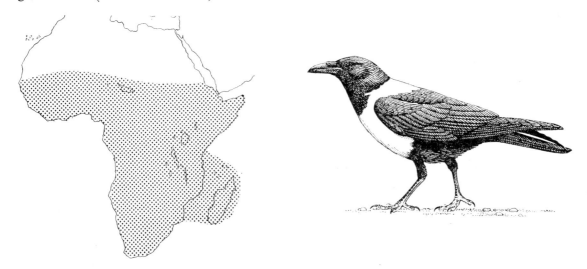

Commonly in pairs or small parties but large numbers gather at good feeding places, at communal roosts, and sometimes to soar on thermals.   General behaviour, so far as recorded, very similar to that of Carrion and Hooded Crows, *Corvus corone*, and like them often plays with sticks etc. while in flight, but it more often circles and soars high in the air.

Where not persecuted shows little fear of man and scavenges around human dwellings but soon becomes shy and wary if shot at.   Frequently mobs birds-of-prey.   Dekeyser & Villiers observed that around Dakar it does not usually interfere with the numerous Black Kites but mobs less familiar species when they are on passage, including Ospreys and Snake Eagles, neither of which are likely to harm it or its young.

Holds large food objects under one or both feet to break or tear with the bill.   A captive has been seen to store food, and wild ones probably do also.   I never saw this captive, at the London Zoo, dunk food in spite of my efforts to elicit this behaviour, although a Collared Crow, to which it was paired, did so regularly.

Habitually flirts up its folded wings as a flight-intention movement after alighting or when slightly alarmed, in this resembling the Collared and Carrion/Hooded Crows and differing from the ravens *C. corax* and *C. albicollis*.

Nesting   Nests in trees, often quite small ones.   In some areas regularly nests on the cross supports of telephone poles.   Nest of sticks with thick inner lining of soft materials such as fibres, hair, wool, torn-up rags, paper, or fibrous bark.   A nest dissected by Dekeyser & Villiers had a layer of flattish materials immediately above and inside the outer shell, then a layer of sand (possibly mud when originally placed there?) and then the thick lining of hair and other soft materials.

Eggs 3 to 6, pale blue or greenish blue, spotted, flecked or streaked with olive brown and sometimes purplish brown and yellowish brown, and with underlying lilac or greyish markings.   Usually less heavily marked than many *Corvus* eggs and very like those of *C. ruficollis*.   Nests with eggs found in October in South Africa, in October and November in Madagascar, in September in Uganda, Sudan and in late February and March in Eritrea and Abyssinia.

Both sexes build.   Female incubates and broods young, fed by the male, who often covers the nest but probably without really incubating, for short periods if the female leaves the nest (Lamm).   Incubation sometimes, perhaps usually, begins with the first or second egg.   Number of young reared is sometimes considerably fewer than the number hatched.   Incubation period 18–19 days, possibly sometimes longer.   A young bird in Ghana fledged at 43 days (Lamm).   Both sexes feed and care for young.

Voice A captive individual (believed male) frequently uttered a harsh 'ar! ar! ar!' or 'karh! karh!' in an upright posture, with a slight upward movement of the head at each call. The individual calls were a little longer-drawn than those of a Raven and much less croaking in character. In definite alarm a harsher, rather longer 'aarr! aarr!' was given.

The same bird very frequently uttered odd sounds like series of hollow knocks, apparently equivalent to similar and clicking sounds of other species, 'klok, klok, klok' or 'kla-kla-kla'. Usually these calls were suggestive of the tapping of a woodpecker (not its drumming) but were very loud and deep in tone. If one was not watching the bird it would be hard to believe the sound was vocal and not instrumental. Typically the bird uttered this in a rather upright posture; with each series of 'kloks' it spread its folded wings at the shoulders, fanned out and closed its tail, opened its bill widely and threw up its head. There was a rapid up and down movement of the lower mandible in time with each knocking sound. Benson and Penny record a long nasal 'wonk woo' given with similar posturing.

Except for a 'soft gulping call' (Rand) descriptions of this bird's calls by others seem to refer to the above calls or variants of them.

Display and social behaviour When giving its knocking call the London Zoo bird usually erected the head feathers in an apparent self-assertive display very similar to those of the Carrion Crow and Raven. It also often strode about with lifted head and erected head feathers without calling. Benson & Penny observed a chin-up threat display and an apparently submissive ruffling of head feathers with bill held down at an angle of about 30 degrees. Allo-preening occurs between members of a pair.

REFERENCES

BENSON, C. W. & PENNY, M. J. 1970. The land birds of Aldabra. *Phil. trans. Roy. Soc.* B **260**: 417–527.

BROOKE, R. K. & GROBLER, J. H. 1973. Notes on the foraging, food and relationships of *Corvus albus* (Aves, Corvidae). *Arnoldia.* **6**, 10: 1–13.

CHEESMAN, R. E. 1936. On a collection of birds from North-western Abyssinia. *Ibis* (13) **3**: 163–197.

DEKEYSER, P. L. & DERIVOT, J. 1958. Étude d'un Type d'Oiseau Ouest-Africain: *Corvus albus*. *Initiation africaines* **16**: 1–58. Dakar.

——— & VILLIERS, A. 1952. Sur une nichée du corbeau blanc. *Notes africaines* **56**: 124–127.

ELGOOD, J. H., FRY C. H., & DOWSETT R. J. 1973 African migrants in Nigeria. *Ibis* **115**: 375–409.

GOOD, A. I. 1952. The birds of French Cameroon. *Mem. Inst. Français d'Afrique noire*, Série: Sci. Nat. **2**: 127.

LAMM, D. W. 1958. A nesting study of the Pied Crow in Accra, Ghana. *Ostrich* **29**: 59–70.

RAND, A. L. 1936. Distribution and habits of Madagascar Birds. *Am. Mus. Nat. Hist. Bull.* **72**: art. **5**: 495.

SMITH, K. D. 1955. The winter breeding season of land birds in Eritrea. *Ibis* **97**: 480–507.

——— 1957. Birds of Eritrea. *Ibis* **99**: 326.

BROWN-NECKED RAVEN   *Corvus ruficollis*

Corvus ruficollis Lesson, 1830/1831, Traité Orn., p. 329.

Description Between Raven and Hooded Crow in size. Proportions like Raven but wing usually slightly more pointed and bill not so stout; but there is much individual and local variation in size and depth of bill. Short feathers immediately around eye and between eye and bill dull black. Face, forehead, throat and front of breast brownish black with an oily purple gloss. Rest of head, and hind neck, slightly browner and with little or no purple sheen, underparts purplish-black to blue-black with brownish fringes to feathers. Rest of plumage black strongly glossed with blue, purple or purplish blue. Bases of neck feathers medium grey to greyish white. Plumage tends to fade rapidly and to become much browner, even the blue-black feathers often bleaching to a rusty brown. In life head and neck may, in some lights, show a coppery gloss. Irides dark brown. Bill, legs and feet black. Juvenile duller. Some descriptions of supposed differences between adults (brown) and immatures (black) seem to have been based on birds in worn and others in very new adult plumage.

The Somaliland race, sometimes called Dwarf Raven or Somali Crow, *C. ruficollis edithae*, is usually appreciably smaller (but measurements may overlap), being about the size of a Hooded Crow or a little smaller, and has a proportionately shorter bill.   The bases of its hind neck feathers are usually snow-white but sometimes greyish white.   See introductory chapter for discussion of status of this and other forms.

Field characters   Distinguished from Raven by higher-pitched, more 'crow-like' usual calls.   The brown neck is not a good field character.   Longer tail at once distinguishes it from Fan-tailed Raven (q.v.) and entirely dark plumage from Pied and Hooded Crows.

Distribution and habitat   Cape Verde Islands, North Africa in the Sahara south to northern Nigeria, Egypt, desert and arid parts of the Sudan, Red Sea districts, Ethiopia south to Kenya, Somaliland, Sinai Peninsula, Palestine, Arabia, Socotra, southern Iran in the Zagros to Fars and probably Kirman, islands of the Persian Gulf, Persian Baluchistan to western Sind, Seistan, Afghanistan in the Paropamisus and probably in the south also, Transcaspia, plains and parts of the desert between the Amu and Syr Daryas.

Inhabits desert and arid country but will come into desert oases, cultivation on the desert edge, and palm groves.   In the Cape Verde Islands habitually in cultivated as well as desert areas which suggests that ecological competition with other species, such as the Raven and Hooded Crow, may affect its choice of habitat elsewhere.

Feeding and general habits   As Raven so far as known, allowing for habitat differences.   Known foods include carrion, wounded birds, lizards, small snakes, grasshoppers, locusts, stranded fish, maize, rice (obtained by tearing open bags laden on pack animals), ticks and possibly other ectoparasites picked from domestic animals, unidentified grains from animal droppings and dates.

Hiding and subsequent recovery of the hidden food recorded from captive birds (Koenig, 1920) and no doubt practised in the wild also.

Where not persecuted by man can be bold and fearless but wary and suspicious if it sees attention fixed on it and it becomes very shy where shot at.

Nesting   Nest similar to that of Raven, to judge from descriptions although these are less detailed than some available for nests of *corax*.   In densely populated regions rags and bits of clothing are very often incorporated in the nest.   Like Raven may nest either in trees, cliffs, or buildings.   The small Somaliland form always nest in thorn trees or palm trees (*fide* Archer & Godman).

Eggs 1 to 6, usually 4 or 5.   Like those of Raven but smaller, and bright or pale blue types with only light spotting and others (either lightly or heavily marked) in which the markings tend to form longitudinal streaks, are proportionately more abundant than with *corax*.   Nests with eggs found in January and February in Saudi Arabia; in late February, March, and early April in Egypt; in mid-April in Palestine and in April and early May in Somaliland.   In north-western Africa eggs found in January, February and March, except in southern Mauretania where laying occurs in autumn (Heim de Balsac & Mayaud).   In the Cape Verde Islands eggs may be laid from mid-November to mid-April but most often from late January to mid-March, (Bannerman; Naurois).   Incubation by female only.

In Kyzylkums (USSR) eggs laid in late March and April.   Incubation 20–22 days; young leave nest at 37 or 38 days; can fly at 42–45 days (Lakhanov).

Voice   Most or all calls less deep and croaking than those of *corax*.   I noted 'a harsh crow-like "karr karr karr" ' from an adult female when I was near her young.   Koenig recorded 'korr-korr' and 'kuerk kuerk' from flying birds and also a variety of guttural, gurgling and cawing calls from captive birds. Some field observers describe the calls usually heard as suggestive of those of the Rook or Carrion Crow rather than those of the Raven.   North & McChesney (1964) have published a gramophone record on which the Somaliland form is heard calling.

Display and social behaviour   From König's description it is evident that the self-assertive and pre-copulatory displays of the male are similar or identical to those of *corax*.   A captive pair did not begin to breed until their 6th year (König).

Other names   Desert Raven, Desert Crow, Rufous-necked Raven, Brown Crow, Somali Crow, Edith's Raven, Edith's Crow (these last three for the Somaliland form).

REFERENCES

ARCHER, G. F. & GODMAN, E. M.   1916.   *The Birds of British Somaliland and the Gulf of Aden*, vol. 4.   London.
BANNERMAN, D. A.   1968   *History of the Birds of the Cape Verde Islands*.   Edinburgh.
ETCHÉCOPAR, R. D. & HUÉ, F.   1967.   *The Birds of North Africa*.   London.
GOODWIN, D.   1946.   Odd hours with Brown-necked Ravens.   *Avicult. Mag.* **52**: 90–97.
HARTERT, E.   1915.   In Algeria 1914: 2: Notes on some birds and their nests and eggs.   *Nov. Zool.* **22**: 61–79.
HEIM DE BALSAC, H. & MAYAUD, N.   1962.   *Les Oiseaux du nord-ouest de l'Afrique*.   Paris.
KÖNIG, A.   1905.   Das Bruten von *Corvus umbrinus* in der Gefangenschaft.   *J. Orn.* **53**: 259–260.
—— 1920.   Die Rabenartigen Vögel (Coraces) Aegyptens.   *J. Orn.* **68**: 126–141 (note: in this paper the same author's name is spelt Koenig).
LAKHANOV, ZH. L.   1967.   K biologii pustynnogo vorona v yugo-zapadnykh Kyzylkumakh.   *Ornitologiya* **8**: 364–366.   (English summary in *Bird Banding* **39**: 137.)
MACKWORTH-PRAED, C. W. & GRANT, C. H. B.   1960.   African Handbook of Birds, ser. 1, vol. 2: 671–672.
MEINERTZHAGEN, R.   1954.   *Birds of Arabia*.   London.
NAUROIS, R. DE.   1969.   Notes brèves sur l'avifaune de l'archipel du Cap-Vert.   *Bull. Inst. Fond. Af. Noire* **31**: **1**: 143–218.
NORTH, M. E. W. & MCCHESNEY, D. S.   1964.   *More voices of African birds*.   Boston, U.S.A.

AMERICAN WHITE-NECKED RAVEN   *Corvus cryptoleucos*

Corvus cryptoleucos Couch, 1854, Proc. Acad. Nat. Sci. Philadelphia **7**: 66.

Description   About size of Hooded Crow but shaped like Raven, with relatively pointed wings, graduated tail and heavy bill.   The bill is, however, relatively shorter than Raven's and has profuse nasal bristles which reach about two-thirds down the culmen.   Plumage glossy black, the gloss predominantly purplish and purplish blue in most lights.   Back and sides of neck often with a brownish tinge.   Bases of neck feathers snow white.   Irides brown.   Bill, legs and feet black.   Juvenile duller.

Field characters   Easily confused with Raven although smaller in size, with proportionately shorter bill.

Usual calls less loud and penetrating. Habitat typically differs but in some places both occur. Large flocks or gatherings are typical of *cryptoleucos*.

From American Crow distinguished by slightly larger size and more graduated tail. The white bases to the neck feathers are seldom visible in the field.

Distribution and habitat Southern North America in the western United States and Mexico. From south-eastern Arizona, southern New Mexico, north-eastern Colorado, and south-central Nebraska south to Guanajuato and Tamaulipas.

Inhabits deserts, open plains and arid farmlands, extending into the foothills.

Feeding and general habits Insects, especially grasshoppers and beetles, and cultivated grains, mainly sorghums, form a large proportion of its food, at least in those places where intensive studies have been made (Bent). Also takes other invertebrates, small reptiles, fruits, especially of cacti, carrion, scraps of human food when available, other cultivated grains such as maize, eggs and young birds. Hides surplus food and one was seen apparently digging a hole in which to do so (Bendire).

Frequently in large flocks outside the breeding season. Where not molested may show little fear of man but wary where persecuted by him. Often forms large communal roosts in trees in canyons and gulches.

Nesting Nests in trees, shrubs, and old buildings; often in low scrubby trees. Sometimes colonial but from the little information available it seems that this is, perhaps, a response to a relative sparsity of nesting sites in a particular area.

Nest with base and outer part of sticks, twigs and sometimes bits of wire; the inner cup lined with wool, fur, rags and, almost always, with cow hair.

Eggs 3 to 8, usually 5 to 7. Pale green or pale bluish green, often nearly white, with dark olive brown, light drab, grey and lilac markings. They are, on average, rather more sparsely marked than is usual with *Corvus* eggs and differ more noticeably in that most of the markings usually consist of more-or-less longitudinal streaks. This is particularly the case with the underlying grey or lilac markings. The much less profuse (sometimes almost absent) dark markings usually take the form of spots or small blotches.

Eggs are laid in mid-May, late May or June, although a nest with well-feathered young was found in late May in New Mexico, when others in the same area had eggs (Ligon). This late breeding is probably an adaptation to the food supply for the young. At least in much of its range the rains begin in late May after which insect life becomes more plentiful.

Voice Some observers describe its 'call' as higher-pitched, others as lower-pitched than that of Raven! Some recorded calls I have heard (Kellogg & Allen, 1962) were croaks very like those of the Raven but a little higher-pitched than usual 'pruk' croaks of *corax*. Further and more detailed observations are needed but it seems probable that its most usual calls are less loud than those of the Raven and its typical vocabulary less extensive since many agree on these points.

Display and social behaviour Evidently has a display very similar to self-assertive display of Raven (q.v.), in which the erection of the head and neck feathers causes their white bases to become startlingly visible. Johnston, who described this display in captive birds, thinks it occurs only in hostile and not in sexual contexts. In view of what is known of the behaviour of the Raven and some other species further studies, involving observation of pair-formation, would be necessary to prove this.

Other names White-necked Crow.

REFERENCES

BENDIRE, C. 1895. Life histories of North American birds 402–405. *U.S. Nat. Mus. Spec. Bull.* 3.
BAILEY, A. M. & NIEDRACH, R. J. 1965. *Birds of Colorado.* Denver.
BENT, A. C. 1946. Life histories of North American jays, crows and titmice. *U.S. Nat. Mus. Bull.* **191**: 215–225.
BLAKE, S. F. 1957. The function of the concealed throat patch in the White-necked Raven. *Auk* **74**: 95–96.
BRANDT, H. 1951. *Arizona and its Bird Life:* 264–266. Cleveland, Ohio.
JOHNSTON, R. F. 1958. Function of cryptic white in the White-necked Raven. *Auk* **75**: 350–351.
KELLOGG, P. P. & ALLEN, A. A. 1962. *Field Guide to Bird Songs of Western North America.* Boston.

LIGON, J. S. 1961. *New Mexican Birds* 202–203. New Mexico.
PHILLIPS, A., MARSHALL, J. & MONSON, G. 1964. *The Birds of Arizona* 106.
ROBBINS, C. S., BRUUN, B. & ZIM, H. S. 1966. *A Guide to Field Identification of Birds of North America.* New York.
SCLATER, W. M. 1912. *A History of the birds of Colorado:* 293–294. London.

RAVEN   *Corvus corax*

Corvus corax Linnaeus, 1758, Syst. Nat., ed. 10, 1, p. 105.

Description The largest all-black species. Tail graduated. Large bill with curved culmen. Feathers of throat and upper breast long, lanceolate and highly glossed. Black, glossed with greenish and greenish blue on upper throat, cheeks, underparts and outer webs of wing quills and with blue, purplish blue and purple elsewhere but amount and hue of iridescence varies both individually and with incidence of light. Bases of hind neck feathers light grey. Irides dark brown. Bill, legs and feet black. Juvenile duller with, at first, bluish grey irides.

The above description is of birds from Britain and north-western Europe which belong to the nominate subspecies. Many other races have been described. The general trends of geographical variation are as follows: Ravens from the northern parts of the species' range, and from high altitudes in the Himalayas, are, on average, larger than the nominate form and tend to have proportionately slightly larger bills, this latter feature being most marked in Greenland specimens. Those from the southern parts of the species' range tend to be smaller or similar in size to the nominate race and to have proportionately smaller bills. They also tend to have a brownish tone about the head and neck when in worn plumage;

this is most marked in populations from the Indian regions (Afghanistan, Sind, Rajputana and the Punjab) many of which are intermediate in colour between other forms of *corax* and *ruficollis*. Many have the bases of the hind neck feathers whitish grey, as have also many from the Arctic and Iceland, whereas elsewhere these feather bases are usually light to medium grey.

That Arctic Ravens tend to have larger rather than smaller bills than southern representatives, in opposition to Allen's rule, is probably due to their feeding to a greater extent on fairly large live prey in the Arctic than elsewhere.

Field characters The hoarse resonant croaks which are the most commonly-heard calls are diagnostic. Much larger size distinguishes Raven from all other European *Corvus* species if seen with them but size is useless as a field character if the bird is seen alone. In flight more graduated tail, proportionately longer wings, larger bill and *longer-looking neck* distinguish from Carrion Crow and other species. If seen in profile long throat feathers often form a conspicuous 'dewlap'; this character is shared by Jungle Crow (and several other species not sympatric with Raven) and is therefore not valid in some eastern parts of its range. See under Brown-necked and American White-necked Ravens for differences from those species.

Distribution and habitat Holarctic: Europe and Asia from Greenland (mainly or entirely coastal areas), Iceland and northern Scandinavia eastward to the Pacific, south to northern Manchuria, Hokkaido, central Asia to the Himalayas and north-western India, Iranian region and near East, north-western Africa and Canary Islands. North and Central America south to north-western Nicaragua.

Resident; but some wandering and local migration of immature and non-breeding birds. In high arctic, and possibly elsewhere, some breeding pairs do not remain resident throughout the year (Salomonsen).

Occurs in many types of country but most often in open, mountainous or coastal regions. Not usually in extensive woodlands or, in Africa and the middle East, in hot arid deserts where it is replaced by allied species. In many countries past and present persecution by man probably have more effect on its distribution than the bird's own choice of habitat.

Feeding and general habits Most food taken from the ground. Eats carrion, afterbirth of ewes and other large mammals, small mammals, reptiles, frogs, young and wounded birds, eggs, insects and other invertebrates including mollusca. Stomach contents suggest that when it visits rotting carcasses it sometimes feeds chiefly or entirely on the blowfly maggots and beetles in and around them (Nelson). Also takes some vegetable foods: cultivated grains, beechmast, acorns and cherries have been recorded as well as unidentified vegetable remains in its castings. Readily learns to eat bread and other human foods.

Often a bold scavenger about human dwellings and encampments, especially those of nomadic or semi-nomadic herdsmen. Quick to take alarm and become shy of man where persecuted. Often robs feeding vultures of pieces they have torn from a carcass (Schäfer). Appears readily to recognize and attack sick or injured individuals of species it does not otherwise interfere with. Holds large food objects under one or both feet. Sometimes carries objects in feet.

Habitually hides surplus food in typical manner. Gwinner's (1965) observations show that tame Ravens store food most intensely when they are themselves hungry; that they hide fat in preference to other foods (even to those that they prefer to eat), except that birds with small young store most eagerly foods such as insects which are suitable for the young. The use of such preferential storing is obvious and there is little doubt that wild Ravens behave similarly. Ravens learn to hide food out of sight of other Ravens and out of *reach* of humans who have robbed them (Lorenz, 1931).

Breeding pairs are territorial. The members of a pair may forage separately. Territories are more extensive than those of other British *Corvus* species but vary in size, probably in relation to the food supply (Holyoak & Ratcliffe). Immature birds, that have left their parents, form flocks, probably sometimes together with non-breeding and territoryless adults. Such flocks tend to roam about, they are always loose-knit and straggling and within them pairs or at least apparent pairs are clearly evident. Large numbers may gather at carcasses, garbage tips, open-air slaughtering yards, battlefields and other sources of abundant food but typical flocks of non-breeding birds form irrespective of food supplies or roosting sites (Coombs; Franz; Mylne).

Roosts on cliff ledges or in trees. Large numbers may gather at communal roosts, sometimes in company with other *Corvus* species. Many of the birds coming to such roosts arrive in ones and twos at the gathering place. Territory-owning pairs sometimes, and perhaps usually, roost in their own territories.

Appears to be much more vulnerable to human persecution than some other crows. Probably this is largely due to its fidelity to its territory and, within it, to a limited number of nest sites. However wary the old Ravens may be, to destroy their young each year is usually easy enough.

Walks and (less often) hops on the ground. Flight direct and strong with rather slow wing beats. Frequently glides, soars and performs various aerobatics, especially diving with closed wings, and suddenly turning over back downwards in the air. Calls very frequently in flight as well as at other times.

Nesting   Nests on ledges and in recesses of both inland and sea cliffs, also in trees; usually fairly high up, but will use quite small trees or low cliffs where necessary; occasionally nests on buildings, in some places may do so regularly. Cliff nests are usually sheltered by an overhang even when not in a recess. The same nest site may be used in successive years but most pairs have two or more sites which are used alternately.

Outer part of nest of sticks or stick-like stems of heather, gorse etc., reinforced with lumps of earth, clumps of grass or moss. Thinner sticks are used for the nest rim; the central part of the nest is of thin sticks, twigs, clumps of earth, wool, hair and similar materials, the deep inner cup lined with finer strands of wool, hair, fur and fine stems. Large sticks are carried one, or rarely two, at a time; other material is bundled. Wool and other material for the final inner lining (but not for the outer part of the lining) is finely teased out or pulled to shreds or strands before being carried to the nest (Gwinner, 1965).

Both sexes build but in any particular pair either the male or female may do more work at some, or all, stages than the other. The nest may be completed from one to four weeks before eggs are laid (Gwinner, 1965a).

Eggs 3 to 6, rarely fewer and very rarely 7. They show much variation in both ground colour and type and density of markings. Light blue, greenish blue, green or brownish green; speckled and/or spotted or blotched with various shades of dark brown or olive brown. They often have underlying purplish or greyish markings but these tend to be a less prominent feature than on eggs of many *Corvus* species. They are usually laid in the morning and on consecutive days.

Incubation by female only, beginning with penultimate or last eggs, although female usually spends most of her time on the nest (but without truly incubating) from the first egg. She is fed by the male, sometimes on the nest, sometimes she leaves it to take food from him nearby. Incubation period 18 or 19 days, rarely 20 (Gwinner). Before incubation the eggs are sunk into the nest lining, this being deliberately done by the female probing beneath them and opening her bill, and pulling up material between and around the eggs. Female turns hatching eggs so that the bill of the young one is always uppermost and visible to her when she looks into nest. She eats the eggshell, cleans the newly-hatched young and places its neck so that it rests on an egg (Gwinner).

Eggs are laid early in the year. In Britain usually in late February and early March (Holyoak, 1967), in Tibet and Greenland in April, in northern India as early as January. Surprisingly, in North Africa eggs are often, perhaps usually, laid in April. Probably, in high latitudes, the need for the young to be strong and self-supporting by winter, as well the availability of food in the breeding season, has influenced breeding times.

Both sexes feed and tend the young. Only the female broods them, but when she leaves the nest for a period the male will cover the young, standing or crouching over them without actually brooding them (Ryves; Gwinner, 1965a). Gwinner found that his captive and semi-captive tame Ravens fed their young on insects (mealworms and crickets), sometimes with a little curd, for the first two days; from the third day (and sometimes as early as the second day) they began also to give them small pieces of mice and day-old chicks. While the young were small they did not give them meat or liver of large mammals although still readily eating it themselves. At first they carefully killed and crushed even small insects before feeding them to the young. They removed all hard parts and bits of bone when preparing food for young but often gave them small bits of mouse or chick-skin, sometimes apparently preferentially. The parents often, especially when the young were 3 to 10 days old, drank after filling their throat pouches and before feeding them, thus giving them soaked food. Water alone was brought to the young, and offered with the usual food-offering call, on hot days when the young were panting. Wild Ravens have also been seen to bring water to their young (Hauri).

The female will also wet her underparts and cover the young while she is still wet if they appear to be suffering from heat, or bore a hole through the nest so that the young are ventilated from underneath. In cold weather small nestlings are half buried in the soft nest lining by the female (Gwinner, 1965a).

While there is no doubt that Gwinner's Ravens behaved normally and that their behaviour reflected that of wild Ravens in most parts of the species' range, it is unlikely that those breeding in the Arctic could obtain insects for their newly-hatched young and they must, presumably, feed them on vertebrate food from hatching.

The female broods the young until they are about 18 days old (Gwinner, 1965a). At wild nests one or other of the parents, probably the female, usually spends much of its time at or within sight of the nest until the young have left it. Young fledge at about 6 weeks old. At a nest I observed in Wales one of the 4 young left 2 days before the next 2 and the last a day after them. Although able to fly, newly-fledged young are often awkward and clumsy and very vulnerable to human and other predation. They remain more or less under parental care for about $5\frac{1}{2}$ to 6 months.

Voice Very loquacious. Most of the more common calls are deep-pitched with a hoarse croaking tone and a more or less pronounced 'r' sound and, in spite of their variability, are at once distinguishable from the calls of all other European crows. They can, however, easily be confused with some calls of *C. albicollis* (q.v.).

As with some other corvids but perhaps to a greater extent than with most of them, descriptive listing of the Raven's calls is difficult because there is much individual variation; certain calls may be used in situations different from those 'normally' eliciting them; copied sounds may be incorporated and combined with, or used instead of, specific innate calls; and young Ravens, especially when singing, may use any or all of the innate calls even when none of the stimuli that normally elicit them appear to be present. Gwinner (1964) has described the apparently innate calls and given sound spectrograms of them. The descriptions below are derived and condensed from Gwinner's except where otherwise indicated.

The 'kra' call, which Gwinner speaks of as the 'typical Raven call' is given in many situations, all of which involve some real or imagined threat from an enemy other than another Raven. A possible exception to this is the version given in flight but, as Gwinner says it is particularly used during 'wild flight chases' and I think here it is possible that some element of escaping or enemy-attacking motivation is present even if the enemy is absent. This is the call that is often written in English as 'pruk' or 'krok'. Gwinner gives a detailed description of its usual variants. The version given by a female, uneasy because I was watching her nest and (later) her fledged young, sounded to me like 'pruk-pruk-pruk' (the 'u' as in 'but'). She uttered it both when perched and in flight and also, perhaps a little quicker and more vehemently, when warding off attacking Herring Gulls. When perched she often gave a very husky and faint variant that sounded like a common call of *C. albicollis*. Although this call is so frequently heard from wild Ravens that many people imagine they constantly give it, it seems likely that in most cases the disturbing human presence is the factor eliciting it. Dr Kenneth Simmons (*pers. comm.*) informs me that, when in Algeria, he never heard it from the numerous Ravens that scavenged around the hotel where he stayed.

Gwinner's 'gro' call is, I think, one that I have less precisely transcribed in my notebooks as 'a deep, low throaty note'. Gwinner describes it as being more uniform and softer in tone than the 'kra' call. It is evidently equivalent to the appeal call of jays of the genus *Garrulus* and, like it, used in many social contexts. Slightly different variants are used as a contact call between paired birds and between parents and flying young, when offering to feed young, and when offering to feed the mate.   When the female is fed on the nest by the male she will, if she has young, give this call also, even when she does not in fact give any food to the young herself (Gwinner).

A soft, tender version of the 'gro' call, sounding like 'gru', 'gri', 'gwee' etc. is called by Gwinner the whining call (Winsel-laute).   It seems to have similar social functions to the 'gro' call and is given especially by young birds when preened by their parents and by tame hand-reared young Ravens to humans.   It has a prominent place in the song of young birds and one form of song consists entirely of variants of this call.   It is, perhaps, equivalent to the chirruping notes of *Garrulus*.

What Gwinner describes as the 'rüh' call is given in loud form by fledged young as a location call. All other forms of it are rather soft.   Other forms of it are given: as a nest call which functions to stimulate the mate to join in nest-building; as an appeasement call in response to actual or implicit threat from a dominant individual or sometimes to dominant individuals in apparently friendly situations; and by the female while laying.   It would thus seem that a common factor of all situations eliciting this call is that the calling bird feels in a submissive or dependent mood and, usually, also somewhat ill at ease.

A very soft, somewhat rattling call, with a complaining sound, is often given by one of two Ravens when the other is, apparently, slightly rough when allo-preening or feeding it.   It indicates low-intensity threat or protest.   It intergrades with the 'gro' call (see above).

Gwinner transcribes as 'krä' (which might be anglicized 'kray') the call given in defensive threat.   It is loud but variable and is given by Ravens that are cornered, defending the nest, or food, or in other similar situations.   It is strongly dependent on the apparently very specific mood eliciting it and, unlike other calls, is never incorporated in the song of juveniles.

In the self-assertive bowing display the male utters a choking-sounding call ('Wurgelaute') that Lorenz (1940) writes (my anglicization) as 'ow', 'row' or 'krrooa' and of which Gwinner gives a sound spectrogram.   The female gives, especially in her first year, squeaking or squealing calls in this display but she may give the 'krrooa' call and often gives clicking, knocking or clappering calls that are very mechanical in sound.

Gwinner thinks that clicking or clappering sounds, which are, rarely, also given by males, are copied sounds, as they were not given by those of his Ravens that had little or no opportunity to learn them either from White Storks or other Ravens.   He shows, however, that although males may learn such clappering sounds they utter them much less often than females do.   It seems, therefore, that female Ravens must at least have an innate tendency to learn such sounds and to incorporate them in their self-assertive display.   I have heard guttural clicks and knocking sounds from Ravens in Britain.

Ravens are very apt to use or incorporate copied sounds in the bowing display.   Established pairs may use personal variants of various innate calls and displays.   These may function to facilitate immediate recognition at a distance as well as, presumably, to enhance the emotional bond between them (Gwinner and Kneutgen, *pers. obs.*).   When one of a pair of Ravens is lost (or removed by a human) the other will often or usually utter particular calls or variants of calls that were habitually used by the lost partner (but not by itself).   This has an attractive effect on the partner and, if it is within hearing and a free agent, results in its immediate return.

The begging call of fledglings and recently fledged young Ravens, that I heard in Wales, was a husky 'kra-kra-kra' or 'kreh-kreh-kreh' with a pronounced 'r' sound.   It was essentially 'Raven-like' and although having something of the imploring tone of a begging Rook, Carrion Crow or Jay was much less like any of them than their respective begging calls are to each other.   Gwinner implies that the begging call of the female is like that of the fledged young, as is to be expected.

Display and social behaviour   Gwinner (1964) describes in detail the Raven's displays and postures and illustrates all of them with sketches or photographs.   Some especially fine photographs of the male's pre-copulatory display are given by Lorenz (1940).   The descriptions here are based largely or entirely on those of Gwinner (with which most other less detailed information in the literature and my own much briefer observations agree) unless otherwise stated.

In the self-assertive display ('*Imponieren*') the Raven usually begins by erecting the feathers immediately above the eye so that they look rather like two small ears; the remaining head feathers are not much erected, the flank feathers are positioned to give a 'trouser-like' appearance, the feathers of the throat, neck and breast are sufficiently erected to form a more or less smooth surface together with the long flank feathers. The feathers of the hind neck and mantle also form a continuous line; the wings are slightly opened at the shoulders so that the carpal joints stand a little away from the body. There is a copious flow of saliva, causing frequent swallowing and consequent movement of the long shining throat feathers. The bird strides about in an intense impressive manner and after a time may give a soft 'ko' or similar sound in the same rhythm as its steps.

From this the bird goes into a posture in which all the head feathers are fully erected, giving it a thick-headed and shaggy-throated appearance with the shining lanceolate throat feathers fully displayed. Similar calls may be uttered as in the 'feather-ears' display. At higher intensity the bird holds itself horizontal and makes forward bowing or retching movements during which it utters 'kro', 'krua' or some personal equivalent (see voice). The more intensely the bird is motivated the more intense and strained-looking the movements and the more it leans or reaches towards its 'partner'. Between series of the bowing forward movements and calls it usually stands more upright but still otherwise in full display. As it bows and calls the bird usually spreads its tail and often draws the white nictitating membranes over its eyes.

The female version of these displays differs slightly but constantly from that of the male (Gwinner, 1964). Her 'feather ears' are not so long as the male's and she gives this display with her other head feathers slightly erected so that the 'ears' are much less conspicuous. She remains silent both in this and the next ('thick-headed') phase of the display. In the intense bowing or forward-reaching phase she bows lower, inclining towards the partner with tail spread and wings lifted well away from the body; and usually utters either a series of squeaking calls or clicking or clappering sounds, giving upward movements of her previously more or less down-pointed bill as she does so, and drawing the nictitating membranes over her eyes. Her tail is inclined upwards and her head, as she calls, raised above the line of the back so that her outline tends to be rather u-shaped, whereas the male at this stage has head, back and tail in a more or less straight line.

The self-assertive display may be shown either towards rivals of the same sex or towards the mate or potential mate. Gwinner suggests that this indicates that it may be differently motivated, in the first by a combination of aggression and escape (anger and fear) but in the second by sexual tendencies unmixed with fear or anger. In the first situation although, under normal conditions, it appears to be fear which inhibits an outright attack and thus elicits the display, if a Raven that is known to have no fear of another is physically prevented from attacking it, for example, by a wire netting barrier, it will go into the self-assertive display.

In sexual contexts the self-assertive display of the male may be followed by display in which he stretches his neck forward, raises his tail which is somewhat spread, partly spreads and stretches back his wings and utters, whilst drawing the nictitating membranes over his eyes, a soft high nasal-sounding 'krooyoo-yoo'. This intermediate display goes over into the actual pre-copulatory display in which the wings are half spread and held drooping but well away from the body, the tail spread and raised, all the contour feathers except the 'trousers' sleeked down, and the head raised on stretched neck with the bill either horizontal or inclined downwards and the nictitating membranes continually drawn over the eyes for periods of several seconds.

If the female then invites coition by crouching, slightly or markedly opening and extending or drooping her wings and shaking or quivering her (at high intensities) slightly raised tail, mating may follow. If not, the male normally goes from the male pre-copulatory display into the typical female pre-copulatory posture. As in some other corvine birds this display is also used in submissive or appeasing contents, especially by tame individuals towards humans.

Feeding of the female by the male takes place in the usual manner. Gwinner (1964, p.683) implies that some individual females always beg with flapping wings when fed and others not. If so this is in contrast to most other corvine birds whose behaviour is known, in which, according to circumstances and her physical or psychological condition, the same female may or may not show juvenile-type begging when fed.

A slightly different version of the 'feather ears' display is shown in more intensely aggressive situations, usually after self-assertive display and immediately before actual attack. In this all the plumage except the 'feather ears' is sleeked down, the bird adopts an upright posture and moves with quick, light steps and bounds. In actual fighting, which occurs fairly often in captivity but seldom in a wild state, the eyes are never harmed. The fighting birds often lie on the ground with interlocked claws, directing their pecks chiefly at each other's bills and carpal joints. In captivity weak or injured individuals may be killed by others, there being evidently no inhibition against inflicting serious injury except to the eyes (Gwinner, 1964).

The eyes are important indicators of mood and intention in the Raven as in man. Captive Ravens often respond at once to a friendly, intimidating, or aggressive look with appropriate calls or gestures. Gwinner makes the point that although it is difficult to define differences of eye expression even people not at all familiar with Ravens can tell at once whether the bird's look is hostile, appeasing or loving. All that can be said in written description is that in hostile contexts the eyelids tend to be widely open and the pupils dilated, in friendly contexts the eyelids to be slightly closed and the pupils somewhat contracted.

Ravens that feel submissive or inferior tend to retract the neck and depress the plumage, making themselves look small and thin. The bill is raised towards but held at a lower level than the bill of the dominant bird. Turning the head away from the partner or looking down towards the feet ('Herabstarren') may also be shown in apparently appeasing situations. The tail-quivering display in appeasing situations occurs only between mates or other more or less trusted individuals. In all appeasing situations the bird may give juvenile-type calls. Begging is used not only in connection with connubial feeding but also spontaneously and with the intention to appease the dominant bird. Both sexes may show such begging behaviour.

Allo-preening occurs between birds that are on friendly terms with one another, and between mated pairs. Sick captive birds that sit about with head feathers fluffed up are frequently preened by others, including their social inferiors. An allo-preening bird very commonly lifts up the long throat (and other) feathers of its partner and then looks intently at the feather bases as if for possible parasites (*pers. obs.*). Even between paired and allo-preening birds some individual distance is maintained (except of course during copulation), the preening bird standing a little away and not in bodily contact with its partner.

What Gwinner terms the head forward threat posture is very variable: the Raven threatens with open bill, sometimes lifting or drooping its wings, and snaps its bill. A mere inclining of the bill towards a social inferior is usually sufficient to keep it at a distance or drive it from food.

In frontal threat, which Gwinner states is seen in a pure form only in nest defence, the Raven erects its plumage, especially on the head (to judge from Gwinner's photographs), and opens its bill. Gwinner distinguishes from this the defensive threat display in which the plumage of the back and mantle are so fully erected as to present a jagged or ruffled profile and a hump-backed posture is often adopted. The bill is open as in the frontal threat display, of which this appears to be merely a more intense version or a version involving greater fear and thwarting of the tendency to flee. Calling and bill snapping accompany these defensive displays. The full defensive threat is very common from captive birds that cannot escape from the vicinity of dominant individuals.

Other names   Corby (used also for the Carrion Crow).

REFERENCES

Bowles, J. H. & Decker, F R.   1930.   The Raven in the State of Washington.   *Condor* **32**: 192–201.
Coombes, R. A. H.   1948.   The flocking of the Raven.   *Brit. Birds* **41**: 290–294 and 386.
Cushing, J. E.   1941.   Winter behavior of Ravens at Tomales Bay, California.   *Condor* **43**: 103–107.
Fielden, H. W.   1909a.   Some Sussex Ravens.   *Brit. Birds* **2**: 279–280.
——— 1909b.   Ravens as scavengers.   *Brit. Birds* **3**: 57–58.

FRANZ, J. 1943. Uber Ernahrung und Tagesrhythmus einiger Vögel im arktischen Winter. *J. Orn.* **91**: 156.

GOTHE, J. 1963. Zur Droh- und Beschwichtigungsgebärde des Kolkraben (*Corvus corax* L.). *Z. Tierpsychol.* **19**: 687–691.

GWINNER, E. 1964. Untersuchungen über das Ausdrucks und Sozialverhalten des Kolkraben (*Corvus corax corax* L.). *Z. Tierpsychol.* **21**: 657–748.

—— 1965a Beobachtungen über Nestbau und Brutpflege des Kolkraben (*Corvus corax*) in Gefangenschaft. *J. Orn.* **106**: 145–178.

—— 1965b. Über den Einfluss des Hungers und anderer Faktoren auf die Versteck-Aktivität des Kolkraben (*Corvus corax*). *Vogelwarte* **23**: 1–4.

—— 1966. Der zeitliche Ablauf des Handschwingen-mauser des Kolkraben und seine funktionelle Bedeutung. *Vogelwelt* **87**: 129–133.

GWINNER, E. & KNEUTGEN, J. 1962. Uber die biologische Bedeutung der 'zweckdienlichen' Anwendung erlernter Laute bei Vögeln. *Z. Tierpsychol.* **19**: 692–696.

HAURI, R. 1955. Beiträge zur Biologie des Kolkraben (*Corvus corax*). *Orn. Beobachter* **53**: 28–35.

HOLYOAK, D. 1967. Breeding biology of the Corvidae. *Bird Study* **14**: 153–168.

—— 1968. A comparative study of the food of some British Corvidae. *Bird Study* **15**: 147–153.

—— & RATCHIFFE, D. A. 1968. The distribution of the Raven in Britain and Ireland. *Bird Study* **15**: 191–197.

HURRELL, H. G. 1956. A Raven roost in Devon. *Brit. Birds* **49**: 28–31.

HUTSON, H. P. W. 1945. Roosting procedure of *Corvus corax laurencei* Hume. *Ibis* **87**: 455–459.

JONES, F. M. 1935. Nesting of the Raven in Virginia. *Wilson Bull.* **47**: 188–191.

KRAMER, G. 1932. Beobachtungen und Fragen zur Biologie des Kolkraben (*Corvus corax* L.). *J. Orn,* **80**: 329–342.

LORENZ, K. 1931. Beiträgen zur Ethologie sozialer Corviden. *J. Orn.* **79**: 67–127.

—— 1940. Die Paarbildung beim Kolkraben. *Z. Tierpsychol.* **3**: 278–292.

MYLNE, C. K. 1961. Large flocks of Ravens at food. *Brit. Birds* **54**: 206–207.

NELSON, A. L. 1934. Some early summer food preferences of the American Raven in south-eastern Oregon. *Condor* **36**: 10–15.

RYVES, B. H. 1948. *Bird Life in Cornwall*. London.

SALOMONSEN, F. 1950. *The Birds of Greenland*. Copenhagen.

SCHÄFER, E. 1938. Ornithologische Ergebnisse zweier Forschungsreisen nach Tibet. *J. Orn.* **86** Sonderheft: 260–261.

VAURIE, C. 1959. *The Birds of the Palearctic Fauna: Passeriformes:* 174–177. London.

WHISTLER, H. Manuscripts and notes in library of the Sub-dept. of Ornithology, British Museum (Nat. Hist.).

WITHERBY, H. F. *et al.* 1938. *The Handbook of British Birds*, vol. 1. London.

FAN-TAILED RAVEN *Corvus rhipidurus*

Corvus rhipidurus Hartert 1918, Bull. B.O.C., 39, 21, new name for *Corvus affinis* Rüppell.

Description About size of Hooded Crow but with proportionately thicker bill, rather smaller body, much larger wings with very long secondaries, and much shorter and more rounded tail. Nasal bristles forming a fan-shaped patch at base of culmen and covering nostrils. Throat hackles shorter than in most 'ravens' and mostly bifurcated. Shining slightly bluish or purplish black, sometimes with a faint coppery brown tinge on head and throat; in worn plumage the brownish tinge on these parts becomes more pronounced and other parts of the plumage may fade to brownish black, but this species is seldom or never so brownish as Brown-necked Raven in comparable plumage. Bases of feathers on upper part of hind neck white, those on lower part of hind neck and elsewhere are grey at base. Irides dark brown. Bill, feet and legs black. Juvenile duller black.

Field identification In flight the large broad wings and very short tail give a batlike silhouette which, together with the all-black plumage, is diagnostic.

Distribution and habitat The Middle East and north Africa: in Syria, Palestine, Jordan, Arabia (the eastern coast probably excepted), Sinai, Egypt, Ethiopia and Somaliland, south to the Sudan and Kenya; also in the Air Massif in the Southern Sahara. In desert or other open country with cliffs or crags, from which it may travel some distance in search of food. Often at high altitudes.

Feeding and general habits Feeds on the ground. Known to take insects and other invertebrates, grain pecked from animal droppings, carrion, and scraps of bread, meat and other human foodstuffs. Also takes ectoparasites from camels (Mountfort). Has very little fear of man where not molested and habitually scavenges around camp sites, garbage heaps and similar places. Meinertzhagen observed it refusing meat but taking bread and fruit; this was probably a preference due to the local conditions and consequent needs of the individual birds concerned, as the species is known to take meat readily at times.

Often in parties, sometimes in pairs. Fond of soaring and playing in thermals, perhaps even to greater extent than other ravens. Sometimes associates, and roosts in palm trees, with *Corvus ruficollis* (Bates).

Nesting Nests in holes and recesses and on sheltered ledges on cliffs and crags. In Somaliland tree nests have been found (Archer & Godman) but only exceptionally. Nest of sticks, woody stems and twigs with lining of wool, hair, bits of cloth or other soft materials. Said sometimes to nest colonially, but this may be erroneous as Professor Mendelssohn of Tel-Aviv University has found nesting pairs to hold extensive territories.

Eggs 2 to 4, greenish blue splashed, streaked and speckled with light and dark olive brown and with underlying lilac or grey markings. Nests with eggs have been found in early and late April in Palestine; and in Somaliland from mid-April to early June, but most nests have fresh eggs in early May (Archer & Godman). Sometimes parasitized by the Great Spotted Cuckoo, *Clamator glandarius*.

Voice I know of no detailed study. The various and sometimes conflicting descriptions indicate that this species has a great variety of calls, among which a high-pitched call would appear to be common. 'Raucous cries and guttural croaks' (Archer & Godman) have also been described. Recorded calls I have heard (North) were a high, falsetto croaking very like that of *C. albicollis* but perhaps even higher-pitched, and from singing individuals a medley of such high-pitched croaks, varied with soft clucks, high-pitched squeals, and odd trills suggestive of the calls of some frogs.

Display and social behaviour No information.

REFERENCES

ARCHER, G. & GODMAN, E. M. 1961. *The Birds of British Somaliland and the Gulf of Aden* 4: 1391–1395.
BATES, G. L. 1936. On the birds of Jidda and Central Arabia. *Ibis* 6, 13th ser., v. 541.
CHEESMAN, R. E. 1936. On a collection of birds from North-western Abyssinia. *Ibis* (13) 6: 163–197.
JOURDAIN, F. C. R. & LYNES, H. 1936. Notes on Egyptian birds. *Ibis* (13) 6: 39–47.
MEINERTZHAGEN, R. M. 1954. *Birds of Arabia* 75–76 and 590–591. London.
MOUNTFORT, G. 1965. *Portrait of a Desert.* London.
NORTH, M. E. W. 1938. *Voices of African Birds.* New York.
SMITH, K. D. 1957. An annotated check-list of the birds of Eritrea. *Ibis* 99: 326.

WHITE-NECKED RAVEN   *Corvus albicollis*

Corvus albicollis Latham, 1790, *Index Orn.*, **1**: 151.

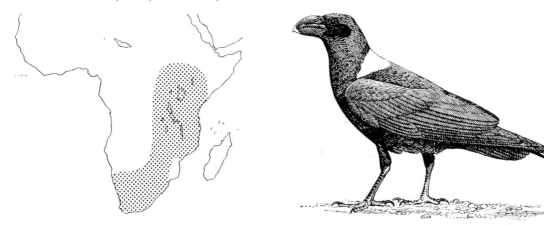

Description   About size of Raven or very slightly smaller (than nominate form of Raven) but with proportionately much shorter and much less graduated tail and much deeper bill with high, strongly-arched
culmen and deep nasal groove.   Feathering immediately around base of bill and eyes, and rictal bristles,
blackish.   Rest of head, upper part of hind neck, sides of neck, throat and breast blackish brown with
a faint purplish gloss, fading to dark vandyke brown; the somewhat elongated feathers of the throat and
upper breast are strongly bifurcated.   Some or most of the feathers bordering the brownish areas of the
neck and breast may be fringed with white to form a delicately laced and individually-varying pattern on
the living bird.   Feathers that are wholly or largely white may occur in this area.   A large and conspicuous
white patch on hind neck.   Rest of plumage deep black with only a slight silvery or greenish iridescence
in some lights, fading to dull and slightly brownish black in worn plumage.
   Irides dark brown.   Bill black with white or yellowish white tip.   Legs and feet black.   Juvenile
duller, with very woolly-textured contour feathers on underparts, and often with many white or partly
white feathers forming a band across lower breast.

Field identification   Shape of bill, if seen in profile, at once identifies it from all sympatric species.   Otherwise combination of white on hind-neck and dark lower breast equally diagnostic.

Distribution and habitat   Eastern and southern Africa from Uganda and Kenya south to Namaqualand
and Cape Colony.   Primarily a bird of open mountainous country, including openings in mountain forest.
Over much of its range a common bird about towns, villages and camp sites in many types of country,
even in some places, such as Usumbura, at quite low elevations.   It is, however, usually based on mountains or cliffs for breeding and roosting.

Feeding and general habits   Seeks food mostly on the ground but sometimes in trees where it will take
insects from among the leaves (Brooke).   Has been recorded eating locusts, grasshoppers, grubs and
other insects, tortoises and lizards, small mammals, carrion, young birds, eggs, maize, peanuts and
fruit.   Readily takes many kinds of human food when available.   Where not persecuted has little fear
of man and scavenges around huts and houses, in courtyards and so on.   Visits highways to feed on
creatures killed by motorists.
   Food objects requiring tearing or breaking up are held under one or (less often) both feet.   Four
captive birds, to whom I often gave peanuts, always bit and tore at the shells but did not hammer them.
A wild bird was seen to drop a tortoise onto rocky ground (Uys) and there is circumstantial evidence that
this is regularly done.   Dunking of sticky food by captive birds has been observed.
   Usually in pairs but large numbers may associate, especially at suitable feeding places.   It is probable
that breeding pairs are territorial but further observations are needed.   Kunkel (*in litt.*) informs me that

in the towns and villages where he has watched it 'It does not form flocks but (shows) no tendency to establish territory or keep a distance from conspecifics, in a dirty courtyard you can find six to eight of them'.

Glides, soars and performs various aerobatics similar to those of Raven. Also very like Raven in other movements and postures.

Nesting Nest of sticks, lined with softer materials, on a ledge or in a recess of a cliff, exceptionally in a tree. Eggs 3 to 5, bluish green, pale green or greenish white, speckled and/or spotted, mottled and streaked with dark brown and olive brown and usually with greyish, mauve or brownish mauve underlying markings. Very similar to although slightly larger than common forms of eggs of *C. corax*.

Breeding has been recorded from August to November in South Africa, September to November in Malawi, October in Tanzania, October to December in Kenya, and February in Ruwenzori, but further information on breeding biology much needed.

Voice Most, perhaps all, calls of this species are similar to and probably homologous with calls of *C. corax* but differ in having an odd, high-pitched and yet husky and whispering tone. They suggest a Raven that has 'lost its voice'.

The usual call is a croak, very variable but very similar to the croaking of *C. corax* except for the high, whispering tone. Another common call is a hoarse, throaty whisper 'hurch' or 'haa'.

The begging call I wrote as 'aaa, aaa'. It is essentially similar in character to the begging notes of many other *Corvus* species and rather longer-drawn than the begging calls of juvenile *corax* but with the same husky 'lost voice' tone as other calls of *albicollis*; at high intensity it may have a frantic-sounding screaming character.

The alarm call is a high, falsetto, screaming 'kroorh' or 'kroorch'.

A rattling 'kl kl kl kl . . .', given with lowered head (Holyoak, *in litt.*), is probably homologous with similar mechanical-sounding calls of other species.

The above is based on observations of four captive individuals, believed to be two males and two females, at London Zoo. The briefer descriptions in various standard works do not appear to refer to calls other than those here described.

It should, perhaps, be added that *C. corax* can croak in exactly the same husky, falsetto tone as *C. albicollis* but does so relatively seldom.

Display and social behaviour When giving the rattling call a captive bird erected its neck and body feathers, partly spread its tail and lowered its head.

Allo-preening common between paired individuals. Dr J. Nicolai (*in litt.*) noted that the white neck patch was a particularly favoured place for allo-preening but the London Zoo birds seem just as often to preen the black parts of each other's heads and are perhaps particularly liable to pay attention to the throat of the partner. Very commonly the throat feathers (and others) are lifted up with the 'flat' of the bill and the preener then peers intently at the exposed feather roots. At other times one bird will make gentle lunges into partner's feathers with closed or only very slightly-opened bill and make swallowing movements though I have not been able to see if any objects such as ectoparasites or scurf are actually eaten.

Feeding of presumed female by presumed male seen in captive pairs.

Other names Cape Raven, African Raven.

REFERENCES

BROOKE, R. K. 1965. Ornithological notes on the Furancungo district of Mozambique. *Arnoldia* No. 10: 2: 10.
MACKWORTH-PRAED, C. W. & GRANT, C. H. B. 1960. *African Handbook of Birds*, ser. 1, vol. 2: 676. London.
MCLACHLAN, G. R. & LIVERSIDGE, R. 1957. *Roberts Birds of South Africa*. Cape Town.
SCLATER, W. L. & MOREAU, R. E. 1933. Taxonomic and field notes on some birds of north-eastern Tanganyika
UYS, C. J. 1966. At the nest of the Cape Raven. *Bokmakierie* **18**: 38–41.
    Territory. *Ibis* (13) **3**: 205–206.

THICK-BILLED RAVEN   *Corvus crassirostris*

Corvus crassirostris Rüppell, 1836, Neue Wirbelthiere . . . Abyssinien, Vög., p. 19, pl. 8, 1835.

Description Like previous species, *albicollis*, but averaging slightly larger, with proportionately much longer and more graduated tail, and much larger bill with very deep nasal grooves and the broad, flattened ridge of the culmen not at all covered by the nasal bristles. Feathering of head, back and sides of neck and, to a lesser extent, of throat and foreneck very short, some throat feathers bifurcated but not to the extent of those of *albicollis*. Throat, upper breast and sides of neck blackish brown to dark vandyke brown with an oily-looking but not colourful gloss. Rest of plumage black to glossy black, fading to dark drab in worn plumage, except for a large white patch on the nape that extends medially onto hind neck.

Irides dark brown. Bill black with white or creamy tip. Legs and feet black. Juvenile like adult but duller and with usual difference in feather texture.

Field identification The very large, deep, arched bill and consequent profile at once distinguish it from all other crows, and the white nape from other sympatric crows. Does not occur within range of *C. albicollis* but should it do so the much longer and wedge-shaped tail would identify it.

Distribution and habitat Eritrea and Ethiopia, has occurred in Somaliland and the Sudan.

In mountains and on high plateaux, usually at elevations of about 1500 to about 2400 metres.

Feeding and general habits Seen to take grubs, probably beetle larvae, from cattle dung, carrion, scraps of meat, offal, and other human foods. When seeking food in dung uses its bill to scatter it with a neat scything movement (Brown). Has been seen taking the ears of standing wheat (Cheesman). Regularly comes to seek scraps if a sheep or other animal is slaughtered within sight of it. A captive bird regularly dunked its meat in water and hid surplus food (Stewart).

Usually in pairs but sometimes in large or small parties. Such flocks probably consist either of landless non-breeding individuals or of birds gathering at a likely feeding ground or roosting place.

Nesting Nests in trees and on cliffs. I can find no description of the nest and eggs; they are probably very like those of *C. albicollis*. Nests with well-feathered young have been found in north-western Ethiopia in mid-February and late March (Cheesman).

Voice Cheesman describes a harsh nasal croak, and Brown 'a low, wheezy croak "phlurk-phlurk", a most obscene sound'.

Display and social behaviour Cheesman says that territorial fighting and magnificent aerial displays take place but does not describe either in detail. Feeding of one member of a pair by the other seen (Schüz).

Other names Great-billed Raven, Abyssinian Raven.

REFERENCES

BROWN, L. 1965. *Ethiopian Episode*. London.

CHEESMAN, R. E. 1936. On a collection of birds from north-western Abyssinia. *Ibis* ser., 163–197. (13) **6**: 163–197.

MACKWORTH-PRAED, C. W. & GRANT, C. H. B. 1960. *African Handbook of Birds*, ser. 1, vol. 2: 677.

SCHÜZ, E. 1967. Ornithologischer April-Besuch in Äthiopen, besonders am Tanasee. *Stuttgarter Beiträge zur Naturkunde*. Nv. 171.

SMITH, K. D. 1957. An annotated check-list of the birds of Eritrea. *Ibis* **99**: 326.

STEWART, T. 1913. The Great-billed Raven in captivity. *Avicult. Mag.* (3) **4**: 137–139.

VAURIE, C. 1962. *'Peters' Check-list of Birds of the World*, vol. 15: 282.

The choughs

The choughs, genus *Pyrrhocorax*, have black plumage with red, orange or yellow bills and legs. Their bills are more slender than those of *Corvus* species of comparable size. One species has the bill curved, the other has a slightly curving culmen only. Their nostrils are closely covered with dense, stiffened nasal plumes. Their tarsi are 'booted' (covered with an unbroken lamina in front and behind) in the adults but in young birds they are more or less divided into scutes. They have long large wings and are strong flyers.

Amadon says that *Pyrrhocorax* is 'intermediate between *Nucifraga* and *Corvus* in some respects' but does not describe connecting features. Except in size, and in characters that both share with other corvids, I cannot see any suggestion of close relationship in either appearance or behaviour between nutcrackers and choughs. I have, however, not seen Clark's Nutcracker alive, only the European species. I concur with Amadon in thinking *Pyrrhocorax* to be probably an offshoot from '*proto-Corvus*' stock. Both in appearance and in many aspects of behaviour the choughs seem nearest to *Corvus*, especially to the jackdaws, subgenus *Coloeus*. Although very distinct, the Alpine Chough, *P. graculus*, at least in its bill shape, serves to link the *Corvus* species with the more highly divergent Chough. However, as has been said when discussing *Corvus*, there is a possibility that the resemblances between choughs and typical crows are convergent.

The Alpine Chough is a montane bird almost throughout its range, the Chough occurs also on and about coastal cliffs. Although the two species may breed and feed at the same altitude the Alpine Chough is, on the whole, a bird of higher elevations. It is possible that where both habitually occur together, as in parts of Europe, this may be due to alterations of the environment brought about by man.

The Alpine Chough, since it evolved into its present form, has almost certainly always been a high mountain species. With its relatively slight bulk, large long wings, and small slender bill it shows the same kinds of structural differences from typical lowland species of *Corvus* as do, to a greater or lesser degree, some other montane forms such as the Grandala, *Grandala coelicolor*, and the Wall Creeper, *Tichodroma muraria*, in comparison to their lowland relatives. Its present distribution suggests that the Chough also evolved in inland montane areas and subsequently spread, at least in the western parts of its range, to some coastal cliffs, rather than that it originated as a coastal species and then extended to inland mountains. Both choughs seem to require rocky walls with caves, holes or fissures, and open ground (whether stony or pasture) that is not covered with rank or high vegetations and is not snow-covered in winter. This latter requirement may be obtained by daily flights or local migration to lower elevations, or may be provided by snow-free slopes and rock faces at high elevations.

The Chough has decreased in or entirely vanished from much of its former range in the British Isles and other parts of Europe. In Cornwall, where as late as the 1940s its position was thought secure by an observer long familiar with it (Ryves), it is now (1971) extinct. The marginal increase in its numbers that has been 'suspected' in Ireland and Wales (Rolfe) may, unfortunately, merely reflect increased interest in the bird by local and visiting birdwatchers.

Competition with the Jackdaw in coastal regions and with the Alpine Chough in the Alps has been suggested as a possible factor in its decline. That there could be competition with the Jackdaw has been strongly denied by many ornithologists (e.g. Ryves) on the grounds that the Chough and the Jackdaw do not normally feed or nest in the same situations. This may be largely true in Britain, although the Jackdaw in many places certainly does seek food in types of terrain which in Cornwall were, according to Ryves, virtually the Chough's prerogative. There is, however, some evidence to suggest that where the Jackdaw and the Rook either do not occur or are restricted in numbers and distribution the Chough may be able to exploit a wider range of feeding places than it can where they are abundant (Cullen, Schäfer). I have only watched Choughs feeding in the Isle of Man, in September. Here, at this period, both feeding methods and prey taken differed from the Jackdaw's although there was some overlap of feeding areas.

In view of its very different and specialized Hoopoe-like bill it is unlikely that, before man came on the scene, there can have been any significant competition for food with the Jackdaw or, for that matter, with any other corvid. It is possible, however, that where man's activities have resulted in either a distributional or numerical increase (or both) of the Jackdaw there may be some competition between it and the Chough. The same may possibly apply to the two choughs in the Alps. Here the Alpine Chough has shown some local increase in numbers and this is almost certainly due to its not now being entirely dependent on natural food sources but feeding largely in winter on food supplied by man.

Although it is thus just possible that some competition may exist or have existed between the Chough and other corvids, I doubt if it is or has been a major factor in the former's decline. Rolfe has shown that the period of cold winters from 1820 to 1880 coincided with the Chough's disappearance from or decrease in many parts of Britain. Although the species endures colder winters elsewhere its range in Britain is, and was, in areas that tend to have relatively mild winters. It seems likely also that the Chough is more sensitive to and suffers relatively more from human predation than the commoner corvids. In the last century it was a popular candidate for the ornamental case of stuffed birds. Up to the present day some gamekeepers and farmers readily shoot any crow or crow-like bird that gives them opportunity and the Chough is often less distrustful of man than other species and so falls an easier victim. At least up to the early 1940's rare birds were being keenly collected both privately and for sale (Harrison). It is often assumed that an unusual bird would only be shot for gain, to protect game, or by scientific collectors. This is not the case. As most aviculturists who have lost brightly coloured birds know, some people shoot any strange bird they see out of mere curiosity. As the Chough has become rarer it is probable that relatively more have been shot as more shooters would be unfamiliar with the species. When rabbits were abundant and the gin trap was the usual means of catching them for market, gins set on and about cliff tops caught some Choughs and many more than was generally assumed may have been destroyed in this way.

Such predation would have little or no effect on the numbers of a thriving species but might well constitute an extra and irreparable drain on a less successful one. There is some evidence to suggest that disease may have been a factor in the Chough's decline in some areas (Rolfe; Ryves).

In much of Tibet the Chough is, or at any rate was (Schäfer), more abundant and widespread than the Alpine Chough. The Chough is, so far as known, very sedentary and shows, even for a sedentary species, a surprising apparent lack of inclination to colonize new areas, although it obviously must have done so during its evolutionary past. In Britain its low or declining numbers might well account for its failure to spread. This can, however, hardly be the case in the Canaries where the Chough is extremely abundant on Palma but completely absent from the other islands, some of whose cliffs are clearly visible only 40 km away (Bannerman).

The name Chough was formerly used for the Jackdaw, notably by Chaucer and Shakespeare. Failure to realize this leads some people to suppose the Chough was formerly more widespread in Britain than, in all probability it ever was.

The Alpine Chough appears to be a more thriving species in the western parts of its range and may possibly be elsewhere. In places where it seems less abundant than the Chough this may be due to its keeping more to higher elevations. In parts of the western Himalayas it scavenges about camp sites for food and follows climbers high into the mountains. In the Alps its partial dependence on man may be one of the factors in its present success. Although some hotel owners object to its presence, notably its habit of visiting the windows of hotels for handouts, their guests are often more benevolent.   It is usually tolerated or actively befriended by man in contrast to the behaviour often shown by him towards typical crows.

REFERENCES

AMADON, D.   1944.   The genera of Corvidae and their relationships.   *Amer. Mus. Novit.* No. 1251.
BANNERMAN, D. A.   1953.   *The Birds of the British Isles*, vol. 1.   London.
CULLEN, J. M. *et al.*   1952.   Birds on Palma and Gomera (Canary Islands).   *Ibis* **94**: 73–74.
HARRISON, J. M.   1968.   *Bristow and the Hastings Rarities Affair.*   St Leonards-on-Sea.
ROLFE, R.   1966.   The status of the Chough in the British Isles.   *Bird Study* **13**: 221–236.
RYVES, B. H.   1948.   *Bird Life in Cornwall.*   London.
SCHÄFER, E.   1938.   Ornithologische Ergebnisse zweir Forschungsreisen nach Tibet.   *J. Orn.* **86** Sonderheft: 265–270.

CHOUGH   *Pyrrhocorax pyrrhocorax*

Upupa pyrrhocorax Linnaeus, 1758, *Syst. Nat.*, ed. 10, 1, p. 118.

Description   From slightly smaller than to slightly larger than House Crow but differently shaped (see sketch) with proportionately longer wings, rather shorter tail and characteristic long curved bill.   General plumage deep glossy black, the body plumage having, although shiny, a somewhat velvety quality and usually a bluish or purplish gloss, the gloss on wings and tail is predominantly greenish or bluish.

Irides brown or dark brown.   Bill usually bright orange-red to crimson red, sometimes dark crimson or pink.   Legs orange-red to purplish red, usually bright red; the feet sometimes a little deeper red than the legs, claws black.   Female averaging a little smaller than male and usually with noticeably smaller bill, especially in the rather long-billed North African and Himalayan populations.

Juvenile a little duller.   Bill (of fledglings and recently-fledged juveniles) purplish-brown to blackish, whitish to salmon pink at tip and along cutting edges, with yellowish white to pale orange-yellow gape flanges.   Bills of older juveniles are at first orange rather than red.   Legs purplish brown to black with the scutes visible and the interstices between them salmon-pink to orange pink, as are the soles.

Six and seven day old nestlings were pinkish flesh, blackish (growing feathers showing?) on down tracts, with greyish brown down on head, back, wings and upper part of legs.   Bill mauve, whitish at tip and cutting edges.   Gape flanges pale yellow.   Inside mouth orange pink with white spurs on palate and tongue bases yellowish.   Legs and feet flesh pink (Williamson, 1939).

Many geographical races of the Chough have been described.   They differ chiefly in size, the British population being smallest and the Himalayan populations the largest, and to a lesser extent in bill length, wing and tail proportions and intensity and tone of plumage gloss.   These racial differences have been described by Vaurie.   The description given above is composite and covers all forms of the species.

Field characters   Combination of long curved red bill and black plumage distinguish it from all other species.   Recently-fledged juveniles have shorter bills and might possibly, when not in company with their parents (which they usually are), be confused with Alpine Choughs.   Usual flight silhouette is very different from Alpine Chough's due to shorter tail.   When flying high in air might be mistaken for a Rook (if profile of head and bill not visible) but usually shows more widely and conspicuously separated primary tips and has a rather shorter and less rounded tail.   Most of its calls are sufficiently distinctive to attract the attention of any interested person not familiar with them.

Distribution and habitat   Ireland, Wales, Isle of Man, Islay and possibly still some other parts of western Scotland, Alps, Pyrenees, Iberian Peninsula, Canaries (on Palma only), Brittany, Abruzzi mountains in Italy, Sicily, Sardinia, Crete, Asia Minor, Caucasus and the Near East eastward through the Iranian region to Russian Turkestan, Sinkiang, and the Himalayas; China and Manchuria to northern Mongolia, and southern Siberia to western Altai.   Also in north-west Africa (Morocco to Algeria) and Ethiopia (Semien Mountains and the Araenna mountains of the Bale Province).

Local and patchy in distribution throughout much of its range.   Within the past hundred years it has considerably declined throughout many of the European parts of its range.   Until relatively recently it bred in south-western England and the Channel Islands but now (1971) no longer does so.   Rolfe has discussed in detail its status in Britain.   Possibly there has been a comparable decline elsewhere.   Koslova found it common in Ulan Bator, Mongolia, in the 1930's whereas in 1960 Grummt did not even see it there.

Inhabits mountainous regions with rocky walls, hills with crags or quarries, rocky river valleys, and rocky sea cliffs; also fields and pasture lands adjacent to such areas for feeding purposes.   Locally may breed in buildings or isolated rocks or eminences in otherwise open steppe (Schäfer).   Frequents human habitations and breeds in and about houses in some eastern parts of its range and, exceptionally, elsewhere. On Palma, in the Canaries, a characteristic bird of the cultivated fields although found also in other and wilder habitats (Cullen *et al.*).   Inland in Europe usually from about 900 to 1800 metres but in eastern Tibet and Nepal it is (*fide* Diesselhorst) absent from apparently suitable areas below 3600 metres.

Feeding and general habits   Feeds largely on insects; including beetles and their larvae, caterpillars, larvae of flies, especially of crane flies, ants and/or their grubs and pupae (Cowdy, pers obs.), crickets and other orthoptera.   Has also been recorded taking spiders, worms, molluscs and crustaceans.   Weed seeds and grain are sometimes eaten and in north-eastern Tibet (and possibly elsewhere) are the main winter food (Schäfer).   Locally may scavenge for scraps of human food but seldom, to any appreciable extent, where the Jackdaw or Alpine Chough are established in their common role of part-scavengers. Takes oranges and figs on Palma (Cullen *et al.*).

Feeds on the ground, very seldom, if ever, in trees except in the Canary Islands (Palma).   Typical feeding places are areas of short grass or bare earth above or on the slopes of coastal or inland cliffs, stony ledges and slopes, pasture lands, and cultivated fields.   Coastal populations sometimes feed along the shoreline, especially in winter.   Usually feeds in open areas but a pair that were feeding young, on the second day after an unseasonable snowfall, sought food inside a wood where the ground was free of snow (Schifferli & Lang).

Habitually probes, digs, and turns over stones, mammal droppings and other objects when seeking food, as well as picking from the surface.   The bill movements of Choughs that I watched taking leatherjackets on the Isle of Man struck me as very similar to those of the Hoopoe, *Upupa epops*.   There was a repeated quick pecking (shallow probing?) of the substrate, then the bird would suddenly thrust its bill in deeply, often jump half round, thrust again (sometimes first tearing up a little earth or grass but more often not) more deeply with some apparent levering and withdraw its bill with a crane fly larva held in it.   Schäfer describes the Chough's method of turning stones by thrusting the bill between the stone and its substrate, the former being then pulled or pushed towards the bird's body or tipped sideways.   On a narrow ledge (Schäfer, pers. obs.) the bill is usually inserted on the 'inside' and the displaced earth or stone then falls freely.   Captive Choughs hide food in typical manner (Castle-Sloane; Turner); probably wild ones do also if a surplus is available.

Not very wary even in Britain, and where it constantly sees people who do it no harm, as is (or was) the case in Tibet, it has little fear of men and will follow close at the ploughman's heels and nest readily in inhabited buildings.

Usually walks on the ground with steps that appear rather shorter than those of Rook or Carrion Crow and gait like but a little less brisk than Jackdaw's. Runs and hops at times. Flight often leisurely in appearance with alternate flapping and gliding; when flying some distance the flapping is more continuous and flight appears very Rook-like. Often uses a spectacular flight in which it bounds through the air in a series of dives and inverted arcs. I saw this from presumed males, and less markedly from presumed females, of pairs in or near their breeding areas and think that it is a form of display flight. Gliding, soaring and swooping aerobatics are common. Perches chiefly on rocks, cliffs, walls and buildings but in some areas regularly in trees (Holyoak; Cullen et al.).

Commonly in pairs or family parties. Often in flocks where numerous but, as with other corvids, the pair appears to be the basic unit. Members of a flock seldom show close cohesion. Does not nest colonially but where it is numerous, or suitable nest sites are few and concentrated, several pairs may breed close together. Elsewhere, as in Wales and the Isle of Man, nesting pairs are territorial and nest sites wide apart. May breed among Jackdaws or Alpine Choughs. Breeding pairs, and the male while the female is sitting, may feed in company with others when away from nest area.

Largely sedentary but may winter at lower elevations than the breeding areas. Roosts communally outside the breeding season (and sometimes during breeding season also) in caves, on sheltered ledges, in rock fissures, or equivalent sites on buildings. Individual pairs may, however, roost by themselves even in winter. Anting once recorded (Holyoak).

Nesting Nests on ledges in caves or under overhangs of rock, and in recesses, holes and crevices in cliffs, rock faces and quarry sides, and in equivalent places in buildings. Sometimes the nest is in some very deep, gloomy and inaccessible situation but it may be easily reachable. The same nest site is frequently used year after year, sometimes for long beyond the possible life-time of any pair of birds.

Nest of small sticks, twigs, woody plant stems etc., with a thick inner cup of wool, hair, dead grass, fibrous roots or similar materials. A pair in the Alps included felt from an old carpet and coconut fibre in the lining. Both sexes build, the female sometimes, perhaps usually, doing more work on the interior lining than the male. The same site may be used repeatedly year after year, the old nest being repaired or a new one built on its remains.

Eggs usually 3 to 5, most commonly 4, exceptionally 2, 6 or 7. Cream, buff, pinkish buff, very pale greenish grey, very pale green or off-white, speckled, spotted and (sometimes) blotched with dark brown, yellowish or reddish brown and with underlying grey or (in eggs with pinkish ground colour) lilac markings. Eggs of a pair that were closely observed were laid at regular 30 hour intervals (Schifferli & Lang). Eggs appear usually to be laid in April or May throughout most of the birds' range, mainly from about the second week of April to mid-May, but from early April in southern Europe. Eggs found in June and July probably represent late or repeat clutches, not true second broods.

Incubation by female only, fed by male. Male brings food in gullet and may call the female off the nest and feed her outside or go to the nest site. The former seems more frequent but it is possible that at times fear of the watcher or hide may make the male less ready to bring food to the nest than he might otherwise have been. Female may also leave nest on her own iniative, especially in early stages and for as long as 50 minutes (Schifferli & Lang). The female spends much time on the nest from laying of the first egg, observers differ as to when true incubation starts, whether with first (Witherby et al.), second (Schifferli & Lang) or last (Ryves) egg. Possibly there are individual differences. Incubation period usually stated to be 17–18 days, but Schifferli & Lang recorded 21 days. Eggshells are carried out by the female, not (ever?) eaten, although she eats any remnants of membrane adhering to chicks or to the inside of the shell (Schifferli & Lang).

Both parents feed the young and remove faeces but only the female broods, cleans and preens them (Schifferli & Lang). Ryves, however, records allo-preening of fledged young by both parents. At the nest watched closely by Schifferli & Lang the male first fed the young (as distinct from feeding the female and leaving her to feed the nestlings) on the second day and was not feeding them as often as the female until the 11th day. For the first three days the female ate some faeces of the nestlings and removed others, afterwards she removed them all after having, in some cases, first placed them on the nest rim until she was ready to leave the nest. For the first three days she fed the young by inserting her bill into their throats with a single movement but thereafter food was disgorged into their throats with a repeated shaking movement while the bill was still deeply inserted, although at this time some young were still only newly-hatched. Any food morsels spilled were eaten again and once more regurgitated. All food given to the nestlings was thus mixed with saliva.

The young beg most intensively in response to the food call of the adult or an imitation of it, both in their early stages and later, when also responding to visual stimuli. They fledge at 36 to 41 days, but keep in or near cover of cliffs, overhangs, caves etc. for some days after leaving nest. Fledglings watched by Cowdy began tentatively to follow their parents 6 days after leaving the nest and by 8 days were accompanying them. Schifferli & Lang give very full details of development of the nestlings they observed.

Voice The most characteristic call is a loud explosive 'keeah!' or 't'cheea!' subject to much variation. It is somewhat like a common call of the Jackdaw but clearer, more explosive and rather higher pitched. It would appear to be used as a contact call, as a self-assertive call (combined with an upward wing flick) and possibly in other contexts. Soft conversational variants have been heard from pairs sitting quietly together.

Witherby et al. describe the alarm call as 'keeaw' changing to a loud harsh 'kwarr' when nest or young are in danger. Holyoak transcribes the (? same) alarm call as 'harsh, scolding "ker ker ker"'. I heard a screaming 'kreeaa' from fighting birds. The mobbing call of three captive Choughs, shown an Eagle Owl's head, was a long loud screech 'chaaaaay', rather like the alarm screech of a Jackdaw but clearer and higher-pitched. When shown a Jackdaw in my hand they showed less fear and uttered a shrill 'tchaik-aik!'

Schifferli & Lang record a Buzzard-like call when soaring; a Jackdaw-like 'dya' or 'dyo'; and several variants of a cry of fear or combined fear and anger whose characteristics are that they are always hard and short. These calls are given by individuals when seized hold of, when diving in attack at Buzzards and Kestrels and when angry. They describe the begging call of the female as a whimpering 'veeaygaygay-gaygay' and the food-offering call, used by both sexes, as 'croa' or 'graa'. I have here anglicized the transliterations of calls given by Schifferli & Lang.

The young utter a peeping cry from before hatching, at first very weak, later louder when food begging and softly after being fed as an apparent note of contentment ('Zufriedenheitsausserungen'). On the 8th and 9th day young watched by Schifferli & Lang were silent, even when begging. On the 10th they began to beg with a noise very like that of young Starlings; later this gradually changed to a begging call like that of the adult female. Holyoak transcribes the begging call of fledged young as a high-pitched 'kee kee kee'.

Witherby et al. describe also a soft 'k'chuf' and a rapid 'kwuk-uk-uk'. Holyoak emphasizes that he, like me, has never heard any call sounding like 'chuf'. He describes what is probably song as a medley of low warbling, chittering and churring notes.

Display and social behaviour In sexual solicitation the female partly opens her wings and quivers her tail (Holyoak). Ryves saw what was probably another form of this quivering display in which the male opened and quivered his wings towards the female after feeding her. He also saw this done at very full intensity with wings widely spread and 'a series of indescribable notes' uttered by a male while his mate was in the act of laying. I saw, but only once, a similar display given by a Chough, immediately before it turned and fled from another that was swooping at it.

Food begging as in other corvids, with fluttering wings and juvenile-like begging call.

Holyoak observed two forms of threat display. In one, body and neck feathers are erected and the bird threatens frontally with open bill. This is often used when displacing another bird at a feeding place. In the other the bird adopts an upright posture with downward-pointing bill and sleeked plumage. This form often leads to serious attack and fighting.

A presumed courtship display in which one Chough hops towards another, stops when about 30 cm from it and bows with upraised tail and upward flirting wings, was seen by Holyoak from birds in feeding flocks.

Schäfer observed very intense display from two presumed males to a presumed female. They had all their body feathers fully erected, wings held slightly opened and drooped, tail erected so that at times it almost touched the back, and head lowered with bill at right angles to the ground. The back feathers were so fully erected as to give a serrated profile. In this posture they tripped rapidly, and in silence, around the female. This display is, perhaps, a more intense version of that seen by Holyoak and has much in common with the precopulatory display of the male Rook.

Allo-preening between paired birds and feeding of the female by the male is usual. Guichard records the alleged pairing together, in the wild, of a Chough and a Jackdaw.

Some observers of Choughs in Britain have considered them relatively peaceful although Holyoak observed attacks on and driving away of trespassers in nesting territory. Schäfer had a very different impression of the species in north-eastern Tibet. Possibly there are more occasions for aggression where the species is abundant. Two birds fiercely fighting on the ground were collected by Schäfer and were both females.

An upward-flirting of the wings is a flight intention movement, the tail usually moves upwards with the wings. It accompanies mobbing and self-assertive calls and other situations when there is some motivation to take wing or leap upward.

Other names Red-billed Chough, Cornish Chough, Red-legged Crow, Fire Crow, Keg, Keeog.

REFERENCES

BANNERMAN, D. A. 1953. *The Birds of the British Isles.* vol. 1. London.
BROWN, L. H. 1967. The occurrence of the Chough *Pyrrhocorax pyrrhocorax* in the Mendebo Araenna Mountains of the Bale Province, Ethiopia. *Ibis* **109**: 275–276.
CASTLE-SLOANE, C. 1905. The Red-billed Chough. *Bird Notes* **4**: 1–4.
COWDY, S. 1962. Post-fledging behaviour of Choughs on Bardsey Island. *Brit. Birds* **55**: 229–233.
—— 1973. Ants as a major food source of the Chough. *Bird Study* **20**: 117–120.
CULLEN, J. M., GUITON, P. E., HORRIDGE, G. A. & PIERSON, J. 1952. Birds on Palma and Gomera (Canary Islands). *Ibis* **94**: 73–74.
DIESSELHORST, G. 1968. Beiträge zur Ökologie der Vögel zentral- und ost- Nepals. in *Khumbu Himal*, **2**: published in Munich.
GUICHARD, G. 1962. Le Crave à bec rouge. *Oiseau* **32**: 1–4.
GRUMMT, W. 1961. Ornithologische Beobachtungen in der Mongolei. *Beitr. Vogelk.* **7**: 349–360.
HOLYOAK, D. 1972. Behaviour and Ecology of the Chough and the Alpine Chough. *Bird Study* **19**: 215–227.
KOSLOVA, E. V. 1933. The birds of south-west Transbaikalia, northern Mongolia and central Gobi. *Ibis* 2, (14) **2**: 64.
ROLFE, R. 1966. The status of the Chough in the British Isles. *Bird Study* **13**: 221–236.
RYVES, B. H. 1948. *Bird life in Cornwall.* London.
SCHÄFER, E. 1938. Ornithologische Ergebnisse zweier Forschungsreisen nach Tibet. *J. Orn. Sonderheft:* 265–268.
SCHIFFERLI, A. & LANG, E. M. 1941. Beitrag zur Naturgeschichte der Alpenkrähe *Pyrrhocorax pyrrhocorax erythorhampus* (Vieillot). *J. Orn.* **88**: 550–575.
TURNER, B. C. 1959. Feeding behaviour of Ravens and Choughs *Brit. Birds* **52**: 129–131.
VAURIE, C. 1954. Systematic Notes on Palearctic Birds No. 4 the Choughs (*Pyrrhocorax*). *Amer. Mus. Novit* No. 1658.
WHISTLER, H. Unpublished notes in the library of the Sub-dept. of Ornithology, British Museum (Nat. Hist.).
WHITTAKER, I. 1947. Notes on Welsh Choughs. *British Birds* **40**: 265–266.
WILLIAMSON, K. 1939. Down plumage of nestling and soft parts of the juvenile Chough. *British Birds* **33**: 78.
—— 1959. Observations on the Chough. *Peregrine* **3**: 8–14.
ZIEGER, R. 1967. Kleine Beobachtungen aus der Mongolei. *Beiträge zur Vogelkunde* **13**: 116–124.

ALPINE CHOUGH   *Pyrrhocorax graculus*

Corvus Graculus Linnaeus, 1766, Syst. Nat., ed. 12, 1, p. 158.

Description About size of Chough but more slender and with longer, somewhat rounded tail and shorter bill. Plumage coal black with a slight greenish gloss on wings and tail. Bill bright yellow, sometimes approaching yellowish orange or golden, and usually with a slight greenish tinge near base of bill. The bills of captive birds in zoos (and probably of wild ones under certain conditions) may fade to nearly white. Feet and legs orange-red, light orange, salmon-orange or yellowish orange; legs of captive birds may fade to pale yellow. From descriptions, it seems the legs may sometimes be deep red. Irides dark brown or dark greyish brown.

Juvenile a duller black, with no highlights at all except on tail and wings. Bill at first a dusky horn tinge. Mouth yellow. Legs and feet olive brown, mottled with dark brown or blackish. In winter and early spring, birds of the previous year, have the legs more or less blackish with some orange or red markings but they become red or orange later in the same spring.

Newly hatched nestlings examined by Voisin (1968) had a little down on head, rump and wings. Their mouths were flesh pink, later yellow.

Alpine Choughs from the Lebanon eastward average a little larger than western European specimens and have been separated as *P. g. digitatus*.

Field characters Very characteristic silhouette when seen from below in flight with (for a corvid) small head pulled well into shoulders, large broad wings and rather long tail, giving a very hawk-like outline. The commonest call, a high-pitched short trilling whistle, is distinctive. Habitually indulges in spectacular aerobatics, perhaps even more so than Jackdaw or Chough.

At close quarters the short, Blackbird-like, yellow bill distinguishes it from all other corvids except young juvenile of Red-billed Chough, whose parents should be in evidence and which has different tail/wing proportions. At a distance in sky, if the observer is behind the bird and its head is not seen, it might be mistaken for a Raven. Bill may look white at a distance.

Distribution and habitat Mountains of Europe and Asia, the Alps and Pyrenees, mountains of Spain, Corsica, possibly the Carpathians, the Abruzzi mountains of Italy, Yugoslavia, Greece, Bulgaria, Crete, Asia Minor, Caucasus, Lebanon, Iran, Transcaspia, Afghanistan, northern Baluchistan, Russian Turkestan to western Altai and western Sayan, and the Himalayas and southern Tibet to eastern Sikang. In north west Africa, in Morocco in the Atlas Mts and possibly elsewhere.

Inhabits the alpine zone of high mountains. In summer usually above the tree line but in winter (and sometimes locally in summer also) descends to valleys, slopes or villages well below the tree line for feeding purposes. In Europe usually breeds from about 1260 to 2880 metres, in Morocco between 2280 and 3900 metres and in the Himalayas from 2880 to 4800 metres. Has been recorded at 8100 metres in the Himalayas, when following mountaineers for scraps. Locally in south-eastern Europe may breed at elevations of only about 600–900 metres or less (Reiser).

Feeding and general habits   Takes insects, including beetles (remains of *Otiorrhynchus morio* and *Corymbites aeneus* found in pellets), some snails and other invertebrates.   Also berries and small fruits especially rose hips, juniper berries, and fruits of *Celtis australis* and *Hippophae rhamnoides*.   May kill small vertebrates, as it will carry off dead mice put out for it (Rothschild, in Allan).   In many places an habitual scavenger about human dwellings, camp sites, picnic places and garbage tips, especially in winter. Thus, in many parts of its range, human foods such as bread, meat, cheese, cooked fruits etc. now form part of its diet.   Sometimes takes cultivated cherries and mulberries (Reiser), fallen apples, pears, and fresh putty (Strahm 1960).   Seeks food on the ground; on alpine pastures, snow-free slopes and ledges, in cracks and crevices among rocks, open mountain tops (where these support some invertebrate life or are used as eating places by wasteful or generous people) and around human dwellings.   Tends to avoid areas that are wooded or surrounded by trees; in one instance this avoidance appeared to be complete (Rothschild, 1957).   The species does, however at times perch in trees (Strahm, 1960; pers. obs.) and perches on or clings to shrubs or bushes when feeding on berries, although Schäfer noted that it tends to be rather awkward when so-doing, alighting on the outer twigs and balancing itself with much wing-flapping.   The belief that it cannot grasp a branch is incorrect although it certainly perches 'flat-footed' more often than, for example, the Jay does.

Hides food in typical manner, covering it carefully.   Observations of this in the wild (e.g. Strahm, 1960) involve bits of human food pushed into crevices of rocks, buildings or tree trunks and then carefully covered.   Two captive birds, that I often watched in a large aviary in London Zoo, showed a definite preference for hiding food either in crevices of a rock wall or in a part of the ground that was stony and overhung by a bridge although they would sometimes hide food in grass or at the base of a shrub.   Probably this choice of rock crevices or stony ground under an overhang would serve in a natural state to increase the chance of food being hidden where it would not be covered by snow.   When putting food in rock crevices they made a rapid two-and-fro movement of the bill when covering, suggestive of some nest-building movements.   They also, while clinging to the face of the wall by the crevice, often collected bits of dirt, old spider webs etc. from the wall by an odd 'scissoring' movement of the bill, which was held almost parallel to and moved over the rock face.   When hiding in the stony area they often used stones about 5 cm in diameter, which they could only lift with difficulty, to cover the food.

Holds large food morsels in or under one foot, possibly both feet may be used at times, as with *Corvus* species, but I have not seen this.   Often the food is held in the foot, which rests on the ground and is thrust somewhat forward so that it is well in front of, not on a level with, the other foot as the bird feeds; a position I have not seen other corvids use.   Several observers have noted that this species appears to show little or no quarrelling over food, even in winter at artificial food supplies.

Walks and runs actively on the ground, ledges and roof tops.   Sometimes, when hurrying, makes a kind of half hopping 'polka step' (Kunkel).   Flight strong, light and bouyant; habitually glides, soars and indulges in spectacular aerobatics.   High-flying Alpine Choughs, when attacked by a bird-of-prey, plunge downwards at great speed (Strahm 1958).   They often do the same in apparent play or as a prelude to alighting.   Members of a flock descending to seek food will often dive down steeply, checking and then dashing about just above the ground before settling.

Where it can obtain food, may winter high in the mountains but usually, and perhaps where not scavenging from man always, it comes down into valleys or onto slopes below the tree line to feed in winter.   An Alpine Chough that accidentally injured itself and died, in mid-winter at 1200 metres, had eaten over 20 snails of a species that lives in rock crevices (Rothschild, *in litt.*).   Flies back up into the mountains to roost even when feeding by day at much lower elevations, in this resembling some other montane species, such as the Snow Pigeon.   The time at which birds feeding at lower levels return to their roosting area varies greatly, from before mid-day until shortly before dusk.   Factors that appear to induce an early return are fine weather, visibility of the roosting place from the feeding grounds, and probably the possibility of obtaining some natural foods near the roost.   Sometimes, perhaps usually, roosts communally in caves, grottos or extensive rock crevices in winter, at lower elevations than the usual breeding sites.

Highly gregarious, commonly in small or large flocks, sometimes in pairs or family parties. The pair seems to be the basic unit within the flock. When travelling to or from winter feeding areas usually does so in large flocks which split up into smaller groups when at or near their destination. Where both species occur may associate with Choughs. Rothschild (1957) observed that about one Swiss village Alpine Choughs and Carrion Crows each showed mutual avoidance of areas used by the other species, the Crows keeping to the vicinity of trees and the Alpine Choughs to open areas, although in summer, when the Choughs no longer visited the place, the Crows foraged everywhere. Further observations on relations between the two species, indeed on relations between their respective genera everywhere, would be of much interest.

Nesting Nests on ledges and in nooks in caves, crevices and 'chimneys' in cliffs and rocks; also, at least in the Alps, quite often in equivalent situations in chalets or other buildings. The nest site is often, perhaps most usually, in semi-darkness, sometimes in complete darkness (Codourey 1968).

A nest found by Codourey (1966) was of sticks and dry roots, becoming finer towards the inside, and lined with fine dry grass. One examined by Voisin (1968) was built of coarse grass, lichens and rather few twigs, lined with a compact cup of fine grasses. Sharpe and Dresser describe the nest as a bulky structure of twigs, grasses and roots, intermixed with lichens and mosses and lined with leaves, hair and fine roots.

Reports of colonial nesting appear to have been based on incorrect assumptions that caves used for communal roosting were also breeding caves. Several pairs may, however, breed in the same general neighbourhood and it is possible that colonial nesting might occur locally if, for example, there were many nest sites available close together and few or none elsewhere.

Eggs 3 to 6, most often 4; warm buff through cream and off-white to light greenish, speckled, spotted and/or blotched with reddish brown, dull brown or greenish brown and with grey or lilac underlying markings. Throughout most of its range eggs appear to be laid from early May to early June but laying early in April occurs (usually?) in southern Russia, and from the condition of birds collected, Whistler thought April laying might occur in the Himalayas, although clutches were collected in May. Nests with eggs have been found in late June and early July, probably these were repeat layings by birds whose first attempts had failed.

Incubation certainly at times by female only; fed at nest by male who may come in company with other birds on his feeding visits (Ferguson-Lees). At a nest watched by Voisin (1968) the male was usually accompanied by a third individual, which did not feed the female and only once went into the building where the nest was. Incubation by both sexes is claimed by Sharpe & Dresser but, if it ever occurs, is probably an exception. Fledged young are sometimes fed by birds other than their parents (*fide* Rothschild 1960).

Voice One of the most common and characteristic calls is a musical, whistling 'trree' or 'sree'; a rather high-pitched sound suggestive of a football whistle. It is given by members of a flock when in flight, by single birds when flying or about to take flight, and by a bird apparently looking for its mate or young. I had the impression, when watching this species in the Austrian alps, that individuals could instantly recognize their own mate or young by voice.

A harder-sounding, less musical version of this call, that I transcribed as 'chrrurr', is given in apparent alarm.

A somewhat squeaking, nagging-sounding 'pee (a),pee(a)', suggestive both of the squeaking of a young pigeon and of the mewing call of the Black-headed Gull, was given by flying young waiting near their parents. These calls were speeded up and increased in emphasis when actually begging the parents for food.

Rothschild (1957) also distinguishes the 'arrival cry' of birds coming to and arriving at their daily feeding grounds, which she describes as 'a series of shrill double notes without any cadence', and the 'departure cries,' uttered when returning to roost or preparing to do so, which 'somewhat resemble the hurried chattering of Jackdaws in flight but louder and more sustained.'

Display and social behaviour Warncke observed nest-site selection in which the male flew to the future nest site, calling loudly as he alighted.   The female repeatedly flew past him without alighting but later the site was used.   He also saw males displaying by making nest-shaping movements with pieces of stem, uttering unceasing calls while so-doing.   This took place at the communal roosting site.

Allo-preening occurs and, at least in captive birds, may not always be confined to members of a pair.

Other names   Yellow-billed Chough, Mountain Chough.

REFERENCES

ALLAN, R. M.   1961.   Fleas collected by Miriam Rothschild in the Bernese Oberland, Switzerland.   *Parasitology* **52**: 169–175.

CODOUREY, J.   1966.   Nid de Chocard dans un chalet.   *Nos Oiseaux* **28**: (**304**): 177.

—— 1968.   Sur la nidification du Chocard à bec jaune dans les Préalpes fribourgeoises.   *Nos Oiseaux* **29 (321)**: 338–341.

FERGUSON-LEES, I. J.   1958.   Chough and Alpine Chough.   *Brit. Birds* **51**: 99–103.

HENDERSON, G. & HUME, A. O.   1873.   *Lahore to Yarkand* 243–244.   London.

KUNKEL, P.   1962.   Zur Verbreitung des Hüpfens und Laufens unter Sperlingsvögeln (Passeres).   *Z. Tierpsychol.* **19**: 417–439.

MURR, F.   1957.   Zur Kulturfolge der Alpendohle *Pyrrhocorax graculus* im Berchtesgadener Gebiet.   *Anz. orn. Ges. Bayern* **4**: 556–558.

PRAZ, J. C.   1967.   Les Chocards à Sion.   *Bull. de la Murithienne, Société valaisanne des Sci. nat.*, face. 84.

REISER, O.   1926.   Zur Fortpflanzungsbiologie der Alpendohle.   *Beitr. z. Fortpflanzungsbiol.* **2**: 81–82.

ROTHSCHILD, M.   1956.   Diurnal movements of the Mountain Chough in the Wengen and Kleine Scheidegg (Bernese Oberland) areas during the months of January, February and March.   *Int. Orn. Congr.* **11**, 1954 (1955): 611–617.

—— 1957.   L'augmentation du nombre des Chocards à bec jaune en hiver, dans la région de Wengen (Oberland bernois), et l'extension de leur terrains de pature.   *Nos Oiseaux* **24 (250)**: 1–6.

—— 1960.   Collecting Fleas in Switzerland.   *Entomologist*, July 1960: 139–140.

SCHÄFER, E.   1938.   Ornithologische Ergebnisse zweier Forschungsreisen nach Tibet.   *J. Orn.*, Sonderheft 269–271.

SHARPE, R. B. & DRESSER, H. E.   1871–1881.   *A History of the Birds of Europe* **4**: 445–448.

STRAHM, L.   1958.   Les déplacements des Chocards à bec jaune hôtes d'hiver de Bulle.   *Nos Oiseaux* **24**: 177–184.

—— 1960.   Observations hivernales de Chocards *Pyrrhocorax graculus* dans la haute vallée de la Sarine.   *Nos Oiseaux* **25**: 265–271.

—— 1963.   Observations hivernales de Chocards *Pyrrhocorax graculus* en Valais: Loeche-les-Bains, Viege et Saas-Fee.   *Nos Oiseaux* **26**: 179–195 and 207–303.

VOISIN, R.   1963.   Une année de transhumance chez les Chocards de Monthey.   *Nos Oiseaux* **27**: 164–171.

—— 1968.   Neuf jours au nid du Chocard à bec jaune *Pyrrhocorax graculus*.   *Nos Oiseaux* **29**: 286–292.

WARNCKE, K.   1968.   Zur Brutbiologie der Alpendohle.   *J. Orn.* **109**: 300–302.

WHISTLER, H.   Unpublished notes and manuscripts in the Bird Room, British Museum (Nat. Hist.), Library.   Library.

The nutcrackers

The nutcrackers are medium to large-medium sized corvids with rather large long bills with the culmen straight or nearly so, and a hard ridge on the inside of the basal third of the lower mandible, which is used, at least in the Eurasian species, to crack seeds.   They have short nasal bristles, and the body plumage is less lax and soft than that of most other corvids.   This difference in plumage texture is especially noticeable if they are compared to the jays of cold temperate regions, which live in similar climates.   Nutcrackers lack any bright plumage other than the rather slight iridescence on the black parts of their wings and tails. They have well-developed sublingual pouches for carrying food (Bock, *et al.*; Jung; Turcek and Kelso; Balda, *in litt.*).

Nutcrackers inhabit coniferous woods in the Holarctic region.   Although to some extent omnivorous, their main foods are the seeds of conifers or hazel nuts.   The Eurasian species shows much geographical variation in size and relative thickness of its bill.   These differences are probably adaptations for dealing most efficiently with the primary food.   Thus those forms which feed principally on the seeds of the Arolla Pine, *Pinus cembra,* have more slender bills than those whose basic food is hazel nuts.   There are, however, some apparent exceptions to this correlation (Turcek & Kelso, 1968). It is likely that the species evolved in symbiosis with *Pinus cembra* and/or allied conifers, which appear to rely largely on the Nutcracker for seed dispersal, and that the reliance of some populations on hazel nuts is, in an evolutionary sense, much more recent.

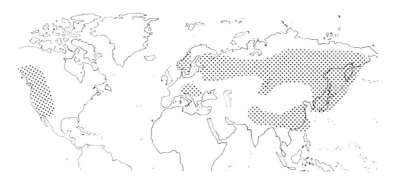

Nutcrackers have the food storing habit highly developed. Some populations are known to rely on their stores for winter food and, to a large extent, for food for their young also. It is highly likely that the same will prove true for all nutcrackers, as is suggested by their early breeding, relative to the nesting seasons of sympatric species. When their main food supply fails, many nutcrackers wander far from their normal range. It is not known to what extent, if any, the actual individuals that take part in such irruptions survive and return to their original homes, although it is known that some apparently attempt to return. It is possible that such behaviour might be useful rather to the population as a whole than to the irrupting individuals, by lessening the pressure on food supplies during times of shortage and so at least ensuring the survival of part of the stock; provided that it is not shown by all related individuals.

The Eurasian nutcrackers are usually all considered races of the one species *Nucifraga caryocatactes*. This seems, on present knowledge, most likely to be correct. As compared with the western and northern populations the forms found from the Himalayas east to China are somewhat longer-tailed, with different tail markings, and less profusely spotted. An exception to this generalization is *N. c. multipunctata* of Lahul, Kashmir and some adjacent areas, which is a long-tailed, slender-billed form but with large and profuse white spots. It thus differs rather strikingly from the form geographically nearest to it, *H. c. hemispila*. It seems probable that *multipunctata* is approaching specific level and it is treated here as a form of *caryocatactes* with some reservation, mainly because of Vaurie's findings that, although the ranges of the two forms are separated by the Pir Panjal Range, there is evidence of hybridization, presumably where a pass connects their respective living areas.

The American or Clark's Nutcracker, *Nucifraga columbiana*, is sometimes considered to be a more primitive form that has survived near the periphery of the original distribution of the genus and been displaced in the Old World by the supposedly more highly specialized *caryocatactes*. This may be so, but I think it more likely that it and the Eurasian species diverged from a common ancestral form after a population of the latter had reached the New World. The colour pattern of *columbiana* could well be derived, by simplification of pattern and increase of white in wings and tail, from one similar or even identical to that of present-day *caryocatactes*.

I do not think the resemblance in coloration between *Nucifraga columbiana* and *Zavattariornis* is of any phylogenetic significance. A mainly grey body with mainly black wings and tail occurs as a fairly frequent general colour pattern in many unrelated birds. What may be of some distributional or evolutionary significance is the resemblance in the differences between the Old World and New World forms of both *Perisoreus* and *Nucifraga*, in both of which the Old World forms have brown or rufous colours which are replaced in the New World forms by grey with no trace of pure brown or rufous.

Nutcrackers may well represent transformed Old World jays, as suggested by Amadon, if one uses the term 'jay' in a general sense for any presumably rather primitive corvid. The similarity in form of the rictal bristles to those of *Podoces* may, as Amadon suggests, be adaptive to the rather cold climates that both endure.   I also concur with Amadon in thinking that the resemblance of *Nucifraga* to the Piñon Jay, *Gymnorhinus*, is due to convergence.   Amadon's suggestion that the nutcrackers, typical crows and choughs might have derived from a common ancestor subsequent to the latter's having diverged from other Old World corvids or their ancestors seems likely.

REFERENCES

AMADON, D. 1944. The genera of Corvidae and their relationships. *Amer. Mus. Novit.* No. 1251.
BOCK, W. J., BALDA, R. P. & VANDER WALL, S. B. 1973. Morphology of the sublingual pouch and tongue musculature of Clark's Nutcracker. *Auk* **90**: 491–519.
JUNG, E. 1966. Eine biologisch bedingte Besonderheit des Sibirischen Tannenhähers. *Der Falke* **7**: 238–239
TURCEK, F. J. & KELSO, L. 1968. Ecological aspects of food transportation and storage in the Corvidae. *Comm. Behav. Biol.*, Pt. A, **1**: 277–297.
VAURIE, C. 1954. Systematic notes on Palearctic Birds. No. 5, Corvidae. *Amer. Mus. Novit.* No. 1668.

NUTCRACKER   *Nucifraga caryocatactes*

Corvus caryocatactes Linnaeus, 1758, Syst. Nat., ed. 10, 1, p. 106.

Description   A little larger than Jay, with shorter tail and much longer and larger bill.   Nasal plumes dull white with inconspicuous dark brown bases and fringes to the individual feathers.   Loral region predominantly dull white or creamy white.   Front of forehead very dark chocolate brown to blackish brown shading to a slightly lighter dark chocolate brown on crown and nape.   Lower rump and upper tail coverts brownish black.   Under tail coverts white.   Rest of body plumage dark chocolate brown, profusely spotted or streaked with white.   The individual feathers on face, throat and neck have longitudinal white tips; those on underparts, mantle, back and scapulars have drop-shaped white spots near the tip, each white spot being edged with brownish black.   Wings black with slight bluish or greenish gloss lesser wing coverts tipped white, sometimes small white tips on median and greater coverts and minute white pointed tips to secondaries and primaries; these latter often soon wear off.   Sixth and seventh primaries with white crescentic mark near base on inner web; sometimes smaller white mark on fifth primary.   Tail glossy black, central feathers narrowly and outer ones broadly tipped white.   Underwing coverts blackish, tipped white.   Irides dark brown.   Bill, legs and feet black.

Juvenile much paler, a pale dull milk-chocolate in body colour with the white spots smaller and less contrasted.   Wings and tail less glossy and with conspicuous whitish tips and fringes to greater coverts. Bill and legs full horny brownish.   Irides greyish.   Nestlings have some whitish down and by the time they are about half grown, the inside of the mouth is red, purplish at back, with pale yellow gape flanges.

The above description is of nominate *N. c. caryocatactes*, which is the form breeding in the European parts of the species' range east to the central Urals. *N. c. macrorhynchos* has a more slender and pointed bill and usually more extensive white ends to the outer tail feathers. It averages a little smaller in size than Scandinavian specimens of the nominate form, which are a little larger and larger-billed than those from central Europe. *N. c. macrorhynchos* is found from north-eastern Russia and the northern Urals eastward across the Siberian Taiga to Manchuria, Kamchatka, Sakhalin and the northern Kuriles. It occurs far outside its normal range during eruptions, sometimes reaching Britain. *N. c. japonica*, from Japan (Hokkaido and Hondo) and the central and southern Kuriles, is similar but has a shorter and proportionately stouter bill. *C. n. rothschildi*, from the Tian Shan, is larger than *macrorhynchos*, being a little larger even than Scandinavian specimens of *caryocatactes*, but has an absolutely as well as proportionately shorter bill, with more curved culmen.

N. c. hemispila, from the western Himalayas in western Nepal and Kumaon, south of the Pir Panjal Range to southern Kashmir and Murree, has the top of the head very dark, almost black in fresh plumage, and the wings a very glossy bluish or greenish black. The white spots and streaks of its body plumage tend to be smaller and to be either few in number or entirely absent on the lower throat and again on the underparts below the breast. The two central tail feathers often have no white at their tips but the outer tail feathers have very extensive white areas, the outermost two on each side being predominantly white. Its bill is similar to that of *rothschildi*, and its tail is a little longer than that of *caryocatactes*. Juveniles of *hemispila* are a rather warmer brown ground colour than those of *caryocatactes* and other previously described forms and have the pale tips to the feathers larger and buff, not whitish in colour (except when worn and bleached).

N. c. yunnanensis, from the mountains of Yunnan, is similar to *hemispila* but a little smaller and darker in ground colour, its body colour being a very dark blackish chocolate when in fresh plumage. The populations of eastern Bhutan, south-eastern Tibet and adjacent areas are similar but tend to be a little less dark and to have the white spots extending more over the belly and upper throat. *N. c. macella*, of western China, is similar to *yunnanensis* but averages a little paler in ground colour and has a rather shorter and less massive bill. *N. c. interdicta*, from northern China in the mountains of northern Hopeh, is said to be similar to *macella* but a little paler in colour. I have seen no specimens from Hopeh but specimens from Shansi, which are probably referable to this race, agree with this description but also have rather smaller bills than most specimens of *macella*, or indeed than any other forms of the species. *N. c. owstoni*, from Formosa, is like *hemispila* but has the white spotting more restricted and the individual spots smaller.

N. c. multipunctata is very distinct from other forms and has sometimes been considered a good species (see col. pl. 1). It is found in Lahul, and possibly western Ladak, west through Kashmir, north of the Pir Panjal Range, to Baltistan, Gilgit, Hazara, North West Frontier Province, northern Baluchistan and eastern Afghanistan in the Safed Koh and south of the Hindu Kush. The ground colour of its plumage is blackish brown, with a grey rather than a chocolate tinge. All the white spots and streaks are much longer and larger than those of other forms so that, seen even at only a few feet distance, it appears to be white with darkish streaks on the body rather than dark with white spots. The white spotting extends onto the upper tail coverts. The tail is rather longer than in *hemispila* and much longer than in the nominate form. The amount of white on the outer tail feathers is intermediate between that of *caryocatactes* and *hemispila*, but the central tail feathers are more extensively white-tipped than either, as are the wing quills. The bill is very slender but not usually so long as that of *macrorhynchos*. The ground colour of the juvenile is light greyish buff and its white markings are smaller and less well-defined than those of adults.

Field characters In flight the broad dark wings, shortish tail, short-looking neck and large bill are distinctive. White under tail coverts and the white tips to tail feathers are often very conspicuous. At a distance the body plumage often appears pale and nearly uniform; at close quarters the white spotting on the dark brown ground is diagnostic.

To those familiar with the Jay's calls, the Nutcracker's harsh alarm screech attracts attention by being very *but not quite* like that of the Jay.

The above remarks apply to the nominate form, the only one I have seen wild. Except for their longer tails with more white on outer tail feathers, the Himalayan and Chinese forms probably look very similar in the field, as the Siberian form certainly does.

Distribution and habitat   Europe and Asia.   Found in Scandinavia, the Alps, and the mountains of central and eastern Europe; eastward through northern Europe through the Taiga and mountain forest regions to eastern Siberia, western Anadyrland, Kamchatka, Sakhalin, Kuriles, Manchuria, China and Formosa.   Also in northern Burma, Yunnan, west to the western Himalayas and northern Baluchistan. Irruptive vagrant to western Europe and Britain.

Inhabits coniferous woodlands or mixed woods dominated by conifers.   May make feeding trips away from the conifer woods where it breeds and roosts.   After eruptions it may occur in almost any type of country but appears seldom, if ever, to survive for long away from its normal habitat.   As a resident breeding bird it is closely tied to conifer habitat with or near trees that produce its main foods.

Feeding and general habits   The most important foods are seeds of conifers and hazel nuts, which are fed upon from their early 'milky' stages onwards, stored extensively, and usually provide the main food throughout the winter and early spring.   Where they occur the conifers *Pinus cembra* and *Pinus korayensis* are the most important food trees but seeds of *Pinus pumila*, *Pinus mugo*, *Picea excelsa*, *Picea obovata*, *Picea yezoensis*, *Picea schrenkiana*, *Picea morinda* and possibly other conifers are also taken, and in some areas, or at times when the crops of *P. cembra* or *P. korayensis* have failed, they may constitute the principal food.   The Scandinavian and some other European populations feed chiefly on hazel nuts; the nuts of 'a kind of hazel' are also taken in the Indian Himalayas (Whistler).

Also takes beetles, wasps, grasshoppers and other insects; berries, walnuts, eggs and young of small birds, small mammals, beech nuts and, it is said, acorns.   Probably acorns are taken only rarely or in default of other food; they are certainly sometimes refused when offered to Nutcrackers feeding in gardens. Sometimes catches insects on the wing (Latzel).   In parts of Siberia makes a nuisance of itself to trappers by taking the meat or fish (or getting caught in attempting to do so) from the traps set for fur-bearing mammals.   Has been seen to dig out wasps' and bumblebees' nests (Glause; Röthing).

Seeks food both in trees and shrubs and on the ground.   Green pine cones, that cannot be wrenched off, may be opened on the trees but when possible the cones are removed, carried to a convenient perch such as a large branch, projecting root, or tree stump, and held under one foot while the seeds are extracted by hacking, biting and probing.   In probing the bird inserts the closed bill between the scales and then opens it ('Zirkeln', p.19).   Sometimes the cone may be placed or wedged in a depression or fork and there dealt with.   I think this probably happens most often when it is sticky with resin.   When eating seeds, or preparing them to feed to young, the bird takes them into the basal part of the bill and cracks them with the aid of the ridge on the inside of the lower mandible.   If too hard, as fresh (or dried) hazel nuts often are, they are held under foot and hacked open (Löhrl).

Food storage starts usually in late summer, as soon as the conifer seeds or hazel nuts begin to ripen, and continues as long into autumn as supplies are available.   During the peak storing periods the Nutcrackers may fly continually to and from the feeding places.   Seeds are carried in the sublingual pouch, sometimes a final one in the bill, back from the gathering place to the bird's territory or living area.   Food is hidden in a Jay-like manner in the ground or (less often) in trees.   Typically the Nutcracker hides food where the ground is rather bare, such as in moss or lichen on rocky surfaces; on a slight prominence such as among the roots of a tree stump; in the rotted wood still surrounded by less rotting bark of a tree stump, and in similar places.   Frequently food is stored near the upper edge of the tree line and in other places where there are only scattered trees.   The choice of site for hiding food is probably determined largely by the Nutcracker's need to have a clear view all round so that it cannot easily be surprised by a Goshawk or other predator when on the ground.   It results, however, in those seeds which the Nutcracker does not recover being often 'planted' in ideal situations.   In the central Alps, for example, the Nutcracker has brought about extensive re-establishment of *Pinus cembra* in areas where this tree had been extirpated by man and his domestic stock (Holtmeier).

Nutcrackers may fly up to about 15 km (possibly at times further) to and from their living areas when collecting seeds.   Distances of a few miles are, however, probably more usual.   From three to nine hazel nuts or from five to fifteen seeds of *Pinus cembra* are usually hidden together. The Siberian form, when storing seeds of *Pinus cembra*, first conceals them in temporary hiding places where up to forty seeds are put together. These seeds are later removed and hidden in smaller numbers elsewhere. The function of this behaviour is clearly to save time while the ripe seeds, for which there is competition not only with other Nutcrackers but also with squirrels and many other creatures, are available. It is not certain whether this two-stage storing is invariable or whether its use depends on local conditions.

The Nutcracker remembers where it has hidden food, even after snow has covered the ground, and also appears to remember which food stores it has already made use of. Swanberg (1951) found that, as shown by diggings through the snow, it was exceptional for the bird to dig through the snow cover and not find nuts, as would often happen if it did not know which stores it had already emptied. It is quite possible indeed that when nutcrackers and jays appear to have made a mistake the food has previously been removed by some other creature. Like other corvids, nutcrackers will often rob a food store, if they see it being made.

Adult Nutcrackers in Sweden, and probably elsewhere, live in pairs in territories which seem not to be defended by actual fighting or attacking of trespassers. Young birds and possibly adults without breeding territories may lay up food stores and spend the winter and following spring in areas with (initially) good food supplies but without suitable nesting habitat. In Siberia loose flocks of up to two hundred or more birds have been recorded in summer, apparently searching for good feeding areas.

Established pairs are highly sedentary, except possibly in times of food shortage. Young, unestablished birds appear to wander to some extent. Periodic large-scale eruptions occur, especially from Siberia. They appear to be caused mainly, and perhaps entirely, by failure of the food trees to produce adequate seed crops. At such times, as in the summer of 1968, great numbers of Nutcrackers may invade western Europe. To what extent, if any, established adult pairs with territories take part in these eruptions, appears not to be known.

Flight rather Jay-like but shape in flight very different from that of Jay. On ground usually hops in a heavy but quite Jay-like manner but may walk or run a few steps, especially when approaching some close objects or when threatening a conspecific (Kunkel).

The Goshawk is a main predator on the Nutcracker, at least in the northern parts of its range. The Jay is treated by Nutcrackers as a potential nest predator, being attacked and driven from the vicinity of the nest but ignored out of the breeding season. Many creatures are potential food competitors. Steinfatt has suggested that Red Deer, by destroying or preventing regeneration of hazel, may adversely affect the Nutcracker's numbers and distribution.

Nesting Throughout its range an early nester, incubation usually beginning when the country is still snow-covered, in central Europe in March (Bartels). In the Himalayas nests with young have been found as late as June and July but this probably represents second or third attempts after earlier nests were predated. Nest usually in a conifer, 2·5–9 metres above ground but Siberian form said sometimes to nest in broadleaved trees (Grote) and it is possible that other forms may do so exceptionally. Bartels found that in the Alps nests were usually on the sunny side of the trees, possibly for protection from wind, as in American Nutcracker.

Nest built of twigs and sticks, then a thick layer of rotten wood, earth, tufts of earthy roots, or weeds; thick inner cup of grass stems, lichen, fibrous bark, fibrous roots, grasses or similar materials. Fur, wool, and feathers are sometimes used in the lining of the exterior (Crocq, with photograph). In appearance and construction more like the nest of a crow, *Corvus*, than that of a jay, *Garrulus*. Both sexes build.

Eggs 2 to 4, rarely 5; pale bluish, bluish green or off-white, speckled or, less often, spotted or blotched, with olive brown; with underlying grey or lilac markings. Usually more sparsely marked than most corvid eggs. Swanberg found, in the population he studied in Sweden, that when ample food stores were available 4 eggs were laid but never more than 3 when the food supply was poor. The first egg is laid early in the morning, the others at intervals of about 26 hours. Incubation period usually 18 days, rarely 19. Both sexes incubate and brood the young in turn by day but the female sits for a long unbroken spell from late afternoon until just after dawn next day.

Both sexes feed the young, as a rule largely with seeds or nuts from their stores. Some other food for them may, however, be collected from outside the territory. Whole but shelled seeds of *Pinus cembra* were fed, together with spiders and insects, to a brood of ten day old young (Crocq). The parents swallow faeces and remove and swallow the debris of disintegrating feather sheaths from the young in the usual way (Steinfatt). Food is brought at intervals of fifteen minutes to about two hours. Young fledge at 23 days (perhaps sometimes a little earlier, and sometimes later). They stay in their parents' territory for 2 to 3 weeks after fledging; then follow the parents, and the whole family may spend the day, often in deciduous woods, far from their home to which, however, they return to roost each evening. The parents may feed them when as old as 105 days, probably still later in some cases (Swanberg 1956). Frightened nestlings crouch with half-open bills like young Jays.

Voice The alarm call is a loud, harsh 'kraak', very like the alarm screech of the Jay but a little less sharp and strident; often rapidly repeated. Subject to some variation and perhaps, even when given at same intensity, varying geographically, as is suggested by differing descriptions, 'kro(e)', 'kra', 'kree' etc. A tame bird of the Siberian race gave this screech in apparently pleasurable excitement (or momentary frustration?) when it saw its favourite foods being brought to it, as well as when mobbing predators (Beaufort).

The loud harsh cries that are given at the commencement of the breeding season and which seem to be a proclamation of territory (Swanberg 1951) are similar in sound to the alarm screech, but probably not identical.

A mechanical-sounding, rather Nightjar-like, rattling call has been heard from both European and Himalayan forms but the circumstances in which it is used are uncertain. Possibly it is homologous with the rattling notes of jays and crows.

The song consists of various piping, whistling, and whining notes interspersed with clicking sounds. It is given, so far as is known, only by the male but has no territorial significance. When singing the bird inclines its bill upwards and dilates its throat (Swanberg 1951). Vocal mimicry was practised by a hand-reared individual (O. & M. Heinroth) and it seems highly likely that it is by wild birds also, during their songs or among the many different notes that are heard at ceremonial gatherings.

A tame (but wild-caught) captive bird regularly begged for food with 'a short, soft, plaintive note' that varied in pitch (Beaufort). What would appear to have a rather louder and more screeching type of begging call was heard from a wild female by Bartels and Bartels, who also heard a short, soft call (probably the same as that of Beaufort's tame bird and homologous with the food appeal call of Jay) from a male bird when arriving with food near the nest.

Display and social behaviour Ceremonial gatherings of up to ten birds often take place within the territory of an established pair. The territory owners may either participate or else watch with no sign of hostility. The primary function of such gatherings seems to be to enable unpaired birds, especially young ones, to meet (Swanberg 1956a). If food is placed in a territory, any other Nutcracker that tries to take it is attacked by the owners.

At nest relief the sitting bird often or usually gapes open its bill but feeding of the mate on the nest does not normally occur. Feeding of presumed female by presumed male has been *heard*, but apparently not seen, away from the nest (Bartels & Bartels). A tame bird begged for food with flapping wings in juvenile manner (Beaufort) but feeding of the female by the male, if it occurs at all in the wild, would seem to be rarer than in other corvids.

Other names Thick-billed Nutcracker (the nominate race), Slender-billed Nutcracker (the Siberian race).

REFERENCES

BARTELS, M. & H. 1929. Zur Brutbiologie des dickschnabligen Tannenhähers *Nucifraga caryocatactes* (L). *J. Orn.* **77**: 489–501.

BARTELS, M. 1931. Verzogerung des Brutgeschaftes durch Schneefall und Kalte beim Tannenhäher. *Beitr. Fortpfl. biol. Vög.* **7**: 129–130.

BEAUFORT, L. F. DE. 1947. Notes on the behaviour of a Slender-billed Nutcracker. *Ardea* **35**: 226–230.

BRANDT, H. 1962. Bemerkenswerte Lautäusserungen des Tannenhähers (*Nucifraga caryocatactes*). *Vogelwelt* **83**: 81–82.

CROCQ, C. 1974. Notes complémentaires sur la nidification du Casse-noix. *Nucifraga caryocatactes* dans les Alpes françaises. *Alauda* **42**: 39–50.

GLAUSE, J. 1969. Tannehäher plundern Hummelnester. *Vogelwelt* **90**: 66.

GROTE, H. 1947. Ueber die Lebensweise des Schlankschnabligen Tannenhähers in Siberien. *Orn. Beobachter* **44**: 84–90.

HEINROTH, O. & M. 1931. *Die Vögel Mitteleuropas* vol. 4: 13–14.

HOLTMEIER, F. K. 1966. Die Ökologische Funktion des Tannenhähers im Zirben-Lärchenwald und an der Waldgrenze des Oberengadins. *J. Orn.* **107**: 337–345.

JUNG, E. 1966. Zur Lebensweise des sibirischen Tannenhähers. *Der Falke* **13**: 408–411.

—— 1968. Eine biologisch bedingte Besonderheit des Sibirischen Tannenhähers. *Der Falke* **7**: 238–239.

KINZELBACH, R. 1962. Schnurren des Tannenhähers. *Vogelwelt* **83**: 187.

KUNKEL, P. 1962. Zur Verbreitung des Hüpfens und Laufens unter Sperlingsvögeln (Passeres). *Z. Tierpsychol.* **19**: 417–439.

LATZEL, G. 1968. Zur Nahrungsaufnahme Sibirischer Tannenhäher. *Vogelwelt* **89**: 231–232.

LÖHRL, H. 1970. Der Tannenhäher (*Nucifraga caryocatactes*) beim Sammeln und Knacken von Nüsschen der Zirbelkiefer (*Pinus cembra*). *Anz. Orn. ges. Bayern* 9, 3: 185–196.

PFEIFER, S. 1953. Stimmlaute des Tannenhähers. *Vogelwelt* **74**: 216–217.

PIECHOCKI, R. 1956. *Beitragen zur Avifauna Nord und Nordost Chinas* (*Mandschurei*). Dresden.

RÖTHING, H. 1969. Tannenhäher gräbt Wespennest aus. *Vogelwelt* **90**: 146–147.

SCHÄFER, E. 1938. Ornithologische Ergebnisse zweier Forschungsreisen nach Tibet. *J. Orn.* **86**, Sonderheft.

SCHWAMMBER, K. 1962. Tannenhäher plundert Wespennest. *Vogelwelt* **83**: 186.

STEGMANN, B. 1931. Die Vögel des dauro-mandschurischen Uebergangsgebietes. *J. Orn.* **79**: 146–147.

STEINFATT, O. 1944. Beobachtungen über den Tannenhähers, besonders über seine Jungenpflege. *Orn. Monatsber.* **52**: 8–16.

SUTTER, E. & AMANN, F. 1953. Wie weit fliegen vorratsammelnde Tannenhäher? *Orn. Beobachter*, **50**: 89–90.

SWANBERG, P. O. 1951. Food storage, territory and song in the Thick-billed Nutcracker. *Proc. 10th Int. Orn. Congress* 1950 (1951): 497–501.

—— 1952. The Nutcracker. *Brit. Birds* **45**: 60–61.

—— 1956a. Territory in the Thick-billed Nutcracker. *Ibis* **98**: 412–419.

—— 1956b. Incubation in the Thick-billed Nutcracker, *Nucifraga c. caryocatactes* (L). *Bertil Hanström, Zoological Papers in honour of his sixty-fifth birthday.* Lund. Sweden.

TURCEK, F. J. & KELSO, L. 1968. Ecological aspects of food transportation and storage in the Corvidae. *Comm. Behav. Biol.*, Pt. A, **1**: 277–297.

WHISTLER, H. Unpublished manuscripts and notes in library of Bird Room. British Museum (Nat. Hist.).

CLARK'S NUTCRACKER   *Nucifraga columbiana*

Corvus columbianus Wilson, 1811, Amer. Orn., 3, p. 29, pl. 20, fig. 2.

Description A little smaller than the Old World Nutcracker, about size of Jay but with typical nutcracker proportions. Nasal plumes, lores and chin whitish grey. Ring of soft, dense feathers around eye creamy white to greyish white. Rest of head and body light ash-grey except for darker grey rump, greyish black upper tail coverts, and white under tail coverts. When worn and bleached the plumage, especially on forehead and (to a lesser extent) on crown, mantle and back may be largely or entirely pale creamy grey. Wings glossy black with broad white tips to most of the secondaries which form a conspicuous white patch in flight. Tail white except for the two central feathers and a varying amount of the inner webs of the next pair which are glossy black.

Irides dark brown. Bill, legs, and feet black. Inside of mouth blackish. Juvenile a dingier and more brownish grey. At fledging time has grey irides, legs and feet; inside of bill and mouth pale salmon-red to whitish. The soft parts gradually change colour during the first moult. As with *Garrulus* small black areas appear on the inside of the mouth, spread and coalesce. Newly-hatched nestlings have sparse white down on their principal feather tracts (Mewaldt 1956).

The sublingual pouch is formed of loose tissue of the entire floor of the mouth, in front of the tongue.

It can form a very large sac.   It has no single opening but is completely open to the mouth cavity (Balda, *in litt.*).

Field identification   Light grey bird with long bill and conspicuously black and white wings and tail. Often suggests 'a cross between a crow and a woodpecker'.   White in wings and tail at once distinguishes it from the similarly-shaped but blue Piñon Jay.

Distribution and habitat   Western North America from central interior British Columbia, south-western Alberta, western Montana, and south-eastern Wyoming south to northern Baja California, eastern Arizona and western New Mexico.   When not breeding may wander to central Alaska, southern Yukon, southern Saskatchewan, south-western Manitoba, western British Columbia including Graham and Vancouver Islands, western Washington, south-western California, and southern Arizona, east to South Dakota, Nebraska, Kansas and south-western Texas.

Found in mountains at altitudes of from 900 to 3900 m but breeding range mainly between 1800 and 2400 m between the lower limits of coniferous forest and its upper limits at the timber line.   Large-scale eruptions out of the usual range occur when there are severe shortages of conifer seed.   (Davis & Williams, 1957 and 1964.)

Feeding and general habits   Usually in pairs or small parties.   Large numbers may gather at good feeding grounds, or during eruptions.   Adult birds appear to live in pairs in their breeding territories, from which trespassers may be, but are not always, driven out.   Territorial adults frequently seek food outside their territories.

Flight often undulating and woodpecker-like but when flying some distance rapid, straight and with regular wing-beats.   Most observers say or imply that it hops on the ground (like previous species) but Pettingill (in Wetmore) says that it 'walks sedately about much as a crow does.'   If it does sometimes walk in this manner, this suggests a parallel (but less advanced) development to that of the Piñon Jay, which walks although almost certainly rather recently derived from hopping ancestors.

Feeds primarily on the seeds of conifers, especially *Pinus edulis, P. ponderosa, P. monophylla, P. flexilis* and *P. albicaulis*.   Also takes cicadas, grasshoppers, crickets, beetles and their larvae, ants, bees, wasps, moths, caterpillars and other insects; spiders and ticks; grains and berries; small mammals (and rarely flesh from the carcasses of large mammals); eggs and young of small birds.   Readily learns to take such foods as peanuts, bread and suet when available.

Feeds both in trees and on the ground.   Very agile at manoeuvring among peripheral twigs.   Cones may be broken open without removing them but rather more often are plucked or hacked loose, taken to a firm perch and held under one foot while the seeds are prized out.   Hacks and probes in rotten logs for beetle larvae. Digs in loose substrate with sideways flicks of the bill in usual passerine manner. Tips over dry cowdung and other objects to look for hidden insects.

Habitually stores pine seeds. Two females shot while carrying seed to store had, respectively, 72 pinyon seeds and 65 white-bark pine seeds in their throats. Food is stored in typical manner, both in the ground and (probably less often) in trees. French noted birds storing food on ledges and slopes where snow accumulation was slight, even in winter. It has, however, been observed to dig through snow cover to retrieve hidden food. When feeding from bird tables, peanuts, lumps of suet etc. are regularly stored. Recovery of such items has also been seen (Davis & Williams 1957 and 1964).

Observations by Mewaldt (1956) and Dixon seem to indicate that stored food is not used during the breeding season as it is by *N. caryocatactes*. Further observations are needed, however, as probably much depends on the food situation of individual pairs. In the case of the birds watched by Mewaldt pine nuts were still available on the trees. There is, in any case, no reason to doubt the opinion of Davis & Williams (1957) that the main function of the storing behaviour is to get the average nutcracker safely through the average winter. They also plausibly suggest that in years of pine seed failure the birds may be stimulated to erupt from the area if they find insufficient pine seed when they begin their storing.

Nesting Nest in a Juniper or conifer, often at or near the end of a horizontal branch. Dixon (1934) found nests on steep slopes in the coldest spots where the snow lay longest, and concluded that such places were chosen because they were relatively free from strong winds. The actual nest site also seems usually wind-sheltered. Nest externally of twigs and sticks, sometimes intermixed with strips of fibrous bark. Outer portion of nest cup of strips of fibrous bark and/or wood pulp, with an inner lining of dried grass, fine strips of fibrous bark, fibres and similar material. Mewaldt found that the nests he examined had a layer of mineral soil about half an inch thick at the bottom of the cup between the wood pulp and the grass lining. The nest cup is deep and thick-walled. Both sexes bring material and build, but in the few pairs that have been closely watched the female did more actual building than the male.

Nests early, while snow still on the ground; eggs usually laid in March or early April. Usually 3 eggs, often 2, sometimes 4 and very rarely 5 or 6. Eggs pale green, pale greyish green, or greenish white, spotted and flecked with brown, grey and olive. Usually the markings are small and rather scanty.

Both sexes incubate, and brood the young. In pairs observed closely by Mewaldt the male sat for about 25% of the daylight hours. The members of a pair watched by Dixon changed over about every half hour and incubated for about the same amount of the time.

Nest-probing by the adults has been observed. At one nest a female apparently helped to break open the eggs. She was seen to appear to peck repeatedly and, when she was flushed from the nest, one egg had a series of indentations in line with the break 'pipped' in the eggshell by the young bird inside. Egg-shells are eaten after the young hatch. Both parents either swallow or carry away the faeces of the young. The young are fed with regurgitated food which often, probably usually, consists from the first largely of shelled, partially broken-up conifer seeds.

Information on incubation and fledging periods is a little conflicting but it seems probable that incubation normally takes from 16 to 18 days and the young, if well-nourished, fledge at about 22 days old. They are fed by the parents for some time after leaving the nest.

Incubating or brooding birds sit very close. When approached by a human they often refuse to leave the nest, gaping defensively but apparently inhibited from any less passive defence. Dixon shows an excellent photograph of a sitting bird gaping in this manner.

Voice Mewaldt (1956), from whose observations the notes in this section are taken, described the following calls.

(1) *Regular call.* This has been variously written as 'khaaa', 'khraa', 'char-r-r', 'kra-a-a', 'kar-r-r-r-ack' etc. It is harsh and usually given in series of three calls. The version used by juveniles has a squalling tone. It is used frequently by both sexes at all times of year. Apparently used as a contact call but from the contexts in which it is often given, may also, I think, indicate alarm or disquiet.

(2) *Musical call.* Similar in some respects to the *regular call* but liquid and soft. Heard most often in

late winter and spring during the pre-nesting and nesting periods.   Used by both sexes.   Apparently used as a contact call between paired adults, also to indicate readiness to feed nestlings, which gape for food on hearing it.

(3)   *Shrill call.*   A high-pitched and penetrating screech.   It has a metallic version that Mewaldt terms the *trumpet call.*   These calls are given, in apparent excitement, by both sexes at all seasons.   Used at times when mobbing flying birds of prey but also when no predator is evident.

(4)   *Squalling call.*   A squalling, prolonged version of the *regular call.*   Uttered by both sexes at all seasons.   Used when mobbing predators.

(5)   *Bullfrog call.*   A slow rattle, sounding much like the croaking of some species of frogs.   Uttered by adults of both sexes and, at least, by females in their first year.   Probably this call is homologous with the rattling calls of jays; it is interesting that this is one of the few species in which it is known to be given by both sexes.

(6)   *Crackle and whistle call.*   Alternating crackles and wheezing whistles scarcely audible at 22 m, accompanied by bowing and neck-stretching.   Given by both sexes but only in March and April and appears to be associated with nesting.

(7)   *Hunger call.*   Very similar to the squalling call and with a similar tone to the begging notes of young crows (and other young corvids).   Given by young birds when begging food, and sometimes by the adult female during courtship (presumably when soliciting food).   Said to be given by young in nest 'when being fed or when disturbed', but it seems unlikely that the begging call should not differ *at all* from the call of frightened young.

(8)   *Conversational squalling.*   A subdued musical version of the *squalling call.*   Heard from adults of both sexes when both parents were present at a nest with young nestlings.

(9)   *Nestling calls.*   Soft peeping calls, hardly audible ten feet from the nest, were uttered almost continually during the day (no night observations) by nestlings from one day to one week old.   The peeps increased in tempo when they were being fed.   At about a week old the peeping was gradually replaced by squealing calls which were given only during feeding.   The pitch of these squealing calls became lower and they developed into the *hunger call.*

Display and social behaviour   Long flights, often culminating at or near the starting point, in which presumed male follows presumed female, occur in the early part of the nesting season.   During such flights the male may carry a twig.   Birds also seen to carry twigs in flight when the mate was nearby but did not join in the flight.

Food-begging with fluttering wings, seen from females, and from brooding birds of either sex when the mate returns to the nest to feed the young.   Usually, however, the begging adult is not fed in this situation although a *female* was once seen to feed a *male* (Mewaldt 1956).   Feeding of the female by the male has been seen on a few occasions away from the nest.

Other names   Clark's Crow, Woodpecker Crow.

REFERENCES

Bent, A. C.   1946.   Life histories of North American jays, crows, and titmice.   *U.S. Nat. Mus. Bull.* **191**: 310–322.

Cahalane, V. H.   1944.   A Nutcracker's search for buried food.   *Auk* **61**: 643.

Cottam, C.   1945.   Feeding habits of the Clark Nutcracker.   *Condor* **47**: 168.

Davis, J. & Williams, L.   1957.   Irruptions of the Clark Nutcracker in California.   *Condor* **59**: 297–307.

—— 1964.   The 1961 irruption of Clark's Nutcracker in California.   *Wilson Bull.* **76**: 10–18.

Dixon, J. B.   1934.   Nesting of the Clark Nutcracker in California.   *Condor* **36**: 229–234.

French, N. R.   1955.   Foraging behavior and predation by Clark Nutcracker.   *Condor* **57**: 61.

Mewaldt, L. R.   1952.   The incubation patch of the Clark Nutcracker.   *Condor* **54**: 361.

—— 1956.   Nesting behavior of the Clark Nutcracker.   *Condor* **58**: 3–23.

—— 1958.   Pterylography and natural and experimentally induced molt in Clark's Nutcracker. *Condor* **60**: 165–187.

Wetmore, A.   1964.   *Song and Garden Birds of North America:* 151. Washington.

The typical and azure-winged magpies

The typical magpies of the genus *Pica*, with their long tails and beautifully glossed black and white plumage, are among the best-known birds wherever they are found. Past familiarity with the bird in England is indicated both by the now virtually obligatory addition of the familiar 'Mag' to the original (Norman French?) 'Pie' and latter's use as an adjective to describe anything that, like the Magpie, is 'pied' in colour-pattern.

The typical magpies have a wide, but in some places rather patchy, distribution in the northern temperate regions of both Old and New Worlds. In some places they extend north of the Arctic circle and they are found as far south as Indo China and have an isolated population in south-western Arabia. The forms within the genus *Pica* are remarkably homogeneous, suggesting either a relatively recent spread over their present wide range or else a considerable resistance to variation. Within the Corvidae only the genus *Corvus* has a much wider distribution and of other genera only *Perisoreus* comes 'a good second' in this respect but the component forms of both these genera (especially *Corvus*) show greater diversity.

The typical magpies are the only long-tailed corvids to have an extensive world range. They are also less arboreal than most other long-tailed corvids. They feed mainly on the ground and need tree or scrub cover only for nesting, roosting and to take shelter from some enemies. They also differ from their presumed nearest relatives, and nearly all other corvids, in building nests that are normally roofed over with a canopy of sticks, leaving only a small opening which can be relatively easily defended. There can be little doubt that this type of nest greatly reduces predation, particularly by crows of the genus *Corvus*. It is likely that its nest has been an important factor in the success of *Pica*, enabling it to co-exist with *Corvus* species in relatively open habitats.

The typical magpies probably evolved as inhabitants of more or less open and scrub-covered country and/or forest edge and riparian woodland in otherwise open and dry country. It is possible that, as I think was the case with some species of *Corvus*, *Pica* early became a scavenger around human habitations and hunting camps, as it was at Red Indian encampments during the period of White settlement in western North America. Later, in many parts of the world, human agriculture and livestock farming almost certainly improved conditions for Magpies in many areas and created suitable habitat for them where none had been before. It is likely that man's activities permitted at least considerable local expansion of the Magpie's range and was perhaps a decisive factor in its successful colonization of many rather wet areas, such as Ireland which it only reached during the 17th century.

It is usual to treat all the black-billed forms of *Pica* as races of one species, *Pica pica*, and this seems the best decision on present evidence. Some of them, such as the American *P. p. hudsonia* and the Arabian Magpie, *P. p. asirensis*, are, however, completely isolated from any congeners and it is possible that they have reached species level in spite of their morphological similarity to other forms. The Tibetan Magpie *P. p. bottanensis* has also been suspected of specific distinctness by some observers, but no detailed comparisons of its voice or behaviour with those of other forms have been made.

The Yellow-billed Magpie, *Pica nuttalli*, is usually given specific rank. It is convenient to do so, and is possibly justifiable as it not only possesses a strikingly conspicuous character in its yellow bill and yellow post-orbital skin, which might well function as an isolating mechanism if it ever came into contact with black-billed forms, but also shows some behavioural divergence in its colonial nesting habits and apparent insistence on tall trees as nest sites.

On the basis of a fossil tarsometatarsus whose measurements and characters agree with those of *Pica pica*, and which was believed to date from the early Pleistocene, from Texas (Miller & Bowman), Voous suggests that the Yellow-billed Magpie of California represents a relict population derived from an early invasion of America by *P. pica* and that the Black-billed Magpies of North America, *P. p. hudsonia*, represent a second invasion from Asia. How safely magpie bones from the early or late pleicestocene can with certainty be ascribed to one of two presently-existing species (whose measurements overlap) I am not competent to judge. I think, however, that it is likely that, in spite of their differently coloured bills and different average size, *hudsonia* and *nuttalli* are phylogenetically closer to each other than either is to the old-world forms of *Pica*.

In details of plumage colour-pattern and proportions of bill, wings, tail and legs, *P. p. hudsonia* resembles *P. nuttalli* more closely than it does the eastern Asiatic forms of *pica*. As *nuttalli* shows divergence from *hudsonia* not only in its yellow bill but also, to some degree, in ecology and habitat choice, it seems rather unlikely that the details in which they so closely resemble each other are due to convergence. Also Brooks has stated that the calls of *hudsonia* and *nuttalli* are identical and that both differ from those of Old World forms of *Pica*. This is partly corroborated by the recorded calls I have heard (Kellogg & Allen, 1959 and 1962) of *hudsonia* and *nuttalli*. On the other hand in its comparatively less specialized or more adaptable ecology *hudsonia* certainly resembles the Old World forms. Detailed comparative studies of voice and behaviour of all the more distinct forms of *Pica* from both Old and New Worlds would prove of much interest.

The typical magpies show some resemblances to the genus *Corvus*. I think, however, these represent convergent adaptations to ground feeding in relatively open country and do not indicate that *Corvus* and *Pica* shared a common ancestry subsequent to their splitting off from other corvids. The nearest relative of *Pica* seems to be the Azure-winged Magpie, *Cyanopica cyana*, which is similar in shape, and has some very similar displays and nest-building techniques, although it does not erect a canopy over its nest and does not usually, if at all, walk when on the ground. More distantly *Pica* seems related to the blue and green magpies, *Cissa*, and tree pies *Crypsirina*, on one hand and the American jays, *Cyanocitta* etc., on the other.

The genus *Cyanopica* contains only one species, the Azure-winged Magpie, *Cyanopica cyana*. It differs from *Pica* in not having the specialized first primary, in the shortness of the juvenile tail feathers, and in replacing the juvenile wing quills at the first moult. In this latter character it seems to differ from all other corvids. I think the Azure-winged Magpie is most closely related to the typical Magpies on one hand and to the blue and green magpies on the other, and is a link between them. It is, however, a very distinct form and the possibility cannot be excluded that it may be closest to the American jays and be the Old World representative of the stock that, in America, developed into the various blue jays.

The Azure-winged Magpie is found only in eastern Asia and in the Iberian peninsula. Very few other birds show such a disjunct distribution. It has often been suggested that the Iberian population might be a feral one and owe its origin to escaped or liberated captives brought back to Spain or Portugal by early traders with the Far East. This theory is usually discounted on the grounds that there are distinct racial differences between the far-eastern and Iberian forms of the Azure-winged Magpie. These differences are, however, not very great (see Description), and in view of the amount of geographical divergence known to have taken place in the House Sparrow in less than a hundred years since its introduction to North America (Johnston & Selander), it cannot be considered impossible that the differences of the Iberian Azure-winged Magpie could have arisen subsequent to introduction, if this took place long ago.

A more cogent objection to the introduction theory is that, contrary to popular opinion, successful introductions of birds to new areas, though often attempted, seem only to have been achieved where quite large numbers of individuals in good condition have been liberated together. Usually successive batches of birds have been released in different years. It seems unlikely either that so many Azure-winged Magpies were once imported into Iberia or that a considerable number of both sexes escaped or were liberated or, alternatively, that the escape of only a few individuals would have led to their establishing their species.

That the Azure-winged Magpie may be a declining species that once inhabited a much larger range is suggested also by the fact that within its present ranges it is absent from many areas that appear suitable. At least in the Far East this seems unlikely to be due to human persecution and even in Iberia, although its recent decrease is probably due to persecution by man, its patchy distribution seems due to rather rigid habitat and/or temperature requirements (Dos Santos).

Although no other corvid shows a comparably disjunct range, that of the Chough, *Pyrrhocorax pyrrhocorax*, is of interest in this connection. A glance at its distribution map will show that, were the Chough to become extinct in the central parts of its range and in the western parts north of the Pyrenees (and in central Europe and the British Isles it may well be in the process of so-doing) its range would then show similar disjunction to that of *Cyanopica*. The two have, of course, entirely different ecological needs but it is possible that both might be affected, at least to the extent of being restricted in habitat, by competition from more successful species.

REFERENCES

BROOKS, A. 1931. The relationships of American magpies. *Auk* **48**: 271–272.
DOS SANTOS, J. R. 1968. The colony of Azure-winged Magpies in the Barca d'Alva region. *Cyanopica* **1**: 1–28.
MILLER, A. H. & BOWMAN, R. I. 1956. A fossil Magpie from the Pleistocene of Texas. *Condor* **58**: 164–165.
JOHNSTON, R. F. & SELANDER, R. K. 1964. House Sparrows: Rapid Evolution of Races in North America. *Science* **144**, No. 3618: 548–550.
KELLOGG, P. P. & ALLEN, A. A. 1959. *A Field Guide to Bird Songs of Eastern and Central America*. Boston.
——— 1962. *Field Guide to Bird Songs of Western North America*. Boston.
VOOUS, K. H. 1960. *Atlas of European Birds*. London.

MAGPIE   *Pica pica*

Corvus pica Linnaeus, 1758, Syst. Nat. Ed. 10, 1, p. 106.

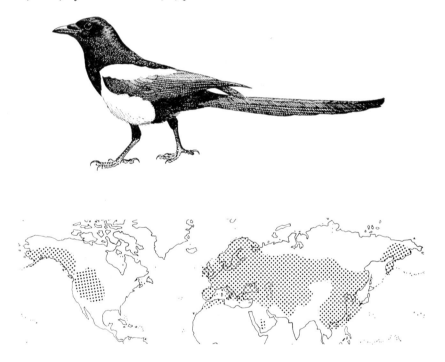

Description Outermost primary characteristic; very narrow and somewhat sickle-shaped. Head and body plumage, except where otherwise stated, deep velvety black. Usually with a slight bronze or bronze-green sheen on the top of the head and sometimes with a slight bronze or, more usually, purplish lustre on the hind neck, mantle, back and upper tail coverts. Throat feathers have a rather hairy texture, greyish shafts and usually white or whitish bases. Upper part of rump dull white, brownish white or pale brown, often with dusky or dull black tips to feathers. Underparts below breast, but excluding under tail coverts, tibial feathers and those immediately around vent, pure white, Scapulars and greater part of inner webs of primaries, except at their tips, also white. Lesser and median wing coverts black with slight greenish or bluish gloss. Greater coverts more brightly glossed green or greenish blue. Inner secondaries shining dark blue or greenish blue; outer secondaries same but with basal half (approximately) a bronzy dark green edged with shining blue. Primary coverts and outer webs of primaries greenish black to dark bronze green; most of inner webs of primaries, except for about half an inch at tip, white. Those parts of the wing feathers not visible when wing is folded (and not white) are dull black. Central tail feathers a rich dark green, bronze green or, less often, bluish green; about two and half inches from tip this green shades through golden-red or purple-red into a more or less V-shaped purple area, which in turn shades through purple-blue into dark bluish green or black, more or less glossed with bluish or greenish on the last inch or more of tail. Outer webs of outer tail feathers similarly patterned and coloured but the outermost pair have their outer webs purple or purple-red at base, rest greenish or greenish blue. The inner webs of outer tail feathers mainly dull black as is underside of tail.

Irides dark brown. Bill, legs and feet black. Nictitating membrane whitish with an elliptical bright orange patch. Juvenile like adult but outer primary less narrow and pointed, duller black on head and body. Wings and tail only slightly duller than adult's. Irides at fledgling stage pale grey to greyish blue; mouth deep pink or purplish-pink, gape-flanges yellow. Newly-hatched young are naked with translucent skin that soon turns flesh-coloured or yellowish. Some or all of the tail feathers may be shed and renewed at the first moult, although the primaries and secondaries are not shed at this moult. The juvenile usually shows a bare patch behind the eye homologous with that of adults of the North African and Californian forms but not conspicuously coloured.

The above description is of nominate *Pica p. pica* from most of northern and central Europe, the British Isles and southern Scandinavia, eastern and south-eastern Europe. *P. p. galliae*, from Belgium, Rhineland Germany, France, Switzerland, Italy, Sicily, and Dalmatia south to Macedonia and Greece tends to be a shade smaller, with less extensive white areas on the wings and less whitish on the rump. *P. p. melanotos*, from Spain and Portugal, is similar to *galliae* but has the rump either entirely black or with only an obscure greyish patch or band.

P. p. mauretanica, from north-western Africa, is rather distinct but most like *P. p. melanotos*, from which it differs in having proportionately shorter wings and rather longer tail, less extensive white areas on the wings, and a conspicuous patch of bare blue skin behind the eye. Its rump is always black. Its tail tends to be rather darker green and purple than in the nominate form but is otherwise the same in colour and pattern. In weathered plumage the central tail feathers turn blackish bronze (as do those of other forms, although seldom to the same extent) but bronze tail feathers are certainly not a racial character of *mauretanica*, as has been claimed.

P. p. fennorum, from northern Scandinavia, the Baltic countries and western Russia, averages a little larger than nominate *pica*, a little more extensively white in the wing and more often bronze green rather than dark green on the tail. *P. p. bactriana* is found from central and eastern Russia, the Caucasas, Transcaucasia, Iran, including Azerbaijan and southern Caspian districts to eastern and northern Iraq, Transcaspia, Russian Turkestan north to western and central Kirghiz Steppes east to Semipalatinsk and Zaisan, south-western Tarbagatai, Afghanistan, Baluchistan, Gilgit and Baltistan to Ladak, and possibly western Tibet, also in the Ferghana Valley but not in the surrounding mountains where replaced by *hemileucoptera*. It is a little larger than *fennorum*, with more extensive white in the wing. The green areas on its outer secondaries are more extensive and the inner secondaries often more green than blue. The green parts of its tail may be dark green as in some specimens of the nominate form but are most often a beautiful bright bronze-green, with a golden tinge. The upper part of the rump is clear white and forms a conspicuous band contrasting with the black back and lower rump.

P. p. hemileucoptera, from western and central Siberia north and east of the range of *bactriana*, the mountains of Russian Turkestan, to the Sayans, north-western and western Mongolia, western and central Altai, Sinkiang; and *P. p. leucoptera* from southern Transbaicalia east to about Sretensk on the Shika, south to central and eastern Mongolia; are very like *P. p. bactriana* but slightly larger and with a little more white in their wings. *P. p. camtschatica*, from Anadyrland, northern Okhotsk Sea area, and Kamchatka, much resembles them but has even more extensive white on its wings, the entire inner webs of most primaries usually being white, and the wings and tail usually as green as in the greenest individuals of *bactriana*, *hemileucoptera*, and *leucoptera*.

P. p. sericea, from Amurland and Ussuriland, south through Manchuria, Korea and China to Tonkin, northern Laos and west to Yunnan and northern Burma, is very similar to nominate *P. p. pica* from western Europe, but has proportionately longer wings and a slightly shorter tail. In the southern populations of *sericea*, the tail is usually rather dark and often has a bluish purple tinge on the part that is green in other populations, in weathered plumage it becomes predominantly purplish black. The blue on the wings is usually tinged with purple and the green areas on the secondaries are darker and less extensive. These features are less marked in the northern parts of *sericea's* range, as given here, and birds from these areas have sometimes been separated racially as *P. p. jankowski* and *P. p. anderssoni*. I concur with Vaurie in thinking it best to include all these intergrading and slightly differentiated forms under *sericea*.

A very large form, *P. p. bottanensis*, is found from north-eastern Tsinghai, south through central Sikang to south-eastern Tibet and the eastern Himalayas in Assam, Bhutan, and Sikkim. It has proportionately much larger and longer wings even than *sericea*, usually very rich green and blue on the wings and a very vivid bronze and purple zone on the tail.

The American form, *P. p. hudsonia*, is very like nominate *pica* but has rather longer wings and tail and usually a very distinct white, or white and greyish, band across the rump. The bronze-green sheen on its crown is more pronounced, as a rule, than in most individuals of Old World forms. Its iris has (always?) a whitish outer ring (Brooks).

Pica p. asirensis, from Arabia, is a very distinct form. It has a large bill and appears very dark. The glossy parts of its wings are very dark purplish blue with hardly a hint of green; its tail is very dark greenish purple or bronzy purple. In weathered plumage the exposed parts of the wings and tail bleach to a dull bronzy brown. The white areas are smaller than in other races. In juvenile plumage the white on its belly and scapulars is strongly suffused with greyish brown.

Field characters Combination of black and white plumage and long tail diagnostic. In flight the primaries appear mainly white. Tail when spread is a somewhat elongated wedge-shape.

Chattering call often betrays its presence when unseen, but Jay can mimic this perfectly so caution needed where both are likely to occur.

Nest (q.v.) characteristic and in winter gives sure proof of previous presence of Magpies in the area.

Distribution and habitat Much of Europe and Asia (see map), including a presumably, but probably relatively recently, isolated population in Anadyrland, northern Okhotsk Sea area and Kamchatka; north-western Africa; western Arabia, in the Asir mountains south and east of Mecca, probably south to the Yemen; and western North America.

Typically inhabits country that gives a combination of scrub, large bushes, or trees for cover and nesting; and open ground with short, scattered, clumped or grazed vegetation, or exposed earth, for food seeking. Where there is little or no effective human persecution it can sometimes maintain itself in almost treeless places.

Commonly in or near partially scrub-covered hills or downland; in agricultural or stock-raising country with patches of scrub, tall hedges, clumps of trees or similar cover interspersed; in open woodland and along wood edges (but seldom or never in extensive dense woodland); around villages and farmsteads. In Britain often breeds or feeds (respectively) on bush-grown or grassy parts of sea cliffs. In the eastern parts of its range, and to some extent in the west where not too keenly persecuted by man, lives immediately around human dwellings, in towns and villages and even about human habitations in nearly treeless areas.

Sedentary, except for dispersion of some young birds and possibly occasional eruptive wandering. In some of the North American populations, however, 'fall and winter movements are noted regularly . . . . . . and in some years well-defined migrations occur outside (the normal) range' (Bent).

Feeding and general habits Feeds mainly on the ground but sometimes in trees or shrubs. Often forages on the ground in small open spaces, narrow paths or between clumps of high grass or other herbage. Insects and other invertebrates, including beetles and their larvae, among them the harmful Colorado Beetle, grasshoppers, crickets, crane-flies, wasps, bees, snails, slugs, millipedes, woodlice and spiders probably form the bulk of the food, except in winter, of most Magpie populations. Grain and some seeds, cherries, elder-berries and other fruits, soft-shelled almonds, small mammals, lizards, eggs and young birds, and the flesh of larger creatures that have been killed by man (especially by traffic on roads) or other predators are also taken.   Acorns, nuts, peas and potatoes are also recorded foods, but seem not usually to be eaten extensively.   Magpies sometimes damage large domestic animals by eating or trying to eat the flesh from branding wounds, saddle sores or other injuries caused by human cruelty or folly.

Readily takes many human foods, such as all kinds of cooked meat and bread, when available.   Where not persecuted by man (and sometimes even where it is) scavenges around houses or tents and on garbage heaps, or comes to bird tables, especially in winter.   Attacks predators from behind in usual corvine manner.   Pairs often successfully rob Black Kites of food by such tactics.

Large food objects are held under one or (less often) both feet.   When seeking food on the ground, turns over or throws to one side mammal droppings and other objects in search of invertebrates.   Catches grasshoppers with great agility.   Will often attack birds, of species that it normally ignores, if they show signs of weakness or injury, especially if they make apparently uncoordinated, helpless-looking fluttering movements.   The speed with which it can fly up or dodge enables it to take great apparent risks when mobbing predators or when feeding at the same carcasses as dogs, wolves, coyotes or foxes.

A tame bird regularly dunked any meat given to her before eating it.   She did the same with mice and sparrows and such behaviour has been recorded from a wild Yellow-billed Magpie.   It appears to make the subsequent plucking of fur or feathers simpler and quicker.   How common this habit is in wild Magpies appears to be unknown.

On ground or other level surfaces walks most of time but frequently hops quickly to catch prey or when in haste.   As Kunkel has described, it only hops with feet held parallel when in a great hurry, more often the hops are a sort of Polka-step with the legs spread and lifted from the ground one after the other.   Flight usually direct, weak-looking and with rather rapid wing beats, but often interspersed with short glides, and spectacular swoops and dives with partly-closed wings.   The flight of the large-winged Tibetan form appears stronger and it is said more often to fly long distances over open country (Schäfer).

Hides food in typical manner.   Has been seen to recover hidden food (Hayman).   Often said to hide bright non-edible objects.   I have not seen this, however; none of my tame Magpies did so; and Mr Ray Connor, who has made an intensive study of this species, informs me (*pers. comm.*) that he also has never seen a Magpie hide an inedible object.

Usually in pairs or small parties.   Large numbers may congregate at roosts or at sources of food. Some pairs remain all year within or in the immediate vicinity of their breeding territory; others desert the breeding place in summer or autumn and re-occupy it early the following year.   Where suitable cover is scarce and localized occupied nests may be as little as 18 metres apart (Connor, 1965).

Communal roosts are often in fairly dense thickets of young trees, scrub, or tall bushes.   They may be used throughout the year but by fewer birds during the breeding season.   Magpies using a roost usually come in pairs or small straggling parties.   They may gather on trees near the feeding ground until large numbers have collected, but tend to straggle and break up into smaller groups on their way to the roost.   Some pairs roost in their breeding territories throughout the year, even when these are near to a communal roost.   Building pairs often roost near the nest site but the male no longer does so, as a rule, after incubation starts.

Roosting in nests has often been recorded but appears not to be very frequent in Britain.   K. G. Spencer (*in litt.*) observed a pair roosting in late winter, one inside and one underneath an old nest.   Sometimes this pair would go to the communal roosting place but return later the same evening to roost in their nest.   Schäfer states that the Tibetan Magpie *Pica p. bottanensis*, in north-eastern Tibet, builds large roosting nests in which as many as ten Magpies may roost regularly.   One which he examined was a honeycomb-like stick structure suggestive of several small Magpie nests built together.

Where not persecuted by him the Magpie shows little fear of man but where, as in Britain, much shot at, it is timid and wary.   Of natural predators the Goshawk, *Accipiter gentilis*, kills many Magpies at and near their roosting places in the early morning (Bährmann).   The Carrion Crow is a nest predator, especially of undomed nests (see esp. Raspail 1908); the American Crow, *Corvus brachyrhynchos*, and

Great Horned Owl, *Bubo virginianus*, have been observed to attempt nest predation (Erpino) and are probably successful at times. The Raccoon is an important nest predator of Magpies in America. Where their ranges overlap the Magpie is extensively parasitized by the Great Spotted Cuckoo, *Clamator glandarius*.

Ants in typical active manner. It sometimes applies ants to its rump and the base of the tail, both above and below, as well as to the wing feathers.

Lehmann (1953) gives details of how a female, who lost two thirds of her upper mandible in a trap in winter, not only survived (without any human help) but successfully bred the following spring.

Nesting Nests usually in a tree, bush or shrub; much less often on a building, ledge of cliff or bank, or on the ground among bushy cover. In some parts of Europe now nests frequently on electricity pylons and similar structures. The nest may be either low or high; in Britain sites between 2 and 6 metres high in large Hawthorn or Blackthorn bushes are perhaps most frequent, although nests in the tops of tall elms and oaks often appear to be more numerous because of their conspicuousness.

Nest large and usually unmistakeable. An outer framework of sticks and large twigs, inside which is a heavy cup of mud, damp earth, cowdung or similar stuff more or less intermixed with vegetable material. The inner cup is lined with fine roots or fine wiry plant stems, sometimes also with fibrous bark, hair or grass stems. An open-work canopy of sticks which, like those of the outer framework, are often thorny, in which there are one or two side openings for the bird to pass through, is usually built above and partly around the nest. Sometimes, and quite often when the nest is built in small, thornless shrubs, the canopy is absent. I think in most or all of such cases the site has not permitted the builders to make a canopy owing to lack of suitable branches in which to lodge the first sticks for its framweork. Others have, however, recorded canopy-less nests in sites in which it seemed to them that the Magpies could have built a canopy had they tried to.

Both sexes build, the male often bringing more sticks than the female. Either male or female is capable of building a nest unaided (Bhärmann; Goodwin; Latchford). When building Latchford's tame female dipped each billful of mud in water before taking it to the nest. Bährmann found that the first materials placed in the site are torn up grass clumps, roots and mud or earth. Twigs are used to broaden this base, then the surrounding stick framework and the mud or earth cup are built up more or less simultaneously. As with other birds, unfinished nests are readily deserted if the builders are frightened at them. This and the rare occurrence of a 'difference of opinion', which may cause male and female to work at separate sites for a period, seem responsible for the legend that one pair of Magpies builds several nests in order to fool potential nest-robbers.

Usually a new nest is built each year, or for any new breeding attempt. Rarely, if ever, is an old nest simply refurbished and re-used. A new mate may take over a partly-built or completed nest together with the widow or widower whose mate has been killed. New nests are often built on top of the remains of old nests, or adjacent to an old nest, and such cases may give the false impression that an old nest is being re-used. In England, carrying of material to existing nests may occur in autumn (Spencer, *in litt.*). Nest building, in Britain, central and western Europe, commonly begins in February or March. In England, in mild winters, nests may be nearly completed before the end of January (Spencer *in litt.* and *pers. obs.*). Spells of hard weather usually put a temporary stop to such early ventures. Eggs are usually laid in April, rarely in late March, in England and comparable latitudes of Europe. In Burma and southern China eggs are laid in March or even late February. In Tibet May appears the usual month for egg-laying. In most or all areas replacement clutches may be found much later, up till June or July. In America also, first clutches are usually laid in April.

Normally single-brooded but pairs will nest and lay a second, third, possibly even a fourth time, if they have lost eggs or nestlings. Clutch of 2 to 8, usually 5 to 7. The American form, *hudsonia*, tends to have larger clutches, often 8 or 9, and up to 13 recorded. The eggs are bluish green, greenish blue, pale greenish, greenish yellow or cream-coloured; speckled and/or spotted or blotched with dull brown, olive brown or greyish, and with underlying pale grey or violet markings. Usually the ground colour is fairly densely covered with spots or speckles. There is evidence (Holyoak, 1968) that all the eggs of a clutch may not be laid on successive days, as is normal with most passerine birds, but that two or three days may elapse between the laying of successive eggs. The reason for this is unknown and it is certain that the eggs are often laid daily.

Incubation and brooding by female only, fed by male. Female spends much time on nest from laying of first egg. Young fed by both sexes. A tame female offered food (in her gullet) to her nestlings with low guttural calls, and if they did not respond she would tap the nestling's head and prise open its bill (Latchford). Incubation period 17 to 18 days; much shorter and longer periods recorded exceptionally, from 'perhaps as little as 14 days' to 23 days' (Evenden).

Young are usually brooded by day until ten or eleven days old. After fledging they keep in or close to cover near the nest site for at least several days. Bährmann has known instances where fledged young returned to roost in the nest, but this seems unusual. When the young can fly well the family may wander away from the nesting territory.

There is good circumstantial evidence that the canopy over the nest serves to protect its contents from predators, in conjunction with the defensive attacks of the parents. Raspail (1908) noted that un-canopied Magpie nests were more often successfully robbed by Carrion Crows than were normal nests.

Magpies appear usually to begin breeding in their second year but first-year birds do so at times. Probably this usually occurs through deaths of older birds leaving territories vacant or older birds mateless. Non-breeding birds sometimes hold territory (Holyoak).

Voice The well-known and characteristic rattling chatter, sometimes written as 'ka-ka-ka-ka-ka...' or 'shak-shak-shak-shak...' is primarily an alarm call. It is also used in apparent frustration or anger; probably in any situation which involves considerable excitement and conflict, especially between fear and aggression, or fear and curiosity. Short bursts of chattering that appear somewhat more deliberate and less violent in tone seem rather characteristic of social gatherings. Panic-stricken Magpies do not chatter. Sometimes each chattering phrase is prefaced by two longer notes: 'skaa! skaa! ka-ka-ka-ka..'. In a tame female this version always indicated the sudden appearance of some alarming object. Observations on a limited number of individuals of known sex suggest that at comparable levels of excitement female Magpies utter higher-pitched chattering than males.

A harsh two-syllabled 'shrack-ak', often repeated at short intervals but not run together to suggest a chatter, appears to be given when the bird is ill at ease but has no visible object on which to focus its alarm.

The appeal call is a very common call that seems based on the hunger call of the fledged young. It has numerous variants but most typically is an eager-sounding two-syllabled 'cheeuch' or a three-syllabled 'cheeuch-uch' ('ch', at end of words, hard as in the Scottish word 'loch'). Shorter, lower-pitched and more or less monosyllabic versions are very often uttered. Apart from its use by the dependent juvenile, this call is also used as a greeting between paired birds, by the female when begging her mate for food, and by tame birds on the appearance of a human with whom they are on friendly terms.

The low guttural or crooning call, which parent Magpies give when offering to feed nestlings (Latchford; Brown), is probably a variant of the appeal call.

A throaty, explosive, almost snorting 'tchurch!', jerked out as head and tail are jerked up and wings slightly lifted, seems often correlated with sexual or territorial rivalry. When used by tame birds towards humans it is accompanied by aggressive display and is commonly a prelude to attack.

The 'tchurch' call also has a peaceable form. It is given softly and gently by Magpies in company with their mates and by tame birds to people for whom their feelings appear entirely affectionate or submissive. I have known it to be given in an apparently begging context to a human but when nesting material, not food, was desired.

An individually variable clicking 'k'tk', 'kittik', or short explosive 'tchuk!' with a suggestion of a guttural click in it, is given by tame female Magpies when spoken to by someone to whom they are sexually attached or attracted. It is accompanied by a quick downward bow of the head, upward jerk of the tail and the wing-flirting display; the last usually at low intensity. It is frequently used by wild Magpies, perhaps by females only, at cermonial gatherings, and is possibly homologous with the guttural clicking notes of many jays and crows.

A prolonged, hoarse call, continued for up to half a minute or more without intermission, not harsh or sharp enough to be described as a screech, but loud and with an intense urgent almost despairing tone, is often given at the nest site.   Tame birds of both sexes sometimes give this call when they appear to want a human to join them or stay with them at their nest site.   It is given when the person the bird is responding to is at a little distance or begins to go away after having been with the bird.   The Magpie then flies to its nest-site, or a potential nest-site, and utters this call with somewhat lowered head and raised tail, while tugging, pushing, pulling or manipulating nest material, wire netting or other objects in a manner suggestive of great emotional tension.   Sometimes the bird may wing-flirt when giving this call.   It is often uttered by wild Magpies in late winter and early spring, either at or near the nest site. It seems likely that its function is to stimulate the mate to join the calling bird or to participate in nest-building.   It is possible that some element of frustration (perhaps only frustration when the bird is in a nest-building mood) may be involved, as some *Corvus* species give similar-sounding calls when the stick which they are adding to the nest gets temporarily stuck in a wrong position.

A possibly related call, which I have not heard, is that described by Bährmann as a long-drawn 'tschirrl', sometimes uttered in flight, particularly by Magpies disturbed at a roosting place.   He thinks it may stimulate other Magpies to flee with or follow the calling bird or indicate to them that the caller intends to flee or at least to fly away.

A soft protesting 'tsrae(e)', a quiet note that dies away in a pathetic-sounding manner, is sometimes uttered by juvenile Magpies (and possibly adults) when approached threateningly by a social superior. A tame adult female Magpie would utter this note whenever I pushed her away from something that she was investigating, or otherwise thwarted her.

A variety of soft low-pitched sounds were uttered by my tame female when she was perched close to my face, in response to my talking to her in an affectionate tone.   These calls are frequently used between the members of a pair of Magpies, especially when they are at or near the nest-site.   Possibly they are low-intensity variants of the appeal note (q.v.).

A warbling sub-song, which usually incorporates low-intensity variants of all the recognizable calls as well as other sounds, is frequently uttered by juvenile and first-autumn birds.   Bährmann records such singing also from adults visiting their nesting sites in late winter and early spring.

Tame Magpies that have been hand-reared often mimic the human voice as well as the calls of poultry and other birds.   I do not, however, know of any certain instance of vocal mimicry from a wild Magpie.

The above notes on the voice of the Magpie are based on my own observations on tame and wild Magpies in England, except where otherwise stated.   The information available does not, allowing for differences of transliteration, seem to indicate any significant vocal differences between at least the British, European and Chinese populations.   Stegmann states that the voice of the Magpie in Amurland is 'simpler and less hissing' than in Europe but gives no precise comparison.   Schäfer says that the voice of the Tibetan form, *bottanensis*, is much louder and harsher and that besides the well-known chattering it has a soft rattling call suggestive of that of the Nightjar, *Caprimulgus europaeus*

Descriptions of the calls of the American Magpie, *hudsonia* (see esp. Bent) suggest some differences, especially in the alarm chatter or its equivalent.   Brooks states that the voices of the American and European forms differ greatly from each other but does not give information as to how they differ beyond saying that the calls of *hudsonia* are identical with those of the Yellow-billed Magpie, *Pica nuttalli*. Some long whining calls of *hudsonia* that I have heard recorded (Kellogg & Allen, 1962) are unlike any call of the British Magpie that I know.   Some calls on another record (Kellogg & Allen, 1959) are similar or identical to those of British Magpies, but the (presumed) alarm chatter is slower in tempo and more like that of *nuttalli* (as recorded by Kellogg & Allen, 1962).

Display and social behaviour   When socially or sexually excited, and not frightened, the Magpie fluffs out its plumage in such a way as to increase the amount of white visible.   It also tends to hold its wings with the secondaries slightly spread and somewhat flattened in a dorsal plane, so that they present, to one looking down on the bird, two rectangles of brilliant colour.   A Magpie at rest also usually fluffs out its plumage and shows much white.   A frightened Magpie shows relatively little white plumage.

In the wing-flirting display the bird, with head somewhat lowered, suddenly lifts its folded wings so that the 'squared' secondaries are, together with the rest of the wing, tilted forward at an angle of about 30 to 40 degrees above the back.   As the wings are lifted they are fluttered, and may be slightly opened. This wing movement is usually accompanied by a forward bow of the head and an upward movement of the tail but these may be hardly perceptible.   The 'tchuk', the peaceable 'tchurch' or some form of the appeal call is usually uttered at the moment of displaying.   The head feathers are usually erected. This display is given by Magpies of both sexes to their mates.   It may be given when the two are foraging near each other but more often by a bird that is foraging or perched alone, when its mate rejoins it or appears in sight.   It is given at very full intensity by paired (or pairing?) Magpies perching close to one another in couples at ceremonial gatherings.   It is also given at potential nest sites by the male, probably at times also by the female, and then appears to function as a 'nest-calling' display.   Tame Magpies give this display to humans to whom they are sexually attached or attracted.

Aggressive wing-flirting differs from the peaceable form in that the wing movement is usually slight and without fluttering, the tail is jerked upward far more vigorously, and the head feathers, especially on the crown, are depressed.   As the tail is jerked up there is an upward movement of head and body and, usually, the aggressive 'tchurch' is uttered.   This display is seen often at ceremonial gatherings, where it sometimes prefaces an attack by the displaying bird.   It is given by tame Magpies in apparent threat to human beings, often as a prelude to attack.   A tame hen Magpie, who considered herself paired to me, never gave this display to me but frequently directed it at other people in apparent threat or defiance.

In the tilting display the bird approaches with its secondaries displayed as above described.   It tilts its body, slightly raises the further wing without unfolding it, and tilts its tail towards the creature at which it is displaying, the tail forming an angle of about 130 degrees with the body.   The bird usually holds the head high and utters low-pitched, monosyllabic calls.   Some observers have heard subsong uttered in this situation.   This display is shown by male (and female?) Magpies towards their mates, possibly also at times towards other birds; it was shown by my tame female both to me and to people to whom she was not, apparently, much attached.   It appears to be a self-assertive display used in sexual contexts.

Very similar to the tilting display is an aggressive display in which the feathers on the mantle are erected and, as the tail is switched sideways, the lateral feathers on its near side are spread, the head is lowered and held somewhat forward.   This display is often used when threatening or attacking another Magpie or some other creature.   Usually the attacking bird shows some signs of fear and it is likely that the feather raising and the usually side-long approach indicate conflict between impulses to escape and to attack.

Begging is essentially the same as in crows and jays.   The wings are lifted and fluttered or flapped with a 'loose at the shoulders' appearance; often they are raised high above the back.   The appeal call 'cheeuch' is given loudly.   This display is used by young birds, by the female to solicit feeding from her mate, by tame birds towards humans, and probably also in other situations where some response on the part of the mate or parent is wanted.

As with *Corvus* species, a rapid and frequent drawing of the nictitating membrane over the eye is common in sexual and agonistic situations.   My tame female when 'talking' affectionately to me would often droop her head forward, with crown feathers erected, draw the nictitating membrane across rather slowly and hold it over the eye for a second or two so that I could plainly see its brilliant orange patch.   It is probable that the visual reaction of a Magpie is quick enough for the membrane's coloration to be appreciated even when it is drawn more quickly over the eye, as it usually is.

Allo-preening of adults by their mates and of a fledged juvenile by one of its parents has been observed (Holyoak, *pers. obs.*) but appears to be infrequent.   It involves nibbling movements, a Raven-like insertion and subsequent opening of the bill and apparent ingestion of some small particles

Bährmann (1952) describes copulation as taking place sometimes on the ground or on a branch; the female may either quiver or spread her wings, or do both; or spread both wings and tail.   The male displays before copulation with heavily flapping or else slightly drooping and quivering wings.   Clegg gives a detailed description of a mating he saw in which the female adopted a flattened posture with body and tail flat on the ground her head slightly raised and wings held half open and quivered. He particularly noticed that the tail was not quivered. The male hopped towards her with tail tilted towards her and slightly raised, and wings open, held stiffly out from the body and vibrating rapidly. After two or three hops in this attitude he mounted the female from behind and copulated.

Display flight in which the bird appears to stop and hover with fanned tail occurs at ceremonial gatherings, usually accompanied by a distinctive bubbly or chuckly call and another form of display flight, in which the bird alternately beats its wings and floats with wings and tail outspread (Ward).

'Ceremonial' gatherings occur, especially in late winter and early spring. Established pairs may join these gatherings (*pers. obs.*, Bäsecke) but one of their functions seems to be to enable unpaired birds to meet potential partners. In the early part of the breeding season the killing of one member of a nesting pair is often followed within 24 hours or less by a gathering in the area, after which a pair, apparently the bereaved bird and a new mate, are together in the territory (see esp. Raspail, 1901).

The Magpie hammers with closed bill, as well as pecking and tugging at inanimate objects, when in a state of tension, especially when inclined to attack but apparently fearing to do so.

Although the contrary has been stated, young Magpies taken as nestlings and reared in isolation from others of their species may imprint on man or another species as firmly as any Jackdaw.

Other names Pie, Pyet, Black-billed Magpie (in America).

REFERENCES

BÄHRMANN, U. 1952. Ein Beitrag zur Biologie der Elster (*Pica pica pica* L.). *Bonn. Zool. Beitr.*, **3**: 289–304.
—— 1968. *Die Elster.* Wittenberg, Germany.
BÄSECKE, K. 1952. Fruhjahrversammlungen der Elster. *Vogelwelt* **73**: 57.
BENT, A. C. 1946. Life histories of North American jays, crows, and titmice. pp. 133–155. *Bull. U.S. Nat. Mus.* No. 191.
BROOKS, A. 1931. The relationships of American magpies. *Auk.* **48**: 271–272.
BROWN, R. H. 1924. Field-notes on the Magpie, as observed in Cumberland. *Brit. Birds* **18**: 122–128.
CLEGG, T. M. 1962. Pre-coital display of Magpies. *Brit. Birds* **55**: 88–89.
CONNOR, R. J. 1965. Notes on the nidification and oology of the Magpie (*Pica pica*) in a locality on the Middlesex/Buckingham border during 1965. *Ool. Rec.* **39**: **4**: 4–9.
ERPINO, M. J. 1968. Nest-related activities of Black-billed Magpies. *Condor* **70**: 154–165.
EVENDEN, F. G. 1947. Nesting studies of the Black-billed Magpie in southern Ihado. *Auk* **64**: 260–266.
GOODWIN, D. 1951. My Magpies past and present. *Avicult. Mag.* **57**: 10–15.
—— 1952. Notes and display of the Magpie. *Brit. Birds* **45**: 113–122.
HAYMAN, R. W. 1958. Magpie burying and recovering food. *Brit. Birds* **51**: 275.
HOLYOAK, D. 1968. Breeding biology of the Corvidae. *Bird Study* **14**: 153–168.
—— 1974. Ecology, Behaviour and Territory in the Magpie. *Bird Study* **21**: 117–128.
HUGUES, A. 1936. Simples notes sur la Pie Bavarde, *Pica pica* L. *Alauda* **7**: 535–540.
KELLOGG, P. P. & ALLEN, A. A. 1959. *A Field Guide to Bird Songs of Eastern and Central North America.* Boston.
—— 1962. *Field Guide to Bird Songs of Western North America.* Boston.
KUNKEL, P. 1962. Zur Verbreitung des Hüpfens und Laufens unter Sperlingsvögeln (Passeres). *Z. Tierpsychol* **19**: 417–439.
LABITTE, A. 1953. Quelques notes sur la biologie et la reproduction de la Pie bavarde *Pica p. galliae*. *Oiseau* **23**: 247–260.
LATCHFORD, S. 1960. In *Cage Birds* for 6 October, 318.
LEHMANN, E. VON 1953. Ein Beitrag zur Biologie der Elster. *Vogelwelt* **74**: 205–208.
LINSDALE, J. M. 1937. The Natural History of Magpies. *Pacific Coast Avifauna*, No. 25. Berkeley, California
LORENZ, K. 1931. Ethologie Sozialer Corviden. *J. Orn.* **79**: 67–127.
OWEN, D. F. 1956. The food of nestling Jays and Magpies. *Bird Study* **3**: 257–265.
RASPAIL, X. 1901. Cérémonie de secondes noces chez les Garruliens *Pica pica* et *Garrulus gl. glandarius* (L.) *Bull. Soc. Zool. France* **26**: 104.
—— 1908. Sur l'enlèvement des oeufs d'Oiseaux par la Pie. *Bull. Soc. Zool. France* **33**: 149.
RINGLEBEN, H. 1953. Beobachtungen an der Elster (*Pica pica*) im nordwestlichen Teil der Sowjetunion in Freileben und Gefangenschaft. *Zool. Gart. Lpz.* **19**: 1952, 288–294.

SCHÄFER, E. 1938. Ornithologische Ergebnisse zweier Forschungsreisen nach Tibet. *J. Orn.* **86,** Sonderheft: 270–274.
SHANNON, G. R. 1958. Magpie's rapid replacement of dead mate. *Brit. Birds* **51**: 401–402.
STEGMANN, B. 1931. Die Vögel des dauro-mandschurischen Uebergangsgebietes. *J. Orn.* **79**: 137–236.
STUBBS, F. J. 1910. Ceremonial gatherings of the Magpie. *Brit. Birds* **3**: 334–336.
VAURIE, C. 1954. Systematic Notes on Palearctic Birds. No. 5 Corvidae. *Amer. Mus. Novit.* No. 1668: 10–12.
WARD, E. 1952. Some observations at a Magpie Roost. *Brit. Birds* **45**: 403–405.
WITHERBY, H. F. *et al.* 1938. *The Handbook of British Birds*, vol. 1, pp. 26–28.

YELLOW-BILLED MAGPIE   *Pica nuttalli*

Corvus nutalli Audubon, 1837, Birds Amer. (folio), 4, pl. 362, Fig. 1. (corrected to *Corvus nuttalli* in Audubon, 1838, Orn. Biogr., 4, p. 450).

Description Like Magpie, but slightly smaller and more slender in build than nominate *P. pica*, and with yellow bill, patch of bare yellow skin behind eye and yellowish soles of feet. The bill tends to be, proportionately, a very little shorter, with a slightly more curved culmen. The nasal bristles are a little less extensive, leaving more of the culmen ridge exposed. Legs and feet (except soles) black. Irides dark brown. Nictitating membrane with orange spot as in *P. pica*. Iridescent parts of plumage exactly as in the American form of the Magpie, *Pica p. hudsonia*, (q.v.).

Field characters Yellow bill distinguishes from Magpie; pied plumage and long tail from other birds.

Distribution and habitat Western North America: in California west of the Sierra Nevada. Mainly in the Sacramento and San Joaquin valleys and adjacent foothills from Shasta County south to Kern County, and from San Francisco Bay area south-east to Ventura County.

Inhabits park-like country, pasture lands, and cultivated areas with tall trees. Does not inhabit areas with long hard winters, frequent strong winds or very hot and dry summers.

Feeding and general habits Much as Magpie (q.v.) but more consistently sociable. Commonly in small flocks of which, however, the pair is the basic unit. Pairs for life and adult pairs hold territory throughout the year. Territory defence is weakest, and the territories therefore then tend to shrink in size, between mid-June and mid-September. Verbcek (1972), from whose work most of the information here has been derived found the average size of territories was 1.2 hectares.

Feeds much in communal feeding areas, where birds from different colonies freely mingle, but the territory is an important source of food for its owners in the early part of the nesting period, especially shortly before and during egg laying. Food varied: like *P. pica* it feeds largely on insects, including moth larvae, tipulids and pupae but appears on the whole to be less of a scavenger and predator on small vertebrates than the Magpie sometimes is; acorns are often eaten. Hides food in usual manner. Dunking of a mouse by a wild Yellow-billed Magpie has been recorded (Blackburn 1968). When two birds were successively poisoned within sight and sound of their companions, the whole flock deserted the area, where they had been accustomed to feed, although they continued to live nearby (Wiggins).

When not breeding usually roosts communally but adult pairs may begin to roost in their breeding territories as early as October. In summer and autumn large roosts may be formed by the birds from several different breeding colonies. Birds coming to a communal roost first gather in particular tall trees at some distance, and show much caution when entering the roost proper. All roosting places found by Verbeek were in live oaks.

Nesting Breeds colonially in the sense that many pairs have adjacent breeding territories but normally, probably always, each pair nests in its own territory and there is seldom if ever more than one active nest in any one tree. Nest like that of *P. pica* but usually in a tall tree, only rarely in a medium sized tree and apparently never in a small tree or bush. Usually builds a new nest each year but sometimes re-uses or builds on top of an old nest. Yellow-billed Magpies of all ages show an interest in nests of their species, both their own and those built by others (Verbeek 1973).

Both sexes build. Building may start in December or January but is interrupted in bad weather. There is usually a period of about 10 days between the completion or near completion of the nest and the female starting to lay, which she usually does in late March or early April. Eggs like those of *P. pica*, 5 to 8 in number. Incubation is by the female only and begins before the clutch is complete. The male feeds the sitting female but she also comes off and collects some food for herself, mainly towards evening.

The young are fed by both sexes, at first with food brought by the male, later the female, who alone broods the nestlings, also collects food for them. The young remain in the nest tree for 4 or 5 days after fledging; they follow their parents to feeding places at from 10 to 14 days after fledging but are fed, at least in part, by them for about 7 weeks after leaving the nest.

Voice Hunt and Linsdale (in Bent 1946) list the following calls:

(1) 'Qua-qua-, qua-qua-qua', given in a series of two to six. Loud and raucous but sounds 'good-natured or well-disposed'. This appears to be the equivalent of the chatter of the European Magpie and is presumably the same as the 'excited 'check-check-check'' calls described by Verbeek from mobbing individuals.

(2) 'Quack?' a single note, mild yet querelous in tone.

(3) 'Queck' or 'kek'. A note with an 'absurdly weak tone'. In addition they mention a 'primitive song, similar to that of other corvids', probably the same or similar to the 'courtship song' described by Verbeek as sounding like 'wock, wock, wock,-a-wack, wock, pjur, weer, weer'. Verbeck describes the begging call of the female as a questioning, repeated 'quay'. This begging call is mentioned by Linsdale (1937) who also records mimicry from captive individuals.

Kellogg & Allen (1962) have made a record featuring the 'qua-qua' calls and a rather *Garrulus*-like screech. Brooks (1931) states that the calls of the Yellow-billed Magpie are identical with those of the American Black-billed Magpie and that both differ from those of European Magpies. This statement seems confirmed by recorded calls of the two American forms that I have heard. See remarks and references on the previous species.

Display and social behaviour From the descriptions of Verbeek (1972 and 1973) and others it appears that the displays of this form are closely similar or identical to those of *P. pica* (q.v.). Verbeek noticed that in the aggressive wing-flirting display, or 'tail up' as he names it, the bill is pointed downwards if the rival is below the displaying bird.

Allo-preening occurs between the members of a pair (Linsdale) but Verbeek saw it only on a very few occasions. Paired birds often nibble or tug at each others' bills or indulge in a tug-of-war with some small inedible object that the male has initially offered to the female. Soft warbling calls accompany such behaviour (Verbeek 1972).

Feeding of the female by the male is regular but (*fide* Verbeek) only occurs in response to typical juvenile type begging by her. In precopulatory display (Verbeek 1972) the male moves around the female with his head held high, his tail twisted towards her, forming an angle of about 120 degrees with his body, utters the soft warbling song and periodically flaps his wings while holding them fully open with the underside facing forward. The precopulatory display of the female consists of wing-flirting while head, body and tail are held close to the ground. The tail is not quivered.

REFERENCES

Bent, A. C. 1946. Life histories of North American jays, crows and timice. pp. 155–183. *Bull. U.S. Nat. Mus.* No. 191.

Blackburn, C. F. 1968. Yellow-billed Magpie drowns its prey. *Condor* **70**: 281.

Brooks, A. 1931. The relationships of American magpies. *Auk* **48**: 271–272.

Kellogg, P. P. & Allen, A. A. 1962. *Field Guide to Bird Songs of Western North America.* Boston.

Linsdale, J. M. 1937. *The Natural History of Magpies. Pacific Coast Avifauna*, No. 25. Berkeley, California.

Verbeek, N. A. M. 1972. Comparison of displays of the Yellow-billed Magpie (*Pica nuttalli*). *J. Orn.* **113**: 297–314.

—— 1973. The exploitation system of the Yellow-billed Magpie. University of California publications in Zoology, vol. 99.

Wiggins, I. L. 1947. Yellow-billed Magpies' Reaction to Poison. *Condor* **49**: 213.

AZURE-WINGED MAGPIE   *Cyanopica cyana*

Corvus cyanus Pallas 1776, Reise d. versch. Prov. Russ. Reichs, 3, p. 694.

Description A little larger than a Blue Jay. Like Magpie, *Pica*, in shape but more slightly built, with proportionately smaller legs and bill, and very soft, silky-textured plumage. All top of head, including nape and face, black with a slight blue or purplish sheen. Throat white, shading to off-white or pale greyish fawn on breast and underparts. Mantle and back light silvery grey to light greyish fawn, paler on rump and upper tail coverts. Wings and tail, except where otherwise stated, a beautiful soft light azure blue. Two outermost primaries (not usually visible) blackish; the next six have varying amounts of white on the outer web, forming a more or less longitudinal silvery white patch near the end of the folded wing. Those parts of the wing quills not visible when wing is folded are blackish. The two central tail feathers have broad white tips; the remaining tail feathers usually have only a slight margin of white at the ends or none at all. Underside of tail, where not white, bluish grey.

Irides dark brown to brownish black. Bill, legs and feet black. Juvenile has most of body plumage darker and browner, with pale fringes to most feathers. Its cap is dull black with pale buffish edges to feathers giving a scaly effect. Wing coverts and innermost secondaries greyish brown to brownish blue with conspicuous buff tips. The outer tail feathers are narrowly but conspicuously tipped with white. The two central tail feathers of the juvenile plumage are relatively narrow and weak in texture and grow to only about half the length of the next pair instead of being an inch or more longer as they are in subsequent plumages. Stegmann, who seems to have been the first to describe this phenomenon, states that the two central tail feathers and the inner secondaries are replaced at the first moult. This is so, but the only juveniles in full moult that I have examined are also renewing their primaries. It thus seems likely that renewal of all the wing quills at the first moult is normal in this species.

Newly-hatched young naked and pink, later dark lead colour (in captivity). Mouths of fledglings crimson, pinkish at gape (Porter 1941).

Many slightly differing races have been described from eastern Asia and the above is a composite description that covers them all. The main trend is from larger, paler and greyer forms in the northermost parts of the range (see col. pl. 1) to smaller and slightly browner forms in the more southerly parts. Vaurie gives the differences, real or supposed, on which the races *pallescens, koreensis, stegmanni, jeholica japonica, swinhoei, interposita* and *kansuensis* have been separated from nominate *cyana*.

The Iberian form, *C. cyana cooki* (see sketch), is smaller than most Asiatic forms. It overlaps with some eastern Chinese specimens in size, but its tail is usually shorter. Its body plumage is darker and browner, being a soft but relatively deep greyish fawn with a slight pinky tinge on the upper parts and, except for the white throat, a lighter tinge of fawn below. Its wings and tail are an appreciably deeper and slightly brighter blue. It usually has no white tips to any of the tail feathers when adult although the juvenile has narrow white tips to the outer tail feathers and, exceptionally, an adult may have them. In all Azure-winged Magpies the upper parts tend to be browner in worn plumage, unless much bleached, when they become very pale; these differences due to wear are more marked in the browner western form than in far eastern birds.

Field characters Pale grey or fawn bird with long blue tail, shortish blue wings and mainly black head. In Europe the blue tail alone distinguishes it from all other species. In the Far East its black bill, white throat and entirely black crown and nape at once distinguish it from the much larger and much longer-tailed Red-billed Blue Magpie. In zoos the unbarred wings and tail and small black bill distinguish it from Lanceolated Jay.

Distribution and habitat Occurs in eastern Asia in eastern, central and northern China, northward to Transbaicalia and Mongolia, the Amur Basin, Korea and Japan; and in western Europe in the central, western and southern parts of the Iberian Peninsula. Within both the western and eastern parts of its range it is absent from some areas which appear, at least to ornithologists who have visited them, to be suitable for it.

Inhabits open woodland, both coniferous and deciduous; cultivated or open country with groves of trees, thickets, orchards, hedges or other cover; riparian woodlands and thickets; gardens, and parks. In its European range it is essentially a bird of the warmer valleys, and local populations are often widely separate from one another, (Dos Santos). In Japan, however, it occurs in some areas of heavy snowfall (Hosono 1969)

Largely resident but apparently indulges in some local migrations or wanderings, as it may be absent from breeding places during the winter.

Feeding and general habits Usually in small parties, even in the breeding season. Sometimes in larger flocks of up to 30 individuals. Feeds both in trees and bushes and on the ground. Food consists largely of insects and other invertebrates, especially beetles and their larvae, and includes, in Europe, the Colorado Beetle; also soft fruits and berries. Readily learns to take various human foods when given the opportunity and sometimes scavenges around houses, garbage tips etc. Hides food in usual manner in captivity. Said to feed on and store seeds of *Pinus pinea*, acorns and olives in a wild state (Valverde, in Turcek & Kelso).

Very agile and graceful. Hops on the ground, usually with short but very quick hops. I have seen captive birds make an occasional 'polka-step'.

Large food objects are held under one foot and torn or dissected with the bill.

When anting (in captivity with *Formica rufa*) uses the same wing movements as the Jay, but picks up ants in the bill and applies them to the insides of the primaries in usual way. Several ants are used, one after another, without discarding those first picked up, so that the bird soon has a large clump of ants in its bill tip, just as the Magpie does.

Often roosts communally. In Japan, and probably elsewhere, large communal roosts form in winter; at other seasons smaller roosting groups are usual (Hosono 1967).

Nesting Nests in small colonies, usually only one nest in any one tree or bush and individual nests often forty to one hundred yards apart. Nest normally placed in tree or bush, from 0·5 to 12 metres or more high; in the Ussuri region, and perhaps elsewhere, sometimes under or among piles of driftwood lodged in trees or bushes (Vorobiev). Nest of sticks and twigs with an inner wall of intertwined plants, roots, fibres etc; usually (perhaps always) with mud in the foundations; lining of fine roots or other vegetable fibres, hair or wool. Both sexes build but further information needed as to the extent to which each does so.

I watched a pair in a zoo that were trying to build on an unsuitable site (they had no other). After taking up one or more sticks (separately), the male tore up stems and roots of grass in his bill till he had a bundle, then keeping them held there, he picked up damp sand (no mud available) from the shaded part of the floor by partly opening and stabbing in his bill until he had both wet sand and the grass. He then took the billful to the nest site and tried to plaster it down. The collecting procedure was thus similar to that of the Swallow, *Hirundo rustica*, when building, and doubtless serves under natural conditions to secure mud bound with grass, roots or other material as a foundation. I only saw the female of this pair (who, unlike her mate, was of the Iberian form) take one or two sticks but she was timid and afraid of my watching her which the male was not. The usual nest-building movements were used.

Eggs 5 to 9, usually 6 to 8, buff, greenish buff, light green, greyish green or greenish white, spotted or speckled with dark brown to olive brown and with underlying grey or violet markings. The underlying greyish spots, and less often all the markings, sometimes form a zone around one end (usually the larger) of the egg. None of the many clutches of eggs of the Iberian form I have seen had the greenish ground colours often found in eggs of the far eastern form. Nests with eggs once recorded as early as March in Iberia; commonly found in May or June throughout most of the species' range; and often in July, possibly sometimes second broods.

Incubation, by female only, 15 days, in captivity in England; hatching dates suggested that true incubation began with the third or fourth egg (Porter). Captive birds, of the Chinese form, were double-brooded and continued to feed the young of the first brood while incubating a second clutch of eggs. Young fed by both parents. Sometimes parasitized by the Short-winged Cuckoo, *Cuculus micropterus* (Shaw 1938).

Voice 'Krarraah! kwink-kwink-kwink' the first note very loud, harsh and upward-inflected; the 'kwinks' quick, metallic-sounding, upward-inflected notes. This appears to be an alarm call and may correspond to the chatter of *Pica*. I have heard it from captive birds when I have shown them some object that apparently aroused both fear and curiosity.

'Wee-we-wee-u', sometimes 'wee-we-we-wee-u', a soft, sweet but high pitched whistling call with the final 'u' sharply inflected upwards; given, I think in self-assertion or threat, by a tame male to me. Usually accompanied by the tail-tilting and wing-fluttering display.

'K'we' or 'k'we(it)', a soft note, very like some of the softer variants of the appeal call of *Garrulus* but upwardly inflected. Given in various situations, especially when bird has food in its gullet and seems undecided whether, or where, to store it.

'Tschrreeeeeh', a long-drawn, rather husky and sibilant call. Usually, and perhaps always, uttered with apparent effort, in an upright posture with bill raised somewhat above the horizontal and a very slight opening and sometimes also quivering of the folded wings. I have heard this call from captive birds on many occasions. When (twice) it was given by female of a pair out of sight of her mate, he immediately flew to her. This is probably the same call as that which Mountfort describes as 'a hoarse, rising "shree"' and found to be the most characteristic sound heard from wild birds in Spain in the breeding season.

I once heard faint, soft, high-pitched chattering calls from a captive male displaying to a female; a rather sharp series of chirrupping notes from the same male just afterwards when he was in his nest-site making building movements; and a single harsh note, suggestive of the aggressive 'tchurch' of *Pica*, from a tame male as he broke off a threatening or self-assertive display that he had directed at me.

The above descriptions are all of calls I have heard from various captive birds in zoos, about a dozen individuals in all. Most descriptions by others evidently refer to the same calls except for the following: A predator-mobbing alarm call which consists of a nasal screech beginning with a metallic guttural rattle. Simms tape-recorded this call from Spanish birds mobbing a stuffed Eagle Owl. An alarm call of the Chinese form is evidently similar as Swinhoe describes it as 'nasal and guttural'. Mountfort also heard 'a quiet "ker"' from birds offering food to their young.

Display and social behaviour A captive male repeatedly used towards me (on other side of the wire of his aviary) a display very similar to the tilting display of the Magpie. The tail was partly spread, on both sides not only on side nearest to me as in *Pica*, the body tilted towards me, and the folded wings slightly lifted and fluttered, the far wing being raised more than the near one. The bird gave the 'wee-we-wee-u' call. There was a very slight 'squaring' of the secondaries but much less so than in *Pica*. This seemed to be a self-assertive display used in a threatening context, as the bird was hostile to me.

Azure winged magpie: (1) sexual display; (2) giving the long husky call

In what was probably a sexual version of the above display, the male hopped around his mate, just after having fed her, with head a little lowered, tail only slightly tilted towards her, wings partly open and fluttering. This performance was suggestive of the pre-copulatory display of the male Rook. The head feathers were not erected.

The male (and female?) sometimes erects the feathers of its head so that its appearance is greatly changed and it seems to be wearing a black busby. This display was shown by a male when approaching or near his mate, sometimes in association with feeding her, although feeding of the female often takes place without such display. Allo-preening probably occurs as a human-imprinted bird would solicit substitute attempts from its owner's fingers by elongating its neck and erecting all its head and neck feathers.

Feeding of female by male and, much less often, of male by female, seen in captivity. A pair that wanted to build but had no facilities for so-doing often passed twigs (which I had given them) to one another in crouching posture and with slightly opened and fluttering wings.

Other names Blue-winged Magpie, Blue Magpie, Blue-tailed Magpie.

REFERENCES

COVERLEY, H. W. 1933. Nesting notes from Portugal. *Ibis* (13) **3**: 783.
DEMENTIEV, G. P. & GLADKOV, N. A. 1970. Birds of the Soviet Union, 5. English translation published by Israel Program for Scientific Translations, Keter Press, Jerusalem.
DOS SANTOS, J. R. 1968. The colony of Azure-winged Magpies in the Barca d'Alava region. *Cyanopica* **1**: 1–28.
HOSONO, T. 1967. A life history study of the Blue Magpie. *Misc. Rep. Yamashina Inst. Orn.* **5**: 34–47 and 177–193.
—— 1969. A life history study of the Blue Magpie. *Misc. Rep. Yamashina Inst. Orn.* **5**: 659–675.
JAHN, H. 1942. Zur Oekologie und Biologie der Vögel Japans. *J. Orn.* **90**: 75–77.
LA TOUCHE, J. D. D. 1932. *A Handbook of the Birds of eastern China* **1**: 14–15.

MOUNTFORT, G.   1958.   *Portrait of a Wilderness*, 53–56.   London.
PORTER, S.   1941.   Breeding the Chinese Azure-winged Magpie.   *Avicult.* Mag. (5) **6**: 3–8.
SHAW, T. H.   1938.   Nord-chinesische Blauelstern als Pflegeeltern von *Cuculus micropterus*.   *Orn. Monatsber.*
   46: 154–155.
SIMMS, E.   1951.   Communications in *Animals* B.B.C. Record R.E.S.R. 11.
STEGMANN, B.   1931.   Die Vögel des dauro-mandschurischen Uebergangsgebietes.   *J. Orn.* **79**: 142–144.
SWINHOE, R.   1861.   Notes on Ornithology between Takoo and Peking, North China.   *Ibis* (1) **3**: 336.
TURCEK, F. J. & KELSO, L.   1968.   Ecological aspects of food transportation and storage in the Corvidae.   *Comm.*
   Behav. Biol., Pt. A, **1**: 277–297.
VAURIE, C.   1959.   *The birds of the Palearctic Fauna* **1**: 146–148.
VOROBIEV, K. A.   1954.   *Birds of the Ussuri Area* (translation by G. Reed).   Moscow.
YAMASHINA, Y.   1961.   *Birds in Japan* 62.   Tokyo.
ZIEGER, R.   1967.   Kleine Beobachtungen aus der Mongolei.   *Beitr. Vogelk.* **13**: 116–124.

The blue, green and Whitehead's magpies

In his review of corvine genera, Amadon (1944) included the blue magpies, the green magpies or hunting crows, the Ceylon Magpie and Whitehead's Magpie all in the genus *Cissa* (formerly *Kitta*).   Later, however, Vaurie in 'Peters' check-list (1962) placed Whitehead's Magpie, *whiteheadi*, and the Ceylon Blue Magpie, *ornata*, together with the Yellow-billed, Red-billed and Formosan Blue Magpies, *flavirostris*, *erythrorhyncha*, and *caerulea*, in the genus *Urocissa*, leaving only the green magpies in the genus *Cissa*.

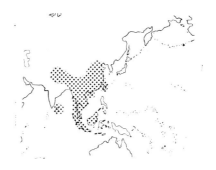

Although a very distinct species, the Ceylon Magpie partly bridges the gap between the green and blue pies.   It agrees with the former in size and in having enlarged, bright, fleshy eye-rims; in coloration it is nearer to the blue pies (although of a brighter blue) and in the length of its tail it is intermediate. It is also marginally closer to the blue pies in the colour pattern of its outer tail feathers but these are very similar in the two groups.   It may be mentioned here that, although the difference in head markings has sometimes been given as one criterion for separating the blue from the green magpies, juveniles of some forms of both *erythrorhyncha* and *flavirostris* have head markings very similar to those of the green magpies.

Whitehead's Magpie agrees with the blue magpies in size, or rather slightly surpasses them, but is shorter tailed and has no trace of green or blue in its plumage.   It also has black legs unlike the bright red or yellow legs of its congeners and differs in some details of pattern from the other forms.   It seems to me to be likely to stand as far from '*Urocissa*' as does *ornata* from *Cissa*.   The alternatives are either to put both it and the Ceylon Magpie in monotypic genera or to follow Amadon's example and put all these forms in the one genus *Cissa*, and this latter seems to me much the better course.

The blue magpies are graceful, elegant birds about the size of a Magpie, *Pica pica*, but with longer tails, due to elongation of the two central tail feathers.   They are predominantly mauvish blue in colour with black and whitish or all-black heads, bold white and black markings on the outer tail feathers and bright red, orange or yellow bills and legs.   In life *flavirostris* usually has more or less of a green and primrose yellow tinge but this colour is fugitive as in the green magpies (q.v.).   The webs of the ends of their

outer tail feathers turn up at the edges so that in profile a cross section of the tail tip is concave.   They
are birds of woodlands and thickets, usually keeping in or near thick cover, but are often found in cultivated
country, gardens or fairly open hillsides so long as there is plenty of cover nearby in the form of clumps
of trees, thick hedges, bamboo thickets and so on.   On the ground they take long bounding hops, only
exceptionally walking a few short steps when they wish to turn aside towards some object.   They carry
the long tail somewhat lifted so that its end falls in a graceful arch and does not get soiled.

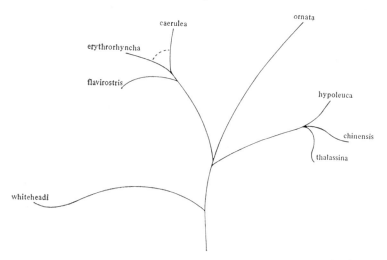

FIG. D.3.   Presumed relationships of species in the genus *Cissa*.   In this and subsequent dendrograms a dotted line connects
members of the same superspecies.

The Red-billed and Yellow-billed Blue Magpies, *Cissa erythrorhyncha* and *C. flavirostris*, are very closely
related and similar species.   They have a wide geographic overlap in range but within it appear usually
to be ecologically separated, *flavirostris* keeping to higher altitudes than *erythrorhyncha*.   Whistler (MSS)
noted that where both species occurred *flavirostris* was always rarer and that they seldom, if ever, inhabited
the same valley.

Some specimens of *C. flavirostris cucullata*, from parts of the Punjab (Simla, Murree, Khoteghur,
Mandi State), have the pale head patch more extensive than usual, reaching nearly as far back as in
C. erythrorhyncha, and have pale tips to many of the crown feathers.   Other birds from the same area
have the small nuchal patch typical of the species and in some it is intermediate.   Thus in these areas,
where both *erythrorhyncha* and *flavirostris* occur, some specimens of the latter approach closely to the
former in head markings.   These specimens appear all to have had yellow bills in life and, in those instances
where they have been named by the collector, do not seem to have appeared to him as other than normal
specimens of *C. flavirostris cucullata*.   The type of *cucullata*, from Kulu, Punjab, is in fact one of these
birds with a large nuchal patch.

Other morphological differences between the two species are of rather indefinite character and their
measurements overlap, although *erythrorhyncha* averages larger in length of wing (189–206 mm as against
178–195 mm) and tarsus (48–55 mm as against 45–50 mm).   If, therefore, any hybridization were to
take place it is very likely that the hybrids would not be readily recognizable as such.   The possibility
of hybridization between the two forms cannot, I think, be entirely excluded; but the alternative hypothesis of a remarkable convergence in appearance in this area of overlap is, on present evidence, perhaps
more likely.

The Formosan Blue Magpie, *C. caerulea*, is a geographical representative of *C. erythrorhyncha*.   It
has, however, diverged considerably from the mainland form in acquiring its deep blue body colour,
entirely black head and pale yellow eyes.   It seems best considered as forming a superspecies with *C.
erythrorhyncha*.

Whitehead's Magpie, *Cissa whiteheadi*, lacks all trace of blue in its plumage and has extensive white or yellow markings on the wings, unlike any of its congeners. Those parts of the plumage which are yellow in life fade in cabinet skins, and probably in some cases in the living bird also, to white only slightly, if at all, tinged with yellow. The predominantly black and white coloration of such faded specimens suggest affinities with *Pica* but the plumage pattern is quite different. Its appearance, geographical range and what is known of its habits all suggest that *whiteheadi* is most closely related to the blue magpies and best considered congeneric with them.

The Ceylon Blue Magpie, *C. ornata*, is a very distinct species that, as has been said, is in some respects intermediate between the blue and the green magpies. It may represent the surviving branch of some stock ancestral to both or, and more probably in my opinion, of some form once existing on the mainland of India but which has since become extinct there.

The green magpies differ from the blue magpies in having shorter tails; the bare eye-rims much more developed and in life very conspicuous; a different head pattern and predominantly green and chestnut-red coloration. The green and yellow colours change to blue and white in museum skins, in captive live birds and, in many instances, in free-living wild individuals also.

Ticehurst has shown that green feathers taken from skins will turn blue in 72 hours if exposed even to a northern light. Blue wild specimens have been taken, in more open country than the species typically frequents (Lowe); wild specimens in a similar state of plumage wear may differ in the extent to which their green, yellow and red tints have changed into blue, white and dull brown (Deignan). Blue captive birds, if kept in a large aviary and given an abundance of varied live food, regain their green, yellow and red colours at the next moult but these are often subsequently lost (Delacour, 1929; pers. comm. from various aviculturists).

Green magpies are typically birds of evergreen forest or second growth jungle, sometimes occurring in more open woods or scrubland, but never far from cover. They are widely distributed in the Indo-Malayan region from the lower Himalayas in north-central India south-east to Indo-China, Hainan, Java and Borneo. Delacour (1929), in his revision of the genus, recognized six species: *chinensis* (races *chinensis*, *minor*, *robinsoni*, *klossi* and *margaritae*), *hypoleuca* (races *hypoleuca* and *chauleti*) and four monotypic species *jefferyi*, *katsumatae*, *concolor* and *thalassina*. In the latest world checklist Vaurie recognized only two species, treating *hypoleuca*, *jefferyi*, *katsumatae* and *concolor* as races of *thalassina*.

Vaurie's conception of *thalassina* thus includes two rather different groups of green magpies, one of which occurs in Indo-China and Hainan and one in Java and Borneo. Both differ from *chinensis* in the colour pattern of their inner secondaries and both show some geographical overlap with *chinensis*. They also, however, differ from each other and on present evidence there is little other than the fact that they are allopatric to suggest that they are more closely related to one another than either is to *chinensis*.

I think it is best to give both these populations specific rank and to treat as three species the forms which show the following constant differences.

The Green Magpie, *C. chinensis*, with a relatively long tail and large whitish terminal spots, bordered posteriorly with black, on its inner secondaries.

The Short-tailed Green Magpie, *C. thalassina*, with a much shorter tail, the light and dark markings at the ends of the outer tail feathers small and obsolescent, and the pale tips to the outer tail feathers differently shaped, more extended on the inner webs and more narrowly margined with black. *C. chinensis* and *C. thalassina* both occur in North Borneo but appear to be ecologically and altitudinally separated. On Mount Kina Balu *chinensis* has been collected at heights up to a little over 360 metres and *thalassina* at 1200–2400 metres.

The Eastern Green Magpie, *C. hypoleuca*, with the tips of the inner secondaries green or blue with only very faint and ill-defined dark posterior borders; the tail rather shorter than that of *chinensis* but similar in pattern, and appreciably longer than the tail of *thalassina*.

Both *chinensis* and *hypoleuca* occur in central and northern Annam (Vaurie), and Delacour & Jabouille (1931) record both in Saravane Province in southern Annam. There does not, however, appear to be any proof of the two occurring in precisely the same locality. There are not specimens of both species from any one locality in the British Museum (Natural History) collection.   The populations in the areas of possible overlap in central and southern Annam differ in colour, *chinensis* having a yellow forehead and forecrown, green breast and conspicuous pale markings on the wings, and *hypoleuca* having a green forehead, yellow breast and green or blue markings on the wings.   These colour differences might function as isolating mechanisms, no doubt in conjunction with other differences, to help prevent interspecific pairing.

Oates has sometimes been criticized for using the name 'Green Jay' for *Cissa chinensis*, on the grounds that it was closely related to the blue magpies and, therefore, not a jay.   In so far as the names 'jay' and 'magpie' are assumed to indicate relationship with *Garrulus* and *Pica* respectively, I think Oates was a better judge of corvine affinities than his critics.   The blue and green magpies resemble the typical jays more than they do the magpies in several characters.   The tail patterns of all species, except the aberrant *C. whiteheadi*, and the pattern on the inner secondaries of *C. chinensis*, closely resemble those of *Garrulus lidthi* and *G. lanceolatus*.   They agree with *Garrulus* also in freely indulging in vocal mimicry in a wild state.   Many of the apparently innate calls of *C. erythrorhyncha* are very similar to innate calls of *Garrulus*.   In their hopping gait on the ground, in their anting postures, and in using the wing-quivering appeasing posture, *C. erythrorhyncha* and *C. chinensis* (and probably also other *Cissa* species) agree in detail with *Garrulus glandarius*.

Apart from the rather superficial character of their long, graduated tails, the *Cissa* species resemble *Pica* rather than *Garrulus* in having a polysyllabic 'chattering' alarm cry rather than a monosyllabic screech. Such vocal differences depend largely on the relative duration of individual notes and the speed with which they are repeated and may not be of much phylogenetic importance in some cases.   Comparable differences are sometimes found between the alarm calls of closely-related and congeneric species, as in the blue waxbills, *Uraeginthus*.

The green and blue magpies appear to be most closely related to the Old World jays *Garrulus* and to the tree-pies *Crypsirina*.   They may also be related to *Pica*, via *Cyanopica*.   I think, however, that the gap between the blue magpies and *Cyanopica* is greater than that between *Cissa* and *Garrulus*.

REFERENCES

AMADON, D.   1944.   The genera of Corvidae and their relationships.   *Amer. Mus. Novit.*, No. 1251.
DEIGNAN, H. G.   1938.   Plumage change in wild Siamese Hunting Crows.   *Ibis* **1938**; 769–772.
DELACOUR, J.   1929.   Revision du Genre *Cissa*.   *L'Oiseau* **10**: 1–12.
—— & JABOUILLE, P.   1931.   *Les Oiseaux de l'Indochine Française* **4**: 280–284.   Paris.
LOWE, W. P.   1938.   The plumage of the Green Magpies (*Cissa chinensis*) *Ibis* (14) **2**: 536–537.
OATES, E. W.   1883.   *A Handbook to the Birds of British Burma including those Found in the Adjoining State of Karennee* 406–407.
TICEHURST, C. B.   1938.   Footnote in *Ibis* (14) **2**: 771.
VAURIE, C.   1962.   *Check-list of Birds of the World* ('Peter's Check-list'), vol. 15, pp. 242–244.
WHISTLER, H.   Unpublished notes in library of Bird Room, British Museum (Nat. Hist.).

WHITEHEAD'S MAGPIE   *Cissa whiteheadi*

Urocissa whiteheadi Ogilvie-Grant, 1899, Bul. Brit. Orn. Cl., 10, p. 18.

Description   A little larger than Magpie, with proportionately larger and heavier body, bill and legs, and slightly shorter tail.

Head, neck, mantle, back and breast brownish black, the feathers of forehead and crown with greyish brown fringes, giving a slightly scaled effect.   The black of the breast shades to grey tinged with buff on lower breast and flanks, and yellowish buff on the belly and under tail coverts.   Wings black, boldly patched with white.   The lesser wing coverts are mainly white, the greater coverts have broad white tips, and the inner secondaries have most of their outer webs and a small part at the tip of the inner web white, the amount of white decreasing on successive feathers to a narrow white fringe on the outer secondaries.   The primaries have the basal third of the inner webs tinged silver grey, and very small white tips except on the outermost two primaries. Rump blackish grey, with white tips to some feathers; upper tail coverts with broad white tips. Central tail feathers silver grey with broad white tips and broad black sub-terminal bands; the amount of white increases outwards until the two outermost pairs of tail feathers on each side show more white than black.

Irides straw yellow. Bill red, brownish yellow at base. Legs and feet dark brown. The above description is of the nominate form, from Hainan, and is based on only two specimens, a male and female. It is likely that in life the white parts are more or less tinged with yellow.

The mainland form, *C. whiteheadi xanthomelana*, differs in being, on average, slightly larger in size, dull coal black rather than brownish black above and in having the dark parts of the tail feathers black with at most some suffusion of grey near their bases. Its irides are pale clear greenish yellow; the patch of bare skin behind the eye brownish-green and the legs and feet black with some orange at the joints. All the 'white' parts of its plumage are pale yellow, or tinged with pale yellow, in life.

Immature birds have the dark parts of the plumage ashen grey, tinged with yellow in life, except on the back, secondaries and outer wing coverts and tail feathers, where, however, the black is less intense than in the adults. The feathers of crown and forehead are blackish brown with broad, pale grey fringes. The irides are yellowish brown; the bill brownish grey with reddish orange tip and greenish base, sometimes entirely reddish, and the legs black. Delacour (1927, 1931) describes this as the juvenile plumage, but birds in this phase that I have seen are certainly not in their juvenile (first) plumage unless, which seems unlikely, the juvenile plumage of this species is unlike that of other corvids in being like the adults' in texture. It is not known how long the young take to acquire adult dress but as some immatures are darker than others and immatures appear more numerous than adults in the wild, it is probably at least their second year before they obtain the dark adult dress.

Field characters   Black or grey and yellow or white plumage, large size and long tail distinctive. Lack of any blue or green distinguishes it from any other *Cissa* species, the parti-coloured tail and yellowish or reddish bill from the Magpie.

Distribution and habitat   Indo-China, in Tonkin, northern and central Annam and central Laos; and Hainan island. Found in forest and at the forest edge, particularly near watercourses.

Feeding and general habits   Said to take insects and berries. Probably eats other small creatures also. Social and noisy but little is apparently known in any detail about its habits.

Nesting   A nest of the nominate form was a concave platform of dry stems of creepers and roots firmly interwoven.   It contained 6 eggs, now in the British Museum (Natural History), which are pale greenish blue, flecked and spotted with brown.

Voice   Has many different calls, some very loud and piercing, but there appears to be no detailed information.

Display and social behaviour   No information.

Other names   Whitehead's Hunting-crow, Grey Magpie.

REFERENCES

DELACOUR, J.   1927.   New birds from Indo-China.   *Bull. B.O.C.* **47**: 163–165.
—— & JABOUILLE, P.   1931.   *Les Oiseaux de l'Indochine Francaise* **4**: 278–280.
GRANT, W. R. O.   1900.   On the birds of Hainan.   *Proc. Zool. Soc.* **1900**: 475–504.

RED-BILLED BLUE MAGPIE   *Cissa erythrorhyncha*

Corvus erythrorynchus (*sic*) Boddaert, 1783, Table Pl. enlum., p. 38.

Description   About size of Magpie but with a much longer and less rigid tail.   Tail strongly graduated, the outermost pair of tail feathers being only about a fifth the length of the central pair.   Feathering at base of bill bristly and semi-erect but not conspicuously so.   Nostrils only partly covered by nasal bristles.

Head, neck and breast black except for a large pale bluish mauve patch extending from the hind crown to the hind neck, and spots of the same colour (pale tips to black feathers) on the crown.   Back and rump dull mauvish blue, suffused with grey.   Wing coverts rich bright mauvish blue.   Inner secondaries, outer webs of outer secondaries, and most of outer webs of primaries mauvish blue with white tips.   Parts of outer webs of outer primaries bluish white, forming a stripe along the closed wing.   Inner webs of primaries and outer secondaries and undersides of wing quills greyish.   Upper tail coverts mauvish blue with narrow bluish white subterminal bars and and broad black tips.   Central tail feathers mauvish blue, broadly tipped with white.   Outer tail feathers mauvish blue with broad black subterminal bands and broad white tips; on the inner webs, which are duller, there are narrow white bars before the black areas.   Underparts below the breast pale mauvish grey shading to cream-coloured on belly and nearly white on under tail coverts.   In fresh plumage the creamy and white parts are usually tinged with salmon pink or pinkish buff, but this colour is apparently soon lost even in wild birds.

Irides reddish brown, dark reddish brown, yellow-orange, or red.   Eye rims red, orange-red, or yellow. Legs and feet vermilion, orange-red or pinkish orange, with paler and duller claws.   Bill bright orange-red, vermilion, or reddish pink, usually with the tip a little paler than the rest of the bill.   These colours are taken from specimens of most subspecies.   The data suggest individual rather than geographical variation but too few collectors have recorded soft part colours and more information is needed.   All live birds that I have seen had dark reddish brown eyes.   The bills and feet of captive birds (in England) are usually orange or yellow-orange in colour even when they appear in perfect health and plumage.

Juvenile duller and paler with dull grey back and usually having the pale head patch, which is nearly white in the juvenile, extending to the forehead, and throat and malar regions grey to greyish white, so that the bird's head pattern is strongly suggestive of a green magpie's.   The juvenile's irides and bill are at first pale bluish and its legs dull yellowish.

The above plumage description is of the nominate form which is found in central and southern China and northern Indo-China.   Northern Chinese specimens average slightly paler in colour and greyer on the back.   They have been racially separated as *C. e. brevivexilla*.   Those from northern Yunnan and north-eastern Burma, *C. e. alticola*, tend to be bluer, less grey-tinged on the back.   The form from Assam and most of Burma, Thailand and Indo-China, *C. e. magnirostris*, has the pale patch on the head smaller and whiter and the mauve-blue of the upperparts darker and brighter with no grey tinge (except in very worn plumage).   The form from the western Himalayas, east to Sikkim, *C. e. occipitalis*, is very like *magnirostris* but is paler blue, with broader white tips to the secondaries and almost pure white nape patch and underparts.   The juveniles of *occipitalis* have darker, usually blackish grey, throats and less extensive white on the top of the head.   Juveniles of *magnirostris* and *alticola* seem intermediate but I have seen very few juveniles of these forms.

Field characters   Cannot be confused with any other species except the Azure-winged Magpie and the Yellow-billed Blue Magpie.   From the former distinguishable by larger size, longer tail, orange or red bill and black breast.   Much more easily confused with Yellow-billed Blue Magpie but adult separable, if clearly seen, by red or orange bill.

Distribution and habitat   Western Himalayas from the Punjab (Simla and Mussooree areas) east to northern China, the Indo-Chinese countries and south-east to Assam, Burma (not Tenasserim) and Thailand (Siam).   Has been said to occur in Kashmir and Tibet but proof seems lacking and confusion with the Yellow-billed Blue Magpie is possible.   May extend into south-eastern Manchuria but no recent evidence.

Inhabits jungle, scrub, and forest; also cultivated country and gardens, provided plenty of tree or shrub cover is available.   Most typically in hilly or mountainous country but also on plains where conditions are suitable, although not at the western end of its range.   When in true forest it occurs mostly or, at least in most abundance, at the edge or in and near clearings.   In some places a typical bird of camping grounds and hill cultivation.

Feeding and general habits   Seeks food both on the ground and in trees.   Takes insects, molluscs, centipedes, young birds, eggs, small mammals and small reptiles, fruits, nectar and, at times, scraps of human food and edible offal.   Said to eat seeds and may do so, or these may be seeds of fruits found undigested in its stomach.

Usually in pairs or in parties of 4 to 12 or more, which follow one another at intervals, like Jays, when crossing any open space.   Flight graceful, with alternate wing-beating, and gliding with the tail feathers spread.   When descending does so in graceful curves.   On the ground it moves in long hops with the tail carried somewhat raised so that the drooping end is clear of the ground.   Sometimes takes a few short sideways steps if it wants to investigate some object to one side, but it does not usually walk.

Anting postures of captive birds, with Wood Ants, *Formica rufa*, were identical with those shown by the Jay, *Garrulus glandarius*, but at high intensity the tail may be spread behind the bird and quivered over the ants.

Food that requires tearing up is usually held under one or, less often, both feet.   Like *Garrulus* it dislikes holding wet or even slightly sticky food under foot and places it in a crotch or fork, in a depression or even on a flat surface, and tries to dissect it with bill alone.   Hides food in typical manner, like *Garrulus*, but it is not known to what, if any, extent it relies on food stores in the wild.

It is said to be able to rob successfully nests of the Magpie but the observers (Vaughan & Jones) do not describe how it goes about this feat which, in view of the Magpie's strength and agility and its covered nest, would seem likely to be both risky and difficult.

Sometimes shy and wary of man, but where he is abundant and does not persecute it, becomes bold and indifferent to his presence.

Nesting Nests in trees or shrubs, more often in the top of a sapling or at the periphery of a large branch than in a main fork. Commonly from 2·5 to 6 metres high. A shallow nest of twigs, tendrils and roots, the shallow inner 'cup' of roots (especially where available the aerial roots of the False Banyan) and sometimes also of fine pliable twigs and thin tendrils. The eggs are creamy white, light to dark buff, buffish grey or very pale olive green, profusely speckled, and usually also spotted and blotched, with reddish brown, dull brown or olive brown and with underlying pale greyish markings. From 3 to 5 is the usual clutch.

Nests with eggs have been found in April, May and June in southern China, in June in northern China; from March to June (inclusive) in Burma, and April to June in India. In south China Vaughan and Jones found it breeding from late March, when nest-building started, until August. They state that 'it is undoubtedly double-brooded in most cases' but do not give the evidence on which this statement is based, except in one case where the previous brood of young were observed around the new nest when their parents were building. Both sexes build and feed the young; probably only the female incubates.

Vaughan and Jones found that when disturbed by man the incubating bird would usually leave the nest quietly, sometimes chattering at a distance or flying overhead, but when there were young in the nest both parents would come very close to mob the intruding human.

Voice Has a variety of calls and freely indulges in vocal mimicry (Ali) in a wild state. Vaughan and Jones say its calls 'range from a flute-like whistle to harsh, guttural cluckings and at times almost amount to a song, being continued with various modulations as much as five or ten minutes'. Boosey records a 'low and surprisingly sweet song' from the male of a captive pair. This song accompanied the jumping display. I have heard the following calls from captive birds in zoos.

Chirrupping notes very like those of the Jay but higher pitched, and rather louder and more 'chinking' in tone. These have been given by individuals when I spoke to them in an affectionate tone, by individual birds when shown a tit-bit, before taking it, and (single instances only) by a bird offering food to its mate and by a bird giving the wing-fluttering display.

A *harsh chatter*, very like the alarm chatter of the Magpie but with a more 'scratchy' tone. This was given when mobbing the head of an Eagle Owl that I showed the birds and is, undoubtedly, the usual alarm call.

The female of a pair repeatedly gave one to three *liquid whistling notes* followed by a harsh grating rattle, 'kwit, krrrreh!', 'kwit, k'yu-k'yu, krrreh-ah' with many minor variants. Comparable calls of the male were without the final grating or rattling note.

Other calls heard were a loud harsh sharp 'kwee-ick' or 'kweeek!' and softer versions of the same.

Display and social behaviour Has a display in which the wings are slightly or half-opened (perhaps fully extended at high intensity?) and quivered. The tail was shaken and quivered also on two occasions when I saw this display but not on the third. This is almost certainly homologous to the quivering display of the Jay (q.v.); on the occasions that I saw it, it accompanied passing or offering of food from one bird to another. The wings may be fluttered in a begging display like that of other corvids; but I have only seen this a few times, at rather low intensity.

Rickett (La Touche & Rickett) saw a striking display from the presumed male of a pair in a tree. The displaying bird 'puffed out the feathers of the head and neck, raised the tail which was spread like a fan, and turned its body slowly from side to side'. Boosey saw the male of a pair (which successfully bred in captivity) leap to and fro, singing, over the female as she crouched on a perch.

When offering food to a female, a captive male repeatedly flirted his wings upwards, without tail movements and without fluttering or opening them. In threat or defensive display the tail may be partly spread and tilted sideways towards the rival. This display is very suggestive of that of a Pheasant, *Phasianus*. It is probably also shown in courtship.

Other name Occipital Blue Pie.

REFERENCES

ALI, S. 1949. *Indian Hill Birds*. Oxford.

BAKER, E. C. S.   Notebook on his egg collection.   In the Sub-dept. of Ornithology of the British Museum (Natural History).

BOOSEY, E.   1950.   The Keston Foreign Bird Farm comes of age.   *Avicult. Mag.* **56**: 214–215.

LA TOUCHE, J. D. & RICKETT, C. B.   1905.   Further notes on the nesting of birds in the province of Fohkien, S.E. China.   *Ibis* (8) **5**: 25–67.

OATES, E. W.   1883.   *A Handbook to the Birds of British Burma* **1**: 400–401.

SCHÄFER, E.   1938.   Ornitholologische Ergebnisse zweier Forschungsreisen nach Tibet.   *J. Orn.* **86**, Sonderheft: 265.

VAUGHAN, R. E. & JONES, K. H.   1913.   On the birds of South-Eastern China.   *Ibis* (10) **1**: 17–76.

FORMOSAN BLUE MAGPIE   *Cissa caerulea*

Urocissa caerulea Gould, 1863, Proc. Zool. Soc. London, 1862, p. 282.

Description   Size and proportions similar to Red-billed Blue Magpie but a shade heavier in build, and tail not quite so long and curving.   Head, neck and breast black.   Plumage elsewhere generally a rich dark purplish blue; the underparts slightly paler but not noticeably so except on the under tail coverts, that are tipped whitish.   White markings on wing and tail as in Red-billed Blue Magpie (q.v.) but grey of inner webs darker, nearly black.

Irides light yellow.   Bill, feet and legs bright coral red.   These soft part colours are based on only a few museum specimens.   The only living bird of this species I have seen, a captive specimen, had the irides a clear, pale yellow; the bill a deep but bright orange-red (more red than orange) and legs and feet a slightly paler orange-red.

Juvenile duller and greyer, underparts below the blackish breast almost entirely grey.

Field characters   Predominantly deep blue coloration together with long tail and red bill diagnostic.

Distribution and habitat   Formosa; inhabits mountain forest.

Feeding and general habits   I can find nothing more detailed than Swinhoe's observations; most subsequent notes in the literature appear to be derived, with or without acknowledgement, therefrom.   He found it in parties of 6 or more, shy of man.   Flight with short, quick flaps of the wings, presumably interspersed with glides, with the body and tail held nearly horizontal.   Swinhoe observed it feeding on wild figs, berries and insects, the latter chiefly melolonthine beetles.

The single captive bird I have observed, at the London Zoo, uses its feet (and refrains from using them for slightly sticky food), and hides food, in exactly same manner as *C. erythrorhyncha* (q.v.).

Nesting   An egg in the British Museum (Nat. Hist.) collection is similar to a common type of egg of *E. erythrorhyncha*, being creamy white with a faint greenish tinge, blotched and spotted with dark brown and with underlying pale grey markings.   It is said to have been taken from a nest containing five other well incubated eggs, on May 22nd.

Voice   Alarm call, given also in conflict and frustration, a high-pitched cackling chatter 'kyak-kyak-kyak-kyak'.   In tempo not unlike the chatter of the Magpie but a little slower and much higher-pitched.   When sitting quietly the captive bird often uttered a soft 'kwee-eeep' or 'swee-eee'.

Display and social behaviour   Has a begging display in which the wings are raised and fluttered with a rather 'floppy' action, similar to that of many other corvids when food begging.

When its mate, a Red-billed Blue Magpie in the next aviary, which was feeding it through the wires, paused before passing food (because it had seen something which slightly alarmed it), the Formosan bird erected all its head feathers, making its head look very large and intensely black in contrast to the yellow eyes.

Other names Formosan Blue Pie.

REFERENCE

SWINHOE, R. 1863. The Ornithology of Formosa or Taiwan. *Ibis* (1) **5**: 377–345.

YELLOW-BILLED BLUE MAGPIE   *Cissa flavirostris*

Psilorhinus flavirostris Blyth, 1846, Journ. Asiat. Soc. Bengal, 15, p. 28.

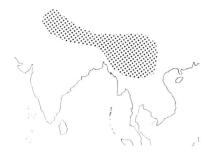

Description Size, proportions and colour pattern very like Red-billed Blue Magpie from which it differs as follows: pale patch on nape smaller, not extending forward to the crown or back to the mantle; upperparts often tinged with olive; underparts and the pale tips to the wing and tail creamy-yellow, primrose yellow or yellowish green. In museum skins and, to some extent apparently in live birds in worn plumage, the yellow and green are lost, the underparts become pale mauvish grey and the wing and tail tips white.

Irides yellow, yellow-brown, brown, or dark brown. It has been claimed that males have yellow, females brown eyes, but, unless there are very many wrongly-sexed specimens in collections, this is not a regular sexual difference. Eye rims yellow or yellowish brown. Bill pale yellow to deep yellow; yellow-orange once recorded. Legs and feet usually orange or yellow-orange, sometimes yellow, claws duller.

The above description is of the nominate form, *C. f. flavirostris*, from the eastern Himalayas. The form from the Chin Hills, Burma, *C. f. schäferi*, is slightly smaller in size. The form from north-western Tonkin, *C. f. robini*, is said to be much more green and yellow in tone so that in life its upperparts are predominantly a yellowish olive-green. In museum skins, however, all trace of green and yellow is lost. The form from the western Himalayas, *C. f. cucullata*, is much bluer above and whiter on the underparts and sometimes has the whitish head patch more extensive and many of the crown feathers tipped with bluish white. From descriptions it would appear that, even when in new plumage, it is seldom so strongly tinged with green and yellow as are the eastern forms. It is thus much closer in appearance to *C. erythrorhyncha* than are other forms of the species.

Juveniles are duller and greyer (but perhaps in life greener-looking?), with the usual lax, woolly body plumage of most young corvids. A juvenile of the form *cucullata* has the entire central area of crown and nape and the malar regions whitish, but juveniles from further east do not show more extensive whitish areas on the head than do the adults. The juvenile has dull legs and the bill is at first dark with some yellowish areas.

Field characters Bluish or greyish and greenish yellow or whitish coloration together with long tail, yellow bill and orange or yellow legs distinguish it from all but the Red-billed Blue Magpie. Information on valid field characters (if any) to distinguish these two is lacking but the present species probably looks duller and greener, and bill colour, when typical for the species, is probably diagnostic.

Distribution and habitat   Western Himalayas from Hazara, Murree and Kashmir east to Assam, southern Tibet, northern Burma and western China in northern Yunnan.   Also in the Chin Hills of western Burma and north-western Tonkin.   Typically at higher altitudes than the related Red-billed Blue Magpie; in the Himalayan regions normally between 1500 and 3150 metres but has been recorded as low as 900 metres in central Nepal (Ripley); Stevens found it wintering at 3000 metres on the Sikkim-Nepal frontier.

Inhabits many types of hill and montane forest, freely coming into clearings, alpine meadows, rocky slopes and other open areas.   Often regular in cultivated areas (terrace cultivation) and about camp sites.

Feeding and general habits   Recorded observations do not suggest any significant differences from Red-billed species.   Like the latter feeds both in trees and on the ground.   Diesselhorst (1968) says it is one of the few species known to eat land leeches.   In the Chin Hills (Stresemann & Heinrich) extremely wary and shy but in some places it is, if anything, an even bolder camp scavenger than its relative.   In Sikkim Stevens had Yellow-billed Blue Magpies come around his tent door and take food within 'one or two paces' of his feet.

Stevens observed that the individuals he fed would grip three or four large pieces of raw flesh before flying off; it seems almost certain, therefore, (from analogy with corvids whost behaviour is better known) that this species hides food in a wild state.

Nesting   Nest and eggs similar to those of Red-billed Blue Magpie (q.v.) but nest often lined with fine grasses (Baker MSS).   Usually lays in May or June, at least in the Himalayan region, but eggs have been found in August (Marshall, in Whistler, 1923).

As with *C. erythrorhyncha*, the possibility that sub-adult birds may sometimes associate with, and even play a rôle in the breeding activities of established pairs, is suggested by observations of the species being often in small parties even in the breeding season.   Such behaviour is known to occur in some American jays that inhabit somwhat comparable biotopes.

Voice   Evidently much as that of the Red-billed Blue Magpie and likewise an habitual and accomplished vocal mimic.   Heinrich (in Stresemann & Heinrich) describes the voice of the two as similar but with a small difference in nuance.   Stanford & Mayr list 'a single loud pipe . . . its alarm chatter and a shrill whistling call'.

Display and social behaviour   No information.

REFERENCES

ALI, S. 1962. *The Birds of Sikkim*. Oxford.
BAKER, E. C. S. MS Notebook on his egg collection. In the Sub-dept. of Ornithology of the British Museum (Natural History).
DIESSELHORST, G. 1968. Beiträge zur Ökologie der Vögel zentral- und ost- Nepals. in *Khumbu Himal*, vol. 2. Munich.
STANFORD, J. K. & MAYR, E. 1940. The Vernay-Cutting Expedition to Northern Burma. *Ibis* (14) **4**: 697–698
STEVENS, H. 1923. Notes on the birds of the Sikkim Himalayas. *Journ. Bombay Nat. Hist. Soc.*, 29 **(1)**: 503–518.
STRESEMANN, E. & HEINRICH, G. 1940. Die Vögel des Mount Victoria. *Mitt. Zoolog. Mus. Berlin* 24, 2: 166–167.
RIPLEY, S. D. 1961. *A Synopsis of the Birds of India and Pakistan* 307. Bombay.
WHISTLER, H. 1923. A note on the Corvidae of the Punjab. *Journ. Bombay Nat. Hist. Soc.* 29 **(1)**: 161–168.
——— Unpublished notes in library of Bird Room, British Museum (Natural History).

CEYLON BLUE MAGPIE   *Cissa ornata*

Pica ornata Wagler, 1829, Isis von Oken, Col. 749.

Description   About size of Magpie.   Head, neck and upper breast a deep rich chestnut-red.   Back and upper breast rich cobalt or purplish blue shading to sky blue with a slight tinge of green on rump and belly. Lesser wing coverts purplish blue; median and greater coverts a darker and duller purplish blue. Outer webs of primaries and secondaries chestnut, not quite so dark and reddish as on the head. Inner webs of inner secondaries purplish blue, forming a broad stripe on inside edge of closed wing. Inner webs of outer secondaries and primaries blackish, the former have a small amount of dark blue on the outer web, adjacent to the shaft. Undersides of wing quills mostly with pale chestnut fringes. Central tail feathers greenish blue, sometimes tinged with purple, with broad white ends and black subterminal bands. Outer tail feathers similar but with their outer webs more purplish blue, the inner webs duller, and the white terminal area becoming progressively more extensive on the outer webs, towards outside of tail; on the two outermost feathers on each side the black subterminal band does not usually extend on to the outer web.

Irides light to medium brown; the conspicuous, serrated-edged, fleshy eye-rims bright red. Bill, legs and feet bright coral red; claws reddish yellow with dusky tips.

Juvenile duller and paler with underparts and rump much suffused with grey. Eye-rim brownish; bill, legs and feet paler and duller.

Field characters Blue and chestnut plumage and long tail diagnostic. Combination of the above with red bill and legs distinguish it from any other bird in the world.

Distribution and habitat Ceylon; inhabits evergreen forests in the hill zone and parts of the low country wet zone at altitudes above 180 metres. Sometimes comes into gardens and plantations but in general a bird of the jungle. Believed to have decreased greatly in numbers through the destruction of the forests.

Feeding and general habits Feeds both in trees and undergrowth and on the ground; but when on the ground is particularly alert and at once flies up if disturbed (Legge). Eats insects and other small creatures, fruits and probably eggs and young birds. Foods known to be taken are various chafer beetles, tree-crickets, tree-frogs, lizards (*Calotes*), hairy caterpillars, which are rubbed long and vigorously on a perch to remove the hairs, and the fruits of the Climbing Screw-pine, *Freycinetia*.

Commonly in parties of about 6 but sometimes in pairs or singly. Flight appears weak and is seldom long sustained. In flight the tail is carried closed except when vol-planing, when it is widely spread. When flying any distance the bird usually drops from its perch to within a few feet of the ground, rising again at the end of its flight. The parties move about a good deal but each adheres to a definite although extensive area.

Nesting Two nests (Legge; West, in Henry, 1955) were in, respectively, a fork in the top branch of a tall young tree at about 13 metres high, in jungle, and in the top of a small tree growing in a strip of forest bordering a stream in a tea garden. Four nests found by Jenkins (in Baker MSS) were all on small branches of small trees, 4·5–6 metres high. The nest is built of sticks, with a cup-shaped lining of fine roots and, in one instance, of 'old man's beard' lichen. Nests with eggs have been found in all months from January to April inclusive.

Clutch of 3 to 5 eggs (Henry, 1955) but most clutches seem to consist of only 3 eggs. The eggs are whitish, speckled, flecked and spotted with brown, usually so profusely as almost to obscure the background colour.

Voice   Would appear to have many calls that are probably innate as well as indulging in vocal mimicry both in the wild and in captivity.   Henry (1954, 1955) distinguishes a ringing, metallic 'crink-crink-rink' suggestive of the jingling of a gigantic bunch of keys and uttered with the bill wide open; a loud, rasping 'crakrakrakrak'; a plain, loud 'whee whee'; 'tweewi-kraa', and various low conversational croaking, chattering and sucking noises.   Recognizable vocal mimicries include calls of raptors, babblers and jungle fowl.

Display and social behaviour   No information.

Other names   Ceylon Jay, Ceylon Hunting-crow.

REFERENCES

BAKER, E. C. S.   1922.   *The Fauna of British India, Birds* **1**: 46–47.   London.
—— MSS notebook on his egg collection.   In the Sub-dept. of Ornithology, British Museum (Nat. Hist.).
LEGGE, W. V.   1879.   *A History of the Birds of Ceylon* **2**: 553–554.
HENRY, G. M.   1954.   The Ceylon Blue Magpie.   *Avicult. Mag.*, **60**: 151–153.
—— 1955.   *A Guide to the Birds of Ceylon.*   London.
WHISTLER, H.   1944.   The Avifaunal Survey of Ceylon.   *Spolia Zeylanica* **23,** pts 3 and 4: 128.

GREEN MAGPIE   *Cissa chinensis*

Coracias chinensis Boddaert, 1783, Table Pl. enlum., p. 38, based on Daubenton pl. 620, 'Rollier de la Chine'.

Description   About size of Jay, or very slightly smaller.   Tail rather long and graduated; the two central feathers about two inches longer than the next pair.   Feathers of hind crown and nape elongated.

General coloration vivid bright green, slightly paler on the underparts, and yellowish green to greenish yellow on forehead and face (except where black).   Tips of central tail feathers whitish.   A broad black stripe from bill across side of head, enclosing the eyes and meeting at the nape.   Wings (except for some greenish lesser coverts) rich dark maroon or chestnut-red, the inner secondaries with broad whitish tips and black subterminal bands.   Outer tail feathers green with broad white tips and broad black subterminal bands.

Irides brownish red to crimson; conspicuous fleshy eye rims bright orange-red to crimson or yellowish brown edged with bright red.   Bill, legs and feet bright orange-red to bright deep blood red, claws sometimes paler and duller, and tip of bill often a little paler than rest of bill.

The green parts of the plumage may change to light blue, the yellow to whitish and the red to dull olive or greyish brown (see p.190).

Juvenile duller and paler with pale brownish or yellowish bill, legs and irides.

The above description is of the nominate form, which is found from India and Burma east to northern Laos, Tonkin and northern Annam. The form from Sumatra and N. W. Borneo States, *C. chinensis minor*, is smaller but resembles the nominate form in colour although a minority of specimens approach the Malayan form in wing markings. *C. chinensis robinsoni*, from the Malay States is similar in size to *C. c. minor* or a little larger and usually has the whitish tips to the inner secondaries more extensive, more elongated in shape and with only narrow and obscure posterior margins. The form from the Langbian Peak in southern Annam, *C. chinensis margaritae*, is very distinct and of extreme beauty. It is about the size of the nominate form or a very little smaller but tends to have a slightly longer tail. It has the entire forehead and crown a bright golden yellow with only a tinge of green on the long feathers of the hind-crown and nape. *C. chinensis klossi*, from central Annam and central Laos, is intermediate in appearance between the nominate form and *margaritae*, having a golden yellow forehead but the crown suffused with green.

Field characters Apart from other green magpies, the only bright green Jay-like bird with red wings and conspicuous black eyestripe. In areas of possible overlap green, not yellow, underparts would distinguish from Eastern Green Magpie, and at least under favourable conditions, longer tail and spotted or barred pattern on inside edge of folded wing from Short-tailed Green Magpie. When in blue plumage, the black eyestripe on a pale head and the entirely pale blue breast distinguish it from the blue magpies.

Distribution and habitat The Indian lower Himalayas from the Jumna Valley eastward through Assam and Bengal to northern Laos, Tonkin and Annam and south to Tenasserim (Mergui), the Malay States, Sumatra and north-western Borneo. Typically in evergreen forest, bamboo jungle or other dense cover but also in more open scrub, tea gardens, the secondary growth on old clearings and similar places.

Feeding and general habits Seeks food both in branches and on the ground. Probably feeds chiefly on insects and other small creatures; recorded foods include grasshoppers, beetles, praying-mantises, lizards, small snakes, frogs, young birds, and the flesh of mammals killed by large predators. Probably also takes some fruits and other vegetable foods and the eggs of small birds.

Usually in small parties or pairs, often in company with other birds, such as jay-thrushes, *Garrulax*, and drongoes, *Dicrurus*, when seeking food. Very active, with the same bouncing elegance in its movements as the Jay. Usually shy of man.

Hides food in typical manner in captivity and a caged individual also hid bright, inedible objects (Vernon).

Captive birds given Wood Ants, *Formica rufa*, anted exactly as Jay, *Garrulus glandarius*, without picking up ants in bill. Captive birds in India have, however, been seen to hold a Peach Worm in the bill and ant with it apparently in typical active manner.

Nesting Nests in trees, shrubs and vine tangles commonly, or at any rate most often discovered, near the tops of small trees. Nest of twigs, often with tendrils roots, moss and leaves intermixed; the inner cup mainly of fine roots and fibres. Eggs 3 to 7, usually 4 to 6, white to pale greenish or buff, profusely speckled with brown and usually with underlying grey markings. Often the speckling is so dense as to obscure the pale ground colour; sometimes the markings at one (either) end coalesce to form a darker zone; more rarely the eggs are only sparsely speckled or have larger spots and blotches.

In the Indian parts of its range nests with eggs have been found chiefly in May and June but at all times from late April to August (inclusive). It is uncertain whether the species is ever truly double-brooded but almost certain that it will sometimes nest and lay again after loss of young as well as after loss of eggs. In Burma eggs have been found in April. In north Borneo many nests with young in March (Whitehead).

Voice Stevens and Ali both record a harsh, repeated 'peep, peep' and a 'whistling chatter'. Whitehead says the Bornean form, *C. chinensis minor*, has many calls 'the most peculiar being a three-syllabled whistle, from which it gets its Dusun name of "Ton-ka-kis" '. The predator-mobbing alarm call of a captive bird, when I showed it an Eagle Owl's head, was a chatter very like that of the Magpie, *Pica*, but slower and more uniform in tempo, and higher-pitched.

Display and social behaviour No information.

Other names Green Jay, Green Pie, Hunting Cissa, Hunting Crow. Yellow-crowned Cissa (the race *C. c. margaritae*).

REFERENCES

ALI, S. 1962. *The Birds of Sikkim*. Oxford.
DEIGNAN, H. G. 1945. The birds of northern Thailand: 303. *Bull. Smithsonian Inst. U.S. Nat. Mus* No. 186.
OATES, E. W. 1883. *A Handbook to the Birds of British Burma*, **1**: 406–407. London.
STEVENS, H. 1923. Notes on the birds of the Sikim Himalayas. *Journ. Bombay Nat. Hist. Soc.* 29 **(1)**: 515–516.
VERNON, W. 1913. A tame Hunting Cissa. *Avicult. Mag.* (3) **5**: 62–63.
WHISTLER, H. Unpublished notes in library of Bird Room, British Museum (Nat. Hist.).
WHITEHEAD, J. 1893. *Exploration of Mount Kina Balu, North Borneo:* appendix 205–206. London.

EASTERN GREEN MAGPIE   *Cissa hypoleuca*

Cissa hypoleuca Salvadori and Giglioli, 1885, Atti R. Accad. Sci. Torino, 20, p. 427.

Description Very like preceding species, *C. chinensis*, from which it differs as follows: tail rather shorter, the bright green of the upperparts perhaps a little darker; entire underparts pale yellow to light golden yellow, tinged with green on the throat, at least in some individuals; tail olive green, tipped with grey (with black subterminal bands on all but central pair as in *chinensis*); inner secondaries broadly tipped with grass green. Colour changes as in previous species.

The above description is of nominate *C. h. hypoleuca* from southern Annam, southern Laos, eastern Thailand (Siam) and Cochin-China. *C. hypoleuca chauleti*, from central Annam, has the underparts a deeper yellow, the green parts, especially on the head and neck, strongly tinged with yellow and the tail tinged with brownish buff, especially on the tips of the outer tail feathers. *C. hypoleuca concolor*, from northern Annam, is similar to *chauleti* but has the upper parts of a rather darker and less yellowish green and the underparts light green tinged with yellow. *C. h. jini*, from the Yaoshan Massif, in Kwangsi, south China, is similar to *concolor* but less tinged with yellow and with a proportionately rather longer tail. *C. hypoleuca katsumatae*, from Hainan, is similar, also with the underparts green or yellowish green.

Field characters As *Cissa chinensis* (q.v.). Green, or in faded plumage blue, ends to inner secondaries and (in the races *chauleti* and *hypoleuca*) yellow or whitish underparts should serve to identify it from *chinensis*.

Distribution and habitat Annam, eastern Thailand (Siam), Cochin-China, the Yaoshan Massif in Kwangsi, southern China; and Hainan Island. Apparently inhabits similar types of wooded country to its relatives.

Feeding and general habits The little that I can find recorded about this species in the wild does not suggest any difference of feeding habits or general behaviour from those of *C. chinenesis*.

Nesting A captive pair built a nest of sticks, lined with dry grass and feathers. Both sexes built but only the female incubated (Ezra).

Voice No information.

Display and social behaviour No information.

REFERENCES

DELACOUR, J. 1927. The Yellow-breasted Cissa. *Avicult. Mag.* series 4, **5**: 313–314.
—— & JABOUILLE, P. 1931. *Les Oiseaux de l'Indochine Française* **4**: 283–284.
EZRA, A. 1927. Untitled notes on his captive *C. hypoleuca*, forming an additional section to Delacour 1927.

SHORT-TAILED GREEN MAGPIE   *Cissa thalassina*

Kitta thalassina Temminck, 1826, in Temminck and Laugier, Pl. Col., 401, livr. 68.

Description Similar to the nominate form of *C. chinensis* (q.v.) except in the following characters: tail much shorter in proportion; feathers of crown and nape much less elongated; two innermost secondaries entirely or largely pale green to greenish white; next with outer part of outer web red and the pale part margined with black, following pair with a large whitish to green, black-bordered spot on the inner web and a small one on the outer web; these marks forming a broad pale stripe, rather than a barred pattern as in *chinenesis*, on the inner edge of the folded wing; tail green with ill-defined small pale green to whitish tips on some outer feathers and rather larger pale tips on the four outermost pairs.

The above description is of nominate *C. t. thalassina*, from Java. The form from the mountains of north-western Borneo, *C. t. jefferyi*, differs in having more red on the outer webs of the inner secondaries; the pale tips to the outer tail feathers more clearly defined and usually with some indication of blackish sub-terminal bands; a deeper green general coloration with little or no yellow tinge in the green areas even on the forehead; the irides white with a very light blue outer edge instead of red as in the nominate form and the bill and feet a darker red ('deep lake red') than those of *C. chinensis minor* (Whitehead).

Field characters As *chinensis* (q.v.), but tail much shorter and with different pattern on inner edge of closed wing.

Distribution and habitat Java and the mountains of northern Borneo. Inhabits forest; in Borneo on mountains between 900 and 2400 metres.

Feeding and general habits Probably much as *chinensis* but snails (Whitehead) and insects, including caterpillars (Harrisson, in Smythies), appear to be the only foods actually recorded. Whitehead thought that it also fed on small frogs. On Mount Kina Balu he found it on and about twisted and moss-covered trunks near the ground.

Nesting On Mount Kina Balu, Whitehead found flying young in company with their parents in April, there were two young in the broods he saw. The only description I can find (Kuschel) suggests that its eggs are identical in appearance with those of *C. chinensis*.

Voice Whitehead recognized this as a separate species from *C. chinensis minor* by its different call which he describes as 'not nearly so clear as that of *C. minor* but . . . still a feeble attempt at "Ton-ka-kis" '.

Display and social behaviour No information.

Other names Short-tailed Green Jay, Short-tailed Hunting Cissa, Short-tailed Hunting Crow, Whitehead's Cissa.

REFERENCES

KURODA, N. 1933. *Birds of the Island of Java* 31–32. Tokyo.
KUSCHEL, M. 1895. Zur Oologie Javas. *Ornith. Monatsber.* **3**: 153–154.
SMYTHIES, B. E. 1960. *The Birds of Borneo.* London.
WHITEHEAD, J. 1893. *Exploration of Mount Kina Balu, North Borneo, appendix:* 205–206. London.

The tree pies and the Black Jay

The tree pies of India and south-eastern Asia are long-tailed corvids with thick bills with strongly-curved culmens. They range in size from about as large as a Jay, but with a much longer tail, to rather smaller than a Blue Jay. They appear to be most closely related to the Black Jay (q.v.) and to the blue and green magpies, *Cissa*, to which they have some resemblances of plumage pattern although they completely lack the bright colours characteristic of *Cissa*. They are clad in various shades of brown or grey, black, and white, and have black bills and feet.

They are largely arboreal although some of them also feed readily on the ground. The heavy bill with arched culmen and curved commissure is presumably adapted to their feeding habits, but it does not appear to be known in what way the foods taken, or the means by which they are taken and prepared, differ from those of other partly arboreal corvids such as *Garrulus* and *Cissa*.

Vaurie in the current world check-list recognizes three genera of tree pies, *Dendrocitta*, *Crypsirina* and *Temnurus*. Amadon earlier 'lumped' these genera in *Crypsirina* but maintained, with some misgiving, the Black Jay in the monotypic genus *Platysmurus*. I agree with Amadon's opinion on the apparent close relationship of all the tree pies and include them all in *Crypsirina*, giving *Dendrocitta* and *Temnurus* only subgeneric rank.

The tree pies in the subgenus *Dendrocitta* form a rather homogeneous group of closely-related species. The Grey Tree Pie, *Crypsirina formosae*, the Southern Tree Pie, *C. leucogastra*, the Sumatran Tree Pie, *C. occipitalis* and the Bornean Tree Pie, *C. cinerascens*, have similar and probably homologous plumage patterns with the wings entirely black except for a small white patch and whitish upper tail coverts. They are allopatric and best treated as members of a superspecies.

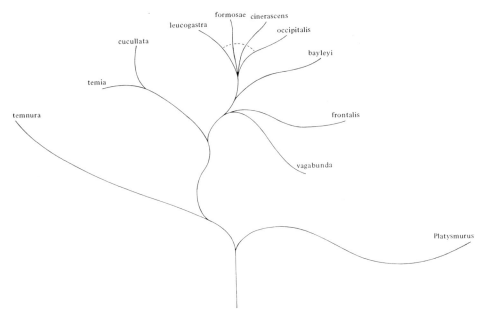

FIG. D.4.   Presumed relationships of species in the genera *Crypsirina* and *Platysmurus*.

The Rufous Tree Pie, *C. vagabunda*, overlaps in range both *C. formosae* and *C. leucogastra*. It differs from them in being slightly larger and has a rather different colour pattern, with the wing coverts and large areas of the secondaries pale grey and nearly concolorous head and neck. Its geographical variation is similar to that of *C. formosae*.

The Black-faced Tree Pie, *C. frontalis*, (often misleadingly called Black-browed Tree Pie, a name which would better fit *C. formosae*) overlaps in range both *formosae* and *vagabunda*. Its colour pattern is at first sight very suggestive of that of *C. leucogastra* but it lacks the pale upper tail coverts and white wing patch of *leucogastra*, the black on its breast is less extensive and the rufous on its ventral regions more so, and it has grey wing coverts. It is much smaller than the species previously discussed and has a proportionately deeper bill with much more strongly curved culmen and commissure. It seems therefore almost certain that its feeding habits, at least in some respects, must differ from those of the larger tree pies with which it is sympatric.

The Sumatran Tree Pie, *C. occipitalis*, and the Bornean Tree Pie, *C. cinerascens*, are commonly treated as races of one species under the English name Malaysian Tree Pie. It is likely, on geographical grounds, that these two forms are most closely related to each other and the colour pattern of *cinerascens* could well represent a rather degenerate version of that of *occipitalis*. On the other hand the colour pattern of *occipitalis* suggests a rather degenerate version of that of the Southern Tree Pie, *C. leucogastra*, and that of *cinerascens* might equally well be derived from that of the Grey Tree Pie, *C. formosae*. It seems best, therefore, to treat both *occipitalis* and *cinerascens* as species. Together with *C. leucogastra* and *C. formosae* they form a superspecies, within which *C. bayleyi* ought probably to be included.

The Andaman Tree Pie, *C. bayleyi*, is smaller in size but very similar to *C. vagabunda* in coloration, but has wings marked like those of the *formosae* superspecies. It may perhaps represent an ancestral form but I think it most likely that it is the geographical representative of *formosae* and its allies. Its colour pattern seems to represent a somewhat simplified version of that common to the *formosae* group, whose tendency to develop a generally tawny rufous coloration when isolated on islands is seen, it to a lesser degree, in *C. occipitalis* and *C. cinerascens*. In particular its grey lower rump and upper tail coverts, contrasting with the rufous back, and the fact that its black face is slightly more contrasted than that of *vagabunda*, also suggest affinities with the *formosae* group rather than with *C. vagabunda*. Its small size is at first surprising in an island form but may reflect the lack of any sympatric species.

The two species in the subgenus *Crypsirina*, the Hooded Raquet-tailed Tree Pie, *C. cucullata*, and the Black Raquet-tailed Tree Pie, *C. temia*, agree with one another in having spatulate central tail feathers; velvety frontal feathers which cover the nostrils, taking the place of nasal bristles and forming a dense matt-black band from eye to eye across the forehead which contrasts with the glossy greenish black of the rest of the head, and being small in size. It is likely that *temia* and *cucullata* are more closely related to each other then either of them is to any other species. They also differ from the other tree pies in having 10 instead of 12 rectrices. The field observations available on them suggest that they are more exclusively arboreal than the '*Dendrocitta*' species and that their spatulate tails may function as highly-developed balancing organs.

The subgenus *Temnurus* contains the Notch-tailed Tree Pie, *Crypsirina temnura*, which has the black frontal band of rather less velvety and more bristly feathers backed by slightly stiffened but otherwise 'normal' glossy feathers, thus showing a condition intermediate between other *Crypsirina* species and *Platysmurus*, and is otherwise dull black in colour almost without iridescence. It has remarkably shaped tail feathers which are incised along the edges and truncated at the tips. Very little is known about its habits.

The Black Jay, *Platysmurus leucopterus*, differs from the tree pies in being more heavily built with a proportionately shorter tail. Its nasal bristles are stiffened and curve forwards as a continuation of a short bristly crest formed by similar feathers on the front of the forehead; immediately behind this, across the forecrown, is a band of elongated, broad, glossy stiffened feathers that form a second short crest. There is a conspicuous white wing patch involving white areas on both coverts and secondaries. It seems likely that the tree pies are this bird's nearest relatives; indeed in coloration, length of tail and head feathering *C. temnura* might be a connecting link between the other tree pies and the Black Jay. The possibility of convergence cannot be ruled out, however, especially in view of how often similar frontal crests have developed in different genera of Corvidae as well as in other passerine families.

REFERENCES

AMADON, D. 1944. The genera of Corvidae and their relationships. *Amer. Mus. Novit.* No. 1251.
VAURIE, C. 1962. '*Peters' Check-list of Birds of the World*, 15. Cambridge, Mass.

RUFOUS TREE PIE   *Crypsirina vagabunda*

Coracias vagabunda Latham, 1790, Ind. Orn., 1, p. 171.

Description A little smaller than a Magpie and slimmer in build with proportionately shorter wings, longer tail, deeper and more curved bill and shorter legs. As in the blue pies the tail is graduated but with the central pair of feathers considerably longer than the next pair. Head, neck and upper breast a rather dark but soft slate-grey or brownish grey, darkest around the base of the bill and around the eyes. Scapulars and mantle a rather dull and slightly reddish tawny-brown shading to a lighter and brighter orange-tawny on rump and underparts. Wing coverts greyish white. The three innermost secondaries have their outer webs almost entirely pale grey, very slightly darker than the wing coverts, the next three secondaries have decreasing areas of grey on the outer webs. Rest of wing black. Central tail feathers light bluish grey, becoming paler for an inch or more before the broad (4–5 cm) black terminal bands. Outer tail feathers similarly marked but with the black tips covering proportionately more of the feather until the outermost pair have the end half black.

Irides dark reddish brown, dark red or brown. Bill dark grey, bluish black or blackish with, usually, a paler area at base, around the gape. Legs and feet dusky or horn-coloured with whitish soles.

The juvenile is slightly duller and paler in body colour and has a sooty brown head and neck which usually fade to light drab before the onset of the first moult. Its tail feathers have grey and buff tips, often vestigial or lacking on the central pair, which fade to near white, and narrow buffish tips and fringes to most of the dark wing feathers. The wing and tail quills are not, or at least not usually, shed at the first moult so that the bird retains its juvenile tail pattern for about a year.

The above description is of the nominate form, *D. v. vagabunda*, from eastern India. *C. v. pallida*, from north-western India, has the tawny parts paler, its back being a beautiful clear golden-tawny colour. *C. v. parvula*, of south-western India, is like nominate *vagabunda* but smaller. *C. v. vernayi*, from south-eastern India, is also smaller but is paler and brighter than the nominate form although not usually as pale as *C. v. pallida*. *C. v. sclateri*, from western Burma, has the back a little darker than the nominate form and the grey of the hind neck tending to merge more into it. The form from southern Burma, the Shan States and north-western Thailand, *C. v. kinneari*, is similar but a little darker. *C. v. saturatior*, from Tenasserim and south-western Thailand, is a shade smaller and the darkest of all, having a deep reddish earth-brown back. *C. v. sakeratensis*, from eastern Siam, is very like the nominate form in colour but has the head and neck a darker grey and more sharply contrasting with the golden brown back. Most races intergrade with one or more others so that many specimens are intermediate. Plumage wear and individual variation also account for some differences; others have been over-emphasized in the original descriptions of some races.

Field characters Tawny body and large pale grey or whitish area on wings distinguish it from other tree pies and from blue magpies; size and shape from all other birds.

Distribution and habitat India, Assam, Burma south to Tenasserim, and Thailand (Siam). Inhabits open forest, scrub, plantations, gardens and clumps and groves of trees in otherwise open country. A typical species of human-inhabited country provided cover is available.

Feeding and general habits Arboreal; taking food from branches, leaves and trunks of trees, shrubs and creepers, and sometimes from the ground. Can hop, cling and clamber with great agility. Known to eat fruits, berries, insects, including wasps, carpenter bees and caterpillars, spiders, small lizards and snakes, eggs and young of smaller birds, and is said sometimes to feed on the remains of large mammals killed by predators. It may not be so bold and determined a nest robber as is popularly imagined as nests of it and an oriole, both with young, have been found in the same tree (Whistler MSS). Osborn watched a pair taking pieces, at intervals, nearly all day, from a joint of meat hung in a tree. He presumed the birds were feeding young but they may, I think, have been storing the surplus food.

Usually in pairs or small parties whose members follow one another in loose order.   Often a member of 'bird parties', particularly liable to seek food in company with babblers, *Turdoides striatus*, and Racket-tailed Drongos, *Dicrurus paradiseus*.   Keeps much to cover but will forage around human habitations and enter verandahs or rooms in search of wasps and lizards.

Flight dipping with alternate wing-beating and gliding on spread wings.

Nesting   Nests in trees, bushes or shrubs, rarely in cactus clumps.   Nest of stick foundation, which varies much in size according to situation.   On this is built a shallow cup of twigs and roots lined with finer roots and sometimes, it is said, grass and wool also.

The 2 to 6, usually 3 to 5 eggs are white to pale green or deep buff, most often creamy buff or greenish white, spotted, speckled and sometimes blotched with reddish brown, drab brown or greenish brown and with underlying grey or lilac markings.   Rarely, unmarked eggs may be laid.   Whistler found clutches averaged larger in size in northern than in southern India.

Breeding season prolonged but egg laying begins in February and March in southern parts of the species' range and in April and May in the north.   It seems uncertain whether very late nestings are genuine second broods or repeat attempts after nesting failures.

Voice   Has a variety of calls, some quite musical, others harsh, but its voice does not appear to have been studied in detail.   A frequent call is a musical 'bob-o-link'.   The alarm call of a captive bird, mobbing an Eagle Owl's head that I showed it, was a chatter much like that of the Magpie, *Pica pica*, but deeper, harsher and in slower tempo.

Display and social behaviour   No information.

Other names   Indian Tree Pie, Wandering Tree Pie, Common Tree Pie, Plains Tree Pie.

REFERENCES

ALI, S.   1941.   *The Book of Indian Birds*.   Bombay.
BAKER, E. C. S.   1922.   *The Fauna of British India: Birds* 1: 48–51.   London.
DEIGNAN, H. G.   1945.   The Birds of Northern Thailand.   *Bull. U.S. Nat. Mus*. No. 186: 304–306.
OATES, E. W.   1883.   *A Handbook to the Birds of British Burma*.   London.
OSBORN, W.   1902.   Habits of the Indian Tree Magpie.   *Journ. Bombay Nat. Hist. Soc*. **14**: 164–165.
RIPLEY, S. D.   1961.   *A Synopsis of the Birds of India and Pakistan*.   London.
WHISTLER, H.   1949.   *Popular Handbook of Indian Birds*.   London.
—— Unpublished notes in British Museum (Nat. Hist.) library.

BLACK-FACED TREE PIE   *Crypsirina frontalis*

Dendrocitta frontalis Horsfield, 1840, Proc. Zool. Soc. London, 1839, p. 163, ex. McClelland MS.

Description   A little smaller than a Blue Jay in body size but shape and proportions as in other species formerly placed in the genus *Dendrocitta*, except that the bill is a little deeper in proportion and more strongly curved.   Forehead, forecrown, face, throat and part of upper breast black.   Nape, neck, upper mantle and breast silver grey to light bluish grey, palest at the line of demarcation with the black head, especially at sides of neck where the demarcation line is often white.   Mantle (below grey part) and back dark tawny brown or tawny chestnut with a slight olive tinge, shading to a brighter paler rufous tawny on the rump and chestnut on the upper tail coverts.   Most wing coverts bluish grey, forming a large grey patch on 'shoulder' of wing.   Primary coverts, primaries, secondaries and tail feathers black.   Tibial feathers grey, tinged with tawny.

Irides reddish brown or dark red.   Bill, legs and feet black.   Juvenile duller, with brownish tips to many of the feathers of the grey parts.   There appears to be a tendency for males to have the grey parts a little paler and the brown parts a little brighter than females but this may be coincidental as I have been able to examine only a few sexed specimens from the same areas in comparable plumage state.   Specimens from the eastern part of the species' range average a little duller and darker in coloration; those from north-eastern Tonkin have been separated as *C. f. kurodae* but the difference is very slight.

Field characters Black head sharply contrasting with pale grey nape, neck and breast distinguishes it from all sympatric tree pies except the much smaller Hooded Racket-tailed Tree Pie from which the reddish brown back and belly and black outer tail feathers at once separate it. Chestnut rump and upper tail coverts also distinguish it from Grey Tree Pie and entirely black tail from Rufous Tree Pie (and from Grey Tree Pie in western parts of its range).

Distribution and habitat Indian Himalayas from eastern Nepal to Assam and Manipur, northern Burma and northern Tonkin. Inhabits forest, most usually but not always at high elevations. Freely comes into open glades and about the forest edge and is probably more regular in such places than in denser forest. Tends to be rare or very local in much of its range.

Feeding and general habits Recorded taking caterpillars and other insects, fruits and berries. Habits apparently much as other tree pies but little recorded in any detail. Has been observed hawking for flying termites from the tops of bamboo clumps (Stevens).

Nesting Nest described as like that of Grey Tree Pie (q.v.) but smaller, neater and more compact. It is placed in bamboo clumps, small trees or bushes, usually at the edge of forest. Breeding season April or May to July. The only eggs I have seen are a clutch of 3 taken on May 29th in Dibrugarh, Assam. They are creamy white, rather profusely speckled and blotched with drab brown and with underlying greyish markings.

Voice Has a variety of notes, some metallic and musical, others discordant. All who have written on it appear to agree that its calls are similar to those of other tree pies but can be at once distinguished from them, although they do not describe the distinguishing features.

Display and social behaviour No information.

Other names Black-browed Tree Pie, Black-browed Magpie, White-naped Tree Pie.

REFERENCES

ALI S. 1962. *The Birds of Sikkim.* Oxford.
BAKER, E. C. S. 1922. *The Fauna of British India* **1**: 54–55. London.
DELACOUR, J. & JABOUILLE, P. 1931. *Les Oiseaux de l'Indochine française* **4**: 288–289. Paris.
MACKINTOSH, L. J. 1915. *Birds of Darjeeling and India* **1**: 158. Calcutta.
STEVENS, H. 1914. Note in *Journ. Bombay Nat. Hist. Soc.* **23**: 237.

GREY TREE PIE   *Crypsirina formosae*

Dendrocitta sinensis, var, *formosae* Swinhoe, 1863, Ibis, p. 387.

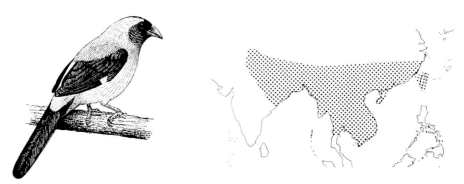

Description   A little smaller than the Rufous Tree Pie (wing about one half to one inch shorter, tail about one to two inches shorter) but similar in shape except that the ends of the outer tail feathers are square or nearly so.   Forehead and stripe above eyes jet black, rest of face and throat sooty black to sooty brown, shading to glossy greyish brown on ear coverts.   Sides of neck and breast brownish grey shading to pale grey on belly and ventral regions.   Under tail coverts light yellowish chestnut.   Crown and nape deep silvery grey shading into a warm and slightly reddish earth-brown on mantle and back.   Lower rump and upper tail coverts pale grey to greyish white.   Wings glossy black with white patches near the bases on both webs of the primaries that form a small white patch when wing is closed and a bar across it when opened.   Outer tail feathers black; two central tail feathers bluish grey for half to two thirds from base, ends black; lesser amounts of grey on next two pairs of feathers.   Irides reddish brown, red, vinous brown or brown.   Bill black.   Legs and feet black or brownish black.

Juvenile paler, duller on the grey parts and with light rusty brown tips (when in fresh plumage) to most of the cover feathers.   Bill and legs paler.   Inside mouth probably pink or red, not blackish as in adult.

The above description is of the form from the western Himalayas, *C. formosae occidentalis*.   The form from the eastern Himalayas east to Assam and northern Burma, *C. f. himalayensis*, is slightly smaller, that from eastern India and southern Madras, *C. f. sarkari*, is similar but tends to have a slightly shorter bill; *C. f. assimilis* of southern Burma, Tenasserim and Siam tends to be duller, especially on the underparts, and to have a heavier, more stumpy-looking bill.   It is also rather smaller and with a proportionately shorter tail.   All these forms are, however, very similar in appearance.

The far-eastern forms (see sketch) differ more markedly; *C. f. sinica*, from eastern and south-eastern China, is rather darker in general colour with, as a result, the more nearly pure white lower rump and upper tail coverts more contrasting.   It has a proportionately shorter and entirely black tail and its bill is usually a little smaller in proportion.   *C. f. insulae*, from Hainan Island, is similar to *C. f. sinica* but a little smaller and duller in colour.   Nominate *C. f. formosae*, from Formosa, is very similar to *C. f. insulae* but rather browner on the underparts and, as a rule, with the bases of the central tail feathers more or less tinged with grey.   Populations from central Tonkin are intermediate between *C. f. sinica* and *C. f. assimilis* and are sometimes separated as *C. f. intermedia*.

The main geographical difference within the species is from paler, more clearly marked, long-tailed birds with greyish rumps in the west to duller, darker, shorter-tailed, white-rumped birds in the east; these latter being replaced by yet slightly darker and grey-rumped populations on Hainan and Formosa.

Field characters   Dullish, grey, brown and black bird with long tail.   Duller brown back and contrasting pale grey or whitish rump and the black wings with small white patch distinguish it from Black-faced and Rufous Tree Pies.

Distribution and habitat   Northern and eastern India, Nepal, Assam, Burma and Tenasserim, Thailand, the Indo-Chinese regions, southern China, Hainan and Formosa.   Inhabits forest and wooded areas, usually in hilly or mountainous country.   Often common in and around terraced hill cultivation but not otherwise typically a bird of human-inhabited regions.

Feeding and general habits   Arboreal; but feeds to some extent on the ground, both within woods and in harvested terrace fields.   Takes caterpillars, moths, grasshoppers and other insects, fruits, berries, nectar, grain and some seeds, lizards, eggs and young birds.   Often seeks food in company of other birds, particularly laughing-thrushes, *Garrulax* spp.

Salim Ali (1962) describes its flight as undulating with alternate rapid noisy wing-flaps and glides. 'When alarmed or agitated these undulations become curiously syncopated and steeply saw-edged with the bird shooting down rocket-like on closed wings at every dip.'   Usually in small parties or pairs.

Nesting   Builds a rather shallow nest of twigs, tendrils and roots; the inner cup, of finer roots, fibres etc., is shallow and slight.   Nests in trees, bushes, shrubs or clumps of bamboo.   In Sikkim nests were found in scattered cover in cleared and cultivated areas at heights of 2·5 to 6 metres, but nests as low as 1·2 metres above ground have been found elsewhere.   Eggs usually 3 or 4 to a clutch, occasionally 2 or 5. They are creamy white to deep buff, more rarely white or greenish white, spotted and blotched with brown, red-brown, or olive brown and with underlying greyish or pinkish-mauve markings.   Nests with eggs have been found from May to July in the Indian Himalayan regions and in May and June in Burma.

Voice   Has a variety of loud calls, some harsh and grating, others melodious.   Ali (1962) says that a commonly heard call sounds like 'kokila-ka-ka', and that a 'throaty kr-r-r' is often given by a bird perched alone in a tree top.   Rickett noted that the Chinese form also has 'a great variety of notes', two frequent calls sounding like 'tootle-leetle-too' and 'tee-poo-lik'.

Display and social behaviour   No information.

Other names   Himalayan Tree Pie, Hills Tree Pie.

REFERENCES

ALI, S.   1949.   *Indian Hill Birds.*   Oxford.
—— 1962.   *The Birds of Sikkim.*   Oxford.
DEIGNAN, H. G.   1945.   The birds of northern Thailand.   *Bull. U.S. Nat. Mus.* No. 186; 306–307.
LA TOUCHE, J. D. D.   1925–1930.   *Handbook of the birds of Eastern China* 1: 17–18.
OATES, E. W.   1883.   *A handbook to the Birds of British Burma* 1: 403–404.   London.
RICKETT, C. R.   1908.   *Notes on the Birds of Fohkien Province.* (MSS volume in library of the Sub-dept. of Ornithology, British Museum (Natural History)).

SOUTHERN TREE PIE   *Crypsirina leucogastra*

Dendrocitta leucogastra Gould, 1833, Proc. Zool. Soc. London, p. 57.

Description   About size of Grey Tree Pie but with longer and broader tail, with the ends of the two long central feathers more rounded, and slightly deeper and more heavily-curved bill.   The upward inclination of the webbing at either side of the shaft towards the end of the long central tail feathers, which gives a concave plane to the end of the tail, is usually more pronounced in this species than in other tree pies.

Forehead, crown, face, throat and central area of upper breast black.   Nape, hind neck, lower parts of sides of neck and all underparts, except the black tibial feathers and bright light chestnut under tail coverts, snow white. Back light reddish tawny or yellowish chestnut. Rump and upper tail coverts white, the longest tail coverts sometimes with black tips. Two long central tail feathers silvery white or silvery grey for about two-thirds or rather less of their length, then black at ends. Outer tail feathers black. Wings glossy black, marked with white as in Grey Tree Pie.

Irides reddish brown, dark red or brown. Bill black. Legs and feet black or brownish black. Juvenile like adult but with pale brownish fringes to many of the contour feathers and with shorter and narrower tail (as in young of other tree pies). See col. pl. 3.

Field characters Striking black, white and bright brown bird with very long tail. White hind neck, rump and underparts at once identify it from Rufous Tree Pie, the only sympatric species with which it could possibly be confused.

Distribution and habitat Southern India: from north Kanara south to Travancore, and Mysore east to Chittoor district in Madras but mainly on west side of peninsula. Inhabits rain forest, overgrown cultivated areas, neglected plantations and similar places from the base of the hills to above 105 metres. Replaced by Rufous Tree Pie in deciduous woodland and nearby inhabited areas. Where deciduous and evergreen woodlands are intermixed or adjacent the two species may be found 'side by side', each usually keeping to its preferred habitat.

Feeding and general habits Feeding habits presumably much as other tree pies but they do not seem, perhaps for that reason, to have been much recorded. Commonly in pairs or small parties. Often seeks food in mixed bird parties, particularly in company with the Racket-tailed Drongo.

Nesting Nests in trees and tall bushes. Nest and eggs similar to those of the Grey Tree Pie (q.v.); 2 to 4 (most often 3) to a clutch. Eggs have been taken from February to May. Eggs in the British Museum collection were found in March and April. Stewart (in Baker) says the species is double-brooded and that he has collected eggs in August. Further observations on this point are needed.

Voice Ali says the 'call notes' are 'loud and more metallic' than those of *C. vagabunda*. A call often heard while the bird is seeking food among foliage he describes as a 'subdued castanet-like "kt-kt-kt-kt-kt-kt" ending in a short croak'. What is, perhaps, a mobbing or alarm call he describes as 'a throaty "chough-chough-chough" like some cheap Japanese clockwork toy'. Ali notes that some of its calls are like those of the Racket-tailed Drongo; it seems probable that this and other tree pies are habitual vocal mimics.

A captive bird that I watched at the London Zoo repeatedly uttered a series of clicking sounds, each series of clicks being usually, but not always, followed by two or more very melodious cooing notes of a dove-like or owl-like quality but with a more liquid tone than most dove or owl calls. These calls seemed to form an integral part of a display (see below). It also gave a dove-like 'kó-kó', or 'kóo-kóo', with a marked upward inflection and a simple upward movement of head and body.

Its alarm (?) call was a harsh 'kra' or 'kror' repeated either two or three times before pausing. It was given in rather quicker time than the double screech of the Jay but the individual notes not so quickly run-together as to suggest chattering of the Magpie.

Display and social behaviour A bird at London Zoo adopted a posture very similar to that of the Jay in one form of its self-assertive display. The tail was held low, the feathers of head, neck and the black part of the breast sleeked down but those of rump, belly and flanks erected. In a tense, strained posture it gave its clicking notes (see under Voice) with a movement of the mandibles for each click; then, as it gave the cooing notes, it made a forward and slightly downward movement of its head and the mandibles opened and shut more slowly with each coo.

It was also seen while in the same posture, to flutter its nearly closed wings while giving a short husky call.

Ali describes a raising of the tail, with horizontal stance, and jumping up and down on perch uttering the 'chough-chough' call. This sounds like predator-mobbing behaviour and also closely parallels that of *Garrulus*.

Other names White-bellied Tree Pie.

REFERENCES

ALI, S. 1953. *The Birds of Travancore and Cochin.* Oxford.
BAKER, E. C. S. 1922. *The Fauna of British India: Birds* **1**: 51–52. London.
WHISTLER, H. Unpublished notes and MSS in British Museum (Natural History) Bird Room Library.

SUMATRAN TREE PIE   *Crypsirina occipitalis*

Glaucopis occipitalis S. Müller, 1835, Tijdschr. Natuur. Gesch. Phys., 2, p. 343, pl. 5.

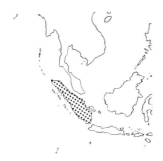

Description   Similar in size and shape to the Southern Tree Pie but with a slightly shorter and stumpier-looking bill and very slightly narrower central tail feathers.   Forehead and crown dark dull chocolate brown, face, sides of upper neck and central part of upper breast a very slightly paler tone of same colour.   Rest of underparts light tawny rufous shading to bright orange-tawny on under tail coverts and a duller brown hue immediately adjacent to the darker neck and upper breast.   Nape white or greyish white; hind neck silvery grey.   Mantle and back a darkish tawny brown.   Lower rump and upper tail coverts greyish white with faint sandy brown tips to feathers in fresh plumage.   Wings and tail as in *C. leucogastra* but the silver grey on tail feathers not so pale, and more extensive.   Irides reddish brown, post-orbital skin bluish grey.   Bill black, greyish at base.   Legs and feet dark grey.   These soft part colours are based on only one record and further information is needed.

  Juvenile has top of head blacker, with whitish tips to feathers of hind crown.   Face and throat more sooty.   Pale buff or rusty buff fringes and tips to most contour feathers and inner secondaries.

Field characters   Long pale grey and black tail, mainly tawny-brown body and white nape and rump.   Not sympatric with any similar species.

Distribution and habitat   Sumatra; apparently inhabits wooded mountains.

Feeding and general habits   No information.

Nesting   No information.

Voice   No information.

Display and social behaviour   No information.

Other names   Malaysian Tree Pie.

REFERENCE

HARTERT, E. 1902. Aus den Wanderjahren eines Naturforschers. *Novit. Zool.* **9**: 215.

BORNEAN TREE PIE   *Crypsirina cinerascens*

Dendrocitta cinerascens Sharpe, 1879, Ibis, p. 250, pl. 8.

Description   General size and shape similar to Sumatran Tree Pie, with which it may be conspecific, but tail a little shorter and bill, proportionately, a little larger.   Rictal bristles dark brown; smaller feathers at back of nostrils and base of bill light dull tawny-brown.   Band across forehead and contiguous stripe above eye brownish black.   Crown and nape silvery grey.   Mantle and upper back dull tawny brown more or less intermixed and overcast with dull silvery grey, shading to pure or nearly pure silvery grey on scapulars and upper rump and whitish on lower rump and upper tail coverts.   Throat and face light, dull tawny brown with paler shaft streaks to feathers, becoming a rather darker shade on sides of lower neck and breast, and paling to a light, bright tawny-rufous on lower breast, belly and under tail coverts. Wings and tail as in *C. occipitalis* but grey parts of tail a little darker.

Irides chestnut-red, dull red, dark chestnut or hazel.   Bill and feet black.   These soft part colours are based on labels of only two specimens and on statements by Harrison & Hartley and Whitehead. I have not seen a juvenile of this species or a description of one.

Field characters   Tawny brown and grey bird with black, white-marked wings and very long grey and black tail.

Distribution and habitat   Borneo; chiefly, but not only, in the mountains.   Inhabits woodland, both forest and second-growth jungle on abandoned cultivated areas.   On Kina Balu, Whitehead found it at all elevations from about 300 to about 2700 metres.

Feeding and general habits   Apparently much as other tree pies.   Foods recorded (in Smythies) are large beetles, fruits and small mammals.   Doubtless many other insects besides beetles are taken.   Usually in pairs or small parties.

Nesting   The only information I can find is that of Whitehead who found a nest on a low tree in scrub jungle on March 13th.   It was a shallow nest of fine twigs and contained two eggs which were greenish white dotted all over with brown markings which increased in size to form a nearly complete ring of blotches at the large end.

Voice   Whitehead heard it utter a 'bell-like note' and a cackling (chattering?) cry like that of the Magpie. Smythies records 'a harsh corvine chatter of six to ten notes uttered rather faster than one can count', which is presumably the same as the 'cackling cry' noted by Whitehead, and a 'three-note whistle . . . a short, high-pitched staccato "pip" followed by two lower prolonged notes of a peculiar hoarse tone'. He notes that it has 'an enormous range of voice' and 'also definitely mimics other birds'.   It seems likely that all the tree pies are, like *Garrulus*, habitual vocal mimics.

Display and social behaviour   No information.

Other names   Malaysian Tree Pie.

REFERENCES

HARRISON, T. H. & HARTLEY, C. H.   1934.   Descriptions of ten new sub-species from mountain areas of Borneo.
        Bull. B.O.C. **54**: 156–157.
SMYTHIES, B. E.   1960.   *The Birds of Borneo.*   London.
WHITEHEAD, J.   1893.   *The Exploration of Mount Kina Balu, North Borneo*, appendix: 205.   London.

ANDAMAN TREE PIE   *Crypsirina bayleyi*

Dendrocitta bazlei (lapsus) Blyth, 1863, Ibis, p. 119, ex Tytler MS.

Description   Appreciably but not greatly smaller than Blue Jay, with usual tree pie shape and proportions. Forehead and lores deep black, ear coverts and chin greyish black, rest of head dark iron grey shading into medium grey on upper mantle and upper breast.   Lower breast rather dark greyish tawny; rest of underparts bright tawny rufous shading to a darker, more chestnut hue on under tail coverts.   Mantle and back dark tawny brown, usually with an olivaceous tinge, shading to a more rufous tone on the rump and dull grey on the upper tail coverts.   Wings black with white patch as in Grey Tree Pie; the lesser and median coverts are very dark grey but this is only evident on close inspection.   Tail black, the basal half of the two long central feathers being greyish black to dark grey although, again, this is not very noticeable.

Irides bright golden yellow or bright clear yellow.   Bill, legs and feet black.   The juvenile has the grey parts of head and neck replaced by a rather sooty, dark reddish brown.   The brown of the back darker and redder, the feathers of rump and upper tail coverts with rusty fringes and the wing coverts not quite so dark a grey and with brownish fringes to the lesser and median coverts.   Tail greyer and shorter than adult's.   Irides (*fide* Butler) at first olive green, changing through bright green to yellow, the yellow first appearing as an inner ring and gradually spreading.

Field characters   Slender and drongo-like in shape and flight but its largely rufous body and white wing patch at once distinguish it from drongos.

Feeding and general habits   Little recorded.   Apparently often or usually in small parties, commonly in company with drongos.

Distribution and habitat   Andaman Islands: inhabits wooded country.

Nesting   Osmaston (in Baker's notebook) described a nest he found 4·5 metres high in a sapling in forest as a flimsy cup-shaped structure of bents and fine sticks, lined with rootlets; it contained 3 eggs on May 21st.   Other eggs have been found in March and April (Baker, 1922).   The eggs are creamy white, spotted and speckled with olive brown and with underlying mauvish grey markings.   Butler found flying young in June.

Voice   Butler records a harsh, constantly repeated note of alarm.

Display and social behaviour   No information.

REFERENCES

ABDULALI, H.   1965.   The birds of the Andaman and Nicobar Islands.   *Journ. Bombay Nat. Hist. Soc.* **61**: 554.
BAKER, E. C. S.   1922.   *The Fauna of British India: Birds* **1**: 55–56.   London.
—— (MSS Notebook on his egg collection in the Sub-dept of Ornithology of the British Museum (Natural History).
BUTLER, A. L.   1899.   The birds of the Andaman and Nicobar Islands.   *Journ. Bombay Nat. Hist. Soc.* **12**: 390.

HOODED RACKET-TAILED TREE PIE   *Crypsirina cucullata*

Crypsirina (Temia) cucullata Jerdon, 1862, Ibis, p. 20.

Description   About a third smaller in body size than Blue Jay, typical tree pie shape (see sketch) but with the spatulate ends of the two central tail feathers much more developed.   Forehead and lores velvety black, rest of head glossy greenish black.   Areas of neck immediately adjacent to the black parts, except at front of neck, white or greyish white, shading into grey of body.   Body plumage a clear silvery grey, slightly tinged with fawnish mauve except on upper back and mantle where it is a more bluish grey. Wing coverts pale fawnish grey, the outer webs of the outer greater coverts edged white.   Inner secondaries fawnish grey; outer ones dark grey to black with greyish white to white (progressively towards centre of wing) edges to outer webs forming a whitish stripe along wing.   Primaries, primary coverts and the two long, spatulate-ended, central tail feathers black.   Outer tail feathers mainly pale fawnish grey.

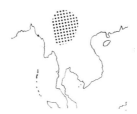

Irides dark blue; eye-rims leaden grey or blackish.   Bill black.   Legs and feet blackish brown or black.   One female specimen, that is in fully adult plumage (taken in January), has a pale area, presumably orange or yellow in life, at gape, like on an immature bird.

Juvenile paler and browner, with blackish brown head and narrower and less markedly spatulate central tail feathers.   Bill with a large orange patch around gape, rest black or brownish black; inside of mouth orange (Oates) and eyelids pale blue with orange edges.   The irides of juveniles are presumably different in colour also but do not appear to have been recorded.

The juvenile bird moults from the plumage described above into a second plumage in which it differs from the adult by being a darker grey, especially on neck and mantle, with no whitish collar between the grey and black areas.   The black on the head is less intense and shiny than the adult's.   The light patch on the bill, around the gape, is retained; the appearance of museum specimens suggests it may be rather paler than in the juvenile, in the only specimen in which the collector noted the soft part colours it was yellow, not orange.   The juvenile wing and tail quills are retained until the second moult, when the bird acquires its full adult plumage.   One specimen taken in August and two taken in September are in this moult and one taken in November just completing it.   This moult takes place when the bird is probably about 13 to 16 months old, as a juvenile in August is in its first moult although others taken in September (presumably later hatched) have not begun to moult.

Field characters   Black head, pale grey body and long spatulate tail are, in combination, diagnostic.

Distribution and habitat   Northern and central Burma.   Inhabits scrub and forest, including bamboo jungle and secondary growth.

Feeding and general habits   Both Jerdon and Roseveare (1949) found it usually singly (mate on nest?) or in pairs, although Roseveare also encountered family parties from July to October.   The only definite observations on its feeding habits that I can find are those of Jerdon who noted it as feeding on grasshoppers, locusts, mantises and flying termites.   No doubt it takes other insects also and probably some vegetable foods.   Makes a whirring noise with its wings in flight (Smythies).

Nesting   Smythies says it nests in a small tree or shrub and that the nest is 'neatly made'.   Baker (1922) implies that the nest is very like that of other tree pies, built of twigs, tendrils and roots.   However, Major Harington, who collected eggs for Baker, described two nests, almost certainly of this species, as being 'with a thorny foundation to nest and sides going slightly over the lips of nest proper very like a miniature *P. rustica* (Magpie) inverted' which suggests a more elaborate nest than descriptions of those of other tree pies indicate.   Eggs 2 to 4 (from 3 clutches only); creamy to greenish white, profusely speckled and flecked or blotched with brown, and with underlying mauvish grey markings.   The markings tend to coalesce at the larger end of the egg.   Eggs have been taken in May and (at Prome) in July.

Voice   Harsh discordant calls and a mewing call like the excitement cry of the Collared Dove (perhaps an imitation of it?) have been recorded.

Display and social behaviour   No information.

Other names   Hooded Spatulate-tailed Tree Pie, Grey Racket-tailed Tree Pie, Hooded Racket-tailed Magpie.

REFERENCES

BAKER, E. C. S. 1922. *The Fauna of British India: Birds* **1**: 57–58. London.
—— MSS notebooks on his egg collection, in Bird Room, British Museum (Natural History).
HARINGTON, H. H. (in Baker MSS notebook, see above).
JERDON, T. C. 1862. Notice of some new species of birds from Upper Burma. *Ibis* (1) **4**: 20.
OATES, E. W. 1883. *A Handbook of the Birds of British Burma* **1**: 405–406. London.
ROSEVEARE, W. L. 1949. Notes on birds of the irrigated area of Shwebo District, Burma. *Journ. Bombay Nat. Hist. Soc.* **48**: 516.
—— 1950. Notes on birds of the irrigated area of Minbu District, Burma. *Journ. Bombay Nat. Hist. Soc.* **49**: 245–246.
SMYTHIES, B. E. 1953. *The Birds of Burma*. London.

BLACK RACKET-TAILED TREE PIE   *Crypsirina temia*

Corvus temia Daudin, 1800, Traité Orn., p. 244.

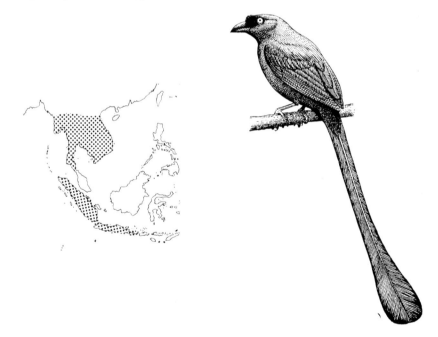

Description   A little larger than the previous species, *C. cucullata*, similar in shape but with the bill proportionately a little longer and the spatulations at the ends of the central tail feathers a little less pronounced. Forehead, lores and a narrow ring of feathers round eye, plush-like in texture and velvety black. Rest of plumage a very dark oily green, appearing black in a poor light or at a little distance, except for the wing and tail quills which are black with some green tinge or gloss on those parts visible when wings and tail are folded. In worn plumage, and sometimes to a minor degree in fresh plumage, there is a bluish hue on head and back and, in some lights, a bronzy tone. The body plumage is soft and silky in texture and is usually described as glossy or iridescent but it is a subdued iridescence compared with that seen, for example, on a Starling, *Sturnus vulgaris*, or Magpie.   Both the dark green colour and its degree of gloss are reminiscent of the Shag, *Phalacrocorax aristotelis*.   Irides turquoise blue or light blue, darkening to ultramarine blue or blackish blue near pupil; sometimes recorded as entirely light or dark blue.   Bill, legs and feet black.

The juvenile has the forehead and lores not quite so intense a velvety black as adult; rest of body plumage greyish black with little or no green lustre, and the usual woolly texture of juvenile corvids.   The tail is narrower, with the spatulations on the central feathers hardly more than indicated and the gloss on the outer webs brownish bronze rather than greenish.   The concealed (when wing is closed) parts of the wing quills are greyish black rather than the deeper black of the adult.   Iris colour probably differs from that of the adult and, at least in fledged juveniles, is no doubt similar to that of the first year bird.   The juvenile moults into a plumage like that of the adult except for being, on average, a little less intensely green, especially on the underparts.   First year birds can, however, only be certainly distinguished by the juvenile wing and tail quills which are, as usual, retained until the second moult.   The irides of immatures are brown but it appears not to be known at what age they turn to blue; one taken in December still had dark brown eyes.

Field characters   All-black coloration distinguishes this species from other tree pies; unforked, graduated tail with broad-ended *central* feathers from drongos.

Distribution and habitat   Southern Burma and Tenasserim, Thailand (Siam), Indo-China, Sumatra, Java and Bali.   Inhabits scrub, secondary growth, bamboo groves, gardens, open country with scattered bushes or bamboo clumps and open forest.   Often common in scrub jungle near villages.

Feeding and general habits   Arboreal, not known to feed on the ground but has been seen on ground bathing (Deignan).   Hops and clambers with great agility among the branches, using the long mobile tail as a balancing organ.   Feeds largely on insects, said also to take fruit.   The bird that Deignan saw bathing at a small rain pool carried its tail forward over its back at an angle of about 45°.   Sometimes singly or in pairs; sometimes in small, loose-knit (family ?) parties.

Nesting   Builds a more or less cup-shaped nest of twigs, and sometimes creeper stems and tendrils; lined with tendrils and/or fine roots.   Nest placed in shrubs, bushes and bamboos; very commonly in clumps of thorny bushes or bamboos growing in open grassy areas; usually about 2 to 3·5 metres above ground but sometimes lower.   Eggs 2 to 4, greenish white, greenish buff, white or cream, profusely speckled and spotted with dark brown, reddish brown or olive brown, usually with some underlying greyish markings. Less often the eggs may be more sparsely marked, in which case the spots and blotches are usually larger. Nests with eggs have been found from April to August (inclusive) in Burma and Siam and in April in Tonkin.

Voice   Deignan records parties of birds uttering a 'characteristic whining call'; Smythies 'a harsh, swearing note of three syllables' and Decoux, who kept a tame specimen, says that its voice was harsh and disagreeable but seldom heard.

Display and social behaviour   No information.

Other names   Bronzed Racket-tailed Tree Pie, Black Spatulate-tailed Tree Pie, Bronzed Spatulate-tailed Tree Pie, Black Racket-tailed Magpie.

REFERENCES

BAKER, E. C. S. 1922. *The Fauna of British India: Birds* **1**: 56–57. London.
—— MS Notebook on his egg collection; in Bird Room, British Museum (Nat. Hist.).
DECOUX, A. 1929. La Pie bronzée, *Crypsirina varians*. *Oiseau* **10**: 764–766.
DEIGNAN, H. G. 1945. The Birds of Northern Thailand. *Bull. U.S. Nat. Mus.* No. **186**: 307–308.
OATES, E. W. 1883. *A Handbook to the Birds of British Burma* **1**: 404–405. London.
ROBINSON, H. C. & CHASEN, F. N. 1939. *The Birds of the Malay Peninsula.* **4**: 346. London.
SMITH, H. C. 1943. *Notes on Birds of Burma*: 9–10. (Privately printed?).
SMYTHIES, B. E. 1953. *The Birds of Burma.* London.

NOTCH-TAILED TREE PIE   *Crypsirina temnura*

Glaucopis temura Temminck, 1825, in Temminck and Laugier, Pl. Col., livr. 57, pl. 337.

Description   About size of Blue Jay or a shade smaller, usual tree pie shape but tail shorter than in other species and with ends of tail feathers remarkably notched on the insides and with the ends of the webs, especially on the outer sides, elongated.   Forehead feathers stiffened and bristly in texture and deep black.   Feathers on crown immediately behind this area are slightly stiffened and glossy at tips.   Rest of plumage greyish black with very slight iridescence on head, wings and tail.   Irides brownish red, brown or wine-red.   Bill, legs and feet black.

I have not seen the juvenile of this species or a description of it.   Some specimens I examined appeared to be first year birds still retaining juvenile wing and tail quills.   From these it would appear that the juvenile's tail is very similar to that of the adult, differing only in the feathers being somewhat narrower and their modifications slightly less pronounced, this being most apparent with the two short outermost tail feathers (one on each side) which are smaller and shorter, with rounded ends, and only a slight indentation.

Field identification   All black coloration distinguishes it from other tree pies.   Information on field characters to distinguish it from drongos, when unusual shape of tail feather ends is not visible, is needed.   The voice (q.v.) is apparently distinctive.

Distribution and habitat   Tonkin; northern and central Annam; and Hainan island.   Said to inhabit both forest and open woodlands (Delacour).   In northern Tonkin Stevens found it only in 'open forest composed of single bamboos of huge dimensions;'.   It tends, apparently, to be local in distribution. Found at low elevations.

Feeding and general habits   Presumably largely insectivorous but I can find no detailed information. Sometimes in small parties and then often in company with Paradise Drongos, *Dicrurus paradiseus* (Stevens in Kinnear).

Nesting   No information.

Voice   Stevens noted that it had 'striking and distinctive call notes that unfortunately cannot now be given from memory'.

Display and social behaviour   No information.

Other names   Black Tree Pie.

REFERENCES

DELACOUR, J. & JABOUILLE, P.   1931.   *Les Oiseaux de l'Indochine française* **4**: 291–292.
KINNEAR, N. B.   1929.   On the birds collected by Mr H. Stevens in Northern Tonkin.   *Ibis* (12) **5**: 340–341.

BLACK JAY   *Platysmurus leucopterus*

Glaucopis leucopterus Temminck, 1824, in Temminck and Laugier, Pl. Col., 265, livr. 45.

Description   About size of Magpie but with shorter and more rounded tail and deeper bill with strongly-curved culmen.   Short, bristly crest on forehead and immediately behind it an area of rather broad-ended, glossy, stiffened feathers.   Large white stripe on wing, formed by white areas on most greater coverts and on three secondaries.   Plumage otherwise jet black.   There is some bluish or greenish iridescence on the crown feathers; the wing and tail feathers have a somewhat shining appearance but do not show more than a trace, if any, of blue or green sheen.

Irides bright vermilion, scarlet or crimson red.   Bill, legs and feet black.   I have not seen a juvenile of this form but it probably differs from the adult in precisely the same degree as does the Bornean form (q.v.).   The juvenile primary coverts are sometimes tipped whitish and they and the wing and tail quills, which are retained until the second moult, are not quite so intensely black as the adult's.

The above description is of the nominate form *P. l. leucopterus*, from Tenasserim, the Malay Peninsula and Sumatra.   The Bornean form, *P. l. aterrimus*, has the crest feathers, especially on the crown, much longer, and has no white in the wing, being entirely black. Its juvenile body plumage is greyish black and of the usual loose and woolly texture.   In both forms adults and birds hatched the previous year, or some of them, are moulting in July, August and September and completing their moult in October.

Field characters   Jay-like but black with conspicuous white in wing (nominate form) or all black. Longer tail than that of any typical crow.   Frontal crest may give characteristic profile.

Distribution and habitat   Tenasserim north to Tavoy district, Malay Peninsula, Sumatra and Borneo. Inhabits forest and scrub jungle.   In Borneo often near human habitations.

Feeding and general habits   Said to take caterpillars, beetles and other insects, small mammals and fruit. Arboreal; forages both high and low in trees and scrub.   Would appear not to have been seen on the ground.   Often in small parties, the individuals following one another at intervals, like Jays.   Described as flying with short wing beats and partly-spread tail, producing a soft 'boobooboo' sound from the feathers (Harrisson, in Smythies).   Much of the information on its habits, nesting etc., seems to originate from W. R. Davison, a keen collector and observer who apparently gave much information to Hume, Oates and others but did not publish his observations.   He is quoted in Oates and the other references given here.

Nesting   Nests in bushes, small trees, shrubs or palms; the few nests so far found have been 1·8 to 2·4 metres above ground.   The nest is a large, coarsely-built structure of sticks with a shallow cup lined with fibres and strips of bark.   Nests of the nominate form found in February, March and April; the only record for the Bornean form is of one egg, in the British Museum (Natural History) collection, taken at Baram on 21 June.   Eggs 2 to 3, white or creamy white, finely speckled with brown and grey, the markings often forming a zone at either the large *or* the small end of the egg.

Voice   Davison heard a 'deep, rolling, metallic note' from the nominate form.   Smythies records, from the same individual, a harsh chatter of six to ten notes and 'a three-note whistle, consisting of a short, high-pitched staccato *pip*, followed by two lower prolonged notes of a peculiar hoarse tone'.   He quotes Harrisson as saying that this species has an enormous range of voice and also mimics the calls of other birds, especially barbets.

Display and social behaviour   No information.

Other names   White-winged Jay (nominate form only), Black Crested Magpie (Bornean form), White winged Black Magpie (nominate form).

REFERENCES

BAKER, E. C. S.   1922.   *The Fauna of British India: Birds* **1**: 58–59.   London.
—— MS Notebook on his egg collection; in Bird Room, British Museum (Natural History).
OATES, E. W.   1883.   *A Handbook to the Birds of Burma* **1**: 409.   London.
ROBINSON, H. C.   1927.   *The Birds of the Malay Peninsula* **1**: 265–266.
SMYTHIES, B. E.   1960.   *The Birds of Borneo*.   London.

The typical jays

   The typical jays of the genus *Garrulus* number only three species; one of them polytypic and with an extensive range, the other two with relatively tiny ranges.   They are characterized by similar and un-doubtedly homologous blue-and-black barred feathers on the wings and/or tail, traces of similar barring on the head feathers in most cases, and a strong resemblance in movements, ecology, voice and, at least in two species, of display patterns also.

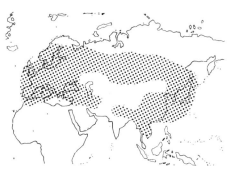

   They are omnivorous but feed largely on acorns, although some forms may occur outside the range of oaks and rely on other foods.   They are persistent food hoarders and some (probably all) forms rely very largely on previously hidden food at certain times of year.

   They appear most closely related on one hand to the green and blue magpies of the genus *Cissa* and on the other to the boreal jays of the genus *Perisoreus*, to which they seem to be linked by the Sooty Jay *P. internigrans* which is, as is discussed in the section dealing with the grey jays, in some respects intermediate between other *Perisoreus* species and *Garrulus lanceolatus*.

   Over the greater part of their combined ranges the species of *Garrulus* are completely allopatric but the Jay, *G. glandarius*, and the Lanceolated Jay, *G. lanceolatus*, overlap in the western Himalayas.   It is of interest that the form of *G. glandarius* that overlaps *G. lanceolatus*, although strikingly different in plumage and especially in the colour pattern of the head, is the most like it in bodily proportions and eye colour. This suggests that similar environmental factors may have influenced these characters.

The Jay, *Garrulus glandarius*, has a much more extensive range than either of its congeners or, indeed, than any other corvine bird except the Magpie, *Pica pica*, and some species of *Corvus*. Within this range it shows considerable geographic variation. Some populations now appear to be completely isolated from their nearest relatives by sea or unsuitable terrain which is not, or at any rate not normally, crossed by any individuals. As, however, at least as far as their taxonomic characters are concerned, the most diverse forms are connected by intergrades and no instance is known of two forms coming together and not interbreeding to form a mixed population, they seem best all treated as members of a single polytypic species.

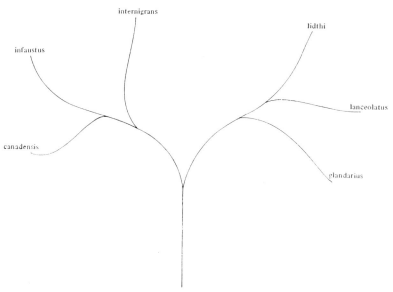

Fig. D.5. Presumed relationship of species in the genera *Garrulus* and *Perisoreus*.

Within each major group of the more diverse forms, numerous races, or one might better say micro-races, of the Jay have been named and recognized. Sometimes, it seems, those who have done so had an ability to recognize geographical variation in inverse relation to their ability to recognize individual variation. Most authorities recognize 7 or 8 major racial groups within the species (see esp. Stresemann; Vaurie, 1954). I think, however, that these can best be reduced to five rather more comprehensive major groups which can be defined as follows:

(1) *Glandarius* group: Crown of head streaked or black; white patch on secondaries; cheeks white or brownish. Irides usually purplish, mauve or bluish but sometimes dark. Range: Europe, western Asia, north-western Africa. Includes the *cervicalis* and *atricapillus* groups of Vaurie and other authors.

(2) *Brandtii* group: Crown of head streaked; head and neck rufous, contrasting with the greyish back; white patch on secondaries. Bill tending to be rather smaller than in (1). Range: north-eastern Russia through Siberia to Manchuria, Korea, and northern Japan (Hokkaido). Intergrades (or interbreeds) with *glandarius* group in the Urals (Johansen; Stresemann), the race *G.g. severtzowi* being intermediate.

(3) *Japonicus* group: Loral region black and contiguous with the black malar stripe; edges of crown feathers nearly snow-white, giving a very bright black and white appearance to top of head with consequent much greater contrast than in any other Jays with streaked crowns. Range: Japan (except Hokkaido).

(4) *Bispecularis* group: Crown of head immaculate; blue patch on secondaries; bill rather small; irides dark brown (western races) to greyish (eastern races). Range: western Himalayas to Formosa. Intergrades with *brandtii* group in northern China.

(5) *Leucotis* group: Crown of head black; blue patch on secondaries; cheeks white; irides dark brown. Range: Burma, Thailand (Siam), Laos, Annam and Cochin China.   Forms intermediate between the *leucotis* group and the *bispecularis* group occur in northern Burma (*G.g. oatesi* and *G.g. harringtoni*). Both for reasons of convenience, and also because there may possibly be significant behavioural or ecological differences between some of them, these five major groups of the species are dealt with under separate headings in the species section.

Heads of Jays from Japan, Syria, western Europe and northern India, to show major differences of colour-pattern of the head within the species.   Top left to bottom right: *Garrulus glandarius japonicus*, *G. g. atricapillus*, *G. g. glandarius* and *G. g. bispecularius*.

The Lanceolated Jay, *G. lanceolatus*, of the western Himalayas east to Nepal and Lidth's Jay, *G. lidthi*, of the Ruy Kyu (Loo Choo) islands south of Japan, differ in coloration and size, and in the proportional length of the head feathers.   They have, however, very similar proportions and plumage patterns and the differences in coloration result mainly from the more simplified pattern and deeper pigmentation of *G. lidthi*, characters usual in Ryu Kyu forms as compared with their mainland relatives.   Although they have now perhaps diverged too far to be treated as members of a superspecies, these two forms are certainly geographical representatives.

REFERENCES

JOHANSEN, H.   1944.   Die Vogelfauna Westsibiriens.   *J. Orn.* **92**: 18–19.
STRESEMANN, E.   1940.   Discussion and review of A. Kleiner's 'Systematische Studien üben die Corviden',
    Ornith. Monatsber. **48**: 102–104.
VAURIE, C.   1954.   Systematic notes on Palearctic Birds.   No. 5 Corvidae.   *Amer. Mus. Novit.* No. 1668.
—— 1959.   *The Birds of the Palearctic Fauna: Passeriformes* 132–145.   London.
VOOUS, K.   1953.   The geographical variation of the Jay (*Garrulus glandarius*) in Europe: a study on individual
    and clinal variation.   *Beaufortia* 2, No. 30.   Amsterdam.

JAY (*glandarius* group)   *Garrulus glandarius*

Corvus glandarius Linnaeus, 1758, Syst. Nat., ed. 10, 1, p. 106.

Description   Nasal plumes creamy white, with dark or brownish central areas to the individual feathers, which are less bristly in character than the nasal plumes of most corvids.   Forehead and forecrown creamy white, greyish white or very pale vinous fawn, with dark centres forming conspicuous streaks.   The dark centres become less distinct on hind crown and nape, where the feather edges are more or less pinkish grey, vinous pink, pinkish brown or vinous rufous, with a distinct light and darker pattern of fine barring; this barring is not, however, noticeable except at very close examination. Lores and area immediately around eyes off-white to pinkish fawn with, at close quarters, a slightly speckly effect due to the dark centres of the individual small feathers. Throat dull white to creamy white, bordered on either side by a broad black malar stripe.

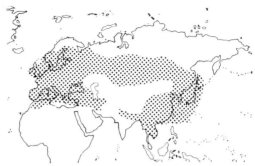

Lesser wing coverts pinkish chestnut with a pattern of fine barring visible on close examination. The alula, outer webs of the primary coverts and outer secondary coverts are barred black and bright light blue; at very close quarters it will be seen that the barring consists of a black bar which shades through dark and light blue to bluish white or snow white, sharply demarcated from the posterior edge of the next black bar. Inner greater coverts jet black. Innermost secondary dark chestnut tipped broadly on outer web and narrowly on inner web with black, sometimes obscurely barred with blue near base of feather where it is never visible in life. Next two secondaries jet black, next with some blue barring at base of outer web. Rest of secondaries with a large white area on outer webs and barred with black and blue on those parts of the outer web not visible on the folded wing. Primaries greyish black with dull white outer webs, or at least greater part of outer webs, except for the short outermost primary which has little or no white edging. Often a trace of blue barring on white parts of primaries. Tail black, the two central feathers and outer webs of the others more or less barred at base with dull silvery blue; sometimes this barring extends to a greater or lesser (usually lesser) extent, to about half way down the tail. The two outermost tail feathers are dull greyish black with ill-defined, narrow, pale tips and edges. Lower part of rump, and upper and under tail coverts white.

Rest of body plumage pinkish fawn, pinkish rufous or pinkish grey, with a strong mauve tinge, usually deepest and pinkest on hind neck and often much paler on underparts. Much minor geographical and local variation. Individuals with more heavily streaked heads, or, to be precise, with the individual streaks on each feather broader, tend to be darker and greyer in general tone than those with paler-looking heads, caused by narrower blackish streaks, which are usually pinker in colour. To some extent such differences are geographical but 'pink' and 'grey' Jays may breed in the same English wood or even, at times, be taken from the same brood.

Irides bluish grey, usually slightly intermixed with reddish and with a narrow brownish, pale reddish or purplish red outer ring, and around the pupil an inner ring of brown or reddish brown. Often more suffused with red when bird is in stress. Bill black or dark horn colour, sometimes a little paler at tip. Inside of mouth greyish black, tinged fleshy grey on tongue and palate. Legs and feet pale fleshy brown.

Juvenile very like adult but with the fawn parts of the plumage of a more rufous or rusty hue with little or no vinous pink tinge, and with the usual rather woolly texture of juvenile corvids. Irides at fledging time a clear pale blue or greyish blue. Inside of mouth bright red to pale mauvish pink, sometimes tinged yellowish, sometimes predominantly dull fleshy yellow with red on tongue and centre of palate only. The black adult colouring starts as isolated spots and marks which spread and coalesce. Bill slate grey, tinged with mauve. Legs and feet tinged yellow as a rule. Newly hatched young are naked, yellowish flesh colour, skin semi-transparent. At about one week skin is much darker and if, as usual in

England, the diet has been largely caterpillars, strongly tinged with olive-yellow. Bill pale mauve grey.

The above description is composite and covers the forms found in Europe and the British Isles, except as hereunder specified. For comparative descriptions of the races recognized by him, see Vaurie 1954; and for detailed discussion of geographical and individual variation Voous (1953).

The form from Cyprus, *G. glandarius glaszneri*, is rather small, with a smaller bill than most others (although bill size and shape is, to some extent, individually variable in all forms) and has the forehead pinkish fawn with dark streaks. *G. g. hyrcanus*, from Lenkoran, eastward along the southern Caspian districts of northern Iran to Gurgan region, has the crown feathers entirely greyish black and those of the forecrown with only narrow pale fringes, so that the top of the head appears predominantly dull black. On close examination most of these black feathers are seen to be finely barred with dark silvery blue; the same is true for the black parts of the head feathers of the streaked-crowned forms.

G. g. krynicki, from Asia Minor (Turkey), but not in the Cilician Taurus, the Aegean Islands east to the Caucasus, Transcaucasia, Azerbaijan and Talych, has the forehead and face white, tinged with mauvy-rufous, and the crown and nape black, with obscure bluish barring on the individual feathers. The form from the Crimea, *G. g. iphigenia*, is similar but a little paler.

G. g. atricapillus, from southern Turkey (Asia Minor) south to Palestine and east to northern and western Iraq and western and southern Iran, is very distinctive, having the forehead and face almost pure white and the white of the throat extending beyond the black malar stripe to meet that of the cheeks. It is paler in body colour than other forms. Its irides are dark purplish grey with a very dark inner ring so that the whole eye looks dark, unlike the eyes of British or western European Jays.

In north-western Africa there are three forms of the Jay which are almost certainly more closely related to each other than any of them is to any non-African form, even although one of them closely resembles the typical streaked-headed forms and another bears considerable superficial resemblance to *atricapillus*. *G. g. cervicalis*, from northern Tunisia and Algeria west to the Department of Alger, has the front of the forehead streaked, the rest of the forehead, crown and nape black, the hind neck and sides of neck deep rufous or chestnut, extending to the black malar stripes, enclosing the white cheeks and forming a not very sharply-demarcated contrast with the vinous grey of the mantle and back, and the breast and under-parts rather greyer than in most other forms. The dull silvery blue barring on its tail feathers is often more extensive than in other forms, frequently extending about two-thirds down on the central tail feathers.

G. g. whitakeri, from northern Morocco to Oran, in western Algeria, is intermediate between *cervicalis* and nominate *glandarius* in appearance, being browner than *cervicalis* in body plumage, the hind neck and sides of neck being deep pinkish brown rather than rufous and this colour suffusing the white cheeks; and the tail barring is usually less extensive. *G. g. minor*, of the Saharan Atlas and the Middle and Great Atlas in Morocco, is smaller than other forms, except *G. g. glaszneri* from Cyprus, and in coloration very similar to *whitakeri*, but with the vinous fawn of the neck less contrasting with rest of body plumage, the head streaked (but more heavily than in most streaked-headed forms) and pinkish fawn cheeks.

Field characters White and blue areas on predominantly black wings diagnostic (and conspicuous when bird seen in flight from above). Combination of pinkish fawn, pinkish grey, or rufous (juvenile) body, white rump and blackish tail suffice for identification if the bird is seen flying away and its wings are not clearly visible. Face-on, from below, black bill and broad black malar stripes against white throat and fawnish or greyish breast equally diagnostic.

At high intensity alarm screech is diagnostic, but Nutcracker's is rather similar and some calls of Starling very like lower intensity versions.

Distribution and habitat British Isles; north-western Africa; Europe east to Palestine, Iraq and Iran, and the larger Mediterranean islands. Intergrades with *brandtii* group in the Urals.

Inhabits woods, copses, spinnies, also often parks, large gardens, and towns, provided there is plenty of tree cover. Usually its range coincides with that of oaks, *Quercus* sp., but in some places, such as northern Sweden (Swanberg, *pers. comm.*), it occurs outside the range of the oaks. Resident, but local dispersion, and periodic eruptions southwards and westwards of birds from northern and central Europe.

Note: map shows distribution of *all* forms of the species.

Feeding and general habits   Feeds both in trees and shrubs and on the ground.   Acorns are usually a staple food.   Insects, especially caterpillars, cockchafers and other beetles, are taken in quantity and form the principle food given to nestlings (Owen).   Also takes chestnuts, beech mast, grain, green peas and beans, cherries, raspberries and other fruit, buds, spiders, slugs and small snails (slugs probably not very readily, judging from their usual refusal by captive Jays), young birds, eggs, mice and other small mammals, lizards, slow-worms, and small snakes.   Keve gives a very full list of recorded foods.   Hunting and killing of recently-fledged young small birds is usually, and perhaps only, practised by adult Jays that are feeding well-grown young.   Individual captive Jays which otherwise ignored small birds that got into their aviary would immediately try to catch them when they had large young of their own.

When seeking food the Jay will dig in dead leaves, loose soil etc. with side-to-side swings of head and bill; try to open crevices, rolled-up leaves or any other seam or small hole by inserting and then opening the bill; and remove loose bark by tugging or levering.   Food that needs breaking up is usually held under both feet, less often under one foot.   The Jay dislikes holding anything at all sticky under foot and food of this description, if it needs further breaking up, is usually held in the bill and rubbed about on the perch or on the ground.   Sometimes dry foods are treated in this way but should they not break up easily they are at once transferred to the feet.

To eat an acorn the Jay holds it between its feet on the perch.   Most often the two outer toes of each foot grip the perch and the innermost one the acorn, but during the meal the bird shifts and re-adjusts its hold and all three front toes are used for either perch or acorn as the need arises.   The Jay seldom, if ever, hammers at an acorn but bites and levers with its bill till the shell is pierced, when it is soon removed.   Pieces of the 'kernel' (cotyledons) may be broken off and swallowed or the Jay may stab the partly open mandibles into the shell-less acorn and, with quick movements of the lower mandible, rasp off a mass of fragments which are held against the inverted upper mandible and swallowed with a backward jerk of the head when enough have been collected.   Whole acorns are carried in the gullet but are always disgorged later either for eating or hiding.

Many distasteful or poisonous insects are habitually ignored by wild Jays.   This is almost certainly due to learning (Goodwin, 1951; Rothschild) Rothschild proved that a Jay was able to distinguish which of two insects, one poisonous, one innocuous, the former eaten shortly before the latter, had caused its discomfort even although both were vomited up together.   Wasps, *Vespa* sp., are, however, readily taken.   The Jay bites hard as it seizes the wasp, then puts it down and bites it near the tip of the abdomen several times before swallowing it.   No attempt is made to remove the sting.   This behaviour appears to be innate (Goodwin, 1952b).

Habitually hides food, usually in the ground, sometimes in trees.   Captive Jays, and wild ones in the London Parks, hide bits of meat and cheese above ground more often than they do nuts and acorns, perhaps through learning that such foods are not improved by being buried.   Food is hidden in the typical manner.   When an acorn is being hidden the Jay usually gives it a few hard blows with the bill after inserting it and before covering it up.   If it is carrying two or more acorns they may all be buried together but more often they are carefully disgorged on to the ground, one only picked up and hidden there, and the others removed to a fresh spot.

Intensive storing of acorns takes place as soon as they are ripe (beginning before they are, as a rule) and while they are still on the trees (Chettleburgh; Schuster).   They are, at any rate by resident adult pairs, carried back to the birds' living areas.   This is very apparent in times of widespread failure of the acorn crop when Jays may fly miles to obtain acorns, and in places, such as inner London, where oaks tend to be scarce and scattered; but much less so under other conditions as, naturally, the Jay collects acorns as near home as it can.   There seems a correlation between the distance the Jay has to fly and the number of acorns it will engorge.   I have seen wild Jays take 6 or 7 acorns into the gullet on some occasions and greater numbers have been recorded by others (e.g. Schuster; Turcek & Kelso), but Jays that are storing in the immediate vicinity of the collecting area usually carry only from one to three acorns in the gullet, and I have never been able to persuade tame Jays to engorge more than four, and very seldom more than two, acorns. Regardless of the number of acorns in its gullet, the Jay often carries a final one in its bill as it flies.

Acorns are habitually recovered. Observations suggest that, at least in south-eastern England, most of the many acorns eaten by Jays in winter and spring have been previously hidden by them. Acorns sometimes form part of the food given to well-grown nestlings (Owen, *pers. obs.*) and Bossema found that, in Holland, they were an important food for the fledged young. Hidden acorns may be regularly recovered from under a foot or more of snow (Swanberg). The Jay retrieves hidden food by flying or hopping straight to the spot. This it does not only when digging up buried acorns but also when retrieving, for example, a bit of meat tucked into a crevice on the underside of a branch. It will often drive off any other bird that it sees near one of its caches, then at once remove the food and hide it elsewhere.

Bossema found that acorns, with their cotyledons still in good condition, were discovered by Jays that investigated baby oaklings and pulled at their stems. He concluded that this was the method by which the Jay found its hidden acorns. He implied that acorns eaten in winter and early spring were found by random searching but this is not the case in England nor, I believe, elsewhere. I think it very likely that Jays may *learn* to correlate baby oaklings with the presence of a hidden acorn, through finding the former when they return for an acorn they have buried or possibly by chance. Comparable learning is apparently shown in relation to birds-nesting. Many Jays, presumably as a result of experience, will at once begin to search for a nest if a Song Thrush or some other passerine starts to mob or attack them. It is at first astonishing to see the way in which the Jay, which may be high in a bare tree or on a garden fence when a Song Thrush or Blackbird begins to mob it, immediately flies to the nearest bush, hedge, clump of brushwood or other likely nesting place and determinedly searches there.

When hiding acorns the Jay shows a strong tendency to bury them in some rather open space; a glade, a grass slope above or adjacent to the tree line, in the ground beneath conifers and similar places. Possibly the Jay, when engaged in food-hiding, is less liable to be surprised by a predator or watched by a potential robber or the hidden acorn may be rather less liable to be found by small mammals or wild swine in such situations. One result of this is to increase the Jay's effectiveness as a planter and spreader of oak-woods.

Jays are usually seen in pairs, small straggling parties or singly (mate sitting) but never in compact groups. When crossing open ground members of a party always go one by one, the second bird not usually breaking cover, even when being forced to leave by an approaching human, until the first is some way across. Pairs flying together are never very close; usually one is at least several yards behind the other.

The Jay's flight appears laboured when in the open, probably owing to its broad wings and rather slow full wing beats but it can swoop and turn quickly. Among trees its flight is extremely agile and graceful. It hops on the ground and in branches.

Observation and circumstantial evidence suggests that adult breeding Jays live in pairs within a territory which is sometimes defended against neighbouring pairs but in which Jays who are not considered as rivals are often or usually tolerated, and that food is obtained both inside and outside the defended area. Information on known, marked birds, in natural woodland as well as in town parks, is needed. In good habitat favourite breeding areas, such as small boggy woods with dense growth of birch and alder much festooned with honeysuckle, may have three or four breeding pairs in about as many acres, some or all of which travel to some distance when seeking food.

Periodic irruptions into western Europe of Jays originating (and in some cases ultimately returning) further east or north take place; as well as irregular movements within western Europe. It seems likely that food shortage, perhaps linked with high population, is the basic cause. This has been denied (Berndt & Dancker) on the grounds that, as the Jay eats a great many foods and occurs in some oakless areas, it could not be affected by failure of the acorn crop, but I do not find this convincing. Küchler has shown that during these eruption years some young Jays may move while others stay near their birthplace. Return migration may take place as late as June (Geyr von Schweppenberg).

Timid and wary of man where persecuted, the Jay readily becomes tame or indifferent in towns where not molested, is less suspicious of strange or new objects than *Corvus* species and easily caught in traps.

When anting the Jay does not pick up ants in the bill although it makes the same movements of the head as species which do. The wings are (at high intensity) spread quite widely and thrust forward like a canopy in front of the anting bird. Usually both wings are thrust forward together. I have seen a great number of both wild and captive Jays anting but, except in one case of a wild bird anting among black ants in a tree, all were doing so with Wood Ants, *Formica rufa*, supplied by the observer(s). Captive Jays invariably bathe in water immediately after anting.

Nesting Nests in trees or shrubs, sometimes in recesses and hollows of trees, rather rarely on sheltered supports, ledges or niches of buildings. Typical nest sites, in Britain, are a main fork of a hawthorn or crab apple; a clump of honeysuckle; the forking branches near the summit of a birch sapling; or against the trunk of a birch or conifer, supported by outgrowing branches. Usually from 3 to 6 metres above ground but sometimes lower or much higher. Nests in dense woods or thickets are usually, perhaps always, near some little glade or other open space or break in the canopy.

Nest made of twigs, small sticks, and sometimes woody stems, with an inner lining of fine roots or root-like fibres, with sometimes a little horsehair or any other fine wiry materials. Roots and fibres of any shade from black to white may be used in the lining, it is not true that only black ones are used. Sticks are broken from trees or shrubs but lining material is sought on the ground. Sticks are taken singly but a number of roots and fibres are collected at each trip. Each piece is, however, picked up singly. If a building Jay is given a bundle of coconut fibres it does not carry it off at once but holds it underfoot and pulls out strand after strand until its bill is full of individually separated fibres.

Both sexes build at all stages, each putting in place the material it has brought. The male tends to take the initiative in nest site selection.

Eggs 3 to 7, usually 4 to 6 and very commonly 5. Light bluish green to dull light yellowish green, with speckles and small flecks of light brown or greenish brown. These markings are usually so dense that they partly obscure the ground colour, less often they form a zone around the larger end and are sparse elsewhere. Most eggs are marked with a few black hair-like markings. Eggs are laid daily, in the early morning. The female may roost on the nest the night before laying the first egg but does not always do so. Incubation and brooding by female only, there are a very few observations of males covering young for short periods. Incubation period 16 to 19 days (usually 16–17). True incubation appears usually to begin with the second or third egg, although the female covers the eggs from the first. Usually the first 2 or 3 eggs hatch on the 19th or 20th day after the laying of the first, the remaining eggs on consecutive days. Young fledge at 21 to 23 days but will jump out as early as 17 days (perhaps sometimes earlier) if badly frightened.

The sitting female is fed by the male who brings food in his gullet. At wild nests watched in southern England males came about once in two hours and showed caution when approaching the nest. Female leaves nest about once in three hours, for periods of 5 to 15 minutes, rarely longer. While off she sometimes obtains food for herself and may be fed by the male. When incubating, fidgetting about and nest probing seem to be largely provoked by hunger or discomfort. Such actions occur most often when the female has been some time without food and, if persisted in, are a sure sign that she will shortly leave the nest for a spell.

When approached by man incubating wild Jays crouch low in the nest, all plumage appressed but the bill partly open. Sooner or later they flee. Tame female Jays (if not regarding the human as a mate) go into defensive threat display. They will often leave the nest to attack but are inhibited from doing so *at* the nest (Goodwin, 1956). Whether this inhibition also prevents attack on non-human predators once they have reached the nest is not known.

The female eats the hatched eggshells and cleans the plumage of the young if soiled or wet. In the Jay apparent probing in and pulling at the nest lining follows what appear to be unsuccessful attempts to catch ectoparasites. Typically the female rises somewhat, backs slightly and looks into the nest. Suddenly she plunges her head down quickly into the cup of the nest and appears to pick up and swallow some minute object. When she, evidently, 'misses' such failure is often followed by nest-probing.

Both sexes feed the young, at first mostly with food brought by the male. Food is carefully prepared for very young nestlings, each insect being pulled to pieces (unless very small) and its hard parts removed. In at least one pair (Goodwin, 1951) this behaviour was initiated by the sight of the young. When feeding young the parent induces them to gape by giving the food call, and inserts its bill deeply into the nestling's throat before disgorging food from the gullet. As the bill is withdrawn food is usually seen in the bill tip; this is either swallowed or offered to another nestling. Both sexes take faecal sacs directly from the young and swallow them. At least after the first week the male habitually disgorges them away from the nest but the female evidently ingests them (Goodwin, 1951). The young are fed for some time after leaving the nest, the parents tiring of them gradually over a period of several days during which young may be fed, ignored, or repulsed when they beg, according to the shifting moods of the parent. In two captive pairs the females ceased to feed their young about a week or more before the male did. During and shortly after this transition period the young frequently try to snatch food from the parents when they are feeding and sometimes succeed in doing so.

When the young are fledged they appear to be recognized as individuals. A parent will often give some food to a young one then leave it, still begging eagerly, in order to seek out and feed another of the brood. The flying young appear to start to follow the parents at the stage when the latter begin to neglect them. The parents will fly from a distance to attack a crow or other predator that they see near where their well-grown, flying young are in cover, just as they would to defend a potentially threatened nest of un-fledged young.

In captivity and, to judge from less detailed and certain observations, in the wild also, the young begin to feed themselves at about five weeks old, although they may pick morsels of food from each other's bills as early as four weeks. They become fully independent, so far as food is concerned, at from six to eight weeks old. In Britain eggs are usually laid in late April and the first half of May but quite often in late May and early June. These later nests are probably often repeats after loss of the first clutch, and the occasional clutches laid in mid or late June almost certainly are. Throughout most of Europe the breeding season is similar. In north-west Africa nests with eggs have been found from early April to mid-May, in Turkey from early April to early June, in the near East in late April.

Only one brood is reared but repeat attempts are often made if eggs or young are destroyed. In southern England (and probably elsewhere) two to four young are most commonly reared although five is the most frequent clutch size. The reduction in numbers takes place, in many cases, at or near hatching time. It is not due to eggs failing to hatch as such eggs are not removed for a week or more, probably then only as a result of breakage. Eggs and small young often disappear from nests with no overt signs of predation (such as are at other times very evident). At least in the case of captive birds it is known that sometimes one of the parents must be responsible (see Goodwin, 1956).

Voice   The appeal call, which develops from the hunger call of the fledged young, may be written 'aaaa', and perhaps better 'oor' or 'choork' for the softer variants which have a decidedly muted kissing sound. There are many intergrading forms, of which the more distinguishable are:

(a)   The typical querulous mewing call, very suggestive of the calling of a hungry domestic cat. Often given when the Jay is hungry and intensified into a frantic scream by very hungry juveniles when their parents are neglecting them. Also used as a contact call.

(b)   The food-offering call: a husky, deeper-pitched, 'throaty' version, usually with a tender affectionate tone. Used when offering food to the mate, sometimes when accepting food from the mate, when a pair are passing objects to each other at nest site, and sometimes in apparent attempts to conciliate the mate; also when offering food to young, then tending to be less husky, very soft, and tender in tone, especially when the young are still small.

(c)   The juvenile-type begging call: an urgent-sounding 'aa, aaa!' breaking into a squawking gabble (apparently due to attempting to call while swallowing) when fed. Used by well grown or fledged young; and by adults, especially the incubating female, when begging.

(d)   A rather high-pitched but not usually loud version, with a very pathetic, yearning tone. Used at spring gatherings and during pursuit flights; also by Jays looking for a hiding place for food they are carrying; and by birds seeking food for their young, but not usually given by Jays seeking food for themselves alone.

(e)   Rather similar to (d) but softer, shorter and lower-pitched.   Used by both sexes on finding a suitable nest site.   Probably functions to attract partner, who is, however, usually at hand.

A short, husky, panting, rapidly repeated call is often given by tame Jays when their young are handled and is always accompanied by attack.   I have heard it from wild Jays dashing up in response to the alarm cries of handled fledglings (but giving way to alarm screeching on seeing man) and once by a breeding pair chasing a Sparrow Hawk.   In sound this call is suggestive of the appeal call, except in its speed of utterance, but it seems to express extreme anxiety or anger.

A short hard grating call is often given when the Jay is attacking a Carrion Crow or other predator or at the moment that it turns to defend itself from attack by a thrush, *Turdus* sp., or some other bird. It intergrades through a Mistle Thrush-like rattle into the panting calls on one hand and into the alarm screech on the other.

What I have termed 'chirruping notes' are a series of soft, stammering calls, usually interspersed with somewhat louder and longer-drawn sounds which appear to be soft variants of the appeal call.   They intergrade especially with the food-offering version of the appeal call and are capable of much variation in tone and inflection.   As each monosyllable is uttered there is a corresponding small jerk of body and tail.   Usually the first longer note (and often subsequent ones also) interjected is immediately followed by a wide yawn-like gaping of the bill.

The chirruping notes seem often expressive of submissive affection and also to be used in apparent perplexity, or relief from tension or fear.   They seem to serve an appeasing function between paired birds by inducing a similar mood in the bird at which they are directed.   Between paired Jays they are used by whichever partner is subordinate, when it apparently fears that its mate is about to drive it from perch or food.   Pairs also frequently hold 'chirruping duets' which either may initiate and to which the mate usually responds at once.

The harsh, rasping screech commonly functions as an alarm call.   Usually the Jay screeches twice in quick succession and then pauses before screeching again.   There are many minor variants, and the Jay sometimes screeches in apparent anger or threat.   Generally, however, screeching, which is the characteristic predator-mobbing call, is used when the Jay appears to be highly excited and somewhat alarmed but with its impulse to flee in conflict with aggressiveness or curiosity.   The thwarting of almost any strong impulse appears at times to elicit screeching.   Screeching intergrades with both the appeal call and the 'kraah' call, although in its most typical forms it is quite distinct from either.

The hawk-alarm is a very soft sad-sounding call, very difficult to pinpoint.   It is given at sight of a flying Sparrow Hawk, *Accipter nisus* (and other birds-of-prey?).   While giving it the Jay 'freezes' in a crouched posture and watches the hawk.

A loud resonant rather crow-like 'kraa-aah' or 'kraah', typically as loud as but more resonant and less harsh than the high intensity variants of the alarm screech, is heard chiefly in connection with spring gatherings.   It usually sounds two-syllabled and has numerous variants, especially two that might be written 'k'yankh' and 'k'ya-arnkh' with a slightly nasal tone.   It is characteristically uttered by some individuals, or sometimes only one individual, taking part in spring gatherings.   It is uttered especially from high perches and in flight, with great apparent effort, and always in a characteristic posture (quite different from that used when screeching) with head bent somewhat downwards and the back of the neck appearing arched or humped in a conspicuous manner.

I have not heard this call from Jays known to be males.   Among my captive Jays it was uttered most freely by unpaired females in late winter and spring.   Paired females gave it seldom and only at low intensity.   I once removed her mate from a captive female, in September, and placed him out of her sight in another aviary.   On the following day she began to utter 'kraah' calls, at first only soft variants but by the third day she was giving very intense 'kraah' calls, each of which was answered, better perhaps 'echoed', by an appeal call (version d) from her mate.   I then re-united them and the female at once ceased to utter 'kraah' calls.   In the related Lanceolated Jay, however, the 'kraah' call is certainly uttered by males, so that the possibility that some males of *glandarius* may give this call cannot be excluded on present evidence.

A variety of squeaking, bubbling and chinking notes, individually variable but not sufficiently so to suggest that they have no innate bases, are uttered by the male when he hops around the female in what appears to be a purely sexual form of the lateral self-assertive display (q.v.).

When giving the self-assertive display males utter individual display-phrases which usually incorporate and are sometimes mainly or wholly composed of peculiar hissing sounds and of vehement 'hissing-crashing' sounds, suggestive of a load of gravel being tipped onto a road.   The display-phrases, of which each male usually has two or more, may consist partly or entirely of copied sounds and are largely individual compilations although the tendency to incorporate or use hissing sounds seems to be innate.   When males utter clicking sounds in display, these are, in my experience, always of a different quality, lighter and more suggestive of scissors snipping, than the guttural clicks of females.

Female Jays usually utter guttural clicking sounds when giving the self-assertive display, or incorporate clicking or castanet-like sounds in their display-phrases.   There is much individual variation and some Jays, believed to have been females, have uttered grating rather than clicking sounds.   Some females may also use copied sounds, not involving clicks, as alternative display-phrases.

Soft 'rambling' warbling or singing, which usually seems to consist mostly of muted variants of the appeal calls interspersed with various copied sounds, is characteristic of young unpaired Jays in their first year of life, although not entirely confined to them.   Such soft singing is usually by a Jay that is alone, either sitting quietly or seeking food in a desultory manner.   Louder imitations may also be uttered in such circumstances.

Apparently inconsequential vocal mimicry, and the learning of many new sounds, occurs mainly in the first year.   To judge from tame birds, adults that have paired and bred do not thereafter learn many new sounds although, at least in the case of captive individuals, they do not entirely cease to do so.

Copied sounds are frequently uttered in situations that seem appropriate.   Thus a Jay will often imitate the call of a Grey Heron or a Carrion Crow when it sees one of these birds flying over (in silence).   When mobbing a Tawny Owl it may intersperse its screeching with imitations of the Owl's hooting or its 'ker-wick' call.   When mobbing a human who is at their nest (usually this only happens if the nest contains young) Jays often mimic the calls of nest predators, such as the Carrion Crow and Tawny Owl or the *alarm* calls of other birds.

Besides such sounds as the calls of crows and herons, and the hooting of owls, Jays can also mimic the songs of some smaller passerines, often so well that one would never suspect the singer's identity if one did not see the Jay.   For fuller details of the vocal mimicry of some individual Jays see Goodwin (1951).

Jays often defy conspecifics with imitations of their own display-phrases.   A wild Jay defied a captive with an imitation of one of the latter's display phrases, which consisted entirely of whistling that the captive had learned from me.

Display and social behaviour   In the self-assertive or lateral display the feathers of the rump, belly and flanks are erected more fully than other body feathers, thus giving a characteristic outline (see p.232).

The wings are folded with the secondaries slightly spread, and usually the inner greater coverts droop so as to interpose a solid black area between the blue wing coverts and the white patch on the secondaries, which is thus accentuated.   The crest may be either erected or flat.   The displaying bird usually presents itself laterally, reaching forward and uttering a display-phrase.   If on the ground it may walk a few tottering steps as it does so, the only situation in which I have seen Jays walk.   Often it also tilts itself towards the creature displayed at.

This display is used by the male to the female and also to other males, especially in territorial boundary disputes.   Raising of the crest seems sometimes to indicate an increased degree of conflict and sometimes more purely sexual motivation.   A Jay displaying with crest fully erect is less likely to switch immediately to either attacking or fleeing than is one with its crest lowered.

In its most clearly sexual context this display is often shown by the male towards his mate in the early stages of the breeding cycle.   He hops around her uttering the characteristic squeaking, chinking and bubbling calls.   Every so often he hops nearly or quite up to the female, either gives her a little food or makes intention movements of doing so, and hops away again.   This display may end in the male attempting to mount the female, probably sometimes in actual copulation although I have not seen this.

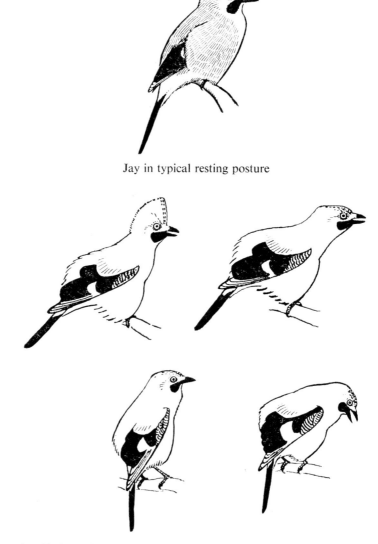

Jay in typical resting posture

(1) Male Jay in self-assertive display, with crest erect (L) and flat (R); (2) Female Jay giving guttural clicking notes with self-assertive display, high (L) and low (R) phases of movement (see text)

The self-assertive display of the female is similar but differs in that the feathers on the back are more fully raised and those on flanks and rump often less so, giving a rather different outline (see sketch, above). Her crest is held flat or only partially erect.   As she utters her (usually clicking) display-phrases she starts from a more upright position and moves downward rather than forward, so that her head is pointing down at a steep angle, often nearly at a right angle, at the end of the movement.   This display is given both to sexual rivals and to the mate.   Self-assertive display between members of a pair occurs often during or immediately after hostile encounters with neighbouring pairs.

Self-assertive display is seen chiefly in late winter, spring and early autumn. It may, however, be shown even by Jays in full moult.

In the quivering or submissive display the Jay adopts a rather horizontal posture. The tail and rump are often slightly raised, and are jerked and quivered violently. The wings are spread and slightly arched so as to present them somewhat frontally, and are quivered. At lower intensities of this display, which are far more often performed, the wings are only slightly extended. Sometimes only the wings are quivered, at others they may be slightly extended without any visible movements and only the tail quivered.

This display is the female's invitation to coition. It is sometimes used by both sexes of a pair when exchanging food or inedible objects. It may also be shown towards social superiors and, in this context, by tame male Jays to humans. Jays give this display towards social superiors in situations where their impulses to escape and to attack appear to be in conflict (Goodwin, 1956). In my experience, tame female Jays only give this display to humans in sexual contexts whereas males do so in apparent appeasement and at all times of the year.

Begging with flapping or fluttering wings and juvenile-type begging call is characteristic of the female soliciting food during the laying and incubation periods. It can be induced simply by hunger. Tame Jays of either sex will, if very hungry, beg from their keeper at any time of year. Sometimes begging occurs in other situations that apparently, induce a feeling of dependence on the partner or desire for it to perform some action. Males may beg to attract their mates to the nest site although more often the nest call (q.v.) is used in this context. A two year old captive male persistently begged to and was fed by his mate during their first spring together. He then showed no interest in her nest building and ate her eggs as soon as laid. In subsequent years he behaved in a completely normal manner, fed the (same) female and successfully reared young with her. I once saw a wild male beg towards his mate, who was several yards away from him. She went to him, fed him, then solicited with quivering wings and coition took place.

A rudimentary version of the Lanceolated Jay's chin-up display is often given with the chirruping notes.

In the defensive threat display most or all of the contour feathers are erected. The wings are held uncovered by the body feathers and may be slightly spread and drooped, the tail may be slightly spread. At very high intensity the wings may be fully spread. The defensively displaying Jay tries constantly to face its enemy and usually keeps its bill open. In high intensity forms this display is used mostly when defending the nest or when attacking a predator that is near the nest or young. Less intense forms may be seen away from the nest, in social contexts, and sometimes towards birds of other species.

Audible snapping of the bill is often used in threat, especially by a dominant Jay towards an inferior. Sometimes, in reference to the mate, the typical method of threatening an inferior, by slightly stretching the neck towards it and giving a single bill snap, may be replaced by thrusting the bill towards the mate but giving a soft version of the appeal call instead of a bill snap.

Young that have recently left the nest may rest or sleep in contact but adults maintain an individual distance of, usually, a metre or so. Even the members of a pair seldom come to within about a metre of each other without showing appeasing or threatening behaviour. The preludes to courtship feeding and copulation fall, of course, within these categories.

Feeding of the female by the male, much less often of the male by the female, occurs mainly in spring before and during nesting and incubation. It takes three main forms, although intermediate types often occur. (1) Food is passed from male to female, rarely from female to male, with the food-offering version of the appeal call. No marked posturing is shown but the rump feathers and those of the black malar stripes are usually somewhat erected. Either sex may initiate such feeding, most often the male. (2) Food is received and/or solicited with juvenile-type begging. Feeding of the mate in this context has been discussed above. (3) The submissive quivering display, especially a version in which the wings are only slightly extended, may accompany food giving. This seems to occur most in the pre-building stages of the breeding cycle. Quite often it is the female who gives food to the male, who also goes into the quivering display on receiving it.   The food may then be passed back and forth several times before one swallows it.   It is often presented in the tip of the bill.   Inedible objects may be used instead of food in this form of courtship feeding.

Food given by one bird to another is usually, and when the male gives it almost always, prepared ready for swallowing and held in the mouth or gullet, being ejected with the help of the tongue as the bills come together with the birds' heads at right angles to each other.   One bird, usually the male, turns its head sideways during the food-passing for this purpose.

Excited gatherings take place in late winter and spring ('spring gatherings').   In southern England they are most frequent from late February until late April.   They take place especially on fine mornings but may occur at almost any time of day in almost any weather.   From three to twenty or more Jays may be involved, so that it seems unlikely that all such assemblages consist of only one female and the males courting her.   That one or more Jays may fly in from a distance, giving the 'kraah' call in flight, to join a gathering where the 'kraah' call is already being uttered, also suggests that more than one female may be involved.   Some of the smaller gatherings do, however, appear to consist of one female who is followed and displayed to by two or three males.

To summarize present knowledge of these spring gatherings (see Geyr von Schweppenburg, 1939, and Goodwin, 1951 for more detailed accounts of some individual gatherings):

They involve intense excitement and the participants move over a considerable area, one bird taking flight and others trailing after it.   The 'kraah' call and version (d) of the appeal call are characteristically heard but many other calls may be uttered as well as vocal mimicry.   Intense self-assertive display occurs; often several apparent pairs will be perched in the same or adjacent trees, each individual nearer to its 'partner' than it is to any of the other displaying birds.   Much chasing takes place, some chases ending with mutual self-assertive display between an apparent male and female.   Fights often occur but are usually brief.   Sometimes established pairs ignore gatherings in their immediate vicinity (compare information on Blue Jay).   Chasing and display may occur between two Jays that appear to be already paired together.   When a gathering comes within sight and sound of captive Jays those of the latter that are *unpaired* try to escape and join it, males uttering version (d) of the appeal call and females the 'kraah' call.   Paired captive Jays display self-assertively at the wild Jays that come near but show no desire to follow the gathering when it moves away.   Social gatherings can sometimes be made to take place by killing one member of an established pair (Raspail).   When studying Jays in an area where I tried to locate every nest, I found that gatherings, or even excited chasing and display between two birds, late in the nesting season (mid-May to early June), always indicated that one or more nests had recently lost all the eggs or young.

It seems likely that a main function of the social gatherings is to bring together unpaired birds.   They may also aid in local synchronization of breeding, and perhaps also in determining or re-adjusting the territories or living areas of the Jays taking part.

Upward flicks of the tail and, at higher intensity, the closed wings also, are flight-intention movements.   The movement of the tail seems to consist of a quick downward flick followed by an upward movement during which it is partially spread and then closed again.   In agonistic situations these movements, like all others, tend to be performed with great vigour and abruptness.

The flight-intention movements shown when mobbing a predator are rather different.   As the Jay screeches (but sometimes in silence), the head and body are swung downward and sideways with an upward swing of the hind parts and tail, then jerked upwards again with a downward flick of the tail.   The downward movement seems to be the intention movement of leaving the perch with a quick downward dive into cover (Goodwin, 1956).

Bill wiping, pecking at the perch, digging in the ground, and pecking, tugging or tearing any convenient object commonly accompany nervous tension, especially thwarted aggression.   Such actions intersperse boundary disputes between males, for example.   These movements are otherwise all used when feeding or when seeking food but tend, in hostile situations, to be performed with a vigour and ferocity which is not seen in actual feeding or food seeking unless the Jay is extremely hungry.   The element of redirected aggression is thus very obvious. I have only once seen a Jay hammer with the closed bill as do crows, *Corvus* spp., and the Magpie.

The typical 'play' or 'frolicking' of the Jay consists of dashing from bough to bough with a rather small area, ducking, dodging and sometimes uttering low intensity variants of the grating call. It is seen most often in young Jays among which it seems often infectious. The movements are those which are used in earnest when trying to escape from the attacks of a hawk.

REFERENCES

BERNDT, R. & DANCKER, P. 1960. Analyse von der Wanderungen von *Garrulus glandarius* in Europa von 1947 bis 1957. *Proc. 12th Orn. Congr. Helsinki:* 97–109.

BOSSEMA, L. 1968. Recovery of acorns in the European Jay (*Garrulus g. glandarius* L.). *Proc. Koninkl. Nederl. Akad. Wetenschappen. Zool. Ser. C.* 71, No. 1.

CHETTLEBURGH, M. R. 1952. Observations on the collection and burial of acorns by Jays in Hainault Forest. *Brit. Birds* **45**: 359–364.

—— 1955. Further notes on the recovery of acorns by Jays. *Brit. Birds* **48**: 183–184.

HEIM DE BALSAC, H. 1952. Rythme sexuel et fecondité chez les oiseaux du nord-ouest de l'Afrique. *Alauda* **20**: 213–242.

GEYR VON SCHWEPPENBURG, H. F. 1939. Frühlingsversammlungen des Eichelhähers. *Beitr. Fortpfl. biol. Vog.* **15**: 198–199.

—— 1956. Heimzug von Eichelhähern. *Vogelwarte* **18**: 210.

GOODWIN, D. 1949. Notes on voice and display of the Jay. *Brit. Birds* **42**: 278–287.

—— 1951. Some aspects of the behaviour of the Jay. *Ibis* **93**: 414–442 and 602–625.

—— 1952a. A comparative study of the voice and some aspects of behaviour in two Old World Jays. *Behaviour* **4**: 293–316.

—— 1952b. Jays and Magpies eating wasps. *Brit. Birds* **45**: 364.

—— 1955. Jays and Carrion Crows recovering hidden food. *Brit. Birds* **48**: 181–183.

—— 1956. Further observations on the behaviour of the Jay. *Ibis* **98**: 186–219.

HOLYOAK, D. 1967. Breeding biology of the Corvidae. *Bird Study* **14**: 153–168.

KEVE, A. & STERBETZ, I. 1968. Über die Nahrung des Eichelhähers. *Der Falke* **15**: 184–187 and 230–233.

KÜCHLER, W. 1932. Invasionen des Eichelhähers in den Jahren 1932 und 1933. *Vogelzug* **5**: 116–120.

MAYAUD, N. 1948. La mue et les plumages du Geai *Garrulus glandarius*. *Alauda* **16**: 168–179.

OWEN, D. F. 1956. The food of nestling Jays and Magpies. *Bird Study* **3**: 257–265.

RASPAIL, X. 1901. Cérémonie de secondes noces chez les Garruliens. *Bull. Soc. Zool. France* **26**: 104–109.

RICHARDS, T. J. 1958. Concealment and recovery of food by birds, with some relevant observations on squirrels. *Brit. Birds* **51**: 497–508.

ROTHSCHILD, M. 1966. Experiments with captive predators and the poisonous grasshopper *Poekilocercus bufonius* (Klug). *Proc. Roy. Entom. Soc. London* (C) 31, **6**: 32.

SCHUSTER, L. 1950. Über den Sammeltrieb des Eichelhähers (*Garrulus glandarius*). *Vogelwelt* **71**: 9–17.

SWANBERG, P. O. 1969. Jays recovering buried food from under the snow. *British Birds* **62**: 238–240.

TURCEK, F. J. & KELSO, L. 1968. Ecological aspects of food transportation and storage in the Corvidae. *Comm. Behav. Biol.*, Pt. A, **1**: 277–297.

VAURIE, C. 1954. Systematic Notes on Palearctic Birds. No. 5 Corvidae. *Amer. Mus. Novit.* No. 1668.

VOOUS, K. H. 1953. The geographical variation of the Jay (*Garrulus glandarius*) in Europe. *Beaufortia* 2, No. 30.

JAY (*brandtii* group)   *Garrulus glandarius*

Garrulus brandtii Eversmann, 1842, Addenda Pallas Zoogr., **3**: 8.

Description As nominate *glandarius* (q.v.) but tends to have proportionately smaller bill and denser and softer plumage. Head, nape and hind neck deep rufous red to pale rufous tawny; forehead a little paler than crown, sometimes nearly whitish; black streaks on forehead and crown usually narrower and less pronounced than those of *glandarius*, lores and around eyes speckled or suffused with black (black feather bases). Reddish or tawny colour of head usually more or less suffusing the underparts but fairly sharply demarcated from and contrasting with the fawnish grey or vinous grey of the lower mantle and back.   White of throat suffused with grey or tawny rufous, the looser texture of the feathers making their grey bases more readily visible than in other forms.   Coloration otherwise as in nominate form, *G. g. glandarius.*

This form has been subdivided into several races but I agree with Vaurie that these are best lumped together.   The *brandtii* group intergrades with the *bispecularis* group in northern China and south-western Manchuria, probably as a result of recent secondary contact and subsequent interbreeding of the two stocks, as there is a great amount of variation in this area.   It intergrades with the *glandarius* group from the western foothills of the Urals westward (Johansen; Vaurie).

Garrulus glandarius sewerzowii, from Russia north and east of the range of *G. g. glandarius* east to the Urals, represents a population, probably of hybrid origin, that intergrades between *brandtii* and *glandarius*. It may occur as far west as Norway and Sweden in winter.

G. g. kansuensis, of north-western China, is very like *brandtii* but shows some signs of intergradation with the *bispecularis* group, having less black around the eye and more reddish underparts.   *G. g. peking-ensis*, from north-eastern China, represents a variable population, probably of hybrid origin, between the *bispecularis* and *brandtii* groups.

Field characters   As *glandarius* group (q.v.).   Blue and white on wing, white rump, black tail, and black malar stripes, all distinguish it from Siberian Jay, *Perisoreus infaustus*.   When wandering or straggling within normal range of the *glandarius* group, the contrasting reddish head and grey back identify it.

Distribution and habitat   North-eastern Russia in the Pechora region, the Urals east through Siberia; forests of the Salair and Kuznetzk Mountains, the Altai and the Sayans, to Transbaicalia south to north-eastern Mongolia and the Urga, Amurland north to the Stanavoi Range, northern and central Manchuria, Korea, Ussuriland, Sakhalin, Hokkaido and the southern Kuriles.

Inhabits broadleaved, mixed and coniferous woodland.   Also (Johansen) in wooded steppe country, mainly when not breeding.   Like *glandarius* group, not averse to inhabited and cultivated regions, provided there is suitable tree cover.

Feeding and general habits   As *glandarius* group.   According to Johansen, over much of its range it feeds largely on the seeds of *Pinus cembra*.   Where available acorns are, however, a staple food, as with other forms of the species (Dementiev *et al.*; Vorobiev).

Prone to mass eruptions, presumed to be usually due to food shortage, that start in late summer and continue through autumn.   In some areas apparently regular southward migration in autumn.

Nesting   Apparently much as *glandarius* group and, like it, sometimes nests in hollows in trees.   Dementiev *et al.* mention a nest, the only one they describe, as being lined with feathers and lichen.   It would be interesting to know whether this form of the Jay normally uses feathers or similar substances as nest lining, presumably in adaptation to colder temperatures.   If so, this would be a most interesting be-havioural difference between it and other forms of the species.   Eggs often, perhaps most usually, laid in May.

Voice   Apparently as *glandarius* group.   Johansen says the alarm screech is perhaps a little harsher.

Display and social behaviour   No information.   Presumably as *glandarius* group.

Other names   Brandt's Jay, Red-headed Jay.

REFERENCES

DEMENTIEV, G. P. & GLADKOV, N. A.   1970.   *Birds of the Soviet Union* **5**: 81–82.   English translation, published by Keter Press, Jerusalem.
JOHANSEN, H.   1944.   Die Vogelfauna Westsibiriens.   *J. Orn.* **92**: 18–19.
VAURIE, C.   1959.   *The Birds of the Palearctic Fauna: Passeriformes* 132–145.   London.
VOROBIEV, K. A.   1954.   *Birds of the Ussuri Area.*   Moscow.   English translation by G. Reed.

JAY (*japonicus* group)   ***Garrulus glandarius***

Garrulus glandarius japonicus Temminck and Schegel, 1848, in Siebold's Fauna Japonica, *Aves* 83 pl. 43.

Description   As nominate *glandarius*, except as follows: slightly smaller in size.   Feathers on forehead and crown tend to be shorter and broader with their edges nearly pure white; the white-edged feathers extend to the nape and are relatively sharply demarcated from the vinous fawn of the neck and cheeks. Hence top of head appears snow white, spotted or streaked with black.   Blue of wing a little darker (dark bands on individual feathers wider, light blue and white bands narrower) and with a faint tinge of purple in some lights.   White on outer web of most primaries does not extend so far basally, so that the white wing patch is differently shaped.   Black of malar stripe extends over loral regions and suffuses face around eye.   Irides pearly white, at least in some individuals, but more information on soft part colours needed.
   The above description is of *Garrulus glandarius japonicus* from Hondo, Shikoku and northern Kyushu. *G. g. namiyei*, from Tsushima, is similar but has a rather larger bill and averages darker on the head, the black streaks being usually more extensive and continued further onto the hind neck.   *G. g. hiugaensis*, from eastern Hondo (the Izu Peninsula) and southern Kyushu in Kumatoto, Hiuga and Kagoshima, is slightly darker than *japonicus*, especially on the head, and has the nape suffused with pinkish fawn so that the white and black 'cap' is less sharply demarcated.   *G. g. orii*, from Yakushima Island, of which I have not seen a specimen, is said to differ from *japonicus* by being darker, having a smaller and blue-suffused white wing patch and the blue on the wing darker (no white bars on the blue feathers).

Field characters   As nominate *glandarius*.

Distribution and habitat   Japan: found in all the main islands and their major satellites, except the Izu chain and the Riu Kiu Islands.   Replaced in Hokkaido by a jay of the *brandtii* group.   Inhabits forest and wooded areas, from the subtropical lowlands to the lower parts of the montane coniferous woods (Jahn).   Those breeding at high elevations move down into the lowlands for the winter (Yamashina).

Feeding and general habits   As other forms of Jay.   Recorded feeding on acorns, seeds, berries, insects, small reptiles, frogs, eggs and young birds.

Nesting   Nest and eggs as those of *glandarius* group, but nest is usually sited in a conifer.   Several clutches of eggs in the British Museum (Natural History) were all taken in May.

Voice   Evidently very similar to and perhaps identical with that of *glandarius* group; likewise known to indulge in vocal mimicry.

Display and social behaviour   Presumably as in *glandarius* group.

Other names   Japanese Jay.

REFERENCES

JAHN, H.   1942.   Zur Oekologie und Biologie der Vögel Japans.   *J. Orn.* **90**: 78.
YAMASHINA, Y.   1961.   *Birds in Japan*.   Tokyo.

JAY (*bispecularis* group)   ***Garrulus glandarius***

Garrulus bispecularis Vigors, 1831, Proc. Zool. Soc. London: 7.

Description   Slightly smaller than *Garrulus g. glandarius* and slimmer in build.   Head and body, except for the consequently very conspicuous black malar stripes, a beautiful light pinkish cinnamon; with a hint of a mauve tinge in very new plumage but much less vinous and greyish than the body colour of *glandarius*, as well as much paler.   The throat and forehead are slightly paler than elsewhere but not noticeably so.   Wing pattern as in *japonicus* group but black on outer webs of primaries usually rather more extensive and white on secondaries replaced by blue like that on the wing coverts (see description of *glandarius* group) except that the bars on the feathers are more widely spaced.   Chestnut on the inner secondary less extensive.   Irides very dark bluish brown, dark brown or blackish.   In the only two living birds of this form I have seen, the dark 'liquid' appearance of the eye made it very difficult to judge its precise colour, at a little distance it looked quite black.   Eye rims partly bare and deep flesh pink but not very conspicuous.   Legs and feet flesh-coloured or fleshy brown.

The above description is of *G. glandarius bispecularis* of the western Himalayas from Kashmir to Nepal. *G. g. interstinctus*, from the eastern Himalayas, is similar but of a slightly darker pinkish cinnamon colour.   *G. g. persaturatus*, from the Khasia Hills in Assam, is darker and redder.   *G. g. sinensis*, from most of China and north-eastern Burma, tends to have a more purplish tinge to the general pale cinnamon body colour (although not as vinous as nominate *glandarius* usually is) and its nasal plumes and some of the feathers at front of forehead have blackish tips.   It averages a little larger and less slender in build than the more western forms of the *bispecularis* group; its irides are also paler, those of specimens from northern Burma and Yunnan being described as brownish pink, greyish, pinkish grey and greyish yellow. *G. g. taivanus*, from Formosa, is similar to *sinensis* but smaller, paler, more strongly tinged with vinous pink, with black nasal plumes and conspicuous black tips to the feathers of the front of the forehead.

G. g. haringtoni, from the southern Chin Hills, in Burma, is very like *G. g. interstinctus* (see above) but has a larger bill, whitish throat and paler cheeks.   It thus shows the beginning of intergradation in appearance towards the *leucotis* group.

Intermediates, possibly of hybrid origin, between the *bispecularis* and *brandtii* groups occur in northern China and adjacent areas.   The forms concerned usually approximate more closely to *brandtii* (q.v.).

Field characters   Black and blue patterned wings diagnostic.   In flight the combination of pale cinnamon to pinkish fawn back, white lower rump and black tail; and, face on, cinnamon to pinkish fawn head, with black malar stripes, almost equally so.   Reddish fawn head and all-black tail both distinguish it at once from Lanceolated Jay.

Distribution and habitat   Himalayas from eastern Punjab and Kashmir east to China and Formosa; north of the range of the *leucotis* group.   In the western parts of its range in hills from about 1200 to 3000 metres, occasionally higher in summer and lower in winter.   In China mainly in mountains and hilly country, more rarely in large river valleys, and not in the plains.   Inhabits woodland of all types but especially in or near oakwoods.   In Sikang in and around cultivated areas but not in pure jungle or high montane forest (Schäfer).

Feeding and general habits   So far as known does not differ from *glandarius* group (q.v.).   Ali states that pairs or parties often seek food in company with mixed flocks of laughing thrushes, *Garrulax* spp., and blue magpies.   Whistler mentions its being sometimes in company with blue magpies or Lanceolated Jays.

Nesting   Nest and nest site as *glandarius* group but the outer framework of the nest is said sometimes to be composed of green moss as well as twigs.   Lining of roots and fibres as in *glandarius* group.   Some nests have been described as being lined with grasses but possibly this refers to roots of grasses.

Eggs like those of other forms.   Clutch usually 3 to 5.   Nests with eggs found from late April to late June (most in May) in Indian Himalayan parts of its range, early May to mid-June in Assam and April and May in southern China.

Voice   The chirruping calls sound to me identical with those of *glandarius* group, but I have only heard them from two captive individuals.   The alarm screeches of these two captive birds struck me and Dr K. E. L. Simmons as being rather flatter in tone and nearer to typical alarm screeches of the Lanceolated Jay than to those of English *glandarius*.   From the few remarks on its other calls in the literature these would not appear to differ from those of *glandarius*.

Display and social behaviour   Probably as *glandarius* group, but I can find no description and have only seen, from one captive bird, low intensity self-assertive display, which was identical to that of English Jays.

Other names   Sikkim Jay, Red-crowned Jay, Chinese Jay, Cinnamon Jay, Himalayan Jay.

REFERENCES

ALI, S. 1962. *Birds of Sikkim*. Oxford.
BAKER, E. C. S. MSS notes on his egg collection. In the Sub-dept. of Ornithology, British Museum (Natural History).
LA TOUCHE, J. D. D. 1952. *A Handbook of the Birds of Eastern China* 1: 19–20. London.
SCHÄFER, E. 1938. Ornithologische Ergebnisse zweier Forschungsreisen nach Tibet. *J. Orn.* **86,** Sonderheft.
VAURIE, C. 1959. *The Birds of the Palearctic Fauna.* **1**: 136–146. London.
WHISTLER, H. 1949. *Popular Handbook of Indian Birds.* London.

JAY (*leucotis* group)   *Garrulus glandarius*

Garrulus leucotis Hume, 1874, Proc. Asiastic Soc. Bengal: 106.

Description   A little coarser in plumage texture and with contour feathers less long and lax than in nominate *glandarius*. Size similar or a little smaller, with relatively rather large bill. Blue patch on secondaries, and wing pattern in general, like *bispecularis* group (q.v.) but extent of chestnut on inner secondary more nearly as in *glandarius*. Facial pattern very similar to that of *G. g. cervicalis* of the *glandarius* group; forehead white streaked with black, crown and nape black. Throat and cheeks snow-white, bordered posteriorly with dark greyish chestnut, greyish vinous or greyish brown, darker behind cheeks than below throat. This dark area shades into pinkish brown, pinkish grey or mauvish brown on the mantle and lighter pinkish brown or pinkish tawny on the underparts. The lower back is usually paler and more tawny in hue than the mantle. In worn plumage the pinkish mauve tinge is entirely lost and the body colour becomes predominantly tawny grey or light tawny brown.

Irides dark brown. Bill blackish brown to black with paler tip. Legs and feet fleshy brown, claws horny brown to pale brown.

The above description is of *Garrulus glandarius leucotis*, which is found in much of Burma, Siam and the Indo-Chinese countries. *G. g. oatesi*, from the Chin Hills and the Chindwin Valley, resembles *leucotis* in proportions but in colour pattern shows some approach to the *bispecularis* group, having the head pinkish rufous or greyish rufous, streaked with black, and the white of the cheeks and throat suffused with fawnish cream.

Some, but not the majority, of specimens of *leucotis* from Shwebo and the Katha District of Burma show some approach to *oatesi*, having the crown and nape dark grey, tinged with rufous and with darker streaking, rather than black. The description of *oatesi* given above is based on only three specimens: the type, which is a juvenile from Taungdwin, Upper Chindwin; a male from the Tinzai-Kubo Valley, East Chindwin; and a female from Pondaung, Lower Chindwin. It agrees, however, with descriptions of other specimens.

G. g. haringtoni, from the southern Chin Hills, is intermediate in appearance between *G. g. oatesi* and the *bispecularis* group but is closer to the latter and so has been described with it.

Field characters   Blue-patterned black wings and white face with black malar stripes, diagnostic.

Distribution and habitat Burma, Thailand (Siam), central Laos, southern Annam and Cochin China; tends to be local and patchy in distribution though usually common where it does occur. Inhabits, at least in Burma, mainly dry deciduous and conifer forest in the hills and dry dipterocarp forest in the plains. Usually in or near woods of oak or chestnut.

Feeding and general habits Probably much as other forms but detailed studies lacking. Oates found the stomachs of several he dissected full of green grasshoppers. Deignan 'more than once' observed numbers of this Jay gathering at jungle grass fires to catch insects fleeing from the flames.

Nesting As *glandarius* group, but nest said to be often lined with grasses. If so, this may be some grass having a wiry or fibre-like consistency. Harington, who found several nests, noted that they were lined with grass *roots*. Possibly this was the case with the nests other observers have described as being lined with grass? An excellent photograph of a nest of this form, which I have seen, showed this particular nest to be exactly like that of an English Jay. Eggs like those of *glandarius* group but examples without any black hair streaks perhaps more frequent. Clutch 3 to 5, full clutches of 3 or 4 eggs appear more numerous than 5-egg clutches. Nests with eggs found in April and May in Burma (one nest on April 7th but most in late April and early May) and flying young seen in late May in Thailand. Often said to nest colonially. This statement seems based on Harington's finding of seven nests within a hundred square yards but Wickham, who also saw this 'colony', described it as unique and emphasized that he had otherwise always found only single pairs breeding at a distance from each other.

Voice No detailed information. Alarm screech would appear to be similar or identical to that of *glandarius* group. Probably the same is true for other calls.

Display and social behaviour No information; probably as *glandarius* group.

Other names Burmese Jay, White-faced Jay.

REFERENCES

BAKER, E. C. S. 1922. *The Fauna of British India: Birds* **1**: 61–63.
—— MSS notebooks on his egg collection, in the Sub-dept. of Ornithology, British Museum (Natural History).
COOK, J. P. 1913. A list of Kalaw birds with bird-nesting notes. *Journ. Bombay Nat. Hist. Soc.* **22**: 261.
DEIGNAN, H. G. 1945. The birds of Northern Thailand. *Bull. U.S. Nat. Mus.* No. **186**: 301–302.
HARINGTON, H. H. 1911. Some Maymo birds. *Journ. Bombay Nat. Hist. Soc.* **20**: 1003–1004.
OATES, E. W. 1883. *A Handbook to the Birds of British Burma* **1**: 407–408. London.
SMYTHIES, B. E. 1953. *The Birds of Burma.* London.
WICKHAM, P. F. 1929. Notes on the birds of the Upper Burma Hills. *Journ. Bombay Nat. Hist. Soc.* **33**: 804.

LANCEOLATED JAY   *Garrulus lanceolatus*

Garrulus lanceolatus Vigors, 1831, Proc. Zool. Soc. London: 7.

Description Between Jay and Blue Jay in size. Proportions nearest to Jay but more slender, with proportionately shorter and thicker bill. Tail longer and slightly graduated; crest longer. Face and top of head black; the long crown feathers usually show obscure silvery blue barring when examined closely but this is not visible at a little distance. Throat feathers lanceolate, black or greyish black, with conspicuous white shaft streaks; in life the throat looks mainly white except when the bird erects its throat feathers in display.   Beyond this streaked plumage, at the upper breast, is an area where the feathers are bluish grey (finely barred greyish blue and blackish on close inspection) with less conspicuous white shaft streaks or no white at all.   Upperparts pinkish grey with a delicate mauve tinge.   Underparts pinkish fawn, tinged with grey, often with little or no grey tinge on belly and under tail coverts.   Inner and median wing coverts black.   Visible parts of alula mainly barred deep silvery blue and black.   Tips of alula feathers and of most primary coverts white, forming a conspicuous white patch on wing.   Inner three secondaries very broad and, where visible on folded wing, light mauvish grey with broad black subterminal and rather narrower white terminal bands.   Outer secondaries black with white tips and with most of the outer webs barred black and silvery blue or black and dark cambridge blue.   Primaries greyish black, with outer webs, above the emargination, that is for about three-quarters of the visible length of inner primaries and progressively less outwards, barred silvery blue to dark cambridge blue and black, and fringed with whitish on the emarginated areas.   There is an ill-defined dull white patch or spot about the middle of the inner web of most primaries.   The small outermost primary has no blue and the next one to it very little.

Tail silvery blue barred with black, with broad black subterminal band, and tipped with white.   Except on the central feathers the blue and black barring is less pronounced on the inner webs, and the outermost tail feather on each side is mainly greyish blue with only a trace of barring but with the usual black subterminal band and white tip.   When this bird is in good health and unworn plumage it has a beautiful soft bloom, suggestive of that on a ripe peach or plum.   Museum skins or live birds in poor condition do not give an adequate idea of its great beauty.

Irides dark brown or dark reddish brown.   Bill a glaucous horny greyish green, slate grey or greenish grey, often rather darker near the base and usually darker at the tip.   Legs and feet dull bluish grey to fleshy grey.

The juvenile has a dull black head, with much shorter crest and throat feathers.   Its body feathers have obscure reddish fawn fringes, most prominent on rump and ventral areas.   Blue on wings and tail usually duller and greyer than in adult.   A variably-sized white spot or band is interposed between the blue-barred area on the outer webs of the secondaries and primaries and their black tips.   The white tips of the tail feathers are less sharply defined, often clouded with black or greyish.   There is much individual variation in the wing and tail markings of juveniles, probably connected with their food supply and consequent state of metabolism during the growing period.   As is usual in the family, the wing and tail quills are not shed at the first moult but are retained until the second moult when the bird is from 13 to 16 months old.

Field characters   White-tipped tail and black head distinguish from sympatric form of the Jay; blue-barred wings and tail from other species.

Distribution and habitat   Eastern Afghanistan in Safed Koh and region south of Hindu Kush, North-west Frontier Province and Himalayas east to Nepal.   Inhabits wooded country, in fairly open areas about forest edge or openings rather than in dense forest.   Often in scrub-covered hillsides with some trees, in cultivated regions and around human habitations, provided there is tree or scrub cover.   Usually between 1500 and 2400 m, sometimes higher or lower.

Feeding and general habits   Seeks food both on the ground and in trees.   Known to take acorns, caterpillars, beetles and other insects, fruits, eggs and young of small birds, and scraps of human food where available.   A comparison of its feeding habits with those of the sympatric race of the Jay would be of interest, as the two may be in competition.   Often forages in loose association with Jays and Yellow-billed Blue Magpies.

Hides food in same manner as Jay and, at least in captivity, recovers much of what it has hidden.   In a wild state it has been observed storing acorns of *Quercus incanus* and seeds of *Pinus groffithi* (Keve & Kretzoi, in Turcek & Kelso).   When feeding on acorns of the Bang oak is said to open them with 'hammer blows' (Ali), but captive birds (8 in all) invariably opened acorns from English oaks in the same way as Jay, holding them with both feet, biting, levering and tugging to pierce and then remove the shell but never hammering them.

Flight appears more fluttering (due to faster wing beats) than that of Jay and more suggestive, when in the open, of the flight of Blue Jay. I have, however, only seen it flying at full liberty a few times and then not in its native haunts. Among cover or in a confined space, it twists, turns, darts and bounces about with the same wonderful agility as the Jay.

Anting of captive birds, with Wood Ants, *Formica rufa*, was of the usual active type and unlike that of Jay. Captive birds roosted well hidden in a small Cypress, *Cupressus* sp., or in conifer branches. They went to roost early, while it was still perfectly light, and, once on their roosting perches, did not come off again that evening unless greatly disturbed. This behaviour presumably lessens the chance of the roosting place being discovered by crepuscular predators.

Nesting Nests in trees, bushes or shrubs. The upper fork of a young sapling is a favourite site or, perhaps, the type of site where the nest is most easily found by man.

Nest like that of Jay; of small sticks and twigs, lined with roots, fibres and the black horsehair-like rhizoids of fungi. Grass said sometimes to be used for lining, presumably either grass roots or some grass of root-like texture.

3 to 5 eggs, like those of Jay and although a little smaller yet rather larger in proportion to the size of the bird. Breeds from mid-April to mid-June. Probably single brooded if young are successfully reared. Captive birds in England usually laid in early or mid-May; once a pair that had reared young from a rather early nest, the female having laid her first egg on April 13th, nested again. The female laid her second clutch early in June but either ate or hid it after incubating for a week. Eggs laid (by captive birds in England) in early morning between 6 and 8 am. Females went on nest, as if to lay, for one or two mornings before the day of laying and spent much time sitting on the empty nest.

Incubation period (in England) 16 days. Female sits on nest, but probably does not incubate, from laying of first egg or before. Incubation by female only, fed by the male both at the nest and when she leaves it for short periods. Both sexes build; the males of two captive pairs appeared to do rather more work on the nest at all stages than their mates.

Like Jays, captive Lanceolated Jays with eggs or young showed intense aggressiveness towards Jackdaws approaching or perching on the aviary, although almost ignoring them at other times. Both sexes feed the young. Insects are prepared carefully for small young, or for the female if she is brooding small young, by removing hard parts and/or tearing them into small pieces.

Voice All the apparently innate calls that I heard from captive birds were very similar to calls of the Jay.

The appeal call, like that of the Jay, seems used to express almost any need. I could distinguish only three constant variants: (1) the typical mewing appeal call, so like that of *glandarius* as to be difficult to distinguish from it but rather higher in pitch, with a more marked rising inflection and, at same level of intensity, rather less loud. Uttered when the bird is hungry, also used as a contact call; (2) the food offering call; a loud, long-drawn version of the usual appeal call. Given by the male when he has prepared food and wishes to feed his mate or a female he is courting. I very seldom heard a female give this call when accepting food (as the female of *glandarius* does more often than not) and on the few occasions when I did it is possible that she had uttered the call for some other reason at that moment; (3) the juvenile-type begging call similar to the fledgling's food begging call. Used by the female, together with typical juvenile-type wing fluttering, when begging food from the male or receiving food from him, shortly before and during the laying period, when incubating and when brooding young. I have not heard it used by males but it may be under some circumstances. This form of the appeal call resembles the begging call of *G. glandarius* but is perhaps rather higher pitched and shorter.

The chirruping notes are a series of soft stammering sounds, usually interspersed with what appear to be low and muted variants of the appeal call. They are higher pitched and more 'cheeping' in sound than the homologous notes of *glandarius* and could be written 'chip-chip-chip, chip-chip-chip, eea – chip' etc. These calls appear to be appeasing in character. They are given with the appeasing chin-up display and, sometimes, without any accompanying display by a subordinate bird when approached by a dominant individual.

The loud alarm screech is very similar to that of *glandarius* but sounds flatter and lacks, even at high intensity, something of the crispness and incisiveness of that of *glandarius*. A more notable difference is that even when screeching in strong alarm the Lanceolated Jay pauses perceptibly between each screech, instead of giving two screeches in quick succession and then a pause, as *glandarius* usually does. This is the typical predator-mobbing call but is used in many situations of excitement, most of which appear to involve conflict and some thwarting or inhibition of the impulse to escape.

The 'tschrerr' is a peculiar mechanical-sounding call somewhat suggestive of the alarm call of the Mistle Thrush, *Turdus viscivorus*, but always given singly, not in series. It is not loud but impresses because of its suddenness and emphasis, suggesting the release of a spring in some mechanical contrivance. I do not know the function of this call or the stimuli eliciting it. It seems often to be given at moments of possible relief from tension or excitement, for example shortly after there has been a hawk in sight or after a bout of 'playing'. I once heard a Lanceolated Jay give this call as it looked at an aeroplane high in the sky. On the few occasions when I actually saw which bird gave this call, it was always a female.

The 'kraah' call is very similar to that of *G. glandarius* but flatter and less resonant in tone. In captive birds I found the 'kraah' call, and variants thereof, given rather more freely than by *G. glandarius* and (unlike that species) given more by males than by females. Female Lanceolated Jays gave the 'kraah' call less often and less loudly than males. The presence of the mate did not inhibit utterance of this call, as it normally does in the Jay, although the removal of a female from her aviary resulted in her mate (after he had very thoroughly searched through the aviary) giving 'kraah' calls loudly and repeatedly until she was returned to him. This call is given in a characteristic posture and with much apparent effort, as by the Jay, with the bird's body rather upright but with head bent forward and downward. Even when the 'kraah' call is given in flight a similar posture is used.

It is likely that the Lanceolated Jay also possesses a hawk alarm call comparable with that of *G. glandarius*.

Song was uttered by two captive males in early spring. It consisted of a variety of soft, mewing, bubbling and whistling sounds, among which were recognizable both low intensity versions of innate calls and vocal mimicry.

Wild-caught captive birds habitually indulge in vocal mimicry and there can be little doubt they do so in freedom. Two wild-caught males, that were fully adult when they came into my possession, had extensive repertoires of bird calls unknown to me. They later learnt and used other sounds, such as the calls of the Golden Pheasant, human whistling and the barking and whining of my neighbour's dog, that they could not have heard in the wild. Copied sounds are usually rendered with great fidelity but in a softer and 'purer' tone than the originals in some cases. Sometimes this species, like *G. glandarius*, will produce what appears to be a 'symbolic interpretation' of a sound or series of sounds.

When giving the self-assertive display captive males usually uttered either a husky mewing call, perhaps homologous to the loud hissing sounds that the male Jay often gives in this display, or a sibilant piping 'tsee-tsee-tsee-up'. Less often, vocal mimicry would accompany this display.

Display and social behaviour All the displays I have seen from this species are clearly homologous with and very similar to those of the Jay although, owing to the different colour pattern, the appearance of the displaying bird is very different.

In defensive threat the Lanceolated Jay erects all its head and body plumage more or less uniformly. The wings are held uncovered by the body feathers and may be slightly spread, as may the tail. At high intensity the wings may be fully spread, usually only for a moment. I have seen this display from nesting birds towards Jackdaws alighting on or near their aviary, and once from a male bird shown a stuffed Jackdaw.

In the lateral self-assertive display, that is used both in courtship and in apparent symbolic threat or competition between males, the plumage is differentially erected, as in the Jay, except that the Lanceolated Jay does not spread or otherwise make especially prominent its secondaries, which, in view of their beautiful markings, is rather surprising. Otherwise the behaviour of the self-assertively displaying bird is similar in both species. It presents itself laterally to or hops round or to and from the object of its display and calls as it reaches forward.   In the Lanceolated Jay, I have seen this display used by females on only a few occasions and never at full intensity.   In each instance, when I saw it used by a female, her mate and a rival male were displaying intensely at one another.   This display, in which the throat feathers are erected and their diffuse blackish edges thus fully exposed, is the only situation in which the living bird even partly justifies its other name of Black-throated Jay.

Some displays of the Lanceolated Jay: (1) Self-assertive. (2 & 3) Versions of chin-up display; (4) Giving kraah call

   In the chin-up display the bird often adopts a crouching posture and always has the belly plumage more or less erected.   It holds its head at about right angles to the substrate and moves it with little jerking movements from side to side.   The head feathers are sleeked down and the bird usually presents its throat, whose plumage is tightly appressed and thus presents an almost completely white surface, towards the bird it is displaying to.   It utters the chirruping calls (q.v.) while giving this display.   The chin-up display seems to be appeasing or conciliatory in character.   It is a common response from the female when her mate, or a male in whom she is interested, gives the self-assertive display to her; when her mate offers to feed her; when accepting food from him and, especially in the early part of the breeding cycle, in an apparent attempt to get food from him.   The male uses it, but rather rarely, when approaching the female with intent to feed her and (even more rarely) when hopping round her after having fed her.
   The quivering display is like that of the Jay.   The bird usually adopts a rather horizontal posture with rump and tail somewhat raised, extends the wings from the body in a strained-looking manner, arching and spreading them, and quivers both wings and tail.   I have seen this display given by captive male Lanceolated Jays towards superiors who were robbing their food caches and, with tail only quivered, by a female joining her building mate at the nest site.   It is almost certainly the female's invitation to

coition but, if the male is eager, coition may take place without the quivering display, or without sufficient intensity for it to be perceptible to a human observer a few yards away.

On the seven occasions when I saw coition in captives of this species it took place at dawn, immediately after the male and female had left their roosting places. The male hopped up to and/or around the female, in self-assertive display, sometimes giving her a little food or making intention movements of doing so, then mounted her and apparently achieved coition without her having given further prior indication of willingness than not attempting to move away or resist.

Begging for food, with typical juvenile-type begging calls and flapping or fluttering wings, was shown by two captive females before and during the laying period and during incubation; also by a third who was in ill health but who showed no indication of breeding activity although she was paired. I have not seen begging by a male of this species.

Bill snapping may be used in threat, especially to conspecifics. The posturings when mobbing a predator are identical with those of the Jay.

Other names Black-headed Jay, Black-throated Jay, Himalayan Jay, Indian Jay.

REFERENCES

ALI, S. *Indian Hill Birds*. Oxford.

BAKER, E. C. S. Notebook on his egg collection. In the Bird Room, British Museum (Natural History).

BATES, R. S. P. & LOWTHER, E. H. N. 1952. *Breeding Birds of Kashmir*. Oxford.

GOODWIN, D. 1952. A comparative study of the voice and some aspects of behaviour in two old-world jays. *Behaviour* **4**: 293–316.

—— 1953. Observations on captive Lanceolated Jays. *Avicult. Mag.* **59**: 122–133.

—— 1954. Lanceolated Jays breeding in captivity. *Avicult. Mag.* **60**: 154–162.

TURCEK, F. J. & KELSO, L. 1968. Ecological aspects of food transportation and storage in the Corvidae. *Comm. Behav. Biol.* Pt. A, **1**: 277–297.

WHISTLER, H. 1941. *The Popular Handbook of Indian Birds*. London.

LIDTH'S JAY   *Garrulus lidthi*

Garrulus lidthi Bonaparte, 1851, Consp. Av., 1 (1850) p. 376.

Description Slightly larger than Jay, with proportionately more massive bill and longer and more rounded tail. Except for heavier build and lack of crest its shape is very like that of Lanceolated Jay, its closest relative. Feathers of forehead and loral regions somewhat stiffened and velvety black. Throat black, shading to dark blue on lower throat, with narrow white shaft streaks. Rest of head, neck, upper mantle and upper breast dark rich purplish blue. The blue on the upper breast shades through dark reddish purple to a slightly lighter reddish purple or purplish rufous on belly, flanks, and under tail coverts. Upperparts (except where otherwise stated) deep purplish chestnut; the tips of the feathers are most strongly purplish so that in worn plumage the back is more rufous. Lesser wing coverts dark purplish blue somewhat tinged with rufous. Most parts of the wing feathers, that are visible when the wing is folded, are dark rich purplish blue, barred with black on the alula, greater coverts and, to some degree, on the secondaries also. Ill-defined black subterminal bands and conspicuous white tips to secondaries, rather narrower white tips to primaries. Some white on tips of alula feathers, usually confined to outer webs. Outer webs of primaries, below the emargination, and inner webs of primaries and most secondaries and underwing dull black. Tail feathers dark purplish blue with blackish subterminal areas and white tips, broadest on the outer tail feathers, which are largely black on their inner webs.

Irides dark violet-blue. Bill light glaucous green to ivory white, usually shaded darker near base. Legs and feet grey. I have not seen a specimen in juvenile plumage. This has been described (from a captive-bred individual) as being brownish black or greyish brown on head and neck where the adult is blue, dull brown where the adult is purplish chestnut, and lacking the white tips on the wing quills.

Field characters Combination of *dark* blue and *dark* purplish chestnut distinguish it not only from all sympatric species but from all other corvids. The only other corvine bird at all similar in colour is the Ceylon Magpie, which is lighter blue and lighter chestnut and has a red or orange bill.

Distribution and habitat Found only on Amami Oshima and Tokinoshima, in the northern Riu Kiu (Loo Choo) Islands. Inhabits subtropical woodland, also, especially outside the breeding season, pine woods, cultivated regions and around villages.

Feeding and general habits Feeds largely on acorns of *Quercus cuspidata*; also known to take insects, small reptiles and small sweet potatoes. General behaviour very like that of Jay and, except for the longer tail, said to have a similar outline in flight (Jahn). Now shows little fear of man, perhaps as a result of legal protection. Formerly it was hunted intensively for its plumage and at, or shortly after, that time was apparently much more timid (Taka-Tsukasa). Commonly in pairs or small parties. In autumn sometimes in flocks of a hundred or more (Jahn); perhaps this represents dispersal of young birds or gathering at a good food source.

In captivity hides food in the same manner as the Jay and it is known to store acorns when wild (Udagawa, in Turcek & Kelso). Ants in typical active manner, like Lanceolated Jay and unlike Jay.

Nesting In large holes and cavities in trees, usually from 1 to 4·5 metres above ground. Nest like that of Jay (q.v.). Eggs 3 or 4, pale greenish blue, usually unmarked but sometimes with pale brownish speckles. Breeding season February to May (Yamashina); young have been found in nests in March. Single brooded.

Voice Calls, or at least some of them, evidently very like Jay's but I can find no detailed descriptions. Indulges in vocal mimicry in captivity and probably when wild also.

Display and social behaviour No information.

Other names Purple Jay, Loo Choo Jay.

REFERENCES

JAHN, H. 1942. Zur Oekologie und Biologie der Vögel Japans. *J. Orn.* **90**: 80–82.
KURODA, N. 1925. *A Contribution to the Knowledge of the Avifauna of the Riu Kiu Islands and the vicinity.* Tokyo.
OLIVER, T. C. 1964. Breeding of the Loo Choo or Lidth's Jay. *Avicult. Mag.* **70**: 212.
TAKA-TSUKASA, PRINCE. 1937. Le Geai de Lidth *Lalocitta lidthi. Oiseau* **7**: 1–2.
TURCEK, F. J. & KELSO, L. 1968. Ecological aspects of food transportation and storage in the Corvidae. *Comm. Behav. Biol.*, Pt. A: 277–297.
YAMASHINA, Y. 1961. *Birds in Japan.* Tokyo.

The grey jays

The grey or boreal jays of the genus *Perisoreus* (formerly *Cractes*) inhabit the northern coniferous forest regions of both old and new worlds, extending further south in montane conifer forests in America and with a population in the montane conifer forests of western China and eastern Tibet. They are characterized by their small bills, soft dense plumage and predominantly greyish coloration with no trace of bright blue or green.

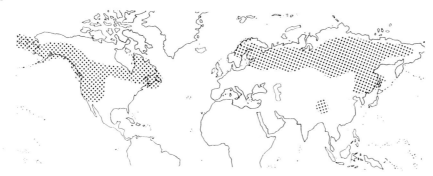

They are omnivorous, feeding largely on seeds and insects but very readily taking scraps of human food when available. They are habitual food storers and it is probable that they rely much on food they have previously hidden. They usually show little fear of man, often none at all. It is this trait, one common to many other birds of the far north, that is largely responsible for the 'un-jay-like' impression that they have made on many people. They are probably more closely related to the typical jays, *Garrulus*, and possibly also to the American jays than they are to any other forms.

The Grey Jay or Canada Jay, *Perisoreus canadensis*, inhabits the northern and some more southernly montane coniferous forests of North America. The Oregon Jay, *P. obscurus*, was formerly considered a good species, characterized by smaller size, entirely white underparts and white shafts to the mantle feathers. Intermediate populations exist, however (Aldrich), and it seems rightly now considered as a form of *P. canadensis*.

The Grey Jay is replaced in the old World by the Siberian Jay, *P. infaustus*. Although it has a similar, if more simplified, plumage pattern to that of the Grey Jay it differs strikingly from that species in having extensive orange-rufous areas on wings and tail, and some suffusion of rufous elsewhere. It is an odd fact that the only widespread Old World form of *Perisoreus* has partly reddish plumage, like *Garrulus*, whereas neither the American blue jays nor the American forms of *Perisoreus* have any trace of rufous in their plumage. If, which I think unlikely, the Grey Jay has evolved from the American jays after the latter, or rather their ancestor(s) became separated from the Old World jays, then its resemblance to Old World *Perisoreus* species would be an extreme example of convergence.

These two species of *Perisoreus* are allopatric and are clearly geographical representatives, although they have perhaps diverged too greatly to be treated as members of a single superspecies.

The Sooty Jay or Szechwan Jay, *Perisoreus internigrans*, is often spoken of as if it represented a relict population of *P. infaustus* stock. In coloration it bears great resemblance to the juveniles of the darker forms of *P. canadensis* but lacks any trace of the latter's white tips to wing and tail quills. I do not concur with Voous in thinking that it directly connects *canadensis* with *infaustus*. Its colour pattern could well represent a simplified and melanistic derivation from that of *P. infaustus* but it could equally well be derived from some colour pattern similar to that of *Garrulus lanceolatus*. This is particularly apparent if juvenile specimens of *G. lanceolatus*, with their duller and shorter head feathers, are used for comparison. The bill of *P. internigrans*, or at least the bill of the only specimen of it that I have been able to examine, is almost exactly intermediate in shape and proportions between the bill of *P. infaustus* and that of *G. lanceolatus*. In the dried skin the bill colour is almost identical with that of *G. lanceolatus* and in all probablility they are alike in life also. If the wings of *P. internigrans* are looked at from an oblique angle they show 'water-mark' barring on the secondaries of similar pattern to the blue and black barring on the secondaries of *G. lanceolatus*.

Thus, so far as one can judge from its external taxonomic characters, *internigrans* is a connecting link between *Perisoreus* and *Garrulus*. It is, however, rather closer to the former and seems best included in that genus. A detailed comparison of its biology and behaviour with those of *Perisoreus infaustus* and *Garrulus lanceolatus* would be of great interest but seems unlikely to materialize soon in view of political and geographical factors.

REFERENCES

ALDRICH, J. W. 1943. Relationships of the Canada Jays in the northwest. *Wilson Bull.* **55**: 217–222.
VOOUS, K. H. 1960. *Atlas of European Birds*. London.

GREY JAY   *Perisoreus canadensis*

Corvus canadensis Linnaeus, 1766, Syst. Nat., ed. 12, 1, p. 158.

Description About size of Blue Jay but with proportionately longer tail and wings and much smaller bill.

Around eye, hind crown and nape dull black or blackish brown, bordered in front by an ill-defined greyish area on crown. Forehead, face, throat, sides of neck and upper breast white. The white at sides of neck extends across behind the black nape but is here tinged with grey and sometimes interrupted by a greyish median area. Lower breast and rest of underparts light dull grey or brownish grey, paler on centre of belly and under tail coverts than on sides. Rest of plumage slate grey with a faint bluish tinge on wings and tail. Tail feathers, primaries and secondaries tipped with dull white as, more narrowly, are the greater wing coverts. Outer primaries narrowly edged dull white on outer webs. Inner webs of wing quills and underwing darker grey.

Irides dark brown. Bill, legs and feet black. Juvenile has the underparts, and those parts of the head and breast that are white in the adult, sooty grey except for an ill-defined whitish grey stripe on the malar region and some traces of whitish grey on the ear coverts and 'collar'. There are light areas on the juvenile's bill (see col. pl. 3).

The above description is of nominate *Perisoreus c. canadensis*, from much of Canada and the northern United States. *P. c. nigricapillus*, from northern Quebec and Labrador south to south-eastern Quebec, Anticosti Island, Newfoundland and Nova Scotia, is darker, with the black on the head extending further forward on the crown. Its white parts are often suffused with grey, except on the forehead, but appear in as great contrast owing to the darker grey of its lower breast and upperparts. The juvenile of this form is very dark, appearing almost uniform sooty black on head and foreparts.

P. c. pacificus (formerly *P. c. fumifrons*), from north-central Alaska, northern Yukon and north-western Mackenzie, is like nominate *canadensis* but has the white parts suffused with grey and, especially on the forehead, with buffish. *P. c. arcus*, from the Rainbow Mountains area in the central coast range of British Columbia, is very similar to *pacificus* but darker and with no trace of buff on its greyish white forehead. *P. c. capitalis*, from the Rocky Mountains from south-central and south-eastern Idaho and south-western Montana south through western and southern Wyoming, eastern Utah and western and central Colorado to central eastern Arizona and north-central Mexico, is very pale grey above and has the dark parts of the head dark grey, restricted to the nape and not, or only obscurely, extending to the eye. Its juvenile is also much paler than those of other forms. *P. c. albescens*, from north-eastern British Colombia and north-western Alberta south-eastward, east of the Rocky Mountains, to western South Dakota and north-western Nebraska, is very like *capitalis* but even paler and with the dark areas on the head less restricted.

P. c. obscurus, from the coastal belt of north-western United States from Washington south through western Oregon to Mendocino County, north-western California, is appreciably smaller than nominate *canadensis*, has the dark parts of the head extending further forward and more suffused with brown, the white of the throat continued, with only a slight increase of creamy tinge, over the lower breast and belly, and the grey upperparts more tinged with brown and with conspicuous white shafts to the mantle feathers. It has a very clearly demarcated white collar dividing the brownish black of the nape from the brownish grey of the mantle. This form and its allies were formerly reckoned a distinct species (see Aldrich).

P. c. griseus, from south-western British Columbia and Vancouver Island, south through central Washington and central Oregon to north-central and north-eastern California, is slightly larger and greyer than *obscurus*, with less prominent white shafts to the mantle feathers, thus showing an approach to the *canadensis* type of colour pattern. Populations from the mountains of central northern Washington, central British Columbia and central western Alberta show this intergradation to a rather greater degree. They were formerly separated as *P. canadensis connexus* but are now usually considered not racially separable from *griseus*.

The juveniles of *obscurus* and its allies are much like those of *canadensis* but predominantly sooty brown in hue.

Field characters Mainly slate-grey (adult) or sooty grey (juvenile) bird with longish white-tipped tail and conspicuous white forehead and throat (adult). Lack of any blue in plumage distinguishes it from all other sympatric jays; blackish nape and crown from Great Grey and Loggerhead Shrikes.

Distribution and habitat North America from north-central Alaska, northern Yukon, western Mackenzie, south-western Keewatin, northern Manitoba, northern Ontario, northern Quebec, northern Labrador and Newfoundland south to northern California, central Arizona, south-western Colorado, northern New Mexico, South Dakota, northern Minnesota, northern Wisconsin, northern Michigan, south-central Ontario, north-eastern New York, northern New England, New Brunswick and Nova Scotia. Has occurred occasionally south of its normal range.

Inhabits coniferous forest, sometimes in nearby mixed or deciduous woodland. Will come into open spaces adjacent to woods. Usually sedentary but some move to lower elevations for the winter. Large scale movements have been recorded (Bent).

Feeding and general habits Feeds both in trees and on ground. Has been recorded eating caterpillars, beetles, grasshoppers and other insects, conifer seeds, berries, young birds, small mammals, moths' eggs, carrion, lichen (in times of food shortage) and 'fungi' or 'mushrooms'. Also habitually takes meat and fat from carcasses of large mammals, when available, and many human foods, including bread, biscuits, oatmeal, baked beans, bacon, cheese and dried fish. Two observers who tested wild Grey Jays with a variety of foods found that cheese and baked beans were the favourites. Fish is sometimes refused, at others taken; no doubt much depends on the bird's condition and what, if any, natural foods are available. Sometimes catches flying insects on the wing.

Habitually stores food for future use. Usually each billful or gulletful of food is hidden separately but both wild and captive Grey Jays sometimes hide a considerable amount of food in one place. Food thus stored may be removed to a fresh hiding place if the bird is aware that a human has discovered it (Brewster, in Bent). Food to be hidden is usually first formed into a bolus, coated and permeated with saliva by means of the tongue and the specially developed mandibular salivary glands. This coating of saliva causes the food bolus to stick firmly in position when hidden among conifer foliage or twigs (Dow).

Food may be stored among conifer needles, in a fork among branches, in any crevice or hole, or in the ground. When hiding food in the ground the behaviour is like that of *Garrulus*, even to the final placing of a leaf, fircone or some other object on the cache. The Grey Jay, however, appears to prefer to hide food above ground. In winter (which lasts long in its habitat) it must necessarily do so; and the production of the adhesive saliva is clearly an important adaptation to food storing in trees. Such enlarged salivary glands are not, so far as is known, possessed by any other jay, but it would seem highly likely that the Siberian Jay also has them.

Food is often held under one foot and pulled to pieces but the Grey Jay does not hammer at hard objects and (*fide* Dow) is unable to break open sunflower seeds. It has been seen to carry large food objects in its feet (Simpson, in Bent; Allen). Dow found that his captive birds were able to pick up and swallow mealworms while retaining a bolus of other food in the throat, an ability that appears to be absent, or at least not recorded, in other corvids.

Very active and agile when feeding or seeking food. Flight silent and usually consisting largely of gliding on spread wings, except when flying upwards. Usually shows little or no fear of man, is attracted by gunshots and other noises and also by the smoke of camp fires. Comes freely about and even inside tents and buildings in search of food. Will carry off and presumably eat soap; also many inedible objects, but it is likely that these are taken because the bird assumes they may prove edible rather than from curiosity or desire to possess them for other reasons. Will often settle on humans, especially if encouraged by offers of food. It seems possible that scraps from the kills of large mammals, including 'primitive' man, have long been an important source of food for this species and that its behaviour towards modern man is but the persistence of an innate or, less probably, traditional tendency to approach any large noisy creature in its domain.

Many of the people who come in contact with the Grey Jay regard it with tolerance or even affection, in spite of its 'thievish' habits. This is, however, not always the case. Turner (in Bendire) noted that, in Ungava and Labrador, the American Indians 'wage war on every Whisky Jack that comes in sight', although, like the Alaskan Indians, they thought that bad luck would result if they interfered with its nest or eggs or even looked at them. It is of interest that a similar superstition exists among the Lapps in reference to the Siberian Jay. Taverner suggests that the fact that the Grey Jay disappears 'as soon as a camp becomes a permanent settlement' might be because sedentary civilized men are intolerant of wildlife and soon kill off this tame but troublesome bird.

Nesting Breeds early. Nest-building may begin in February and in most parts of its range it lays in March or April, when the woods are still snow-covered and the temperature often considerably below freezing point. It would be of interest to know what the newly-hatched young are fed on. Warren, whose early observations on the nesting of this species still seem the most detailed, could only ascertain that the food appeared to be in 'a soft partially digested state'.

The nest is placed in a conifer. Sometimes well hidden in the crown of the tree or at the end of a branch but sometimes in a relatively exposed position. Usually from 1·5 to 3·5 metres above ground, sometimes up to 9 metres. Nest like that of Siberian Jay; of twigs, strips of bark and sometimes stems or grass, intertwined and padded with moss, lichen and other soft materials, and the inner cup thickly lined with dried grass, soft moss, vegetable down, catkins, feathers, hair, fur or similar materials. Spider nests and cocoons also used, especially on the outside of the nest, presumably for camouflage. Readily uses string and other artificial materials when available. Unlike many birds it often picks up any material dropped when building (Grinnel, in Bent; Warren) although this behaviour is not always shown (Mercier, in Bendire).

Eggs 2 to 5, usually 3 or 4; pale pearl grey to greenish white, speckled or spotted, usually profusely, with dull brown and greyish brown, and with underlying markings of grey and lilac.

Both sexes build. In the pair watched by Warren the female did more actual construction work. Female alone incubates. An observation of two Grey Jays incubating one on top of the other in the same nest was most probably, in my opinion, a case of two females paired together (Lawrence). Female sits on nest from time first egg is laid. Incubation period between 16 and 18 days. Both sexes feed the young, the male bringing most of the food for the first few days (Warren).

Voice Has a number of different calls, some or most of which intergrade, and is also a vocal mimic. A whistling call is common and what are probably different intensity variants of this call may be a soft 'whee-ah' or 'whee-ooh' and one suggestive of a loud human whistle. A harsher call, used when mobbing predators, has been described (for the Oregon form) as a 'swearing Ke-weep'. A soft trilling song of 'sweetly modulated notes' was given, especially on fine days, by the male of a nesting pair (Warren). A squawking call, similar to but not identical with the begging call of the female, is used with appeasing or submissive display, and a soft piping call with the highest intensity form of this display (Geist, 1968 and *in litt.*). A soft 'ca-ca-ca' is often uttered when flying down to investigate possible sources of food. Recorded calls (Kellogg & Allen), that I have heard, were screeches, whistling calls and a very deep, harsh 'throaty' chatter.

Display and social behaviour Female begs for food with calls similar to or identical with those of fledglings (these calls do not seem to have been described in any detail, which suggests they are similar to the begging calls of most other corvids) and with flapping wings.

In the presence of a dominant individual, subordinates fluff out their body plumage, erect the spread tail, and hop around uttering a call like that of the begging juvenile. At higher intensity, shown often in response to being looked at by a very dominant individual, the subordinate spreads its wings and tail and buries its bill in the snow, thus presenting the black hind crown, and utters soft piping cries. An apparently intermediate stage of intensity is shown by the bird crouching, flapping *and* quivering the wings, and screeching at the dominant bird (Geist, 1968 and *in litt.*). Professor Geist thinks that these displays function to allow a number of Grey Jays to gather around and each obtain some food from a carcass (or bird table) in winter when food sources may be few and far between, instead of all others being driven away by the most dominant male or pair.

Other names Canada Jay, Whisky Jack, Moose-bird, Meat-bird, Grease-bird, Hudson Bay Bird, Camp Robber, Caribou Bird, Oregon Jay, Labrador Jay, Rocky Mountain Jay.

REFERENCES

ALDRICH, J. W. 1943. Relationships of the Canada Jays in the Northwest. *Wilson Bull.* **55**: 217–222.
ALLEN, C. R. K. 1965. Unusual behaviour in Gray Jays. *Canad. Field Nat.* **79**: 211.
AMERICAN ORNITHOLOGISTS' UNION. 1957. *Check-list of North American Birds*, 5th ed.: 366–369.
BENDIRE, C. 1895. Life Histories of North American birds: 385–396. *U.S. Nat. Hist. Mus. spec. Bull.*
BENT, A. C. 1946. Life histories of North American jays, crows and titmice: 1–32. *U.S. Nat. Mus. Bull.* **191**: 118–128.
DEVITT, O. E. 1961. An example of the whisper song of the Gray Jay. *Auk* **78**: 265–266.
DOW, D. D. 1965. The role of saliva in food storage by the Gray Jay. *Auk* **82**: 139–154.
GEIST, V. 1968. On the interrelation of external appearance and social behaviour and social structure of Mountain Sheep. *Z. Tierpsychol.* **25**: 212.
KELLOGG, P. & ALLEN, A. A. 1962. *Field Guide to Bird Songs of Western North America*. Boston.
LAWRENCE, L. DE K. 1947. Five days with a pair of nesting Canada Jays. *Canad. Field Nat.* **61**: 1–11.
MILLER, A. H. 1933. The Canada Jays of Northern Idaho. *Trans. San Diego Soc. Nat. Hist.* **7**, No. 25: 287–298.
PETERS, J. L. 1920. A new jay from Alberta. *Proc. New England Zool. Cl.* **7**: 51–52.
PETERSON, R. T. 1961. *A Field Guide to Western Birds*. Cambridge, Mass.
TAVERNER, P. A. 1938. *Birds of Canada:* **304**, London.
WARREN, O. B. 1899. A chapter in the life of the Canada Jay. *Auk* **16**: 12–19.

SIBERIAN JAY   *Perisoreus infaustus*

Corvus infaustus Linnaeus, 1758, Syst. Nat., ed. **1**: 107.

Description About same size and proportions as Grey Jay (q.v.). The full soft nasal plumes are pale fawnish brown to yellowish cream, same colour at extreme top of 'chin' and front of malar region. Top of head and face sooty brown to dark drab brown, the lores slightly darker, and the forehead and ear coverts usually slightly paler than elsewhere. Mantle, back and breast light ashy grey or ashy grey suffused with tawny, shading through tawny grey to pale tawny rufous on lower back, upper part of rump, ventral regions and under tail coverts. Wings ash-grey with dark brownish grey inner webs to primaries, and outer secondaries with a conspicuous tawny orange to light chestnut patch formed by the outer webs of the primary coverts, outer secondary coverts and basal areas of the outer webs of the inner and central primaries. Underwing coverts tawny orange, and basal parts of undersides of most primaries tinged with same colour. Two central tail feathers grey; outer tail feathers tawny orange to light chestnut-red with or without some pale grey on tips of outer webs. Lower rump and upper tail coverts tawny orange to light chestnut-red. Bill and legs blackish. Irides brown or blackish brown.

   Juvenile usually slightly browner on the grey parts but otherwise like adult except for the usual shorter and woollier-textured body plumage. The juvenile retains its wing and tail quills until its second moult at about 12 to 16 months old. Adult birds moult in late spring and summer; an adult taken in Yeniseisk, Siberia, on May 25th and two taken in Russian Lapland in early June are in full moult.

   The Siberian Jay shows some minor geographical variation, mostly clinal, in size, nuances of colour, and the size of the reddish wing patch. This geographic variation has been discussed in detail by Johansen and more succinctly by Vaurie. On the whole, the species is remarkably homogeneous in appearance throughout its enormous range. The above description covers all forms.

Field characters Greyish, dark-headed bird with bright reddish wing patch and outer tail feathers. The redstart-like bright reddish outer tail feathers at once identify it. In the field, or rather in the forest, it usually appears much brighter (as do the redstarts with their similar tail coloration) than it does in the hand.

   Blomgren's splendid photographs of this species illustrate both his book (Blomgren, 1964) and his paper in *British Birds* (Blomgren, 1971).

Distribution and habitat Northern Europe and Asia, from central and northern Scandinavia and Russia east across Siberia to Anadyrland, Sakhalin and Ussuriland and south to the Altai and northern Mongolia. Inhabits coniferous forest and, to a very limited extent, deciduous woodland adjacent to coniferous forest.

Feeding and general habits Commonly in pairs, sometimes in small rather loose parties. Blomgren's (1964, 1971) studies on the Siberian Jay in Scandinavia show that there paired birds are sedentary. The usual territory size for a pair is about one and a half square kilometres.   One female, observed for twelve years, was always in the same territory at all seasons of the year.   In summer pairs that have bred successfully are accompanied by their young.   These may remain in their parents' territory until well into the following breeding season.   Territory-less and unpaired individuals may possibly form loose flocks at times.

Feeds both in trees and on ground; sometimes hangs upside-down in tit-like manner.   Recorded foods include insects, especially beetles and caterpillars, berries, especially *Vaccinium* species, seeds of conifers and, but to a smaller extent, small mammals, young birds, eggs and remains of mammals killed by larger predators.   Said to eat tree-growing lichens in winter (Franz).   Very readily takes human foods around camp-sites, especially meat, and often comes to grief in traps set for fur-bearing mammals.

Flight like that of Jay but quieter and lighter.   When flying long distances, quick, regular wing beats alternate with short glides on outspread wings and tail.   Very agile and active when seeking food.   Habitually hides surplus food.   Food stored for winter consists largely of berries, which are hidden behind loose bark or in beard lichen on trees (Blomgren).   These food hoards are scattered about the territory.   A captive bird, carrying food in its throat, when offered some more favoured tit-bit, would disgorge the food it was carrying carefully onto a branch, swallow the tit-bit, then re-engorge the food pellet (Meade-Waldo).   I have several times seen similar behaviour from the Jay.

Usually shows little fear of man, approaching him at once when he appears, either out of curiosity or in expectation of food.   Generally tolerated and often regarded with affection or as an omen of good luck by sympatric humans but sometimes, and very easily, shot by visitors from further south.   In Ussuriland, Vorobiev noted that it fed extensively on the wood and bark-boring bettles *Rhegium inquisitor*, *Sachalinobia holtzei*, *Elater compactus*, and *Ips subelongatus*, which are considered harmful to forestry.

Nesting   In a tree or bush, most often between 1·8 and 6 metres high, against the stem, in a conifer.   The nest varies in size but is usually very thick-walled with the inner cup extremely soft and thick.   Outer framework of twigs and sometimes roots also, intertwined and padded with beard lichen and sometimes feathers, plant down, fibrous bark, moss and soft rotten wood.   Lining of feathers and/or plant down, fine grass stems, soft lichens, hair and fur.   Most commonly the lining is largely of feathers and the often discredited belief that it collects and hides feathers in autumn for this purpose ought not perhaps to be dismissed without investigation, in view of its food-storing activities.   Both sexes bring materials but only female actually builds (Blomgren).

Eggs 3 to 5; pale greyish green, off-white or pale greenish buff, spotted, freckled and blotched with dark olive brown or drab brown and with underlying grey or lilac markings.   Sometimes the markings coalesce at the large end.

Nests early.   In northern Scandinavia building begins in mid to late March or early April, sometimes a little later; eggs usually laid in April, often early in that month.   In Russia, near Archangel, complete clutches found from mid-April to early May.   Incubation by female only, who covers nest from first egg, and is fed at nest by male.   True incubation begins with the third egg (Blomgren).   Incubation period 19 days; young fledge at 21 to 25 days.   Both parents feed young, male bringing all food for first week or so.   Young remain with parents until the winter and sometimes in their territory until well into spring.

Juveniles in the British Museum, taken in July, are in full moult, others taken in August have nearly completed the first moult.

A brooding bird, discovered by Carpelan (1929), flew from the nest when he struck the supporting branch but returned, while he was climbing to the nest, to cover the nestlings and would not leave until lifted from the nest.   This behaviour is so like what I have observed from a tame female Jay as to suggest that both species may have an innate fleeing reaction to a jarring of the nest supports.   Other observers (see esp. Dresser) have found incubating Siberian Jays equally bold, sitting tight until removed by hand from the nest and then returning again at once.

Both the Lapps in Finland and the Alaskan Indians have, or did have, similar beliefs that bad luck would result from molesting or even looking at the nest of a *Perisoreus*.

Voice The commonest calls are a loud scream and a Buzzard-like mewing call, but many other quieter calls are also uttered (Blomgren). Song, of various soft notes and vocal mimicry, is used mainly in sexual contexts (Blomgren). Some of its calls have struck many people as sounding wild, musical and mysterious. Meade-Waldo, who observed it both wild and in captivity, wrote 'Its own voice is delightfully wild and musical; it has, however, a great variety of cries, some of which are perhaps rather the reverse'. Habitually practises vocal mimicry both when wild and in captivity (Blomgren; Carpelan; Meade-Waldo).

Display and social behaviour In sexual display the male makes a series of excited hops, bows and turns in front of the female. Afterwards he flies away with a peculiar swooping flight (Blomgren).

Other names Boreal Jay, Northern Jay, Red-tailed Jay.

REFERENCES

BLAIR, H. M. S. 1936. On the birds of East Finmark. *Ibis* **6** 13th ser., 280–308.
BLOMGREN, A. 1964. *Lavskrikan*. Stockholm.
——1971. Studies of less familiar birds 162. Siberian Jay. *Brit. Birds* **64**: 25–28. (Plates 1 to 8, in same volume, are splendid photographs of this species and its habitat, all but one taken by Blomgren).
CARPELAN, J. 1929. Einige Beobachtungen über Lebensweise und Fortpflanzung des Unglückshähers (*Perisoreus infaustus*) im nördlichen Finnland. *Beitr. Fortpfll-biol. Vög.* **5**: 60–63.
DRESSER, H. E. 1871–1881. *A History of the Birds of Europe* **4**: 471–477.
FRANZ, J. 1943. Ueber Ernährung und Tagesrhythmus einiger Vögel im arktischen Winter. *J. Orn.* **91**: 154–165.
JOHANSEN, H. 1944. Die Vogelfauna Westsibiriens. *J. Orn.* **92**: 20–22.
MEADE-WALDO, E. G. B. 1889. The Siberian Jay. *Avicult. Mag.* **5**: 101–102.
STEGMANN, B. 1931. Die Vögel des dauro-mandschurischen Uebergangsgebietes. *J. Orn.* **79**: 145.
VAURIE, C. 1959. *The Birds of the Palearctic Fauna: Passeriformes*. London.
VON HAARTMAN, L. 1969. The nesting habits of Finnish birds. *Comm. Biologicae Soc. Sci. Fenn.* **32**: 38–40.
VOROBIEV, K. A. 1954. *Birds of the Ussuri Area*. Moscow. (Translation by Gervais Reed in library of British Museum (Natural History), London).

SOOTY JAY   *Perisoreus internigrans*

Boanerges internigrans Thayer and Bangs, 1912, Mem. Mus. Comp. Zool., 40: 200, pl. 6.

Description Slightly larger than Canada Jay and similar in proportions except for the bill, which is intermediate in shape and depth between that of Canada Jay and that of Lanceolated Jay. General colour a medium-dark grey with no tinge of either brown or blue. Head and throat dull black, the grey feathers of the lower throat and upper breast edged with dull sooty black, giving an obscurely laced effect. Greater wing coverts, primaries and tail a slightly darker grey than the rest of the plumage and with a very faint brownish tinge.

Irides brown. So far as can be judged from the appearance of the only specimen I have been able to examine, the legs are blackish in life and the bill similar in colour to that of the Lanceolated Jay.

Field characters A grey jay with blackish head and no bright or contrasting colours except the palish bill.

Distribution and habitat   Northern and north-western Szechuan west to eastern Sikang.   Inhabits sub-alpine coniferous forest.

Feeding and general habits   No information.

Nesting   No information.

Voice   A vocal mimic, heard to mimic calls of buzzards, woodpeckers and laughing-thrushes (Kleinschmidt & Weigold).

Display and social behaviour   No information.

Other names   Szechuan Grey Jay.

REFERENCES

KLEINSCHMIDT, O. & WEIGOLD, H.   1922.   Zoologische Ergebnisse der Walter Stötznerschen Expedition nach Szetschwan, Osttibet und Tschili.   *Abh. v. Ber. Mus.* Dresden **15**: 3–7.
LÖNNBERG, E.   1924.   Notes on some Birds from Kansu, China.   *Ibis* **6,** 2nd ser.: 308–328.
SCHÄFER, E.   1938.   Ornithologische Ergebnisse zweier Forschungsreisen nach Tibet.   *J. Orn.* **86**: Sonderheft.

The American jays

The American jays or blue jays are a numerous group of small to large sized jays confined to the Americas.   In South America they are the only members of the Corvidae.   They show much divergence in size, relative lengths of wing and tail and in size and shape of the crest (where present).   Many have beautiful and striking colour patterns on the head and neck (some to some extent elsewhere) but these are all obvious permutations of one or two basic patterns.   They are predominantly blue in colour, usually in combination with black and/or white, although two are partly yellow or yellow and green and one species lacks any bright colours and is mainly dull brown.   Some of them have brilliant golden or yellow eyes that add much to their beauty.   See col. pl. 2.

In spite of their adaptive radiation and consequent divergences they are all, even the aberrant Piñon Jay, almost certainly representatives of a single stock, and are all more closely related to one another than to any species in any other group. They probably derived from some jay that reached America early, perhaps before the separation of the ancestral Old World stock into such relatively distinct forms as modern *Garrulus*, *Cissa* etc. As has been mentioned when discussing the grey jays, it is an interesting fact that both the blue jays and the New World forms of *Perisoreus* differ from Old World forms of *Garrulus* and *Perisoreus* by lacking any rufous, vinous or fawn plumage.

In general the American jays fill similar niches to those filled by the typical jays, blue magpies, green magpies and tree pies in the old world, although some have succeeded in rather more arid and sparsely-wooded areas than have these old world relatives. This, however, probably reflects not a greater potential adaptability in the New World stock but that they have not had time to develop such strongly differentiated forms as, for example, the ground jays, *Podoces*, or magpies, *Pica*. An interesting point of ecological agreement is that many of the New World jays feed, like the Old World *Garrulus* species, largely on acorns. Many (probably all) of them store food in typical manner but present observations suggest, possibly incorrectly in some cases, that none of them, except the Piñon Jay, relies so much on previously hidden food as some Old World forms do. In some of them it is usual for several individuals to cooperate in rearing a brood of young.

Leaving aside the very distinct Piñon Jay, the American jays pose a problem as to how many genera they are best divided into. Most workers have favoured an abundance of genera but have, in many instances, disagreed as to which species should be included in which genera. Amadon, in his review of the Corvidae, kept the two long-tailed and long-crested magpie-jays in the genus *Calocitta*, the Brown Jay in the monotypic genus *Psilorhinus*, and distributed the remaining species between *Cyanocitta* and *Cyanocorax*. The latter genus he re-defined as being 'like *Cyanocitta* but in general more specialized; crest usually present but extremely variable; throat, breast, and usually large areas on sides and top of head black; the black breast more sharply demarcated from the remainder of the underside . . . lower breast and abdomen and large areas in the tail characteristically white or yellow but sometimes blue or purple; size averaging larger and body form, legs and feet more robust than in *Cyanocitta*.' He added, very truly, 'The problem for one who would like generic characters to be more stable and substantial than specific characters is not whether to unite the above species in *Cyanocorax* but how to keep *Cyanocorax* separate from *Psilorhinus*, *Calocitta* and, for that matter, *Cyanocitta*'.

In Peters' Check-list, Blake (1962) recognizes seven genera: *Cyanocitta*, *Aphelocoma*, *Cyanolyca*, *Cissilopha*, *Cyanocorax*, *Psilorhinus* and *Calocitta*; and, of course, the very distinct *Gymnorhinus*, which has been left in its monotypic genus by all revisers. Hardy (1961 and 1964) separated the American jays into two tribes, Aphelocomini and Cyanocoracini, on the grounds that the former group (genera *Aphelocoma* and *Cyanolyca*) had a less extensive vocabulary and more simplified colour patterns. At least one species of *Cyanolyca* was, however, found to be vocally intermediate (Hardy 1967) and later he (Hardy 1969a) recognized only four genera: *Cyanocitta*, *Aphelocoma* (syn. *Cyanolyca*) and *Cyanocorax* (syns. *Cissilopha*, *Psilorhinus* and *Calocitta*).

The seven genera recognized by Blake undoubtedly represent groups of species, each of which is more closely related to its congeners than it is to any species placed by them in a different genus. The differences between the two least mutually divergent forms in any two of these genera are, however, slight. On the other hand, to reduce the number of genera might be misleading unless all, with the possible exception of *Cyanocitta*, were placed in a single genus, *Cyanocorax*. I think, for example, that some forms in *Aphelocoma* may, in spite of their vocal differences (Hardy), be as close phylogenetically to *Cyanocitta* as they are to some forms of *Cyanolyca*.

To lump all the American jays except *Gymnorhinus* in one genus has much to commend it, in spite of the difficulty of defining such a varied assemblage. It would, however, make difficulties for the reader when looking up other works on the group. Also, as genera are to some extent units of convenience, there is much to be said for using the generic names in the world check-list (Peters) where feasible. I have, therefore, provisionally used the genera recognized by Blake. This is done largely for convenience and it must be emphasized that all these genera, and their component species, are very closely related.

The genus *Cyanocitta* contains the Blue Jay, *Cyanocitta cristata* and Steller's Jay, *C. stelleri*. Both are of smallish to medium size with similar types of crest (although the crests of most forms of Steller's Jay are longer than those of Blue Jays) and black barring on the wings and tail. Alone among the jays, the *Cyanocitta* species use mud or earth in their nests. They are almost, if not entirely, allopatric and can be considered as geographical representatives. Their nearest relatives appear to be on the one hand mostly very similarly proportioned but crestless jays in the genera *Aphelocoma* and *Cyanolyca*, and on the other the much larger and longer-tailed magpie-jays of the genus *Calocitta*.

The jays in the genus *Aphelocoma* have more simplified colour patterns and are crestless. They have no black barring on the wings and tail although, at certain angles, their tails and secondaries often show a pronounced 'watermark' barring, the 'fundamental barring' as it is sometimes called, that is to be seen on the otherwise unpatterned tails of many birds. They are found from western North America through Mexico to El Salvador and Honduras, with an isolated population in Florida. A detailed study of the taxonomy and ecology of this group has been made by Pitelka (1951), to which readers are referred for fuller details than can be given here.

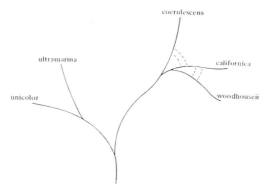

FIG. D.6. Presumed relationships of species in the genus *Aphelocoma*. Two dotted lines connect very distinct subspecies.

Woodhouse's Jay, *A. woodhouseii*, and the Californian Jay, *A. californica*, are now usually thought to be conspecific with the Florida Jay, *A. coerulescens*, and all are given the comprehensive and descriptive English name of Scrub Jay. I concur in thinking that these forms are best regarded as races of a single species. As, however, there may be some behavioural divergence between *californica* and *woodhouseii* and between both of these and *coerulescens*, these three forms of the Scrub Jay are dealt with under separate headings.

The Scrub Jay is primarily a bird of the chaparral-woodland complex, to which it is often largely or wholly confined in areas where it is, in a geographical sense, allopatric with other jay species and, particularly, with the other two species of *Aphelocoma*. It seems likely that this adaptation to chaparral scrub has come about through its being unable to compete successfully in areas of richer vegetation.

The Mexican Jay, *Aphelocoma ultramarina*, and the Unicolored Jay, *A. unicolor*, are similar in size and in their simplicity of plumage pattern but they differ in colour and habitat choice. They are allopatric throughout most of their respective ranges but overlap in a small area of south-eastern Mexico. The Unicolored Jay overlaps rather more widely with the Scrub Jay than it does with *A. ultramarina*. The Mexican Jay overlaps with the Scrub Jay throughout its range. Both Mexican and Unicolored Jays are largely separated from the smaller species by their keeping mainly, although not entirely, to different habitats.

The species within the genus *Cyanolyca* appear closely related to *Aphelocoma* and to connect that genus with *Cyanocorax*. They have predominantly blue, purplish blue or greenish blue body plumage and a usually conspicuous head pattern, with pale crown and/or frontal band and superciliary stripes, and either a pale throat contrasting with black cheeks or else the face and throat entirely black. As with some *Cyanocorax* species, and many other birds, different degrees of melanization on head and throat may give rise to considerable differences of appearance which are not likely to be correlated with other divergences between the forms in question.

The four small species: the Dwarf Jay, *Cyanolyca nana*, the Black-throated Dwarf Jay, *C. pumilo*, the White-throated Jay, *C. mirabilis*, and the Silver-throated Jay, *C. argentigula*, are closely allied and allopatric. The last two seem best given specific rank within the superspecies. It is possible that when more information is available it may indicate that they should be treated as conspecific.

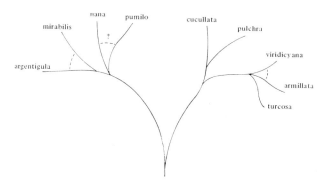

FIG. D.7.   Presumed relationships of species in the genus *Cyanolyca*.

On their taxonomic characters I would place *C. pumilo* and *C. nana* in the same superspecies but for the fact that Hardy (1964) thinks that the calls and ecology of *pumilo* indicate that it is further from *nana* than the latter is from *mirabilis*. On its plumage characters *C. pumilo* seems to form a link between *C. mirabilis* and *C. argentigula* on one hand and *C. nana* on the other but to be closest to the latter. Its black throat, in which *C. pumilo* differs from the other three, is at best a specific character and a rather trifling one at that. In view of the alleged vocal and ecological differences I hesitate to put *nana* and *pumilo* in the same superspecies but they are certainly geographical representatives.

In coloration and plumage pattern the Beautiful Jay, *C. pulchra*, of western Colombia and Ecuador, is largely intermediate between the Collared Jay, *C. armillata,* with which it is partly sympatric, and the Hooded Jay, *C. cucullata*, of Mexico and Central America. In appearance it is rather closer to *cucullata*. Hellmayr treated them as conspecific but most later workers on the group have given *pulchra* specific rank This is, I think, the better course but it can be considered as forming a superspecies, together with *cucullata*.

The Collared Jay, *C. armillata*, and the White-collared Jay, *C. viridicyana*, are usually treated as conspecific. They differ chiefly in *armillata* having a black band across the upper breast and no white on the forehead, whereas *viridicyana* has a narrow white band and a white or bluish white area on the forehead. The Turquoise Jay, *C. turcosa*, has sometimes been treated as conspecific with them (e.g. Blake, in Peters' Check-list) but it overlaps with the Collared Jay in south-eastern Colombia and, probably, also in north-eastern Ecuador (De Schauensee). It differs from *C. armillata* in having a shorter tail, more greenish blue general coloration and a paler blue throat. Thus the difference between them is less striking than that between the Collared and White-collared Jays. As, on present evidence, it seems likely that *turcosa* and *armillata* are specifically distinct, it seems better to give *armillata* and *viridicyana* specific rank within the same superspecies rather than to treat them as races of one species.

The jays within the genus *Cyanocorax* all appear to be closely related. The Tufted Jay, *Cyanocorax dickeyi*, the White-tailed Jay, *C. mystacalis*, the Cayenne Jay, *C. cayanus*, the Plush-capped Jay, *C, chrysops*, and the White-naped Jay, *C. cyanopogon* are, with a possible exception to be discussed later, allopatric. All have similar plumage patterns. They differ chiefly in the form and length of their forehead and crown feathers, and the precise shade of coloration and extent of their contrasting nuchal, supra-orbital and malar regions. They are best considered as members of a superspecies and their affinities discussed within this grouping.

C. dickeyi, of western Mexico, bears a striking likeness to *C. mystacalis* of western Ecuador and western Peru, from which it differs in appearance only by being a little larger, having much longer forehead and crown feathers (and hence a much more fully-developed crest), larger supra-orbital spots, different tail pattern and slightly darker blue upperparts. Their very close affinity can hardly be doubted and it seems worth pointing out that in its entirely white outer tail feathers, *mystacalis* differs from all other American jays except the Green Jay, *C. yncas*, whose yellow outer tail feathers also lack melanin pigment.

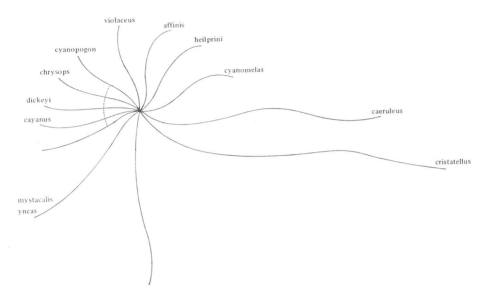

C. cayanus, from the Guianas, parts of Venezuela and northern Brazil, seems also very close to the above forms. In some of its characters it is intermediate between them. Its tail pattern is like that of *dickeyi*, except that the white areas are less extensive, its supra-orbital spots are like those of *mystacalis*, but it has head feathers even shorter than the latter's, a less extensive white nuchal area, and more brownish purple upperparts than either *dickeyi* or *mystacalis*. Hardy (1969a), however, believes that *cayanus* is most closely related to *C. heilprini* and *C. cyanomelas*.

The Plush-capped Jay, *C. chrysops*, and the White-naped or Blue-bearded Jay, *C. cyanopogon*, are sometimes treated as conspecific on the basis of an intermediate specimen from Alagoas (Pinto). I agree with De Schauensee that this bird may well have represented a chance hybrid rather than an intermediate population. Other specimens, claimed to be of this allegedly intermediate form, were examined by Hardy (1969a), who considered them to be worn subadult specimens of *cyanopogon*. I therefore prefer to treat *chrysops* and *cyanopogon* as separate species.

The Black-chested Jay, *C. affinis*, of north-western South America, may be a member of the same superspecies. I do not include it, however, because not enough is known of the ethology and anatomy of these jays to indicate relationships among such closely allied forms and, on its plumage characters, it might equally well be more close to the Azure-naped Jay, *C. heilprini*, whose range appears to overlap that of *C. cayanus* (De Schauensee).

The Azure-naped Jay, *C. heilprini*, of extreme southern Venezuela and adjacent regions, agrees with *affinis*, *mystacalis* and *dickeyi* in having the pale nuchal area extending forward to the crown, but in the rest of its plumage pattern and in its predominantly purplish coloration it either resembles *affinis* or is intermediate between *affinis* and *cyanomelas*. The Purplish Jay, *C. cyanomelas*, has a simplified colour pattern, apparently caused by an invasion of melanin over the (originally) pale or bright facial and nuchal areas. These latter can, however, still be seen in suitable angles of light, owing to the differing texture of the feathers, although they appear only as slightly differing tones of the general brownish black. It is probable that *affinis*, *heilprini* and *cyanomelas*, which are allopatric, are more closely related to one another than to other species, but in view of the close relationship of all forms of *Cyanocorax* I hesitate to treat them as members of a superspecies at present.   Hardy (1969b) considers *cyanomelas* a close relative of *caeruleus*.   Lester L. Short (*in litt.*) concurs with this opinion and tells me that he found these two species allopatric in northern Argentina.

The Violaceous Jay, *C. violaceus*, appears more closely related to the members of the *cayanus* super-species than to any others.   It has a more simplified colour pattern, apparently caused by an increase and spreading of melanin pigments so that the underparts are purplish blue, like the back, and the face is entirely black.   It still retains, however, a contrasting pale nuchal area.   In distribution it overlaps *C. cayanus, C. affinis* and possibly also *C. heilprini*, and it is probable that its simpler coloration and larger size serve as isolating mechanisms in reference to these species.   It is perhaps significant that it does not overlap the other two large South American forms of this genus, *C. careuleus* and *C. cristatellus*.   Hardy (1969a) places *C. dickeyi, C. mystacalis, C. chrysops* and *C. affinis* in one species-group and *C. cayanus, C. heilprini* and *C. violaceus* in another.

The Azure Jay, *C. caeruleus*, and the Curl-crested Jay, *C. cristatellus*, have more simplified plumage patterns than most other species of *Cyanocorax* and are larger in size, with rather large bills and well-developed frontal crests.   In these characters they resemble the still more simply-patterned Brown Jay, *Psilorhinus morio*, as they do also in the malar patch being of a similar blackish brown to the rest of the face but distinguishable at close inspection by the different texture of the feathers composing it.   They differ from *Psilorhinus* in their relatively short tails.   They may be more closely related to *Psilorhinus* than they are to other *Cyanocorax* species as Hardy (1961) has suggested.   I think it more probable, however, that *caeruleus* and *cristatellus* are more closely related to other South American forms of *Cyanocorax* than they are to *Psilorhinus*, and that their resemblances to the latter are due to convergent evolution although they certainly emphasize the undoubted very close relationship between *Cyanocorax* and *Psilorhinus*.

C. caeruleus and *C. cristatellus* are of similar size and agree in their relatively simplified plumage pattern and similar frontal crests.   The crest of *cristatellus* is much longer and more specialized in the adult but the crest of the young is similar to that of adult *caeruleus*.   They differ, however, in some details of colour and colour pattern; that of *cristatellus* suggests relationship with such forms as *C. dickeyi* and *C. cayanus*. On the other hand the colour and pattern of *caeruleus*, although it may represent a more simplified derivation from this stock, is also very suggestive, especially in the shades of blue, of possible relationship with the genus *Cissilopha*.

C. caeruleus and *C. cristatellus* are allopatric except for a possible marginal overlap in the Sao Paulo region of Brazil.   They may possibly be geographical representatives and most closely related to each other but it is also possible that, being much of a size, they have somewhat similar ecological requirements and that competition has tended to keep them geographically apart.   Hardy's (1969b) observations suggest that the longer-winged *cristatellus* frequents more open country but further information on ecology of both, especially *caeruleus*, is needed.   Hardy (1969a) considers *caeruleus* most closely related to *cyanomelas*.   This may be so, but I think their similar colour patterns are due to convergence (within a closely-related stock) and that *cyanomelas* is closer to *affinis* and *heilprini* than to *caeruleus*.   I agree with Hardy, however, in thinking *caeruleus* probably closer to *cyanomelas* than to *cristatellus*.

The green jays were formerly placed in the genus *Xanthoura*.   Apart from the possession of yellow pigment which, except on the head (in most forms), gives them a green and yellow instead of bluish and white general coloration, they agree with the more typical *Cyanocorax* species in colour pattern as well as in form and are, I think, now rightly included in that genus by most ornithologists.   The green jays were formerly treated as two species, *C. yncas*, of Mexico and Central America, and *C. luxuosus*, of north-western South America, but are now all treated as forms of a single, polytypic species *C. yncas*.   On their taxonomic characters this seems justified, as the ill-named *C. yncas guatimalensis*, from northern Venezuela, is intermediate in plumage characters between nominate *yncas* and the northern forms formerly separated as *C. luxuosus*.   The two groups show, however, some ecological differences and they are, therefore, treated here under separate headings, but as groups of a single species.

The genus *Cissilopha* includes four forms which, were they allopatric, might well be considered members of a superspecies or even as conspecific. They have a simple colour pattern in which the head, breast and (usually) underparts are black and the back, wings and tail some shade of blue. Some have wispy crests similar to although smaller than those of the magpie-jays. They range in size from rather larger than a Magpie (but with a shorter tail) to about the size of a Blue Jay. They have rather long, somewhat graduated tails, and rather large bills, legs and feet.

It is questionable which of the other American genera these jays are most closely allied to. Their colour patterns could well be simplified derivatives of those of *Cyanolyca* or *Cyanocorax*. I think, however, that their nearest relatives may be the magpie-jays, *Calocitta*. They show some approach to the latter in shape and, in some cases, in their crests and the colour patterns of their juvenile plumages.

Beechey's Jay, *Cissilopha beecheii*, and the smaller San Blas Jay, *C. sanblasiana*, are largely allopatric but have an area of sympatry in Nayarit and appear to be distinct species (Selander & Giller). *C. sanblasiana* and the Yucatan Jay, *C. yucatanica*, are allopatric and often considered conspecific. They are geographical representatives but differ in their coloration as juveniles (largely white in *yucatanica*), as well as in other less striking features, and I prefer to treat them as species. Hartlaub's Jay, *C. melanocyanea*, seems also properly considered a member of the same superspecies as *sanblasiana* and *yucatanica*.

The Brown Jay, *Psilorhinus morio*, of eastern Mexico and Central America is dull brown in colour, and has an apparently unique furcular pouch of the intraclavicular air sac, but in its other characters connects *Cyanocorax* with the magpie-jays of the genus *Calocitta*. It is likely that it is closely related to the latter, in spite of their different coloration, as an apparent hybrid between them was collected in one of the few places where both *Psilorhinus* and *Calocitta* occur (Pitelka *et al.* 1956).

The Magpie-jay, *Calocitta formosa*, and Collie's Magpie-jay, *C. colliei*, are often considered forms of a single species. Dr R. K. Selander informs me (*in litt.* 1968) that he found both forms in the same narrow valley in Colima; the populations here show no signs of intergradation, and the frequency of *colliei*-like characters in (some) individuals of *formosa* is no greater where the two forms are adjacent. I therefore treat these two magpie-jays as specifically distinct, although some specimens from Jalisco certainly *appear* to be hybrids or intergrades.

It is interesting that whereas the Magpie-jay has a facial pattern like that of the Blue Jay, *Cyanocitta cristata*, that of Collie's Magpie-jay resembles those of typical *Cyanocorax* species, a clear indication that the different colour patterns found within the American jays, even at their most divergent, do not necessarily imply any comparable phylogenetic gap between them.

The Piñon Jay, *Gymnorhinus cyanocephala*, is nutcracker-like in shape, highly social, and walks in a crow-like manner on the ground. For these reasons it is often thought to be closely related to *Corvus* or *Nucifraga*. I concur with Amadon in thinking that it is an offshoot of the American jays and that its structural and behavioural resemblances to crows and nutcrackers are due to convergence.

In coloration *Gymnorhinus* would readily pass for an *Aphelocoma* and is quite unlike either species of *Nucifraga* or any species of *Corvus*. From the former genus (and most of the latter) it also differs in having exposed nostrils. Like the nutcrackers it feeds largely on conifer seeds, hence their similar bills; but its way of life differs in many respects from a nutcracker's. Indeed, allowing for differences in habitat, much of its behaviour suggests a convergent resemblance to that of the Old World Rook, *Corvus frugilegus*. Its phylogenetic relationships are, in my opinion, with the other American jays.

REFERENCES

AMADON, D. 1944. The genera of Corvidae and their relationships. *Amer. Mus. Novit.* No. 1251.
BLAKE, E. R. 1962. *Peters' Check-list of Birds of the World* vol. 15. Cambridge, Mass.
DE SCHAUENSEE, R. M. 1966. *The Species of Birds of South America.* Pennsylvania.
HARDY, J. W. 1961. Studies in behaviour and phylogeny of certain New World jays (Garrulinae). *Univ. Kansas Sci. Bull.* **42**, pp. 13–149.
—— 1964. Behaviour, habitat, and relationships of jays of the genus *Cyanolyca*. *Occ. Papers C.C. Adams Center for Ecological Studies*, No. 11.

—— 1967.   The puzzling vocal repertoire of the South American Collared Jay, *Cyanolyca viridicyana merida.* *Condor* **69**, pp. 513–521.

—— 1969a.   A taxonomic revision of the New World Jays. *Condor* **71**: 360–375.

—— 1969b.   Habits and habitats of certain South American jays. *Cont. Sci. Los Angeles County Mus.,* No. 165.

HELLMAYR, C. E.   1934.   Cat. Birds Am., pt. 7. *Publ. Field Mus. Nat. Hist., zool. serv.,* vol. 13, pt. 7.

PITELKA, F. A.   1951.   Speciation and ecologic distribution in American jays of the genus *Aphelocoma.* *Condor* **47**: 229–260.

PITELKA, F. A., SELANDER, R. K., & DEL TORRO, M. A.   1956.   A hybrid jay from Chiapas, Mexico. *Condor* **58**: 98–106.

PINTO, O. M. DE O.   1954.   *Papeis Avulsos, Dept. Zool., Sao Paulo* **12**: 75.

SELANDER, R. K. & GILLER, D. R.   1959.   Sympatry of Jays *Cissilopha beecheii* and *C. san-blasiana* in Nayarit. *Condor* **61**: 52.

BLUE JAY   *Cyanocitta cristata*

Corvus cristatus Linnaeus, 1758, Syst. Nat. Ed. 10, 1, p. 106.

Description   See col. pl. 2.   Nasal plumes pale mauvish blue to off-white, with black shafts.   Narrow black band across forehead, contiguous with black marking at sides of front of crest and loral regions. Forehead (behind black band), crown and crest light violet-blue, bluish mauve or sky-blue tinged with violet.   Face and throat dull mauvish white to very pale greyish mauve with narrow dark shafts to many feathers giving a slightly streaky appearance at close quarters.   A narrow black stripe extends from behind the eye and joins a black necklace-like band encircling the neck but largely or quite hidden on nape when the crest is depressed.   Mantle, back, and lesser wing coverts light to medium bluish mauve to (less often) violet blue, shading to a brighter blue, with little or no mauve tinge, on rump and upper tail coverts.

Median wing coverts mauvish blue with faint dusky barring.   Greater wing coverts and secondaries bright rich blue with black bars; the blue on the outer webs of the inner secondaries is usually lighter and brighter and that on the outer webs of the outermost secondaries much darker than elsewhere.   All these feathers have broad white tips, those of the greater coverts forming a white bar across the folded wing.   Alula and primary coverts dull blue or mauvish blue with obscure blackish barring.   Outer webs of primaries light blue or greenish blue.   Tail sky-blue to light sky-blue, barred with black, this barring being less distinct on the outer feathers.   All but the two central tail feathers have conspicuous white tips, broadest on the outermost feathers.   Inner webs of wing quills, where not visible when wing is folded, dull greyish.   Underside of wing quills dull grey with silvery central area.   Underside of tail (where not white) dull grey.   Underparts a dingy, dirty-looking, medium to very pale mauvish grey, except on central area of belly and under tail coverts which are white.   In very worn and bleached plumage the crest and back may become pale grey rather than mauve or blue.   The forehead feathers are sometimes tipped with white or silvery blue.   A few individuals have feathers in which some or (rarely) all of the bars are obsolescent, or abnormally broad or narrow, presumably owing to food deficiencies or other factors affecting metabolism at the time of feather growth.   Irides dark brown.   Bill, legs and feet black.

Juvenile duller with greyish blue crown and crest and dull grey back and mantle. The barring on the wing coverts and alula is absent or only slightly indicated, that on the secondaries and tail more often (but by no means always) aberrant or distorted than in the adult and the white tips on wing and tail feathers are usually less extensive. Nestlings hatched entirely naked and pinkish. Rand has described the growth and development of young in detail.

Four races of this species are usually recognized (Blake). They intergrade and the differences in coloration are very slight. The description above is composite and covers them all. In general the Blue Jay shows a north to south cline in size, those from southern Florida, *C. cristata cyanotephra*, being smallest.

Field characters Predominantly bright blue and mauve (adult) or blue and grey (juvenile) jay with white markings. Broad white tips to blue tail feathers are diagnostic and prevent confusion with any other sympatric jay.

Distribution and habitat North America: in Canada and the United States from central Alberta, central Saskatchewan, southern Manitoba to central Ontario, southern Quebec and Newfoundland, south through the Dakotas, eastern Wyoming, Nebraska, eastern Colorado, the Texan Panhandle and the eastern states south to central Texas, the Gulf Coast and southern Florida. Some, but not all, of the more northern populations are migratory, wintering south of their breeding areas. There is much evidence that, at least in some such areas (perhaps in all), birds of the year migrate south for the winter whereas adults, or most of them, usually remain throughout the year (Pitelka; Laskey; Hardy). Individuals may, however, migrate after having once wintered 'at home' (Laskey).

Inhabits woodland, especially mixed woodland containing oaks or beeches (or, formerly, American chestnuts). Also regularly in wooded parks, gardens, suburbs, and some towns; including city parks such as Central Park, New York, where it is plentiful.

Feeding and general habits Seeks food both on the ground and in branches. Has been recorded taking a great variety of foods, including acorns, beech nuts, chestnuts (before the virtual extermination of the American Chestnut), seeds of the Palmetto and of many weeds, grain (usually only locally and in small quantities), fruits, berries, insects and other invertebrates, eggs and young of small birds, mice, and many kinds of foodstuffs given or discarded by man, such as peanuts, sunflower seeds, bread, meat, cheese and suet. An examination of the contents of 292 Blue Jays' stomachs (Beal) showed that, exclusive of the considerable amount (14%) of mineral matter that had been eaten, 76% of the food consisted of vegetable matter. It is possible, however, that the quicker digestion of animal food may have influenced this finding.

Acorns and, in Florida, Palmetto seeds seem to be among the most important vegetable foods; caterpillars, grasshoppers and beetles among the most important animal foods. Both stomach content analysis and the observations of many unbiased bird-watchers suggest that the Blue Jay does not prey on eggs and nestlings to anything like the extent that many of its detractors have claimed (see esp. Laskey). Large or hard food objects are held under the feet and hammered or torn with the bill. Large seeds, nuts etc. may be engorged whole for transporting but are shelled and broken up before eating them.

Habitually hides acorns, nuts and other food items. It has been stated (Bendire) that only resident individuals do this and that migratory Blue Jays do not. This seems unlikely to be entirely true but it is possible that the urge to store food is stronger in adult or territory-owning birds than it is in young or landless individuals. Blue Jays that I watched hiding food items in the grounds of the Bronx Zoo, New York, did so in exactly the same manner as *Garrulus*, pushing the morsel into the ground or ground vegetation and then carefully covering it up. As with *Garrulus*, food may also be hidden above ground in tree crevices and similar places. Hardy (1961) thought that the function of food hiding in this species is not to provide a future or reserve food supply but, probably, by removing a temporary surplus of food, to remove temptation for other individuals to enter a territory with the possiblity that they might stay and compete with the residents when food was no longer superabundant. I think this hypothesis unlikely. Wild Blue Jays have been seen regularly recovering food that they had hidden several days previously (Dadisman). Hardy observed Blue Jays shelling acorns before carrying them off to hide and appears to imply that this is usual, but it is not mentioned by Brewster who describes acorn-gathering Blue Jays carrying one acorn in the mouth or throat and another in the tip of the bill (Brewster, in Bent).

Usually associates in couples or small parties in winter and in family parties or larger groups in summer and autumn. Breeding pairs are more or less alone in their territories once nesting has started. Flocks, if such they can be called rather than mere aggregations in good feeding areas or at some centre of interest, are at all times loose. The individual rather than the group is the deciding unit and individual distance between birds is usually maintained. On migration commonly in small loose flocks but often in large, although again only loosely cohesive flocks, especially when bad weather or reluctance to cross a large sheet of water has resulted in a build-up of numbers.

When travelling any appreciable distance usually flies very straight, with body and tail horizontal, bill pointed somewhat downwards, using regular wing beats in rather quicker time than those of *Garrulus glandarius*. May glide, especially when flying short distances but does so less than *G. glandarius*. Very agile and graceful among branches, like all jays. I noticed that birds I watched did not flick up the tail on alighting as the Jay so often does. They did, however, make the same head and body movements as *Garrulus* and flick the tail when mobbing predators. When crossing open ground parties trail behind one another, leaving the cover one or two at a time, in the same manner as other jays, and many woodland passerines do.

Habitually mobs predators, often taking great apparent risk when mobbing the small and dangerous hawks of the genus *Accipiter*, another point in which its behaviour is like that of *Garrulus*. Very reluctant to cross large sheets of water on migration, doubtless because of the danger from birds-of-prey, and will often delay long before doing so and then rise high in the air before setting off (Bent). Ants in typical 'active' manner. Where not much molested by him shows little fear of man but where persecuted by him the survivors soon become wary and shy.

Nesting Nest in tree, bush or shrub, at varying heights but most often between 3 and 12 metres. Has nested inside buildings (Dubois, in Bent). Nest built of twigs, usually with the addition of strips of bark, roots, grass stems and often paper, especially crepe paper when available, bits of rags and feathers. Mud is used, but not always according to some authorities (see Bent), to bind the materials together, and the inner lining is of fine roots or similar fibrous materials. Both sexes bring materials and build, Hardy found that, in the pairs he watched, males sometimes brought much less than their mates and appeared awkward and inefficient at building, most of the real construction being done by the females.

Prior to nest-building and sometimes during its early stages, pairs indulge in 'false nesting' (Hardy), the male habitually bringing twigs and giving them to the female while she crouches at a particular site. She may arrange these twigs beneath her but no proper nest results. The false nest never becomes the true nest of its owners, although sometimes a different pair may build a true nest on the foundation of such a false nest.

Eggs 2 to 6, usually 4 or 5 in northern parts of its breeding range and 3 or 4 in Florida. Very variable; light olive, buff, pale green, pale brown, pale bluish green, pinkish buff, greyish white or some intermediate shade; spotted or speckled and flecked with various shades of brown, and with paler underlying greyish markings. First clutches usually laid from late March and April to May and June in the more northerly parts of its range but repeat or second nestings may be laid later and there is one remarkable record of apparently recently-fledged young, still with short tails and being fed by the parents, in December in Arkansas (Marshall).

Incubation is normally by the female only, fed both on and off nest by the male. There is, however, one apparently valid record of a pair in which both individuals took part in incubation, 'relieving [each other] at more or less regular intervals', and *each* brought food for the other during its 'off-duty' periods (Thayer). Appears usually not to breed until its second spring, when nearly two years old, but some individuals of both sexes are known to have bred in their first year. Probably much depends on the local social and territorial situation and it is doubtful if first-year birds breed except when, perhaps usually through having been widowed, they pair with an established older bird. Behaviour towards man at nest is variable. Some females sit passively and allow themselves to handled without fleeing or fighting.

In the more northern parts of its range commonly one brood only (per year) appears to be reared although repeat nests are built if the eggs or nestlings are destroyed. Elsewhere, as at Nashville, Tennessee, a second brood may be reared even if the first has been successful. One pair nested a third time when the young of the second brood (one had been fully reared in the first) was removed from the nest when nearly ready to fly (Laskey). In Florida Nicholson found three broods a year to be usual.

Incubation period 16 to 18 days. Young fledge at 17 to 21 days; sometimes as early as 15 days in Florida (Nicholson), but this perhaps represents premature fledging due to disturbance. Both sexes feed and tend the young. The female alone broods them (but see above remarks on incubation). Young begin to find their own food about three weeks after fledging but are fed for longer by the parents who may still give them some food two months after fledging (Laskey).

Voice The alarm and assembly calls are variously transliterated 'jay', 'jayer', 'peer' and so on, the differences probably being due as much to geographical or individual variation in the calls themselves as to the vagaries of the observers. As heard from Blue Jays in New York state between early May and mid-June I wrote it down as 'a loud, rather gull-like scream, variable but not unlike the "kraah" call of *Garrulus glandarius* although higher-pitched, and both higher-pitched and less harsh than the intense versions of the alarm screech of *Garrulus*'. Hardy distinguishes three variants: 'jayer', given at a lower and 'jaay', repeated rapidly, at higher intensities of alarm or excitement; and 'jeer jeer' given immediately after a real or feigned attack on a predator. I thought I could distinguish a difference in tone, comparable to but less marked than that between the 'kraah' call of *Garrulus glandarius* and its alarm screech, between the versions of this call I heard uttered by displaying birds at courtship gatherings and those uttered when mobbing predators or in obvious alarm. Hardy (p.22) confirms this difference, saying that the assembly calls 'are, however, less intensely given and do not connote danger'.

These calls are given when mobbing predators, perhaps in many forms of intense excitement or conflict and, at least the version which I think may be homologous to the 'kraah' call of *Garrulus*, in display. I heard this call given by perched Blue Jays during the bobbing display as well as during the display flight.

Hardy says the 'jay' calls of the adult are derived from the begging call of the nestlings and, as given by juveniles in late summer and early autumn, are somewhat intermediate and more nasal in quality than the equivalent calls of the adults.

I several times heard Blue Jays utter a soft, low 'cheuh-cheuh-cheuh', in tempo not unlike the chatter of a Magpie, *Pica pica*. Perhaps this was a variant of the low, conversational 'kut', 'kuet' or 'kut-kut-kut' described by Hardy. These low, conversational calls are given by members of the pair when together in the early part of the nesting cycle and also when bringing food to the mate. They would thus seem equivalent to the food-offering versions of the appeal call of *Garrulus glandarius*. A captive Blue Jay in the Bronx Zoo, which had just been fed by another, flew restlessly about calling a soft but rather sharp 'yek' or 'tyek', varying this with a lower-pitched, less sharp and more mewing 'aaaa', very like some appeal calls of *Garrulus*.

The 'cleeop, cleeop' which Hardy terms the pump-handle call, is, presumably, the call described elsewhere (in Bent) as 'the creaking, wheel-barrow call, commonly written "whee-oodle"'. It is described by Hardy as bell-like and liquid. It is given with the bobbing display and seems equivalent to a display phrase of *Garrulus*. Hardy says that it is given in low-intensity predator intimidation as well as to intimidate fellow jays and in territorial skirmishes. Possibly a similar self-assertive mood may be elicited by a predator, that does not arouse much fear, as by a conspecific rival. On the other hand, I think it possible that when some individuals of a group of jays gathered around a predator give displays and calls that are typical of intraspecific conflict these may, perhaps, be a response to the presence of one or more of the other jays, not to that of the predator.

Besides the 'cleeop' call, I heard, from Blue Jays in courtship parties, a liquid musical 'pooly-oo, tootoo' and shorter variants of it, a musical 'pee-e' and a high-pitched 'pwilly-pwilly'. These were all given with the bobbing display. Hardy distinguishes another rather similar call as 'wheedle-ee', resembling the sound made by a clothes line on a pulley, which he says seems always to be associated with uncertainty or suppressed excitement and to express 'the anxiety of the males' at courtship gatherings.

It seems highly likely that these liquid and musical or creaking calls are subject to individual variation, possibly sometimes involving vocal mimicry, and that this accounts for the number and variety of transcriptions of them in the literature.

Hardy describes what he terms the 'solicitation call' of the female as 'kueu kueu kueukueukueu'. It is given when begging food from the male as well as when soliciting copulation. Other observers (e.g. Nicholson) have stated that the female's call when food-begging is exactly like that of the young. Hardy, however, describes the food call of the young as harsh, squealing 'squrreesh' changing to a 'rich chortling call' as food is received. It thus seems possible that the Blue Jay, like *Garrulus*, may solicit food either with a juvenile-type call or with a different (but related) call. The 'rich chortling' described as given by young receiving food is doubtless similar or identical to the sounds made by the young of *Garrulus*, *Corvus* and *Pica* when accepting food. I have the impression that it is caused by the bird trying to give the begging call and to swallow food at the same time. Very young nestlings utter a high-pitched squealing 'squee, squee' (Hardy).

After being fed, nestlings utter a series of twittering notes (Hardy), another feature in which behaviour of this species is like that of *Garrulus*. Flying juveniles also utter a call that Hardy writes as 'chur chur' which is only rarely given. He describes as a harsh 'cuz cuz' another rare call of the young that they utter sometimes after feeding and which is accompanied by restlessness.

The song, perhaps better subsong as it seems in this and other jays to be uttered in similar circumstances to the subsongs of some other passerines, has been described (Bent, p.47) as 'a potpourri of faint whistles and various low, sweet notes, some in phrasing and pitch, suggesting a Robin's song . . . . But as the song goes on one realizes that most of the notes are clearly in the Blue Jay's repertoire but are disguised by being jumbled together and delivered gently and peacefully'. Other descriptions of the song agree with that given above. It is usually given when the bird is alone, or at least not engaged in any social activity, and in cover. It seems likely that vocal mimicry may sometimes be involved in the song.

A mechanical-sounding low guttural rattling 'trrrrrrrrrr', very like the guttural clicking call of female Jays, *G. glandarius*, but soft and longer-drawn. Others have described it as 'a rattling "brrrrr"'; 'a grating, pebbly "r-r-rt"'; and 'a dry, wooden rattle, almost a growl'. Probably, as with the apparently equivalent call of *G. glandarius*, there is some individual variation. In the Blue Jay this call is given by both sexes (Hardy). In every case when I both heard and saw a Blue Jay giving this call it performed the bobbing display as it did so, but Hardy (p.21) implies that this is not always the case.

I heard this guttural, rattling call given by members of courting parties and by individuals perched alone, but with others nearby and in sight; also by a bird at the Bronx Zoo just after a large and noisy aeroplane had passed over. Hardy considers this call associated with anxiety but is unable to categorize it; he has heard it at all times of year. I had the impression that it was self-assertive in character. The reason that this species and some other corvids, such as the Lanceolated Jay and Pied Crow, sometimes give similar mechanical-sounding rattling calls immediately after an alarm, or in the presence of apparently mildly frightening stimuli may be because performing a self-assertive act at such a time is psychologically helpful. Men who whistle in the dark and pigeons who indulge in self-assertive display on, apparently, recovering from an alarm, are perhaps comparable phenomena. Calls of this species are on a gramophone record by Kellogg & Allen.

There is some difference of opinion as to what extent the Blue Jay is a vocal mimic. Some observers describe it as an habitual mimic of the calls of many other species (Baird *et al.*; Nehrling), others (see Bent) imply that it either does not mimic or confines its mimicry to the calls of species of *Buteo* (Nicholson). Probably there is much individual and geographical variation but the evidence suggests that at least some wild Blue Jays mimic other species. The idea that vocal mimicry is restricted to the calls of *Buteo* species may, perhaps, be due to these calls being rendered more faithfully, or being more readily identified by the human listener.

Display and social behaviour   The bobbing display consists of a sudden upward thrust of head and body, by flexing and extending the legs at the ankle joint. The movement is straight up and down, not forward as in the equivalent, and perhaps homologous, lateral self-assertive display of *Garrulus*. Hardy (p.21) says that the tail is fanned and the crest erected, but his sketch (p.24) shows the displaying birds with their crests down and tails only slightly spread and this was the feather posture of most of the many Blue Jays I saw give this display. The feathers of face and neck seem to be somewhat erected, making the facial markings prominent, the body feathers are tightly appressed everywhere, in striking contrast to *Garrulus*. I noticed, although this does not seem to have been mentioned by other observers, that the folded wings seemed to be somewhat flattened in a lateral plane, like those of a displaying Magpie, *Pica*. On one occasion, I clearly saw that a presumed male, who was below and to one side of the presumed female he was displaying to, had his flattened wings tilted towards her in a Magpie-like manner.

This bobbing is a characteristic courtship display but appears to be used in other situations most or possibly all of which involve self-assertion in reference to conspecifics (see remarks under 'Voice').

In display flight (at high intensity) the wings are beaten rather more slowly and through a wider arc than usual, this alternating with gliding with wings widely spread, the tail spread and the bill pointed straight forward, not somewhat downward as is otherwise commonly the case. Except when performed at high intensity with fully spread tail the differences between display flight and normal flight seemed to me less noticeable than in *Garrulus glandarius* or many *Corvus* species. Display flight is commonly shown by males (and females?) in courtship parties, and probably also by sexually active birds in other situations.

Hardy describes and figures (p.28) the begging display of female in which, in a crouching posture, she partly opens and quivers her wings and partly raises and spreads her tail. The invitation to copulation is a more intense version of this, in which the wings are fully spread out and the tail erected more steeply and more fully spread. Hardy describes the wing movements sometimes as 'quivering', at others as 'fluttering', but does not draw any distinction between them, thus implying that this species does not have a begging display distinct from a quivering display, as do *Garrulus* and *Corvus*.

Feeding of the female by the male is frequent from early stages of courtship onwards. The precopulation posture of male is upright, with crest erect, body feathers sleeked down, and bill pointing down towards the female.

Noisy and excited social gatherings in late winter and spring are concerned with courtship. Such courting parties usually consist of one female and two or several males who follow her and display to her (Hardy). In the earlier part of the year only adult birds form these courtship parties but later, when the adults are nesting, they consist mostly of yearling birds that will not, in most cases, breed that year. In the courtship 'flocks' courting displays, directed at the female, are interspersed with aggression between the males, display flights, and straggling after the female if she flies away. Presumably the strongest and most persistent male in each group succeeds in pairing with the female. Hardy found that paired birds did not join these parties. Many of the displaying parties of Blue Jays that I watched in New York seemed to consist of males and one female, as described by Hardy; a few, however, seemed to include more than one female. At such gatherings, and at other times, redirected aggression occurs, involving pecking, tearing and hammering at the perch or other inanimate objects.

Nesting pairs hold territory but territorial boundaries appear to be rather ill-defined and the territory is not usually, if ever, defended against all other Blue Jays but only against those individuals who seem, by their sexual or self-assertive behaviour, to be potential rivals (Hardy).

REFERENCES

BAIRD, S. F., BREWER, T. M. & RIDGWAY, R. 1874. *A History of North American Birds* 2: 273–277. Boston.
BEAL, F. E. L. 1897. The Blue Jay and its food. *Year Book of the U.S. Department of Agriculture for 1896*: 197–206.
BENDIRE, C. 1895. *Life Histories of North American Birds* 356–362. Washington.
BENT, A. C. 1946. Life histories of North American jays, crows, and titmice: 32–56. *U.S. Nat. Mus. Bull.* **191**: 118–128.
BLAKE, E. R. 1962. In *Peters' Check-list of Birds of the World* vol. 15.
DADISMAN, A. J. 1918. Feeding the Blue Jays. *Bird Lore* **20**: 352–353.

GESELL, A. 1939. What did the Blue Jay do with the nut? *Science* **89**: 35.
HARDY, J. W. 1961. Studies in behaviour and phylogeny of certain New World jays (Garrulinae). *Univ. Kansas Sci. Bull.* **42**, No. 2.
KELLOGG, P. P. & ALLEN, A. A. 1959. *A Field Guide to Bird Songs of Eastern and Central North America.* Boston.
LASKEY, A. R. 1958. Blue Jays at Nashville, Tennessee; movements, nesting, age. *Bird Banding* **29**: 211–218.
MARSHALL, T. 1949. Late Blue Jay nesting. *Wilson Bull.* **61**: 189.
NICHOLSON, D. J. 1936. Observations on the Florida Blue Jay. *Wilson Bull.* **48**: 26–33.
PITELKA, F. A. 1946. Age in relation to migration in the Blue Jay. *Auk* **63**: 82–84.
RAND, A. L. 1937. Notes on the development of two young Blue Jays (*Cyanocitta cristata*). *Proc. Linn. Soc. New York*, No. 48: 27–58.
THAYER, H. C. 1901. Our Blue Jay neighbours. *Bird Lore* **3**: 50–53.

STELLER'S JAY   *Cyanocitta stelleri*

Corvus stelleri Gmelin, 1788, Syst. Nat., 1 (1), p. 370. Based on Steller's Crow of Latham, 1781, Gen. Synop. Birds, 1 (1), p. 387.

Description Steller's Jay shows much geographic variation. Very many, possibly too many, different races have been described and named. The main tendency is from black-headed, grey- or black-backed birds in the northern parts of its range to blue-headed, blue-backed birds in Central America, at the southern extremity. The situation is, however, quite complex and has been discussed in detail elsewhere (Moore; Brown, 1963b). In central Mexico a circle of about 450 km in diameter, through west-central and eastern Michoacán, north-eastern Guanajuato, Hidalgo, Veracruz, Puebla and central Guerrero, has several breeding populations of blue-crested Steller's Jays but enclosed within it, chiefly on the higher mountains, are black-crested populations. Also, intergrades are found in some areas. In this Mexican part of its range the blue-crested forms are found at altitudes of from 1500 to 2500 metres, but the black-crested forms go as high as 3900 metres (Moore).

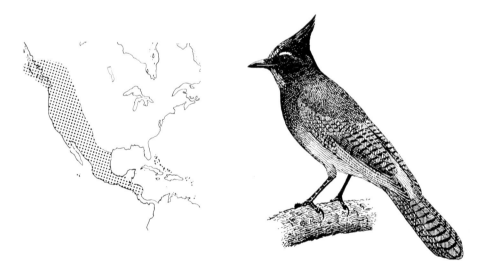

Nominate *C. s. stelleri* is a little larger than a Blue Jay and similar in proportions but with a conspicuously longer crest and slightly longer legs and more slender bill. Head, including crest and extreme upper breast, brownish black or black, with slight gloss; light blue streaks on forehead formed by blue tips to some feathers; throat feathers with greyish white central parts, giving a pale, streaky throat. Mantle, back and sides of neck dark brownish grey to greyish black, not usually contrasting noticeably with black of head. Lower breast a dark slightly greenish blue, becoming brighter and more silvery on flanks, under tail coverts and rump. Lesser wing coverts and primary coverts dull blue with obscure darker barring. Outer webs of primaries (the only parts visible when wing is folded) deep blue to silvery greenish blue, dullest and palest near ends of outer primaries. Rest of wings deep rich blue to purplish blue, the inner secondaries with usually conspicuous narrow black bars and the other feathers with obscure or vestigial bars. Tail dark rich blue or purplish blue, inclining to silvery greenish blue on fringes of basal half of outer feathers, and narrowly barred with black. Black barring on the tail very variable but usually conspicuous towards end of tail and obscure elsewhere. Inner webs of wing quills dark grey or blackish; undersides of wing and tail similar but with a silvery sheen. As with other predominantly blue birds appearance varies much with the incidence of the light; seen against the light Steller's Jays can look very dull. Irides dark brown. Bill, legs and feet black. Sexes alike.

Juvenile has underparts and rump a dark smoky grey, not greenish blue; crest shorter and without blue frontal streaks; wings and tail a little paler and less purplish blue. Bill at first pale but darkens before or (at latest) at onset of post-juvenal moult.

The above description is of nominate *C. s. stelleri*, from southern Alaska and coastal British Columbia south to western Washington and north-western Oregon. *C. s. carlottae*, from the Queen Charlotte Islands, British Columbia, is the largest race, between Blue Jay and European Jay in size, and darker in colour, especially on the back and mantle which are almost coal black. *C. s. annectens*, from the interior of British Columbia and south-western Alberta south through eastern Washington, northern Idaho, and western Montana to north-eastern Oregon and north-western Wyoming, is like *stelleri* but has a cluster of pale-tipped or pale-edged feathers forming a silvery spot above the eye and is slightly paler in colour, with the dark grey back, mantle and neck contrasting more with the black head and crest.

C. s. carbonacea is a little smaller than *annectens*, has a rather longer crest, lacks the white spot over the eye, has the pale markings on the throat less prominent and the sides of the neck and upper parts of a more brownish grey. It is found in the central coastal belt of California from Marin and Contra Costa Counties south through Montery County. *C. s. frontalis*, from central Oregon south through the mountains of California (except central segment of the coastal belt and the south-eastern desert area) and central western Nevada, is very like *carbonacea* but is slightly smaller and paler, and duller in colour. Its head and crest are dull greyish black, with the blue streaks on the forehead extending to some degree over the crown, and a bluish tinge to the long crest feathers. Its mantle and back are dull smoke grey, tinged with greenish blue on the lower back. The blue parts of the plumage are also paler, especially on rump and upper tail coverts.

C. s. macrolopha, is found in the Rocky Mountain district of the United States and the Sierra Madre Occidental of Mexico, from eastern and southern Nevada, Utah, south-eastern Wyoming, south-western South Dakota, and western South Dakota, and western Nebraska south to northern Sonora, northern Chihuahua, and south-western Texas. Its forehead is conspicuously streaked with silvery white. It has a white stripe over the eye and a white fleck below and adjacent to it. Its mantle, back and hind neck are brownish grey and contrast strongly with the deep black face and very long glossy black crest. *C. s. diademata*, of the Sierra Madre Oriental of Mexico, is very similar (see sketch). The juveniles of these forms differ from the adults in comparable manner to those of nominate *stelleri*.

C. s. azteca, from Mexico, in the mountains of eastern Michoacán, State of Mexico, Distrito Federal, Morelos, Puebla, and west-central Veracruz, is very like *macrolopha* but has the grey of the upperparts strongly tinged with blue, the white marks above and below the eye more extensive, the crown feathers tipped with dull blue and the long crest feathers more or less tinged with dark blue at their tips. *C. s. coronata*, of much of south and east Mexico, has a blue or purplish blue crest which is usually a little shorter than that of *azteca*, its back and mantle are a deep, soft and only slightly greyish blue. *C. s. purpurea* of the Highlands of western and central Michoacán is said to be of a richer and more purplish blue with a darker throat. *C. s. teotepecencis*, from the high mountains of central and southern Guerrero, is said to resemble *purpurea* but to have a richer blue crest and conspicuous white throat patch. As has been stated in the introduction, intergrades between blue and black-crested forms also occur in Mexico.

C. s. ridgwayi, of Central America, from the highlands of Chiapas and western Guatemala south to El Salvador and Honduras (where it intergrades with *suavis*) tends to be rather shorter-crested than *coronata*, and a richer blue in colour, with the streaks on forehead less whitish, a distinct greyish white throat and very conspicuous white patches above and below the eyes. It tends also to have a rather larger and coarser-looking bill. *C. s. suavis*, from the highlands of Nicaragua, is very similar to *ridgwayi* but has a smaller and more greyish throat patch, shorter crest, larger bill and is generally of a slightly darker blue. The juveniles of these blue races have the body colour predominantly greyish blue. They either lack the pale or white markings on forehead and about the eyes or have them only slightly indicated.

Field characters Darkish blue or blackish and blue jay with conspicuous erectile crest and no white on wings and tail. Crest distinguishes at once from all *Aphelocoma* species; lack of white on wings and tail from Blue Jay and most others. If seen, barring on wings or tail diagnostic, as the only other American jay with wing and tail bars is the conspicuously white-tipped Blue Jay.

Distribution and habitat Western North America and Central America: southern Alaska (except Alaska Peninsula and Aleutian Islands), western and southern British Columbia, south-western Alberta, western Montana, Wyoming, south-western South Dakota and western Nebraska south through southern California and Mexico to El Salvador and northern Nicaragua; east to east-central Colorado, eastern New Mexico and south-western Texas.

Inhabits coniferous and mixed coniferous and broadleaved woodlands. In extensive forest it is more numerous near breaks in the forest than deep within it. Often in comparatively open woodland, parks and inhabited areas with tree cover. Altitudinally, over much of its range, it is replaced by Clark's Nutcracker at higher elevations and by the Scrub Jay at lower levels, but often occurs in same places with them at the higher and lower limits of its range, respectively.

Feeding and general habits Feeds both on ground and in trees. Flicks aside leaf litter and digs in ground in usual manner with sideways strokes of bill, pries under or tears off loose bark and so on. Takes seeds, nuts, fruits, berries, insects and other invertebrates; also eggs and young of smaller birds. Acorns and seeds of conifers are important foods when available. Of the invertebrates taken quite a number are wasps and wild bees, as well as beetles, caterpillars, moths, grasshoppers and spiders. Readily takes many foods supplied by man such as bread, biscuits, peanuts, sunflower seed, suet, meat scraps and cheese. Often regularly visits picnic sites and bird tables.

Acorns and other hard or large food items are held under one or both feet and opened with the bill. Brown (1964) observed this behaviour closely and discovered that only the lower mandible is used to make the initial incision. The blows are delivered with the bill slightly open so that the lower mandible strikes the object and the upper mandible glides over its outer surface. Habitually stores food, especially such things as acorns and sunflower seeds, in usual jay manner (Abbott). Brown's (1964) observation that in winter acorns are no longer 'commonly utilized' suggests that such stores may not be an important source of food. Further observations on this point are needed, particularly in view of Brown's own findings (1963a) that, when storing sunflower seeds given by him, each jay took them back to its own area of dominance and hid them there. Has been noted to eat quantities of snow even when water was available (Abbott).

Commonly in pairs or small parties, the latter often consisting of paired birds that have joined neighbours for mutual display, to mob a predator, or to visit a food source. Larger numbers may aggregate in good feeding areas. Adult paired birds appear to be often, and perhaps nearly always, resident in or near their breeding areas but some birds (possibly mostly birds of the year?) evidently winter at lower altitudes than they frequent in summer (Bent). There are also local migrations or eruptions, perhaps connected with overpopulation or failure of food supplies. Brown found that, in the area of California where he studied them, the main dispersal of birds of the year took place in September and there seemed to be little tendency for them to return later to the areas where they had been reared.

Usually gives way to other jay species where their living areas overlap. Is dominated by Scrub Jays except in the immediate vicinity of an active Steller's Jay's nest (Brown, 1964). Typically rather shy of man even, or perhaps especially, in thinly populated regions, but readily becomes tame where it constantly sees people who do not harm it.

Nesting Nests in trees, usually in conifers; sometimes in shrubs or bushes or in hollows or cavities in trees (Goss).   Nesting inside buildings evidently rare, but may locally be regular and extensive in spite of deliberate destruction of such nests by man (Bryant, in Bent, p.67).   Nest similar to that of Blue Jay. Usually from 2·5 to 5 metres above ground but heights of 0·6 to over 30 metres recorded.

Eggs 2 to 6, like the bluish and greenish types of Blue Jay eggs.   Nests with eggs have been found in mid- and late April in central America; in April, May and June in California; and in May and July in Alaska.   The later dates probably represent second attempts.   Both parents build.   Incubation usually (perhaps almost always) by the female only; fed on and off nest by the male.   It has, however, been claimed that, at least in Alaska, both sexes incubate (Gabrielsen & Lincoln).   Young fed by parents for a month or more after fledging.

Voice By far the most intensive study of the voice of Steller's Jays I have read is that of Brown (1964), from which the information given here has (except where otherwise stated) been compiled.   It has, of necessity, been condensed and I have in some cases given my own interpretations as to the functions of a particular call or its relationship to those of other species, deduced from the very full data Brown gives on the situations in which the call is given.   Brown's names are used here for the various calls.   There is evidence of some geographic variation in voice but the other less detailed descriptions I have read do not suggest any very basic differences.

Song is of low amplitude and consists of a medley of whistled, harsh or gurgled notes and snapping or popping sounds run together; with frequent repetitions.   It resembles the songs of many other American jays.   It is given in courtship, especially by the male when *courtship-circling*; also by birds of either sex when alone.   The songs of first-year birds in autumn tend to be louder than those of adults and to include other calls in imperfect form.   When singing alone Steller's Jay adopts a characteristic near-vertical posture with head stretched slightly forward and turning slowly from side to side as it sings, giving the sounds a ventriloquial effect.   Sometimes, as with many other passerines, song is uttered when the singer appears mildly anxious or slightly alarmed.

The *guttural* notes could be written 'ut' when given at lower and 'aap' or 'amp' when given at high intensity.   The latter are given with open and the former with nearly closed bill.   The *guttural* notes are given in many contexts, especially in connection with the early stages of the breeding cycle.   They are uttered by both sexes.

The *ow* note is very similar to the high-intensity form of the *guttural* but higher-pitched, more nasal, and louder.   It is often repeated in short series.   It is given mainly, perhaps entirely, by females; during encounters between pairs and in courtship parties.

The *rattle* is a mechanical-sounding call with a rolling quality.   It resembles the rattle of the Scrub Jay except for having, usually, a change in tone quality from a long 'o' sound to an 'ee' sound about half-way through the call.   This change accompanies a gradual opening of the bill.   It is given by females only.

The *rattle* is not always accompanied by a stereotyped display as are the presumably homologous rattling calls of *Aphelocoma* and *Garrulus*.   It may be given either from a perch or in flight.   It is uttered at all times of year but most frequently in the pre-incubation stages of the breeding cycle.   It is usually given in response to other jays and is used in both hostile and sexual contexts.   It seems primarily a self-assertive call.   It also indicates the sex of the bird giving it and thus seems to be equivalent to the homologous calls of many other corvids.

The *musical* note lacks the loud, harsh quality of most calls.   It is a high, muted whistle usually all on one pitch and ending abruptly with a short popping sound audible only at very close range.   It is subject to much individual variation; the *musicals* of three different males were transcribed as 'oot', 'woot' and 'toodle-oot'.   Given by males only.   It is uttered both perched and in flight.   It is given chiefly in aggressive contexts, when threatening or supplanting other males that have trespassed into the caller's territory.   Sometimes given when courting a female, especially if she utters the *rattle*.   Sometimes appears to be used in hostile contexts towards other species, in one instance to a human being near the nest.

The *too-leet* call appears to be given in the same situations as the *musical*; although some individuals seem never to use it. It is a shrill, whistling call, rather high-pitched, and with the second syllable higher than the first. Sometimes a tri-syllabic version is uttered. Usually it is repeated two to four times, sometimes more.

The *wah* is a harsh, nasal call that lacks an abrupt beginning or end. It is given by both sexes at all times of year. This is the typical predator-mobbing call and it is given in other contexts that appear to involve conflict or alarm. It is also (surprisingly) given in submissive begging and food begging and while performing aggressive sidling. Possibly under these different circumstances versions are given that are distinguishable to the garruline if not to the human ear. As with other predator-mobbing calls, conspecifics at a little distance are usually attracted to approach and investigate the cause of the outcry. I think this is the call recorded by Kellogg & Allen as the 'shack' call. Their recorded version sounds very like the alarm screech of *Garrulus* but less sharp.

The *growl* (which Brown says is, perhaps, an inappropriate term as the sound does not much resemble the growling of a mammal) is like an intense version of the *wah* call. It is generally given in phrases of two notes, down-slurred with the initial higher-pitched part of each having a musical quality and the lower-pitched end part a rasping or grating quality. It is given, but rarely, by the male in aggressive contexts.

The *shook* is a loud repeated call, sometimes up to five 'shooks' per second being uttered. It is given by both sexes and there seems to be a slight sexual difference, the *shook* calls of the female being slightly higher-pitched. This is apparently the 'wek-wek' call of Kellogg & Allen, on whose record it sounds a rapid chatter, rather like that of a European Magpie but in quicker tempo and less loud.

The basic use of this call, or at least of one version of it that consists of three or four very loud abrupt 'shooks' and then silence, is as a hawk-alarm. This version is given at sight of a nearby *Accipiter*, sometimes while the caller is diving headlong into cover.

The *shook* call is also given as a response to sudden disturbances such as loud noises or low-flying aircraft and sometimes in hostile situations, both towards other species, as when attacked by American Robins, *Turdus migratorius*, and when attacking conspecifics. It is commonly heard when a group of mobbing or courting jays is dispersing, from individuals or pairs flying from the scene or about to do so. It is rarely heard during predator-mobbing.

The *tee-ar* call is a clear whistled call resembling the scream of the Red-tailed Hawk, *Buteo jamaicensis*. It is given in situations where it seems likely that the jay is mildly alarmed and also, in at least one instance, in response to the sight of a Red-tailed Hawk (Brown, 1964, p.302). I think it likely that this call is an example of vocal mimicry even although it may now, as Brown suggests, be transmitted from one jay to another. The situations in which it is given (Brown, 1964) closely parallel those in which *Garrulus glandarius* mimics the calls of its predators.

The *squawk* is a loud, noisy but variable call given, usually only once, when the jay is either being closely pursued by another jay or by some other species; or when diving to within a few inches of a predator while mobbing. It is not usually given unless body contact has either just been made or seems imminent. It is thus uttered in the same context as the grating note of *Garrulus glandarius*.

Various other calls were heard by Brown on relatively few occasions. Some of them were similar to calls of other birds and of squirrels and may, I think, have been imitations of them. Brown is of the opinion that vocal mimicry plays only a small part in the behaviour of Steller's Jay (Brown, 1964, p.305). Pettingill (in Wetmore) on the contrary states that it is 'a superb mimic'.

Display and social behaviour   These (and other) aspects of this species have been intensively investigated by Brown (1963, 1964), from whose works the information here has been compiled and condensed and whose terms are used for the displays and calls he describes.

In the *wing-spreading* display the wings are jerked in and out, folding and unfolding the primaries. At high intensity the primaries (but not the secondaries) are fully spread; at low intensity, which is more frequent, the wings are only lifted slightly away from the body. The wings are not fluttered or quivered but jerked in and out. The body may be held at a variety of angles but very rarely horizontally. The displaying bird usually faces the individual eliciting the *wing-spreading*.

Wing-spreading is given by both sexes but most often by males, very rarely by unpaired individuals and never, so far as has been observed, by territory-less individuals. It is given in a great many situations whose common factors seem to be conflict between two opposing impulses (e.g. to continue feeding or to attack an intruder) or temporary frustration through the uncooperativeness of another individual or environmental factors. When giving the wing-spreading display the *guttural* note is given or sometimes if the bird is a female, the *ow* note.

Wing-flicking, in which, as in many other passerines, the wings are jerked quickly off the back and on to it again, and the tail is flicked up at same time, appears to be a flight-intention movement as with other species.

Brown describes as '*gaping and appeasement begging*' an apparently rather rare display which seems equivalent to the wing and tail-quivering displays of *Garrulus* and *Corvus* but which in form and movements does not differ significantly from the begging of the fledged juveniles except for being characterized by withdrawal from, rather than approach to, the bird at which it is directed. In this display the bird usually crouches; if on the ground or a flat surface the tail is pressed against the substrate. The head and neck are retracted and the juvenile-type begging call is uttered with open bill. The wings may be fluttered but not so intensely as in genuine food-begging. This display was seen from two males and two females low in the dominance hierarchy when approaching other jays at an artificial food source and in response to attack from a dominant jay that had been too closely approached. In the latter case 'the short retreat followed by crouching, gaping, and giving the *wah* call was often apparently successful in inhibiting the dominant bird's attacks'.

That this display, or what appears to be a form of it, can approximate very closely to the quivering display of *Garrulus* is shown by Brown's observation that 'An unmated male who persistently remained in the territory of another male was several times seen fluttering his wings silently, with his bill closed and *vibrating his tail rapidly up and down* . . . while [the territory owner] called aggressively and bill-rapped a few feet away' (my italics).

The begging of the mated female differs from the appeasement begging described above in that *wah* calls are never given. If, in fact, the female Steller's Jay never (even when very hungry) begs for food with juvenile-type calls, this is a remarkable difference from the behaviour of *Garrulus*, *Corvus* and *Pica*.

Aggressive sidling appears equivalent to, and possibly homologous with, the self-assertive lateral display of *Garrulus*. The displaying bird typically aligns sideways on to its opponent, often reversing its direction by a jump through 180 degrees. The tail may be partly spread and/or tilted towards the other bird so as to show its dorsal surface. The body and wings may also be tilted similarly. The crest is usually raised, often fully so, the body is held nearly horizontal, and the legs may be strongly flexed. The head is frequently extended, probably to facilitate calling, and may be lowered in a sudden bow. While performing *aggressive sidling* both sexes may give the *shook* call, males may give the *musical* call, and females the *rattle* call. The display is often interspersed with vigorous pecking, digging and other feeding and food-seeking movements. It is much more frequently given by males than by females.

This display is typically used by two birds that are, in the place where they display, of nearly equal status. It commonly follows or, less often, precedes actual fighting. Usually both birds utter the same calls. It is not, so far as is known, given by unpaired or immature individuals.

Sexual sidling differs from *aggressive sidling* in that the crest is kept flat or only slightly erected, the head is held upright, the body less horizontal, the *shook* call is not uttered, *song* being the usual vocal accompaniment, redirected aggression rarely occurs, the birds taking part are of opposite sex, and the female generally remains still.

Sexual sidling follows or precedes *courtship circling*. In this the male circles round the female, about 15 cm from her, with his wings and tail more or less (according to intensity of display) tilted towards the female so as to show their dorsal surfaces. This courtship circling may culminate in mounting and copulation. More rarely the female may display to the male in this way by circling around him.

Erection of the back feathers, not including those of the rump, is sometimes seen in aggressive contexts. Usually the bird doing this is in a more or less horizontal position and has the crest lowered. The tail is often spread. This would seem to be homologous to the defensive threat posture of *Garrulus* and *Corvus*.

The crest is raised (apart from situations, such as bathing, which involve erection of most or all of the contour plumage) in situations involving aggression or alarm but not, or only to a slight degree, in sexual contexts. In general the degree of agonistic arousal seems indicated by the degree of crest erection. Tail flicking is shown as an apparent flight-intention movement. Brown (1964, p.254) concludes that 'tail-flicking in the Steller's Jay may be interpreted as the result of low-level activation of the neural pathways controlling vertical movements of the tail which find their primary function during jumps, take-offs, and landings'.

Displacement behaviour is shown in agonistic contexts. It involves a good deal of redirected aggression, and the movements used are those normally used in feeding and food-seeking (and fighting?) such as pecking, hammering, and digging.

Self-assertive displays take place between pairs at territorial borders. Resident pairs appear deliberately to visit the border areas to provoke such meeting and mutual threatening with one or more neighbouring pairs. This is usually followed by courtship between the pair after they have withdrawn further into their own territory. Brown did not observe courtship parties involving unpaired birds. The adult birds are paired and centred on their own territories at all seasons but territories are ill-defined. The defended area is centred on the nest, in whose vicinity each paired male Steller's Jay is dominant over all other Jays throughout the year. In the same area his mate is dominant over all other females. As the distance from this area is increased the number of jays subordinate to the nest-owners decreases and the number dominant to them increases. These concentric zones of decreasing dominance result in a complex dominance structure, and dominance relationships are continually undergoing readjustment. Defence of the immediate vicinity of an active nest is usually intense and conspicuous but defence of further areas of dominance is variable; the same bird (according to its demeanour?) may be attacked at some times and ignored at others. Females do not take their mates' ranks in the dominance hierarchy. Neither males nor females intervene in quarrels between their mate and another jay of the same sex. Males are dominant over their mates although there is usually no visible dominance (supplanting attacks etc.) in April, May and June. Brown (1963a) recorded only 7 cases of a female supplanting her mate, out of 5632 such encounters, and 6 of these involved the same female.

REFERENCES

ABBOTT, C. G. 1929. Watching Long-crested Jays. *Condor* 31: 124–125.
BENT, A. C. 1946. Life histories of North American jays, crows, and titmice. *Bull. U.S. Nat. Mus.* 191 : 118–128.
BROWN, J. L. 1963a. Aggressiveness, dominance, and social organisation in the Steller Jay. *Condor* 65: 460–484.
—— 1963b. Ecogeographic variation and introgression in an avian visual signal: the crest of the Steller's Jay, *Cyanocitta stelleri*. *Evolution* 17: 23–39.
—— 1964. The integration of agonistic behavior in the Steller's Jay *Cyanocitta stelleri* (Gmelin). *Univ. Calif. Pub. Zool.* 60: 223–328.
GABRIELSON, I. N. & LINCOLN, F. C. 1959. *The Birds of Alaska* p. 612. Pennsylvania and Washington.
GOSS, N. S. 1885. *Cyanocitta stelleri frontalis* nesting in holes in trees. *Auk* 2: 217.
KELLOGG, P. P. & ALLEN, A. A. 1962. *Field Guide to Bird Songs of Western North America*. Boston.
MOORE, R. T. 1954. A new jay from Mexico. *Proc. Biol. Soc. Wash.* 67: 235–237.
PITELKA, F. A. 1958. Timing of molt in Steller Jays of the Queen Charlotte Islands, British Columbia. *Condor* 60: 38–49.
WETMORE, A. 1964. *Song and Garden Birds of North America* p. 141. Washington.

SCRUB JAY (*californica* and *sumichrasti* group)   *Aphelocoma coerulescens*

Garrulus californicus Vigors, 1839, in Zool. Beechey's Voy., p. 21, pl. 5.

Description About size of Blue Jay but crestless and with proportionately longer and rather more graduated tail and slightly shorter and more rounded wings. Forehead, crown, nape and sides of neck deep and usually slightly purplish blue. Face and ear coverts dark grey, suffused with blue on lower part of face. Narrow white stripe above eye dividing greyish face from blue crown. Throat and central part of upper breast dull white with ill-defined grey streaks (grey feather bases, and central shafts on some feathers). Blue of sides of neck extends as a band, often narrow or obsolescent at median part, around the whitish breast area, a combination of blue and partly blue feathers giving this effect. Underparts medium to very pale creamy grey, shading to white on ventral regions, under tail coverts sometimes tinged blue. Back light to medium greyish brown or brownish grey; rump similar but more or less tinged with blue. Wings, tail and upper tail coverts a fairly bright blue, brightest and palest on the upper tail coverts and darkest on the tail. Inner webs of wing quills (where not visible when wing folded) dark grey. Underside of wings and tail dark silvery grey. Irides dark brown. Bill, legs and feet black.

Female usually a little paler and duller than male, often with some reduction of the blue pectoral band. Juvenile has back, head, face, sides of neck and pectoral band greyish brown, without blue except for a tinge on top of head. Wings and tail paler blue than adult and with brownish tips to greater coverts; lesser and median wing coverts bluish grey, edged buffish brown. Bill, legs and feet brown or brownish black. Newly-hatched young naked.

The above description covers *C. coerulescens californica* and several generally recognized but very slightly differentiated races (see especially Pitelka who describes the geographical variation in this and other *Aphelocoma* species in great detail). *A. c. insularis*, from Santa Cruz Island, off southern California, is larger and much darker, deep hyacinthine blue and dark greyish brown above, darker creamy grey below, with a very contrasting dark blue pectoral band, and light blue under tail coverts. It also has a proportionately longer bill, with a tendency for the female's bill to be markedly smaller than the male's.

A. c. sumichrasti, from south eastern Mexico, is a lighter blue on head, wings and tail. It has only a suggestion of a blue pectoral band at sides of breast and its underparts are a very pale greyish cream. The white eyestripe is smaller and less extensive. *A. c. remota*, from south-western Mexico, is similar but a shade duller and paler.

Field characters Crestless blue and grey jay with white throat and blue 'necklace'. From above, grey back contrasting sharply with blue head and tail.

Distribution and habitat Western U.S.A. in extreme south-western Washington, the Williamette Valley of interior western Oregon, south-central and south-western Oregon, California, Baja California and Santa Cruz Island of the Santa Barbara group off southern California. Mountains of the south-western part of the Mexican Plateau, and south-western Mexico, in the Sierra Madre del Sur.

Inhabits scrub, shrubbery and woodland, most commonly in broken ground along streamsides, forest borders and other places with extensive scrub cover. Also in desert vegetation of cacti, mesquites etc.; mangrove swamps, and sometimes in orchards and other cultivated areas.

Feeding and general habits Feeds both on the ground and in the branches. Takes many kinds of insects and other invertebrates, including beetles, grasshoppers, crickets, bees, wasps, caterpillars and spiders, eggs and nestlings, mice, small reptiles and small frogs. Of vegetable foods acorns are probably the most important but it also takes almonds, green walnuts, cultivated grain, elderberries, cherries, plums, blackberries, raspberries and other fruits. Habitually hides food and is an important agent in spreading oakwoods uphill (Grinnell). Has been known to take eggs and young of domestic fowls. Methods of breaking up and hiding food almost certainly identical with those of the Florida race of the species (q.v.).

When mobbing domestic cats (and other predators?) may approach from behind, peck their tails and then immediately flee in similar manner to Magpie or some typical crows (*Corvus* sp.).

The pair appears to be the basic social unit but it is also found in small parties and numbers will gather to any attraction or disturbance. Where not much persecuted usually bold and will closely approach humans; at other times, and especially when near nest, wary and suspicious.

Hops on the ground. Flight sometimes appears slow and laboured. Often flies down slopes in a series of long shallow curves. Probably much of the behaviour of *A. c. woodhouseii* (q.v.) is shared by this group of the species.

Nesting Nests in trees, bushes or shrubs, usually fairly low down. Typical jay nest of twigs with inner lining of fine roots, fibres and sometimes horsehair. The twigs of the foundation are said sometimes to be mixed with moss, straw and other materials.

Eggs 2 to 6; clutches of 2 or 3 most usual in the arid parts of its range. Usually greenish blue to pale olive green, spotted, speckled and sometimes blotched with darker and lighter shades of drab or olive brown, with underlying grey or lilac markings. Less often the eggs are whitish, buff or light green with reddish markings.

Both sexes build but only the female normally incubates and broods. Both sexes feed and tend the young. Incubation probably 14 to 16 days (Bent).

Voice Within the *californica* group of this species there would appear to be either some geographical variation in voice or, which is perhaps more likely, this has been suggested by individual differences of the birds or their transcribers. Grinnell & Storer (in Bent) describe, for *C. c. superciliosa* (now considered a synonym of *C. c. oocleptica*), a staccato 'cheek, cheek, cheek' repeated three to ten times; a slow 'chú-ick, chú-ick, chú-ick' usually repeated three times; a still slower 'schwee-ick' repeated two to six times; a series of 'mildly harsh' notes sounding like 'kwish, kwish, kwish', usually three to five times in quick succession; a softer 'kschu-ee' or 'jai-ee', usually given singly, and a subdued guttural 'krr'r'r'r' given by members of a family party. When attending young in the nest the parents utter a low crooning call (presumably a food offering call and homologous to the very similar-sounding call of *Garrulus glandarius*).

Mrs Bailey (in Bent) describes the voice of nominate *californica* as strikingly different from that of Steller's Jay, 'having a flat tone and being uttered with unseemly haste'. A frequent call 'used apparently to arouse attention' (Alarm call?) is a 'quick "quay-quay-quay-quay-quay-quay-quay" ', another is a more emphatic 'boy'ee boy'ee', another an inquiring 'quay-kee?'. Other descriptions of its calls seem to refer to slightly differing transcriptions of the above. Vocal mimicry has been claimed and would seem likely but I have not seen evidence of it.

The Santa Cruz race has been described as having a Magpie-like chattering and also an exquisite warbling song.

Display and social behaviour Presumably as those of other forms of the species (q.v.) although probably resembling *woodhouseii* rather than *coerulescens* where these two differ.

Other names California Jay, Long-tailed Jay, Nicasio Jay, Belding's Jay, Xantus' Jay, Santa Cruz Jay.

REFERENCES

BAIRD, S. F., BREWER, T. M. & RIDGWAY, R. 1874. *A History of North American Birds* **2**: 288–291.
BENT, A. C. 1946. Life histories of North American jays, crows, and titmice. *U.S. Nat. Mus. Bull:* **191** 118–128.
GRINNELL, J. 1936. Uphill Planters. *Condor* **7**: 80–82.
MARSHALL, J. T. 1957. Birds of pine-oak woodland in Southern Arizona and adjacent Mexico, *Pacific Coast Avifauna* No. 32, published by Cooper Orn. Soc.
PETERSON, R. T. 1961. *A Field Guide to Western Birds.* Cambridge, Mass.
PITELKA, F. A. 1951. Speciation and ecologic distribution in American Jays of the genus *Aphelocoma*. *Univ. Calif. Publs Zool.* **50**: 195–464.

SCRUB JAY (*woodhouseii* group)   *Aphelocoma coerulescens*

Cyanocitta woodhouseii Baird, 1858, in Baird, Cassin and Lawrence, Rept. Expl. and Surv. R. R. Pac., 9, pp. 584–585.

Description   Like *A. coerulescens californica* (q.v.) but bill tending to be more slender and less hooked at tip.   Colour pattern similar but blue parts lighter and less bright.   The brownish grey of the back is strongly suffused with light blue, and not sharply demarcated from the blue nape and hind neck.   Predominantly greyish blue feather edges form conspicuous streaks on the bluish white throat.   Underparts, below the breast, ashy grey tinged with blue and not contrasting with the light blue pectoral band so strongly as these parts do in other forms of the species.   Iris brown.   Bill, legs and feet black.   Age and sex differences comparable with those in other forms of the species.   The races *woodhouseii*, *nevadae*, *texana*, *grisea*, and *cyanotis* are referable to this group.

Field characters   As previous group but grey of back clouded with blue and not sharply demarcated from deeper blue head and tail.

Distribution and habitat   South-western U.S.A. and Mexico: in south-eastern Oregon, southern Idaho, Utah and southern Wyoming, south through Arizona, extreme south-western New Mexico (Sierra Hachita), western and southern Colorado and western Oklahoma, Texas and northern and east-central Mexico south to Jalisco and central Guanajuato.

Habitat as *californica* group but this form is perhaps even more prone to inhabit open arid country with (compared with other jay habitats) relatively little cover.   Isolated pairs occur on almost bare canyon sides and in dry foothills with Piñon Pine, *Pinus edulis*.

Feeding and general habits   As other forms of the species, so far as known, except that many observers have emphasized that the seeds of the Piñon Pine are often an important food, except for the race *cyanotis* which, like those in the *californica* group, relies rather on acorns as a staple vegetable food (Pitelka).

Usually much more shy of man and wary than are other forms of the species.   'Flight more laboured than that of Mexican, Blue and Steller's Jays.   Immediately upon launching into the air, *woodhouseii* resembles in flight the thrashers (*Toxostoma*), the path of flight being up and down, the tail flitting from side to side . . . a peculiar sound (like that of the Mourning Dove) is made by the wings . . . .   If the jay flies a long distance, it eventually moves more easily, it may alternately glide and flap its wings' (Hardy). Lives in pairs (presumably in family parties immediately after breeding) and is highly territorial, although some areas may be frequented by several pairs and not defended by any, and, as with other territorial species, trespassing quite often occurs.

When either member of a pair is seeking food or nest material on the ground or in low cover, the other usually perches on top of a shrub or some other vantage point, where it functions as a 'sentry'.   This behaviour is thought to be correlated with the relatively open habitat (Hardy).

Nesting   Nest as in other forms of the species but appears more often to consist of grass or weed stems as well as of twigs and the usual inner cup of rootlets, fibres, hairs and similar materials.   Eggs like those of the *californica* group but rather more often with purplish or reddish brown markings.   Nests with eggs are commonly found in April and May, recently-fledged young in late May and early June.

Both sexes build.   Hardy found that a pair that he watched when building took turns in collecting material, one bird always perching high, apparently 'on guard', while its mate collected material.   When they brought material from a distance both birds would collect some, separately, before flying to the nest. Both sexes feed the young. Incubation and brooding probably by female only. Young that have recently left the nest and are active respond by instantly 'freezing' and remaining perfectly quiet for about a minute if the parent gives a single (alarm?) call (Linsdale). When the observer squeaked the parents at once came and mobbed noisily, the young remaining silent.

Voice The calls appear to be the same as or similar to those of the *californica* group, although descriptions suggest that the 'accent' of *woodhouseii* may be less harsh and loud. Hardy distinguishes a loud, repeated 'kwesh, kwesh' which is the usual alarm call, and a suppressed, begging 'greer greer' used when food begging, sometimes by the feeding male as well as by the begging female. Homologous with, and perhaps the same in sound as the hiccup note of the Florida Scrub Jay, is what Hardy describes as 'a rattling br'r'r'r''. He considers it is often given 'in situations of seeming anxiety'. He did, however, hear it given in territorial situations in which other interpretations seem possible. He implies that in *woodhouseii* it is not always given with an accompanying upward movement, which latter he interprets as a flight-intention movement, and that it is uttered by both sexes. Future studies may prove whether or not *coerulescens* and *woodhouseii* show such differences in use, and presumed significance, of their rattling or hiccup calls as this suggests.

Display and social behaviour An upward bobbing movement, similar to that of the Florida form, may accompany the rattling call (q.v.). Hardy considers this likely to be an intention-movement of flying, but although this may well have been its origin, I expect it will prove to have self-assertive or sexual significance.

Territorial disputes observed by Hardy involved brief chases, 'br'r'r'r'' calls accompanied by the upward bobbing, and what he terms the 'flitting display', in which head is held erect, the contour feathers closely appressed, the whole attitude is one of alertness and the bird hops vigorously about switching tail and body from side to side.

Other names Woodhouse's Jay, Texas Jay, Blue-grey Jay, Blue-cheeked Jay.

REFERENCES

BENT, A. C. 1946. Life histories of North American jays, crows, and titmice. *U.S. Nat. Mus. Bull.* **191**: 118–128.

HARDY, J. W. 1961. Studies in behaviour and phylogeny of certain New World jays (Garrulinae). *Univ. Kansas Sci. Bull.* XLII, No. 2.

LINSDALE, J. M. 1938. Environmental responses of vertebrates in the Great Basin. *Amer. Midland Nat.* **19**: 93–95.

PITELKA, F. A. 1951. Speciation and ecologic distribution in American jays of the genus *Aphelocoma*. *Univ. Calif. Publs Zool.* **50**: 195–464.

SCRUB JAY (Florida race)   *Aphelocoma coerulescens*

Corvus coerulescens Bosc, 1795, Bull. Sci. Soc. Philom. Paris, 1, (1791–1799), p. 87.

Description Generally similar to other forms of the species, especially the *californica* group (q.v.), but tends to be slightly smaller and with proportionately longer and more strongly-graduated tail. Feathers at base of bill and extreme front of forehead bluish white or very pale blue, shading to deep powder blue on crown, nape, back and sides of neck. White or bluish white stripe over eye. Loral region very dark greyish blue shading to a lighter shade of dull blue on cheeks and ear coverts. Throat and central part of upper breast dull white streaked greyish blue, blue of sides of neck extend around this area in a pectoral band that is narrowest at median part, as in other forms. Underparts below breast light fawnish grey with faint darker streaks (darker shaft streaks on feathers). Flanks and tibial feathers a little darker and tinged with blue; under tail coverts predominantly light blue. Back light greyish fawn, sharply demarcated from the blue hind neck and shading to a silvery powder blue on upper tail coverts. Tail and wings a rather darker and slightly duller blue than head and upper tail coverts.   Irides dark brown.   Bill, legs and feet black.

Female averages a little paler and duller, and often has the median part of the pectoral band less well defined.   The juvenile has those parts of the head that are blue in the adult drab brown to brownish grey, wing and tail quills a little duller and paler, and wing coverts greyish blue with brownish fringes.

Field characters   Small slender blue and greyish jay with long and often drooping tail.   Lack of any white on wings and tail and greyish back contrasting with blue head and tail at once distinguish it from Blue Jay, the only sympatric species with which it might possibly be confused.

Distribution and habitat   Peninsular Florida, from Dixie, Gilchrist, Alachua, and coastal Duval Counties south on the west side to Collier County, and along the east coast to Dade County (Rockdale).   Absent in the east-central parts of the interior from Osceola County southwards.

Inhabits low thicket or scrub where the individual trees are seldom more than about 3 metres high and the dominant species are oaks, *Quercus geninata*, *Q. catesbei* and *Q. myrtifolia*, Saw Palmetto, *Serenoa serrulata*, Dwarf Wax Myrtle, *Myrica pumila*, stunted pines, *Pinus clausa* and *P. caribaea*, and Rosemary, *Ceratiola ericoides*.   Usually found near or around small openings or at the edge of the scrub rather than in dense, uninterrupted scrub.   Readily frequents gardens, roadways and other artificial openings provided there is scrub cover nearby, but has disappeared from areas where the scrub has been eliminated by man (see Grimes).

Feeding and general habits   Takes many kinds of insects and other invertebrates, including grasshoppers, locusts, crickets, beetles, flies, moths, wasps, dragonflies, termites, caterpillars, spiders, millipedes, ticks and molluscs.   Also small reptiles and frogs, fruits and seeds, especially acorns and the seeds of the Saw Palmetto, and at times also eggs and young of small birds.   Readily learns to eat bread, peanuts and other human foods when given the chance.

Seeks food largely on the ground, especially in open spaces near to cover, but also in vegetation. Catches insects flying near the ground by a series of quick hops ending in a leap.   Hops when on the ground.   Digs in loose soil, sand, or similar substrates with the usual side-to-side movements of head and bill.   Acorns and other foods that need to be opened or torn up are held underfoot.   Amadon found that it appeared to need a solid perch to hold acorns down on.   Pieces of wood sticking out of the (soft) soil were commonly used; at least 125 acorns had been taken to one projecting root for opening.

Acorns and other foods are stored in typical manner, as by Jay.   Much circumstantial evidence suggests that the Florida Scrub Jay recovers many of the acorns it buries.   It has been seen picking ticks from cattle.

Usually shows little fear of man, soon becomes tame enough to feed from the hand, if encouraged, and many individuals allow themselves to be handled on the nest.   This tameness is unusual in a corvid but is paralleled, to a lesser degree, by the Grey and Siberian Jays.   Naïve birds readily enter traps but experienced individuals soon become wary of them.

Usually in pairs or small parties but many individuals may come to sources of food or other interest. Adult breeding pairs are territorial but usually (at least where intensively studied by Professor Glen E. Woolfenden, in Highlands County, Florida) permit one or more immature birds to share their territory. These immatures assist in territorial defence and often also in rearing young.   They are usually offspring of the pair whose territory they share.   Territories are large, averaging 12 hectares.   Where a superabundance of food is supplied by man such 'feeding stations' may, and probably usually do, become common property, visited by very many individuals but territorially defended by none.

The flight consists mainly of quick glides from one bush to another, but longer flights of several hundred yards are also made, in which flapping and gliding alternate.   Very agile on the wing in cover, like most jays, and can fly almost vertically upward.   Amadon (1944) implies that its flight is, or at least looks, weaker than that of the Blue Jay or the Mexican Jay.   Sedentary.

Nesting   Nests in trees, shrubs, bushes and vine tangles; usually 1 to 3 metres high.   Nest of twigs, the inner cup lined with palm fibres, fine roots and sometimes other fibrous materials.   Both sexes bring material and build.   In some cases the female may do much more building than the male but this may be due to individual rather than sexual differences.   Nests with eggs found from late March to mid-June but most abundantly in April.   Single-brooded, but will nest again if eggs or young are lost.

Eggs 2 to 5; light green to greenish blue or pale greyish, spotted, speckled or blotched with brown and/or reddish, and with pinkish lilac underlying markings.   Incubation period 15–17 days (Grimes, in Bent).   Hatching dates suggest that true incubation may not start until the third egg is laid, although the female may sit on the nest from the laying of the first and, at least in some instances, for two days previous to laying.   Incubation and brooding by the female only, fed by the male, who usually brings food in his gullet.   The male may cover eggs or young when a human is at or near nest, especially if the female fears to do so.   Both sexes feed the young.   When they are small the male usually gives some food to the brooding female and then both feed the young together, as in *Garrulus*.   The faeces of the young are usually swallowed (perhaps disgorged later), less often carried away in the bill.

From one to three non-breeding birds commonly assist in territorial defence, defence of the nest and feeding of the young.   Most of these are one or two year old birds that are usually, and, so far as is known, when they actually feed the young always older offspring of the pair concerned that have remained in their parents' territory (Woolfenden, *in litt.*).

Incubating or brooding females, and males that are temporarily covering nests, will often allow themselves to be handled.   In this situation they fluff out the plumage and half open the bill but do not fight or struggle.   A male trapped by its nest (Amadon) was similarly docile.   Birds of either sex trapped away from the nest often defend themselves by biting fiercely but some individuals are always docile when handled (Woolfenden, *in litt.*).   When the sitting bird is handled its mate, and any helpers present, may mob the human.   Two of three jays attending a nest attacked the observer's hands when he covered the young with them (Grimes) and five attacked another observer's head and face when he peered at the nestlings.

Voice   The most detailed published account of the voice of this form seems to be that of Amadon who distinguishes the following calls:

A harsh grating 'ka', repeated several times.   Given when mobbing predators and in many situations where the bird appears excited.   In more intense excitement this call becomes more of a screech: 'ke' or 'kwe'.   This latter form may be uttered when mobbing an intruder at the nest or by a jay dashing after a bit of food thrown to it.   This call thus appears equivalent to the screech of *Garrulus*.

A similar but softer call, with an 'r' sound in it, 'krer', seems to be used in intra-specific situations. A rapidly repeated 'kre' or 'kra' is the commonest note uttered by quarrelling individuals; a little chirp, like that of the American Robin, *Turdus migratorius*, may intersperse a series of 'kre' calls.

What sound like low conversational variants of the above calls, audible only at a short distance, are given by members of a family when seeking food or at the nest together; sometimes also by lone birds when apparently puzzled or curious.

Amadon describes the begging notes of the young as 'of the chipping type common to many passerines'; the begging call of the adult female is similar.   A soft warbling song, given in a whispered or subdued manner, has been described by Wetmore (in Howell) as 'a mixture of sweet low-toned calls, high in pitch mingled with others that were variously trilled or slurred'.   This song is sometimes given when the bird appears quite at ease but also in situations where it seems to be somewhat alarmed or ill at ease.

The 'klok' note or hiccup is a hollow mechanical sound suggestive of that made by rattling two sticks together or tapping a heavy block or wood with a mallet. The bird directs its head and bill upwards, and a series of hiccups is then given as the head is thrust upwards in spasmodic, piston-like thrusts. The bill is opened each time the sound is emitted. The tail is slightly spread and, if the bird is perched on the ground, it is pressed against the ground as a result of the upward thrust of head and neck. Usually about six to twelve hiccups are given in a series, sometimes so rapidly as to sound almost like a roll. Amadon saw a bird hiccup without the upward thrust of the bill, and then the notes were given at irregular intervals.

The hiccup call is given only by the female. She utters it in situations involving antagonism to jays other than her mate. Woolfenden (*in litt.*) tells me 'It is used most often to incite or support territorial disputes by family members'. It thus seems comparable to and probably homologous with the clicking notes and accompanying self-assertive display of the female Jay, *Garrulus glandarius*.

Display and social behaviour The male has a display in which, with head held high and tail spread and dragging on the ground, he hops around the female. Probably this is a sexual form of self-assertive display and the masculine equivalent of the female's posturing when she gives the hiccup call.

Feeding of the female by the male regular and frequent both before and during incubation. The male prepares food for swallowing before giving it to the female.

The female begs for food with flapping or fluttering wings. Amadon saw individuals, that were not paired to it, beg from a male (who did not feed them) in a similar way. Possibly begging is used in appeasing contexts?

Noisy gatherings, which involve much excited chasing and calling, are frequent in the early part of the breeding season. Nesting pairs may sometimes join such gatherings. Woolfenden (*in litt.*) thinks these are usually territorial disputes between two or more families.

Young still in juvenile plumage are often tolerated by other adults when they trespass but are fed only by their own parents. During or after the first moult they are usually driven from neighbours' territories. They then usually live with their parents for a year or more, helping them in territorial defence and sometimes in rearing their subsequent brood. Rarely immatures other than their own young may be allowed to live in the territory of a breeding pair. It is thought that the young usually leave their parents' territory for good when mature, at two or more years old, and then (if all goes well with them) pair with unrelated birds elsewhere (Woolfenden, *in litt.*).

When frustrated, hammers, pecks and pulls at its perch or other objects in the usual corvine manner.

Other names Florida Jay.

REFERENCES

AMADON, D. 1944. A preliminary life history study of the Florida Jay, *Cyanocitta c. coerulescens*. *Amer. Mus. Novit.* No. 1252.

BENT, A. C. 1946. Life histories of North American Jays, Crows and Titmice: 79–88. *U.S. Nat. Mus. Bull.* **191**: 118–128.

GRIMES, S. A. 1940. Scrub Jay reminiscences. *Bird Lore* **42**: 431–436.

HOWELL, H. A. 1932. *Florida Bird Life*. New York.

PITELKA, F. A. 1951. Speciation and ecological distribution in American jays of the genus *Aphelocoma*. *Univ. Calif. Publs. Zool.* **50**: 195–464.

WOOLFENDEN, G. E. 1970. Social organisation of breeding Florida Scrub jays (*Aphelocoma coerulescens*). *Congr. Int. Orn.* – Abstracts.

——— 1974. Nesting and survival in a population of Florida Scrub Jays. *The Living Bird* **12**: 25–49.

——— 1975. Florida Scrub Jay helpers at the next. *Auk* **92**: 1–15.

MEXICAN JAY   *Aphelocoma ultramarina*

Corvus ultramarinus Bonaparte, 1825, Journ. Acad. Sci. Philadelphia, 4 (2), p. 387.

Description About size of Jay but with proportionately smaller body, longer tail and legs and more slender bill. Upperparts, including nasal bristles, a rather dull ultramarine blue, brighter and more silvery on crown, nape, rump and upper tail coverts than elsewhere and dullest on back and mantle where the underlying dark greyish brown tends to show through. Inner webs of primaries and underside of tail feathers dull dark grey. Throat silvery grey with darker shaft-streaks to feathers, breast light grey more or less suffused with blue, shading to pale grey on belly and whitish on under tail coverts. Underwing silvery grey, darker and duller towards tips of wing quills. Loral region blackish. Irides dark brown. Bill black, sometimes with pale horn or whitish areas. Legs black. As with other blue birds its appearance differs greatly according to the incidence of the light; it may appear predominantly bright, silvery blue or dull brownish blue.

Juvenile has upper parts dull greyish brown, more or less tinged with blue except on mantle and back, and with faint rusty edgings to many feathers. Wing coverts similar but greater and primary coverts more strongly suffused with blue except at tips. Primaries, secondaries and tail feathers like adult's but a little duller. Legs and feet brownish. Bill flesh-coloured, tip and base of upper mandible dark. In some populations bill may not turn completely dark until the bird is several years old (Pitelka). The age at which the bill darkens is earlier in populations that are less social and where only one pair of jays attend each nest (Hardy; Brown). Birds with white or pale bill markings may breed (Brown). Newly hatched nestling is naked pinkish. Full details of nestlings' development are given by Gross.

The above description is of nominate *ultramarina* from Mexico in south-eastern Jalisco and north-western Michoacán east through the states of Mexico, southern Hidalgo, northern Morelos, Tlaxcala, and Puebla to central western Veracruz. *A. u. colimae*, from the mountains of north-western Jalisco south-eastward to south-central Jalisco and north-eastern Colima, is similar but a little paler and with the mantle often more grey than blue. *A. u. potosina* (formerly *A. u. sordida*) from the mountains of east-central Mexico is appreciably smaller but with a proportionately larger bill. It is paler in colour, being more silvery blue on the head and light to medium greyish blue on the back and mantle, which later becomes more grey than blue in worn plumage, and with more contrast between the blue of the hind neck and grey-blue of the mantle. *A. u. couchii*, from the mountains of extreme south-western Texas and north-eastern Mexico, south-eastward through Coahuila to southern Nuevo Leon and west-central Tamaulipas, is similar. In these forms the bill of the juvenile becomes black (Pitelka; Brown) before completion of the first moult. *P. u. arizonae*, from Arizona, New Mexico and north-western Mexico, is much paler, with the head, wings and tail a pale dull blue or silvery azure blue (according to angle of light), pale bluish grey back, grey breast and nearly white throat and belly. Its bill is proportionately smaller and more slender. *A. u. wollweberi*, from the mountains of western Mexico, is very similar. *A. u. gracilis*, from the mountains of central-western Mexico in eastern Nayarit and much of northern Jalisco, is smaller and has the back less tinged with blue.

Field characters Lack of white streak above eye distinguishes it from Scrub Jay; also more nearly uniform blue upperparts and greyish underparts. Light greyish, not deep blue, underparts distinguish from Unicoloured Jay and lack of crest and grey underparts from Steller's Jay.

Distribution and habitat Mountainous districts of southern U.S.A. in Central Arizona, southern New Mexico and south-western Texas, and Mexico from Chihuahua south along the Sierra Madre Occidental and eastern coastal mountains to Colima, northern Michoacán, Mexico, central Puebla and Central Veracruz. Inhabits woodland dominated by oaks or mixed oak and pine woodland, somtimes venturing into adjacent pure pine woods or more open scrub. The presence of live oaks in its home range seems essential. Pitelka concluded that either rocky, broken terrain with fairly steep slopes or else the presence of tall pines rising above the main canopy were essential features of its habitat.

Feeding and general habits Seeks food both on ground and in trees; also catches flying insects on the wing. Takes acorns; beetles, caterpillars and many other insects; lizards, seeds, fruits, and (but perhaps not to the extent that some of its human enemies proclaim) eggs and young birds. Said to hold acorns down with one foot only when breaking them (Marshall). Readily eats bread and other human foods when available. Stores acorns and other food items in typical manner, in ground or in some nook or crevice of a tree. Brown (1963) found no evidence that the populations he watched intensively fed on acorns in late winter and early spring, thus suggesting that stored acorns are not an important food source. Hardy thought that food-storing played a much smaller part in the life of this species than in that of the Blue Jay, but Brown (1963) observed intensive storing of (man-given) food supplies.

The most detailed studies on this species have been made on the form *A. c. arizonae* in southern Arizona, by Gross, Hardy and, on colour-banded flocks, by Brown (1963, 1970). Except where otherwise stated the information given here applies to this population.

Highly social, associating in flocks of from 5 to 20. The home ranges of different flocks are largely exclusive and do not overlap although trespassing by outsiders may occur, especially to visit a good feeding area or to join in mobbing a predator. Usually little evidence of friction between flocks, but attacking and/or chasing off of intruding strangers has been seen (Brown, 1963) and it seems likely that as a rule the individuals from different flocks are mutually hostile.

Flight stronger in appearance than that of allied species: often takes long, direct flights, and rises high in the air to swoop down on half-closed wings. Hops very actively on ground and among branches. Flock members readily seek food within a few inches of each other, unlike most corvids. Habitually mobs predators. One bird often perches on a high tree overlooking the area where the rest of the flock are seeking food, thus acting as a sentinel (Pitelka). An integrated flock may temporarily break up and travel in smaller groups. Brown could observe no dominance hierarchy within the flock although he suspected it from the nest-robbing behaviour (see 'Nesting'). Hierarchies develop in captive Mexican Jays.

Often bold and unsuspicious towards man, unusual objects and new food supplies presented by him (Gross; Hardy); at other times (probably due to different experience or environment of the individuals concerned) wary and suspicious. Brandt says that it can always be attracted by squeaking or hissing sounds and that the same individual will sometimes return again and again to a partially concealed human, as often as he squeaks. This returning after having once seen the human author of the squeaking is in very strong contrast to the behaviour of *Garrulus glandarius* in England.

Hardy found that, at least in early spring and late summer when he made his observations, the small flocks of Mexican Jays were highly integrated, all the component individuals of a flock behaving in a similar manner at the same time. When not engaged in nesting the birds begin calling about half an hour after dawn, then fly to some exposed place on an eastward-facing slope and sit, fluffed out, on tree tops, in the rising sun. Such sunning is most prolonged in cool weather; typically the birds spend up to an hour in this manner before they begin to forage actively, moving down the hillside as the air warms, to the canyon floor. There is another resting period at mid-day. In the evening the jays move back up the hillsides along small ravines and gullies. Circumstantial evidence indicates that they roost in trees in such hillside gullies, not in the larger trees lower down. A lateral wagging of the tail is shown, in captive birds, just before settling down to sleep. Captive birds did not bathe or ant, although given facilities for both (Hardy), but bathing by a wild individual has been observed (Marshall).

Nesting In tree, usually a live oak, from 1·8 to 15 metres or more above ground but most commonly between 4·5 to 7·5 metres high. Nest of sticks and twigs lined with tendrils, fine rootlets or horsehair. Sticks are broken off trees, not picked from ground. Hair and other lining material is regularly taken from deserted nests as well as collected afresh. Sometimes nests are completed and then deserted for no apparent reason, a fresh nest being built in the immediate vicinity and lined with material taken from the first.

Each nest is built mainly by one pair although sometimes another member of the flock may bring some material to it. Two nests with eggs or young may be present at the same time within the territory of a single flock (Brown, 1970). Both sexes bring material and build but the female takes the greater share, especially in the actual construction of the nest and its lining. Building activity is most intense in early morning and evening. Incubation by the female, fed on nest by her mate and rarely by other members of the flock. Of nine such feedings observed by Brown with his individually marked birds at one nest, eight were by the bird's own mate and one by another female who had lost her own eggs a few days previously; at another 9 different individuals fed the sitting female. At a nest which was closely watched by Gross two birds incubated, changing over at the nest. The possiblity that these were two females cannot, I think, be excluded. At a nest watched by Hardy the incubating bird was not fed at the nest until the young hatched, when it was visited by others, one of which fed both it and the nestlings. These young died when a few days old; those observed by Gross were brooded almost continually until a week old. They were fed by two adults, one of whom always roosted at the nest. Brown (1970, 1972) found that all flock members fed the young. After the young had fledged, parents did not discriminate between their own young and those from another nest. Feeders eat or remove the faeces of the young.

One or both of the breeding pair may spend much time sitting in the nest for several days before eggs are laid. This may function to mitigate nest-robbing. Other jays, including and perhaps usually members of the same flock, visit nests, often interfering with or attacking the owner or stealing nest-lining material from around or under it. Usually the owner shows no resistance, but crouches in the nest and gives the apparently submissive wing-quivering display. Sometimes, however, an owner will fight back and drive off the robber. Eggs may also be taken (Brown, 1963). Young fledge at 24 to 26 days old. The flying young are a centre of interest to the group.

A. u. couchii, from Texas is less social and, so far as is known, only one pair is involved with each nest.

Eggs 3 to 7, most often 4. Pale greenish blue to yellowish green, spotted, speckled and/or blotched with light or dark brown; those of the Arizona race, *A. u. arizonae*, are, however, immaculate. In the northern parts of its range eggs are usually laid in April and May; populations breeding at high elevations lay later than those breeding lower down.

Sometimes incautious and noisy at the nest (Gross; Hardy) but sometimes, at least in reference to man, cautious, shy and silent (Brandt).

Voice   The alarm and assembly call has been variously written as 'weet', 'wheat-wheat', 'a rough querulous "wink? wink?" ', 'a finch-like "rink" ' and so on. It is subject to much variation of pitch and inflection and is given in rapid phrases. The equivalent call of the Texas population of the species, *A. u. couchii*, is given more slowly and evenly and in a higher pitch. This call seems equivalent to the screech of *Garrulus*. It is used when mobbing predators and in many other situations where the bird is apparently both highly excited and alarmed, frustrated, or angry.

Hardy also heard a softer, conversational 'kwot, kwot', 'whut, whut' or a low 'kwa kwa kwa', which would appear to be the calls defined as *guttural* by Brown who describes them as 'low amplitude, single syllable sounds something like *cuck, cluck, uh, quick, up*, and so on'. These calls are used by birds foraging in company and may serve to keep them in contact with each other. They seem equivalent to some of the versions of the appeal call of *Garrulus* and, as in *Garrulus*, there is, apparently, a version sometimes given when about to receive (and when offering?) food which Hardy describes as a 'ree kwa kwa kwa'.

The begging call is described by Hardy as a soft 'kwaa kwaa kwaa' and by Brown as 'aah'. It is given when begging for food sometimes with fluttering or flicking wings and also, with the appeasement or submissive display, in response to attempts at nest-robbing by other jays. The begging call of the young is a high-pitched whistle 'shree', changing in later life to 'choree', with an appended 'itch-eeitch' as food is accepted (Hardy). Gross described calls of the young in the nest as 'rasping' and implied that these were food-begging calls. If so they were possibly given at higher intensity than the calls heard by Hardy. Further observations seem desirable, as the young of *Garrulus* give rasping cries when terrified but not when begging.

The song (Brown) is very like that of Steller's Jay (and most other jays). It consists of 'garbled, run-together series of *weet* notes and others similar to normal calls in quality and pitch, but subdued in volume and with various inflections'. It is given in the usual singing posture, rather upright, with bill near horizontal and head turned slowly from side to side. It is, like the songs of many other birds, often given when there seems reason for the singer to feel slightly alarmed or ill-at-ease.

The Arizona population of this species appears not to possess the mechanical-sounding rattle that (in only slightly differing form) is common to so many jays, although the Texas form, *A. u. couchii*, utters it (Brandt, in Hardy; Van Tyne).

Display and social behaviour The male's courtship, as described by Brown, is similar to the *sexual sidling* and *courtship circling* of Steller's Jay (q.v.), but the bill is pointed downwards, the belly feathers may be conspicuously fluffed out and the neck feathers may be ruffled. The displaying bird thus has a hunch-backed appearance. In two instances, out of four, the displaying bird carried food in the bill.

Feeding of the female by her mate occurs but has been rather seldom seen in the wild. In captivity a female may feed a male over whom she is dominant. Incubating females may, but relatively rarely, be fed by individuals other than their mates.

Typical food-begging with loud juvenile-like calls and fluttering of the wings occurs. It is not quite clear from descriptions (see esp. Brown, 1963, pp.145 and 146) whether this intergrades with or is distinct from the submissive or appeasing display in which the wings are quivered 'slightly to vigorously without spreading them'.

A tame bird *strutted* on the ground with head and body held bolt upright and tail pressed on the ground until a third of it was dragging 'whenever it was angered and wished to show fight'. Some wild birds were seen posturing in the same manner in the presence of a rattlesnake (Swarth). It seems likely that this is normally an intraspecific display rather than a reaction to predators since the usual predator-mobbing behaviour consists of bowing and tail-flirting, as with other jays.

Displacement bill-wiping, hammering branches or other objects, scattering and plucking leaves, occur in situations of apparent frustration and are commonly performed during predator mobbing. Probably much of the hammering etc. is redirected aggression, as is the occasional chasing of other jays that may occur in this situation. Brown (1963) however, unlike Hardy (p.98), did not observe such behaviour in the wild.

Other names Arizona Jay, Couch's Jay, Ultramarine Jay.

REFERENCES

BENT, A. C. 1946. Life histories of North American jays, crows, and titmice. *U.S. Nat. Mus. Bull.* **191**: 118–128.
BRANDT, H. 1951. *Arizona and its Bird Life* 387–397. Cleveland, Ohio.
BROWN, J. L. 1963. Social organisation and behaviour of the Mexican Jay. *Condor* **65**: 126–153.
——— 1970. Cooperative breeding and altruistic behaviour in the Mexican Jay, *Aphelocoma ultramarina*. *Anim. Behav.* **18**: 366–378.
——— 1972. Communal feeding of nestlings in the Mexican Jay (*Aphelocoma ultramarina*): interflock comparisons. *Anim. Behav.* **20**: 395–403.
GROSS, A. O. 1949. Nesting of the Mexican Jay in the Santa Rita Mountains, Arizona. *Condor* **51**: 241–249.
HARDY, J. W. 1961. Studies in behaviour and phylogeny of certain New World jays (Garrulinae). *University of Kansas Sci. Bull.* **42**, No. 2: 13–149.
MARSHALL, J. T. 1957. Birds of Pine-Oak Woodland in Southern Arizona and adjacent Mexico. *Pacific Coast Avifauna* **32**: 93–95.
PETERSON, R. T. 1941. *A Field Guide to Western Birds*. Cambridge, Mass.
PITELKA, F. A. 1951. Speciation and ecologic distribution in American jays of the genus *Aphelocoma*. *Univ. Calif. Publs Zool.* **50**: 195–464
SCOTT, W. E. D. 1886. On the breeding habits of some Arizona birds. *Auk* **3**: 81–83.
SWARTH, H. S. 1904. Birds of the Huachuca Mountains, Arizona. 30–32. *Pacific Coast Avifauna* No. 4.
VAN TYNE, J. 1929. Notes on some birds of the Chisos Mountains of Texas. *Auk* **46**: 205.

UNICOLOURED JAY   *Aphelocoma unicolor*

Cyanocorax concolor Cassin, 1848, Proc. Acad. Nat. Sci. Philad., 4, p. 26.

Description Very slightly smaller than nominate form of the previous species (*A. ultramarina*) and similar in shape and proportions although bill averages a trifle stouter and more tapered towards tip. Loral region, inner webs of primaries and outer secondaries, and tips of outer primaries blackish. Under-wing dark brownish grey with a silvery sheen. Rest of plumage rich rather dark blue, appearing hyacinthine in some lights and brilliant silvery blue in others. The wings and tail are always less brilliant than elsewhere. Bases of feathers are dark greyish and may show to some extent if plumage much worn or disarrayed. Irides dark brown. Bill, legs and feet black.

Juvenile a general dark, brownish grey with paler shaft streaks and faint, pale brownish tips to most feathers. Most of the median wing coverts similar but washed more or less with blue; its wings and tail are otherwise like the adult's but a little duller. Its bill is partly yellowish buff or greenish yellow. These yellowish areas on the bill are retained at least until the first complete moult when about 13 to 16 months old.

The above description is of nominate *A. u. unicolor* from the mountains of Chiapas, south-eastern Mexico and in Guatemala. *A. u. concolor*, from west-central Veracruz and (formerly) eastern part of Mexico State and Puebla, is very similar but slightly duller and, at least to some eyes, more purplish in hue. *A. u. griscomi*, from El Salvador and western Honduras, is more purplish in colour and has a proportionately larger bill. *A. u. oaxacae*, from the central highlands of Oaxaca, is very similar to *griscomi* but does not have so large a bill and has a relatively slightly longer tail. *A. u. guerrensis*, from the mountains of south-central Guerrero, is the most distinct from *A. u. unicolor* in appearance, being of a distinctly purplish or hyacinthine blue. It also has a proportionately longer tail and shorter wings. The differences between these geographical races are very fully described and discussed by Pitelka.

Field characters Entirely blue plumage with no light areas or markings (except on bill of immature) distinguish it from all other Central American jays.

Distribution and habitat Mountains of southern Mexico, in west-central Veracruz, eastern part of Mexico State and Puebla (perhaps now extinct in these last two areas); mountains of south-central Guerrero; central highlands of Oaxaca; mountains of Chiapas and Guatemala; and the mountains of northern El Salvador and western Honduras. Inhabits cloud forest in high mountains, but may make excursions into more open country. Has been recorded in conifer forest as well as in mixed and broad-leaved forest (Griscom, in Pitelka), but is probably usually dependent on presence of oaks. In Chiapas Griscom (p.358, footnote) found it in all types of mixed oak and pine forest, whether natural or modified by man, but absent from pure pine forests and also from grove-like stands of oak and pine in dry areas.

The currently recognized geographical races of this species are now separated by areas of unsuitable terrain and are presumably no longer in contact (Pitelka).

Feeding and general habits   Little recorded.   Apparently very similar to the Mexican Jay, allowing for differences of habitat, and equally social.   Food is sought both on the ground and in trees.   Pitelka found it particularly prone to forage in dense epiphytic growth along large oak limbs, especially among bromeliads.

Nesting   Pitelka found nests with eggs in the living areas of two groups of Unicoloured Jays and another group were attending two fledglings.

Voice   Pitelka records 'a distinctive, finch-like "rink" ', like what he has heard from *A. ultramarina*.

Display and social behaviour   No information.

Other names   Cerulean Jay, Griscom's Jay.

REFERENCES

BLAKE, E. R.   1953.   *Birds of Mexico:* 383.   Chicago.
DICKEY, D. R. & VAN ROSSEM, A. J.   1938.   The Birds of El Salvador, *Zool. Ser. Field Mus. Nat. Hist.* **23**: 408–410.
PITELKA, F. A.   1951.   Speciation and ecologic distribution in American jays of the genus *Aphelocoma*.   *Univ. Calif. Publs Zool.* **50**: 195–464.

DWARF JAY   *Cyanolyca nana*

Cyanocorax nanus Du Bus, 1847, Bull. Acad. Roy. Sci. Lettr. Beaux-Arts Belg., 14, pt. 2, p. 103.

Description   Very similar to the White-throated Jay, *Cyanolyca mirabilis*, (see p.289) but a little smaller and more slightly built and with proportionately much more slender bill and legs.   Sides of face, including loral region, around eyes and ear coverts black, shading into a bluish black ill-defined gorget that encloses the bluish silver throat.   Forehead bluish white to pale mauvish blue, extending at either side into a pale mauvish blue line over eye and downwards to enclose the black ear coverts.   Rest of plumage dull hyacinthine blue, shading to a brighter purplish blue on crown and nape, a slightly brighter and more silvery blue on outer webs of wing quills and a paler, duller, greyish blue on lower breast, belly and ventral regions.   Those parts of tail and upper sides of wing quills not visible when wing and tail are folded are dull greyish.   Underside of wing quills silvery grey, duller at tips.   Bill, legs and feet black.   Female probably averages slightly duller than male but I have seen too few sexed specimens to be sure of this.   Juvenile duller, with dull greyish blue throat, no pale frontal patch and eyestripe, and top of head dull greenish blue not bright hyacinthine blue.

Field characters   Very small, dullish blue jay with pale throat and forehead contrasting with black face.

Distribution and habitat   Southern Mexico; in the subtropical and temperate zones of the states of Mexico, Veracruz and Oaxaca.   Hardy found it in humid pine-oak forests, both in nearly pure oak forests with only scattered pines and an understory of subdominant broad-leaved trees and shrubs and in forests with nearly equal amounts of pine and oak, scattered fir, *Abies religiosa*, and abundant epiphytic growth.

Feeding and general habits   Little recorded.   In June and early July, after the breeding season, Hardy found it in loose flocks of 5 to 10 individuals.

Nesting   Presumably nests early in the year, as birds observed by Hardy in June appeared to be in post-breeding condition.

Voice   Hardy records that it has 'seemingly . . . only one call-type, a doubly-inflected nasal note that may be written "perzheeup!" '.

Display and social behaviour   No information.

REFERENCES

BLAKE, E. R.   1953.   *Birds of Mexico*.   Chicago.
HARDY, J. W.   1964.   Behaviour, habitat, and relationships of jays of the genus *Cyanolyca*. *Occasional Papers, C.C. Adams Center for Ecological Studies*, No. 11. Western Michigan University.

BLACK-THROATED JAY   *Cyanolyca pumilo*

Cyanocorax pumilo Strickland, 1849, in Jardine's Contrib. Ornith., p. 122 (in text).

Description   Very similar to *Cyanolyca argentigula* (see below), in form and plumage pattern but with a proportionately rather smaller bill.   Front part of forehead of stiffened (but short) velvety black feathers. Face, area immediately above eye, ear coverts and throat black.   A narrow but conspicuous white line extends across the forehead, behind the black frontal region, over and behind the eye, usually so as to encircle the upper half of the black facial area.   Crown, nape, and the areas of neck and breast adjacent to the black face and throat, deep purplish blue or hyacinth blue, shading to a duller and slightly greenish blue on the rest of the body.   Visible parts of wings and tail a rather brighter and less greenish blue than elsewhere.   Those parts of wings and tail not visible when folded dull greyish.

Bill, legs and feet black.   Female tends to be a little duller than male.   Juvenile lacks the white markings on the head and is lighter and duller with dull greyish black face and dark greyish blue throat.

Field characters   Small, dark blue jay with white frontal band and eyebrows and black face and throat.

Distribution and habitat   Mountains of south-eastern Mexico, in Chiapas; western and southern Guatemala, including Sierra de las Minas; El Salvador; and western Honduras.

In Mexico Hardy found it exclusively in cloud forest, where oaks occur only sparingly.   In Guatemala Skutch found it in dense humid forests in sheltered ravines, never in clearings with scattered trees, and only occasionally in open woods of oaks, pines and alders.   Normally at elevations of 1800 to 3000 metres.

Feeding and general habits   Usually in loose flocks of about five to twelve individuals.   Known to take insects in both larval and adult stages and spiders.   Probably takes other foods as well.   Seeks food in trees, bushes and vines, both high and low.   Investigates clumps of leaves, the underside of a branch it is perching on, probes among the lichen on large boughs and holds curled-up leaves under one foot while tearing them apart with its bill in search of hidden prey.   Does not seem to have been observed feeding on the ground but probably does so at times.

Less excitable and suspicious towards man than most jays.

The above information comes mainly from Skutch, although Hardy's observations do not in any way conflict with it.

Nesting   No information.

Voice   Hardy distinguishes a loud, repeated 'kwesh' like that of the Scrub Jay (*woodhouseii* group), used as 'a flock social signal'; and nasal, upwardly inflected 'rink' and 'reek' calls, again similar to homologous calls of *A. coerulescens*, that are used in alarm.   He gives sonograms of these calls.

Skutch heard 'low, whining notes, interspersed with sharper, brisker calls, much like those of the Unicoloured Jay but not so loud' from birds foraging in company; and an alarm note 'typically jay-like' but 'quieter than that of many' (other jay species).

Display and social behaviour   No information.

Other names   Strickland's Jay.

REFERENCES

HARDY, J. W.   1964.   Behaviour, habitat, and relationships of jays of the genus *Cyanolyca*. *Occasional Papers, C.C. Adams Center for Ecological Studies*, No. 11. Western Michigan University.
SKUTCH, A. F.   1967.   Life histories of Central American Highland birds. *Publ. Nuttall Orn. Cl.* No. 7, pp. 107–108.

WHITE-THROATED JAY   *Cyanolyca mirabilis*

Cyanolyca mirabilis Nelson, Proc. Biol. Soc. Washington 16, p. 154.

Description   About one quarter smaller than a Blue Jay, with proportionately shorter and more rounded wings and slightly stouter bill with more strongly curved culmen.   Head and neck black, except for throat and central part of upper breast and a stripe that runs across the forehead, over each eye and encloses the cheeks which are silvery white.   Rest of plumage dull greenish blue or greyish blue with a slight greenish tinge, according to incidence of light.   Those parts of the wing and tail quills that are not normally exposed to view when wings and tail are folded are dark greyish.   Bill and legs black.   I have not seen immature or juvenile specimens of this very local species.   They are said to be duller than the adults but otherwise similar.

Distribution and habitat   South-western Mexico, in the Sierra Madre del Sur, Guerrero.   Although of very small world range it may have a fairly wide habitat tolerance, as it is found in mixed oak and pine woodland, dense humid forest, and coniferous forest (Hardy).   Blake, however, implies that it is restricted to oak forest; possibly the presence of oak trees may prove to be essential, at least at some period of the year.

Feeding and general habits   Little recorded.   Has been observed, in mid-July, both in pairs and (in one instance) in a small party of 3 or 4 individuals (Hardy).

Nesting   No information.

Voice   Has a nasal-sounding, doubly-inflected call, that could be written as 'perzheeup!'.   There are at least three distinguishable variants of this call.   The first is very similar to the homologous call of *C. nana* but less highly pitched and fuller in quality, it is also uttered in couplets, as is the second variant which is not so nasal in quality.   Both these calls are heard from apparently undisturbed birds and appear to function as social signals.   The last variant is very nasal, strongly accented on the first syllable and very querulous in sound.   It is given in apparent mild alarm.   A nasal 'reek', very similar to that of *Aphelocoma coerulescens*, has been heard (once), apparently in extreme fear.   All the above observations are from Hardy who gives sound spectrographs of three calls.

Display and social behaviour   No information.

Other names   Omilteme Jay.

REFERENCES

BLAKE, E. R.   1953.   *Birds of Mexico* 381.   Chicago.
HARDY, J. W.   1964.   Behaviour, habitat and relationships of jays of the genus *Cyanolyca*. *Occasional Papers of the C.C. Adams Center for Ecological Studies*, No. 11. Western Michigan University.

SILVER-THROATED JAY   *Cyanolyca argentigula*

Cyanocitta argentigula Lawrence, 1875, Ann. Lyc. Nat. Hist. New York, 11, p. 88.

Description   Very similar to the previous form, *C. mirabilis*, with which it forms a superspecies.   Colour pattern similar except that the stripe over the eye does not extend to enclose the cheek (see col. pl. 2).   Throat and central part of upper breast silver tinged with mauve, shading to silvery white in worn plumage.   Band across forehead, behind the velvety black frontal feathers, silver tinged with mauve and continuing in a stripe over the eye and extending beyond it.   The edges of the silver areas are mauvish blue and the supra-orbital stripe may be predominantly this colour, although more often silvery.   Head and neck otherwise black, shading to dark and slightly purplish blue (almost Oxford blue) on back, lower breast and underparts.   Wings and tail a slightly lighter and brighter blue with a slight greenish tinge on central parts of tail feathers and secondaries.   Narrow outer webs of outer primaries, below the emargination, dull greenish blue.   Those parts of wing not visible when it is folded, and underside of tail, blackish.

Irides said to have been dark brown in two specimens and dark blue in a third.   Further information needed.   Bill, legs and feet black.   Female sometimes, and perhaps usually, a little duller in the blue and black parts and with the silver areas more suffused with mauve.   I have not seen a juvenile of this species; it is said (Ridgway) to be like the adult but with the pale frontal band and eyestripe lacking or only slightly indicated, and the whole top of the head dusky purplish blue.

The above description is of *C. argentigula albior* from the sub-tropical zone of the Cordillera Central of Costa Rica.   The nominate form, from western Panama and southern Costa Rica, is said (Pitelka) to have the throat darker silvery grey and both throat and eyestripe more suffused with blue.   A coloured plate (Salvin & Godman) drawn from the type specimen of the nominate form does not, however, suggest that the difference is great.   I have not seen any specimens of the nominate form.   There is some individual variation among the specimens of *C. a. albior* that I have examined.

Field characters   Small dark blue jay with large silver throat patch contrasting with black face and neck.

Distribution and habitat   Costa Rica and western Panama.   Inhabits mountain woodlands.

Feeding and general habits   No information.

Nesting   No information.

Voice   No information, probably similar to that of *C. mirabilis*.

Display and social behaviour   No information.

REFERENCES

PITELKA, F. A.   1951.   Race names in the Central American Jay *Cyanolyca argentigula*.   *Journ. Wash. Acad. Sci.* **41**: 114–115.

RIDGWAY, R.   1904.   The birds of North and Middle America.   *U.S. Nat. Mus. Bull.* **50**: 319–320.

SALVIN, O. & GODMAN, F. D.   1879–1904.   Biologia Centrali-Americana.   *Aves* vol. 1, and coloured plate in vol. 4.

AZURE-HOODED JAY   *Cyanolyca cucullata*

Cyanocorax cucullatus Ridgway, 1885, Proc. U.S. Nat. Mus., 8, p. 23.

Description   About size of Blue Jay but rather more heavily built, with more graduated tail and stouter bill with more curved culmen.   Feathers of forehead and loral regions upstanding and plush-like, but short.   Crown and nape light bright blue, this coloured area extending to partly enclose the cheeks. Immediately behind the black forehead the blue is usually paler and more silvery than further back, sometimes, especially in worn plumage, almost forming a silvery white band between the blue and black parts, as in other races of the species.   Rest of head, neck, upper mantle and upper breast black, shading into dark purplish blue on back and lower breast and a slightly lighter, duller and less purplish blue elsewhere.   Tail and, to a lesser extent, wing quills slightly tinged with greenish.   Those parts of wing and tail not visible when folded are black.   Irides reddish brown (based on only one specimen).   Bill, legs and feet black.   Juvenile duller but otherwise (except in plumage texture) like adult in plumage.   Probably has differently coloured irides.

The above description is of nominate *C. c. cucullata* from Costa Rica and western Panama.   *C. cucullata mitrata*, from eastern Mexico to Guatemala, is slightly larger.   It has the black of its forehead extending to about midcrown, and a conspicuous if ill-defined white band between the blue of the hindcrown and the black forecrown.   This white band extends along the sides of the blue patch, and merges into it so that its downwards extension, where it forms a posterior border to face and ear coverts, is more white than blue.   Its juvenile has the head patch a very dull light blue with no white on the forehead and less at the sides.

The populations of the Caribbean slopes of the mountains of western Honduras, *C. cucullata hondurensis*, are said to have the amount of white on the head intermediate between *cucullata* and *mitrata* and the blue on the underparts less purplish.

Field characters   Dark blue and black jay with pale bright blue or blue and white crown, nape and posterior margin to ear coverts.   Bright blue crown and nape diagnostic.

Distribution and habitat   Eastern Mexico, in extreme south-eastern San Luis Potosi and Veracruz, south through east-central Oaxaca and interior Chiapas to Guatemala; the Caribbean slopes of western Honduras, Costa Rica, and western Panama.   Inhabits cloud forest but also ranges into tropical forest in foothills and lowlands, perhaps only when these are contiguous with cloud forest.

Feeding and general habits   Does much of its foraging, at least in June and July, high in the canopy (Hardy).   At this time of year it was found in loose flocks of five to ten individuals.   Often foraged in the same trees as *C. pumilo*, although not in mixed parties with it.

Nesting   No information.

Voice   Hardy records and gives sound spectrographs of two calls of this species.   These are an upwardly-inflected nasal-sounding call, which is usually given singly; and a loud clear whistling call, also upwardly-inflected, which is usually repeated rapidly three or four times.   The first is very similar to the nasal calls of *C. pumilo*, *C. mirabilis* and *Aphelocoma coerulescens* (*woodhouseii* group), and the latter to calls of *A. unicolor* and *A. ultramarina*.

Display and social behaviour   No information.

REFERENCES

BLAKE, E. R.   1953.   *Birds of Mexico.*   Chicago.
HARDY, J. W.   1964.   Behaviour, habitat, and relationships of jays of the genus *Cyanolyca*. *Occasional Papers, C.C. Adams Center for Ecological Studies*, No. 11.   Michigan University.
PITELKA, F. A.   1951.   Central American races of *Cyanolyca mitrata*.   *Condor* **53**: 97–98.

BEAUTIFUL JAY   *Cyanolyca pulchra*

Cyanocitta pulchra Lawrence, 1876, Ann. Lyc. Nat. Hist. New York, 11, p. 163.

Description   Very similar to the Azure-hooded Jay, with which it may be conspecific and which it resembles in size and proportions, although in colour pattern it shows much resemblance to *C. armillata* also. Forehead, loral region, sides of face and ear coverts black.   Throat purplish blue, except at its lower periphery, paler than the general body colour.   Forecrown and crown a silvery bluish white or very pale blue, not very sharply demarcated from a band of bright purplish or violet blue that extends from behind the black ear coverts across the hind neck and shades into the blackish brown mantle and upper breast. Rest of plumage dark purplish blue, a little lighter and brighter on wings and tail than elsewhere.   Undersides of wings and tail, and those parts of wing quills not visible when wing is folded, blackish.   Bill, legs and feet black.   I have not seen a juvenile or a description of one.

Field characters   Dark purplish blue jay with bluish white top of head contrasting with black face.

Distribution and habitat   The upper tropical and subtropical zones of the western slope of the Western Andes of south-western Colombia (north to the headwaters of the San Juan River) and north-western Ecuador.   Inhabits forest.

Feeding and general habits   No information.

Nesting No information.

Voice No information.

Display and social behaviour No information.

REFERENCES

LAWRENCE, G. N. 1875. Description of a new species of jay of the genus *Cyanocorax*. *Ann. Lyceum Nat. Hist. New York* **11**: 163–166.

SCHAUENSEE, R. M. DE. 1964. *The Birds of Colombia*. Pennsylvania.

—— 1966. *The Species of Birds of South America*. Pennsylvania.

COLLARED JAY   *Cyanolyca armillata*

Cyanocorax armillatus Gray, 1845, Gen. Birds, 2, pl. 74.

Description About size of Blue Jay or very slightly larger, but crestless and with longer, more graduated tail, rather more rounded wings and shorter bill with more curved culmen.

Throat and contiguous part of central area of upper breast bright blue, a little lighter than ultramarine blue. Front of forehead, face, including ear coverts, and a band across upper breast, which encloses the bright throat area, black. Forecrown, crown and nape pale bright slightly violaceous blue, not sharply demarcated from the mantle colour which is, like the rest of the plumage, a deep rich smalt blue. The tail feathers and the outer webs of the primaries are a slightly duller blue with a faint greenish tinge. Those parts of the wings and tail feathers that are not visible when wings and tail are folded are mainly or entirely greyish black. Bill, legs and feet black. Juvenile duller, with most body feathers blue only at the tips, and throat greyish.

The above description is of nominate *C. a. armillata* from the eastern Andes of Colombia, and south-western Tachira in Venezuela. *C. a. meridana* from the temperate zone of north-western Venezuela is of a slightly darker and much more purplish blue throughout, although the contrast between its brighter throat and paler crown is similar. The irides of one adult and two juveniles of this form are said to have been blue. *C. a. quindiuna*, of the Quindío Mountains of Colombia south to northern Ecuador is a little larger and has a proportionately larger and stouter bill. Its throat is a slightly darker and rather more mauvish blue than nominate *armillata*; its crown, nape and hind neck are a clear, bright and slightly mauvish blue, shading to a greenish blue on the rest of the plumage, this greenish tinge being most pronounced on wings and tail. I have not seen a juvenile of this form but it probably bears the same relation to the adult as do the juveniles of the other races.

Distribution and habitat North-western South America in north-western Venezuela in the states of Táchira, Mérida and Trujillo; the eastern and central Andes of Colombia and northern Ecuador. Found in temperate and subtropical zones. Inhabits forest.

Feeding and general habits   No information.

Nesting   No information.

Voice   Has a great variety of calls, some of which are homologous with calls of *Cyanocorax* species and others with those of *Aphelocoma* species (Hardy, 1967).   Hardy has discussed its vocabulary and given sound spectrographs of many of its calls.   The following is derived, and somewhat condensed, from Hardy's observations.

The basic calls, each of which is subject to much minor variation, are: an upwardly inflected, nasal, querulous 'schree', similar to but less guttural and sharply-rendered than the 'reek' notes of the *Aphelocoma* species.   A 'reek' call, that is sharp and staccato and sounds much like the presumably homologous call of *Aphelocoma ultramarina* and *A. unicolor*, and has a steep upward inflection.   Soft 'craahs' and snoring calls that are uninflected or have a downward inflection and resemble the alarm calls of some *Cyanocorax* species.   A high-pitched, harsh, staccato chatter and a 'craah-who-op' call in which the harsh first note is followed by a two-syllable, mellow whistle on a higher pitch.   It also has some un-jay-like cheeping or peeping notes suggestive of a small passerine or day-old chicks of *Gallus*.

The functions of or factors eliciting the different calls are, as yet, not known.   Hardy noted that 'the Collared Jay, when vocal at all, often seems to utter its entire repertoire in an almost endless combination . . .'.

Display and social behaviour   No information.

Other names   Armillated Jay, Angela's Blue Jay, Quindio Blue Jay, Merida Blue Jay.

REFERENCES

HARDY, J. W.   1964.   Behaviour, habitat, and relationships of jays of the genus *Cyanolyca*. *Occasional Papers of the C.C. Adams Center for Ecological Studies*. No. 11. Michigan.
—— 1967.   The puzzling vocal repertoire of the South American Collared Jay, *Cyanolyca viridicyana merida*. *Condor* 69: 513–521.
HELLMAYR, C. E.   1934.   Catalogue of birds of the Americas, pt. 7.   *Zool. Ser. Field Mus. Nat. Hist.* vol. 13.
SCHAUNSEE, R. M. DE.   1964.   *The Birds of Colombia*.   Pennsylvania.
—— 1966.   *The Species of Birds of South America*.   Pennsylvania.

WHITE-COLLARED JAY   *Cyanolyca viridicyana*

Garrulus viridi-cyanus Lafresnaye and d'Orbigny, 1838, Synop. Av., 2, in Mag. Zool., 8, cl. 2, p. 9.

Description   Very similar to the Collared Jay, with which it may be conspecific.   Throat and adjacent central part of upper breast very dark greenish blue, hardly contrasting with the black facial regions. Forehead, except immediately above base of bill where it is black, white and extending on each side as a narrow white stripe over and beyond the eye.   On some, but not all individuals, this white line continues round the border of the black facial area to connect with a narrow but conspicuous white band that forms a lower border to the dark throat and upper breast.   Crown and nape a lighter and brighter greenish blue than the rest of the plumage, which is of a nearly uniform greenish blue that is rather dull in most lights though it can appear bright and silvery in some.   Undersides of wings and tail, and inner webs of most wing quills, dull blackish grey.   Irides dark brown or blackish brown (*fide* Taczanowski).   Bill, legs and feet black.   I have not seen a juvenile of this species.

The above description is of nominate *C. v. viridicyana* from western Bolivia.   *C. v. cyanolaema*, from south-eastern Peru, has the throat a definite though rather dark blue, contrasting with the black cheeks. Its general coloration is of a slightly brighter and less greenish blue.   *C. v. joylaea*, from northern and central Peru, is a much brighter blue, tinged only very slightly with green in some lights.   Its chin is pale sky-blue deepening to bright purplish blue on throat and upper breast.   The white on its forehead is less extensive, tinged with blue, and does not usually extend as a stripe over the eye.   In some lights this form can appear largely purplish blue although it does not generally do so.

Field characters   Almost entirely blue or greenish blue plumage with dark face and white on forehead. White breast band diagnostic but probably not visible at a distance.

Distribution and habitat   Temperate zones of northern, central and south-eastern Peru and western Bolivia.   Inhabits montane forest.   Stolzmann (in Taczanowski) found it in those parts of the forest that were interspersed with open, bushy areas.   Hardy found it in luxuriant tropico-temperate cloud forest at 1800 to 2000 metres and the 'ceja' forest of low-growing trees and epiphytes at 2000 to 4000 metres.

Feeding and general habits   Little recorded.   Stolzmann found it in parties composed of a few individuals and noted that it was less noisy than other Peruvian jays but equally bold, or at least unsuspicious, and the others did not flee when one had been shot.   A party, watched by Hardy, when seeking food peered into crevices, pecked into epiphytes and held food under one foot when breaking it up.

Nesting   No information.

Voice   Probably similar to that of previous species but Stolzmann (in Taczanowski) only records a simple, upward-inflected note as its presumed contact call ('voie de rappel').

Display and social behaviour   No information.

Other names   Blue-green Jay, Blue-throated Jay, Joly's Jay.

REFERENCES

HARDY, J. W.   1969.   Habits and habitats of certain South American jays.   *Cont. Sci. Los Angeles Mus.* No. 165
SCHAUENSEE, R. M. DE.   1964.   *The Species of Birds of South America.*   Pennsylvania.
TACZANOWSKI, L.   1884.   *Ornithologie du Pérou* **2**: 400–401.   Rennes.

TURQUOISE JAY   *Cyanolyca turcosa*

Cyanocitta turcosa Bonaparte, 1853, Compt. Rend. Acad. Sci. Paris, 37, p. 830.

Description   Very like the two previous species and with same colour pattern as the Collared Jay but with, on average, a proportionately slightly larger bill and appreciably shorter tail.   Throat rather pale bright blue, shading to a slightly darker and slightly purplish blue near the periphery of the black breast band.   Forehead, above the black frontal band, pale bright blue shading to a little darker but still light blue on crown and nape.   Rest of plumage (except underwings etc.) greenish blue, a little lighter, less green, and considerably brighter than that of the (nominate form of) White-collared Jay.   I have not seen a juvenile.

Field characters   As Collared Jay.   Perhaps distinguishable from that species by much paler blue throat and crown and more greenish tinge.   Shorter tail probably not of use in field identification.

Distribution and habitat   Southern Colombia on both slopes of the Andes of Narino, eastern and western Ecuador and north-western Peru in Piura (El Tambo).   Found in temperate and sub-tropical zones.

Feeding and general habits   Known to eat berries of several species, insects, including beetles, and eggs and young of small birds.   Often, or usually, in (small?) flocks.   This information derived from Good-fellow.

Nesting   No information.

Voice   Goodfellow records 'a harsh cry'.

Display and social behaviour   No information.

REFERENCES

GOODFELLOW, W.   1901.   Results of an ornithological journey through Colombia and Ecuador.   *Ibis* **(8)** 1: 480.
SCHAUENSEE, R. M. DE.   1964.   *The Birds of Colombia*.   Pennsylvania.
—— 1966.   *The Species of Birds of South America*.   Pennsylvania.

TUFTED JAY   *Cyanocorax dickeyi*

Cyanocorax dickeyi Moore, 1935, Auk. 52, p. 275.

Description   About size of Jay but with stiff bristly crest, proportionately slightly more rounded wings and rather broader, longer and round-ended tail.   Crest black with some intermixture of dark blue, chiefly towards bases of feathers.   Dark parts of face, throat and breast black.   Malar and sub-ocular regions and a patch above the eye white, often with some blue or partly blue feathers at edges of the white parts. Mantle, scapulars, most of wings, back, rump and basal third (outer) to half (inner) of tail feathers a dark rich slightly purplish blue, a little darker than Oxford blue. Outer webs of primaries a slightly lighter and less purplish blue. Inner webs of those wing and tail quills whose inner webs are not visible when wings and tail are folded, dull black. Bill, legs and feet black. Irides bright lemon yellow to bright chrome yellow. Immature birds, after the first moult, have shorter crests, lack the white patch above the eye, and have the malar region bright blue, not white. Their irides are dark smoky brown like that of the juvenile but change to yellow early the following year. Juvenile has tail almost entirely white (*fide* Moore, but possibly this description was taken from birds whose tails were not fully grown) and the basal part of the bill is flesh-coloured but this persists only for a few months.

Distribution and habitat Western Mexico, in the Sierra Madre Occidental of south-eastern Sinaloa, central Nayarit and south-western Durango. Inhabits wooded mountain regions. Here the vegetation on the ridges is predominantly oaks, of several species, or mixed oak and pine, giving way to dense mixed deciduous and evergreen woodland in and near the bottoms of the steep-sided ravines ('barrancas') and water courses. The Tufted Jay is found in both types of woodland. It appears mainly to use the low, denser vegetation of the barrancas in the breeding season but to inhabit, or possibly merely to visit for feeding purposes, the pine-oak ridges in autumn. It is nowhere an abundant species and appears to be all too easily extirpated locally by intensive collecting (Crossin).

Field characters The largely white tail is a good field character (Moore). This, and the white hind neck, at once distinguish it from all other Mexican Jays, of which only the much smaller and dark-plumaged Steller's Jay and the very differently-shaped Magpie Jay are known to occur in (some of) its habitat.

Feeding and general habits Known to eat acorns, berries, fruits, (especially the fruits of *Peltostigma eximium*), insects (Orthoptera, Hemiptera, Homoptera, Coleoptera, Lepidoptera and Hymenoptera), spiders, eggs and young birds. Gravel was found in most of 22 stomachs examined (Crossin). Appears to be particularly fond of large green katydids.

Crossin, who watched this species intensively from February to June, found that it was almost entirely arboreal when seeking food. Foraging birds spend much of their time investigating large bromeliads, *Tillandsia* sp., tearing them apart to secure insects and fallen (or previously hidden?) acorns and berries from the leaf axils. They also tear open the *Agave* flowers to obtain either embedded parts of the flower or hidden insects. Large, hard, food objects are held under one foot and struck sharply with the bill. The Tufted Jay will hang upside down, or hover in a trogon-like manner, to pluck berries. Food hiding was practised by tame, hand-reared young birds but appears not to have been seen in the wild. Crossin only once saw a bird come to the ground; however, the gravel in the stomachs of collected specimens suggest that they must do so fairly frequently.

Lives in flocks, which are comprised of birds of varying ages, of from 4 to 16 individuals. Large flocks may break up before the breeding season; one of 11 known to Crossin split up into smaller flocks of 4 and 7, and it is thought likely that small flocks may amalgamate to form larger ones after the breeding season. In February and early March the flocks watched by Crossin foraged mostly in the morning, afternoon and evening and spent several hours preening and resting in large, shady trees at mid-day. After nesting began in late March the flocks often broke up into smaller groups for foraging and made numerous but shorter trips for food from and back to the nesting area. When young were being fed the flock members rested for only about an hour at mid-day, although taking several shorter rest periods throughout the day. The same or similar dense, secluded areas are used for roosting as for the diurnal rest periods. Young captive birds bathed eagerly at least once per day; but after 6 months of age they seldom did so. Wild birds watched by Crossin were never seen to drink or bathe, even in hot weather with water nearby.

Nesting Nests in trees, usually in densely foliaged trees in dark, secluded places, often near the head of a ravine. Nests found by Crossin were from 4·5 to 13 metres high, with an average height of 6·6 metres. Moore apparently found much higher nests as he states they were near the tops of trees which were about

23 metres high.   The nest is usually in the immediate vicinity of the roosting and main resting place of the flock; it is very similar to but rather larger than typical nests of *Garrulus glandarius*, built of sticks and twigs, the inner cup of compactly-woven tendrils and fine roots.

Each nest is a centre of concern for an entire flock, all or most of whom bring materials, although relatively very little bringing and placing of material is done by its first-year members.   Only one pair actually breeds, however, and the female of this pair alone incubates.   This female is believed to be the adult that does a disproportionately large amount of shaping the cup of the nest and arranging of material.   In the early stages green leaves are often brought and placed on the nest rim but during incubation these dry and are blown or knocked away.

The 3 to 5 eggs are dull greenish white with a slight bluish tinge when new, soon fading to pale olive buff; spotted, freckled and blotched with brown, and with underlying lavender grey markings.   Sometimes only one or two young are fully reared.   As with *Garrulus* unhatched eggs appear to be left in the nest until such time as they are accidentally broken.   Incubation is by one adult female only (Crossin).   Another bird, believed to be a male, has been seen to sit on the nest side by side with the female for a few minutes (Moore).   The incubating female is fed by all other members of the flock as well as by her mate.   She leaves the nest for a period during the morning, joining or leaving with the flock, spends twenty minutes or more away and usually returns alone.   While she is sitting her mate (but not other flock members) spends much time perched near and above the nest.

Nest building appears usually to start late in March and often proceeds rather slowly.   The female may roost in the nest for up to three nights before egg-laying.   The eggs are almost certainly laid in the early morning, as with *Garrulus*, and normally at daily intervals.   Nests with eggs or young have been found in late May by Moore; at three of the nests found by Crossin the first egg was laid on April 3rd, April 19th and May 10th respectively.   Incubation period 18 days; true incubation probably begins as soon as the second or third egg is laid.

The newly-hatched young are naked and dark pink with a yellowish tinge.   They probably fledge at about 24 days old (Crossin).   The young are fed by most or all of the flock members although at a nest watched intensively by Crossin only the mother fed them (with food brought to her by the others) until the afternoon of the third day, when her mate also fed them and, after this, the other flock members.

Voice   Appears to have an extensive innate repertoire and to be also an habitual vocal mimic.   By far the most detailed account of its vocabulary is that of Crossin from whose work the following descriptions have been taken.   In his paper Crossin gives sonograms of most of the calls he describes and Moore gives the musical notations of four of them.

A staccato 'rak-rak . . .', 'tuc-tuc' or 'ca-ca-ca-ca' subject to much variation, would appear to be given in alarm or conflict.   A rapid, high-pitched version, in which more than four notes are usually uttered in quick succession, is given when mobbing man or some other predator at or near the nest or young.

A loud, single 'ruk' or 'rook' is often uttered from the nest by the female in the period before laying and during the first few days of incubation.   Crossin states that this does not seem to function to attract mate or helpers to return with food.   Possibly it expresses a conflict between impulses to stay on and to depart from the nest.   Apparently homologous calls of the Brown Jay would appear to attract other flock-members to return with food.

A low-intensity, nasal 'aaagh' (probably this is the call described by Moore as 'a peculiar, plaintive note . . . conveying a sense of uneasiness') appears to be a recognition call.   It is of low pitch and uttered with the bill closed.   Given by a member of the flock when joining others at a resting place, and is answered by one or more of them; by any jay coming to the nest with food or nesting material but not by the incubating female when returning alone to the nest.   Given by tame captive birds to their owner.   It would appear to be comparable to some versions of the appeal call of *Garrulus*.

The begging call of the young and of the sitting female is described by Crossin as like that of 'other young jays, crows or ravens'.

A 'ped-el' or 'pid-it' call, similar in its bell-like quality to the 'cleeop' call of the Blue Jay (Hardy), is used during feeding periods and appears to serve as a signal for flock movement.   One bird in a feeding flock gives the call; others utter the same call and then the birds take flight to a new feeding area in a quiet, orderly manner with no sign of alarm.

A high-intensity 'wheeuh' was heard twice from a bird (different individual) in a flock and once from an incubating female when leaving the nest. Various metallic, clicking and hooting calls were given by males standing guard near incubating females. Duetting calls by both male and female of breeding pairs were heard several times. Perched together at the nest, the female in the cup and the male on the rim, one bird would utter a rapid 'chering-chering' followed at once by a sharply rising metallic 'bling' or 'bring'. The other member of the pair would then repeat these calls. At one nest the female sometimes called a 'double-noted "bsst"' and the male replied with a low-intensity, mellow, double-noted 'ruk'. This duetting may be continued for ten minutes or more. It precedes and follows copulation. When duetting both male and female hold the bills raised and have crests and facial feathers erected.

Display and social behaviour Allo-preening occurs, at least as a response from a presumably dominant individual to a subordinate who invites it by lowering the head and completely raising the feathers of the nape and crown. This posturing, probably an appeasing or submissive display, was shown by young when approached by their mother after they had been fed by other flock members and by tame young birds towards their keeper. In this connection Moore's observation that the young bird has some control over its crest, whereas he thought the adult had not, and that the young bird can raise the white nuchal feathers into a conspicuous crest or lay them completely flat, is of interest, as this display does not seem to have been observed from adult Tufted Jays, although I have seen an apparently identical display from an adult White-naped Jay, *C. cyanopogon*.

Wing-quivering (or low intensity wing-flapping?) is used by the incubating female when food-begging.

Mutual bill-caressing occurs between paired birds at the nest, accompanied by barely audible, whispering duets. Copulation takes place (at least in those instances when it has been seen) at the nest and is preceded by duetting calls (see under 'Voice') given with raised bill and fully erected head and face feathers.

Other names Painted Jay.

REFERENCES

CROSSIN, R. S. 1967. The breeding biology of the Tufted Jay. *Proc. Western Foundation Vert. Zool.* vol. 1, No. 5.
HARDY, J. W. 1961. Studies in behaviour and phylogeny of certain New World jays (Garrulinae). *Univ. Kansas Sci. Bull* 42, **2**: 13–149.
MOORE, R. T. 1938. Discovery of the nest and eggs of the Tufted Jay. *Condor* **40**: 233–241.

WHITE-TAILED JAY   *Cyanocorax mystacalis*

Pica mystacalis Geoffroy St Hilaire, 1835, Mag. Zool., 5, cl. 2, pl. 34.

Description Very similar to the previous species, *C. dickeyi*, from which it differs in appearance as follows: a little smaller in size but with proportionately (and in some individuals actually) rather larger bill. The stiff, upstanding feathers of the forehead and forecrown are much shorter, so that there is only the suggestion of a stiff crest. The dark blue of the upper parts is of a slightly lighter shade. The white spot above the eye is smaller and is sometimes, perhaps always, obtained at the first moult. The tail feathers are white except for the two central ones which are dark blue with broad white tips and the next (from central) pair which have varying amounts of blue and blackish on the basal parts of, respectively, their outer and inner webs. Irides bright lemon yellow. Bill black. Legs and feet black or greyish black. See col. pl. 2.

Juvenile has the feathers of the white malar patch tipped and more or less suffused with purplish blue. It lacks the white spot above the eye, this area being entirely black. So far as one can judge from museum skins, its legs and the base of its bill are less intensely blackish than in the adult. Probably its iris is duller or darker also.

Field characters   White tail and white hind neck both distinguish it from all sympatric or adjacent species. In zoo aviaries the entirely white outer tail feathers are diagnostic. Dark blue, not brown, back, and white malar stripes at once separate it from the more commonly kept White-naped Jay.

Distribution and habitat   From Guayas, in south-western Ecuador, to Libertad, in north-western Peru. Found in the arid tropical zone. Inhabits woodland, particularly thick growth near streams and rivers, but also deciduous forest, cactus steppe woodland, and cultivated regions with trees.

Feeding and general habits   Little recorded. Probably much as Tufted Jay, but said by Stolzmann (in Taczanowski) to feed often on the ground. Hardy, observing it in early August, found it usually in loose groups of 4 to 10 individuals but often in pairs or alone. He had the impression that it was less social than the Tufted Jay. Beetles, ants, other insects and seeds were found by Jelski (in Taczanowski) in the stomachs of specimens he collected. Said to have eaten the eggs of domestic fowls and ducks in former times when it was more abundant. Inquisitive, will approach a shot individual, but with great caution (Jelski, in Taczanowski).

Nesting   The only egg of this species I have seen is pale buff, profusely speckled with drab brown, with underlying greyish markings and a very few blackish brown speckles.

Voice   Jelski (in Taczanowski) says that its (usual?) call is two-syllabled and differs from those of the Green and White-collared Jays, and that it utters a different call (which he does not describe) when approaching a shot individual of its species.

Display and social behaviour   No information.

Other names   Moustached Jay.

REFERENCES

HARDY, J. W.   1969.   Habits and habitats of certain South American jays.   *Cont. Sci. Los Angeles Mus.* No. 165.
SCHAUENSEE, R. M. DE.   1966.   *The Species of Birds of South America.*   Pennsylvania.
TACZANOWSKI, L.   1884.   *Ornithologie du Pérou* vol. 2, pp. 398–399.   Rennes.

CAYENNE JAY   *Cyanocorax cayanus*

Corvus cayanus Linnaeus, 1766, Syst. Nat., ed. 12, 1, p. 157.

Description   Very like the previous species, *C. mystacalis*, but averaging slightly larger, with culmen slightly more curved, the feathers of the crown lying flat or nearly so, not stiffened like those of the forehead. Forehead, face, throat and upper breast black. Malar stripe, contiguous spot below eye, and a spot above the eye (smaller than in *mystacalis*) white, edged and more or less suffused with mauve. Hind crown, nape and hind neck white, shading into dull light purple, more or less suffused with greyish brown, on mantle, back and rump. Upper tail coverts a darker and more bluish purple. Wings dark bluish purple, inner webs of wing quills (where not visible when wing is folded) blackish. Tail very dark bluish purple broadly tipped white. When looked at against the light back and mantle look dull brown and wings and tail black. Underparts below the breast, and underwing coverts, yellowish white, creamy white or dull white. Irides light blue, whitish blue or white. Bill, legs and feet black.

Juvenile duller with the white parts of the tail, especially on the central feathers, suffused with purplish fawn. Malar stripe much more suffused with purple, but fading to nearly white before the first moult. Sometimes has some crown feathers tipped with mauve or mauve and white. Spots above and below the eye very small and bluish mauve in colour. In one specimen the spot above the eye is quite lacking, this area being all black. Bill and legs probably paler, as they are dull, horny brown in fledgling specimens in the British Museum.

Field characters   White nape, malar stripes, tail tips and underparts distinguish it from other sympatric jays. The geographically close *C. affinis* has blue nape and blue facial markings.

Distribution and habitat   South America: The Guianas; Venezuela in tropical zone from northern Bolivar southward to the adjacent parts of northern Brazil in the Rio Negro – Rio Branco region. Inhabits forest and open woodland, including woodland savanna.

Feeding and general habits   Known to eat insects (Coleoptera and Orthoptera), berries and fruit.
   Usually in noisy parties. When on the move tends to take short gliding flights from branch to branch, relatively seldom flapping its wings. Usually wary of man and hard to approach closely; but perhaps is so only where persecuted.

Nesting   Young, very recently fledged, have been collected in late December, January and late March.

Voice   Beebe (in Chubb) states that it has a large vocabulary and that the alarm call is a loud 'keeeow'. Haverschmidt describes 'its call' as a 'melodious "tjeeeoo" ', possibly referring to the same call. Hardy lists and gives sound spectrographs of the following calls: A clear downward whistle, much like presumably homologous calls of the Magpie-jay and Brown Jay. A 'jaaay!' very similar to a common call of the Blue Jay. A 'perk! perk! perk!' very similar to the scolding of an American Robin, *Turdus migratorius*. A very harsh downward whistle. A resonant piping 'penk penk'. A squawking cry, possibly of a begging juvenile. A metallic 'ree', upwardly inflected.

Display and social behaviour   No information.

Other names   Lavender Jay.

REFERENCES

Chubb, C. 1921. *The Birds of British Guiana* vol. 2: 587–588. London.
Hardy, J. W. 1969. A taxonomic revision of the New World jays. *Condor* **71**: 360–375.
Haverschmidt, F. 1968. *Birds of Surinam*. London.
Schauensee, R. M. de. 1966. *The Species of Birds of South America*. Pennsylvania.

PLUSH-CAPPED JAY   *Cyanocorax chrysops*

Pica chrysops Vieillot, 1818, Nouv. Dict. Hist. Nat., nouv. ed., 26, p. 124.

Description   Size, shape and colour pattern very similar to Tufted Jay, *C. dickeyi*, (q.v.) but tail a little longer in proportion.   Feathers on forehead stiffened and somewhat laterally compressed, those of forecrown and crown slightly less stiff and with a very velvety texture at their tips; the whole effect being of a black, plush-like cap (see col. pl. 2).   Head, sides of neck and upper breast intense black except for the deep mauve malar patch, a rather brighter mauvish blue sub-orbital spot which is contiguous with it and a large bright blue spot above the eye.   Sometimes this supra-orbital spot is a very pale greenish blue on its upper portion, sometimes a nearly uniform bright blue; this does not appear to be an age or sex difference.   Nape, below and behind the black cap, pale bright bluish mauve to whitish blue, shading to dark violet on the hind neck.   Rest of upper parts a very dark and not very bright purplish blue. Tail feathers broadly tipped pale yellow to white, the pale tips on the central feathers being about 2·5 cm and some of the outer ones nearly 5 cm in length.   Underparts, below the upper breast, creamy yellow, sometimes fading to nearly white in old plumage (as also in museum skins).

Irides bright lemon yellow to pale yellow.   Bill, legs and feet black or brownish black.   Juvenile has mauve on malar region less bright and extensive and lacks the blue spots above and below the eye.   These are acquired at the first moult but are less bright and extensive than the corresponding spots of the adult. Full adult plumage is obtained at the second moult when the wing and tail quills are first shed.   These remarks on juvenile and first-year plumages are based on only a few specimens and it is possible, though I think unlikely, that there may prove to be significant individual variation in these features.

The above description is of nominate *C. c. chrysops*, from Bolivia, Paraguay, Uruguay, south-eastern Brazil and north-eastern Argentina.   *C. chrysops tucumanus*, from north-eastern Argentine, is very similar but averages a little larger in size.   The form from northern Brazil, *C. chrysops diesingii*, has the head feathers longer, forming a conspicuous erect crest; the blue spots above and below the eye smaller and less brilliant and the malar stripe smaller and less purplish.   *C. chrysops interpositus* is known only from the unique type and may represent a hybrid between *C. chrysops* and *C. cyanopogon*.

Field characters   Black and blue jay with broad yellow or white tips to tail and yellow or off-white underparts.

Distribution and habitat   Brazil, south of the Amazon, from Borba eastward to the lower Rio Tapajóz (Rio Arapiuns), in south-western Pará near the northern Matto Grosso border, in Alagoas, Sao Paulo, Paraná, Rio Grande do Sul west to southern Matto Grosso; Paraguay, Uruguay, Bolivia in Beni, Santa Cruz, Chuquisaca and Tarija; northern Argentina in Salta, Tucuman and possibly La Rioja, eastwards through Formosa and Chaco to Misiones, Corrientes and Entre Rios.

Inhabits woodland, including tropical and temperate rain forest, dense riparian woodland, and forest islands in open country (Pampas).   Sometimes locally or temporarily in fairly open country with trees.

Feeding and general habits   Known to eat insects and fruits and said, no doubt correctly, to take eggs and nestlings of other birds. In Paraguay said to follow natives planting maize and dig up the newly-sown grains (Chubb). Commonly in small parties, often in company with *Cyanocorax cyanomelas* or *C. caeruleus*. Usually shows little fear of man, or perhaps it would be more correct to say treats him as it would any other large mammal, where it has had little or no experience of guns being used against it. Noisy and inquisitive. Sometimes in small loose-knit flocks.

Nesting Nests have been found from 4 to 6 metres high. In Paraguay nests with eggs have been found from early October till early December. Usual clutch, at least in Paraguay, from 2 to 4 eggs, but Goeldi (in Euler) gives clutch size, in Brazil, as 6 to 7. Eggs variable: buff, cream-coloured, greenish white or pale greenish, spotted, speckled and/or blotched with reddish brown, dark brown or olive brown and with underlying grey or lilac markings. Usually the eggs are profusely marked.

Voice All observers agree that the bird is noisy. It seems likely that it may be a vocal mimic. Hardy (1969a) records and gives sound spectrographs of the following calls: A rapid-fire very penetrating 'creech-creech-creech-creech'. He implies (Hardy, 1969b) that this call has several variants. An exclamatory 'eirch!', with a higher-pitched variant, a full-throated mellow 'ooh!' similar to (or mimicry of?) a call of the Laughing Falcon, *Herpetotheres cachinnans*, 'chook!-chook!' and 'chock-chock-chock-chock'; a harsh nasal 'jaay' used as a begging call by one adult to another, a high-pitched 'eee!eee!' and a loud 'clackety-clackety'.

Display and social behaviour Welch saw one of two captive birds open its bill wide and then shake all its plumage rapidly for about 30 seconds. When it was half-way through this performance, the other bird came and put its bill inside that of the shaking bird but did not appear to feed it. Wetmore watched one suddenly jerk up and down on its perch, rising to the full length of its legs and then dropping back, uttering a loud 'kuk kuk kuk' as it did so.

Other names Urucca Jay, Plush-crested Jay.

REFERENCES

APLIN, O. V. 1894. On the birds of Uruguay. *Ibis* (6) 6: 150–215.
CHUBB, C. 1910. On the birds of Paraguay, pt. 4, *Ibis* (9) 4: 572–647.
EULER, C. 1900. Descripçào de ninhos e ovos das aves do Brazil. *Rev. Mus. Paulista* 4: 9–141.
GRANT, C. H. B. 1911. List of Birds collected in Argentine, Paraguay, Bolivia and southern Brazil, with field notes. *Ibis* (9) 5: 80–137.
GYLDENSTOLPE, N. 1945. A contribution to the ornithology of northern Bolivia. *Kungl. Svenska Vetenskapsakademiens Handlingar. Tred. Ser*. Bd. 23, No. 1: 235–236.
HARDY, J. W. 1969a. A taxonomic revision of the New World Jays. *Condor* 71: 360–375.
—— 1969b. Habits and habitats of certain South American jays. *Cont. Sci. Los Angeles County Mus*. No. 165.
SCHAUENSEE, R. M. DE. 1966. *The Species of Birds of South America*. Pennsylvania.
STEINDACHNER, J. 1962. Beiträge zur Kenntniss der Vögel von Paraguay. *Abh. Senckenberg. Nat. Ges.* **502**: 1–106.
WELCH, F. D. 1920. Two Jays. *Avicult. Mag*. (3) **11**: 206–207.
WETMORE, A. 1926. Observations on the birds of Argentina, Paraguay, Uruguay, and Chile. *U.S. Nat. Mus. Bull*. **133**: 365–366.
WHITE, E. W. 1882. Notes on birds collected in the Argentine Republic. *Proc. Zool. Soc. London* June 20th, 1882: 591–629.

WHITE-NAPED JAY   *Cyanocorax cyanopogon*

Corvus cyanopogon Wied, 1821, Reise nach Brasilien, p. 137.

Description Very similar to the previous species, *C. chrysops*, but a little smaller in size, with proportionately slightly longer tail. Feathers of forehead plush-like and stiffened but those of crown only slightly stiffened and not upstanding except when erected. Malar stripe mauve. Small bright blue spot below eye and a rather larger bright blue spot above it. This latter is usually pale brilliant blue or whitish blue in its upper region.   Rest of face, forehead, crown, throat and upper breast black.   Nape mauvish white, shading to a very pale mauvish brown on lower part of hind neck.   The white nape feathers can be erected so as to be far more extensive and conspicuous than would appear from a museum skin. Underparts below the black breast creamy white or cream-coloured.   Captive birds often have pure white underparts, possibly due to lack of carotenoid pigments in their diet.   Mantle and back dark dull brown shading to blackish brown on wing and tail quills.   Tail broadly tipped with white, most extensively on the outer feathers.

Irides bright golden yellow.   Bill, legs and feet black or brownish black.   Juvenile has the mauve malar stripe less bright and only a trace of blue above and below the eye.   Some have described the eye spots as entirely absent from the juvenile plumage but this was not the case in the few juvenile specimens I examined.

Distribution and habitat   Eastern Brazil; in south-eastern Pará, Maranhao, Piaúi, Ceará, Paráiba, Bahía, Goiás, Minas Gerais, western Paraná and eastern Matto Grosso.   Inhabits wooded country, including (*fide* Snethlage) mangroves.

Feeding and general habits   I can find little recorded.   In captivity more or less omnivorous and will take mice readily.   Large food objects are held down on the perch by both feet (Butler, *pers. obs.*).

A captive bird anted in typical active manner.   When so doing it picked up ant after ant until it had a wad of them in its bill (Simmons, pers. comm.).

Nesting   No information.

White naped jay soliciting allo-preening

Voice   Two captive birds in London Zoo, which were moulting but in good condition when I observed them, frequently gave a sharp repeated call, difficult to transcribe but which could, perhaps, be written 'kyup!' or 'chep!'.   The individual notes were not run together in a chatter like that of a Magpie or Beechey's Jay, but followed each other in much quicker time than, for example, the screeches of an alarmed

Jay, *Garrulus glandarius*. Probably these calls are homologous with the 'loud metallic barking notes' mentioned by Butler. Although given with apparent flight-intention movements the calling birds did not seem alarmed and Butler thought that these calls were given by his bird when it wished to attract his attention. One of these captive birds gave a muted call like the food appeal call of Jay. Dr Colin Harrison (pers. comm.) heard one give a long burring, clicking note as it jumped up and down on its perch. Butler's tame bird would give a 'crooning . . . little song', bowing over its perch and 'dancing' as it did so

Display and social behaviour The London Zoo birds, when uttering the 'kyup' call, would jerk up the tail and thrust the head forward, both head and body going slightly downward in this movement. As the tail came up it was partly spread and then closed again. I assume these to have been flight-intention movements but it is possible that they were the homologue, perhaps at low intensity, of the bobbing display of the Blue Jay.

In what appears to be solicitation of allo-preening and is probably also a submissive display, the bird, presenting itself laterally, lowers its head so that the bill points downward and erects the feathers of the hind crown, nape and the white parts of the underparts, the white nape feathers are thus fully exposed and presented to the other bird. I saw this display twice; once the bird at which it appeared to be directed ignored it, on the next occasion it came up to the displaying bird and preened its head feathers. Butler's bird evidently displayed in this manner to him and he notes that it liked being tickled on the top of its head, sides or breast but disliked its feet being touched. It would repulse anyone who tried to touch it except him; probably in a natural state allo-preening is only solicited and accepted from the mate or individuals that stand higher in the social hierarchy.

Other names Blue-bearded Jay, Pileated Jay, White-collared Jay.

REFERENCES

BUTLER, A. G. 1903. The Blue-bearded Jay. *Avicult. Mag.* (new ser.) **1**: 227–230.
HARDY, J. W. 1961. Studies in behaviour and phylogeny of certain New World jays. *Univ. Kansas Sci. Bull.* **42**, No. 2.
REISER, O. 1924. Ergebnisse der Zoolog. Expedition der Akad. Der Wissenschaften nach Nordostbrasilien im Jahre 1903: *Vögel* **173**. Vienna.
SCHAUENSEE, R. M. DE. 1966. *The Species of Birds of South America.* Pennsylvania.
SNETHLAGE, H. 1927. Meine Reise durch Nordostbrasilien. *J. Orn.* **75**: 453–484.

BLACK-CHESTED JAY   *Cyanocorax affinis*

Cyanocorax affinis Pelzeln, 1856, Sitzungsb. K. Akad. Wiss. Wien, math.-naturwiss. Cl., 20 (1), p. 164.

Description Similar to Plush-capped Jay, *C. chrysops*, but a very little larger, on average, feathers on forehead not or much less plush-like but, together with nasal plumes, stiffened and forming a short, more or less laterally-compressed, frontal crest. Feathers of crown not stiffened. Malar stripe less extensive.

Spots above and below eye, and malar stripe, deep rich mauvish blue. Forehead, crown, face, sides of neck, throat and breast black. Nape deep but fairly bright bluish mauve or lavender, shading to dull purple more or less suffused with greyish brown on mantle, back and rump and a brighter and darker bluish purple on the upper tail coverts.   Wings and tail dark purplish blue with broad white or yellowish white tips to the tail feathers.   Inner webs of wing quills, where not visible when wing is folded, and undersides of (dark parts of) wing and tail quills blackish.   Underparts below breast yellowish white or white.   Irides pale silvery yellow to sulphur yellow.   Bill black, legs and feet black or dark grey.   Females are usually, perhaps always, more brownish on mantle and back than males in comparative plumage. The upper parts of both sexes may, however, bleach or fade to a light dull fawn colour in worn plumage.

Juvenile duller and browner, especially on wing coverts, which are predominantly dark purplish brown rather than purplish blue.   Malar stripe duller and less conspicuous, blue spots above and below eye absent or vestigial.   First-year birds, at least in some instances, have the eye spots smaller, of a blackish purple-blue, and hardly visible.   Further information on age and individual differences in immature plumages is much needed.

The above description is of nominate *C. a. affinis*, from Colombia and Venezuela.   *C. affinis zeledoni*, from Costa Rica and Panama, has the blue and purple parts a little brighter (only noticeable if birds of the same sex in same plumage state are compared) and the underparts and tail tips yellower, normally a light creamy yellow.   The populations from those parts of Colombia near the Panama border are intermediate.

Field characters   Dark, purplish blue jay with white or yellowish underparts and tail tips, and blue spots on face.   Lack of any white on nape or malar region would at once distinguish it from the geographically near (but not sympatric) and otherwise similar Cayenne Jay.

Distribution and habitat   Central America and northern South America: Caribbean slopes of southeastern Costa Rica, north at least to the Banana River; tropical and sub-tropical zones of Panama, ascending to 1590 metres near Volcan de Chiriqui; Venezuela, in tropical and sub-tropical zones from Falcón and Zulia southward to Lara, Trujillo, northern Mérida and Táchira; Colombia from the Santa Marta region southward in the eastern Andes to the latitude of Bogotá and southward in Chocó to the middle Rio San Juan.

Inhabits woodland, forest and scrub.   In Darien found in a wide variety of wooded habitats but keeps to well-shaded places (Burton, pers. comm.).   In Santa Marta region of Colombia from sea level to 180 metres wherever woodland exists (Todd & Carriker).

Feeding and general habits   Usually in small parties of 3 to 6 individuals.   Noisy and in some areas wary of man but Dr Philip Burton, who observed it in Darien and to whom I am indebted for much of the behavioural information in this and other sections, found it fairly tame but apt to conceal itself in the shadow of foliage.   When one was shot the others uttered alarm calls but did not move away.

Seeks food at all levels in trees, and on the ground.   Flight similar to that of European Jay; moves in trees largely by long, agile hops.

Nesting   Nests in trees, sometimes at least in an upright fork or towards the end of a branch.   A nest found by Burton on March 24th near Rio Parancho, lower Atrato Valley, Colombia, was in a small isolated tree covered with creeping spiny palms; it was not examined but a jay was sitting on it then and on the 28th.

Nest of sticks and twigs, lined with fine pliable twigs, and probably also at times with tendrils and fibres.

Eggs 3 to 5; pale buff or brownish white, spotted and blotched with olive brown and with underlying lilac or grey markings.   In the Santa Marta region of Colombia nests with eggs have been found from early April until mid-May.   Hardy found a pair with dependent but nearly fully-grown young in Venezuela in July.

Voice   Aldrich & Bole note that this species utters 'a great variety of squeaks and rattling sounds'; Sturgis that an individual which he kept in captivity gave 'an interminable loud monotonous . . . chow chow' and 'a very harsh metallic note like pulling a chain through a hole in a tin can'.   Dr Philip Burton, who observed Black-chested Jays in Darien, tells me that this, or some sound very similar, appears to be used as an alarm call and is usually the first indication of the bird's presence.   Hardy lists and gives sound spectrographs of a begging, whining 'jeer' uttered by full-grown juveniles; a chattering 'che-che-

cheeeh!'; a clearly rendered 'peeooh' used as a 'flock social call' and a 'cheoo' variant of it. Burton found that this species appeared to utter a distinct song; this consisted of squeaking, rattling and liquid fluting calls, and was uttered from a particular perch.

Display and social behaviour Little information. Probably lives in social groups all of whose members are more or less involved in each nest.

Other names Talamanca Jay, Colombian Jay.

REFERENCES

ALDRICH, J. W. & BOLE, B. P. 1937. The birds and mammals of the western slope of the Azuero Peninsula. *Sci. Publ. Cleveland Mus. Nat. Hist.* **7**: 113.

HARDY, J. W. 1969a. Habits and habitats of certain South American jays. *Cont. Sci. Los Angeles Mus.* No. 165.

—— 1969b. A taxonomic revision of the New World jays. *Condor* **71**: 360–373.

SALVIN, O. & GODMAN, F. D. 1879–1904. *Biologia Centrali-Americana, Aves* vol. 1, 504–505. London.

SCHAUENSEE, R. M. DE. 1966. *The Species of Birds of South America.* Pennsylvania.

—— 1964. *The Birds of Colombia.* Pennsylvania.

STURGIS, B. B. 1928. *Field Book of Birds of the Panama Canal Zone.* New York and London.

TODD, W. E. & CARRIKER, M. A. 1922. The birds of the Santa Marta region of Colombia. *Ann. Carnegie Mus.* **14**: 427–428.

AZURE-NAPED JAY   *Cyanocorax heilprini*

Description About size of Jay but typical *Cyanocorax* proportions. Feathers of forehead and fore-crown stiff, forming a short upstanding frontal crest. These feathers are black, more or less tipped with purplish. Face, throat and upper breast black. Hind crown and nape a milky violet-blue, shading to a darker shade of same on hind neck. Ventral region and under tail coverts yellowish white. Rest of plumage dull bluish mauve more or less suffused with brownish grey and with broad white tips to tail feathers. This description is taken from examination of only one female and from others' descriptions.

Distribution and habitat South America, in extreme southern Venezuela and adjacent parts of north-western Brazil in the region of the upper Rio Negro and Rio Vaupés. Inhabits forest.

Feeding and general habits No information.

Nesting No information.

Voice No information.

Display and social behaviour No information.

REFERENCE

SCHAUENSEE, R. M. DE. 1964. *The birds of Colombia.* Pennsylvania.

PURPLISH JAY   *Cyanocorax cyanomelas*

Pica cyanomelas Vieillot, 1818, Nouv. Dict. Hist. Nat., nouv. éd., 26, p. 127.

Description   About size of Jay or a little larger but typical *Cyanocorax* build.   Feathers on forehead and, to a slightly less extent those on lores, malar region and around eye, stiffened and plush-like in appearance and velvety black in colour.   Rest of face, throat and upper breast brownish black.   Crown dark purplish brown, shading into dull purple, suffused with brown, on the nape.   Rest of plumage (except where otherwise stated) dull bluish purple, a little brighter on the visible parts of the secondaries and primaries, and shading to a darker and brighter tint on the upper and under tail coverts.   Tail a dark, fairly bright, purplish blue.   Those parts of wing quills not visible when wing is folded, and underwing, dull brownish grey.   Underside of tail blackish.   In worn and faded plumage the bird is much duller, paler and browner and body contrasts more strongly with the darker, brighter tail.   Irides brown.   Bill, legs and feet black.   Juvenile like adult, except for woollier texture of plumage, but a little paler and duller.

Field characters   Dull, purplish and blackish jay with brighter purple-blue tail and no white or contrasting markings anywhere.

Distribution and habitat   South America in sub-tropical and tropical zones of south-eastern Peru (Cuzco); eastern Bolivia; south-western Brazil in the state of Matto Grosso; Paraguay; northern Argentina, in Misiones, north-eastern Corrientes, northern Santa Fe, eastern Formosa and eastern Chaco.
    Inhabits woodland, both forest and groves or riverside trees in otherwise open country.

Feeding and general habits   Known to eat insects, fruits and berries.   Probably takes much other food and possibly takes meat from carcasses of birds or mammals killed by predators when it gets the opportunity.   Wetmore found that in some remote areas it would approach closely and one such individual eagerly ate pieces of cooked Muscovy Duck that he threw to it.
    Often in small parties of five or six individuals.   Seeks food on the ground and in branches.   Holds large morsels under feet while breaking them up.   Often forages in company with Plush-capped Jays or with large icterids.
    Wetmore noted that the flight, when over any distance, is peculiar in that a number of slow wing beats are followed by about six quicker wing beats, and that every flight ends with a long, upward glide that carries the bird to its perch.   In some areas (probably where much persecuted) shy and wary of man; elsewhere inquisitive and relatively bold.

Nesting   Nests in trees or shrubs.   The only description I have found (Hartert & Venturi) says the nest is placed in low trees covered with creepers, at about 2·7 or 3 metres above ground.   It is built of twigs and creeper stems and lined with leaves.   Confirmation seems desirable.
    Hartert & Venturi state that, in Chaco, Argentina, five or six eggs are laid to a clutch, in November. All the several clutches in the British Museum are from Sapucay, in Paraguay; most are of 3 or 4 eggs, with one of 2 and one of 5.   It is not, however, certain that all these clutches had been completed when taken.   They were found at various dates between early October and early December.   The eggs are white to pale green or pale blue, boldly spotted or blotched with dark brown, chocolate or purplish-brown (often with all three) and with underlying lilac markings.

Voice Wetmore noted that the 'ordinary call' is a loud, crow-like 'car-r-r' but a loud 'chah chah' and 'quaw' are also uttered.

Display and social behaviour No information.

Other names Black-headed Jay.

REFERENCES

GYLDENSTOLPE, N. 1945. A contribution to the ornithology of northern Bolivia. *Kungl. Svenska Vetenskap-sakademiens Handl., Tred. Ser.* Bd. 23, No. 1: 236–237.

HARTERT, E. & VENTURI, S. 1909. Notes sur les oiseaux de la republique Argentine. *Nov. Zool.* **16**: 188.

SCHAUENSEE, R. M. DE. 1966. *The Species of Birds of South America.* Pennsylvania.

WETMORE, A. 1926. Observations on the birds of Argentina, Paraguay, Uruguay and Chile. *Bull. U.S. Nat. Mus.* **133**: 364–365.

VIOLACEUS JAY   *Cyanocorax violaceus*

Cyanocorax violaceus Du Bus, 1847, Bull. Acad. Roy. Sci. Lettr. Beaux-Arts Belg., 14, pt. 2, No. 8, p. 103.

Description A little larger than Jay, typical *Cyanocorax* proportions. Nasal plumes and forehead feathers stiff and erect but quite short, forming a slight frontal crest. Those of lores, malar region and around eye also somewhat stiffened, and plush-like in appearance. Head, throat and upper breast black. Nape mauvish white shading to pale bluish mauve on hind neck. Rest of plumage deep bluish mauve, darkest on tail and wings, somewhat tinged with grey in some individuals, especially some females, on mantle and back, and paler on underparts. Those parts of wing quills not visible when wing is folded, and underside of tail, blackish. Irides dark brown. Bill, legs and feet black. I have not seen a juvenile of this species, it is probably duller and greyer.

The above description is of nominate *C. v. violaceus* which is found throughout most of the species' range. *C. violaceus pallidus*, from the Caribbean littoral of northern Venezuela, is a little paler in colour.

Field characters Largish black and purplish blue jay with pale nape. Lack of white tips to tail and entirely black face distinguish it from related sympatric species.

Distribution and habitat Northern South America: Guiana; Venezuela on the coast of Anzoátegui, and the southern slopes of the Andes of Guárico, Portuguesa, Barinas and Táchira, and south of the Orinoco in Bolivar and Amazonas; Colombia east of the Andes from Meta southwards; eastern Ecuador; northeastern Peru southward to Puno; western Amazoniad Brazil from the Peruvian border eastward, north of the Amazon, to the upper Rio Negro and Rio Branco and south of it to the upper Rio Juruá and the east bank of the lower Rio Purús (Redemçáo).

Inhabits tropical forest and open woodlands, mangroves and, at least sometimes for feeding purposes, plantations.

Feeding and general habits Has been recorded feeding on insects, fruit (mangrove fruits and bananas) and small lizards. Probably largely omnivorous. Sometimes in pairs; Goodfellow found it in pairs at a time when it was moulting. Hardy (1969a) found a flock of 6 to 8 individuals, 2 of whom were still dependent young. Noisy and active. When seeking food sometimes associates with icterids of the genera *Psarocolius* and *Cacicus*.

Nesting A nest found by Cherrie was a little over 9 metres high in the top of a tree at the edge of a grove of mangroves. It was fixed between upright forks, somewhat bulky, of sticks and large twigs with a lining of root-like vegetable fibres. The five eggs, which were laid on consecutive days, were bluish white, thickly speckled all over with various shades of brown from vinaceous to chestnut, the darker markings overlying the others. The clutch was completed in the second week of April.

Voice Hardy (1969b) gives sound spectrographs of two calls, a downwardly-inflected 'jeer' and a 'choppy' juvenal begging and location call. He states (p.366) that this species has only one 'adult call type'!

Display and social behaviour Begging with usual wing flapping seen from fledged young.

REFERENCES

CHERRIE, G. K. 1916. A contribution to the ornithology of the Orinoco region. *Mus. Brooklyn Inst. Arts and Sciences: Sci. Bull.* **2** (6): 212–213.
GOODFELLOW, W. 1901. Results of an ornithological journey through Colombia and Ecuador. *Ibis* **8** (1): 480.
HARDY, J. W. 1969a. Habits and habitats of certain South American jays. *Cont. Sci. Los Angeles County Mus.* No. 165.
—— 1969b. A taxonomic revision of the New World jays. *Condor* **71**: 360–375.
SCHAUENSEE, R. M. DE. 1966. *The Species of Birds of South America.* Pennsylvania.

AZURE JAY   *Cyanocorax caeruleus*

Pica caerulea Vieillot, 1818, Nouv. Dict. Hist. Nat., nouv. ed., 26, p. 127.

Description Rather larger than a Jackdaw, and heavily built with large crow-like bill. The long upward-directed nasal bristles and the stiffened feathers of the forehead form a small bristly frontal crest. Nostrils exposed. Feathers of lores, malar region and around eyes have a plush-like texture. Head and upper breast black or brownish black. Rest of plumage a rich deep smalt blue, mauvish blue, greenish blue or some intermediate shade. The most distinct (mauvish and greenish) of these colour phases were treated at one time as good species, *C. inexpectatus* and *C. heckelii* (see Hellmayr), but are now known to be morphs of *caeruleus*. Underwing, and those parts of wing quills not visible when wing is folded, greyish black. Irides recorded as brown in a few specimens, blue in one; further information on iris colour is needed. Bill, legs and feet black.

I have not seen a juvenile of this species. From descriptions of a moulting specimen, it appears to be much duller and greyer than the adult.

Field characters Large jay with bristly frontal crest, black head and otherwise entirely blue plumage.

Distribution and habitat Southern South America: in south-eastern Brazil, from São Paulo to Rio Grande do Sul; eastern Paraguay; and north-eastern Argentina in Misiones, Corrientes, eastern Chaco and eastern Formosa, Inhabits woodland, sometimes in more open country with some trees.

Captive individuals, offered Wood Ants, anted in typical 'active' manner (Simmons, pers. comm.).

Feeding and general habits I can find little recorded. Commonly in small parties, often in company with Plush-capped Jays. Kerr found that in forest it would approach boldly and close but when in the open was wary and difficult to get near. An injured individual showed complete tameness and lack of fear as soon as it recovered from the first shock of its wound.

Kerr describes the flight as 'very weak and undulating'.

Nesting The eggs are pale bluish green or greenish blue, profusely speckled and blotched with dark brown and olive, and with underlying grey or lilac markings. Sometimes the markings may coalesce and partly obscure the ground colour. A (complete?) clutch of two eggs in the British Museum was taken on October 3rd in Sierra do Mar, Brazil.

Voice Kerr says the harsh screaming 'caa-caa-caa', with which the bird greets human intruders, is the only call he has heard from it. A tame captive individual, in the Bronx Zoo, uttered a wheezing whispered song as it displayed to me in response to my putting my face near to it and talking to it.

Display and social behaviour The captive individual mentioned above displayed to me by hopping up and down on its perch, jerking its head (only) up and then down again through a short arc as it did so. Its frontal crest feathers were erected and more or less vertical but not pointed forwards.

REFERENCES

GRANT, C. H. B. 1911. List of birds collected in Argentina, Paraguay, Bolivia and southern Brazil, with field-notes. *Ibis* (9) 5: 80–137.
HELLMAYR, C. E. 1906. Critical notes on the types of little-known species of neotropical birds. *Nov. Zool.* **13**, No. 2: 305–306.
KERR, J. G. 1892. On the avifauna of the Lower Pilcomayo. *Ibis* (6) 4: 120–152.
SCHAUENSEE, R. M. DE. 1966. *The Species of Birds of South America*. Pennsylvania.

CURL-CRESTED JAY   *Cyanocorax cristatellus*

Corvus cristatellus Temminck, 1823, Pl. Col., livr. 33, pl. 193.

Description Very similar to the previous species, *C. caeruleus*, in size and proportions but averages a little smaller and with proportionately longer wing and slightly shorter tail. The frontal crest is longer and recurved and the nasal bristles partly, perhaps in life wholly, cover the nostrils.

Face, throat, upper breast and crest black, shading to brownish black on nape, hind neck and sides of neck. Mantle and back deep violet, more or less suffused with dull brown, especially in worn plumage. Narrow (past the emargination) parts of outer webs of outer primaries greenish blue. Rather more than end half of all tail feathers snow white. Rest of upper parts deep rich bluish violet. Inner webs and undersides of wing and tail quills black. Underparts below the black upper breast, and underwing coverts, snow-white.

Irides brown or blue; this is based on Reiser's observations on three adults he collected (all brown irides) and the only three specimens with soft part colours on their labels in the British Museum, for which the irides are recorded as blue. Further information is needed. Bill, legs and feet black. Juvenile duller, with obscure brownish tips to feathers of wing coverts and white parts of tail suffused with pinkish mauve. Its crest is much shorter and less curled.

Field characters Very large jay with entirely blackish head and predominantly white tail. Profile of crest probably diagnostic if visible.

Distribution and habitat Brazil: tableland from Maranhão, Piauí, south-western Pará, southward through Goias, western Bahía and Minas Gerais to São Paulo, probably Paraná, and Matto Grosso. Inhabits the rather open 'cerrado' of grassland with low, gnarled trees.   Once seen in dense riparian forest (Hardy, 1969).

Feeding and general habits   When not breeding appears (*fide* Hardy) to be sociable and nomadic.   Flies strongly and when alarmed may fly a considerable distance before alighting.

Nesting   Three eggs taken on November 21st in Chapada, Matto Grosso (Allen), were light pale blue thickly covered with dots and fine streaks of light and dark sepia, these markings being heavier and larger around the big end of the eggs.

Voice   Hardy (1969a) records a 'loud jeering call' and low croaking notes and later (1969b) gave sound spectrographs of them, then describing the latter as a 'soft conversational flock note'.

Display and social behaviour   No information.

Other names   White-tailed Jay.

REFERENCES

ALLEN, J. A.   1891.   On a collection of birds from Chapada, Matto Grosso.   *Bull. Amer. Mus. Nat. Hist.* **3**: 380.
HARDY, J. W.   1961.   Habits and habitats of certain South American jays.   *Cont. Sci. Los Angeles Mus.* No. 165.
—— 1969.   A taxonomic revision of the New World jays.   *Condor* **71**: 360–375.
SCHAUENSEE, R. M. DE.   1966.   *The Species of Birds of South America.*   Pennsylvania.

GREEN JAY (*luxuosus* group)   *Cyanocorax yncas*

Garrulus luxuosus Lesson, 1839, Rev. Zool., 2, p. 100.

Description   About size of Blue Jay but with proportionately shorter and more rounded wings, shorter but thicker bill, and more graduated tail.   Nasal and frontal plumes stiffened and semi-erect but short and not forming a frontal crest, and deep bright blue in colour.   Immediately behind them there is a bluish white band across the forehead.   Crown and nape rich deep blue, in some individuals a lighter blue.   Malar region, a contiguous spot below eye and a spot above eye rich blue; the eye spots may be pale greenish blue in some individuals.   Rest of face, throat and upper breast black.   Mantle, back, rump and those parts of wings visible when folded, bright green, sometimes a paler grey-tinged green, at others strongly tinged with yellow.   In worn and bleached plumage a bluish tinge is often present, as with many other green birds.   Central two pairs of tail feathers dark grass-green, shading to darker bluish green at tips; in worn plumage often entirely bluish green. Outer tail feathers bright yellow with paler yellow inner webs. Underparts below breast pale green, in some individuals more or less suffused with pale yellow, especially on ventral area and under tail coverts. Underwing coverts creamy yellow. Undersides of wing quills greyish, suffused and to some extent edged with creamy yellow. Irides yellow. Bill black. Legs and feet dull brownish. Juvenile paler and duller and with the white on forehead replaced by pale yellow. Although duller than those of the adult the bright facial markings are otherwise fully present in the juvenile plumage.

The above description is of *C. yncas luxuosus*, from eastern and south-central Mexico. *C. y. glaucescens*, from the Lower Rio Grande Valley, south-eastern Texas and northern Mexico in Tamaulipas and Nuevo Leon, tends to be, on average, a little paler and colder in colour and has dark brown irides. *C. y. centralis*, from south-eastern Mexico through northern and eastern Guatemala to British Honduras and Honduras, has the underparts either yellow or very strongly suffused with yellow. *C. y. vividus*, from the Pacific side of southern Mexico and western Guatemala, is like *C. y. luxuosus* but averages a little larger and usually has the under tail coverts entirely yellow. *C. y. maya*, from the Yucatan Peninsula, tends to have a more conspicuous white frontal band and the underparts, below the black breast, entirely bright, light yellow. *C. y. cozumelae* is a questionable race, based on the only two specimens so far obtained on Cozumel Island. They are small with bright yellow underparts and light blue caps. Many of these races intergrade. See col. pl. 2.

Field characters The bright yellow outer tail feathers are very conspicuous in flight and at once distinguish Green Jay from all other jays. When perched the predominantly green, or green and yellow, plumage contrasting with blue and black head and black breast is distinctive.

Distribution and habitat South-eastern Texas; Mexico; Guatemala; British Honduras and Honduras. Inhabits woodland, including rain forest, open woodland, second growth, and brushy thickets. Most common at low elevations but occurs up to 1800 metres in mountains. For combined map, see below, under *yncas* group.

Feeding and general habits Feeds largely on insects; various beetles, bugs, grasshoppers and crickets have been recorded. Also takes acorns and seeds, including cultivated grains. Smith states that Palmetto fruits and Ebony seeds are freely taken and that the latter are an important winter food. Known to take young and eggs of other birds but the extent to which it does so has probably been over-emphasized by some writers. Acorns are probably an important food where available. Readily takes meat and other human foods. Hard or large food items are held under the feet and broken or torn with the bill.

Usually in pairs or small parties. Active and usually rather noisy although some observers consider it less so than other jays.

Nesting Nest in tree, bush or shrub; often in dense thickets, usually from 1·5 to 6 metres high. Built of twigs, commonly thorny ones; with inner lining of fine roots, fine wiry twigs, vine stems, tendrils or fibres. Said sometimes to incorporate dry grass, leaves or moss in lining (Bendire). Nests with eggs have been found in late April, May and June.

Eggs 3 to 5; greyish white, very pale greenish, buff or some intermediate colour, speckled and/or spotted, and blotched with dark and light drab brown or reddish brown and with underlying grey or lilac markings. Incubation (in captivity) by female only, fed by male. Both sexes tend young (Roles). Young about four days old were greenish grey in colour (Friedmann). Possibly, as with *Garrulus*, skin colour of nestlings can vary with different foods.

Voice A variety of calls are uttered. Hardy lists and gives sound spectrographs of the following calls: A syncopated dry rattle. A harsh 'rassh! rassh!' and a rapidly repeated 'rasch-rasch-rasch'. A 'rapid-fire bell call' and 'a clear rolling bell call'. An 'eek eek eek!'. A rarely-uttered 'rapid-rasping' call. A 'wheedle wheedle' suggestive of a squeaking gate and a 'jeer jeer'. The female of a captive pair gave the rattling call in self-assertive display; the male uttered soft chirps, whistles and vocal mimicry in sexual display (Roles). Some of the above calls are on a gramaphone record (Kellogg & Allen) which also includes a grating, burring call very like the grating clicking notes of some females of *Garrulus glandarius*.

Display and social behaviour In self-assertive display female fluffs out plumage, bobs up and down and gives rattling call. In sexual version of this display male sleeks down feathers on head, neck and upper breast and fluffs out those of belly and flanks. Solicits allo-preening by approaching partner, 'freezing' and erecting nape and head feathers, those of nape rising first (Roles).

Other names Rio Grande Jay.

REFERENCES

BAIRD, S. F., BREWER, T. M. & RIDGWAY, R. 1874. *A history of North American Birds* vol. 2: 295–297. Boston.

BENDIRE, C. 1895. Life histories of North American birds. *Special Bull. U.S. Nat. Mus.* No. 3: 383–385.

BENT, A. C. 1946. Life histories of North American jays, crows, and titmice. *U.S. Nat. Mus. Bull.* **191**: 128–133.

COTTAM, C. & KANPPEN, P. 1939. Food of some uncommon North American birds. *Auk* **56**: 138–169.

FRIEDMANN, H. 1925. Notes on the birds observed in the lower Rio Grande Valley of Texas during May 1924. *Auk* **42**: 537–554.

HARDY, J. W. 1969. A taxonomic revision of the New World jays. *Condor* **71**: 360–375.

KELLOGG, P. P. & ALLEN, A. A. 1962. *Field Guide to Bird Songs of Western North America.* Boston.

NEHRLING, H. 1883. *Our Native Birds of Song and Beauty* **2**: 326. Milwaukee.

PAYNTER, R. A. 1955. The ornithology of the Yucatan Peninsula. *Bull. Peabody Mus. Nat. Hist.* **9**: 214–217.

ROLES, D. G. 1970. The Breeding Mexican Green Jay at the Jersey Zoological Park. *Avicult. Mag.* **77**: 20–22.

SMITH, A. P. 1910. Miscellaneous notes from the lower Rio Grande. *Condor* **12**: 93–103.

SMITHE, F. B. 1966. *The Birds of Tikal.* New York.

SUTTON, G. M. 1951. *Mexican Birds: First Impressions.* Oklahoma.

ROSSEM, A. J. VAN. 1934. Notes on some species and subspecies of Guatemala birds. *Bull. Mus. Comp. Zool.* **77**: 395–398.

GREEN JAY (*yncas* group)   *Cyanocorax yncas*

Corvus yncas Boddaert, 1783, Tabl. Pl. enlum., p. 38.

Description As *C. y. luxuosus* but a little larger. Nasal and frontal plumes longer, stiffened and erect, forming a short, bushy frontal crest. Forecrown, crown and nape yellowish white, white or creamy yellow, the yellow tinge usually strongest on hind crown and nape, where the feathers are more or less tinged on their tips with pale mauvish blue, sometimes to such an extent that the nape looks predominantly bluish. The yellow coloration and blue tips are usually most apparent in fresh plumage. Entire underparts below breast bright yellow, fading to pale creamy yellow in worn plumage. Green of upperparts tending to be a little paler than in the *luxuosus* group. Irides brown in birds from Ecuador, yellow in those from

Puño district of Peru. Bill black. Legs and feet light reddish brown. Juvenile duller and paler with top of head primrose yellow with most feathers more or less suffused and tipped with pale bluish green. Irides dull violet in one specimen that had just begun its first moult.

The above description is of *C. y. yncas*, from the subtropical zones of south-western Colombia, eastern Ecuador and Peru to central Bolivia. *C. yncas longirostris*, from high altitudes (900–2400 metres) in the Rio Marañon Valley in northern Peru is very similar. *C. y. galeatus*, from the subtropical zone of Colombia west of the eastern Andes, is like *C. y. yncas* but has a much larger frontal crest. It has yellow irides. Its juvenile is like that of *C. y. yncas* and has a smaller frontal crest than the adult.

C. yncas cyanodorsalis, from the subtropical zone of the Eastern Andes of Colombia and north-western Venezuela, also has a large frontal crest but it is a little smaller than *C. y. galeatus*, the white on its head is confined to a band behind the deep blue frontal crest, and its crown and nape are a dark, bright and very slightly mauvish blue, a little paler than the blue of the frontal crest. Its upper parts are usually a slightly darker green than those of *galeatus* and *yncas* and tend to be more strongly tinged with blue; in worn plumage its mantle may be predominantly greenish blue. Its irides are yellow and its legs and feet often, perhaps always, rather darker than those of the white-headed forms. Its juvenile is duller and paler. *C. yncas guatimalensis*, from the mountains of northern Venezuela (not Guatemala!), is very like *C. y. cyanodorsalis* but tends to have a slightly smaller crest, to be less tinged with blue on the back, and to have a narrower white band behind the frontal crest.

Field characters As *luxuosus* group. The yellow outer tail feathers and green back distinguish it from all other South American jays.

Distribution and habitat South America: in the subtropical and tropical zones of the mountains of Venezuela north of the Orinoco; the Andes of Colombia (but not in Santa Marta or on the Pacific slope south of the Rio Patía); eastern Ecuador; eastern and central Peru; and northern Bolivia in La Paz and Cochabamba. Inhabits woodland and scrub.

Feeding and general habits Known to eat insects and fruits, especially wild guavas and the Peruvian plum (*Spondias*). Said to dig up freshly sown maize and to take eggs and young of Domestic Fowls. Both Stolzmann in Peru and Wyatt in Colombia found it in small parties of up to 6 or 7 individuals, in eastern Ecuador Goodfellow found it in parties of from 20 to 30. Wary and shy, at any rate where persecuted by man, but otherwise inquisitive and tending to approach the traveller in its haunts. Attracted, like other corvine birds, by the distress calls of an injured or seized individual. The above observations, like those on its voice (see under), are mostly taken from Stolzmann (in Taczanowski).

Nesting Three eggs of *C. y. galeatus*, obviously laid by different females, resemble eggs of the *luxuosus* group but are more profusely marked than most of the latter that I have seen, and also, as would be expected, slightly larger.

Voice Stolzmann records a trisyllable call 'quien-quien-quien' that is evidently uttered as an alarm call and in tone much resembling the (alarm?) call of the European Jay. He heard one give a bizarre sound, like that of some hard object striking a metal plate, bowing ('en s'abaissant') at each note. The same individual gave perfect imitations of the cry of the Roadside Hawk, *Buteo magnirostris*. No doubt vocal mimicry is practised by most or all individuals. Goodfellow noted that parties of this species uttered 'an incessant chattering' but did not describe any calls. Schwartz has made a record which includes many calls of this form: a loud sharp 'peea-peea-peea', a rather crow-like 'aar aar', a grating burring sound, a series of bubbling clicks and musical repeated calls.

Display and social behaviour Stolzmann (in Taczanowski) observed a bowing movement with each note of the metallic call.

Other names Inca Jay, Galeated Jay, Blue-headed Jay, Blue-backed Jay (a rather misleading name for the form *cyanodorsalis*).

REFERENCES

GOODFELLOW, W. 1901. Results of an ornithological journey through Colombia and Ecuador. *Ibis* **(8)** 1: 458–480.

SCHAUENSEE, R. M. DE. 1966. *The Species of Birds of South America.* Pennsylvania.
SCHWARTZ, P. *Bird Songs from the Tropics.* No. 1. Venezuela.
TACZANOWSKI, L. 1884. *Ornithologie du Pérou* **2**: 396–398.
WYATT, C. W. 1871. Notes on some of the birds of the United States of Colombia. *Ibis* **(3)** 1: 319–335.

BEECHEY'S JAY   *Cissilopha beecheii*

Pica beecheii Vigors, 1828, to 1829, Zool. Journ. 4, No. 15, p. 353.

Description About size of Magpie but tail appreciably shorter (though much longer than Jay's) and much less steeply graduated. Nasal and frontal feathers stiffened, plush-like and extending as a circle of plush-like feathers above, in front of and, to some extent, under eye. These feathers above the eye contrast in texture with those of the central part of back of forehead and crown between them, and can be erected independently of the other head feathers.

Entire head, neck and underparts, except for the dark purplish blue under tail coverts and tibial feathers, jet black. Mantle, back, wings and tail dark rich purplish blue or hyacinthine blue; brightest on mantle, back and rump and a little darker and duller on wings and tail. Inner webs of wing quills, where not visible when wing is folded, and underside of wings and tail, blackish. Irides yellow. Bill black in adults. Legs and feet yellow or fleshy yellow.

Juveniles bred in captivity (Sutcliffe) were sooty black on head, neck and underparts and bluish grey above. They had the feathers of frontal part of the forehead and above the eyes developed into a strikingly conspicuous frontal crest. At about three and a half months old two of them still retained this crest and their legs and bills were pale flesh colour. I have not been able to find descriptions of wild juveniles of this species. Some observers (e.g. Grayson, in Lawrence) say that the sexes differ, the female having a yellow bill and greyish iris. This is presumably due to their having seen instances where fully mature males were paired to or courting immature females. The bills of immature museum specimens are deep straw yellow and were probably yellow or flesh-coloured in life. On the other hand bill colour of immatures may depend on carotenoid pigments taken in the food and the flesh-coloured bills of Sutcliffe's young may have been due to their being reared largely on mice and not, as is usual with jays, largely on vegetarian insects. Birds in full adult plumage may still have pale tips to their bills and it seems probable that two or more years are required before the bill becomes fully black, if this depends on age and not on the individual's physical state or its social position.

Distribution and habitat North-western Mexico, in Sonora, Sinaloa and Nayarit. Found in lowlands and foothills, is said to prefer areas of low scrubby forest to richer growth but more information on habitat is needed.

Feeding and general habits Hardy found it highly social but does not give very full details. Known to take insects and fruit and such foods as meat and cultivated maize when available. A captive bird at the London Zoo, when given Wood Ants, *Formica rufa*, anted in the typical 'active' passerine manner.

Nesting I can find no descriptions of wild nests. Hardy (Jan., 1971, pers. comm.) believes the breeding unit is a single pair, not a flock as in other *Cissilopha* species. Sutcliffe's captive pair built a typical jay nest of twigs and honeysuckle tendrils lined with fibrous roots. They discarded all other materials given to them. Two eggs in the British Museum, taken in Mazatlan in May, are a dark rich buffish pink spotted with chestnut and lighter brown and with underlying greyish lavender markings. It appears (Hardy, *in litt.*) that the ground colour is sometimes pale pinkish buff. Sutcliffe describes the eggs laid by his bird as 'a beautiful russet-brown colour, marked with darker spots and blotches'. She laid two clutches of 3 eggs (and one clutch that was not examined so the number not known) and re-nested after two failed broods, finally hatching and rearing young in late summer and autumn. Incubation period, in England, about 15 days; young left nest at 12 to 14 days, possibly prematurely.

Voice The presumed alarm call used by a captive bird when mobbing an Eagle Owl's head which I showed it was a repeated screech, very like that of Jay but with a softer, cackling chatter after every two or three screeches; I transcribed it as 'KAA KAA kaha kaha'. Sutcliffe describes his birds as 'screeching and scolding' when he approached their nest.

Display and social behaviour When mobbing an Eagle Owl head, a captive bird kept the central head feathers flat but erected those at sides above its eyes. Possibly such a feather erection also occurs in intra-specific contexts.

Other names Purplish-backed Jay, Beechey Jay.

REFERENCES

HARDY, J. W. 1961. Studies in behaviour and phylogeny of certain New World jays (Garrulinae) *Univ Kansas Sci. Bull.* **42**, No. 2.

LAWRENCE, G. N. 1874. The birds of Western and North-western Mexico. *Mem. Bost. Soc. Nat. Hist.* 2, pt. 3, No. 2: 283–284.

SELANDER, R. K. & GILLER, D. R. 1959. Sympatry of Jays *Cissilopha beecheii* and *C. san-blasiana* in Nayarit. *Condor* **61**: 52.

SUTCLIFFE, A. 1926. Breeding of the Beechey Jay (*Xanthura beecheii*). *Avicult. Mag.* (4) **4**: 102–103.

SAN BLAS JAY   *Cissilopha sanblasiana*

Pica San-Blasiana Lafresnaye, 1842, Mag. Zool., ser. 2, 4, Ois., pl. 28 and text.

Description Very similar to previous species, *C. beecheii*, but much smaller, between Jay and Blue Jay in size. Fully adult individuals usually or always crestless, but frontal crest, when present, of narrow, rather 'wispy' feathers and showing some apparently individual differences in length and development. First-year birds usually have tall erect crests. Nostrils exposed or partly exposed, not covered by nasal plumes as in *C. beecheii*. Feathers of loral region plush-like and somewhat stiffened, and continuing as a broad 'eyebrow' of such differentiated plumage over and behind eye. Entire head, neck and under-parts, except for the dark purplish-blue under tail coverts and tibial feathers, jet black. Upperparts a deep rich and slightly purplish blue becoming deeper and more hyacinthine on the upper tail coverts and a darker and more definitely purplish blue on the tail. Underwing dark silvery grey; inner webs of wing quills (where not visible when wing folded) and underside of tail blackish. Irides olive brown to yellowish olive green in completely adult males, yellow in adult females, but greenish or brownish yellow in younger individuals (Hardy). Bill black. I can find no information on leg colour of living birds. The legs of museum specimens are a dark yellowish horn, paler round the edges of the scutes than elsewhere and look as if in life they would be darker than the legs of *beecheii* or *yucatanica*.

Juvenile has underparts dull brownish grey. Upperparts dull bluish grey with a strong greenish tinge. Crest feathers a little shorter but broader than adult's, dull black tipped with greenish blue. Crown and nape feathers broadly tipped bluish. Wings a lighter and more greenish blue, wing coverts tinged greyish. Tail a rich blue but not quite so dark and purplish as adult's. Bill mostly horny yellow in museum skin, probably yellow or yellowish flesh in life. This description is based on only one specimen, which had already begun its first moult, so further information is needed. First-year birds like adult but usually with large erect crests and usually some hornish or pale areas on bill. Feathers of crown and nape tipped blue. Juvenile wing and tail quills retained.

The above description is of nominate *C. s. sanblasiana* from south-western Mexico in the central coastal region of Guerrero. *C. s. nelsoni*, from south-western Mexico in western Guerrero, Nayarit, Jalisco, Colima and Michoacán, has the blue parts a little paler and less purplish, often of a definite greenish blue, but with much individual variation besides differences due to age and wear.

Field characters Black and blue plumage distinctive. Entirely black head distinguishes from other sympatric jays except the nearby and possibly sympatric Beechey's Jay which is larger and has different usual call but is otherwise similar.

Distribution and habitat South-western Mexico in Nayarit, Jalisco, Colima, Michoacán and Guerrero. Inhabits mixed deciduous evergreen thickets bordering palm groves and cleared fields. Also sometimes in mangroves but not in regions where both it and *C. beecheii* occur in adjacent areas (Selander & Giller).

Feeding and general habits Known to eat insects, lizards and the pericarp of palm nuts. Apparently sometimes, perhaps usually, in small parties and easily lured within gun range by squeaking or imitated owl calls.

Nesting Nests in trees, shrubs or vines. Nest of sticks and twigs, with lining of coarse plant fibres or similar material (Hardy, *in litt.*). Eggs coloured like those of previous species, *C. beecheii*. Hardy found nests with eggs or young in June and July in Nayarit.

Each nest involves a group of usually about six individuals. Incubation and brooding is by female only, mostly by one female at any one nest but a second female may take over for short spells. At one nest such a female was also the main caretaker of four young that had fledged from another nest a few days before. Females fed by males at nest. Both sexes bring food for young. Two males and two females attendant on one brood were collected (Hardy) and proved to be fully adult with ossified skulls and enlarged but regressing gonads.

Voice To date (March, 1974) no published information but Hardy tape-recorded the calls of the birds he studied.

Display and social behaviour No information, except as under 'Nesting' above.

Other names Acapulco Jay, Blue-and-black Jay.

REFERENCES

BLAKE, E. R. 1953. *Birds of Mexico*. Chicago.
HARDY, J. W. 1971. Studies on the reproductive behaviour and ecology of the San Blas Jay, *Cyanocorax sanblasiana*. *Report to the Chapman Committee of the American Museum of Natural History*.
SELANDER, R. K. & GILLER, D. R. 1959. Sympatry of jays. *Cissilopha beecheii* and *C. san-blasiana* in Nayarit. *Condor* **61**: 52.

YUCATAN JAY   *Cissilopha yucatanica*

Cyanocitta yucatanica Dubois 1875, Bull. Acad. Roy. Sci. Lettr. Beaux-Arts Belg., ser. 2, 40: 797.

Description   As previous species, *C. sanblasiana*, with which it may be conspecific, but differs as follows. Slightly larger in average size and with proportionately longer and more graduated tail.   Feathers of central part of top of head elongated but no definite crest.   Blue of upper parts a little lighter and more bright and silvery, inclining to greenish but never to purplish except, slightly, on tail.   Irides very dark brown.   Bill black.   Legs and feet yellow-orange.

The juvenile differs strikingly from that of *sanblasiana*.   It has the entire head and underparts white. Its upperparts, except for the wings and tail, are a light greyish blue, the parts that the feathers first grow on, scapulars and rump, being predominantly grey, but bluish feathers soon partly obscure or replace these.   The wings and tail are like those of the adult but a little duller, and the outer tail feathers are tipped with white.   Iris hazel brown.   Bill orange-yellow.   Legs and feet pale yellow.   At 16 weeks captive specimens (Beebe & Crandall) had moulted nearly all their white feathers and had dark slaty grey eyes.   As with other jays the juvenile wing and tail quills are retained until the second moult.   See col. pl. 3.

The majority of the many specimens in the British Museum (Natural History) with yellow bills have juvenile tail and wing quills and must, therefore, be not more than about 16 months old.   There is, however, one specimen in otherwise adult plumage with a partially yellow bill and another that has moulted its juvenile wing and tail quills but whose tail, although of the deep blue adult colour, has narrow white tips.   This bird also has a partially yellow bill.

The above description is of nominate *C. y. yucatanica*.   *C. y. rivularis*, from Tabasco and south-western Campeche, is said to be larger and a little brighter in colour.

Field characters   Entirely black head and underparts and bright blue back and tail distinctive, but would not separate *yucatanica* from the two previous species if they should ever occur together with it.

Distribution and habitat   South-eastern Mexico and northern Central America: in Yucatán, Campeche, Tabasco and Quintana Roo, south to north-eastern Guatemala (Petén district) and British Honduras. Inhabits woodland, including pinewoods, deciduous forest and scrub.   Usually in or close to dense cover but will forage in more open country nearby.

Feeding and general habits   I can find little recorded.   Apparently usually in parties of about 6 to 12; said sometimes to form larger flocks of up to 100 (Salvin & Godman).   Wary where much persecuted or when in fairly open country, but in forests will often approach man very closely.   Said to be destructive to maize and fruit.

Nesting   A nest with eggs and one just completed were found in British Honduras in late May (Russell).

Eggs cream-coloured to deep pinkish fawn, speckled, spotted and blotched with dark brown and reddish brown and with underlying lilac or grey markings. Very variable in amount of spotting.

Voice Hardy lists and gives sound spectrographs of: A rapid-fire rasping chatter. A downwardly inflected 'crooo', which he says is a 'food expectancy' call. A resonant 'clok! clok!' and a resonant 'crook-crook'. A 'bell-call' like that of the Blue Jay and a 'tin-horn piping note' very like an homologous call of Beechey's Jay.

Display and social behaviour No information.

Other names Blue-and-black Jay.

REFERENCES

BEEBE, C. W. & CRANDALL, L. S. 1911. The undescribed juvenile plumage of the Yucatan Jay. *Zoologica* **1**: 153–156.

BLAKE, E. R. 1953. *Birds of Mexico*. Chicago.

CHAPMAN, F. M. 1896. Notes on birds observed in Yucatán. *Bull. Amer. Mus. Nat. Hist.* **8**: 271–290.

HARDY, J. W. 1969. A taxonomic review of the New World jays. *Condor* **71**: 360–375.

PAYNTER, R. A. 1955. The ornithogeography of the Yucatán Peninsula. *Peabody Mus. Nat. Hist. Yale Univ. Bull.* **9**: 217.

RUSSELL, S. M. 1964. *A distributional study of the birds of British Honduras.* Ornithological Monograph No. 1 (American Ornithologists' Union).

SALVIN, O. & GODMAN, F. D. 1879–1904. Biologia Centrali-Americana, *Aves* **1**: 498. London.

SMITHE, F. B. 1966. *The Birds of Tikal.* New York.

HARTLAUB'S JAY   *Cissilopha melanocyanea*

Garrulus (Cyanocorax) melanocyaneus Hartlaub, 1844, Rev. Zool., 7, p. 215.

Description Very similar to *C. sanblasiana*, but a little smaller, only slightly larger than Blue Jay although with the usual (in *Cissilopha*) coarser bill and larger legs and feet. Head, neck, upper mantle and entire breast coal black. Underparts below breast dull greenish blue. Upperparts greenish blue, slightly greener and duller on outer webs of primaries than elsewhere. Looks mauvish blue in some lights. Tail feathers (where visible when tail folded) a brighter, darker and more mauvish blue, shading to greenish blue at edges (outer edges only in outer tail feathers). Underwing silvery grey; underside of tail and inner webs of primaries blackish. Irides bright greenish yellow. Bill, legs and feet black.

Juvenile much duller, with the head and underparts dull greyish but with the wing and tail quills, which as usual are not shed at the first moult, only a little less bright than the adult's. Irides blackish. Bill yellowish or horn-coloured. First-year birds have yellow or olive-yellow bill and dark brown irides. The bill becomes black at about ten months, the irides yellow at a little over one year old (Hardy).

The above description is of nominate *C. m. melanocyanea* from Guatemala. *C. m. chavezi*, from the mountains of northern Nicaragua, tends to be a darker and less greenish blue above and very mauvish blue on the underparts. The populations in Salvador are intermediate, the only two I have seen from Honduras (Paraiso) are as dark as any from Nicaragua. Some specimens of *C. m. chavezi* are partly or entirely blackish on the underparts.

Field characters Entirely black and blue jay. Blue belly would distinguish it from Yucatan and Blue-and-Black Jays should it ever overlap with them.

Distribution and habitat Central America, in mountainous parts of Guatemala, El Salvador, Honduras and northern Nicaragua. Inhabits woodland, scrub and plantations. The original habitat was woodland dominated by oaks but over much of its range this has been largely replaced by coffee plantations to which the bird has adapted. Rare in mature forest and thrives only where clearings are present (Hardy).

Feeding and general habits Seeks food both among branches and on ground where it forages among the leaf litter. Takes grasshoppers and other insects, seeds and fruit such as figs (Hardy). Usually in noisy parties but quiet and secretive when breeding (Dickey & Van Rossem).

Nesting Nests in thick bushes, vine tangles on trees and similar sites. Nest of twigs, lined with fibres, rootlets, fine pliant twigs or similar materials. The 3 or 4 eggs are bright pinkish-buff to pale brick red, spotted and blotched with shades of dark reddish brown and with underlying lilac and pinkish-mauve markings. Nests with eggs have been found in Guatemala in late April and late May and a nest with young about three days old in El Salvador on May 7th. A whole flock is involved in the care of one or two nests. Only one female is believed to lay eggs in each nest but two females may share in incubation and brooding. Four young in one nest were fed by at least eleven adults. Juveniles from earlier nests may also feed nestlings, and sometimes apparently incubate or brood (Hardy).

Voice No information.

Display and social behaviour No information. See above for reproductive behaviour.

Other names Bushy-crested Jay.

REFERENCES

DICKEY, D. R. & ROSSEM, A. J. VAN. 1938. The Birds of El Salvador. *Zool. Ser. Field Mus. Nat. Hist.* **23**: 411–414.
HARDY, J. W. 1969. Report in *Proc. Amer. Phil. Soc. Year Book* 305–307.
OWEN, R. 1861. On the nesting of some Guatemala birds. *Ibis* (1) 3: 63.
SCLATER, P. L. & SALVIN, O. 1859. On the ornithology of Central America. *Ibis* (1) 1: 21.

BROWN JAY   *Psilorhinus morio*

Pica morio Wagler, 1829, Isis von Oken, col. 751.

Description About size of House Crow or a little smaller, in shape nearer to Magpie but with larger, coarser-looking bill and shorter and less strongly graduated tail. Short bristly frontal crest. Rather plush-like feathering on lores and around eye. General colour a dull dark sepia brown, darkening to near black on the head, palest on the underparts and with a greenish grey semi-sheen on the wing and tail quills that is only noticeable in fairly fresh plumage. Malar patch of only slightly paler colouring is, nevertheless, noticeable at close quarters owing to the different texture of the feathers composing it. Irides brown or dark brown. Eye-rims and a small area of skin below the eye black. Legs and feet black. Bill black or black and yellow.

The above description is of the brown or dark morph or colour phase. The white-tipped morph differs in having broad white tips to the outer tail feathers, and the underparts below the breast yellowish white or cream-coloured, the brown of the breast shading through pale brownish grey to cream on the lower breast.

Juvenile a little paler. Irides grey; eye-rims yellow, greenish yellow, yellow and black, or all black; skin below eye yellow or greenish yellow. Bill yellow, or yellow and black. Legs and feet yellow, greenish yellow, or yellow and black. Soft parts of nestlings usually, perhaps always, entirely yellow but soon partially darkening. There is much apparently individual variation in the age at which dark soft parts are acquired. Some adults and most or, more probably, all first-year birds retain a partially yellow bill and often partially yellow legs. It seems likely that in this species individual differences of bill colour pattern serve to aid personal recognition. Newly-hatched young are naked with yellow or olivaceous skin (Skutch).

Several very slightly differing races have been recognized (see esp. Selander; Vaurie). The general trend is for a slight north-south decrease in size. The brown morph occurs alone in north-eastern Mexico; both all-brown and white-tipped individuals occur together in south-eastern Mexico, and only the white-tipped morph occurs from eastern Tabasco and south-western Campeche south to Panama.

Field characters Large dull brown, or dull brown and white jay with no blue in plumage.

Distribution and habitat Mexico and central America: from north-eastern Mexico in Nuevo Léon and Tamaulipas south through south-eastern Mexico and Yucatan south and east through Central America (but not in El Salvador) to western Panama. Inhabits woodlands of many types, forest edge, plantations, and cultivated or pastoral areas with clumps or lines of trees. Not usually, if at all, in dense primeval forest. Abundant in man-altered environments provided suitable tree cover is available.

Feeding and general habits Seeks food largely in the branches but also on ground. Takes insects, spiders, lizards, nectar of banana flowers, and fruits, especially those of *Castilloa elastica*, *Passiflora* and the catkin-like fruits of *Cecropia*. In some parts of its range habitually takes nestlings of smaller birds but Skutch, to whose observations most of the more detailed knowledge of its habits is due, found that in areas where other foods were apparently abundant, it never robbed nests. Adult birds feed largely on fruit and nectar but give much animal food to the young.

Usually in small flocks of five to ten individuals, sometimes more. In the breeding season such flocks consist of a breeding pair and younger or mostly younger 'helpers'. Two or more groups will readily join to mob a predator or because of any similar disturbance. It is not known whether nesting flocks are comprised only of related individuals. Often follows and mobs human intruders and thus gets itself disliked by shooters and some birdwatchers.

Flight, when going any distance and not alarmed, is with regular crow-like wing beats. When fleeing in alarm or descending a steep hillside it opens and closes its wings with each beat and spreads and closes the tail 'which gives its body a rocking motion and makes its progress appear headlong and reckless' (Skutch). Bathes in wet foliage, probably also in surface water when available.

Nesting Nest in a tree or shrub, built of sticks, twigs and sometimes vine stems, the inner cup or lining of fibrous roots, probably also at times of fibrous tendrils and pliant fine twigs. A common site is far out on the slender bough of a tree from 7·5 to 22·5 metres high. Less often the nest may be against a tree trunk, or in the crown of a banana plant from 3·6 to 6 metres above ground.

Both sexes build, usually arriving separately with material and each arranging what it has brought. Rarely, but perhaps more often at unwatched nests, one of the younger 'helpers' may bring material. In a group the breeding pair appear, from their darker bill and eye-rim coloration, usually to be the oldest individuals. Eggs frequently 3 but a clutch of 6 has been found (Sutton & Pettingill); greyish white to light bluish grey, profusely speckled and blotched (small blotches) with dark brown and olive brown, and with underlying greyish markings.

The adult breeding female alone incubates, and broods the young, but at one nest the male was once seen to cover the eggs for a short period and at another one of the helpers once briefly brooded the young. The female incubates from two to nearly four hours at a stretch. She is brought food by her mate and by some or all of the helpers. She also, however, leaves the nest for periods of up to about twenty minutes while her mate stands on or near the nest rim. Sometimes he will leave before she has returned. If the female leaves the nest when her mate is not present she does not stay away so long as when she has left him 'on guard'.

Both parents and helpers feed the young. Often the bird bringing food will give it to an adult or to another helper and the latter will feed the young. Food given to the young is usually torn into pieces and carried in the gullet; rarely some food object may be brought held in the bill. If the nestling does not at once swallow the food placed in its mouth the giver will remove and re-engorge it, then offer it to another young one. At 4 nests watched by Skutch there were, respectively, 1, 2, 3, and 5 helpers that fed the young, besides the breeding pair. At the nest with 5 helpers, but not at the others, whichever of 6 of the 7 attendant birds brought food would wait, guarding the nest until another arrived before flying away, but the 7th individual never stayed on guard after feeding the young. Only the breeding female brooded the nestlings.

Incubation period 18 days at one nest, 20 at another where the female was often disturbed and spent much time away from the nest. An incubating female allowed a human to approach fairly close but then slipped quietly off the nest if he remained near showing interest. The helpers frequently mob a human intruder near the nest. When re-nesting after a failure, the failed nest is torn to bits and its materials used for the new nest.

In Caribbean Guatemala one nest was found in February but otherwise, at least in Guatemala and Costa Rica, April is the month when nests with eggs are most commonly found. If a nest is robbed or otherwise fails, the birds usually soon nest again, but only one brood per year is reared.

Voice A usually loud but rather low-pitched 'pee-ah' or 'pay-ah' appears to be the most frequent call and is probably largely equivalent to the appeal call of the Jay (q.v.). It is capable of much variation and often has a complaining tone. This call is used as an apparent contact call between members of the flock, and as a begging call by the female when nesting, incubating or brooding. It will probably be found to be used by both sexes in many contexts involving the need for some response from another individual.

The alarm call apparently intergrades with the 'pee-ah' call but is louder, higher-pitched, and more excited and screaming in tone. Sutton & Gilbert transcribe it also a 'pee-ah' but Skutch, although stating that 'the various utterances . . . are all rather similar in form and differ chiefly in loudness and intonation', transcribes the alarm call as 'a loud, harsh chaa or chay'. The alarm call may be accented by the hiccup note (see below) being given at the beginning or (*fide* Sutton & Gilbert) end of the alarm scream.

The hiccup note is a popping or snapping sound made, or at least presumed to be made, by the sudden expansion or deflation of the unique furcular pouch or cervical sac (Sutton & Gilbert), although, as Hardy has emphasized, many other corvids that have no such pouch utter very similar sounds. Hardy (1969) gives sound spectrographs of its calls.

The hiccup does not appear, from the evidence so far available, to be associated with sexual display as with the similar notes of some other jays. Sutton & Gilbert deduced that it was 'a signal for quiet, for a stealthy approach, for close attention to some not quite solved problem'. They found that it could be elicited by keeping quite still and allowing approaching Brown Jays to examine them closely. If they moved at such a time the jays would at once utter the alarm scream, as well as the hiccup note. Selander, however, thinks that the primary function of the hiccup note is that of accenting the alarm call.

The Brown Jay appears to have a more limited vocabulary than most jays and not to practise vocal mimicry. It apparently lacks the liquid and melodious calls (some of them vocal mimicry) that most other jays utter.

Display and social behaviour Skutch records a possible display in which one jay, perching beside or in front of another, stretches up on its legs and makes feints with its bill at the other 'now here, now there, bobbing up and down, twisting and turning from side to side in a spirited manner'. The bird at which these movements are directed turns its bill towards the other and erects the feathers of its head.

Vibrating (quivering?) of the wings may accompany begging for or reception of food.

REFERENCES

HARDY, J. W. 1961. Studies in behaviour and phylogeny of certain New World jays (Garrulinae). *Univ. Kansas Sci. Bull.* **42**, No. 2.
—— 1969. A taxonomic revision of the New World jays. *Condor* **71**: 360–375.
SELANDER, R. K. 1959. Polymorphism in Mexican Brown Jays. *Auk* **76**: 385–417.
SKUTCH, A. F. 1960. *Life Histories of Central American Birds* vol. 2: 231–257. Pacific Coast Avifauna No. 34. Berkeley, California.
SUTTON, G. M. & GILBERT, P. W. 1942. The Brown Jay's furcular pouch. *Condor* **44**: 160–167.
—— & PETTINGILL, O. S. 1942. A nest of the Brown Jay. *Wilson Bull.* **54**: 213–214.
VAURIE, C. 1962. *Peters' check-list of birds of the World.* vol. 15. Cambridge, Mass.

MAGPIE-JAY   *Calocitta formosa*

Pica formosa Swainson, 1827, Philos. Mag., N.S., 1, p. 437.

Description About size of Magpie but with longer tail, especially the four central tail feathers; the feathers of the forehead forming a long, recurved, erectile crest; and longer bill with more deeply curved culmen. Median part of forehead, including crest, black with bases of feathers sometimes, especially in males, more or less barred or intermixed with white and pale blue. Visible parts of crown feathers medium to dark blue, sometimes intermixed with black. Central part of malar patch black, edges blue or of blue-tipped white feathers. Small feathers in front of eye blackish, those around eye blackish tipped with silvery blue. Rest of face, including broad superciliary stripe, throat and upper breast white, divided from the white underparts by a black pectoral band that extends right around sides of neck and nape. Ear coverts, especially in females, may be partly blackish and connect the malar patch to the black collar at sides. Hind neck immediately posterior to nuchal collar deep blue. Mantle and back light greyish blue, slightly tinged with greenish. Wings, especially the outer webs of the primaries and secondaries, a slightly brighter and more violet blue. Those parts of the wing quills not visible when wing is folded are dark greyish. Rump and upper tail coverts a rather dark greyish blue or greenish blue. Tail a dark rich violet-blue, looking in some lights very purple, in others with a greenish tinge. All but the four central tail feathers with broad and (towards outermost) progressively extensive white tips. Inner webs of outer tail feathers more or less suffused with black. Undersides of primaries silvery grey; underwing coverts white. See col. pl. 2.

Irides dark brown. Bill, legs and feet black. Females tend to be slightly but noticeably duller on the back and shorter-tailed than males, and to have narrower pectoral bands and more pronounced or profuse dark facial markings; and they often have the hind crown predominantly black. Juvenile duller, with shorter tail and crest and most of the crest and forehead feathers tipped with blue and white. Bill and legs horny grey. Half-grown juveniles have the bill largely pale, dull orange in museum specimens but possibly fleshy or pinkish in life.

The above description is of nominate *C. f. formosa* from southern Mexico, in Colima, Michoacán and Puebla, south to Oaxaca where it intergrades with *C. formosa azurea*, from the pacific slopes of Chiapas and Guatemala, which is a brighter blue on the upperparts, especially on the nape and hind neck. Its black pectoral band does not usually extend over the back of the neck; it usually has the malar region a pale violet-blue and the upper breast, above the pectoral band, is usually tinged with violet-blue. The white areas on its tail feathers are more extensive and it is slightly larger. *C. f. pompata*, from interior eastern Oaxaca, interior of Chiapas and Atlantic side of Guatemala south through El Salvador and Honduras to Costa Rica, is slightly smaller. The blue of its back is paler, duller, and more greenish than that of *azurea*. Its face is usually pale, as in *azurea*, but some individuals, especially but not exclusively females, show black around or over the eye and on the ear coverts (Dickey & van Rossem). Males, and some females, of this form tend to have much bluish white in the crest feathers.

Field characters Large blue and white jay with long tail. The long blue and white tail at once distinguishes it from all other species except the closely related, and possibly conspecific, Collie's Magpie-jay (q.v.).

Distribution and habitat Southern Mexico from Colima, Michoacán, Puebla, Oaxaca and Chiapas, Guatemala, El Salvador and Honduras to Costa Rica. Throughout most of its range, in the interior and on the Caribbean side, in arid regions; but on the Pacific side of southern Chiapas and northern Guatemala it is found in areas of heavier rainfall. Inhabits all kinds of woodland and scrub, provided there are some fair-sized trees at hand, preferring more open woodlands to dense forest. Abundant in coffee plantations and in cultivated and pastoral regions with plenty of trees or adjacent woodland.

Feeding and general habits Known to take fruits and berries, especially mangoes when available, also caterpillars and other insects. Does not seem to have been recorded taking acorns although it is abundant in oak and pine woodlands and it would be unusual for a jay not to eat acorns when available. Dickey & van Rossem noted that, although other birds mob it, they had no evidence that it robbed nests.

Commonly in small parties. Dickey & van Rossem imply that in the breeding season it lives in pairs but Skutch found it social when breeding as well as at other times. Usually wary of man but habitually mobs him, following him through the woods with loud calls and thus warning other creatures of his approach.

Nesting Nests in trees. Skutch (to whom most of the observations under this heading are due) found nests at various heights from 6 to nearly 30 metres. Nest built of sticks and large twigs, the inner cup lined with roots and fibrous materials. Usual clutch probably 3 or 4 eggs but further information needed.

Eggs of one clutch were grey, finely, densely and evenly flecked with brown. Nestlings found by Dickey & van Rossem were infested with maggots in cysts under the skin.

Incubation sometimes, probably always, by female only. At a nest watched by Skutch the female was fed on the nest by at least two, and probably three different jays. This bird often left the nest for short periods, usually just after she had been fed. She did not seek food for herself while off the nest. If one of the birds that fed her, or any other conspecific, approached the nest while she was off it she would at once return and cover her eggs. Some jays, presumed not to be members of the same group, were driven away from the vicinity by the incubating bird or her helpers.

Nests with eggs or nestlings have been found in late December and early January in Guatemala (near Colomba) and in mid-April in El Salvador. On the Caribbean side of Guatemala (Motagua Valley) and on the Isthmus of Tehuantepec nests with eggs were found in June and July at a time when young from earlier broods were already on the wing. It is not known whether the same pair may breed more than once in the course of a spring and summer. More probably the later nests are of birds that were later coming into breeding condition or whose previous attempts at breeding met with disaster.

Voice Alarm calls have been variously described as 'chattering and screaming', a loud, grating 'kree-up' etc. Skutch notes that besides 'scolding notes, painfully loud and harsh' the Magpie-jay also utters 'a variety of mellow, liquid calls, one of which sounds like "weep weep weep" '. The begging call of the incubating female he described as loud and harsh but with a pleading tone and almost identical to the 'pee-ah' call of the Brown Jay. Griscom remarks that 'It croaks, screeches, mews, growls and whistles'. When I spoke to a tame captive bird in the Bronx Zoo it responded by fully 'erecting' its crest and giving a soft series of whispering but rather musical sounds. Hardy (1969) gives sound spectrographs of twelve different calls, one of which has six variants. This species may prove to be a vocal mimic.

Display and social behaviour The incubating female begs with fluttering wings in usual manner When uttering its whisper song to me a tame captive bird (sex unknown) erected its crest so that the ends of the longest feathers hung in front of and *below* the tip of its bill. Plath states that the male of a captive pair he kept 'usually' carried its crest in this position whereas the female did not. Possibly in any sort of sexual or aggressive excitement the male of this species may erect the crest in this manner, just as both sexes of *Garrulus glandarius* erect the malar feathers in such situations.

Has a display flight in which the wings are stiffly extended and widely spread, the head directed straight forward and the tail spread, like the display flight of the Blue Jay (Hardy, 1961).

Other names White-throated Magpie-jay, Plumed Jay.

REFERENCES

BLAKE, E. R. 1953. *Birds of Mexico* 376–377. Chicago.
DICKEY, D. R. & ROSSEM, A. J. VAN. 1938. The birds of El Salvador. *Zool. Ser. Field Mus. Nat. Hist.* **23**: 414–416.
GRISCOM, L. 1932. The distribution of bird-life in Guatemala. *Bull. Amer. Mus. Nat. Hist.* **64**: 401–402.
HARDY, J. W. 1961. Studies in behaviour and phylogeny of certain New World jays (Garrulinae). *Univ. Kansas Sci. Bull* **42**, No. 2.
—— 1969. A taxonomic revision of the New World jays. *Condor* **71**: 360–375.
PLATH, K. 1930. The Plumed Jay. *Avicult. Mag.* (4) **8**: 250–251.
SKUTCH, A. F. 1953. The White-throated Magpie-Jay. *Wilson Bull.* **65**: 68–74.

COLLIE'S MAGPIE-JAY   *Calocitta colliei*

Pica colliei Vigors, Oct. 1828 – Jan. 1929, Zool. Journ., 4, No. 15, p. 535, pl. 12 (1829).

Description Very similar to *Calocitta formosa*, with which it is sometimes considered conspecific (see p. 261), but differs as follows: crest feathers broader and less, or not recurved. Bill usually slightly longer. Tail relatively much longer. Face, throat and upper breast black except for patches immediately above and below anterior part of eye which are blue, or blue and white, and adjoin the malar patch, which is violet-blue with its lower edge partly or entirely white.   Forehead and crest feathers black.   Upper parts deep hyacinthine blue, brightest on nape and dullest on mantle and back which show a slight green tinge in some lights.   Some specimens, especially in the northern part of the range, may have varying amounts of white on throat and breast (*fide* van Rossem, 1942).

Immature birds retain the juvenile wing and tail quills in the usual manner.   They have the feathers of the crest and crown broadly tipped with white.   Many or most of the feathers of throat and breast are more or less grizzled white and blue at their tips, except those at the anterior border of this area, so the bird appears to have a predominantly pale upper breast and blackish pectoral band.   The blue of the upper parts is paler, duller and more tinged with greenish.   I have not seen a juvenile of this species. From descriptions it would appear to resemble the immature but to lack the blue patch above the eye. It seems uncertain whether and to what extent white-tipped head feathers may be retained, or rather re-grown after the first complete moult; some birds with small white tips on otherwise blue-tipped feathers may perhaps be two-year olds.

Distribution and habitat   Western Mexico, from southern Sonora and western Chihuahua south to Nayarit, Jalisco and possibly Guanajito.   Specimens that, on appearance, seem to be hybrids or intergrades with *C. formosa* occur in Jalisco.   They may, however, possibly be variant individuals of *C. formosa* (see p. 261).   Inhabits forest in the hot, coastal regions (Lawrence).   In Sonora van Rossem (1945) found it in deciduous and riparian woodlands in the south-eastern tropical zone foothills.

Field characters   Black throat and face (of most adults) distinguish it from *C. formosa*; their very long blue and white tails and long crests distinguish both forms from all other jays.

Feeding and general habits   Apparently similar to those of *C. formosa* but little recorded.   Known to feed on insects.   Commonly in small parties, foraging in company with Double-crested Orioles, *Cassiculus melanicterus* (Grayson, in Salvin & Godman).

Nesting   Nest probably like that of the previous form, said sometimes to be lined with moss as well as roots and fibres.   Often, perhaps usually, in thorny trees.   The nest must be rather large if Grayson is correct in saying that it is as big as a Magpie's.   Builds in March.   The above observations are taken from Grayson (in Salvin & Godman).

Eggs greyish white to greyish cream colour, spotted or speckled, blotched and clouded with dark brown, greyish brown and grey and with underlying pale grey and lilac markings.

Voice   Apparently as Magpie-jay but details lacking.

Display and social behaviour   No information; probably as Magpie-jay.

REFERENCES

LAWRENCE, G. L.   1874.   Birds of western and northwestern Mexico.   *Mem. Boston Soc. Nat. Hist.* **2**, pt. 3, No. 2: 284–285.

SALVIN, O. & GODMAN, F. D.   1879–1904.   Biologia Centrali-Americana.   *Aves*, **1**: 507–508.

ROSSEM, A. J. VAN   1942.   Notes on some Mexican and Californian birds, with descriptions of six undescribed. races.   *Trans. S. Diego Soc. Nat. Hist.* **9**: 377–384.

—— 1945.   A distributional survey of the birds of Sonora, Mexico. *Occasional Papers Mus. Zool. Louisiana State University*, No. 21, 171–172.

PIÑON JAY   *Gymnorhinus cyanocephala*

Gymnorhinus cyanocephalus Wied, 1841, Reise Nord-Amer., 2, p. 22.

Description   Between Jay and Blue Jay in size but nutcracker-like in proportions with long wings and bill and rather short tail.   It has exposed nostrils very unlike a nutcracker's.   See col. pl. 2.

Throat dull white, streaked greyish blue (individual feathers have whitish centres and greyish blue edges). Lores dark greyish, feathers tipped dull white near bill, especially in first-year birds.   Malar regions and lower part of ear coverts a soft but quite bright blue.   Rest of head dark hyacinthine blue, a little paler and much brighter on the forehead and forecrown than elsewhere.   Inner webs of wing quills dark greyish; underside of wings and tail dark grey with a silvery sheen.   Rest of plumage soft greyish blue, palest on rump and a little brighter and bluer on breast than elsewhere.   In very worn plumage the upperparts become almost slate grey and the crown and nape (but not the forehead) a dark mauvish grey.

Irides brown.   Bill, legs and feet black.   Males usually have rather longer bills than females.   Female tends to be paler in body colour than male but this difference, said to be recognizable in life (Cameron), is barely discernible in museum skins.   Juvenile dull smoke grey, tinged with blue on forehead, bluish grey on wings and tail.   Bill, legs and feet lavender grey in fledgelings (Cameron, 1907).   First-year plumage predominantly grey like juvenile's, the adult blue plumage not being attained till the second summer moult (Balda & Bateman).   Nestlings are at first naked.

Field characters   A blue or greyish bird with long bill, short tail and longish wings; usually feeding and flying in flocks.   Different proportions and walking gait distinguish it from other jays; lack of white on wings and tail from Clark's Nutcracker; bluish colour from crows.   When flying in *close* formation this habit distinguishes it from all other American corvids.

Distribution and habitat   Western North America; from central Oregon, east-central Montana, and western South Dakota south through central California to northern Baja California, central Nevada, central and eastern central Arizona, central New Mexico and western Oklahoma. Wanders to central Washington, north-western Oregon, northern Idaho, north-western Montana, south-western Saskatchewan, throughout the Great Basin, Nebraska, Kansas, central western and south-western California, south-eastern Arizona, central Texas and northern Mexico in Chihuahua.

Typically inhabits the foothills and lower mountain ranges where Piñon (or Pinyon) Pines, *Pinus edulis*, occur and, together with Juniper, commonly form the dominant vegetation. Occurs in other habitats when adjacent to Pinyon country and at times of failure of the Piñon nut crop.

Feeding and general habits   All information on the social behaviour of this species is based on the comprehensive studies by Balda & Bateman, and on information received from Professor Balda, unless otherwise indicated.

Piñon Jays commonly fly and seek food in large flocks; although smaller groups, especially of parents and flying young, often occur. A flock of about 250 individuals had a home range of about 21 square kilometres. The Piñon Jay is locally nomadic in response to fluctuating food supplies but present evidence suggests that each flock confines its wanderings to within its own home range, except in times of failure of the local piñon seed crop. There is no evidence of exchange of individuals between different flocks. When marked individuals were taken distances of 18 to 34 kilometres from home and released in the home ranges of other flocks, most of them (18 out of 22) returned home. A feeding flock is commonly surrounded by 4 to 12 birds perched on vantage points. These individuals call loudly if they see a predator and thus function as sentries.

When available the seeds of the Piñon Pine, *Pinus edulis*, are the species' staple food. It also takes seeds of Yellow Pine, *Pinus scopulorum*, Ponderosa Pine, *P. ponderosa*, and some other conifers, tender young cones of Piñon and other pines, fruits and berries, especially the berries of the Red Cedar, grasshoppers, beetles and other insects and other invertebrates and other small creatures. The nestlings are given pine seeds as well as animal food. It readily takes foods given by man, especially sunflower seeds, and will come in flocks to gardens where sunflowers are seeding (Braly). Sometimes carries or catches prey with its feet (Balda, *in litt.*).

Habitually hides food, in the ground or in crevices in bark, commonly on or to the southern side of a tree trunk. Large quantities of piñon seeds are carried to and stored in or near the traditional nesting area. Individuals have been seen to remove food previously hidden by mate or parent. Sometimes prepares a cache site by a single backward scratch with one foot, before using its bill (Balda, *in litt.*). Previously hidden seeds are relied on extensively for food when breeding. Has been seen to eat salt put out for cattle. Food is sought both in trees and on the ground.

Walks when on the ground. When travelling some distance forms compact flocks, the individual birds often flying as close to one another as many waders do. Flights of more than about 1·5 km are prefaced by loud calling from a few individuals, followed by a general gathering and calling from high perches before taking wing. Flocks sometimes fly at night but this may possibly be a response to previous disturbance. Flight said to be crow-like but swifter than that of the American Crow.

When not persecuted the Piñon Jay is usually tame or at least indifferent to man, but soon becomes wary when hunted and then will not fly over a human (Miller & Stebbins). Mobs eagle owls and other predators vigorously. When threatened by a flying bird-of-prey, the flock members at once gather into a compact mass, in silence, and dash headlong into the nearest dense cover (Ligon). Flocks roost in various places within the home range. They often fly from 1·5 to 5 km to the roosting place and very seldom, probably never, roost near to where they have last fed that day. Individual flock members roost in clumps of 2 to 5, probably these roosting groups represent pairs or family parties.

Ringing returns suggest that, if they survive to become adult, Piñon Jays may have a life expectation of 6 or more years (Whitney).

Nesting   Nests colonially, but seldom more than one nest in a tree and sometimes the individual nests may be scattered over a considerable area. One flock nested every year within the same 160 hectares within its home range. The nest is placed in a tree or shrub, most often juniper, pine or live-oak, usually from 1 to 6 metres above ground, sometimes higher.   Trees growing in dense thickets are avoided and nests are sited in the southern half of the tree.   Nest of sticks, weed stems and similar materials with a deep inner cup of strips of fibrous bark, sometimes also of other vegetable fibres, roots, hair, wool and grasses. The male usually initiates nest site selection, enticing his mate to the site by carrying sticks to it and feeding her if she follows him there.   Both sexes bring nest lining materials (which get blown away) to the site for 3 to 5 days before serious building starts.   Nesting usually begins in early spring but the time depends largely on the food situation; nests with fresh eggs have been found from February till October (Ligon, 1961).   Ligon (1971) observed failure to breed successfully in the spring of 1969, after failure of the 1968 piñon seed crop, followed by the birds, which were already in the last stages of their moult, beginning to breed in mid-August in response to a bumper crop of piñon seeds.   The moult was halted while breeding took place.   In Santa Fé, New Mexico, Jensen observed that, after a good crop of piñon seed, Piñon Jays nested in February or early March.   Then came three 'lean years' in which they nested, respectively, in late March, early April, and May.   Single-brooded, but repeat attempts are usually made a second or even a third time after failures.

Eggs 3 to 6, most often 3 or 4; pale bluish, bluish white, or pale greenish, speckled with dark brown and black, or reddish brown.   Incubation is by the female only, fed by the male.   Males commute between their nests and the foraging flock, usually in small groups of about 6 to 8.   On coming back with food in his gullet the male often perches in a tree some distance from the nest, calls the female to him and feeds her there (Braly).   Cameron was convinced that both sexes took part in incubation but did not give evidence for this belief.

Incubation period 16 days, the young fledge at about 3 weeks (Bendire).   Both sexes feed the young. Only their parents normally feed nestlings under 12 days old but older nestlings and fledged young are sometimes also fed by other adults.   The young from neighbouring nests, and their parents, form tightly knit feeding aggregates within which the same adult may feed the young from more than one nest.

Braly found much individual difference in the reactions of incubating females when he visited them. Some flew right away, others remained near calling, and two refused to flee and allowed themselves to be lifted from their nests.   In no instance did a male return from the feeding flock in response to the calls of females thus disturbed.

First-year birds do not usually breed although there are some authentic records of their doing so.

Voice   Has a variety of calls (see esp. Bent).   Balda & Bateman describe: (1) a rhythmic 'krawk-kraw-krawk' repeated two or three times, which is used as a warning call at sight of approaching danger and which causes other individuals to cease feeding and fly up into the trees.   (2) A soft 'kraw-kraw' or 'kaw' which increases in loudness to a crescendo of din.   This causes pairs which have separated from the flock for courtship or other activities to fly back and join in, preparatory to flying to a new area. (3) The begging call of the young, and of incubating females, described as harsh and squawking, and by Braly as 'a screeching series of calls'.   (4) A low 'cluck' given by birds during pursuit flights that appear to be predominantly sexual in character.   (5) A 'near-ering' call, constantly given by building birds, possibly the same as the 'peculiar whistle-like note' that Braly recorded as being given by the male when a man was near the nest.

Others have described a call, commonly uttered in flight, a mewing or nasal-sounding 'wi-ar whack', the first two notes long and high-pitched and the last short; a mewing 'queh-a-eh'; and rattling calls.

Display and social behaviour   When begging for food the female flaps or flutters her wings and utters juvenile type calls but if she is actually sitting on the nest such begging is 'abbreviated and silent'.   Feeding of the female by her mate occurs to some extent throughout the year, sometimes in silence and with unprepared food.   During winter connubial feeding occurs much more frequently when the flock are visiting the nesting area than when they are elsewhere.

In submissive display the wings are held close to the body (perhaps not so close when the display is given at high intensity?) and rapidly quivered.   This quivering display is shown by individuals seeking food near presumed social superiors.   Another appeasing display resembles the chin-up display of some other species, the bird presenting its whitish throat feathers frontally.

Especially before nesting, groups of up to 12 individuals fly through and over the trees, performing steep dives and sharp turns and uttering low clucks and drawn-out caws. These flights, in which grey-plumage yearlings may take part, usually occur on or very near the traditional nesting area.   Observations on ringed individuals show that these flights often (and probably always) involve the pursuit of an un-paired female by one or more unpaired males.   They probably function in initiating pair formation.

Flocks have also been observed performing aerobatics high in the air. Possibly these are basically hawk-escaping movements which, although often performed spontaneously, function to keep the per-formers able to perform them in earnest should need arise.

Pairs or prospective pairs usually move a little way from the flock to indulge in courtship behaviour. The male picks up a piece of nesting material, walks slowly to the female, gives it to her and flies to a nearby tree. If she follows him they then fly off to sit together or indulge in other courtship behaviour. Sites similar to nest sites are selected by the male who lures the female by carrying a stick to them, placing it down and feeding her if she follows him.   These sites are used for courtship activities but only 28% of such courtship sites were later used as nest sites.

It has only been possible here to summarize from Balda's and Bateman's fine studies which should be read in full by anyone seriously concerned with this species.

Other names   Blue Crow, Piñon Crow, Maximilian's Crow.

REFERENCES

BALDA, R. P. & BATEMAN, G. C.   1971.   Flocking and annual cycle of the Piñon Jay, *Gymnorhinus cyancoce-phalus*.   *Condor* **73**: 287–302.
—— 1973.   The breeding biology of the Piñon Jay.   *The Living Bird* **11** (1972): 5–42.
BATEMAN, G. C. & BALDA, R. P.   1973.   Growth, development, and food habits of young Piñon Jays.   *Auk* **90**: 39–61.
BENDIRE, C.   1895.   *Life Histories of North American Birds:* 424–426.
BENT, A. C.   1946.   Life histories of North American jays, crows and titmice: 302–310.   *Bull. U.S. Nat. Mus.* **191**: 118–128.
BRALY, J. C.   1931.   Nesting of the Piñon Jay in Oregon.   *Condor* **33**: 29.
CAMERON, E. S.   1907.   The birds of Custer and Sawson counties, Montana. *Auk* **24**: 389–406.
JENSEN, J. K.   1923.   Notes on the nesting birds of Santa Fe County, New Mexico.   *Auk* **40**: 452–469.
LIGON, J. S.   1961.   *New Mexico Birds and Where to Find Them* 204–205.   New Mexico.
—— 1971.   Late summer-autumnal breeding of the Piñon Jay in New Mexico.   *Condor* **73**: 147–153.
MILLER, A. H. & STEBBINS, R. C.   1964.   *The lives of desert animals in Joshua Tree national monument* 142–146. California.
NERHLING, H.   1896.   *Our Native Birds of Song and Beauty* **2**: 314–315.   Milwaukee.
WHITNEY, M. R.   1963.   Results of Pinyon Jay banding in South Dakota.   *Bird Banding* **34**: 219.

The ground jays

The ground jays or ground choughs, sometimes called desert choughs (jays) or running-jays (-choughs), are a very distinct group of corvids inhabiting high semi-desert country in central Asia from Iran (Persia) to Mongolia.   They have long strong legs on which they run quickly and leap onto rocks or bushes and long, heavy, more or less curved bills with which they dig and probe.   As their names indicate, they spend much time on the ground although they readily perch on rocks, shrubs and (when present) trees. They nest in bushes, shrubs or in cavities and one species, *Pseudopodoces humilis*, excavates its own nest site.   They are predominantly pinkish fawn or (one species) silver grey in colour, marked with glossy black and white, except for the aberrant and more dully-coloured *P. humilis*.

Their short dense nasal plumes, large bills and rather short tails suggest relationship to the nutcrackers but parts of their colour pattern are nearer to those of jays, *Garrulus*, and magpies, *Pica*.   On present knowledge any of these resemblances might be due to convergence.   It is, however, possible that their nearest living relatives are represented by *Garrulus* or *Nucifraga* and they are almost certainly not at all closely allied, as corvids go, to the true choughs, *Pyrrhocorax*, to one species of which their curved bills give them a slight superficial resemblance.   The ground jays show some convergent resemblances in appearance and habits to certain unrelated birds that live in rather similar terrain, such as the Hoopoe Lark, *Alaemon alaudipes*, and the Australian quail-thrushes, *Cinclosoma*.

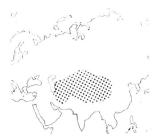

Henderson's Ground Jay, *Podoces hendersoni*, and the White-tailed Ground Jay, *P. biddulphi*, are similar in size and colour pattern except that the former lacks the black facial markings of *biddulphi* and has a black instead of a predominantly white tail.   It also has a shorter and less curved bill, this probably being correlated with living on, and digging and probing in, more stony and hard soil.   To some extent the geographical ranges of *biddulphi* and *hendersoni* overlap but I can find no records of both occurring in the same habitat.   Ludlow found that in Chinese Turkestan *hendersoni* had a peripheral distribution in the Piedmont gravel zone and *biddulphi* a central distribution in the interior sandy zone.   The two are perhaps best treated as members of a species group and are certainly very closely related.

The second species group consists of the Grey Ground Jay, *Podoces panderi*, and the Persian Ground Jay, *P. pleskei*.   Both are rather smaller in size than the previous species and have short instead of very long upper tail coverts.   They are alike in plumage pattern but differ in ground colour, that of *pleskei* being sandy fawn and that of *panderi* silver-grey.   They show a comparable difference in bill length to that between *hendersoni* and *biddulphi*, the Persian Ground Jay having a longer and more curved bill than the Grey Ground Jay.   Their ranges are adjacent and they do not appear to overlap although their bill differences suggest adaptation to different types of soil.

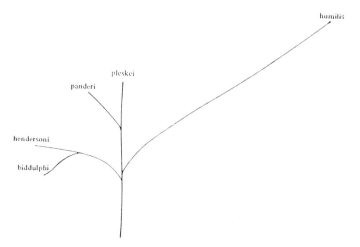

FIG. D.8.   Presumed relationships of species in the genera *Podoces* and *Pseudopodoces*.

Hume's Ground Jay, *humilis*, is currently placed in the monotypic genus *Pseudopodoces*.   There seems justification for this.   It is much smaller and has a duller and, presumably, more cryptic plumage with black *Podoces*-type markings only shown in obsolescent form on lores, alula and tail, and it differs in some other characters.   Thus it excavates a nesting burrow for itself instead of building in a bush or using an existing cavity.   It lays pure white eggs, suggesting that its hole-nesting is of fairly long standing. Some observers who have seen both it and other ground choughs in the field have emphasized that it appeared very different and although these impressions were subjective they are perhaps not less valuable for that.   I therefore provisionally maintain the genus *Pseudopodoces* for Hume's Ground Jay.

REFERENCES

AMADON, D.   1944.   The genera of Corvidae and their relationships.   *Amer. Mus. Novit.* 1251.
LUDLOW, F. & KINNEAR, N. B.   1933.   A contribution to the ornithology of Chinese Turkestan, Pt. 2, *Ibis* **(13)** 3 : 445–447.
VAURIE, C.   1959.   *The Birds of the Palearctic Fauna: Passeriformes.*
ZARUDNY, N. & LOUDON, H. B.   1902.   Über Einteilung des genus *Podoces* in subgenera.   *Orn. Monatsber.* **10** : 185–186.

HENDERSON'S GROUND JAY   *Podoces hendersoni*

Podoces hendersoni Hume 1871, Ibis, p. 408.

Description   About size of Jay but very different in shape, with much shorter wings and tail and long curved bill.   General body colour pinkish fawn, paler on the underparts and shading to almost white on throat.   Lesser wing coverts and scapulars a slightly darker and more rufous shade.   The pinkish fawn fades with wear and bleaching to a pale yellowish buff and the scapulars to a light tawny hue.   The fawn colour on the face extends well above the eye.   The dense short nasal plumes, which completely cover the nostrils, are fawn, rarely suffused with blackish but usually with a narrow ring of black feathers at their base.   Median part of forehead, crown and nape shining bluish black or purplish black.   In new plumage these feathers, especially those on the nape, are often, but not always, tipped with creamy white.   Wings black with a large white patch formed by extensive white areas on the primaries and largely white outer web of outermost secondary.   Some few individuals show varying amounts of white on the inner webs of the three innermost secondaries, or on some of them.   Under surface of wing also black and white but without the rich blue or purple sheen of the upper surface.   Tail black glossed with blue or greenish blue, rarely with some white at tips of outermost feathers.   The long fawn upper tail coverts reach over half-way down the tail.   See col. pl. 1.

   Irides dark brown.   Bill, legs and feet black.   Juvenile like adult but slightly less glossy on the wings, less pinkish on the fawn parts, and with conspicuous buff tips to the otherwise dull black crown and forehead feathers.   Greater wing coverts tipped buff, but these buff tips may soon wear off.

Field characters   Fawn bird with long heavy curved bill, piebald wings and black cap and tail.   Runs on the ground.   Hardly likely to be mistaken for any other species except *P. biddulphi* from which its black tail at once distinguishes it or, if seen head on, its entirely fawn face with no black on malar region.

Distribution and habitat   Central Asia: Inner and Outer Mongolia, northern Kansu, northern Tsinghai in the Zaidam, northern Tibet and Sinkiang westward to Dzungaria, north to the Kara Irtysh and west to the region north of Lake Zaisan.

Inhabits stony or gravelly semi-desert areas with some shrubs or trees. Henderson & Hume found it in areas with hillocks of drifted sand, on which it sought food, and Vaurie states that it is also found in open desert, but both Kozlova in northern Mongolia and Ludlow in Chinese Turkestan found it only in stony or gravelly areas.

Feeding and general habits Sometimes, perhaps usually, in pairs. Runs swiftly on ground. Freely perches on bushes, shrubs or boulders and habitually does so (to get a better view) when somewhat alarmed.

Known to take beetles, and other insects, lizards, grain, melon seeds and some green vegetation; but probably takes a wide range of seeds and invertebrates. On or near caravan tracks picks undigested or only partly digested grain from the droppings of domestic mammals.

Nesting Two nests found, with well-fledged young in mid-April and on May 1st, in Chinese Turkestan, were amongst stones under large boulders. Divnogorskii found a nest under a bush. It was of twigs and rootlets, lined with camel hair (Dementiev *et al.*).

Voice Ludlow describes the 'call note' as somewhat resembling the 'clack, clack, clack' of a wooden rattle.

Display and social behaviour No information.

Other names Henderson's Desert Chough, Henderson's Desert Jay, Henderson's Sand Jay.

REFERENCES

DEMENTIEV, G. P. & GLADKOV, N. A. 1970. *Birds of the Soviet Union* vol. 5. English translation, published by Israel Program for Scientific translations, Keter Press, Jerusalem.
HENDERSON, G. & HUME, A. O. 1873. *Lahore to Yarkand*. 244–247. London.
KOZLOVA, E. V. 1933. The birds of South-West Transbaikalia, Northern Mongolia, and Central Gobi, Pt. 4. *Ibis* (**13**) 3: 63–64.
LUDLOW, F. & KINNEAR, N. B. 1933. A contribution to the ornithology of Chinese Turkestan, Pt. 2. *Ibis* (**13**) 3: 447–449.
VAURIE, C. 1959. *The Birds of the Palearctic Fauna: Passeriformes* 154–155. London.

BIDDULPH'S GROUND JAY   *Podoces biddulphi*

Podoces Biddulphi Hume 1874, Stray Feathers 2, p. 503.

Description Very similar to the previous species, *P. hendersoni*, but with longer and proportionately more slender bill. Coloration very similar but differing as follows: general colour slightly paler, more pinkish on back, and elsewhere in very new plumage; otherwise face, neck and underparts very pale and creamy. Lower part of rump and upper tail coverts pale cream colour. Malar region and a small area just behind eye black with pale fringes to feathers. Throat feathers greyish black with broad creamy tips, usually giving a rather dark, speckly effect, but in the live bird the throat probably appears pale when its feathers not raised. White on wing slightly more extensive than in *hendersoni* and alula mainly white. Tail white but with varying (usually small) longitudinal black areas near shafts of two central feathers; the next two feathers have the shafts blackish as, to some extent, may all but the outermost pair. In no case (in the specimens I have examined) does the black pigment extend to the ends of the feathers, but stops about a centimetre from end of tail.

Sexes alike in colour but the bills of most males are appreciably longer than those of most females; possibly the apparent exceptions are due to specimens being wrongly sexed by collectors. Juvenile paler and duller, with very lax contour feathers. Top of head dull black instead of glossy blue-black. Greater wing coverts with conspicuous buffy brown tips forming a bar across the folded wing. Black areas on tail more extensive but less sharply demarcated. To judge from appearance of specimens the bill and legs of the juvenile are probably brownish or greyish rather than black as in the adult.

Field characters As previous species, from which its white tail and blackish malar patches at once distinguish it.

Distribution and habitat Sinkiang (Chinese Turkestan). Specimens taken in the foothills of the Tian Shan and Kun Lun, Cherchen, Tarim Azne and Lob-Nor. Inhabits sandy wastes and semi-deserts, with some small trees or shrubs.

Feeding and general habits Perches freely in or on trees but probably feeds mainly, if not entirely, on the ground. Has been seen both on open sandy desert (but at no great distance from some vegetation) and in thick scrub jungle (Ludlow & Kinnear). When alarmed sometimes, perhaps usually, flies into trees or shrubs. Runs swiftly on the ground. Flight weak and laboured; only flies short distances.

 Horse dung, small beetles and maize have been found in the alimentary tracts of shot birds. Presumably the maize was obtained either from grain spilled on caravan tracks or picked out of animal droppings.

Nesting Nests in small trees, a metre or so from the ground. Nest has a base and outer shell of twigs and small sticks, above and inside which is deep cup of wool, hair, dead leaves, dry grass and vegetable down. Ludlow, to whom the above information is due, notes that the local people said this species also nests in holes in the ground. Eggs light brownish green to light bluish green, fairly profusely speckled and blotched with light and dark olive-brown and with underlying greyish markings. Three nests, found in mid-March (2) and late March (1) with well-incubated eggs, contained 1, 2 and 3 eggs respectively.

Voice Ludlow notes two quite distinct calls 'a thrice-repeated "chui-chui-chui", the last syllable on a higher note', and 'a succession of low whistles in rapidly descending scale'.

Display and social behaviour No information.

Other names Biddulph's Ground Chough, Biddulph's Desert Chough, Biddulph's Desert Jay, White-tailed Ground Chough, White-tailed Ground Jay.

REFERENCE

LUDLOW, F. & KINNEAR, N. B. 1933. A contribution to the ornithology of Chinese Turkestan, Pt. 2, *Ibis* (**13**) 3: 445–446.

PERSIAN GROUND JAY   *Podoces pleskei*

Podoces pleskei Zarudny, 1896, Ann. Mus. Zool. Acad. Imp. Sci., St. Petersbourg, 1, p. 12.

Description Smaller than the two preceding species, its body size being about that of a Blue Jay, but similar in shape although with proportionately rather longer legs. General colour a bright sandy fawn with a pinkish tinge (probably fading considerably in worn plumage). Nasal plumes buffish, streaked (dark shafts) with blackish. Black stripe from gape to eye. Throat, area above and below facial stripe and around eye white or fawnish white. Black patch on lower throat. Lesser wing coverts as back. Median coverts with obscure blackish sub-terminal bands and broad white tips. Greater coverts glossy blue-black with white tips forming a bar across the closed wing. Primary coverts black tipped with white. Secondaries glossy black with white ends, the white areas being very extensive on the outer secondaries, progressively less so on the inner ones. Innermost primary has the basal half (about) black, rest white; remaining primaries black with broad white band, progressively narrowing towards outermost. Tail black, glossed greenish blue. I have only seen one specimen of this ground jay. It is probable that the differences between juvenile and adult plumages are similar to those of the previous species.

Field characters   Entirely fawn or sandy top of head at once distinguishes it from other predominantly fawn ground jays; sandy fawn, not silver grey, general coloration from Grey Ground Jay.

Might momentarily be mistaken for a Hoopoe, from which its gait, long legs, entirely black tail or crestless head would all distinguish it, or for the Hoopoe Lark, which is smaller, duller, longer-winged and with more or less spotted breast.

Distribution and habitat   Eastern Iran (Persia), in Khorasan, the Dasht i Lut desert and Persian Baluchistan. Probably in similar habitats to those of Grey Ground Jay.

Feeding and general habits   Little recorded; probably very similar to that of Grey Ground Jay (q.v.). Watson (in Sharpe) flushed several pairs from a bush-grown nullah in the desert and later encountered others in similar strips of 'bushy jungle' in desert (or semi-desert?) regions.

Runs actively on the ground and perches freely on shrubs and bushes.

Nesting   No information.

Voice   No information.

Display and social behaviour   No information.

Other names   Persian Ground Chough, Pleske's Ground Chough, Pleske's Ground Jay, Fawn-coloured Chough.

REFERENCE

SHARPE, R. B.   1907.   A note on *Podoces pleskei* Zarudny.   *Journal Bombay Nat. Hist. Soc.* **17**: 554–557.

GREY GROUND JAY   *Podoces panderi*

Podoces Panderi Fischer, 1821, Lettre adressé . . . de la Soc. Imp. Nat. Moscou à . . . Pander, p. 6.

Description   Similar to the previous species, *P. pleskei*, in size but with shorter bill. Upper parts from forehead to rump a beautiful clear light silvery grey. Black stripe from gape to eye, broadening at eye and bordered white above. Throat and around eye (except black area in front) white. A large black oval or half-moon shaped patch on upper breast is narrowly bordered white below. Rest of breast and sides a pale salmon pink or vinous pink, usually slightly tinged with grey, shading to white on ventral regions and under tail coverts.   Wing pattern as in *P. pleskei* but the white areas are more extensive so that the closed wing (see sketch) appears largely white.   Upper tail coverts short and black; tail glossy bluish black.   With wear the plumage becomes very worn and bleached; the upper parts may then be a pale dull creamy grey, with the dark greyish feather bases more or less showing through.

Sexes alike but most females have rather smaller bills than most males.   Irides said to have been brown in one specimen but further information on soft parts needed.   Bill horny grey to black.   Legs and feet greyish.   I have not seen a juvenile.   From Menzbier's description it is similar to adult but of a less silvery grey, with buffish fringes to most feathers, a pronounced sandy buff tinge at back of neck and less extensive white areas on the wings.

Field characters   Silver grey or (worn plumage) creamy grey colour with piebald wings distinctive.

Distribution and habitat   Deserts of Russian Turkestan from Semirechia west to the Aral Sea, the Kyzyl Kum, and the Kara Kum to western and south-western Transcaspia.

Inhabits steppe desert and sandy desert with saxaul or other shrubs but not, *fide* Menzbier & Schnitnikow, found in extensive saxaul thickets.

Feeding and general habits   Known to take insects, including caterpillars, termites, plant bugs, ants, flies, and insect eggs; spiders, woodlice and small vertebrates; also seeds, especially of the grass *Aristida karelini*.   Recorded as regularly scavenging scraps of human food and scattered rice around a railway station in Kara Kum, until some or perhaps all of the individuals so-doing had been snared (Loudon).   Captive birds have been observed hiding food and recovering it later (Loudon); possibly food storage may be important in the wild to this and other desert jays.   Said not to need water or to visit sources of water when wild, although it will drink in captivity (Dementiev *et al.*).   Runs rapidly on ground.   Magpie-like flight; usually flies only a short distance (Dementiev *et al.*, 1970).

Established pairs seem to remain in the same living area and build in or near the same place in succeeding years (Sopyev).

Nesting   Nests in shrubs, usually about one to three feet above ground.   Nesting areas are usually sand dunes with shrubby vegetation.   Less often nests in a building or on the ground.   The nest usually has a canopy over it like that of the Magpie (Menzbier & Schnitnikow; Sopyev); it is made mostly of sticks and twigs with lining of hair, wool or other soft material.   The external wall has many protruding sticks which help to camouflage the nest.   Their appearance suggests that some nests may be re-used in successive years; nests built early in the season usually have thicker walls than those built later (Sopyev).

Eggs 2 to 6; pale greenish or bluish green, when fresh often of a pronounced bluish-grey colour (Sopyev), spotted, speckled and blotched with olive brown and with grey or lilac underlying markings.   Nests with eggs have been found from late February till late May but the latter half of March and the first half of April are the main laying periods, at least in Kara Kum (Sopyev).   Eggs are usually laid daily until the clutch is complete.

Incubation by the female only, beginning with third or fourth egg.   The female is fed at nest by the male, who remains in the vicinity and warns her of danger, but she also comes off nest periodically. An incubating female, watched for nine hours, left the nest five times, sitting for periods of fifteen minutes to over two hours (Sopyev).

Young are hatched blind and naked; their eyes open fully on the 6th day. They fledge at 17 to 18 days. The parents usually bring large amounts of food (in gullet?) and feed 2 or 3 young at each visit (Sopyev). Sopyev collected samples from young and found that the food given to them was 76·8% animal and 23·2% vegetable. The latter consisted mostly of the seeds of the grass *Aristida karelini*, the former of insects (93·9%), although a few small vertebrates, spiders and woodlice were included.

Voice　A pleasant tremulous whistle is evidently a common call. Captive birds were said to give loud cries (not described further) when alarmed by a strange dog.

Display and social behaviour　No information.

Other names　Grey Ground Chough, Pander's Ground Chough, Pander's Ground Jay.

REFERENCES

DEMENTIEV, G. P. & GLADKOV, N. A. 1970. *Birds of the Soviet Union* vol. 5. English translation, published by Israel Program for Scientific translations, Keter Press, Jersualem.
LOUDON, H. B. 1910. Meine dritte Reise nach Zentral-Asien und ihre ornithologische Ausbeute. *J. Orn.* **58**: 53–54.
MENZBIER, M. & SCHNITNIKOW, W. 1921. Der Saxaulhäher des Iligebiets. *J. Orn.* **69**: 527–535.
SNIGIREWSKI, S. I. 1928. Beiträge zur Avifauna der Wüste Kara-kum (Turkmenistan). *J. Orn.* **76**: 588–589.
SOPYEV, O. 1964. On breeding biology of Pander's Ground Jay. *Isvest. Akad. Nauk Turkmen. S.S.R.*, *Ser. biol.* **4**: 56–62.

HUME'S GROUND JAY　　　　　　　　　　　*Pseudopodoces humilis*

Podoces humilis Hume, 1871, Ibis 1, third ser., p. 408.

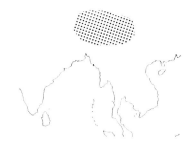

Description　Similar in shape to other ground jays but much smaller, body size being only a little larger than that of House Sparrow. Plumage very soft and lax in texture. General colour above pale earthy brown or greyish fawn with more or less of a tawny-rufous tinge. The wing quills tend to be rather darker greyish brown but have pale buffish edges. The feathers of the alula are brownish black with conspicuous whitish buff tips. Underparts and a broad half collar on hind neck creamy white slightly tinged with fawn. Dark greyish or nearly black stripe from gape to eye. Central tail feathers brownish black with pale rufous or fawn edges; next pair usually brownish black on inner webs, mainly tawny brown elsewhere, sometimes with some white. Outer tail feathers white, often more or less earth-stained.

Irides dark brown or medium brown. Bill horny black, shading to greyish or brownish at base. Legs and feet brownish black or black. Female's bill usually a little shorter than male's. Juvenile like adult but with faint dark bars on feathers of face and upper breast and paler legs and bill. Bill of newly-fledged juvenile much shorter and less curved than adult's. Both adults and young may have the plumage much soil-stained; sometimes this makes the pale parts appear orange or pink. Birds in worn plumage may be very pale through bleaching. See col. pl. 1.

Field characters Brownish bird with conspicuous white outer tail feathers contrasting with dark central tail feathers. Flight weak, straight and low over the ground. Runs and jumps rapidly, and often flees from an approaching observer by running and leaping rather than flying. Rather wheatear-like bobbing and tail-flirting when perched.

Distribution and habitat Southern Kansu and north-western Szechuan, west through Tsinghai and Sikang to Tibet and northern Sikkim; and southern Sinkiang. In open grassy steppe, arid open or cultivated country, sometimes with dwarf bushes but usually away from any dense vegetation or trees. In eastern Tibet Schäfer found it was a characteristic bird of the tree-less grass steppe but did not occur in the highest and coldest steppe desert (Wild Yak steppe).

Feeding and general habits Known to take insects. When seeking food turns over and probes dried yak dung, probes and peers into crevices in rocks, the ground, etc. Runs and hops, or rather leaps. Perches freely on rocks, clumps of earth and other eminences, bobbing up and down as it watches the observer. Flight straight, weak-looking and usually, perhaps always, only for short distances. Schäfer says that even adults gave him the impression of some recently-fledged young bird still weak on the wing.

Schäfer found it wild and timid on the open steppe but tame around Tibetan monasteries where it would scavenge for scraps of meat on the flat roofs.

If wounded and chased by a man (probably also if menaced by a bird-of-prey) it will run into any hole or crevice. Roosts in holes that it excavates itself (*fide* Schäfer). Schäfer implies that the roosting holes do not differ from nest holes; it seems uncertain whether it merely uses old or disused nest holes or whether holes are also excavated for roosting.

Nesting Nest site a hole excavated by the birds in some more or less vertical earth bank, the side of a loose boulder, an earthern wall, or similar place. It is from 0·9 to 1·8 metres long, usually nearly horizontal. The nest at the end chamber is a pad of wool and/or hair on a foundation of grass, fibres, moss or similar materials. Eggs 4 to 6, pure white, the contents giving them a translucent pinkish tinge when fresh. Birds have been seen building in early May but most of the eggs in collections seem to have been taken in June.

The family parties keep together and the young are fed by both parents for some time after fledging.

Voice Schäfer records a rather melancholy-sounding whistling call; no doubt the same as that described by Ali as 'a plaintive whistling "chip (slight pause) cheep-cheep-cheep-cheep"'. Ali also records a 'feeble "cheep" like a munia's but more prolonged', and Schäfer a finch-like two-syllabled call.

Display and social behaviour No information.

Other names Little Ground Jay, Hume's Ground Chough, Little Ground Chough, Tibetan Ground Chough, Tibetan Ground Jay.

REFERENCES

ALI, S. 1962. *The Birds of Sikkim*. Oxford.
MEINERTZHAGEN, R. 1927. Birds collected in Ladak and Sikkim. *Ibis* (12) 3: 374–375.
SCHÄFER, E. 1938. Ornithologische Ergebnisse zweier Forschungsreisen nach Tibet. *J. Orn.* **86**, Sonderheft 275–279.

Zavattariornis

Only one species of this genus is known. Although superficially bearing some resemblance to Clark's Nutcracker (and, for that matter, to some Asiatic starlings!) its affinities are obscure. Its morphological and anatomical characters suggest that it is rightly placed in the Corvidae (Amadon; Ripley) and this is not contradicted by what little is known of its behaviour. Its nest, although unique among the crows, appears not to depart much more from the usual type of corvine nest than does that of the Magpie. It has sometimes been suggested that their nests indicate relationship between them, but Benson's description of the nest of *Zavattariornis* does not suggest that it is really very close to that of *Pica*, even although both have a 'roof' of (different) sorts.

It is possible that *Zavattariornis* may be phylogenetically closer to *Ptilostomus*, the other aberrant African form, than their very different appearance would suggest. The general resemblance of *Zavattariornis* to *Podoces* is, I think, likely to be due to convergence.

ZAVATTARIORNIS   *Zavattariornis stresemanni*

Zavattariornis stresemanni Moltoni, 1938, Orn. Monatsb., 46, p. 80.

Description Slightly larger than Blue Jay but different, rather starling-like, in shape (see sketch). General colour pale bluish grey shading to near white on forehead and to creamy white on face, throat, belly, tibial feathers and under tail coverts. Lesser wing coverts and scapulars grey as back, edge of wing near carpal joint creamy white. Rest of wings and tail glossy black. Feathers, especially at tips on the upper parts, bleach to a paler and browner tint.

Irides brown. Bare skin on loral region and around eyes bright blue. Bill, legs and feet black. Juvenile a browner grey with creamy fawn fringes to most feathers, especially prominent on the lesser wing coverts. Upper tail coverts brownish grey with dark fawn fringes. Underparts predominantly fawnish cream except on throat and belly. This description is based on only two juvenile specimens. Bill and facial skin of young paler than in adult, to judge from appearance of specimens.

Field characters Pale grey bird with black wings and tail. At close range bright blue orbital skin conspicuous.

Distribution and habitat Southern Ethiopia: near Yavello (Javello), Mega and Arero.

Inhabits park-like 'thorn-acacia' country but absent from some areas, such as immediately west of Yavello, in spite of apparently suitable habitat (Hall & Moreau).

Feeding and general habits Little recorded. Known to eat insects. Out of the breeding season usually in small parties but does not nest in colonies.

Nesting Benson found this species breeding, with some nests containing eggs, in March. The usual site is at the top of a thorn tree about 6 metres high. The nest is an untidy-looking, roughly globular structure of thorn sticks and twigs, with an external diameter of about 60 cm. Inside is a globular chamber about 30 cm in diameter; on the floor of this chamber is a mixture of dried cattle dung and short pieces of dried grass. The entrance to the chamber is from the top, and this is protected by a vertical tubular tunnel about 15 cm in height. This superstructure is added to the body of the nest just before the eggs are laid.

One clutch consisted of 6 eggs, other smaller clutches may have been incomplete. Eggs smooth, slightly glossy, cream-coloured with pale lilac blotches; these latter are similar to the underlying markings on most corvine eggs in appearance.

Benson, from whose account the above description is taken, noted that it was 'normal to observe three birds emerge from a single nest, but there is no evidence to suppose that more than one female was responsible for the eggs'. This suggests that *Zavattariornis* may have breeding habits similar to those of some American jays, in which more than one pair of adults attend a single nest.

Voice   A common call is a high-pitched 'chek' (Benson).

Display and social behaviour   No information.

Other names   Abyssinian Pie, Bush Crow.

REFERENCES

AMADON, D.   1943.   The genera of starlings and their relationships. *Amer. Mus. Novit.* No. 1247, 1–16.
BENSON, C. W.   1946.   Notes on the birds of Southern Abyssinia. *Ibis* **88**: 448–450.
HALL, B. P. & MOREAU, R. E.   1962.   A study of the rare birds of Africa. *Bull. Br. Mus. nat. Hist.* (Zool.) **8**, No. 7: 348.
MOLTONI, E.   1938.   *Zavattariornis stresemanni* novum genus et nova species Corvidarum. *Orn. Monatsb.* **46**: 80–83.
RIPLEY, S. D.   1955.   Anatomical notes on *Zavattariornis*. *Ibis* **97**: 142–145.

The Piapiac or Black Magpie

This very distinct African species is the sole representative of the genus *Ptilostomus*. It differs from other corvids in some anatomical characters but these seem to be only of a relatively minor nature (Amadon) and in general its anatomy, appearance and what is known of its behaviour suggest that it is rightly placed in the Corvidae.

Its relationships within the crow family are, however, quite obscure. Its size and long tail give it some superficial resemblance to the typical magpies of the genus *Pica*, but they are not, I think, closely related. Amadon suggests that possibly *Corvus* might be of African origin and, if so, that *Ptilostomus* might be an early offshoot from the same stock. This is quite possible although I think it more likely that *Ptilostomus* is derived from some early form not closer to *Corvus* than to other genera. The parti-coloured bills of subadult *Ptilostomus*, and its tendency to associate in small groups are suggestive of some of the New World jays. These characters, however, could as easily be convergent as the Magpie-like shape and *Corvus*-like plumage colour.

REFERENCES

AMADON, D.   1944.   The genera of Corvidae and their relationships. *Amer. Mus. Novit.* No. 1251.

PIAPIAC   *Ptilostomus afer*

Corvus afer Linnaeus, 1766, Syst. Nat., ed. 12, 1, p. 157.

Description   A little smaller and slimmer than Magpie, with proportionately narrower, more pointed and slightly longer tail and thicker bill with more strongly curved culmen. Plumage dense and rather silky in texture but not very thick. Nasal plumes short and upturned but fully covering nostrils. Only ten tail feathers.

Extreme front of forehead and lores velvety black. Most of plumage black with slight purplish or bluish gloss. Rump and upper tail coverts blackish brown. Primaries and outer secondaries dark drab brown with blackish tips and paler drab on inner webs.   Underwing coverts dull black, undersides of wing quills pale greyish.   Tail feathers blackish brown, soon fading to dull brownish drab, often light drab in very worn plumage.   Irides a beautiful purple, violet, mauve, or pinkish purple, usually with a blue or bluish purple outer ring.   The soft part colours on labels of specimens in the British Museum (Natural History) suggest that the irides of females may usually have the inner ring more tinged with brown or red than is common in males but there appears to be individual variation and more observations on living birds are needed.   See col. pl. 2.

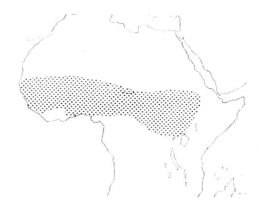

The juvenile is only very slightly duller than the adult; its irides are at first brown or dark brown and its bill pink or pinkish red with a brown or blackish tip.   The irides appear soon to attain the adult coloration or something very near it but the bill remains largely pink or purplish pink for at least about ten months, possibly longer.   Young birds evidently replace their two central tail feathers at or shortly after the first body moult.   It appears, from the limited number of moulting immatures – about ten in all – that I have examined, that the other tail feathers may either be retained for a considerable period before being shed or the next pair may be replaced soon after the central pair.   Thus some immatures taken between December and late March have two new central tail feathers in an otherwise old (juvenile) tail (and new contour feathers) whereas others have new central tail feathers and the next pair already growing.   One taken in mid-November is in body moult and with its two new central tail feathers half grown.   Further observations, especially on living birds, are needed to determine the precise sequence of moults and how long the pink bill is retained.

Field characters   Slender black bird with long pointed brownish tail and brownish primaries.   Thick, and sometimes partly pink, bill distinguishes it from all large, long-tailed starlings; long tail from all other sympatric corvids.

Distribution and habitat   Africa from Senegal to Lagos, eastward to the Sudan and southern Ethiopia; south in eastern Africa to Lake Albert and Lake Edward.   Extensive but irregular migrations occur in some areas (Mackworth-Praed & Grant) but in Ilorin, Nigeria, no seasonal change in numbers was observed.   Inhabits open country, typically cultivated fields and pasture lands and the towns or villages near them.   The *Borassus* palm is usually a feature of its habitat.

Feeding and general habits   Usually in flocks of ten or more individuals.   Breaks up into pairs for breeding but such pairs may, and perhaps usually do, feed with others in communal feeding grounds.   Feeds chiefly on the ground, sometimes to a limited extent on large mammals and in trees.   Food chiefly insects and other invertebrates but also takes the pericarp of the oil palm's fruits.

Walks and runs rapidly and with great agility.   Also hops (Serle).   Flies with rapid wing beats and the long tail trailing behind.   Habitually accompanies goats, sheep and cattle; catching the insects disturbed by them and often perching on them.   Usually it appears not to feed from the animals it uses in this way but it has been repeatedly seen to pick unidentified objects from the sides of elephants (Attwell).

Attwell notes that elephants allow the Piapiac to cling to or perch on them whereas they do not allow oxpeckers, *Buphagus* sp., to do so.

Usually roosts in palms or other trees in or near villages, and flies out into the cultivated fields or pasture lands to feed.   Commonly feeds in the morning and again in the evening, resting in trees during the hot middle hours of the day.   Flocks flying to or from roosting places travel in compact groups and fly low (Hutson, in Bannerman).   Usually has little fear of man; perches freely on huts and houses.   Sometimes colonizes villages in areas where it has not been previously known.

Captive birds anted in typical active manner (Simmons, pers. comm.).

Nesting Nests in palms or other trees.   Nests found by Serle were built of twigs, long strips of palm fibre, and grass stems, with some earth (mud?) in the foundations, and the interior of the deep cup thickly lined with palm fibre.   Other observers record nests built entirely of palm fibre or of palm fibre and only a few twigs.

Eggs 3 to 7; very pale blue or pale greenish blue, sometimes unmarked but usually with a few spots or blotches of tawny brown or olive brown and rather more profuse underlying pale grey or lilac spots or blotches.   The markings, when present, tend to form a zone at the larger end.   Nests with eggs have been found from mid-March to late April.   Serle found a nest with fully-fledged young in early May.

Voice Most observers record shrill squeaking calls as being commonly uttered.   These squeaking calls are evidently given in many situations.   Serle noted a Jackdaw-like quality about them.   Holman (in Bannerman) records a croaking call of alarm or anger, given with a bob of the head.

Display and social behaviour No information.

Other names Black Magpie, African Magpie.

REFERENCES

ATTWELL, R. I. G. 1966. Oxpeckers and their associations with mammals in Zambia. *Puku* **4**: 31.
BANNERMAN, D. A. 1948. *The Birds of Tropical West Africa* **6**: 35–40.
BOUGHTON-LEIGH, P. W. T. 1932. Observations on nesting and breeding habits of birds near Ilorin, Nigeria. *Ibis* **(13)** 2: 457–470.
ELGOOD, J. H., FRY, C. H. & DOWSETT, R. J. 1973. African migrants in Nigeria. *Ibis* **115**: 375–409.
MACKWORTH-PRAED, C. W. & GRANT, C. H. B. 1960. *African Handbook of Birds*, 2nd ed., ser. 1, vol. **2**: 679.
SERLE, W. 1940. Field observations on some Northern Nigerian birds, pt. 2. *Ibis* **(14)** 4: 29–30.

The Crested Jay

The Crested Jay, *Platylophus galericulatus*, was at one time placed with the shrikes, Laniidae, and it is not certain that it is now correctly considered a member of the Corvidae.   Its colour pattern is unusual, but perhaps not more so than that of some unquestionable corvids.   The distinctive crest is quite unlike that of any Old World corvid but bears a distant resemblance to those of some American jays and is, in any case, probably of little phylogenetic significance.   Conspicuously crested forms with completely crest-less, but undoubtedly close, relatives occur in several groups of birds; the Australasian bronze-winged pigeons, for example.   Perhaps of more import is the juvenile plumage which is suggestive of that of some thrush or flycatcher rather than that of a corvine bird.   However, the juvenile plumages of the Azure-winged Magpie and the Nutcracker might be considered in some degree intermediate between the juvenile dress of *Platylophus* and those of other corvids.

On the other hand the external structure of *Platylophus* agrees well with other corvids.   The longer rictal bristles and more strongly hooked bill (which, except for the stronger hook, is very like that of *Garrulus*) are probably adaptive characters; they occur widely among passerines.   Also people who have seen the bird in life appear to have accepted it without question as a jay although, so far as I can discover, they have not recorded any detailed observations on its habits and behaviour.   Provisionally I include the Crested Jay as a member of the Corvidae but with some misgivings.   More detailed studies are needed to be certain about its relationships.

CRESTED JAY   *Platylophus galericulatus*

Corvus galericulatus Cuvier, 1817, *Règne Animal*, **1**: 399.

Description   About size of Blue Jay but more heavily built, with shorter but heavier and strongly-hooked bill, rather shorter tail and more rounded wings.   Very long crest composed of some feathers of the crown and back of head, the greater part of the crest being formed of two very long, broad feathers. Nostrils exposed or only partly covered by nasal plumes; rictal bristles long.

General coloration very dark olive brown above and very dark grey with an olive tinge below, shading to black or nearly black on face, neck, throat and crest.   A broad white band on either side of the neck forms a half collar interrupted narrowly immediately beneath the crest.   There is a small white area above and below the posterior part of the eye (see sketch).   Underwing coverts tipped white.   Irides brownish red, reddish brown or brown.   Bill, legs and feet black or greyish black.

Juvenile very different: reddish brown above and reddish buff below with rather paler tips to feathers. Wings a slightly lighter olive brown than adult's and with buff tips to coverts and secondaries.   The juvenile wing quills and greater and primary coverts are retained after the first moult.   The body plumage attained at this first moult is usually a little paler than that of the adult and the underparts are, to individually varying degrees, tipped or barred with white and/or show pale shaft streaks to the feathers.

The above description is of *P. galericulatus ardesiacus*, which is found in the Malay Peninsula north to southern Tenasserim and south-western Thailand (Siam).   Nominate *P. g. galericulatus*, from Java, is darker, being generally coal black, with a tinge of grey on the back and mantle and of brown on the wings. Its irides are (always?) greyish or brown.   I have not seen a juvenile of this form, it is probably darker than but otherwise similar to that of *ardesiacus*.

P. g. coronatus, from Borneo and Sumatra, is very handsome, being of a general dark rich reddish tawny-brown.   Its crest, which is a little shorter than in other forms, and the parts of the neck adjacent to the white patches, are black.   Its tail is blackish grey.   Its irides are dark brown, sometimes, possibly usually, with a grey outer ring.   Its bill is greyish black or dark grey, its legs and feet dark greyish.   Immature birds have the underparts more or less greyish and with faint light and dark barring sometimes present; their bills are usually horny grey at the base.   I have not seen a juvenile but to judge from the few juvenile feathers on some immatures it is similar to that of *ardesiacus*.   The populations from northern Borneo tend to be, on average, a very little paler in colour than those of Sarawak and southern Borneo.

They are sometimes separated as *P. g. lemprieri*, but such 'splitting' serves, in my opinion, no useful purpose.

Field characters   Combination of conspicuous long broad crest and white neck patches on an otherwise dark bird diagnostic.

Distribution and habitat   Java, Sumatra, Borneo and the Malay Peninsula north to southern Tenasserim and south-western Thailand.   Inhabits tropical forest.

Feeding and general habits   Little recorded.   Known to take insects, including beetles, grasshoppers, cockroaches, cicadas and wasps; also millipedes (Smythies).   Usually met with in pairs or small parties. It appears to have struck several observers as rather tame: from descriptions it seems that it approaches and mobs human observers at fairly close range, as it presumably would other potentially dangerous mammals.

Nesting   Bartels & Stresemann state 'typically jay-like' but give no further details.

Voice   Various whistling and rattling calls have been described but not in much detail or with any reference to their significance.
    While calling it (sometimes?) makes 'weaving' body movements and flicks its crest up and down.

Display and social behaviour   No information.

Other names   Crested Shrike-jay.

REFERENCES

AMADON, D.   1944.   The genera of Corvidae and their relationships.   *Amer. Mus. Novit.* No. 1251.
BARTELS, M. & STRESEMANN, E.   1929.   Systematische Ubersight der bisher von Java nachgewiesenen Vögel. *Treubia* 11, vol. 1: 136.
KURODA, N.   1933.   *Birds of the island of Java* vol. 1: 139–140.
SMYTHIES, B. E.   1960.   *The Birds of Borneo* 506–507.

INDEX OF COMMON NAMES

INDEX OF SCIENTIFIC NAMES